The Age of Milton

The Age of Milton

An Encyclopedia of Major 17th-Century British and American Authors

Edited by ALAN HAGER

Emmanuel S. Nelson, Advisory Editor

GREENWOOD PRESS
Westport, Connecticut • London

Library of Congress Cataloging-in-Publication Data

The age of Milton : an encyclopedia of major 17th-century British and American authors / edited by
  Alan Hager.
       p.   cm.
     Includes bibliographical references and index.
     ISBN 0–313–31008–4 (alk. paper)
     1. English literature—Early modern, 1500–1700—Bio-bibliography—Dictionaries.   2. Authors,
English—Early modern, 1500–1700—Biography—Dictionaries.   3. American literature—Colonial
period, ca. 1600–1775—Bio-bibliography—Dictionaries.   4. American literature—Colonial period,
ca. 1600–1775—Dictionaries.   5. United States—Intellectual life—17th century—Dictionaries.
6. Great Britain—Intellectual life—17th century—Dictionaries.   7. English literature—Early modern,
1500–1700—Dictionaries.   8. Milton, John, 1608–1674—Contemporaries—Dictionaries.
9. Authors, American—To 1700—Biography—Dictionaries.   I. Hager, Alan, 1940–
PR431.A36   2004
820.9'004'03—dc22
  [B]   2003059545

British Library Cataloguing in Publication Data is available.

Library of Congress Catalog Card Number: 2003059545
ISBN: 0–313–31008–4

First published in 2004

Greenwood Press, 88 Post Road West, Westport, CT 06881
An imprint of Greenwood Publishing Group, Inc.
www.greenwood.com

Printed in the United States of America

The paper used in this book complies with the
Permanent Paper Standard issued by the National
Information Standards Organization (Z39.48–1984).

10 9 8 7 6 5 4 3 2 1

To Carol, Stephen, Louisa, and Sophie

❧ Contents

ɜ❧ *Preface*

This encyclopedia is dedicated to the notion that the product of authors in all disciplines of 17th-century culture in Britain, in its American colony, and on the Continent should be taken as a whole. Even in literature, the century is a piece. In science, in music, in painting, in theology, in architecture, and in landscape gardening, there is an acknowledged direct line that combines skepticism with a kind of euphoric hope so as to make one fearful that the world might be producing something like discernible progress.

No one could easily venture that by the late 17th century European culture of the world did not experience an unparalleled flowering of arts and sciences. Continuous and documented scientific discovery went to the development of the Royal Society from the influences of Gilbert and Galileo, Harvey and Newton, and led to England becoming the world's first industrialized nation–state. Renaissance music, taking its cue from Byrd, Douland, and Monteverdi, developed into the magnificent Baroque music of Purcell, Vivaldi, Scarlatti, Handel, and Bach. Shadowy painting of the likes of the works of Caravaggio and Velázquez led to the achievements of Rubens, Van Dyck, Artemisia Gentileschi, Rembrandt, and Vermeer. Architecture from Inigo Jones and the various geniuses of ungeometric landscape gardening flourished beyond all expectations, especially in the gardens in the "town" of London, as did writers of essays, drama, romance, novel, and lyric. The world of art and science had outdone itself in a century.

That English Departments all over the world today make a break in their literature curriculum at the Restoration of the Stuart King Charles II in 1660 creates, I argue, an artificial divide, an unnecessary crack into which many fine literary figures such as Anne Bradstreet, Samuel Butler, John Lilburne, Thomas Hobbes, and John Bunyan normally fall and disappear. Literature in English in the 17th century follows two warring strains—Puritan to Whig and Cavalier to Restoration—with fence-sitters and double agents galore, as we shall see in this modest volume. English Departments in the United States presently also divide British from American Colonial studies, when it could be argued that Chesapeake and, during the so-called Interregnum or Civil War, Massachusetts seemed regions much more in synch with the United Kingdom or the Commonwealth or the Continent than Ireland or even, sometimes, Scotland, soon to invade England at the end of our period.

The title of this encyclopedia, *The Age of Milton*, suggests further paradox. John Milton represents the very yoked opposites that this century in war and peace, and in its curious explosion of competitive creativity, both suffered and enjoyed. Milton himself was hardly a fence-sitter—rather, a fighter on both sides. A Cambridge grad and M.A., like so many of the University Wits of Shakespeare's day, he always had his admirers in both the Cavalier and Puritan camps. And he was often at odds with his age and with himself. He wrote poetry, as he called it with "his right hand," in a tradition that had as its fabric the Olympian myth of Homer and Hesiod, Virgil and Ovid, which is never fully discarded even in *Paradise Regained* and *Samson Agonistes* (his "autobiographical" Greek drama and probable final poetic work). With "his left hand," he wrote some of the most powerful pamphlets in the language (if one could find the period), often pointing to what would be Liberal positions on such emotional issues as tyrannicide (as he saw it), divorce, censorship, liberal humanistic classical education, and religious freedom.

Milton was a dramatist at heart and a student of William Shakespeare and Ben Jonson, producing the remarkable masque now known as *Comus*, as well as his great dialogue-driven international epic and its sequel that had as their origins a kind of operatic Miracle or Mystery play on themes from Genesis and the New Testament. That the definitive version of his *Paradise Lost* did not appear until fourteen years after the Restoration of the Stuart King made him at once England's leading Renaissance and Restoration writer. And his friends from the Royalist camp, like William Davenant and perhaps John Dryden, and from the fence-sitters, like Andrew Marvell, may have saved the head of Cromwell's now largely blind secretary for foreign languages.

At one point in his astonishing *English Literature of the Sixteenth Century: Excluding Drama*, C.S. Lewis admits having gone a quarter of a century out of his ken in a discussion of Francis Bacon's *Essays* of 1625 as "a book (as my successor admirably says) which everyone has read but no one is ever found reading" (537). Only when we go with a hunch to the index to "*Bush, D., 537*" do we realize that Lewis is gently but elvishly passing on the baton in this odd relay race to Douglas Bush, the author of *English Literature in the Earlier Seventeenth Century: 1600–1660*. Bush's volume was something of a thankless task, because going from Lewis to Bush seemed to mean going from the Golden Age through 1603, to what appeared to be an ominous early 17th century of warring factions of Spenserians, now largely forgotten (their works are too long), to Tribes of Ben, to Schools of Donne, and whatnot—I refer only to narrative and lyric. And if we throw in essays (often pamphlets) and drama, *quo vadis* into such a maze? Moreover, coming hard was the world's first fully documented revolution.

I detect, however, far more homogeneity in contrariety, if one will, than one might imagine in Western culture in the revolutionary, the scientific, the musical, the dramatic, the epic, the satirical, the evangelist, the obscene, and the lyrical century. The supposed break between loyalists and Ur-Republicans, between Laudist Oxford and

Puritan Cambridge, and the wars of poets fade. Restoration plays and satire with their love of the independent couplet become an extension of the Cavalier continuum, and the Puritans take off where Sidney, Greville, and Spenser left off; Hobbes and Locke could have talked to each other, and politics is politics.

The 17th century taken as a whole marks the end of the early modern period and places us squarely in modernity, and thus it generated, as we have seen, a huge amount of conflict. There were wars among scholastic, essentially Aristotelian and Thomist thinkers and the moderns in various forms, Protestants, scientists, and Platonists. And there were bloody wars over what seem small differences—in England even over different brands of Protestantism but also over constitutional differences reflected in the tendency to favor autocracy in Hobbes's thought and Republican forms of government in Locke. Bloody protracted wars blotted this century as much as they did the 20th century, though Europe, of course, could not really be seen as at peace at any time since the demise of the Pax Romana in A.D. 180.

In *The Age of Milton*, entries on seventy-nine writers, scientists, and artists, by forty-eight scholars, run alphabetically from Addison to Wycherley, and they range in length from two to three pages to nearly thirty. While the vast majority of the entries focus on British and American writers, some profile European writers and artists who significantly influenced British and American literary culture. Each entry provides a biography, an overview of major works and themes, a review of the author's critical reception by his or her contemporaries and readers over the centuries, a statement of the author's significance in the age, and primary and secondary bibliographies. The theme here is *concordia discors* or *discordia concors*, a unity in opposites. Within each entry, names appearing in **boldface** signal individuals appearing as entries elsewhere in this volume.

Some of the great innovators are not present. William Gilbert, who founded the scientific method of statement and proof, humanistically delivered, that became the hallmark of the Royal Academy, is missing perhaps in part because he was a 16th-century physician. As Dryden said, however, if magnets continue to attract, he will be remembered. Isaac Newton, partly an 18th-century figure, is missing perhaps because of his size and contradictions, but he will hardly go unremembered as well. Adding calculus to his achievements in physics makes him a giant standing on the shoulders of a giant looking backward. Nor will the inventor of the post-Chaucerian heroic couplet, Irishman Sir John Denham, who is missing, be forgotten. This most imitated poet for a century and a half after his death will always be remembered for his simultaneous description of the river Thames and good poetry in the Restoration style that set the stage for Pope and Swift in the next century:

> Though deep, yet clear; though gentle, yet not dull;
> Strong without rage; without o'erflowing, full. (*Coopers Hill*)

May future generations treat this odd group of innovators, with the likes of Cyrano de Bergerac and Increase Mather, better.

This volume, as did the preceding one, *Major Tudor Authors*, contains many more than usual women, especially American authors, Scottish and Irish figures sometimes marginalized, musicians, artists, scientists, and continental writers in all these categories. Figures range from the familiar Shakespeare and Milton to lesser-known authors, such as Sarah Kemble Knight, Robert Boyle, and Samuel Pufendorf.

I would like especially to thank Sara K. Austin of the Newberry Library in Chicago, Janet Lochren O'Hare of the North Shore Public Library, and Terrence J. McGovern of the Memorial Library at Cortland for their help. I add my special appreciation of Sarah Hilsman of the University of Chicago; Bill Kennedy of Cornell University; Richard Strier of the University of Chicago; Frank Fennell of Loyola University, Chicago; Regina Schwartz of Northwestern University; Julie Solomon; Hugh Richmond of the University of California, Berkeley; Ron Levao of Rutgers University; Sheila Cavanagh of Emory University; Andy Weiner of the University of Wisconsin, Madison; Jack D'Amico of Canisius College; Bill Slights of the University of Saskatchewan; Gary Bouchard of Saint Anselm College; Michael Lieb of the University of Illinois, Chicago; and especially Dick Hardin (sine qua non) of the University of Kansas—all gave help above and beyond.

Timeline of Major 17th-Century British and American Authors

1600	William Gilbert's *De Magnete* is published, the first fully documented modern scientific treatise. It explains magnets, the earth being a huge one.
1603	Elizabeth I, the final Tudor monarch, dies. Her first cousin James VI of Scotland, now James I of England, accedes. The age of the Stuart monarchs begins.
1605	The Gunpowder Plot is discovered, the last violent effort of English Roman Catholic extremists before the exodus of 1688–1689. Cervantes publishes the first book of *Don Quixote*, the first modern comic novel of education.
1607	The first English settlers arrive at Jamestown, Virginia. Monteverdi's *Orfeo* is first performed. It combines the elements of modern opera.
1610	Galileo publishes *Siderius Nuncius*, demonstrating the uses of the telescope in analysis of the heavens to include shadows of the mountains of our moon, sunspots, and other moons.
1611	William Shakespeare semiretires from the stage. Kepler suggests the design of the first compound microscope.
1616	Shakespeare dies.
1620	First emigration of the Pilgrims to the section of the New World to be called New England occurs.
1621	Inigo Jones's Banqueting Hall in Whitehall is completed.
1623	The First Folio of Shakespeare's works is published.

1625	James I dies. His son Charles I accedes.
1628	William Harvey publishes *De Motu Cordis et Sanguinis*. It demonstrates the circulation of the blood in animals.
1637	Descartes publishes *Discourse on the Method*.
1641	The English Revolution and Civil War begin. Puritan authorities close the theaters.
1645	The nucleus of the Royal Society begins weekly meetings demonstrating to members scientific discoveries and proofs.
1649	Charles I is executed. The so-called Interregnum (between monarchs) begins. Hereditary rank is abolished.
1651	Thomas Hobbes publishes *Leviathon*.
1653	Oliver Cromwell becomes the Chief Protector.
1657	Cyrano de Bergerac publishes the first work of political science fiction, *Voyage to the Moon*.
1658	Cromwell dies.
1660	The accession of Charles II marks the beginning of the so-called Restoration. The central irregular landscape garden of Westminster in London, St. James's Park, is first designed. The theaters reopen. Hereditary rank is restored.
1664–1666	The Great Plague and Fire of London occur. Isaac Newton invents the integral and differential calculus.
1667	John Milton publishes the first international epic, *Paradise Lost*.
1673	Leibniz independently invents the integral and differential calculus and devises its modern notation.
1674	John Milton publishes the revised *Paradise Lost*. He dies.
1685	Charles II dies. His brother James II accedes.
1687	Newton publishes his *Principia*, the scientific demonstration of gravity, the lunar orbit, and the elements of his quantum physics. John Locke publishes *An Essay Concerning Human Understanding*, the first work of modern epistemology and psychology.
1688–1689	James II, the final Stuart King of England, abdicates and escapes to France on the accession of William of Orange and his wife Mary Stuart as William and Mary in the so-called Glorious Revolution.
1690	Locke publishes *Two Treatises of Government*, in part, attempting to refute Hobbes's absolutism.
1700	John Dryden dies.

The Age of Milton

❧ *Joseph Addison*

(1672–1719)

RICHARD EVERSOLE

BIOGRAPHY

Joseph Addison, whose literary career flourished during the interruption of his more earnest endeavors in political employment, was born in Milston, Wiltshire, on May 1, 1672. After attending for a year the Charterhouse school (at the same time as Richard Steele), he matriculated Queen's at fifteen and resided at Magdalen College, Oxford (B.A. 1691, M.A. 1693). He accomplishes the famous participation with Steele in the periodicals *The Tatler*, *The Spectator*, and *The Guardian*, as well as completion of his tragedy *Cato*, during the four years he is out of office between the loss of position of Secretary to the Lord Lieutenant of Ireland and his appointment to the Secretaryship to the Lords Justices in 1714.

Once the first of a continuous series of Whig administrations resumes power in that year, Addison's success in appointments culminates in his promotion to Secretary of State for eleven months in 1717–1718. He is a moderate Whig, and his early reactions to the more extreme prejudices in his party against the Church attract Tory friends such as Jonathan Swift. But he is ultimately an ambiguous personality. There is a complete absence in his surviving correspondence of any letter he might have sent to or received from his father, brothers, or his wife. (Someone, on the other hand, troubles to save the unpublished correspondence to *The Tatler* and *The Spectator*.) It might be tempting to give the character of him by Alexander Pope in the *Epistle to Dr. Arbuthnot* (1734) a lot of credit. Pope, in fact, sent that character to Addison himself in 1716 as a passage in a fragmentary draft; there he is already the timorous literary arbiter who would "Damn with faint Praise," could "without sneering, teach the rest to sneer" (in which Pope would later substitute "Atticus" for Addison's initials in the finished poem). Another depiction by Pope, as recorded in Spence's *Anecdotes*, a neglected mine of information on Addison, is less tendentious. He

was perfect good company with intimates, and had something more charming in his conversation than I ever knew in any other man. But with any mixture of strangers, and sometimes with only one [or with any man he was too jealous of], he seemed to preserve his dignity much, with a stiff sort of silence. (anecdote no. 148)

Perhaps because of the disappointment his father experienced in ecclesiastical preferments, Addison eliminated the same path upon leaving university by obtaining a dispensation from holy orders. His grant from the Treasury in 1699 for a journey to France expanded into a grand tour lasting four years; he visited the court of the elector of Hanover, who by the Act of Settlement of 1701 seemed likely to succeed Queen Anne. Whatever notice his verse *Letter from Italy* (1703) and book of travels *Remarks on Several Parts of Italy* (1705) actually attracted, his connections in the Kit-Cat Club were more important; it was made up of all the Whig political noblemen along with himself, Steele, William Congreve, and John Vanbrugh, and through it he gained the opportunity to celebrate the victory over the French at Blenheim in the War of the Spanish Succession. His ceremonial poem *The Campaign* was published on the day in 1705 that the Duke of Marlborough returned to London; it immediately benefited Addison with Commissioner of Appeal in Excise, the modest office once accepted by **John Locke**. As an undersecretary who survived a change in administration, he wrote late in 1707 an exposition of Whig policy favoring another expedition in Europe; his opera of *Rosamond* failed earlier that year, though its tale of the mistress of Henry II anticipates his interests in folk ballads in *The Spectator*. He held a seat in the Commons from 1708 that allowed him to oversee in committees the progress of government policies; no less expedient service to the government lay in writing the papers of the *Freeholder* (1715–1716) to support the Hanover succession.

The *Drummer*, a comedy on the triumph of fidelity in marriage, was performed at Drury Lane in March 1716, curiously without acknowledgment of his authorship. He himself had been courting that year the dowager Countess of Warwick and after their marriage in August moved to her commodious house with its splendid library and grounds outside London. Whether because he was overworked (Smithers) or "unequal to the duties" (Johnson), he resigned the position of Secretary of State (for the South) in March 1718. He and Steele quarreled in print over politics and became estranged. Addison died in June 1719 at age forty-seven, six months after the birth of a daughter.

MAJOR WORKS AND THEMES

The Spectator is a work that belongs both to itself and to its authors. Steele acknowledges that he and Addison each contribute 251 numbers, while 35 are by two others and 18 still remain unassigned among the run of the first series, which occurred every Monday through Saturday from March 1, 1711, to December 6, 1712. Addison's own "Papers," as he calls them, are written over the initials C.L.I.O. Isolating these papers brings out a diversity that is hard to reduce under the category of "essay." The enduring poem of his, the version of Psalm 19 temporizing between reason and wonder that begins "The Spacious Firmament on High," completed the discussion of religious belief in no. 465 (August 23, 1712). The most popular (no. 159) in *The Spectator* itself was his orientalized allegory the "Vision of Mirzah" (September 1, 1711), which set a pattern for the ubiquitous Eastern tale in the later magazines. The week of papers on true and false wit is the ground of concepts that appear a year later on the pleasures of the imagination; this series itself in certain papers approaches both a theory of meaning and understanding of words and a philosophy of perception. His own papers depicting the experiences of Mr. Spectator and others of the Club, especially Roger de Coverly, often use situations of georgic poetry, the walk or visit to a location.

Though *The Spectator* pretty much keeps to Addison's promise to avoid party journalism, he and Steele are unashamed in assisting the conspicuous Whigism that trade and finance are the basis of the prosperity of not only Britain but also the world. No statement of globalization and its economic good could be more definitive at the time than Addison's account of a visit to the Royal Exchange in no. 69 (May 19, 1711). It is an instance, too, of the rhetorical tactic of either praise or blame that he favors in poetry. In the *Play-House* (1698/1699), a sardonic inspection of the seedy lives of actors, he writes satire in the mode of **John Dryden** or the later poetry of Swift. The other side of the epideictic coin is the *Campaign* (1705), which also exhibits his own concept of poetry as "Description" (in the papers on the pleasures of the imagination). Though he was congratulated for the six lines in the poem that drape an angelic mantle over Marlborough as being "pleas'd th' Almighty's orders to perform," he is less occupied with the general than with the battle itself. *Cato* (1713) is an epideictic equivocation. People in the original audience of allegiance to either party thought that the play spoke to them in its celebration of "liberty" in Cato and its dread of political egoism in Caesar. What also enables this equivocation is the elimination from the end of the play of expected poetic justice where providence rewards the good and punishes the bad, a convention that Addison had dismissed in *The Spectator* two years before.

In the posthumous *A Discourse on Ancient and Modern Learning*, Addison sides with the sensibilities of the reader during antiquity, yet in his own applications and reactions he is himself a disguised Modern. The closest he comes to literary imitation is the Latin poetry he writes at Magdalen, whose mock-heroic situations could be related to the apocryphal *Appendix Virgiliana*. In the preface he writes to the *Georgics* in Dryden's translation of Virgil (1697), he moves from rather commonplace views of the ornaments of style to a criterion of the effects on a reader that are not rhetorical but perceptual; they go beyond Classical *enargeia* to Lockean "ideas" and the suggestion by Locke that ideas excited by words are on the same level as those produced by objects. He urges this again in *Spectator* no. 416 (June 27, 1712) by what he puts as a "Force in [Words]," whose Lockean animism is not the same thing as a common rhetorical force "of" words. It could even be said that Addison aspires to empower "the Reader" with an inner text of ideas that supersedes the outer one of words on the page. Locke's *Essay Concerning Human Understanding* is a large part of his ambition in *Spectator* no. 10 (March 12, 1711) to have said of him that he has "brought Philosophy out of Closets and Libraries, Schools, and Colleges, to dwell in Clubs and Assemblies, at Tea-Tables and in Coffee-Houses." The genre criticism that he makes accessible to those quarters is not as much directed by values of the ancients as he makes out; he objects, following Richard Bentley, the supercilious Modern, to the "Punns" in *Paradise Lost* and in a telling aside elsewhere says **Milton** built a palace in brick, mere English.

He thought that *The Tatler* and *The Spectator* "had a perceptible influence upon the conversation of the time," as Johnson says. Johnson makes an apposite comparison to the courtesy book tradition to suggest that he did effect a reformation in society to politeness. How much truth there is to all this has yet to be established. Addison likes to assume that his views on a subject, as he declares in beginning the papers on wit, will have an immediate ostensive consequence in the city. Many of the forty-six numbers he also wrote for Steele's *The Tatler* beginning in May 1709 and of the fifty-one for *The Guardian* during 1713 suppose a London that is like a village in circulation of attitudes.

CRITICAL RECEPTION

Addison, unlike some better talents, does not come under much severe scrutiny during the 18th century. **John Dennis** barks at *Cato* after it first appears, and Pope makes use of a line from his own prologue to it to supply the comparison of the "little Senate Laws" of Cato in Utica to the obsequious opinions around him as "Atticus" at Button's Coffee-house. But *Cato* goes on to be repeatedly performed, the *Campaign* admired, *The Tatler* as well as, of course, *The Spectator* reprinted. Though Johnson lets Dennis loose again on the play, his own final words on Addison are an appealing endorsement of his works for "an English style." Hugh Blair had already in lectures at the University of Edinburgh during the 1760s expanded the new approach of literary history to stylistic aspects of *Spectator* no. 411 (June 21, 1712), which introduces the pleasures of the imagination. Meanwhile (with the important exception of Edmund Burke) Addison's theorizing about the imagination of the reader in the preface to the *Georgics* and *Spectator* no. 416 goes on accepted uncritically in criticism.

He is not a collateral victim of the intense antagonistic mythologizing of Pope and Swift during the 19th century. No doubt it is his misfortune that Thackeray (1853) codifies the contrast between him and Steele that will join each to the other as the yin and yang of literary history. But the real damage is that Thackeray makes him into a Victorian prig. This is the Addison that Bonamy Dobrée critically evaluates in "The First Victorian" in *Essays in Biography* (1925) and T.S. Eliot in *The Use of Poetry and the Use of Criticism* (1933). His papers on the imagination are interpreted in the middle of the 20th century as the realization of Lockean mental processes and since then as that of "bourgeois ideology." There still is no proper analytical study of his papers on the imagination, no detailed study together of his poetry, drama, and periodical papers or of his political career and literary purposes. There is no complete collected edition of his works.

BIBLIOGRAPHY

Works by Joseph Addison

A Discourse on Ancient and Modern Learning. London, 1734; Glasgow, 1739.
The Guardian. With Richard Steele. Ed. John Calhoun Stephens. Lexington: University Press of Kentucky, 1982.
The Letters of Joseph Addison. Ed. Walter Graham. Oxford: Clarendon Press, 1941.
The Miscellaneous Works of Joseph Addison. Ed. A.C. Guthkelch. 2 vols. London: G. Bell, 1914.
The Spectator. With Richard Steele. Ed. Donald F. Bond. 5 vols. Oxford: Clarendon Press, 1965.

The Tatler. With Richard Steele. Ed. Donald. F. Bond. 3 vols. Oxford: Clarendon Press, 1987.

The Works of the Right Honourable Joseph Addison. Ed. Richard Hurd (1811). 6 vols. (Bohn) London: G. Bell, 1854–1856.

The Works of the Right Honourable Joseph Addison, Esq. Ed. Thomas Tickell. 4 vols. London, 1721.

Studies of Joseph Addison

Addison and Steele: The Critical Heritage. Ed. Edward A. Bloom and Lillian D. Bloom. London: Routledge, 1980.

Bradner, Leicester. "The Composition and Publication of Addison's Latin Poems." *Modern Philology* 35 (1938): 359–367.

Elioseff, Lee Andrew. *The Cultural Milieu of Addison's Literary Criticism*. Austin: University of Texas Press, 1963.

Ellison, Julie. "Cato's Tears." *ELH: English Literary History* 63 (1996): 571–601.

Johnson, Samuel. "Addison" (1781). In *Lives of the Poets*. Ed. G. Birkbeck Hill. 3 vols. Oxford: Clarendon Press, 1905.

Kelsall, M.M. "The Meaning of Addison's *Cato*." *Review of English Studies* n.s. 17 (1966): 149–162.

Smithers, Peter. *The Life of Joseph Addison*. 2nd ed. Oxford: Clarendon Press, 1968.

Spence, Joseph. *Observations, Anecdotes, and Characters of Books and Men* (folio ms. 1751). Ed. James M. Osborn. 2 vols. Oxford: Clarendon Press, 1966.

Tuveson, Ernest. *The Imagination as a Means of Grace*. Berkeley: University of California Press, 1960.

Walker, William. "Ideology and Addison's Essays on the Pleasures of the Imagination." *Eighteenth-Century Life* 24 (2000): 65–84.

❧ *Lancelot Andrewes*
(1555–1626)

DOUGLAS S. BRUSTER

BIOGRAPHY

Lancelot Andrewes, son of Thomas and Joan Andrewes, was born to a well-to-do merchant family in the London parish of All Hallows, Barking, in September 1555 (a more specific assignment of his birth date to September 25 has probably been influenced by the date of his death: September 25, 1626). Originally slated to follow in his father's footsteps as a merchant, Andrewes so impressed early schoolmasters that he was sent to study at the Merchant Taylors' School in London under headmaster Richard Mulcaster. Andrewes, according to later reports, toiled indefatigably at his studies there, even having to be forced to put his books aside to play with his classmates.

Awarded a Greek scholarship, Andrewes entered Pembroke College, Cambridge, in the fall of 1571. Until 1576, Andrewes would overlap at Pembroke with Edmund Spenser, who had also been a scholar with Andrewes at the Merchant Taylors' School during the 1560s. Andrewes received his B.A. in 1575 and the following year was elected fellow of Pembroke. Nominated to a fellowship at Jesus College, Oxford, he declined to reside there. The year 1580 saw Andrewes ordained deacon at Pembroke and appointed the College's junior treasurer; the next year he was made senior treasurer and incorporated Master of Arts at Jesus College. In 1585 Andrewes received his Bachelor of Divinity at Cambridge.

The following year, in 1586, Andrewes accepted a position as chaplain to Henry Hastings, third Earl of Huntingdon. Hastings was a Puritan sympathizer, as was Sir Francis Walsingham, who had admired Andrewes's abilities—on display since the late 1570s—as a lecturer and scholar. Walsingham had earlier tried to enlist Andrewes on the side of the Puritans; although unsuccessful in his attempt, he bore Andrewes no grudge and secured him a position as vicar of St. Giles, Cripplegate, in 1589. This would be a banner year for Andrewes, one in which his abilities found recognition in several official preferments. It was in 1589, for instance, that, also through Walsingham's efforts, Andrewes was made prebendary of Southwell's Collegiate Church and prebendary of St. Pancras in St. Paul's. That year, too, he was chosen master of Pembroke hall.

During the 1590s, Andrewes's talents for service, administration, scholarship, and preaching saw him advance steadily through the hierarchy of the Elizabethan church. He preached often and to acclaim at Elizabeth's court. Following her death, Andrewes also prospered as a court preacher and religious official during the reign of James. Subsequent to the Hampton Court Conference in 1604, for instance, Andrewes was chosen to lead the scholars of the Westminster Company in translating the first twelve books of the Bible for the Authorized Version. He was persuaded to accept the bishopric of Chichester in 1605, being named the king's almoner in the same year. Later, in 1609, he was made privy councilor for England and was translated to the bishopric of Ely. In 1617 he was made privy councilor for Scotland, and two years later, in 1619, he was translated to the bishopric of Winchester. He died in September 1626, having proved a superb and tireless scholar, churchman, and preacher. His devotion and abilities brought him to the attention of some of the most powerful figures of his day, including the three monarchs whom he served as chaplain; these figures' recognition of his talents allowed him to make an important contribution to the survival and success of the Anglican Church. His labors toward the Authorized Version no less than his many remarkable sermons and his private devotions have greatly enriched English literary history.

MAJOR WORKS AND THEMES

Andrewes is best remembered today for the fascinating prose of his sermons. If we neglect his other writings, however, we are left with an incomplete picture of both his output as an author and his life and interests. Andrewes's publications make us reconsider many stereotypes about religious life and politics in early modern England. From one point of view, for example, Andrewes's interest in religious beauty—his personal chapel at Ely is said to have been tastefully but sumptuously adorned—could lead one to associate him with Catholicism, which similarly stressed the role of decoration in the places and processes of devotion. But several of Andrewes's most important publications remind us of his unswerving commitments to the Anglican Church. For instance, when Cardinal Bellarmine, using the pen name Matthew Tortus, criticized King James's published apology for the oath of allegiance, James directed Andrewes to respond; Andrewes did so in his *Tortura Torti* (1609). After Bellarmine then countered using his own name, Andrewes responded once more in *Responsio ad apologiam Cardinalis Bellarmini* (1610). Each of Andrewes's controversial works was written in Latin and advocated obedience to secular authorities. Together, they added to his domestic reputation and even gathered from the international community.

Beginning in 1592, and prior to his death in 1626, over a dozen imprints brought Andrewes's sermons to the reading public. If his works of controversy—which included two posthumously published responses to Cardinal Perron—force us to see that a churchman with a Catholic aesthetic could be (and staunchly so) anti-*Roman* Catholic, his sermons likewise splinter generalizations about early modern religious life by showing us that a passionate, near-obsessive concern with the Word was not the sole province of Puritan exegetes. Andrewes, who had earned the privilege of preaching before James's court on Christmas, Easter, Whitsunday, and in Lent, wrote festival sermons remarkable not only for their centrality to the devotional life of the court but also for their spiritual, rhetorical, and literary power.

Although there is more variety in Andrewes's sermons than is sometimes alleged, a number of common themes and stylistic patterns can be noted. I have already mentioned Andrewes's interest in the Word. His duties as a translator for the Authorized Version would have squared with the concern for philology, linguistic variety, and verbal plentitude apparent throughout his sermons. Andrewes's sermons begin with the scriptural passage assigned for the day but delve into that passage to a much greater degree than the sermons of his contemporaries. Andrewes takes the verbal level of the biblical text as an absolute reservoir of the sacred work of God: each word, each phrase, reveals to us God's plan.

Andrewes's sermons are thus, among other things, accomplished instances of close reading—instances that themselves offer up condensed and gorgeous passages of English prose. In such passages Andrewes shifts frequently between high and low registers of prose, among words of English, Latin, and Greek origins, and he occasionally puns and engages in other kinds of wordplay. A representative paragraph from his Christmas sermon of 1611, for instance, focuses on Luke 2:10–11, of which the former verse reads, "*Et dixit illis Angelus: Nolite timere: ecce enim evangelizo vobis gaudium magnum, quod erit omni populo*" ("And the Angel said unto them, Fear not: for, behold, I bring you good tidings of great joy, which shall be to all people"). The paragraph in question takes up the word *vobis*, or "you":

We find not any word through all but there is joy in it, and yet all is suspended till we come to this one word, *vobis*; this makes up all. This word therefore we shall do well ever to look for, and when we find it to make much of it. Nothing passeth without it; it is the word of application. But for it, all the rest are loose; this girds it on, this fastens it to us, and makes it ours. But for it, we are but in their case, *Quid nobis et Tibi*, "What have we to do with Thee?" This "Saviour Christ the Lord," in this good time and fit place, *quid ad nos*? "what are we the better"? *Omnio populo*, is somewhat too general, and the hundredth part of them shall not be benefited by Him. We would hear it more particularly. Why *vobis*, "for you it is," born for you. Yea, now ye say somewhat.

The mixture, in this passage, of erudition and purpose, philology and rhetoric, Latin and English, quotation and analysis, question and statement, high style and low—such concentrated variety is characteristic of Andrewes's intriguing sermons, which stress the immediacy of God's will and our pressing need to remain thankful for His gifts.

Finally, no account of Andrewes's writings can afford to overlook his *Preces privatae*, or "private devotions." Andrewes appears never to have intended to publish this work, which was first printed in Oxford in 1675 and many times during the 19th century and after. Written in Latin, Greek, and Hebrew, this text consists of a series of scripts for prayer—morning prayers, evening prayers, prayers for the week, as well as prayers for specific occasions and purposes: "on entering church," "for grace," "of praise." These prayers are pieced together in a mosaiclike fashion, tessellated wholes that Andrewes assembles out of shards gathered from the whole Bible. Thus a typical prayer could have phrases from as many places in the Bible as the prayer itself has lines. Even in translation, it is a beautiful text, full of both generalized devotional language as well as references to things specific to England and even Andrewes's own life.

CRITICAL RECEPTION

Andrewes's reputation suffered an eclipse during the middle and later 17th century, when the staccato variety of his sermons gave way to simpler, more fluid periods and to a less analytical mode of composition. His place in both Church and literary history began to be restored with the publication of his works in eleven volumes from 1841 to 1872, a restoration aided by contemporaneous interest in his *Preces privatae*. Yet no one was more responsible for bringing widespread attention to Andrewes's works than T.S. Eliot, who published his famous essay of homage, "For Lancelot Andrewes," first in 1926, then in a collection of that title in 1928. In his 1927 poem "Journey of the Magi," Eliot also quoted characteristically artful lines from Andrewes's Christmas sermon of 1622. Since the 1920s, Andrewes has been known largely as a stylist to those outside the scholarly community interested in Church and religious history. His sermons have frequently been seen as representing a particularly poetic development in Renaissance prose style.

BIBLIOGRAPHY

Works by Lancelot Andrewes

The Preces privatae of Lancelot Andrewes, Bishop of Winchester. Trans. Frank Edward Brightman. London: Methuen, 1903. Reprint, New York: Living Age, 1961.
Sermons. Ed. G.M. Story. Oxford: Clarendon Press, 1967.
The Works of Lancelot Andrewes, Sometime Bishop of Winchester. Ed. J.P. Wilson and James Bliss. 11 vols. Oxford: Parker, 1841–1854. Reprint, New York: AMS Press, 1967.

Studies of Lancelot Andrewes

Higham, Florence. *Lancelot Andrewes*. London: SCM Press, 1952.
Lossky, Nicholas. *Lancelot Andrewes the Preacher (1555–1626): The Origins of the Mystical Theology of the Church of England*. Oxford: Clarendon Press, 1991.
Macleane, Douglas. *Lancelot Andrewes and the Reaction*. London: Allen, 1910.
McCullough, Peter E. "Lancelot Andrewes and Language." *Anglican Theological Review* 74 (Summer 1992): 304–316.
McCutcheon, Elizabeth. "Lancelot Andrewes' *Preces privatae*: A Journey through Time." *Studies in Philology* 65 (April 1968): 223–241.
———. "Recent Studies in Andrewes." *English Literary Renaissance* 11 (Winter 1981): 96–108.
Owen, Trevor. *Lancelot Andrewes*. Boston: G.K. Hall, 1981.
Reidy, Maurice F. *Bishop Lancelot Andrewes*. Chicago: Loyola University Press, 1955.
Webber, Joan. "Celebration of Word and World in Lancelot Andrewes' Style." In *Seventeenth-Century Prose: Modern Essays in Criticism*, ed. Stanley E. Fish. New York: Oxford University Press, 1971. 336–352.

🍂 *Mary Astell*
(1666–1731)

ERIN MURPHY

BIOGRAPHY

In 1666, Mary Astell was born in Newcastle, England, to a gentry family that had no estate. Her father was a coal merchant who died when she was twelve, leaving the family in extreme financial hardship, which may have inspired her later writings about the precarious situation of the daughters of "fallen gentry." The roots of Astell's staunch royalism grew in Newcastle, which had been a Royalist stronghold during the Civil War, putting up strong resistance before being defeated eventually by parliamentary forces. In addition to the Royalist influences of her surroundings, her mother's Catholic origins may have given rise to her relative lenience toward Catholics, as well as her support for the Jacobite cause. Though Astell was not formally educated, her uncle, Cambridge Platonist Ralph Astell, began tutoring her in French, Latin, philosophy, mathematics, logic, and the arts of poetry when she was eight years old.

Left without a significant dowry, Astell had no prospects in Newcastle and moved to London at age twenty. With no means of support, she desperately appealed to the Archbishop of Canterbury, William Sancroft, who became her first patron. Once settled in Chelsea, she became part of a community of intellectual women, who offered her stimulating conversation, access to books, and financial support.

In these circumstances, she published her first tract, *A Serious Proposal to the Ladies*, in 1694. Immediately causing a stir with her argument for women's education, Astell went on to publish a mix of Tory propaganda, religious contemplations, and philosophical inquiries. In 1709, she founded the Chelsea School for Girls, with the financial backing of her wealthy female friends, which she ran until her death from breast cancer in 1731.

MAJOR WORKS AND THEMES

Astell's first work, the 1694 *A Serious Proposal to the Ladies*, analyzed the way in which the lack of educational opportunities was a source of systematic oppression for women. As a solution, she proposed a "Religious Retirement, and as such shall have a double aspect, being not only a Retreat from the World for those who desire that advantage, but likewise, an institution and previous discipline, to fit us to do good in it." As an escape from the indignities of dancing masters and unworthy suitors, the Retirement would allow women to engage in the life of the mind, in order to advance the life of the soul. For some, the retreat would serve as a place of preparation, but for those who either did not want to marry or who lacked adequate dowries to make a favorable match, it would provide a way for them to avoid choosing between a life of indigence and an unfit marriage. Astell's call for an institution that would provide a means for adult women to live outside of the bonds of marriage may be her most revolutionary idea. In Part II of the proposal, first published in 1697, Astell extends her discussion to a full critique of Lockean (see **John Locke**) epistemology.

Astell's religious writings mirror the depth of her philosophical work. By publishing *Letters Concerning the Love of God* in 1695, John Norris made public the intellectual exchange he and Astell had begun two years earlier. In Astell's self-described "magnum opus," *The Christian Religion, as Profess'd by a Daughter of the Church of England*, published in 1705, she draws upon the recent developments in natural science to insist that reason itself demands faith in God; and in her final work, *Bart'lemy fair, or, an enquiry after wit*, she argues that issues of faith should not be subject to the crude and undisciplined marketplace.

In *Some Reflections upon Marriage*, Astell rails against the inequity of marriage, decrying the unfair subservience of women to men, but does not call for a change in marriage itself. Only if a woman chooses not to marry, like Astell herself, can she be free from the dominance of men. Astell utilizes the analogy between family and state to attack the hypocrisy of Whig claims for freedom, asking, "If all Men are born free, how is it that all Women are born slaves? as they must if the being subjected to the inconstant, uncertain, unknown arbitrary Will of Men, be the perfect Condition of Slavery?" By revealing the contradiction of emerging theories of contractual government by exposing the lack of real choice in the marriage contract, Astell strategically strikes at both those who oppose authority in a state and those who support it in a household without ever resolving the conflict in her own position.

In three political tracts, written for the Tory publisher Richard Wilkin in 1704, Astell's opinions are unmistakably Royalist. In *Moderation Truly Stated* and *A Fair Way with the Dissenters*, she enters the Occasional Conformity debate, defending the Tory policy that the English Constitution requires of its citizens conformity to the Anglican Church. In her *Impartial Enquiry into the Causes of Rebellion and Civil War in This Kingdom*, Astell draws parallels between 1641 and 1688, giving an account of the causes of the Civil War as grounds for her critique of theories of popular sovereignty.

CRITICAL RECEPTION

In her own time, Astell was admired by Royalist divines for her religious thinking, ridiculed by *The Tatler*, lauded by Lady Mary Wortley Montagu for her claims for women's education, and seriously rebutted by Lady Damaris Masham for her supposed philosophical quietism. In 1752, George Ballard included her among other "celebrated ladies" in his *Memoirs of Several Ladies of Great Britain*.

In 1916, Florence Smith wrote the first full-scale study of Astell, which still serves as the most in-depth biographical source. For decades, there was no new work on Astell, but feminist recovery projects of the 1970s and 1980s revived interest in her work on women. Perhaps because only her protofeminist texts were easily available, scholarship on Astell during the 1970s and 1980s focused on the seeming contradiction between her royalism and her arguments for the rights of women. In 1986, Ruth Perry published her invaluable biocritical study.

Patricia Springborg's editions of *A Serious Proposal to the Ladies* and Astell's *Political Writings* add to the critic's previous efforts to broaden the political and philosophical contexts of Astell studies. In similar efforts, Weil shows how Astell strategically uses marriage as a metaphor through which to argue against occasional conformity, and Hartmann argues that *Bart'lemy fair* should be read as part of a broader Tory critique of capitalism. By reconsidering how Astell participated in the early modern public sphere not only as a feminist but also as a philosopher and political pamphleteer, this recent criticism adds to our understanding of the true radicalism of the "celebrated Mary Astell."

BIBLIOGRAPHY

Works by Mary Astell

Bart'lemy fair, or, an enquiry after wit: in which due respect is had to a Letter concerning enthusiasm. London, 1709.

The Christian Religion, as Profess'd by a Daughter of the Church of England in a Letter to the Right Honourable T.L., C.I. London, 1705.

A Collection of Poems Humbly Presented and Dedicated to . . . Lord Archbishop of Canterbury. Published in full as Appendix D to Ruth Perry, *The Celebrated Mary Astell: An Early English Feminist.* Chicago: University of Chicago Press, 1986.

Letters Concerning the Love of God, between the Author of the Proposal to the Ladies and Mr. John Norris. London, 1695.

Moderation Truly Stated: Or, A Review of a Late Pamphlet, Entitul'd, Moderation a Vertue, or, The Occasional Conformist Justified from the Imputation of Hypocricy. London, 1704.

Political Writings. Ed. Patricia Springborg. Cambridge: Cambridge University Press, 1996.

A Serious Proposal to the Ladies for the Advancement of Their True and Great Interest. Parts I and II. Ed. Patricia Springborg. London: Pickering and Chatto, 1997.

Studies of Mary Astell

Ezell, Margaret J.M. "The Politics of the Past: Restoration Women Writers on Women Reading History." In *Pilgrimage for Love: Essays in Early Modern Literature in Honor of Josephine A. Roberts*, ed. Sigrid King. Tempe: Arizona Center for Medieval and Renaissance Studies, 1999. 19–40.

Gallagher, Catherine. "Embracing the Absolute: The Politics of the Female Subject in Seventeenth-Century England." *Genders* 1 (1988): 24–29.

Hartmann, Van C. "Tory Feminism in Mary Astell's *Bart'lemy Fair*." *Journal of Narrative Technique* 28.3 (1998): 243–265.

Kinnaird, Joan. "Mary Astell and the Conservative Contribution to English Feminism." *Journal of British Studies* 19 (1979): 53–79.

Perry, Ruth. *The Celebrated Mary Astell: An Early English Feminist*. Chicago: University of Chicago Press, 1986.

Smith, Florence M. *Mary Astell*. New York: Columbia University Press, 1916.

Smith, Hilda. *Reason's Disciples*. Urbana: University of Illinois Press, 1982.

Springborg, Patricia. "Astell, Masham, and Locke: Religion and Politics." In *Women Writers and the Early Modern British Political Tradition*, ed. Hilda Smith. Cambridge: Cambridge University Press, 1998. 105–125.

Weil, Rachel. *Political Passions: Gender, the Family and Political Argument in England 1680–1714*. Manchester: Manchester University Press, 1999.

John Aubrey

(1626–1697)

KEITH M. BOTELHO

BIOGRAPHY

The eldest child of Richard and Deborah Aubrey, John was born in 1626 in Wiltshire of Welsh descent. Aubrey was plagued with poor health throughout his solitary childhood, nearly dying on a few occasions, yet his powers of observation remained keen; Aubrey himself stated, "I was from childhood affected with the view of things rare." During the summer of 1634, when he was at school in Leigh Delamere under Robert Latimer, Aubrey had a chance encounter with **Thomas Hobbes**, who later became one of Aubrey's dearest friends and the subject of his biography, *Life of Mr. Thomas Hobbes of Malmesburie*.

After only three months at Trinity College as gentleman commoner, Aubrey was summoned by his father to return home due to the outbreak of the Civil War. The Aubrey family had Royalist sympathies, but Aubrey himself was not active in the war. Aubrey returned to Trinity early in 1643, where, after recovering from smallpox, the seeds of his antiquarianism began to develop. In April 1646, Aubrey was admitted as a student of the Middle Temple, but he would never practice law.

In 1649, Aubrey's archaeological interests peaked when he "discovered" Avebury while hunting with friends, later positing his theory that the "segments of rude circles" made with stones were placed there by the Druids. Richard Aubrey died in 1652, leaving John not only the farm at Broad Chalke but also financial woes and lawsuits that ultimately led to his financial ruin some twenty years later. After spending years making "antiquarian remarques" and taking notes on natural phenomena, he began his first serious literary work, the *Natural History of Wiltshire*. He spent a month in Ireland in 1660 but was unimpressed.

In 1663, Aubrey was nominated as Fellow of the Royal Society, which obtained its charter the previous year. The Society had an enormous impact on Aubrey's intellectual life, and through his membership, he met with King Charles II, who called on Aubrey to show him Avebury and later write an account of it. In 1657, Aubrey's fiancée, Katherine Ryves, died; eight years later, he was involved in a disastrous relationship with Joan Sumner that was plagued by court proceedings. Aubrey was never to marry.

Aubrey's friendship with the surly Anthony Wood began in 1667, meeting at Oxford and continuing a close working relationship for over twenty-five years. Aubrey's biographical work for Wood's compilation *Athenae Oxonienses* was to be known as his *Brief Lives*. Financial misfortunes for Aubrey continued in the 1670s. Often in danger of being arrested, he managed to continue his work on *Monumenta Britannica*. In 1677, Aubrey was forced to sell his extensive collection of books. And he considered venturing to Italy, Jamaica, and particularly Pennsylvania (William Penn offered him 600 acres), but these plans never came to fruition.

After his mother died in 1686, having lost his estates, Aubrey stayed at the homes of numerous "good friends" during his final years while beginning work on many different projects. His overriding concern for the protection of his papers led Aubrey to give his collections to the Ashmolean Museum. Aubrey's domestic trouble continued in the 1690s, but a disagreement with his companion Anthony Wood in 1692 strained their friendship forever. Aubrey felt that Wood dealt unkindly with him, particularly in the case of Wood's editing practices for his *Athenae*. A series of letters between the two, as well as bitter commentary contained in Wood's diaries, highlight the fracas—Wood emerges as an insincere individual who, as one contemporary noted, "us'd Mr. Aubrey scurvily." *Miscellanies* was published in 1695, but the effects of old age prevented Aubrey from completing or publishing any of his other work. He died in Oxford in 1697.

MAJOR WORKS AND THEMES

Aubrey is best known for his *Brief Lives*, which he notes he wrote "tumultuarily." His wide-ranging associations and his persistence in securing information helped Aubrey to gather the seeds for the *Lives*. In response to a friend's suggestion that his book was "too minute," Aubrey replied that "a hundred yeares hence that minuteness will be grateful." He produced well over 400 "biographies," ranging in length from a few words to over 20,000. His longest biographies are of Hobbes (King Charles II "was always much delighted in his witt and smart repartees"), Sir Walter Ralegh ("he was damnable proud"), and **William Harvey** ("I remember he was wont to drinke Coffee"). Women were not eliminated from Aubrey's *Lives*: of particular note are his entries on Mary Herbert, sister to Philip Sidney ("the greatest Patroness of witt and learning of any Lady in her time"), and Katherine Philips ("she assures me that she had read the Bible thorough before she was full four yeares old"). Of **Shakespeare** he notes "that when he was a boy he exercised his father's Trade, but when he kill'd a Calfe he would doe it in a high style, and make a Speech." Aubrey's "tapestry of lives" is unparalleled in its merging of fact and anecdote.

Aubrey was influenced by the writings of **Bacon** and **Burton**, as well as **Thomas Browne**'s *Religio Medici*, which he credited with opening his understanding. *Miscellanies* was Aubrey's only work to be published during his lifetime (1695). In his preface, Aubrey comments that " 'tis strange that Hermetick Philosophy hath lain so long untoucht. It is a Subject worthy of serious Consideration." The *Miscellanies* contain fascinating chapters on the occult, including "Omens," "Knockings," and

"Transportation by an Invisible Power," and he intersperses historical accounts of occult phenomenon with personal recollections: for instance, in the chapter "Ostenta, or Portents," Aubrey tells of the phenomenon of a reversed rainbow that appeared at Broad Chalke. Aubrey's accounts (and the ones he quotes and comments upon) are often remarkable reads, filled with coincidence, biography, and historical detail.

An Idea of the Education of a Young Gentleman, the work Aubrey most valued, is his contribution to 17th-century theories on education reform. His liberal curriculum included drawing, studying the Classics, chemistry, mathematics, and even dancing. Aubrey noted that "Schoole should be indeed the house of play and pleasure."

The *Natural History of Wiltshire* has a rambling quality but is filled with agricultural and architectural insights, as well as a history of clothing and clothiers of Wilts. In *A Perambulation of the County of Surrey*, composed in 1673 upon appointment of John Ogilby to survey the county, Aubrey transcribed memorial tablets in parish churches and investigated the intricacies of the county's homes, all the while infusing the work with enlightening personal commentary. *Monumenta Britannica* contains sections on Avebury, Stonehenge, the Druids, Roman towns and walls, and monuments and roads.

There remains a fragment of an unfinished rustic drama Aubrey composed called *The Country Revell*, a precursor to Restoration comedy. His characters include Exceptious Quarrellsome and Sir Surly Chagrin; Aubrey noted that the play is "very satyricall against some of my mischievous enemies."

In his preface to *Remaines of Gentilisme and Judaisme*, Aubrey states that " 'tis a pleasure to consider the Errours that enveloped former ages." The work, containing contributions from his contemporaries, includes excerpts from Classical and modern authors that detail various customs and superstitions. Although not as engaging as the *Miscellanies*, the final chapter of the *Remaines*, "Varia," deserves closer examination for its encyclopedic notes on everything from chimneys to violins to scarecrows.

CRITICAL RECEPTION

"Aubrey tells us . . .": Unfortunately, this is the only way many have come to know the figure John Aubrey. Nonetheless, along with Izaak Walton, Aubrey is often considered the first of England's serious biographers. Modern opinions of Aubrey as unstable and unfocused stem from remarks by his circle of acquaintances; his friend Ralph Sheldon, for example, wrote in 1679 that Aubrey's "head is so full that it will not give his tongue leave to utter one word after another," while John Toland noted that Aubrey was an honest man who was extremely superstitious.

In the century after Aubrey's death, he was generally received as a credulous man who favored superstition—in an age where reason and order flourished, it is no wonder that Aubrey's reputation diminished. Romanticism brought about a new interest in Aubrey's antiquarianism and in his writings of the occult; Lord Byron even quoted from Aubrey's *Miscellanies*. Britton's 1845 biography of Aubrey continued to make an unfavorable case of Aubrey because of his credulity. Richard Garnett's 1885 entry in the *Dictionary of National Biography* notes that Aubrey is "devoid of literary talent, except as a retailer of anecdotes. . . . As a gossip, however, he is a kind of immature Boswell" (716–717). John Buchanan-Brown notes the decline of Aubrey's reputation in the 18th century, for the 1721 republication of *Miscellanies* was aimed at a different readership from Aubrey's intended audience of learned circles (373). Powell agrees with this sentiment, noting that the 18th century remembered Aubrey as "a whimsical amateur of astrology, an amusing if somewhat unreliable gossip," a fact attested to by Samuel Johnson's less than favorable remarks about him.

John Collier, in his 1931 edition of Aubrey, states that Aubrey's name "is now famous," a curious yet flawed statement. Powell states that Aubrey's words are "often half-humorously written, like a remark made in passing conversation" (66). Edmund Wilson, in his foreword to Dick's 1957 edition, calls Aubrey's *Brief Lives* a "source book for historians," and he asserts that one can see a great deal of the 17th century through Aubrey because of his myriad interests and associations.

Oliver Lawson Dick's lengthy essay "The Life and Times of John Aubrey," preceding his edited edition of *Brief Lives*, asserts that Aubrey "had the rare gift of creating, and not just recording, life" (cv). Dick notes that Aubrey was much more of an antiquary than a scientist, and he asserts that Aubrey did not believe everything that he discovered or was told (lviii, lix). I would agree with Dick that Aubrey's talents have been misunderstood, for although he was inaccurate at times, he was not untruthful (c). The trivial details he included in all of his work, much maligned by many of his contemporaries, comprise today some of the most keen (and entertaining) insights into the 17th century.

Michael Hunter attempts to uncover Aubrey's serious contribution to learning, despite Aubrey's numerous discussions of the occult, and he reveals that Aubrey was respected for his intellectual talents by his distinguished acquaintances. He notes that the often inconsistent Aubrey was too busy to arrange the vast amounts of information he collected, yet Aubrey contributed to England's present with his thorough examination of the past.

Aubrey was more of a compiler than a biographer, more a man with roving intellectual interests than a scholar by today's standards—by his own account, his "head was alwaies working; never idle." I would argue that Aubrey's reputation needs to be reconsidered once again as we move into the 21st century, not for his associations or role as biographer but rather as an important contributor to modern science, education, and archaeology (interestingly, the depressions in the ground at Stonehenge that Aubrey surveyed are now known as "Aubrey Holes"). Aubrey called himself the "whetstone against which others sharpened their wits." Aubrey was not just concerned with the past, as Powell argues, but was rather a man poised to compile information so others could make use of it in the present for the benefit of the future.

BIBLIOGRAPHY

Works by John Aubrey

Aubrey's Brief Lives. Ed. Oliver Lawson Dick. Ann Arbor: University of Michigan Press, 1957.
Brief Lives. Ed. Andrew Clark. 2 vols. Oxford, 1898.
Brief Lives and Other Selected Writings. Ed. Anthony Powell. New York: Charles Scribner's Sons, 1949.
Monumenta Britannica: or a Miscellanie of British Antiquities. Ed. John Fowles et al. 2 vols. Sherborne: Dorset Publications, 1980–1982.
Three Prose Works: Miscellanies, Remains of Gentilisme and Judaisme, Observations. Ed. John Buchanan-Brown. Carbondale: Southern Illinois University Press, 1972.

Studies of John Aubrey

Bennett, Kate. "Editing Aubrey." In *Ma(r)king the Text: The Presentation of* Meaning *on the Literary Page*, ed. Joe Bray, Miriam Handley, and Anne Henry. Aldershot, England: Ashgate, 2000. 271–290.

Britton, John. *Memoir of John Aubrey*. London: Wiltshire Archaeological Society, 1845.

Collier, John, ed. *The Scandal and Credulities of John Aubrey*. Ed. John Collier. London: Peter Davies, 1931.

Garnett, Richard. "John Aubrey." In *The Dictionary of National Biography*, ed. Leslie Stephens and Sidney Lee. Oxford: Oxford University Press, 1960. 716–717.

Hunter, Michael. *John Aubrey and the Realm of Learning*. New York: Science History Publications, 1975.

Pinto, Vivian de Sola. *English Biography in the Seventeenth Century*. London: George G. Harrap & Co. Ltd., 1951.

Powell, Anthony. *John Aubrey and His Friends*. London: Heinemann, 1963.

Tylden-Wright, David. *John Aubrey: A Life*. London: HarperCollins, 1991.

?❧ *Francis Bacon*
(1561–1626)

JULIE ROBIN SOLOMON

BIOGRAPHY

Francis Bacon was a Renaissance Englishman of many parts; he served his turn as lawyer, judge, political theorist, statesman, natural philosopher, essayist, historian, rhetorician, and utopianist. He was eminent, however, not only in his ability to forecast the role that empirical science and technology would play in modern European society; he could also conceive a nascent scientific methodology and comprehend the politics and placement of its working institution within the framework of an English monarchy increasingly intertwined with the contributions, needs, and oscillations of mercantile capitalism. The youngest son of Queen Elizabeth's Lord Keeper, Sir Nicholas Bacon, Francis was born with great political prospects. Nicholas Bacon, a well-respected jurist, served Queen Elizabeth alongside his brother-in-law, Sir William Cecil, Elizabeth's Lord Treasurer and principal minister. Francis's mother, Anne Cooke, was Nicholas's second wife. She was the daughter of Sir Anthony Cooke who tutored Edward VI and sister of Cecil's wife Mildred. Both sisters were capable in Greek, Latin, French, and Italian. Anne was a Puritan, to whom Theodore Beza, Calvin's successor in Geneva, dedicated his *Meditations*. Diligently and frequently, she chastised her sons, Anthony and Francis, for neglecting their prayers. While Sir Nicholas Bacon was an architect and defender of Elizabeth's moderate Anglicanism, Lady Bacon directed her sons, with little success, toward a rabid Calvinism.

Following in his father's footsteps, Francis, age twelve, attended Cambridge, where, according to his chaplain and first biographer, Dr. William Rawley, he first came to dislike Aristotelian philosophy in its scholastic form. In 1576, after two and a half years at the university, he was admitted to the study of law at Gray's Inn in London. Later in the same year, he interrupted his legal studies to accompany Sir Amias Paulet on a diplomatic mission to France. Bacon was recalled home after three years' residence in France because of his father's sudden death. Unfortunately, Sir Nicholas had not yet made adequate financial provisions for his youngest son at the time of his death. Francis Bacon continued his legal studies, eventually becoming a bencher at Gray's Inn in 1586. But in addition, the precocious child (whom Queen Elizabeth reportedly dubbed "my little Lord Keeper"), the budding lawyer, and the man who at age thirty-one still wished "all knowledge to be my province" would now struggle to gain political office and titles in order to support himself in the manner to which he had become accustomed. Unfortunately for Francis, his uncle, Lord Burghley, was too taken up with the future of his own son, Robert Cecil, to assist his orphaned nephew substantially.

As an Elizabethan adult, Francis Bacon became a member of Parliament (1584) but also much expended intellectual and emotional capital in efforts to secure the position of solicitor-general. To that and other ends, his elder brother Anthony, who was in clandestine service overseas for Robert Devereux, Earl of Essex, helped enlist Francis as one of the Earl's political counselors. The younger Bacon wrote letters of advice to the ambitious Earl, at times cautioning him against giving full rein to intemperate and brazen efforts to hold sway over Queen Elizabeth. In recompense, Devereux tried to persuade the Queen to appoint Bacon to the newly vacated position of solicitor-general, but she refused, partly on the grounds of Bacon's political and administrative inexperience and possibly because of her displeasure at his speaking out in Parliament against a financial scheme that she advocated. During the Queen's life, Bacon attained the ancillary post of Learned Counsel Extraordinary and the dubious honor of prosecuting his recalcitrant ex-patron, the Earl of Essex, for his treasonous uprising in 1602. Numerous biographers have vilified Bacon as an ingrate and opportunist for this prosecution.

James I's ascension to the English monarchy in 1603 marked a decided turn in Bacon's political fortunes. He was soon knighted and appointed to the position of King's Counsel. In 1607 he garnered the Solicitor Generalship, was subsequently made Attorney General (1613), a member of the Privy Council (1616), and Lord Keeper (1617). In 1618, he was created Baron Verulam and surpassed his father's position by becoming Lord Chancellor of England. From 1604 until 1621, when the Parliament, in lieu of a direct attack on James I, impeached him for bribery, Bacon was a pivotal adviser to the King in his relationship to Parliament and the judiciary, in the King's hopes for the political union of England and Scotland, on religious questions, foreign policy, and royal finances. During the same period, as Chief Justice of the Chancery Court, he wrote important judicial decisions and advocated the reordering and reform of English law; continuously revised and added to his "Essays"; and wrote extensively to James and the public about his programmatic plans for natural philosophy. His *Advancement of Learning* appeared in 1605; his natural philosophic reinterpretation of Greek mythology, *De Sapientia Veterum*, in 1609; the *Novum Organum* in 1620; and his *Historia Ventorum* in 1622. Barred from the verge of the court and the politics for the last five years of his life, Bacon devoted his final years to scientific writing and experiments. His death in 1626 was from pneumonia, reportedly contracted after a foray into winter snows with a chicken carcass to conduct an experiment in refrigeration. Although Bacon married Alice Barnham in 1606, he never had children, presumably preferring to leave his books, rather than his blood, to posterity.

MAJOR WORKS AND THEMES

Bacon's books reveal a mind, gifted with analytic and synthetic facility, that has achieved a fundamental and incisive grasp of the most significant intellectual, social, and political issues of early modernism. Bacon's genius was to formulate a *distinct*, *detailed*, and *conceivable* natural philosophic program out of this rich intellectual brew. Baconian natural philosophy was distinct in understanding its epistemic relation to, and difference from, other competing views; detailed in articulating its working principles and protocols; and politically conceivable insofar as Bacon created his program to be institutionalized under the auspices of a royal government that was increasingly dependent upon technological and commercial developments often beyond its direct control. In *The Advancement of Learning*, Bacon took the measure of the contemporary intellectual scene to pave the way for his distinct contribution to natural philosophy. What he saw was a European intellectual culture in ferment. In some quarters scholastic Aristotelianism had lost preeminence and urgency, giving way to the rhetorical, ethical, and historical foci of humanism. In others, it was challenged by newly popular varieties of Neoplatonism devised by the likes of Marsilio Ficino, Theophrastus Paracelsus, Raymond Lull, and Giordano Bruno, among others. For some, the erosion of a comprehensive and coherent Aristotelianism led to the revival of ancient scepticism, or a fervent belief in the inability to know truly. For others, the protomaterialism of the ancient atomists or the early modern empiricism of Bernardo Telesio held sway. Cognizant of all of these developments, Bacon was also sensitive to the important ways in which artisanal and mercantile cultures promoted technological discovery and invention (witness the compass, the printing press, the silkworm) and pioneered new epistemological stances and attitudes.

In his analysis, Bacon both articulated and cast the weaknesses of each philosophy or development in order to retrieve and incorporate its strengths into his own philosophical program. Rejecting the fossilized and book-driven terminology of Aristotelian natural philosophy with its four causes and elements, Bacon retained an Aristotelian inclination to systemic and foundational thinking and sought to revitalize Aristotelian induction. Although he found humanism limited in its capacity to promote scientific learning, he understood the value of its revival of rhetoric, mastered its stylistic grace, practiced its historical sensibility, and engaged with its ethical issues. He adopted the Neoplatonic belief in the human capacity to cognize and benefit from matter, the lowest gradient emanating from the divine one; yet he repudiated its hypothetical generalizations and a large part (if not all) of its exclusive secrecy. He also—in contradistinction to Neoplatonism—drew a clear distinction between religious faith and natural philosophy, relegating each to its own domain. Bacon respected Telesio's separation of natural philosophy from theology and his advocacy of induction, but he deplored his failure to delineate its actual procedures. Rejecting the pessimism inherent in scepticism, he nonetheless cautioned against uncritical belief in untried hypotheses. Initially attracted to the materialist aspect of ancient atomism, he eventually spurned the metaphysical character of Democritus, opting to view matter instead as a particulate mass whose changing configuration accounted for the kinds of material entities. Finally, Bacon drew solace from the fact that a burgeoning manufacturing and commercial culture had spurred on new discoveries and inventions, as well as an openness to new knowledge, while disparaging the unsystematic, hit-or-miss character of its operations.

Having surveyed this multifaceted intellectual field, Bacon constructed a description—detailed for its era—of his natural philosophic project. Natural philosophy, according to Bacon, had to begin with empirical observation and the painstaking compilation of natural histories. Inductive inquiry and the noting of particulars would be followed by controlled experiments—under natural and artificial conditions—that would yield first-level axioms or generalizations. These in turn would be corrected and refined by further inductive inquiry and experimentation until higher-level axioms—true scientific knowledge—which were capable of producing useful material effects (medical, technological, or other), were attained. Bacon offered his readers rules of thumb—"Prerogative Instances"—and other directives toward the better evaluation of natural philosophic data. To ensure the validity of inductive and experimental findings, the Lord Chancellor required the natural philosopher to recognize and restrain in himself certain ways that the mind naturally and historically had come to process and construct knowledge. These four propensities, or "Idols," included the habit of allowing peculiarities of nature and nurture to distort perception and cognition ("Idols of the Cave"); the habit of injudiciously jumping to conclusions and finding more regularity in nature than actually exists ("Idols of the Tribe"); the "Idols of the Marketplace," or our susceptibility to being deceived and confused by confusing language or terminology; and the "Idols of the Theater," or our tendency to put trust in unproven philosophies and theories. Bacon's intent was not to eradicate human desires and habits. Rather, he sought to delay their incursions into the formulation of scientific knowledge long enough so as to introduce us to new conceptual realms of possibility—or to paraphrase Bacon's own words, to teach a man even what to wish.

While this new scientific philosophy was to expand our powers of intellectual conception, Bacon also took steps to ensure that his program was politically conceivable. His new scientific method was designed to fit within the institutional framework of a Jacobean monarchy purportedly interested in mutually beneficial relations with commercial and artisanal sectors. Bacon imagined the scientific enterprise as a grand public works project that would enlist the energies and ideas of large and ambitious sectors of the society but would nonetheless remain under the auspices of royal government. Working, in Bacon's words, "as if by machinery," the new philosophy's institutional genius would be to reconcile private intellectual ambitions with public interests to the benefit of each. At the same time that Bacon sought James I's patronage for his royal scientific enterprise, he incorporated into his methodology commercial and artisanal modes of thinking, working, and profiting: emphasizing the importance of observation, practical application, and a willingness to temporarily suspend narrow and parochial interests for the sake of larger, future gains. Bacon's science was truly, to use **William Harvey**'s reported phrase, the "Philosophy of a [bureaucratically savvy] Lord Chancellor."

CRITICAL RECEPTION

Francis Bacon never gained financial or political support for his scientific program during his lifetime. James I remained respectfully indifferent to his Lord Chancellor's natural philosophic proposals, and Bacon did not seriously enlist support from other sectors of his society. As early as the 1620s Bacon's importance was understood by Gassendi, Mersenne, and Descartes in France and by Constantijn Huygens and Isaac Beekman in the Netherlands. Intellectual historians, however, have long noted that Bacon's philosophic influence in England was negligible during the first third of the 17th century. By mid-century, however, Bacon's works were increasingly recognized, valued, and republished. The Protestant educational reformists who gathered around Samuel Hartlib in the 1640s took their inspiration in equal measure from Comenius and Bacon. John Wilkins, Samuel Ward, and **John Webster**, among others, followed Bacon in attempting to devise a "real character" or accurate scientific language. Bacon's separation of religious matters from natural philosophic inquiry appealed to Puritan thinkers. Parliamentary opponents of Charles I, including John Pym, admired Bacon's *Novum Organum*. Arguably, the Lord Chancellor's greatest influence was on the early members of England's Royal Society (established 1662). These members, including Walter Charleton, **Abraham Cowley**, **Robert Boyle**, John Evelyn, Joseph Glanville, Robert Hooke, Thomas Sprat, and John Wilkins, viewed Bacon as their intellectual progenitor whose prophetic ideas they hoped to fulfill. Bacon's star rose high into the 18th century but was clouded somewhat in the 19th, when biographers charged him with perfidy in prosecuting his former patron, the Earl of Essex, for treason. Additionally, the growing importance of mathematics brought more reverence for Descartes's early scientific contributions. Nonetheless, the upsurge in published studies of Bacon's life and work at the turn of the 21st century makes evident his continuing role as a seminal figure in the history of early modern science and its institutions.

BIBLIOGRAPHY

Works by Francis Bacon

Advertisement Touching an Holy War. London, 1629.

Certaine Considerations Touching the Better Pacification, and Edification of the Church of England. London, 1604.

De Dignitate et Augmentis Scientiarum. London, 1623.

The Elements of the Common Lawes of England. London, 1630.

The Essayes or Counsels, Civill and Morall. London, 1625. Ed. and intro. Michael Kiernan. Oxford: Clarendon Press, 1985.

Historia Ventorum. London, 1622.

The Historie of the Raigne of King Henry the Seventh. London, 1622.

The Letters and Life of Francis Bacon, Including All of His Occasional Works. Ed. James Spedding. 7 vols. London, 1890.

The New Atlantis. London, 1627.

Novum Organum. London, 1620.

Of the Proficience and Advancement of Learning Divine and Humane. London, 1605. Reprint, *The Advancement of Learning*. Ed. and intro. Michael Kiernan. Oxford: Clarendon Press, 2000.

The Philosophy of Francis Bacon. Trans. and ed. Benjamin Farrington. Liverpool: Liverpool University Press, 1964.

De Sapientia Veterum. London, 1609.

Sylva Sylvarum; or, A Naturall Historie. London, 1627.

The Wisdome of the Ancients. Trans. A. Gorges. London, 1619.

The Works of Francis Bacon. Ed. J. Spedding, R.L. Ellis, and D.D. Heath. 14 vols. London: Longman, 1857–1874.

Studies of Francis Bacon

Anderson, Fulton H. *Francis Bacon: His Career and His Thought*. 1962. Reprint, Los Angeles: University of Southern California Press, 1978.

Bowen, Catherine Drinker. *Francis Bacon: The Temper of a Man*. 1963. Reissue, Boston: Little, Brown, 1993.

Briggs, John. *Francis Bacon and the Rhetoric of Nature*. Cambridge: Harvard University Press, 1989.

Coquillette, Daniel. *Francis Bacon*. Stanford, CA: Stanford University Press, 1992.

Epstein, Joel J. *Francis Bacon: A Political Biography*. Athens: Ohio University Press, 1977.

Farrington, Benjamin. *Francis Bacon: Philosopher of Industrial Science*. 1949. Reprint, New York: H. Schuman, 1979.

Hill, Christopher. *The Intellectual Origins of the English Revolution*. Oxford: Clarendon Press, 1965.

Jardine, Lisa. *Francis Bacon and the Art of Discourse*. London: Cambridge University Press, 1974.

Jardine, Lisa, and Alan Stewart. *Hostage to Fortune*. New York: Hill and Wang, 1999.

Jones, Richard Foster. *Ancients and Moderns*. 2nd ed. St. Louis: Washington University Press, 1961.

Martin, Julian. *Francis Bacon: The State and the Reform of Natural Philosophy*. Cambridge: Cambridge University Press, 1992.

Mathews, Nieves. *Francis Bacon: The History of a Character Assassination*. New Haven, CT: Yale University Press, 1996.

Perez-Ramos, Antonio. *Francis Bacon's Idea of Science and the Maker's Knowledge Tradition*. Oxford: Clarendon Press, 1988.

Rossi, Paulo. *Francis Bacon: From Magic to Science*. Trans. Sacha Rabinovitch. Chicago: University of Chicago Press, 1968.

Sessions, William, ed. *Francis Bacon's Legacy of Texts*. New York: AMS Press, 1990.

Solomon, Julie Robin. *Objectivity in the Making: Francis Bacon and the Politics of Inquiry*. Baltimore: Johns Hopkins University Press, 1998.

Stephens, James. *Francis Bacon and the Style of Science*. Chicago: University of Chicago Press, 1975.

Urbach, Peter. *Francis Bacon's Philosophy of Science: An Account and Reappraisal*. La Salle, IL: Open Court, 1987.

Wallace, Karl R. *Francis Bacon on Communication & Rhetoric; or, The Art of Applying Reason to Imagination for the Better Moving of the Will*. Chapel Hill: University of North Carolina Press, 1943.

Webster, Charles. *The Great Instauration: Science, Medicine and Reform 1626–1660*. New York: Holmes & Meier, 1976.

Weinberger, Jerry. *Science, Faith, and Politics: Francis Bacon and the Utopian Roots of the Modern Age: A Commentary on Bacon's Advancement of Learning*. Ithaca, NY: Cornell University Press, 1985.

Whitney, Charles. *Francis Bacon and Modernity*. New Haven, CT: Yale University Press, 1986.

Wormald, B.H.G. *Francis Bacon: History, Politics, and Science, 1561–1626*. Cambridge: Cambridge University Press, 1993.

Zagorin, Perez. *Francis Bacon*. Princeton: Princeton University Press, 1998.

ɜ❧ *Aphra Behn*
(1640?–1689)

D. SUSAN KENDRICK

BIOGRAPHY

Few details exist about the life of Aphra Behn, "playwright, poet, fictionist, propagandist, and spy," as she is described by biographer Janet Todd (*Life*). Most of the information about her is highly conjectural. The first recognized professional woman writer in English, Behn was popular during her career, and her plays and poems represented the Restoration ideals of political expediency and sexual frankness. Some sources claim that she was Aphra Johnson, a baker's daughter, whereas others claim that her apparent education and access to high-ranking officials in the court of Charles II may indicate a higher-class status. Even her religion is undetermined; she disapproved of religious conflict and wrote approvingly of Roman Catholicism but is buried in the Anglican Westminster Abbey.

Some facts do exist, but details are scarce. Her presence in the West Indies and her espionage in Antwerp for the Crown have been documented. When Lord Willoughby was granted royal permission to explore Surinam in 1663, Behn may have traveled there with her father, the "Lieutenant-General" of the islands. Apparently he died on the voyage, but Behn stayed in the colony. Her prose work *Oroonoko, or, The Royal Slave* describes characters that were historical figures, like William Byam (Lord Willoughby's deputy), John Treffry, and George Marten. Byam, using names from the French romance *L'Astrée* to refer to his subjects, called Aphra Behn "Astrea," a name she used for the rest of her life; the register of Westminster Abbey records the name "Astrea" rather than "Aphra."

After Surinam, she may have visited Virginia, which provided inspiration for her play *The Widow Ranter*. Published posthumously, this was the first English drama to be set in the American colonies. After her return to England she may have married, or "Mr. Behn" is a fiction concocted to ensure respectability. In 1666, she was recruited for espionage in Antwerp on the recommendation of Thomas Killigrew, the manager of the King's Company of players. She was not reimbursed for her service despite repeated requests for financial assistance and had to borrow money to return to England. In 1668, she appealed directly to Charles II when she could not pay the debts incurred in his service and may have been imprisoned for debt. She was able to leave prison, but it is not known how her debts were cleared.

She arrived on the literary scene in 1670, to a changed English theater; a royal decree of 1662 replaced boys with actresses for women's roles, and women were also part of the audience. Todd comments that "the arrival of actresses greatly affected the presentation of female characters, since the body of the woman on stage was heavily sexualized." Criticized for bawdiness, Behn commented in her address to the reader in *Sir Patient Fancy* (1678) that she wrote as men did because she wrote for a living, and wit was ungendered. Behn was not the first woman writing for the theater: Katherine Philips ("the matchless Orinda"), Frances Boothby, and Elizabeth Powhele 'had produced plays—but no more than one or two.

Though early in her career she claimed the right to write for a living, in the prologue to *The Lucky Chance* she declared her wish to be known as a writer of talent: "all I ask, is the privilege for my masculine part, the poet in me . . . to tread in those successful paths my predecessors have long thrived in. . . . I value fame as much as if I had been born a hero."

MAJOR WORKS AND THEMES

Behn's first play, a tragicomedy titled *The Forced Marriage*, was successful, and she wrote prolifically. *The Dutch Lover* (1673) was not well received, and she may have written anonymously until 1676, with the successful tragedy *Abdelazar*. She followed it with comedies that followed the popular taste of fast-paced and bawdy plays. Todd comments that many of these comedies, like *The Roundheads* (1681), were staunchly Royalist and pro-Stuart, attacking Whigs as well as Puritans. Behn's most popular play was *The Rover* (1677), performed before Charles II. She published *Poems on Several Occasions* in 1684, which "investigate the sexual relations between men and women in a pastoral setting." She wrote pindarics, "On the Death of Charles II," "On Desire," "To the Reverend Doctor Burnet," and others. The 1680s produced some of her most "erotic and complex writing": *Love Letters between a Nobleman and His Sister*, for example. Her later works, like *The Widow Ranter* and *Oroonoko*, emphasize political pragmatism, and the character Miranda from *The Fair Jilt* (1688) lives happily after committing crimes with impunity. In her later works, any setting could be a stage for drama—the court, the church, even the gallows.

CRITICAL RECEPTION

Writers turning away from the scandalous Restoration launched attacks on proRoyalists like Behn. Her pro-Stuart policies, combined with her gender and frank expression of sexuality, made her the target of many male writers. Attacked in print during her life, she withstood accusations of plagiarism and prostitution. After 1683, she concentrated on producing novels, poems, translations, and pindarics and, though reduced to poverty and illness, continued to write. After her death in 1689, her work was ignored in favor of texts that followed the ideals of feminine modesty acceptable to 18th- and 19th-century readers. As Janet Todd comments in *The Secret Life of Aphra Behn*:

It would be a long time before a woman would be free to ignore or criticize marriage and motherhood. Or indeed to find death grotesque and funny. Or to display state power and domination as openly erotic. Or to hate commerce and the feckless poor. Or to delight in and mock sex. Or to openly pursue pleasure and ease.

Behn's literary resurrection had to wait until 1915, with Montague Summers's incomplete collection of her work and Virginia Woolf's praise from *A Room of One's Own*: "All women together ought to let flowers fall upon the tomb of Aphra Behn, for it was she who earned them the right to speak their minds."

BIBLIOGRAPHY

Works by Aphra Behn

The Works of Aphra Behn. Ed. Montague Summers. 1915. New York: B. Blom, 1967.

Studies of Aphra Behn

Bernbaum, Ernest. "Mrs. Behn's *Oroonoko*." In *George Lyman Kittredge Papers*. Boston, 1913. 419–435.

Day, R.A. "Aphra Behn's First Biographer." *Studies in Bibliography* 22 (1969): 227–240.

Dhuicq, Bernard. "Further Evidence on Aphra Behn's Stay in Surinam." *Notes and Queries* 6 (December 1979): 524–526.

Duchovnay, G. "Aphra Behn's Religion." *Notes and Queries* 221 (May–June 1976): 235–237.

Duffy, Maureen. *The Passionate Shepherdess: Aphra Behn 1640–1689*. London, 1977. Rev. ed., New York: Morrow/Avon, 1989.

Ezell, Margaret. *The Patriarch's Wife: Literary Evidence and the History of the Family*. Chapel Hill: University of North Carolina Press, 1987.

Ferguson, Margaret. "Juggling the Categories of Race, Class, and Gender: Aphra Behn's *Oroonoko*." *Women's Studies* 19 (1991): 159–181.

Fraser, Antonia. *The Weaker Vessel*. New York: Knopf, 1984.

Gallagher, Catherine. "Embracing the Absolute: The Politics of the Female Subject in Seventeenth-Century England." *Genders* 1 (1988): 24–39.

Goreau, Angeline. *Reconstructing Aphra: A Social Biography of Aphra Behn*. New York: Dial Press, 1980.

Greer, Germaine, Susan Hastings, Jeslyn Medoff, and Melinda Samson, eds. *Kissing the Rod: An Anthology of 17th Century Women's Verse*. London: Virago Press, 1988.

Guffey, George. "Aphra Behn's *Oroonoko*: Occasion and Accomplishment." In *Two English Novelists*. By George Guffey and Andrew Wright. Los Angeles: UCLA William Andrews Clark Memorial Library, 1975.

Hobby, Elaine. *Virtue of Necessity: English Women's Writing, 1649–88*. London: Virago Press, 1988.

Hopkins, Paul. "Aphra Behn and John Hoyle: A Contemporary Mention, and Sir Charles Sedley's Poem on His Death." *Notes and Queries* 239 (June 1994): 176–185.

Huttner, Heidi, ed. *Rereading Aphra Behn: History, Theory, and Criticism*. Charlottesville: University of Virginia Press, 1993.

Jones, Jane. "New Light on the Background and Early Life of Aphra Behn." *Notes and Queries*. Reprinted in Janet Todd, ed., *Aphra Behn Studies*. Cambridge: Cambridge University Press, 1996.

Mendelson, Sara Heller. *The Mental World of Stuart Women, Three Studies*. Amherst: University of Massachusetts Press, 1987.

Mermin, Dorothy. "Women Becoming Poets: Katherine Philips, Aphra Behn, Anne Finch." *English Literary History* 57 (1990): 335–355.

O'Donnell, Mary Ann. *Aphra Behn: An Annotated Bibliography of Primary and Secondary Sources*. New York: Garland Press, 1986.

Payne, Deborah C. " 'And poets shall by patron-princes live': Aphra Behn and Patronage." In *Curtain Calls: British and American Women Writers and the Theater, 1660–1820*, ed. Mary Anne Schofield and Cecilia Macheski. Athens: Ohio University Press, 1991.

Pearson, Jacqueline. *The Prostituted Muse: Images of Women and Women Dramatists 1642–1737*. New York: St. Martin's Press, 1988.

Rogers, Katherine M. "Fact and Fiction in Aphra Behn's *Oroonoko*." *Studies in the Novel* 20 (1988): 1–15.

Sharpe, K., and Steven M. Zwicker, eds. *Politics and Discourse: The Literature and History of Seventeenth-Century England*. Berkeley and Los Angeles: University of California Press, 1987.

Todd, Janet M. *The Secret Life of Aphra Behn*. New Brunswick, NJ: Rutgers University Press, 1996.

———, ed. *The Works of Aphra Behn*. Columbus: Ohio State University Press, 1992–1993.

Wiseman, S.J. *Aphra Behn*. Plymouth: Northcote House, in association with The British Council, 1996.

Woolf, Virginia. *A Room of One's Own*. Harmondsworth: Shakespeare Head Press/Basil Blackwell, 1992.

🎜 *John Blow*

(1649–1708)

THOMAS HOWARD CROFTS III

BIOGRAPHY

John Blow was born at Newark-on-Trent, Nottinghamshire, probably two or three days before his baptism on February 13, 1649. His parents, Henry Blow and Katherine Langworth (a widow), were married on August 20, 1646. John had two siblings, Henrie (baptized May 5, 1647) and Katherine (baptized May 8, 1641). That he died in 1655 without leaving a will is all that is known of Blow's father; nothing of his mother's first marriage is known. Harold Shaw supposes, since the father had no will and is not mentioned in any other wills of the period and locality, that "John Blow's parents and all his near relatives were quite poor people" (*Doctor of Music*).

Nothing certain is known of Blow's early musical education, which must have taken place during the Cromwell's Protectorate. Shaw's educated guess places the young Blow at the Magnus Song School in Newark (founded 1529). At the Restoration, Blow became a chorister at the Chapel Royal (1660) and must have sung at Charles's coronation (April 23, 1661). As a royal chorister Blow received musical instruction from Henry Cooke, Master of the Children of the Chapel Royal, and Christopher Gibbons. The ordinary curriculum included instruction in violin, organ, lute, and harpsichord, as well as in Latin and writing.

The texts of three anthems of Blow's own composition (though the music does not survive) were published in Clifford's *Divine Services and Anthems* (1663). The titles are "I will magnify," "Lord, thou hast been our refuge," and "Lord, rebuke me not." A fourth composition, "I will always give thanks," which was a collaboration between Blow and his fellow students Pelham Humphrey and Turner, also dates from the chorister period. Blow's voice broke in 1664, ending his choir service, but, as was customary, Cooke was allotted a sum of £30 per annum for Blow's continued maintenance.

His first professional appointment was to Westminster Abbey as organist in 1668 (a post he held until 1679). In the following year he was also made "one of his

Majesty's musicians for the virginalls." Thereafter, he continued to accumulate offices, including Gentleman of the Chapel Royal in 1673 and, in 1674, Master of the Children of the Chapel Royal, a post suddenly left vacant by the death in that year of Blow's old choir mate Pelham Humphrey. Blow also succeeded Humphrey as "Composer in his Majesty's private musick for voyces in ordinary." Sometime between October 1676 and December 1677, Blow was also made organist of the Chapel Royal. In 1679 Blow vacated his post as organist at Westminster Abbey, apparently in favor of **Henry Purcell**, who succeeded him; he resumed the post at Purcell's death in 1695.

Blow remained Master of the Children of the Chapel Royal for the remainder of his life, training several generations of choristers. Among his students were William Croft, Jeremiah Clarke, Daniel Purcell, Daniel Roseingrave, and Bernard Gates. Henry Purcell's voice had already broken at Blow's succession to the post, but Purcell stayed as an apprentice and student of Blow, as Blow himself had done under Cooke.

In September 1674 Blow married Elizabeth, daughter of Edward Braddock, Master of the Children of Westminster Abbey. They had five children: Henry (d. 1676), John (d. 1693), Katherine (d. 1730), Elizabeth (d. 1719), and Mary (d. 1738). Mrs. Blow died in childbirth in 1683.

A doctorate was conferred on Blow on December 10, 1677, by the Archbishop of Canterbury, whose power to confer the degree of doctor in music had not previously been exercised. The exact cause of John Blow's death on October 1, 1708, is not known, but references in his will suggest a seven-month period of waning health.

No dependable observations of Blow's personality and behavior survive other than this description, probably given by one of his pupils:

Dr. Blow was a very handsome man, and remarkable for a gravity and decency in his deportment suited to his station, though he seems by some of his compositions to have been not altogether insensible to the delights of a convivial hour. He was a man of blameless morals, and of a benevolent temper, but was not so insensible of his own worth as to be totally free from the imputation of pride. (Shaw, *Doctor of Music* 8)

MAJOR WORKS AND THEMES

Blow's great medium was music for one, two, and three voices, and between his official duties and his private output, he left a great number of compositions both divine and secular. Among the most famous are his *Ode on St. Cecilia's Day* (1684), his musical setting of **John Dryden**'s "An Ode, On the Death of Mr. Henry Purcell" (1695), and the collection of songs and vocal chamber music called *Amphion Anglicus* (published 1700). Unlike many of his contemporaries, he wrote very little music for the stage, but individual songs of his were included in some contemporary plays, for example, **Tate**'s *The Loyal General* (1679), Lee's *The Princess of Cleve* (1681), Durfey's *The Royalist* (1682), and **Aphra Behn**'s *The Lucky Chance* (1686). His only dramatic work was the miniature opera *Venus and Adonis* (1680–1685), which nevertheless holds an important place in the history of English music. Cited as a precursor to Purcell's *Dido and Aeneas*, it is also the earliest extant opera in the English language.

Blow also wrote two theoretical tracts, *Rules for Playing of a Through [sic] Bass upon Organ and Harpsicon* and *Dr. Blow's Rules for Composition*. The dates of composition are unknown, though the latter must have been after 1677.

CRITICAL RECEPTION

If overshadowed both in his own day and now by his pupil and friend Henry Purcell, Blow was not a composer who thrived on experimentation or novelty. He is quite noticeable, in fact, for not imitating fashionable continental styles and for a tone that reflects his education rather than new possibilities. As Shaw writes, "[I]t is impossible to escape the impression of an art in which not gaiety, brilliance or splendour, but sombre dignity, strength and tender pathos are the characteristic ingredients" ("Blow" 772). Nevertheless, Blow was one of the small but significant group of composers of choral music who first wrote with a genuine responsiveness to the rhythms of the English language.

BIBLIOGRAPHY

Works by John Blow

Dr. Blow's Rules for Composition. B.M. Add. MS 30, 933.
Rules for Playing of a Through Bass upon Organ and Harpsichon. B.M. Add. MS 34, 072. Printed in F.T. Arnold. *Art of Accompaniment from a Thorough Bass, as Practised in the XVIIth and XVIIIth Centuries*. London: Holland Press, 1961. 163.

Studies of John Blow

Clarke, Henry Leland. "John Blow: A Tercentenary Survey." *Musical Quarterly* 35 (1949): 412.
Cummings, W.H. "Dr. John Blow." *Proceedings of the Royal Musical Association* 35 (1909).
Shaw, Harold Watkins. "John Blow." In *Grove's Dictionary of Music and Musicians*. London: Macmillan, 1954. 1: 768–772. (Contains an extensive listing of Blow's works.)
———. *John Blow (Newark, 1649–1708), Doctor of Music, a Biography*. London: Novello, 1937.

❧ *Robert Boyle*

(1627–1691)

GERALD EDWARD BUNKER

BIOGRAPHY

What interest for the overstimulated inquirer of the 21st century have the life and works of this 17th-century Anglo-Irish savant, Robert Boyle? First is the intellectual and spiritual adventure that this frail and neurotic man had in planting and cultivating seedlings of the new science during the 17th-century European redirection of thought, method, and ideals, now called the Enlightenment. Second is the historical and novelistic interest of this man's life and relationships. Born to great privilege, driven by such intense sincerity, and creating more by his life than by the actual content of his work, Boyle is the very model in England at least of the new natural philosopher. A few years ago Birbeck College, London, which is the center of the rebirth of Boyle studies, invited a group of psychiatrists—Jungian, Freudian, and other—to discuss Robert Boyle. I have not been able to find the text of their discussions, but certainly Boyle gave them much grist.

Robert Boyle's father, Richard, a sort of carpetbagger who joined the Irish Ascendancy, a Protestant of course, and a Cambridge graduate, went to Ireland at the age of twenty-two as a tax collector (subescheator under the escheator-general). Undergoing various changes of fortune and charges of malfeasance, he proved extremely resilient. In 1602 he bought the vast estates in Munster that Elizabeth I had granted to her sometime favorite Sir Walter Ralegh. There Boyle père nurtured industry and agriculture and became immensely rich. By the time Robert was born in 1627, his father Richard, Earl of Cork, was Lord High Treasurer and once again fending off allegations of malfeasance.

Robert was born in Lismore Castle, Waterford, on January 25, 1627. His mother, Catherine Fenton, daughter of Sir Geoffrey Fenton, Secretary of State for Ireland, was Richard's second wife. His first had died within a year of the birth of their first child. Robert was the fourteenth of Richard and Catherine's fifteen children (and seventh son). The death of the fifteenth (his sister Margaret) left Robert the youngest.

At the time of his birth Richard was sixty-one and lived routinely in his town house in Dublin; Catherine was in her forties. Virtually at birth the young Robert was sent off to be nursed in a rural village, in accordance with the educational theory of his parents. Robert's mother died in bearing his sister Margaret a few days after his third birthday. He always spoke with respect for his father and with affection for his mother, but he had only brief and doubtless formal relationships with them. He had neither maternal love nor paternal guidance.

After his mother's death, Boyle was recalled briefly home from his country nurse and at the age of eight (1635) was sent to Eton College along with his brother Francis. The Earl was a good friend of the provost of Eton, **Henry Wotton** (1568–1639), in turn a friend of **Donne** and **Milton**, and poet. The two boys lived at the house of the headmaster, John Harrison. The two years that Robert studied at Eton with Harrison were his only formal institutional education. Harrison's "strong passion to acquire knowledge" shaped the life course of the boy and the man. When Harrison retired, neither Boyle boy flourished at Eton; the Earl withdrew them in November 1638 when Robert was eleven. He was tutored at home for a year and then, after seeing his father for what was to be the last time, Boyle embarked for a continental grand tour (1639) with his brother Francis and his tutor Isaac Marcombes, who took on the role of parent and friend. The first stop was Geneva.

In that Calvinist city, the sensitive and frail boy underwent a religious conversion experience. This was a culturally encouraged commonplace in the 17th century, but Boyle felt changed for life. It happened during a summer night thunderstorm when he fancied the Day of Judgment had come. He repeated his "consecration of himself to piety" under a clear sky. Nonetheless, despite lifetime piety he strove for an "examined faith"; he was well aware that "usually, such as are born in such a place, espouse the opinions, true or false, that obtain there." He said "distracting doubts about some of the fundamentals of Christianity" disturbed his spirit as a toothache the body.

In Geneva, Boyle studied French, Latin, theology, rhetoric, and especially mathematics—"arithmetic, geometry, the doctrine of the sphere, that of the globe." And he began the study of Italian in preparation for his projected voyage there. Italy was the land of antique culture, the jewel of the grand tour. In September 1641 Marcomes and his two charges visited Venice and proceeded to Florence where they wintered. There Marcomes took the boys to "visit the famousest bordellos" (as part of young men's education?). Robert "not above fifteen" was so deeply shocked by the "impudent nakedness of vice," especially that of two "sodomite squires," that he seems to have decided that sex was not for him. Thus he shared abstinence with the great Newton. Connected to his rejection of the flesh, Robert was drawn to the ancient philosophers, particularly to the stoics, and "he tried his proficiency in their philosophy by enduring a long fit of toothache with great unconcernedness."

As for his advocacy of the "new science," Galileo Galilei was under house arrest at Arcetri near Florence when he died on January 8, 1642. Did the young student fall under the influence of the old savant, study his works, accept his theses that the language of nature is mathematics, that the same physical laws prevail in the heavens as on earth, and that they are revealed by observation and experiment? I believe that Boyle turned to these beliefs later in his life.

Continuing to Marseilles, the trio found that the Earl's check had been held up in the London office and further a letter from the Earl with "two hundred and fifty pounds got together by selling of plate." The British Civil War and the Irish rebellion made further payment unlikely; the Earl urged Marcombes to send the boys to Ireland or to the Prince of Orange to participate in the wars. Francis did return home, but Robert, not at all inclined to be a soldier, accepted Marcombes's offer of hospitality in Geneva. There he met François Perreaud (1572–1657) and was much impressed with his views on demonology. Few in the 17th century doubted the existence of the incorporeal angels and devils, the soul.

The Earl of Cork died on September 15, 1643, so when Boyle returned to England in mid-1644, at the age of seventeen, his inheritance made him independently wealthy. He settled at an estate he inherited from his father at Stalbridge, Dorset, in the southwest of England, some 150 miles from London.

From this time on, his closest friend was his sister Katherine, thirteen years his elder, married to Viscount Ranelagh and with a fine home on Pall Mall, London. When Boyle set himself up as a man of leisure in his country house, he devoted himself to literary projects in poetry and prose, moral and ethical musings, imitations of French popular literature. In 1648 he renewed his vow of chastity in a poem he called "Seraphic Love" comparing the vicissitudes of earthly love of women to angelic love of god. He became a biblical scholar of some note with knowledge of Greek, Hebrew, and Syriac. Boyle, always concerned about his health, dosed himself with horrible medicines in hope of relief. He believed in a very simple diet—"never ate for pleasure, only to keep alive."

Boyle never lost his interest in theological and ethical topics—he was later dubbed by one of his friends as a "lay bishop"—but somehow the experimental bug bit him. He obsessed about obtaining a furnace at Stalbridge, no easy thing in his remote rural location. When it finally arrived he found himself "so transported and bewitched as to fancy my laboratory a kind of Elysium. I there forget my standish [inkwell] and my books and almost all things."

Robert also traveled extensively to Ireland to deal with problems affecting his estates there. He commenced his interest in medicine and physiology by performing animal dissections. Moreover, he traveled frequently to London where his sister Katherine introduced him to Samuel Hartlib (1600–1662), who was a Protestant religious and educational reformer of a group called the "Intelligensers," an intellectual coterie of young unmarried religious intellectuals who met to discuss the new natural philosophy.

Boyle himself became associated with a group centered around John Wilkins (1614–1672); this group with other groups across the country formed the "invisible college," precursor to the Royal Society. Wilkins was chaplain to the Prince Elector of Palatine living in London. John Wallis (1616–1703), the English mathematician who was in many ways Newton's predecessor, wrote that he, Wilkins, Boyle, and others met weekly on a certain day and hour, under a certain penalty, and a weekly contribution for the charge of the experiments, with "certain rules agreed among us to treat a discourse of such affairs."

In 1648 Wilkins was appointed warden of Wadham College, Oxford, and the next year Wallis became professor of geometry. Evidently to continue his association with this group, Boyle took up private quarters in Oxford. He said that those in London continued to meet there as before "and we with them, when we had occasion to be there, and those of us at Oxford and divers meeting in Oxford, and brought those Studies into fashion there."

When Wilkins was at Wadham, he gathered around him a group of "worthy persons inquisitive into natural philosophy and other parts of human learning." His objective was to "gain acceptance for the new science, to bring the work of Copernicus, Kepler, Galileo, Gilbert, Mersenne, to the attention of his countrymen." Among the worthy persons was Christopher Wren (1632–1723), geometrist and architect. Boyle moved permanently to Oxford in 1664, and there he initiated full-fledged experimentation. There is a plaque on High Street to this day marking the lab where he and his brilliant assistant Robert Hooke (see below) conducted their experiments.

Wilkins was married to Oliver Cromwell's sister, so it is not surprising that when Charles II was "restored" to the monarchy, it fell to Boyle to host the group that became subsequently chartered (in 1662) as the Royal Society of London for the Promotion of Natural Knowledge, a group so central to the future development of English science.

In 1668, Boyle moved from Oxford to London to live with his sister Katherine in her mansion, which had plenty of room for his laboratories and assistants. He was close at hand to participate in the work of the Royal Society. Two years later (in 1670) he suffered a stroke. Nonetheless, through the 1670s and 1680s he continued producing a prodigious output of scientific and religious tracts.

From 1689, Boyle's health declined, and he gradually withdrew from public life, no longer communicating with the Royal Society and rarely receiving visitors. He "recruited his spirits, ranged his papers," and proposed chemical experiments as "a kind of Hermetic legacy." His health continued to decline until, desolate at the death of his beloved sister a week earlier, he died on December 30, 1691.

Boyle was buried in the churchyard of St. Martin's in the Fields. The location of his remains is not known. He endowed in his will the Boyle lectures on the harmony of science and religion, which continue; he also left benefactions for biblical translations and propagation of the faith.

MAJOR WORKS AND THEMES

The work of the "Invisible College" (the meaning of the Royal Society) must be seen in contrast to the worldview of Scholasticism (i.e., Aristotle's physics coordinated with the Christian revelation by St. Thomas Aquinas after the 13th century. Whereas none of us feel that there has been "progress" in literature, philosophy, the fine arts, or music since the 17th century (and feel comfortable there except for the orthography), Thomist physics seems bizarre—that all things behave according to their purpose; that there is a "great chain of being" ascending from the grossness of earth to the perfection of the heavens; that stones fall to reach their level, fire rises because of its sublimity. In contrast, Galileo had been silenced because he proposed that natural order behaves according to mathematical laws, heavens as well as earth. Yet Aristotelian physics dominated the universities of Europe until the end of the century.

Robert Boyle and his fellows of the mid-17th century did not have the benefits of modern academic specialties; yet learned and inquisitive men such as Boyle ranged widely through the arts and sciences. I will treat here three topics, representative of the whole. The first is air. The study of this commonplace led him not only to the law for which he is remembered but also to the second topic, corpuscles, his contribution to the development of atomic structure, and to the third, science and religion, which he tried to harmonize as the Christian virtuoso.

It is baffling to recall that the 17th century did not know what air was, or even what a gas was, or a vacuum, which nature was thought to abhor. Yet savants all over Europe were exploring this topic in the mid-17th century. Evangelista Torricelli (1608–1647), who was Galileo's assistant during the last three months of his life in 1643, inverted a mercury-filled glass tube into a dish and observed that some of the mercury did not flow out; above it was the first true vacuum. He also observed that the height of the mercury varied from day to day (the first barometer).

Blaise Pascal (1623–1662) took the next step by having his brother-in-law take a barometer up to the top of the Puy-de-Dome; the observed fall in the mercury from bottom to top of the mountain he interpreted as evidence that we live in an ocean of air. In 1650, Otto von Guericke (1602–1686) invented the air pump and performed many experiments on partial vacuums, the most famous being that of the Magdeburg hemispheres performed before Emperor Ferdinand III. Two copper hemispheres were placed together to make a sphere and the air inside pumped out. That teams of horses could not separate the hemispheres demonstrates the magnitude of atmospheric pressure.

In 1657 Robert Boyle read of the Magdeburg experiment and began his own studies with the aid of then Oxford undergraduate Robert Hooke (1635–1703). Hooke, one of the great scientists of the 17th century, and Boyle spent the next two years improving von Guericke's pump, a "new pneumatical engine." They also spent several years in experimentation demonstrating that the Torricellian barometer falls equivalent to taking it to the top of the atmosphere; that light but not sound would travel in the vacuum; that a robin in the vacuum would perish. Recall that until the Michelson-Morley experiment in 1881, there was no proof that a vacuum—that is, space with nothing in it—could and did exist. Boyle spent time in trying to evaluate the subtle essence (ether) that was supposed to exist. He corresponded on this subject with philosopher **Thomas Hobbes** (1588–1679). Hobbes was a "plenist," believing in the subtle essence that could not be evacuated. In 1660 Robert Boyle published *New Experiments Physico-mechanical Touching upon the Spring of the Air* in which he argued that air particles have little springs on them, that air is compressible—more mercury in the tube will reduce the volume in the closed end, that you can "feel" the spring of air when compressing air with a pump. In 1662 he stated the relationship that made his name eternal among schoolboys: that pressure times volume is a constant, or otherwise stated—each is inversely proportional to the other.

In the history of chemistry, Boyle is most remembered for his "corpuscular or mechanical hypothesis." He attacked the two views that were current in his time: first, the "chymists" or "spagyrists," who believed that all matter was based on the *tria prima*, the principles of salt, sulphur, and mercury; and second, the Aristotelians or Peripatetics, who believed in the four classical elements of earth, air, fire, and water. Of the two, Boyle felt himself more a "chymist." Thus Boyle published his first and most famous chemical work, *The Sceptical Chymist* in 1661 espousing empiric experimentation. And he developed his views that nature is composed of invisible corpuscles in many other works.

There is no question that Boyle was an important pioneer in the road from Greek atomic theory through Lavoisier and others in the next two centuries who discovered chemical elements to the giants of modern particle physics in the century just past. Although we may consider Robert Boyle credulous in joining the alchemists in believing base metals could become gold, we now hypothesize that all elements are resolved from elementary hydrogen in the birth and death of stars.

We may get an idea of the breadth of Boyle's scientific works by surveying his published works, not to mention his voluminous laboratory reports, now available on the Internet. In addition to *Spring of the Air* and *The Sceptical Chymist*, Boyle published *Experiments Touching Colors* (1664), *New Experiments Touching Cold* (1665), *Hydrostatical Paradoxes* (1666), *Origin of Forms and Qualities* (1666–1667), *Rarefaction of the Air* (1670), *Cosmological Qualities* (1671), *Origin and Virtue of Gems* (1672), *Relations betwixt Flame and Air* (1672), *Essays of Effluviums* (1673), *Saltiness of the Sea* (1674), *Hidden Qualities of the Air* (1674), *Mechanical Origin of Qualities* (1675), *Degradation of Gold* (1678), *Producibleness of Chymical Principles* (1680), *Salt Water Sweetened* (1683), *Natural History of Human Blood* (1684), *Experiments about Porosity* (1684), and *Experimental History of Mineral Waters* (1684–1685), among others.

In the same way that it is difficult to put oneself in the mind-set of 17th-century natural philosophy, it is difficult to perceive the depth of religious feeling. Britain had been torn apart by a civil war in which sectarian differences took a crucial part. Boyle's earliest writings expressed religious faith, and he continually wrote both published and unpublished works, including a vast number of notes for a disproof of atheism. Much of his writing—never celebrated for clarity—is difficult to understand, and Boyle does not hesitate to contradict himself as his ideas develop. But the intensity of his belief and the amount of ratiocination that he put into the these important questions are vital to understanding the man.

CRITICAL RECEPTION

During his lifetime, Robert Boyle was lionized first by the Royal Society in its *Philosophic Transactions* (from 1665) and then by the public at large. One author in 1668 declared that Boyle "has done enough to oblige all Mankind and to erect an eternal monument to his memory." He was offered the presidency of the Royal Society (1680) and the headmastership of Eton College, both of which he declined. His wealth, learning, and social standing (albeit that his father was a *parvenu*) gave natural science and his colleagues at the Royal Society new prestige. Scientists (as was Newton to be shortly) became celebrities.

Although Victorian celebration of heroes of science has given way to a more complex understanding, and we cannot claim that Boyle made any single discovery of lasting value, with the exception of Boyle's Law. But he was central in developing the British tradition of experimental empirical science leading to such feats as Cavendish's "weighing the world" in his Cambridge laboratory in 1797.

The last decade has seen a burgeoning of interest in Boyle both as a scientist and as a thinker and study of his philosophical works, previously swept over by scholars as an embarrassment. Comprehensive new editions of all Boyle's works are monuments of scholarship since Boyle himself did not make it easy for his editors. Having a morbid fear of being plagiarized, he often wrote scraps, which he mixed. As noted below, resources available on the Internet open his own words to anyone who wishes to enter the world of this interesting man and of 17th-century thought.

BIBLIOGRAPHY

Works by Robert Boyle

The Correspondence of Robert Boyle. Ed. Michael Hunter and Antonio Clericuzio. London: Pickering and Chatto, 2001.

The Sceptical Chymist. Facsimile reproduction. Available online at http://oldsite.library.upenn.edu/etext/collections/science/boyle/chymist/index.html.

"The Work-diaries of Robert Boyle." Wellcome Trust for the History of Medicine, The Perseus Digital Library. Available online at http://www.perseus.tufts.edu/.

The Works of Robert Boyle. Ed. Michael Hunter and Edward Davis. 14 vols. London: Pickering and Chatto, 1999–2000.

Studies of Robert Boyle

A truly exhaustive and regularly updated bibliography will be found at *The Robert Boyle Project*. Available online at http://www.bbk.ac.uk/boyle/.

Anstey, Peter. *The Philosophy of Robert Boyle*. London: Routledge, 2000.

Hunter, Michel, ed. *Robert Boyle Reconsidered*. Cambridge: Cambridge University Press, 1994.

Principe, Lawrence M. *The Aspiring Adapt: Robert Boyle and His Alchemical Quest*. Princeton, NJ: Princeton University Press, 1997.

Wojcik, Jan W. *Robert Boyle and the Limits of Reason*. Cambridge: Cambridge University Press, 1997.

🪶 *Anne Bradstreet*

(1612–1672)

GAIL WOOD

BIOGRAPHY

Anne Dudley Bradstreet was the first published woman poet of the Americas, and thus her work has been a part of the poetic heritage of American literature. The estimation of her worth as a poet has moved up and down as the critical thinking on American letters has changed through the years since her first published work in 1650. It is assumed she was born in Northampton, England. Her father, Thomas Dudley, served as a page and a soldier. In 1619, he became the steward to the Earl of Lincoln. Her future husband, Simon Bradstreet, was an orphan raised in that household who eventually became a steward to the Earl. Anne was raised in a world of economic comfort. Her father, however, had nonconformist religious beliefs, so despite the access to wealth, family life was devoted to service to God, scriptural study, and a sober approach to living. Though Anne received no formal education, it is conjectured that she had access to an excellent education in the household of the Earl of Lincoln.

Anne Dudley married Simon Bradstreet in 1628, at the age of sixteen. In March 1630, the Dudleys and the Bradstreets set sail for the Americas, on a voyage that would take three months. They sought a life of religious freedom in the Massachusetts Bay Colony, yet found primitive overcrowded conditions on the coast and so moved to Cambridge. Both her father and her husband became prominent in the government of Massachusetts Bay, both serving as Governor. Her first child, Samuel, was born in 1633 or 1634, and she had seven more children between 1635 and 1652. In those years, she was occupied with raising children and running a busy and prosperous household while enduring periods of ill health. At the same time she studied, read, and wrote.

In 1650, her poetry was published in England, brought there by her brother-in-law Reverend John Woodbridge. Published as *The Tenth Muse Lately sprung up in America*, her work was widely read and well received. It is likely that she did not know of its publication beforehand because she began revising and correcting her work immediately after its distribution. The second edition was published in 1678, six years after her death, and was titled *Several Poems Compiled with great variety of Wit and Learning, full of Delight*. This edition includes all the poems of the first along with several others. Her poetry has remained in the Anglo-American canon since that time. Her papers are in the Houghton Library at Harvard.

MAJOR WORKS AND THEMES

Anne Bradstreet was educated at home and had access to one of the great libraries of her time. Her writings reflect a breadth and depth of knowledge of contemporary poetic forms and themes. Poetry such as her elegy to her distant relative Sir Philip Sidney and her tribute to Du Bartas uses the poetic styles of the time and reflects an enormous knowledge and a creative ability. The joy of these poems is in her ability to combine her expertise as a poet with her savvy observations on the literature and history of the time. When her poetry shifts from these more public topics to a more private sphere, however, she shows an even greater ability to communicate. These poems reflect on her marriage, her illnesses, and her children. The private sphere allows her to augment her poetry to a level of emotional authenticity rarely seen. The reader is engaged in her struggles with her love for her husband and children, her illnesses, and her sorrow at the death of family. Her prose writings complement these meditations and reflections when she writes of her struggles to understand God's demands for the Puritan soul living in the wilderness of America.

CRITICAL RECEPTION

Critical analyses of Bradstreet's works have been rich and varied. From the first publication of *Tenth Muse* in 1650, Bradstreet's poetry received abundant high praise, much of the commentary focusing on her technical merits as a poet. In the 19th century, however, scant attention was paid to her poetry. Critics such as Moses Coit Taylor and John Harvard Ellis found her work only occasionally compelling. Interest in her work was revived in the early 20th century when portions of her work were included in the Modern Library edition of *American Poetry 1671–1928*. In the 1940s through the 1960s, Bradstreet's poetry appeared in anthologies with increasing frequency and praise.

Full-scale scholarly attention to Bradstreet began in the 1950s with Elizabeth Wade White's analysis of her place in American poetry. Through the 1950s and 1960s, critical attention to her work placed her in the canon of English-language literature, analyzing her point of view as a woman and a poet. Scholarship also contextualized her in the Puritan world and critiqued her role as a woman in a structured religious society along with her ability to develop spiritual thought. Feminist critics studied Bradstreet's ability to articulate the tension of Puritan life with secular life and the rebellion of an accomplished woman against prescribed and proscribed gender roles. Throughout the centuries, Bradstreet's prose and poems have provided readers and scholars with poetic gold.

BIBLIOGRAPHY

Works by Anne Bradstreet

The Complete Works of Anne Bradstreet. Boston: Twayne, 1981.

A Concordance to the Complete Works of Anne Bradstreet. Ed. Raymond A. Craig. Lewiston, NY: Edwin Mellen Press, 2000.

Several Poems beginning of the Romane Common-wealth to the end of their last King: With diverse other Pleasant and serious Poems (2nd ed. of 1650 publication). Boston: John Foster, 1678.

The Tenth Muse Lately sprung up in America. Or Severall Poems, compiled with great variety of Wit and Learning, full of delight. Wherein especially contained a compleat discourse and description of The Four Elements, Constitutions, Ages of Man, Season of the Year. Together with an Exact Epitomie of the Four Monarchies, viz. The Assyrian, Persian, Grecian, Roman. Also a Dialogue between Old England and New, concerning the late troubles. With divers other pleasant and serious poem. London: Stephen Bowtell, 1650.

Studies of Anne Bradstreet

Blackstock, Carrie Galloway. "Anne Bradstreet and Performativity: Self-Cultivation, Self-Deployment." *Early American Literature* 32 (1997): 222–249.

Cowell, Pattie, and Ann Stanford. *Critical Essays on Anne Bradstreet*. Boston: G.K. Hall, 1983.

Dolle, Raymond F. *Anne Bradstreet: A Reference Guide*. Boston: G.K. Hall, 1991.

Hammond, Jeffrey. *Sinful Self, Saintly Self: The Puritan Experience of Poetry*. Athens: University of Georgia Press, 1993.

Harvey, Tamara. " 'Now Sisters—Impart Your Usefulnesse and Force': Anne Bradstreet's Feminist Functionalism in *The Tenth Muse* (1650)." *Early American Literature* 35 (2000): 5–28.

Nicolay, Theresa Freda. *Gender Roles, Literary Authority, and Three American Writers: Anne Dudley Bradstreet, Mercy Otis Warren, Margaret Fuller Ossoli*. New York: Peter Lang, 1995.

Oser, Lee. "Almost a Golden World: Sidney, Spenser and Puritan Conflict in Bradstreet's "Contemplations." *Renaiscence* 52 (2000): 187–202.

Rosenmeier, Rosamond. *Anne Bradstreet Revisited*. Boston: Twayne Publishers, 1991.

Scheick, William J., and JoElla Doggett. *Seventeenth-Century American Poetry: A Reference Guide*. Boston: G.K. Hall, 1977.

Schweitzer, Ivy. *The Work of Self-Representation: Lyric Poetry in Colonial New England*. Chapel Hill: University of North Carolina Press, 1991.

Stanford, Ann. *Anne Bradstreet: The Worldly Puritan: An Introduction to Her Poetry*. New York: Burt Franklin, 1974.

———. "Three Puritan Women: Anne Bradstreet, Mary Rowlandson, and Sarah Kemble Knight." In *American Women Writers: Bibliographic Essays*, ed. Maurice Duke, Jackson R. Bryer, and M. Thomas Inge. Westport, CT: Greenwood Press, 1983. 3–20.

Wilson, Douglas. *Beyond the Stateliest Marble: The Passionate Femininity of Anne Bradstreet*. Nashville, TN: Highland Books, 2001.

🐦 *Thomas Browne*
(1605–1682)

ADAM KITZES

BIOGRAPHY

Sir Thomas Browne lived the life of a scholar and scientist, as the records of his life bear out. Of his childhood and youth, only a few facts are known. He was born on October 19, 1605, at St. Michael's Parish in Cheapside to a well-established merchant's family. His father died while he was young; his mother remarried Sir Timothy Dutton, a man whose own historical record suggests a notorious lifestyle. Browne's earliest biographer, John Whitefoot, alleges that "he was defrauded by one of his guardians" of an ostensibly large inheritance. Samuel Johnson took this to mean that Dutton had swindled both his mother and Browne himself, but contemporary opinion holds that his mother had transferred the estate over to her brother-in-law (Endicott). Johnson's description of a young Browne being "deprived now of both his parents, and therefore helpless and unprotected" seems doubtful.

Whatever financial troubles there may have been early on, however, they did not prove much of a hindrance in the way of his schooling. He received a scholarship at Winchester College, where he studied for seven years. In 1623 he became a fellow commoner at Broadgates Hall (Pembroke College), Oxford, where he studied, in addition to the traditional curriculum, anatomy and botany, as well as "no less than six languages." His training in medicine continued after he received his M.A. (1629), and he practiced in Oxfordshire for a year. Traveling first to Ireland, then to Montpellier, Padua, and Leyden (where he received an M.D.), he became acquainted with some of the most advanced medical practices known throughout the Continent. His interest in embryology and anatomy probably began in Padua, where he would have known Fabricus of Aquapedente (former adviser to **William Harvey**). More generally, though, his schooling gave him a sense of the methods of scientific experimentation that were emerging at the time.

Browne's sojourn in Leyden, and his subsequent return to England in 1633, meant that he was witness to what one historian describes as "raging controversies between

Arminians, Socinians, and the supporters of Protestant orthodoxy." Such controversies evidently made a major impact on him, since he spent the years 1634 to 1636 working out his religious beliefs in *Religio Medici*, a treatise that asserted his allegiance to the Church of England. It was here that he began to draw a sharp distinction between his natural reason and his faith, as the following statement indicates:

In Philosophy where truth seemes double-faced, there is no man more paradoxicall then my self; but in Divinity I love to keepe the road, and though not in an implicite, yet an humble faith, follow the great wheele of the Church, by which I move, not reserving any proper poles or motion from the epicycle of my own braine. (I, 15)

As the epistle to the reader in the revised (1642) edition indicates, the text had originally been intended as a private work until a corrupt version, which had appeared in print earlier that same year, forced him to put forth a more accurate copy. To be sure, Browne himself had let the treatise circulate among his friends; it seems probable, then, that what began as a private exercise or coterie text evolved into a significantly more elaborate affair. The text itself enjoyed immediate success, although a brief conflict with Sir Kenham Digby, Earl of Dorset, did accompany widespread admiration. Digby allegedly wrote a scathing attack against Browne, but he later retracted what he had written in the so-called *Observations*. After a cordial exchange of letters between the two, along with a further admonition from "A.B." to disregard Digby's remarks, the dispute was cleared up. The entire affair subsequently has been remembered for the sake of anecdote, as the *Observations* along with the letters between Browne and Digby often are printed as appendices to contemporary editions of the *Religio*.

Browne's career during the more turbulent decades of the 1640s and 1650s is not well known. He married Dorothy Mileham in 1641, with whom he had twelve children over a span of twenty years. Browne evidently became active with his experiments in the natural sciences, as *Pseudodoxia Epidemica*, his major work of the period, bears evidence. His living quarters must have been under constant negotiation with his lab work:

There was the dead kingfisher "hung up by the bill" to see whether his veerings showed the direction of the wind; chickens and mice weighed before and after strangulation to see whether their weight increased when the vital spirits left them; the toad "in a glass included with many spiders" to test the belief that there is a natural antipathy between them. Then there were the carcasses of peacocks, turkeys, capons, hares, etc. "suspended freely in the air, and after a year and a half the dogs have not refused to eat them." (Bennett 10)

His love for experimentation evidently did little to shake beliefs that future ages would hold as superstition. In 1655, he served as a witness in a witchcraft trial, and although his expert opinion on witchcraft probably was not the essential component of the case, the defendant did wind up burning at the stake.

Browne also wrote many shorter pieces, generally on natural history. In 1658, the discovery of an ancient burial site in Norfolk provided him the occasion for his *Hydriotaphia, Urne Buriall*, an astonishing study of funeral urns as historical artifacts. He continued to write about such subjects as fossils, mummies, Sphinxes, hieroglyphs, plants mentioned in the Bible, and other subjects that demonstrate a keen historical sensibility. These appeared as short miscellanies and fragments, and they were not published until 1683. All in all, they demonstrate a deep personal interest in historical remains and their significance to contemporary scholars.

Aside from these few details, however, Browne seems to have been more absorbed by his experiments and domestic affairs than by his public persona. Indeed, his public life after the Restoration has an air of reservation about it. He was knighted by Charles II in 1671, but only after the Mayor of Norfolk had turned down that same honor and a substitute had to be chosen hastily. While he was elected a Fellow of the Royal College of Physicians, there is little to show that he was actively engaged with other members of his profession. Instead, his letters from the period indicate a concern with family life and private research.

On October 19, 1682, after suffering from a colic for a week, Browne died. He was laid to rest in the church of St. Peter, Mancroft, where he remained undisturbed for a good 160 years. In 1840, however,

some workmen, who were employed in digging a vault in the chancel of the church . . . accidentally broke, with a blow of the pick-axe, the lid of a coffin, which proved to be that of [Sir Thomas Browne,] whose residence within its walls conferred honour on Norwich in olden times.

It was a fitting accident, and one can only imagine how the author himself might have incorporated it into a revised edition of *Hydriotaphia*.

MAJOR WORKS AND THEMES

Although the range of Browne's interests was immense, a number of problems and themes do recur with remarkable consistency. In his two most important treatises, *Religio Medici* and *Pseudodoxia Epidemica*, Browne draws a sharp distinction between his curiosity in matters scientific and his respect for authority in matters doctrinal. Specifically, he directs his respect toward the Church of England, which he regards as a unifying and pacifying institution. In religious matters he does not want to be regarded as an independent thinker, as he asserts,

In briefe, where the Scripture is silent, the Church is my Text; where that speakes, 'tis but my Comment: where there is a joynt silence of both, I borrow not the rules of my Religion from *Rome* or *Geneva*, but the dictates of my owne reason. (14)

Only in exceptional cases, then, does he allow independent reasoning to determine his religious beliefs—and even then primarily to avoid getting caught up in factional disputes. What is crucial is not some conviction of infallibility but rather a practical way to avoid conflict in matters that tended not to afford peaceful resolutions in the first place.

It should be noted that, as Achsah Guibbory has argued, the idea of a church united in the face of conflict had a particular appeal for Laudians, especially as it left the more rigid tenets of Calvinist theology with little room to operate. Some sense of an anti-Calvinist strain does seem manifest in his writings. For Browne, however, pacifism and acceptance of authority seem grounded in a genuine skepticism. While he maintains as a fundamental axiom that nature does nothing in vain, he is far less assured that human reason could ever fully explain it. Hence, "By acquainting our reason how unable it is to display the visible and obvious effect of nature, it becomes more humble and submissive unto the subtleties of faith" (19). Indeed, Reason contains within it elements of the tragic. As he notes, it is every man's "best Oedipus" (15); meanwhile, it is up to us to remember what became of Oedipus after he solved the riddle of the Sphinx. To that extent, he advocates an early form of empiricism, relying on direct observations of nature but refraining from making too many metaphysical assertions when he can help it. All the more reason to keep a faithful adherence to conventional practices in areas where natural reason cannot penetrate.

His *Pseudodoxia Epidemica* gives us similar ideas in reverse. There, he tries to demonstrate what can be achieved through painstaking observation and experiment. The work is a massive study of a variety of phenomena—so massive that even Geoffrey Keynes concedes in the preface to the complete works that even Browne's most fond admirers probably haven't read it from cover to cover. More generally, his concern lies with showing the bases for our own errors in reasoning. These include deference to authority and antiquity but also something along the lines of false consciousness, wherein people project their personal desires and fears as though they were actualities. Browne's concern with improving methods of knowledge and what he calls the "advancement of learning" invites comparisons with **Francis Bacon**, though he does not quite share the desire to rectify and unite the various branches of learning. Nor is there the sense that knowledge brings power, or that human knowledge could reach the point of mastery over nature.

Browne shows a concern with natural history, particularly insofar as it bolsters his own ethical viewpoints. His best-known example is *Hydriotaphia, Urne Buriall*, a work, as we have seen, occasioned by the discovery of a set of funeral urns in Brampton field, that surveyed as many burial ceremonies as he could think of. The work can be called both an archaeological study and a survey of textual records; by combining these two methods, he attempts to provide an anthropological basis for ceremonial practices. On the one hand, the huge variety of funeral customs suggests something arbitrary about them; on the other, the fact that all cultures have in common a set of arbitrary customs suggests that they fulfill an essential human need, all the same. What is important, then, is not the particular manner of the custom but rather the fact that such a custom exists in the first place.

While the mysterious *Garden of Cyrus* appeared in print with *Hydriotaphia*, a more suitable companion piece arguably would be his *Letter to a Friend*, a detailed study of death and the art of dying. Among the similarities are a suspicion of human reason (particularly its ability to comprehend death), deep misgivings about assigning a chronological date to the end of the world, a vast knowledge of customs pertaining to procreation, birth, disease, and death, and a strong affirmation of private living as an ideal standard of conduct.

Browne's prose style itself has provoked numerous commentaries. The two most recognizable characteristics are his erudition and his mixed tones. His bibliophilic habits may remind one at times of **Robert Burton**; Browne had an extreme fondness for remote knowledge, and he often (mis)quoted texts from memory when making a specific point. As for tone, Browne is known for joining together plain and direct statements with paradoxes, obscure references, and neologisms. Often this has a jarring effect, and his critics have sometimes complained of his dissonant and harsh qualities. Johnson himself described it as "a tissue of many languages." All the same, Browne was conscious of what he described as human rhythm, and his sentence patterns, for all their variety, do suggest that he wanted to recreate some sort of "pulse."

CRITICAL RECEPTION

Although he made some important contributions to botany and embryology, and has enjoyed a considerable reputation as an early modern scientist, Browne owes his current fame to his literary personality, and he is remembered less for what he said than for how he said it. If Johnson's assessment is reliable, *Religio Medici* found its immediate public "by the novelty of paradoxes, the dignity of sentiment, the quick succession of images, the multitude of abstruse allusions, the subtlety of disquisition, and the strength of language" (Patrides ed., *Works* 486). And while Johnson qualifies his own assessment of Browne's style, finding it decadent by comparison to his Elizabethan predecessors, what is not of concern is the actual argument Browne puts forth. Meanwhile, during the 17th century, the *Religio Medici* gave rise to a series of imitations, the most famous perhaps being **Dryden**'s *Religio Laici*; as one recent study has shown, however, many *Religios* were published only on the strength of Browne's reputation, most of them having nothing more to do with their model than a desire to cash in on a successful name.

During the 20th century, when stylistic criticism was in favor, the *Religio* became the subject of numerous studies that largely placed him within Baroque culture. It was through Stanley Fish, whose own theoretical approach called into question the entire basis for stylistic criticism, that Browne's reputation as an eloquent genius underwent its most significant attack. Fish decided that it was justifiable to demand more from Browne than entertaining language, and when he inquired directly into what readers may actually learn from Browne's works, he concluded that the answer was "not much." Browne thus received the unfortunate epithet "The Bad Physician" in contrast to someone like **John Donne** the preacher, whose sermons direct his audience to Lordly salvation by virtue of their verbal "insufficiencies." With the responses that have followed, critics have addressed the ways in which Browne's elusive style does tend to a kind of truth through a process of "working through" his difficult language.

The traditional belief that Browne avoided or was not interested in the political and religious disputes of his age has undergone revision, particularly as critics reconsider the rhetorical techniques of Stuart loyalists. Whereas his "irenic disposition" traditionally implied a lack of interest in the upheavals of the 1640s and 1650s, more recent studies have suggested that his sense of detachment could be taken as a sign of active affirmation of the monarchy. Guibbory has argued that *Hydriotaphia* contains references that suggest a critical attitude toward the Puritans' anticeremonialist habits. Although he certainly was not a polemicist, it is apparent enough that he saw the Stuart monarchy and Church of England, with all their attendant ceremonies, as the most conducive environment for both a life of Christian Morality and a full pursuit of the infinite Aenigmas of the natural world.

BIBLIOGRAPHY

Works by Thomas Browne

The Major Works. Ed. C.A. Patrides. London and New York: Penguin Books, 1977.

The Prose of Sir Thomas Browne. Ed. N.J. Endicott. New York: New York University Press, 1968.

The Works of Sir Thomas Browne. Ed. Geoffrey Keynes. 4 vols. Chicago: University of Chicago Press, 1964.

Studies of Thomas Browne

Bennett, Joan. *Sir Thomas Browne: A Man of Achievement in Literature*. Cambridge: Cambridge University Press, 1962.

Brian, Michael. "The Rhetoric of Urn Burial: The Decomposition of a Text." *English Renaissance Prose* 3 (1989): 18–30.

Colie, Rosalie. *Paradoxia Epidemica: The Renaissance Tradition of Paradox*. Princeton: Princeton University Press, 1966.

Donavan, Dennis, Margaretha Hartley Herman, and Ann Imbrie, comps. *Sir Thomas Browne and Robert Burton: A Reference Guide*. Boston: G.K. Hall, 1981.

Endicott, N.J. "Sir Thomas Browne as 'Orphan,' with Some Account of His Stepfather, Sir Thomas Dutton." *University of Toronto Quarterly* 30 (1961): 180–210.

Engel, William. *Mapping Mortality: The Persistence of Memory and Melancholy in Early Modern England*. Amherst: University of Massachusetts Press, 1995.

Fish, Stanley. *Self-Consuming Artifacts: The Experience of Seventeenth Century Literature*. Berkeley: University of California Press, 1974.

Guibbory, Achsah. *Ceremony and Community from Herbert to Milton: Literature, Religion, and Cultural Conflict in Seventeenth-Century England*. New York: Cambridge University Press, 1998.

Nathanson, Leonard. *The Strategy of Truth: A Study of Sir Thomas Browne*. Chicago: University of Chicago Press, 1967.

Parry, Graham. "In the Land of Moles and Pismires: Thomas Browne's Antiquarian Writings." In *English Renaissance Prose: History, Language, and Politics*, ed. Neil Rhodes. Tempe: Arizona State University Press, 1997.

Patrides, C.A., ed. *Approaches to Sir Thomas Browne: The Ann Arbor Tercentenary Essays*. Columbia: University of Missouri Press, 1982.

Post, Jonathan. "Browne's Life: A Cabinet of Rarities." *English Language Notes* 19 (1982): 313–335.

Preston, Claire. "In the Wilderness of Forms: Ideas and Things in Thomas Browne's Cabinets of Curiosity." In *The Renaissance Computer: Knowledge Technology in the First Age of Print*, ed. Neil Rhodes and Jonathan Sawday. London: Routledge, 2000.

Seelig, Sharon Cadman. "Sir Thomas Browne and Stanley Fish: A Case of Malpractice." *Prose Studies* 11 (1988): 72–84.

Straznicky, Marta. "Performing the Self in Browne's *Religio Medici*." *Prose Studies* 13 (1990): 211–229.

Sununu, Andrea. "Recent Studies in Sir Thomas Browne (1970–1986)." *English Literary Renaissance* 19 (1989): 118–129.

Wilding, Michael. *Dragons Teeth: Literature in the English Revolution*. Oxford: Oxford University Press, 1987.

❧ *John Bunyan*

(1628–1688)

RICHARD F. HARDIN

BIOGRAPHY

John Bunyan's life revolved around two places: Bedford, where his statue now faces the site of the former prison where he languished for so many years, and London, where he successfully published and preached during his last two decades. We know little about his Bedfordshire family except that his father, if religious at all, was probably a conforming believer. His autobiography overlooks conventional details, preferring to dwell on his sinful love of the church bell and similar moments in his spiritual history. The year of his mother's death, 1644, he joined Cromwell's army. Although his military record is obscure, he could not have avoided the New Model Army's Puritan fervor. He married, probably during the year or two following his discharge from the army in 1647. Around this time he worked as an itinerant tinker, perhaps alongside his father and brothers; the trade, which he continued to practice after taking up his ministry, branded him as a "mechanick preacher." A widower whose fourth child had been born before 1658, he married his second wife, Elizabeth, in 1659.

With the restoration of the monarchy came a restoration of the established Church. Bunyan had already been indicted in 1658 for holding meetings as an unlicensed preacher; repeating the offense led to the Bedford jail in 1660, where he remained until his release in 1672, following Charles II's Declaration of Indulgence. Throughout these twelve years his wife worked for his freedom despite the family's poverty; he reports bouts of anguish over a blind daughter. The Bedford church also ceased to meet openly during this period of persecution. On leaving prison, he often preached in London to large, receptive crowds. One witness to Bunyan's fame in the city wrote that he "was fain, at a back door, to be pulled almost over the people to get upstairs to his pulpit." He died in August 1688, four months before the Glorious Revolution. Survived by his widow and six children, he was laid to rest in the Dissenters' cemetery at Bunhill Fields, also to be the burial place of George Fox, Daniel Defoe, Isaac Watts, and William Blake.

Biographers caution against seeing Bunyan as a simple, uneducated man. While he is himself partly responsible for this view, Bunyan not only steeped himself in the Bible, but he studied other writers on religion, especially Luther, whose *Commentary on Galatians* he treasured. His tracts against Ranters and Quakers, whose views on salvation he found reprehensible, show an intimate knowledge of these sects' writings. He recalls that his first wife brought two books when they married, Lewis Bayly's immensely influential *The Practice of Piety* and Arthur Dent's *Plain Mans Pathway to Heaven* (also popular: the earliest known edition, the eleventh, appeared in 1609), a work that surely influenced some of his major writings. His verse, scattered throughout his works, shows an interest in poetry, and it has been credibly argued that he read parts of *The Faerie Queene*. Having written religious tracts as early as 1656, he managed to continue doing so in prison, there completing his great autobiography, *Grace Abounding to the Chief of Sinners*.

MAJOR WORKS AND THEMES

Bunyan wrote *Grace Abounding* as a spiritual autobiography and confession, with the conventional meditation on the author's depraved state before conversion and the intense experiences and visions leading to his rebirth. Traveling to Bedford one day, Bunyan has a vision of a mountain surrounded by a wall. The mountain

signified the church of the Living God; the Sun that shone thereon, the comfortable shining of his merciful face on them that were therein; the Wall I thought was the Word, that did make separations between the Christians and the World; and the Gap which was in the Wall, I thought, was Jesus Christ, who is the Way to God the Father.

Like other moments in this book, the symbols of the door and the wall reappear with similar meanings in *Pilgrim's Progress*. Troubled over his sins, he sometimes hears voices. Sighing, "How can God comfort such a wretch as I?" he hears, "This sin is not unto death." Here he launches into thanksgiving and praise to God for the "fitness of the word, the rightness and the timing of it."

These alternating moments of doubt and confidence reappear as the peaks and valleys that comprise the landscape of *Pilgrim's Progress*. This remarkable allegory divides into two parts, the first begun during a prison stay in 1676, recounting the journey of Christian Hero as seen by the narrator in a dream. Warned to flee the City of Destruction, Christian deserts his family to seek the heavenly Jerusalem. He first must pass through the wicker gate leading to the highway of salvation, and then faces many setbacks before reaching the great walled city, heaven. The second part, probably not originally intended as part of the narrative, describes Christian's wife, Christiana, who undergoes a similar journey with her children, accompanied by Mr. Great-heart, their guide and protector. The strength and character of Bunyan's prose, especially in the first part, has often been traced to the author's profound knowledge of the King James Bible.

The allegory features encounters with character types along the way, the most memorable of them representing religious adversaries or persecutors of the sort the author would have known. The qualities seen in Pliable, Mr. Honesty, and Ignorance reflect thoughtful observation of contemporary life, and Bunyan anticipates later novelists by allowing such figures themselves to reveal their own qualities. Thus these figures transcend mere personification: the Giant Despair argues in bed with his wife; Mr. Talkative exemplifies the loquacious tavern philosopher. The episode of Vanity Fair, a cesspool of worldliness where Christian's companion Faithful is put to death, contains some of the finest writing of the narrative, echoing the Gospel narratives of Christ's passion. The second part eases somewhat the severity of the first, perhaps because of the happier circumstances in which it was written. Christiana's struggles become easier with the assistance of Mr. Great-heart, who takes over the discourse whenever knotty problems of theology surface.

The Life and Death of Mr. Badman recalls in its dialogue form the conversations interspersed in the allegory. Although Bunyan proclaimed it a sequel to *Pilgrim's Progress*, it possesses its own austere charms. Mr. Wiseman informs Mr. Attentive, in the beginning, that an infamous neighbor, Mr. Badman, has just died. The lesson to be gleaned from the book is stated enigmatically by Mr. Wiseman, in that Badman "died that he might die, he went from Life to Death, and from Death to Death, from Death Natural to Death Eternal." He stole, cursed, and skipped church as a boy, deserted his master while an apprentice—though the master, in leaving ribald books around the house, was abetting this delinquency. He entered bankruptcy to avoid paying his debts and married a devout Christian only to obtain her money. Driving that wife to her death, he married another more like himself, but they paid for their sins with penury, ill health, and Badman's death.

Bunyan returns to allegory with *The Holy War, Made by Shaddai upon Diabolus, for the Regaining of the Metropolis of the World. Or, The Losing and Taking again of the Town of Mansoul*. Diabolus somewhat resembles **Milton**'s Satan. Fallen from heaven for envy of the Son's place over him, he is a majestic villain presiding over councils of demons. The infernal spirits soon capture the human city and establish a rule of license, governed by the likes of Mr. Haughty, Mr. Swearing, and Mr. Atheism. Saved by Emmanuel, the town backslides, and the story moves along in rather predictable fashion. This millenarian tome lacks the human element of Bunyan's greater allegory and the interwoven sermons can grow tedious, though the story comes alive with the courtroom scenes—undoubtedly based on many of the author's experiences with English justice.

Bunyan's religious tracts outnumber the stars, but among all his remaining works, perhaps the one most deserving of mention is *A Book for Boys and Girls*, one of the earliest examples of "children's literature" in the language.

CRITICAL RECEPTION

Already in 1692 a folio collection of Bunyan's work appeared, and *Pilgrim's Progress* in particular claimed a high readership, ceasing its hold on English-speaking cultures only in the 20th century. In the 19th it was often mentioned in the same breath as the Bible and **Shakespeare** and among English books was reprinted and read more widely than any book except the Bible. In some Christian communities Bunyan retains authority as a writer and thinker, a status that has guaranteed the availability of his minor works as well as those with wider appeal. By one count Christian's story has seen translation into 108 languages. If Edgar Allan Poe faults what he sees as Bunyan's "metaphysical" allegory, he is mainly concerned with his huge (and deleterious, Poe supposed) influence on Nathaniel Hawthorne. In the 1900s the decline of enthusiasm for Bunyan's theology saw an attendant surge of interest in his literary artistry and psychology. A classic study of *Grace Abounding* occupies one chapter of William James's *Varieties of Religious Experience*, and William York Tindall's work on Bunyan, while sneering at his religion, profitably explores his use of symbol and allegory. F.R. Leavis led the way in viewing *Pilgrim's Progress* as the legitimate expression of a vigorous popular culture—as, in some sense, a novel.

The last forty years have found scholars more understanding of Bunyan's religion, perhaps of religion as such, and better able to consider its relation to his art. Thus Joan Webber can speak of the difference between the style of **Donne** and Bunyan as that between a sacramental and nonsacramental view of reality. Bunyan receives attention in the context of the English emblem books, the 17th-century political crisis, the meditative and confessional traditions in religious history, and the problems of biblical interpretation. Keeble's tercentenary collection, assembling some of the leading Bunyan scholars at their best, is a good measure of the depth and variety of current work on this author.

BIBLIOGRAPHY

Works by John Bunyan

Oxford University Press has published thirteen volumes of the writings, each volume separately titled.

A Book for Boys and Girls, or Country Rhymes for Children. London, 1686.
Grace Abounding to the Chief of Sinners. London, 1666.
The Holy War. London, 1682.
The Life and Death of Mr. Badman. London, 1680.
The Pilgrim's Progress. Part I, London, 1678; Part II, London, 1684.
Some Gospel Truths Opened. London, 1656.
http://www.johnbunyan.org. This site provides access to texts of the collected works in a 19th-century edition.

Studies of John Bunyan

Fish, Stanley E. *Self-Consuming Artifacts: The Experience of Seventeenth-Century Literature*. Berkeley: University of California Press, 1972.

Forrest, James F., and Richard L. Greaves. *John Bunyan: A Reference Guide*. Boston: G.K. Hall, 1982.

Frye, Roland M. *God, Man, and Satan*. Princeton: Princeton University Press, 1960.

Greaves, Richard L. *John Bunyan and English Nonconformity*. London: Hambledon, 1992.

Harrison, F.M. *A Bibliography of the Works of John Bunyan. Transactions of the Bibliographical Society*. Supplement, 6 (1932).

Hill, Christopher. *A Tinker and a Poor Man: John Bunyan and His Church, 1628–1688*. New York: Knopf, 1989.

James, William. *The Varieties of Religious Experience: A Study of Human Nature*. London: Longmans, Green, 1902.

Kaufmann, U. Milo. The Pilgrim's Progress *and Tradition in Puritan Meditation*. New Haven, CT: Yale University Press, 1966.

Keeble, N.H., ed. *John Bunyan: Conventicle and Parnassus*. Oxford: Clarendon Press, 1988.

Knott, John R., Jr. "Bunyan's Gospel Day: A Reading of *The Pilgrim's Progress*." *English Literary Renaissance* 3 (1973): 443–461.

Luxon, Thomas H. *Literal Figures: Puritan Allegory and the Reformation Crisis in Representation*. Chicago: University of Chicago Press, 1995.

Mullett, Michael. *John Bunyan in Context*. Pittsburgh: Duquesne University Press, 1997.

Sharrock, Roger. *John Bunyan*. New ed. London: Macmillan, 1968.

Swaim, Kathleen. *Pilgrim's Progress, Puritan Progress: Discourses and Contexts*. Urbana: University of Illinois Press, 1993.

Tindall, William York. *John Bunyan, Mechanick Preacher*. New York and London: Columbia University Press and Oxford University Press, 1934.

Webber, Joan. *The Eloquent I*. Madison: University of Wisconsin Press, 1968.

❧ *Robert Burton*

(1577–1640)

ALBERT J. GERITZ

BIOGRAPHY

Author of one of the most popular English prose works in the early 17th century, Robert Burton, fourth of nine children, was born to Ralph and Dorothy Faunt Burton at Lindley Hall, Leicestershire, on February 8, 1577. He attended school at Sutton Coldfield and Nuneaton in Warwickshire. At sixteen, he entered Brasenose College, Oxford, as a commoner (he, unlike fellows and scholars, had to pay his own board). In 1599, he was elected a fellow of Christ Church College, Oxford, where he studied with Dr. John Bancroft. There he took the B.A., June 1602; the M.A., June 1605; and the B.D., May 1614. For the rest of his life, he remained at Christ Church as librarian.

In 1615, Burton served as "Clerk to the Market of Oxford"; his duties included checking the accuracy of weights and measures and the quality of food sold in Oxford markets. Although Burton complained of his lack of preferment, he received several church posts. In 1616, he was given the vicarage of St. Thomas Church, Oxford; he received income from the benefice of Walesby in Lincolnshire (although he never lived there); and in 1632, his friend George, Lord Berkeley, granted him a living as rector of Seagrave in Leicestershire, a post he held until his death.

Burton's first recorded literary activity was a contribution to a comedy, *Alba*, but none of it survives. *Philosophaster*, a satiric comedy in the style of **Ben Jonson**, was his next venture. His most significant accomplishment at Oxford was writing and revising *The Anatomy of Melancholy* as a means, he said, of relieving his own depression. A bachelor, Burton seems to have led an uneventful life; as he claims in *The Anatomy*, "I have liv'd a silent, sedentary, solitary, private life . . . penned up most part in my study." Throughout life, he maintained an avid interest in astronomy and astrology. In fact, the date he calculated for his death was so close to his actual death—January 25, 1640—that some suspect he committed suicide; but had he done so, he probably would not have been buried in Christ Church Cathedral. All that is known for sure is that he died alone in his rooms at the college.

MAJOR WORKS AND THEMES

Burton began writing his first extant work, *Philosophaster*, a Latin comedy, in 1606 but did not complete it until 1615. Only performed once on February 16, 1617, it was first published in 1862. His insistence on the early date of composition may have been to avoid charges of plagiarizing from Jonson's *Alchemist*, produced in 1610 and published in 1612. Although both plays feature an alchemist and are satiric, few other similarities exist. The fictional Osuna, a small town in Andalusia, provides the setting for Burton's play, and its inhabitants, who want to found a university, supply the pretext through which Burton exposes false learning, magic, trickery, alchemy, and bad poetry. Although the play is hardly dramatic gold, it exemplifies Burton's ability to write lively satire, so much a part of persona Democritus Junior's wit in *The Anatomy*, as early as 1606.

When Burton began writing his masterpiece, *The Anatomy of Melancholy*, is unknown. In 1621, the first edition appeared, signed with the pseudonym Democritus Junior. During Burton's life, four more editions were issued (1624, 1628, 1632, 1638); a sixth was published posthumously in 1651. Each edition was revised considerably, with Burton adding words and deleting few.

After "The Author's Abstract of Melancholy," a poem on melancholy's positive and negative attributes, *The Anatomy* begins with a lengthy preface, "Democritus Junior to the Reader," in which Burton explains his use of Democritus as a literary convention many readers would recognize. The atomist Democritus of Abdera (5th century B.C.) was known as the "laughing philosopher" (as opposed to Heraclitus, the "weeping philosopher"), and Burton employs Democritus as a satiric persona who deals with problems by laughing at them. Here Democritus Junior catalogs examples of human folly, both ancient and contemporary, and suggests ways to improve society. These utopian ideas satirize 17th-century English politics and customs, but Burton realizes his suggestions for improvement soon vanish in a world inhabited by the madmen his work will describe. Although Burton's book develops this persona, his identity as author was always apparent.

Burton's goal is to "anatomize" melancholy by dissecting and analyzing all its parts. Because anatomies, usually scientific treatises, attempted to be exhaustive, Burton tried to assemble everything ever written on the malady, so he collected a vast number of different, sometimes contradictory, views about its causes and cures. In the 17th century, the term *melancholy* described depression caused by an excess of melancholy, or black bile (never found in an autopsy), one of four bodily humors or fluids thought to determine personality; Burton, however, uses the term more loosely to describe all kinds of mental and emotional vexations.

The body of *The Anatomy* is divided into three "partitions," each with subdivisions into many sections, members, and subsections. The first defines causes, symptoms, and prognosis for melancholy; the second, cures; the third, love melancholy and religious melancholy. Such divisions suggest order; examining the text, however, reveals much disorder. Subjects often overlap; and when a topic does not fit a section, Burton inserts a digression. A wealth of 17th-century medical and psychological knowledge, Burton's work cites more than 1,300 authors.

Listing its contents does not capture the work's essence, because its major appeal lies in Burton's style. Characterized by copia or fullness, sentences often begin with words or phrases played upon at length throughout them. Sentences can be long with their parts loosely connected. Frequently their elements are rhythmic and build to a climax. Contradictions and digressions abound; catalogs are common, along with numerous examples and many uses of metaphor and similes. Sometimes Burton rails at readers. There is abundant quotation in Latin, which posed little difficulty for educated readers in the 17th century.

CRITICAL RECEPTION

Burton's reputation rests, as we have seen, on his most important work, *The Anatomy of Melancholy*, a treasury of Burton's ideas on a wide variety of subjects, a reflection of his mind, and a primary source for students of 17th-century intellectual history. It is also important as the first detailed work on psychology in English. No longer the bestseller it was in 17th-century England, it continues to be read, mainly for its leisurely, anecdotal, informal, and idiosyncratic style. Burton's publisher, who insisted Burton write in English rather than Latin, as he preferred, is said to have made a fortune from the book. Although its popularity declined in the 18th and 19th centuries, Samuel Johnson, James Boswell, Laurence Sterne, Charles Lamb, and John Keats, among others, most admired it. In fact, Sterne's style often reminds readers of Burton.

Near the end of the 19th century, A.R. Shilleto's 1893 edition brought new attention to the work. The new Oxford scholarly edition (1989–), with its projected six volumes (three of which have been issued), should increase critical interest in Burton and provide, for one thing, a useful means of investigating Burton's many revisions. A planned volume with English translations of all Latin will make the work accessible to modern readers. Stanley Fish, Ruth A. Fox, Devon L. Hodges, Ann E. Imbrie, Nicolas K. Kiessling, Bridget Gellert Lyons, Richard Nochimson, Michael O'Connell, David Renaker, and others have contributed to understanding Burton's sophistication as a writer and have inspired new studies about his "voice, his rhetorical and dramatic strategies, his ideas about genre, his originality in reshaping his sources, and [his] poetics of nonfiction prose" (Sununu 248).

BIBLIOGRAPHY

Works by Robert Burton

The Anatomy of Melancholy. Oxford: Printed by John Lichfield & James Short for Henry Cripps, 1621; rev., 1624; rev. again, 1628; rev. again, 1632; rev. ed., Oxford: Printed by Leonard Lichfield for Henry Cripps, 1638; rev. ed., Oxford: Printed by R.W. for Henry Cripps, 1651.

The Anatomy of Melancholy. Ed. A.R. Shilleto. 3 vols. London and New York: Bell, 1893.

The Anatomy of Melancholy. Ed. Thomas C. Faulkner, Nicolas K. Kiessling, and Rhonda L. Blair. 6 vols. projected. London: Clarendon Press, Vol. 1, 1989; Vol. 2, 1990; Vol. 3, 1994.

Philosophaster. Ed. and trans. Connie McQuillen. Binghamton, NY: Medieval & Renaissance Texts and Studies, 1993.

Robert Burton's Philosophaster *with an English Translation of the Same, Together with His Other Minor Writings in Prose and Verse*. Ed. Paul Jordan-Smith. 1931. Reprint, Stanford, CA: Stanford University Press, 1977.

Studies of Robert Burton

Babb, Lawrence. *Sanity in Bedlam: A Study of Robert Burton's* Anatomy of Melancholy. 1959. Reprint, East Lansing: Michigan State University Press, 1977.

Bamborough, J.B. "Robert Burton's Astrological Notebook." *Review of English Studies* 32 (1981): 267–285.

Blanchard, W. Scott. *Scholars' Bedlam: Menippean Satire in the Renaissance*. Lewisburg, PA: Bucknell University Press, 1995.

Colie, Rosalie. *Paradoxia Epidemica: The Renaissance Tradition of Paradox*. Princeton: Princeton University Press, 1966.

Donovan, Dennis G., Margaretha G. Hartley Herman, and Ann Imbrie. *Sir Thomas Browne and Robert Burton: A Reference Guide*. Boston: G.K. Hall, 1981.

Elsky, Martin. *Authorizing Words: Speech, Writing, and Print in the English Renaissance*. Ithaca, NY: Cornell University Press, 1989.

Evans, Bergen, and George J. Mohr. *The Psychiatry of Robert Burton*. 1944. Reprint, New York: Columbia University Press, 1977.

Fish, Stanley. *Self-Consuming Artifacts: The Experience of Seventeenth-Century Literature*. Berkeley: University of California Press, 1972.

Fox, Ruth A. *The Tangled Chain: The Structure of Disorder in* Anatomy of Melancholy. Berkeley: University of California Press, 1976.

Heusser, Martin. *The Gilded Pill: A Study of the Reader-Writer Relationship in Robert Burton's* Anatomy of Melancholy. Tübingen: Stauffenburg, 1987.

Hodges, Devon L. *Renaissance Fictions of Anatomy*. Amherst: University of Massachusetts Press, 1985.

Höltgen, Karl-Josef. "Literary Art and the Scientific Method in Robert Burton's *Anatomy of Melancholy*." *Explorations in Renaissance Culture* 16 (1990): 1–36.

Kiessling, Nicolas K. *The Legacy of Democritus Junior/Robert Burton*. Oxford: Bodleian Library, 1990.

———. *The Library of Robert Burton*. Oxford: Oxford Bibliographical Society, 1988.

Lyons, Bridget Gellert. *Voices of Melancholy: Studies in Literary Treatments of Melancholy in Renaissance England*. London: Routledge & Kegan Paul, 1971.

Mueller, William R. *The Anatomy of Robert Burton's England*. Berkeley: University of California Press, 1952.

Nochimson, Richard. "Burton's *Anatomy*: The Author's Purposes and the Reader's Response." *Forum for Modern Language Studies* 13 (July 1977): 265–284.

O'Connell, Michael. *Robert Burton*. Boston: Twayne Publishers, 1986.

Prescott, Anne Lake. "Is There a Reader in This Response? The Case of Robert Burton." In *Rabelais in Context*, ed. Barbara C. Bowen. Birmingham, AL: Summa, 1993. 181–195.

Renaker, David. "Robert Burton and the Ramist Method." *Renaissance Quarterly* 24 (Summer 1971): 210–220.

Seelig, Sharon Cadman. *Generating Texts: The Progeny of Seventeenth-Century Prose*. Charlottesville: University Press of Virginia, 1996.

Simon, Jean Robert. *Robert Burton (1577–1640) Et* L'Anatomie de la Mélancolie. Paris: Didier, 1964.

Sununu, Andrea. "Recent Studies in Burton and Walton [Robert Burton (1970–85)]." *English Literary Renaissance* 17.2 (Spring 1987): 243–255.

Tillman, James S. "The Satirist Satirized: Burton's Democritus Jr." *Studies in the Literary Imagination* 10 (Fall 1977): 89–96.

Vicari, E. Patricia. *The View from Minerva's Tower: Learning and Imagination in* The Anatomy of Melancholy. Toronto: University of Toronto Press, 1989.

❦ *Samuel Butler*

(1612/1613–1680)

GLENN SUCICH

BIOGRAPHY

"In the mist of this obscurity," wrote Samuel Johnson, "passed the life of Butler, a man whose name can only perish with his language. The mode and place of his education are unknown; the events of his life are variously related; and all that can be told with certainty is, that he was poor." Indeed, compared to his more famous contemporaries, little is known about the details of Samuel Butler's life. What we do know about the author of *Hudibras*, *Characters*, and various other poems and prose tracts comes largely from three sources: the biographer **John Aubrey**, who befriended Butler late in life; an anonymous *Life* attached to a 1704 edition of *Hudibras*; and Anthony à Wood, whose brief 19th-century biography owes much to Aubrey. While these sources provide important biographical information, their inconsistent accounts make any attempt to reconstruct the particulars of Butler's life a labor of speculation.

Butler was born most likely in February 1612/1613 at Strensham on the Avon, a small parish located a few miles south of Worcester. The fifth of eight children, Butler spent his early childhood working the family farm, a hands-on experience that might explain the contempt for abstract philosophical and theological speculation that characterizes his mature thought. His grandfather and father were both fairly prosperous farmers. Upon his death in 1626, the senior Butler bequeathed to his second son "all my Lawe and Latine books of Logicke, Rhetoricke, Philosophy, Poesy, phisicke, my great Dodaneus Herball, and all other my lattine and greeke bookes whatsoever." Judging by the erudition and allusiveness of his later works, the young poet made good use of his inheritance.

In 1622, Butler entered King's School, Worcester, where he likely received a traditional education under the tutelage of Henry Bright. Between the time Butler left King's School in 1627 and his appointment as steward of Ludlow Castle in January 1661, precise information about his experiences is scanty. Despite rumors that Butler attended Oxford or Cambridge, there is no extant evidence of his matriculation in either university. The anonymous *Life* of 1704 and Aubrey both report that he spent "several yeares" as a clerk to various reputable people, including the eminent justice of the peace Leonard Jefferey and the Countess of Kent. During these years, Butler developed an interest in painting, music, and classical literature, befriending the painter Samuel Cooper and the antiquarian John Selden, for whom Butler worked as a translator. Butler eventually moved to London, where he spent considerable time at the Inns of Court. (Aubrey claims that Butler "studied the Common Lawes of England, but did not practise.") One of his employers during this period, the Presbyterian member of Parliament Sir Samuel Luke, is of particular interest to literary historians, many of whom see in Luke the model for Sir Hudibras. While the connection remains unsubstantiated, Butler's tenure with Luke did provide him the opportunity to observe firsthand the Puritanism he vehemently attacks in *Hudibras*. Thus, scholars tend to agree that it was during Butler's service to Luke that the poet's plans for his most famous work were hatched.

When the first part of *Hudibras* appeared in 1662 (Parts 2 and 3 appeared in 1663 and 1677, respectively), Butler was approaching his fiftieth year. Despite Charles's enthusiasm for the poem, Butler never achieved the preferment he spent much of his life seeking. By 1670, he was working for the Duke of Buckingham, accompanying the Duke's entourage on diplomatic embassies to Versailles in 1670 and perhaps to The Hague in 1672. In 1677, the King awarded Butler a small pension, but by then Butler was plagued by poverty and a penchant for alcohol. While in London, says Aubrey, Butler "had a Clubb every night" with John Cleveland and certain lawyers from Gray's Inn. In 1678, two years before Butler's death, the Plymouth physician James Yonge, after seeing Butler at the Wits' Coffee House in Covent Garden, described the poet as "an old paralytick claret drinker, a morose surly man." Samuel Butler died of consumption on September 25, 1680. He was buried in the churchyard of St. Paul's, Covent Garden.

MAJOR WORKS AND THEMES

An acidic skepticism defines the two works on which Butler's reputation primarily rests, *Hudibras* and *Characters*. In both works, Butler takes deadly aim at a wide range of contemporary characters and ideologies, ruthlessly lampooning them until finally the reader senses that "nothing less than a whole culture, its intellectual and moral *modus vivendi* and its great and puzzling divisions, are being buried in the text" (Parker 29). Whereas other satirists of the Augustan age often took as their targets particular groups or currents of ideas, Butler was less discriminating, wielding his pen against anyone whom he perceived to lay false claim to moral or intellectual authority.

Most likely conceived during the political and religious controversies of the late 1650s, *Hudibras* is ostensibly an anti-Puritan mock-heroic; but as the Reverend George Gilfillan put it in 1854, "the author has no objections to take a little sport out of all the parties and persons who come across his path." In fact, if Presbyterians, Independents, and other sectarians suffer Butler's invective, no more fortunate are the scientists, theologians, schoolmen, mystics, and even Royalists of Butler's day, all of whom are ridiculed, often with degrading animal imagery, for their irrational pretensions and self-deluding hypocrisy. The influence of Cervantes, Spenser, Scarron, and Rabelais is evident as Sir Hudibras, a "true blue" Presbyterian who takes his name from a character in the *Faerie Queene*, embarks with his squire Ralpho, an Independent, on various quests that recall the exploits of *Don Quixote*'s eponymous hero and his sidekick Sancho Panza. Near the end of Part I, the two engage in a theological dispute that exposes the equal folly of Aristotelian logic, represented by Hudibras, and the Neoplatonic mysticism espoused by Ralpho. Other characters, too, are mocked for harboring false ideas and for flaunting their useless and deceptive learning. Butler employs octosyllabic couplets with scathing rhymes—the benchmarks of the hudibrastic style—to comic effect, as when he describes the astrologer Sidrophel: "So in the circle of the arts, / Did he advance his nat'ral parts; / Till falling back still, for retreat, / He fell to juggle, cant, and cheat" (2.3.215–218). The conventions of epic and romance literature are also parodied, and several episodes convey Butler's belief, recorded in his notebooks, that "if any man should but imitate what these Heroical Authors write in Practice of his life and Conversation, he would become the most Ridiculous Person in the world."

The impulse to condemn hypocrisy and self-delusion also governs *Characters*, a series of nearly 200 character sketches belonging to the tradition inaugurated by the Greek philosopher Theophrastus (c. 372–287 B.C.). As in *Hudibras*, Butler attacks physicians, philosophers, lawyers, priests, sailors, scriveners, zealots, and a host of other character types, deriding them for their irrational behavior and pedantry. What unites all of Butler's works is a deep-seated contempt for any claim to knowledge that does not rest on Baconian (see **Francis Bacon**) rationality and commonsense empiricism. In terms reminiscent of Pascal, Butler once wrote that "all the Business of this World is but Diversion, and all the Happiness in it that Mankind is capable of—anything that will keep it from reflecting upon the Misery, Vanity and Nonsence of it." Butler's works, perhaps more than anything, bear out this conviction.

CRITICAL RECEPTION

Despite Butler's relative obscurity today, *Hudibras* achieved for itself and its author instant and widespread recognition. Shortly after its publication in 1662, *Hudibras* was, according to Wood, "not only taken into his majesty's hands, and read by him with great delight, but also by all courtiers, loyal scholars and gentlemen, to the great profit of the author and bookseller." That the poem went through nine editions in a single year corroborates one historian's claim that it "became at once the most popular poem in London" (Wilders xix). If James Sutherland would have asked in Butler's own time the question he posed in 1959—namely, "Who now reads Butler?"—the answer would have been almost everybody.

Nearly every major Augustan writer, including **Dryden**, Swift, Prior, Pope, **Shaftesbury**, and Churchill, was influenced by Butler's caustic wit and relentless method. As one recent commentator puts it, "[A]ll those special elements of modernity in English Restoration and eighteenth-century writing—disaffection from ritual, alienated individualism, positivism, mistrust of language, and the cult of taste—may be seen in their infancy in Butler" (Parker 26–27). **Addison** mentions or quotes Butler in fifteen numbers of *The Spectator*, and Butler's influence can be detected in such monumental works as Swift's *A Tale of the Tub*, Shaftesbury's *Characteristics*, **Hobbes**'s *Leviathan*, and Pope's *The Dunciad*.

More recently, critics have recognized a self-defeating circularity in Butler's works, arguing that *Hudibras*, unlike the critiques of metaphysics offered by Bacon, Hobbes, and others, attempts only "to assault the world, not to improve it" (Rothman 34). Because Butler does not engage any new methods of understanding, these critics contend, the satirist becomes one with the objects of his satire, ultimately espousing a dogmatic skepticism that "takes from life any pretense to meaning, fullness, decency, or beauty" (Miner 159). Some critics have argued for the poem's political allegory, while others have aligned *Hudibras* with **Milton**'s *Paradise Lost* as a work that heralds the end of epic and the rise of the novel. However one reads Butler, the fact remains that, in keeping with Dr. Johnson's prediction, neither Butler's name nor his language has perished. In challenging the inherited literary forms and ideals of his age, Butler created new aesthetic and intellectual possibilities for his and later generations. His corpus therefore stands as a significant, if neglected, contribution to the history of modern literature and philosophy.

BIBLIOGRAPHY

Works by Samuel Butler

Hudibras. Ed. with an introduction and commentary by John Wilders. Oxford: Clarendon Press, 1967.

Samuel Butler: Prose Observations. Ed. with an introduction and commentary by Hugh De Quehen. Oxford: Clarendon Press, 1979.

Samuel Butler: Satires and Miscellaneous Poetry and Prose. Ed. René Lamar. Cambridge: Cambridge University Press, 1928.

Samuel Butler 1612–1680: Characters. Ed. Charles W. Daves. Cleveland, OH: Press of Case Western Reserve University, 1970.

Studies of Samuel Butler

De Beer, E.S. "The Later Life of Samuel Butler." *Review of English Studies* 4 (1928): 159–166.

Miner, Earl. *The Restoration Mode from Milton to Dryden*. Princeton: Princeton University Press, 1974.

Parker, Blanford. *The Triumph of Augustan Poetics: English Literary Culture from Butler to Johnson*. Cambridge: Cambridge University Press, 1998.

Richards, Edward Ames. Hudibras *in the Burlesque Tradition*. New York: Columbia University Press, 1937.

Rothman, David J. "*Hudibras* and Menippean Satire." *The Eighteenth Century: Theory and Interpretation* 34 (1993): 23–44.

Seidel, Michael. *Satiric Inheritance: Rabelais to Sterne*. Princeton: Princeton University Press, 1979.

Snider, Alvin. *Origins of Authority in Seventeenth-Century England: Bacon, Milton, Butler*. Toronto: University of Toronto Press, 1994.

Wasserman, George. *Samuel "Hudibras" Butler*. Updated ed. Boston: Twayne Publishers, 1989.

❧ *Thomas Campion*

(1567–1620)

ELLEN THOMPSON McCABE

BIOGRAPHY

Thomas Campion was born to relatively well-off parents, John and Lucy Campion, on February 12, 1567, in London. His childhood was spotted by tragedy in that both his parents died when he was relatively young. His father died in 1576, and his mother remarried in 1577. In March 1580, Campion's mother died, leaving him an orphan. Fortunately, Campion's stepfather, Augustine Steward, undertook guardianship of the Campion children (Thomas had one sister, Rose) and Campion's education, sending him to Peterhouse, Cambridge, which he left in 1584 without a degree. This fact has been used as fuel for the speculation that Campion may have been a Catholic, since Catholics could study at Peterhouse but would not be granted degrees unless they took an oath of allegiance. Campion subsequently studied law at Grey's Inn (1586).

Events of 1588 and the following years distracted Campion from his educational pursuits. In that year he performed in celebrations presented by Grey's Inn at court. These types of performances were often presented by the more affluent (and thus often less serious) students at the Inn. Three years later, five of his songs were appended to a manuscript of *Astrophil and Stella* by Sir Philip Sidney and published under the name of "Content."

From 1591 to 1592 Campion appears to have gone with Sir Robert Carey on Essex's Norman expedition to aid Henry IV against the Catholic League. During the years 1593–1595, Campion composed songs for *Gesta Grayorum*, a court revel, and had a collection of poems, *Thomae Campiani Poemata* (December 2, 1594), published. Again, in 1601–1602, Campion was published: first his *A Booke of Ayres* with Philip Rosseter's musical help, then *Observations in the Art of English Poesie*. The latter caused such a sensation that a rebuttal by Samuel Daniel, *A Defense of Ryme*, was published in 1603. Campion was indeed busy during these years, and he was doing more than publishing, for in 1605 he received a medical degree from the University of Caen in France. It is assumed that he returned to London shortly thereafter to practice medicine, which he continued for the rest of his life.

In 1607 *The Lord Hay's Masque* was performed at court, complete with elaborate staging that included revealing only half of the stage at a time, with two separate scenes. *Two Bookes of Ayres* may have been published in 1613, along with *Songs of Mourning* for Prince Henry's death, with music by Giovanni Coperario. In the same year *The Lord's Masque* was performed for Princess Elizabeth's wedding, *The Caversham Entertainment* was performed for Queen Anne, and *The Somerset Masque* was performed at court. Between 1613 and 1614 Campion indulged in musical theory in *A New Way of Making Fowre Parts in Counter-point*.

Campion was accused of complicity in the murder of Sir Thomas Overbury but was cleared of the charges on October 26, 1615. In 1616 he was allowed to administer a physic to Sir Thomas Monson, his good friend and sponsor who had been imprisoned in the Tower for the aforementioned murder. The year 1617 saw the publication of *The Third and Fourth Bookes of Ayres* as well as a performance of *The Ayres That Were Sung and Played at Brougham Castle by George Mason and John Earsden*, which may have had words by Thomas Campion. Performed for James I, these were published the following year. In 1619, Campion's final work, *Tho. Campiani Epigrammatum Libri II*, was published. Campion died on March 1, 1620. He appears to have remained unmarried and had no children; his life was thus devoted to his written and musical works and to the practice of medicine. He left his limited worldly wealth to his friend and collaborator, Philip Rosseter. Campion was buried at St. Dunstan's in the West, Fleet Street.

MAJOR WORKS AND THEMES

Campion's works consist mainly of poetry (both in English and in Latin) or songs; masques, dramatic performances performed at court; and treatises on subjects relating to poetry and music. His Latin poetry, which comprised about a third of his work, was contained in two volumes, *Thomae Campiani Poemata* (1595) and *Tho. Campiani Epigrammatum Libri II* (1619). The first contained *Ad Thamesin*, the first full-length Latin poem dealing with the Armada. Oddly enough, it only devoted eighteen lines to that actual subject, the rest of the poem consisting of descriptive allegory. Other Latin selections deal with aspects of love, advice and dedications to friends and acquaintances, male-female relationships, and the return of spring.

He also wrote a long and controversial poem, *De Pulverea Coniuratione (On the Gunpowder Plot)*, in which he takes great pains to condemn the Catholic perpetrators of the scheme. The exclusion of this poem in his later issued edition of Latin poems caused speculation that Campion had converted to Catholicism in the meantime.

Campion is remembered widely for his songs or airs, many of which deal with themes of love. The first airs appeared appended, as we have seen, to a pirated edition of Sidney's *Astrophil and Stella* (1591), released by Thomas Newman, signed "Content." He later published *A Booke of Ayres* (1601) with Philip Rosseter, *Two Bookes of Ayres* (1613?), and *The Third and Fourth Bookes of Ayres* (1617?). The earliest airs seem to have been written for a masque as is indicated by the designation of "Canto." The relationship of music to his poetry is essential, which has been a blessing and a bane for his works. The close association of his works to the melodies of the times dated his works prematurely, causing the body of his work to be lost for almost two centuries. This musical element is also the raison d'être for his treatises, *Observations in the Art of English Poesie* and *A New Way of Making Fowre Parts in Counter-point, by a most familiar, and infallible Rule*. In the former, he argued against the use of rhyme in English poetry, advocating instead the quantitative classical Latin style of composition. However, in practice, he continued to write his English poetry and airs with rhyming lyrics and rhythm. In the latter, he addressed the creation of music itself in a series of small primers. Most notable was his insistence that musical combinations are founded on the origins of the bass notes, not the treble line.

Campion is also known for his masques, theatrical-style performances based on the dance, with royalty or aristocracy at their center. His most notable are *The Lord Hay's Masque* (1607), *The Lord's Masque* (1607), and *The Somerset Masque*. *The Lord Hay's Masque* was performed for the marriage of Lord Hayes to Honora Denny. Founded heavily on Olympian myth, the masque included elaborate stage descriptions and diagrams, intricate costume descriptions, and detailed stage directions, music, and song. The intricacy of detail resembles modern-day drama far more than **Shakespeare**'s plays, for example. Inigo Jones, the famous stage and costume designer, worked with Campion on *The Lord Hay's Masque* and *The Lord's Masque*.

The most controversial of Campion's masques was *The Somerset Masque*, performed for the marriage of Frances Howard to Robert Carr. Formerly the Countess of Essex, Howard was responsible for Sir Thomas Overbury's imprisonment and eventual death by poisoning, in which Campion was later implicated. She had arranged for an annulment of her former marriage to wed the now new Earl of Somerset. The masque Campion created for their wedding was not based on Olympian myth, but political reality, and made an effort to exonerate the newlyweds from any guilt. It also included an extensive collection of music. Unfortunately, the stage plans have not survived.

CRITICAL RECEPTION

Once Campion's *Poemata* was published, his reputation soared. Reception was good, with many positive comments made on his works. The one exception was Samuel Daniel, who wrote his *A Defense of Ryme* in response to Campion's *Observations in the Art of English Poesie*. However, even Daniel acknowledged Campion's abilities and in another statement said that it was a shame that Campion was now criticizing the rhyme he had put to such good use in his own poetry.

If imitation is the surest form of flattery, then Campion had many fans of his works. A number of his songs were reprinted in anthologies of songs, both with and without the original music. **Ben Jonson**, while he never uttered words of praise for Campion, parodied *The Lord's Masque* in his *Irish Masque*.

From the Restoration to the later 19th century, Campion was forgotten. Perhaps his lyrics were linked to a particular music, and the music went out of style. However, not much was heard until 1886. In the preceding years, some of his lyrics appeared in anthologies without attribution. *Lyrics from the English Song Books* edited by A.H. Bullen featured some of Campion's works. Three years later Bullen released *The Works of Doctor Thomas Campion*, which included the airs, the masques, and *Observations*. An authoritative edition of Campion's works was published in 1903, edited and with critical comments by Percival Vivian. In addition, modern poets T.S. Eliot, W.H. Auden, and Ezra Pound have acknowledged Campion's contributions to poetry and criticism. Either through imitation of Campion's verses or commentary on his critical works, these authors have expressed a true appreciation of him.

BIBLIOGRAPHY

Works by Thomas Campion

Campion's Works. Ed. Percival Vivian. 1903. Oxford: Oxford University Press, 1966.

Samuel Daniel A Defense of Ryme 1603; Thomas Campion Observations in the Art of English Poesie 1602, Elizabethan and Jacobean Quartos. Ed G.B. Harrison. New York: Barnes & Noble, 1966.

Thomas Campion: De Pulverea Coniuratione (On the Gunpowder Plot). Sidney Sussex MS 59. Ed. David Lindley. Translation and additional notes by Robin Sowerby. Leeds, England: Leeds Texts and Monographs New Series 10, Leeds Studies in English, 1987.

The Works of Thomas Campion. Ed. with introduction and notes by Walter R. Davis. New York: W.W. Norton, 1969.

Studies of Thomas Campion

Binns, J.W., ed. *The Latin Poetry of English Poets*. London: Routledge & Kegan Paul, 1974.

Davis, Walter R. *Thomas Campion*. Boston: Twayne Publishers, 1987.

DeNeef, A. Leigh. "Structure and Theme in Campion's *Lords Maske*." *Studies in English Literature, 1500–1900* 17 (1977): 95–103.

Friedman, Lawrence S. "Words into Power: Renaissance Expression and Thomas Campion." *English Studies* 2 (1988): 130–145.

Irwin, John T. "Thomas Campion and the Musical Emblem." *Studies in English Literature, 1500–1900* 10 (1970): 121–141.

Kastendieck, Miles Merwin. *England's Musical Poet, Thomas Campion*. New York: Russell & Russell, 1963.

Loughlin, Marie H. " 'Love's Friend and Stranger to Virginitie': The Politics of the Virginal Body in Ben Jonson's *Hymenaei* and Thomas Campion's *The Lord Hay's Masque*." *ELH* 63 (1996): 833–849.

Orrell, John. "The Agent of Savoy at the Somerset Masque." *Review of English Studies: A Quarterly Journal of English Literature and the English Language* 28 (1977): 301–304.

❧ *Thomas Carew*

(c. 1595–1639)

THOMAS HOWARD CROFTS III

BIOGRAPHY

Thomas Carew (pronounced Carey) was born in Kent about 1595 to Sir Matthew and
Alice (née Rivers) Carew. He matriculated at Merton College, Oxford, at the age of
thirteen (June 10, 1608), taking a B.A. there in 1611. Around 1613, Sir Matthew lost
all of his money in an obscure real estate transaction, and the remainder of his life
was spent in trying to recover his fortune and place his sons Thomas and Matthew in
lucrative positions. Though Thomas studied law for a while at the Middle Temple,
his professional career began in 1612 or 1613 as secretary to Sir Dudley Carleton on
the latter's embassies to Venice, Turin, and the Netherlands. Carew remained in Carleton's service until 1616, when he was dismissed for making insulting remarks to or
about the ambassador and his wife and for disparaging their horses (the exact circumstances are not known). News of the debacle damaged Carew's prospects for other
employment and caused his father to write to Carleton, "I geue him ouer as vtterly
lost" (Dunlap xxvii). The epistolary record of the poet's disgrace is ample: especially
in the father's letters to Carleton, which reflect both the high publicity that attended
the younger Carew's behavior and the increasing dementia of the elder (Dunlap xxiv–
xxix). Carew and his father remained unreconciled at Sir Matthew's death on August
2, 1618.

Finding no openings in London, Carew in 1619 accompanied his cousin Lord Herbert of Cherbury to the French court. In Herbert's retinue, Carew struck up a friendship
with Sir John Crofts. The connection was to be an important one: Crofts was friends
with **Jonson**, **Herrick**, and **Davenant**, and was himself an accomplished poet (he
composed the three "Hymnes to God the Father, God the Son, God the Holy Ghost,"
set to music and published by Henry Lawes in 1655). Carew composed the lines "To
the King" for Sir John's recitation on James I's visit to Saxham, the Crofts's estate
in Suffolk (1619/1620). Carew himself would be a frequent guest at Saxham and
compose many verses to its master and his family. While in Paris, Carew honed his

famous conversational skill (in which he was said to be **Suckling**'s only peer (Dunlap xxxviii, xliii), read the Pléiade poets, and may have met the Italian poet Giambattista Marino, whose work is known to have made a major impression on the English poet. After a period of travel in Herbert's entourage, Carew returned to England and in 1628 was made a gentleman of Charles I's Privy Chamber and Sewer (or Carver) to His Majesty's table.

At Charles's court, Carew seemed to find his niche, both socially and poetically. He became good friends with Suckling, appearing in the latter's "Sessions of the Poets" and as his interlocutor in the poetic dialogue "Upon My Lady Carlile's Walking in Hampton Court Garden." Carew had a well-deserved reputation for mischief and debauchery that stayed with him all of his adult life. This supposed lifestyle resulted in the poet's complete alienation from his family—his mother, who predeceased him by two years, makes no mention of him in her will—but his reputation was not at all harmful to his career as a poet, soldier, and gentleman. Carew went with King Charles as a cavalier in the first Bishops' War. It was perhaps in the northern cold of that campaign that Carew's health began its decline. He died on or around March 21, 1639, possibly at Wrest, Bedfordshire. At the end of his life, Carew attempted to make amends with the Church and, according to Izaak Walton, summoned the Reverend John Hales, a relative, to his deathbed. Hales granted him absolution "upon a promise of amendment." On his unexpected recovery, Carew apparently resumed his profligate ways. Not long thereafter, Carew relapsed into his sickness; he summoned Hales a second time but was repulsed.

MAJOR WORKS AND THEMES

Carew's earliest known poems are two belonging to the French period in Herbert's retinue: "Upon some alterations in my Mistresse, after my departure into France" and the "Elegie" to Lady Peniston (d. January 1619/1620). Other poems may be dated from this period or just after, such as "My mistris commanding me to returne her letters" and "To my Mistresse in absence." Traditionally grouped with the Sons of Ben, Carew considered himself also a follower of **John Donne**, and his poetry often aspired to the metaphysical. Numerous, though artful, borrowings of Donne's imagery are to be found in Carew's lyrics (as in "Secresie protested," which lifts its opening conceit from Donne's "The Dampe"). The Cavalier poet, however, made his career by displaying his wit rather than wrapping it in thorny conceits. Like Jonson, Carew was devoted to the pleasures of civilization and wrote poetry that embraced both the trivialities and the tragedies of life.

CRITICAL RECEPTION

Carew's kind of poetry was not wholly superficial, but it never, as Yeats would say, gave all the heart. Carew's society verses were very popular, prized especially for their petulant wit. In such pieces as "A Cruel Mistresse" and "Disdain Returned," Carew could execute deftly the amorous parry or riposte. With "To Saxham," Carew made an important contribution to the tradition of the country house poem. In "An Elegy on the Death of . . . Dr. John Donne," the poet wrote perhaps the finest elegy of the period. Remarkable for its dignified, solemn pace, it is also a wonderfully astute appraisal of Donne's contribution to English poetry and (Carew stresses) the English language. Carew also wrote the masque *Coelum Britannicum*, which was produced by Inigo Jones and performed at Whitehall on February 18, 1633/1634 and published later that year. The masque, a blithe adaptation of Giordano Bruno's philosophical dialogue *Spaccio de la Bestia Trionfante*, was a tremendous success with the King and Queen and was also praised highly in letters of the period (Dunlap 273–274).

At his death, the poet had also begun a set of verse translations of the Psalms; these survive but are generally considered inferior. Carew's poems were first collected into an edition in 1640 (reprinted 1642, 1651, 1670, 1772).

BIBLIOGRAPHY

Works by Thomas Carew

The Poems of Thomas Carew with His Masque Coelum Britannicum. Ed. Rhodes Dunlap. 1949. Corrected reprint, Oxford: Clarendon Press, 1957, 1964.

Studies of Thomas Carew

Blanshard, Rufus A. "Thomas Carew and the Cavalier Poets." *Transactions of the Wisconsin Academy of Arts, Sciences, and Letters* 43 (1957): 214–227.
King, Bruce. "The Strategy of Carew's Wit." *Review of English Literature* 5 (1964): 42–51.
Martz, Louis L. "Thomas Carew: The Cavalier World." In his *The Wit of Love: Donne, Carew, Crashaw, Marvell*. Notre Dame, IN: University of Notre Dame Press, 1969.
Rauber, D.F. "Carew Redivivus." *Texas Studies in Language and Literature* 13 (1971): 17–28.
Selig, Edward I. *The Flourishing Wreath: A Study of Thomas Carew's Poetry*. New Haven, CT: Yale University Press, 1958.

❧ *Elizabeth Cary*
(c. 1585–1639)

PAMELA K. SHAFFER

BIOGRAPHY

Linguist, translator, and dramatist, Elizabeth Cary was born the only child of a wealthy Oxford lawyer, Lawrence Tanfield, and his wife, Elizabeth Symondes. As a child, she learned and could read fluently in French, Spanish, Latin, and Hebrew. Precocious and independent, she studied esoteric subjects of her own choosing. At the age of fifteen or sixteen, in 1602, she was married to Henry Cary, who later became 1st Viscount Falkland.

At nineteen, Cary secretly converted to Catholicism, concealing her conversion from her husband and family for twenty years. She bore eleven children between 1609 and 1624; she accompanied her husband to Ireland when he became Lord Deputy of Ireland in 1623. However, when Sir Henry discovered her conversion to Catholicism, he had her sent back to England, tried to get custody of the children, and refused to support her. Having already been disinherited by her father, and placed under house arrest by the King for six weeks, she appealed to the Privy Council, which ruled that Sir Henry must support her with a yearly allowance. Even though he did not adhere fully to the ruling, Elizabeth did not complain. In the early 1630s, Henry and Elizabeth apparently reconciled, but not long after this, Sir Henry died from a riding injury.

In her last years, Cary abducted two of her sons and eventually sent them to seminaries in France; three of her daughters became nuns, one of whom wrote a biography of her mother. Cary died of a lung disease in 1639 and was buried in the chapel of the Catholic Queen Henrietta Maria.

MAJOR WORKS AND THEMES

Cary's biography, written by one of her daughters, a Catholic nun in France, shows Cary as driven by her conscience and persecuted for her conversion to Catholicism. Her own writing echoed the problems she faced in her own life—namely, the conflict between the dictates of religious belief and the necessity of obeying external authority. These writings seem to derive from two periods in her life: first, her early teen years and the first years of her marriage when she lived with her mother-in-law while her husband was on the Continent, and second, the period after her conversion had been made public, when she was living in difficult circumstances in England.

Soon after Cary married, she began writing poetry while living with her mother-in-law. Cary wrote *The Tragedie of Mariam, the Faire Queene of Jewry* in 1605 or 1606, but it was published only in 1613. It is the first extant English drama written by a woman. A Senecan-style tragedy, based on Josephus's *Antiquities of the Jews*, *Mariam* concerns the love between King Herod and Mariam, his wife. It is unique among other dramas of the time that deal with the same biblical account in that it presents the story from Mariam's point of view rather than from Herod's. Cary creates in Mariam a complex character through whom, by contrast and comparison with other female characters, may be seen the ambiguous role of wife.

The History of the Life, Reign, and Death of Edward II, King of England and Lord of Ireland, a work published only in 1680, concerns the abuse of power in both state and family life. In form it is a blend of prose narrative and blank verse. In this piece, as in *Mariam*, Cary focuses on the ways in which the women characters negotiate between the tyranny of a husband and their own integrity.

Cary's translations include *Le Miroir de Monde*, a geographical treatise by Abraham Ortelius. In order to highlight her religious philosophy, Cary chose mainly to translate religious treaties from Europe, including Jacques Davy Dupperon's Catholic polemical writing, especially *The Reply of Cardinal du Perron* to James I. Later in life, she translated the works of Blosius, a Flemish Benedictine monk.

CRITICAL RECEPTION

Recognition of Cary as a learned woman among her contemporaries is provided by the number of works dedicated to her or mentioning her: John Marston, Richard More, and others dedicated works to her and comment on her learning and quality of mind. However, today, the work on which Cary's fame rests is the well-constructed and carefully researched play, *The Tragedie of Mariam, the Faire Queene of Jewry*. Like *The Historie of . . . King Edward the Second*, *Mariam* provides evidence of Cary's interest in the mind-set and position of women. *Mariam* offers an examination of the subject of wifehood, including instances of wifely rebellion against, along with resentful conformity to, patriarchal authority. The focus on Mariam and the complexities of her personality reveal the conflict between a wife's obligation to obey external authority and the moral imperative to resist and challenge that authority. Cary's dramas mirror the conflicts in her own life and the ambiguous and tenuous position of women in marriage in Renaissance England.

BIBLIOGRAPHY

Works by Elizabeth Cary

Certayne Sermons appointed by the Queenes Majestie, to be declared and read, by al Persones, Vycars, & Curates, every Sundaye and holyday in their Churches: where they have curre. London, 1562.

The History of the Life, Reign, and Death of Edward II, King of England, and Lord of Ireland. With the Rise and Fall of his great favourites, Gaveston and the Spencers. Written by E.F. in the year 1627. And Printed verbatim from the Original. London: J.C. for Charles Harper, Samuel Crouch, and Thomas Fox, 1680.

The History of the most unfortunate Prince, King Edward the second: With choice Political Observations on him and his unhappy Favourites, Gaveston and Spencer: Containing several rare Passages of those Times, not found in Other Historians; found among the Papers of and (supposed to be) writ by The Right honourable Henry Viscount Faulkland, some time Lord Deputy of Ireland. In *Harleian Miscellany.* Vol. 1. London: John White, John Murray, John Harding, 1808.

The Tragedie of Mariam, the Faire Queene of Jewry. Written by that learned, virtuous, and truly noble Ladie, E.C. London: Theomas Creede for Richard Hawkins, 1613. Reprint (Malone Society Reprints facsimile), Oxford: Oxford University Press, 1914.

The Tragedy of Mariam, the fair queen of Jewry. With The Lady Falkland: her life. Ed. Barry Weller and Margaret W. Ferguson. Berkeley: University of California Press, 1994.

Trans. *Reply of the Cardinall of Perron to the Answeare of the King of Great Britain.* Douay: M. Bogart, 1630.

Studies of Elizabeth Cary

Beilin, Elaine. "Elizabeth Cary and *The Tragedie of Mariam." Papers on Language and Literature* 16 (1980): 45–64.

Fischer, Sandra K. "Elizabeth Cary and Tyranny, Domestic and Religious." In *Silent But for the Word: Tudor Women as Patrons, Translators, and Writers of Religious Works,* ed. Margaret P. Hannay. Kent, OH: Kent State University Press, 1985.

Fullerton, Lady Georgiana. *The Life of Elisabeth Lady Falkland 1585–1639.* London: Burns and Oates, 1883.

Murdock, Kenneth. *The Sun at Noon: Three Biographical Sketches.* New York: Macmillan, 1939.

Pearse, Nancy Cotton. "Elizabeth Cary, Renaissance Playwright." *Texas Studies in Literature and Language* 18 (1977): 601–608.

Simpson, Richard. *The Lady Falkland: Her Life.* London: Catholic Publishing & Bookselling Company, 1861.

Travitsky, Betty S. "The *Feme Covert* in Elizabeth Cary's *Mariam."* In *Ambiguous Realities: Women in the Middle Ages and Renaissance,* ed. Carole Levin and Jeanie Watson. Detroit, MI: Wayne State University Press, 1987.

Walker, Kim. *Women Writers of the Renaissance.* New York: Twayne Publishers, 1996.

Margaret Cavendish, Duchess of Newcastle

(1623–1673)

PAMELA K. SHAFFER

BIOGRAPHY

Margaret Lucas Cavendish, Duchess of Newcastle, was born in Essex County, England, the youngest of eight children of Thomas Lucas, a wealthy landowner, and Elizabeth Leighton, his wife. Raised by her widowed mother, in a close-knit Royalist family, Cavendish was taught the basics of reading, writing, music, and needlework. With the outbreak of the civil wars in the 1640s, she fled with her family to Oxford, where in 1643 she became a maid of honor to Queen Henrietta Maria, wife of Charles I. In 1644, Margaret accompanied the Queen into exile in France, where she met William Cavendish, then Marquis of Newcastle, a widower thirty years her senior, and they married in 1645.

For the next fifteen years they lived in exile in Paris and Antwerp. Living largely on credit, the Newcastles socialized with well-known European writers and English exiles, perilously maintaining their aristocratic lifestyle. During this time, Margaret came in contact with the ideas of **Hobbes** and Descartes, and she began to write on topics in natural philosophy. When Cavendish and her husband returned to England after the Restoration, they lived quietly away from court. In 1667, Cavendish was invited to attend a meeting of the Royal Society, a recognition of her efforts in natural philosophy. Cavendish continued to revise her earlier writings and to write in a variety of genres, including the work for which she is best known, a biography of her husband. She died on December 15, 1673.

MAJOR WORKS AND THEMES

With a keen interest in the science of her day, Margaret Lucas Cavendish wrote on science and natural philosophy, revealing a skeptical frame of mind unusual for the time. In 1653, she published *Philosophicall Fancies* (1653), a work of scientific speculation, which considers atomist theories, the composition of matter, and the properties of elemental particles. Yet writing in isolation from the general scientific community of the time, she was hampered by her limited resources and lack of a scientific community. Nevertheless, she continued to revise early works and refine her ideas about natural philosophy in works such as *The Philosophical and Physical Opinions* (1655) and *Observations upon Experimental Philosophy* (1666), at the end of which is a work titled *The Description of a New World, Called the Blazing World*, in a blend of fantasy and autobiography.

Her interest in science and natural philosophy informs her poetical works also. *Poems, and Fancies* (1653) offers poems that show a fascination with the natural world, on widely ranging subjects, from the circulation of human blood to the possibilities of multiple worlds. The influence of **John Donne** is evident in her use of unconventional and startling images, to which she gives the label "similizing." Of particular interest to a modern audience is the prefatory material to her poems. In these introductions, she addresses specific audiences and tries to justify and provide a context for her own poems. The persona she presents is full of contradictions: a bashful, politically conservative person who prefers a secluded life yet one who longs for fame and dresses in elaborate clothing.

In 1656, she published a collection of narratives in both prose and verse, *Natures Pictures Drawn by Fancies Pencil to the Life*, presenting heroic female figures engaged in exciting adventure. Included in this collection is a short, autobiographical account of her early life. In 1662, Cavendish published her first folio volume of closet dramas and *Orations of Diverse Sorts*, both of which concern social and gender issues. In the years after 1660, Margaret Cavendish revised her earlier works and attempted to write in new genres. In 1664, she published *Philosophical Letters* and *CCXI Sociable Letters*, two collections that reveal her wit and confidence in herself.

In 1667, she published a biography of her husband, *The Life of the Thrice Noble, High and Puissant Prince William Cavendishe, Duke, Marquess, and Earl of Newcastle*, which proved to be her most widely read work.

CRITICAL RECEPTION

During her lifetime, both in her publications and in her person, Margaret Cavendish gained notoriety. Alongside the praise of her work by notable philosophers and university faculty of her day can be seen the ridicule of her contemporaries for her outlandish ideas and style of dress. To some audiences, her writings seemed undisciplined and wildly imaginative, especially in her speculations about the natural world, contemporary science, and human behavior. The scorn her writings provoked in some measure was due to the fact that she was a woman writing for publication. However, added to the disparaging comments her works received are negative comments about her appearance and extravagant attire.

All her writings show the wide range of interests Cavendish had, including the natural world, human behavior, and natural history. Although her output is remarkable, the few modern editions of her works attest to limited interest in her works. Today, however, she is considered a significant but underrated writer in the history of English literature, and feminists and social historians are examining her work for its complexity and for the context in which it was written.

BIBLIOGRAPHY

Works by Margaret Cavendish, Duchess of Newcastle

The Description of a New World, Called the Blazing World and Other Writings. Ed. Kate Lilley. New York: New York University Press, 1992.

The Life of the Thrice Noble, High and Puissant Prince William Cavendishe, Duke, Marquess, and Earl of Newcastle. London, 1667.

Natures Pictures Drawn by Fancies Pencil to the Life. London, 1656.

Observations upon Experimental Philosophy. To which is added, The Description of a New Blazing World. London, 1666.

The Philosophical and Physical Opinions. London, 1655, 1663. Revised as *Grounds of Natural Philosophy.* London, 1668.

Philosophicall Fancies. London, 1653.

Plays, Never before Printed. London, 1668.

Poems and Fancies. London, 1653, 1664, 1668.

The Worlds Olio. London, 1655.

Studies of Margaret Cavendish, Duchess of Newcastle

Ferguson, Moira. "A 'Wise, Wittie and Learned Lady': Margaret Lucas Cavendish." In *Women Writers of the Seventeenth Century*, ed. Katharina M. Wilson and Frank J. Warnke. Athens: University of Georgia Press, 1989. 305–340.

Grant, Douglas. *Margaret the First: A Biography of Margaret Cavendish, Duchess of Newcastle, 1623–1673.* London: Rupert Hart-Davis, 1957.

Mendelson, Sara Heller. *The Mental World of Stuart Women: Three Studies.* Amherst: University of Massachusetts Press, 1987.

Paloma, Dolores. "Margaret Cavendish: Defining the Female Self." *Women's Studies* 7.1–2 (1980): 55–66.

Rose, Mary Beth. "Gender, Genre, and History: Seventeenth-Century English Women and the Art of Autobiography." In *Women in the Middle Ages and the Renaissance*, ed. Mary Beth Rose. Syracuse, NY: Syracuse University Press, 1986. 245–278.

Sarasohn, Lisa T. "A Science Turned Upside Down: Feminism and the Natural Philosophy of Margaret Cavendish." *Huntington Library Quarterly* 47 (Autumn 1984): 289–307.

Smith, Hilda L. *Reason's Disciples: Seventeenth-Century English Feminists.* Urbana: University of Illinois Press, 1982.

Todd, Janet. *The Sign of Angellica: Women, Writing, and Fiction, 1660–1800.* New York: Columbia University Press, 1989.

❧ *George Chapman*
(1559?–1634)

PAMELA K. SHAFFER

BIOGRAPHY

In 1559 or 1560, George Chapman was born at Hitchin, in Herfordshire, the second son of Thomas Chapman, a yeoman and copyholder, and Joan Nodes, his wife. Not much is known of Chapman's early life. He seems to have attended Oxford in 1574 and was a strong student of Greek and Latin but weak in logic and philosophy, and he did not take a degree. It is known that he served in the household of Sir Ralph Sadler, from at least 1583 to 1585. He is likely to have served in military campaigns in the Netherlands in 1591 and 1592. In 1594, he published his first poetic work, *The Shadow of Night*. This was followed by *Ovid's Banquet of Sense* (1595), printed at a time when he was involved with a group of intellectuals led by Sir Walter Ralegh. He also wrote and published a continuation of Christopher Marlowe's *Hero and Leander* (1598).

In 1595, Chapman shifted his attention to the stage and wrote comedies and tragedies for the next ten years, becoming a successful playwright. However, because he did not receive adequate compensation for his work and because he continually made unfortunate choices in seeking patrons, he was continually short of funds and was even imprisoned for debt in 1599.

He began his translation of *The Iliad* before the turn of the century, eventually dedicating it to Prince Henry, the oldest son of James I, who promised him an annuity and £300. In 1611, Chapman published the twelve books of *The Iliad*. However, when Prince Henry died suddenly in 1612, he did not receive the promised funds and was left once again without a patron.

From 1612 to 1616, he continued to write tragedies and masques, as well as completing his translations of Homer. In 1616, he published *The Whole Works of Homer*, including both *The Iliad* and *The Odyssey*. Unfortunately, in patron after patron, Chapman's hopes for compensation were not realized. Not much is known about his life after his theatrical career. However, after much litigation, in 1621, he was acquitted of the charge of debt that had plagued him for years. He died on May 12, 1634. To honor him, Inigo Jones designed and had placed on Chapman's grave a Roman-style monument.

MAJOR WORKS AND THEMES

Poet, playwright, and translator, Chapman was a Renaissance humanist whose ideas of Platonism and stoicism permeate his poetry, blending seamlessly with his Christian belief. He held lofty goals for literature, believing it could serve as a guide for ethical behavior in private life as well as public policy. In his poetry, including *Ovid's Banquet of Sense* and the continuation of *Hero and Leander*, Chapman continually experimented with contemporary modes. His versatility is shown in his use of metaphysical conceits and, later, heroic couplets and the fourteeners of *The Iliad*.

As a playwright, Chapman set and adhered to high standards for himself, and in his plays, he exhibited a sure theatrical instinct. First, as a member of the Lord Admiral's Men, a company of actors playing at the Rose Theatre, then later, as a member of the Children of the Chapel, a company performing at the Blackfriars' Theatre, and at the Whitefriars' Theatre, Chapman became very successful. He inaugurated the comedy of humors with plays like *A Humorous Day's Mirth* (1597) and *May Day* (1601). Continuing to be an innovator, he moved away from comedies of humor to romantic tragicomedy, in plays like *The Gentleman Usher* (1602) and *Monsieur d'Olive* (1606). Chapman's collaboration with **Ben Jonson** and John Marston on the comedy *Eastward Ho*, in 1605, resulted in his and Jonson's short imprisonment because of some lines offensive to Scotsmen, newly arrived in London, after the accession of James I.

Chapman's tragedies were as successful as his comedies: *Bussy d'Ambois* (1607) and *The Revenge of Bussy d'Ambois* (1613); *The Conspiracy of Charles, Duke of Byron* and *The Tragedy of Byron* (1608); *Caesar and Pompey* (1631). *The Bloody Brother* (c. 1616, published 1639) resulted from collaboration with John Fletcher, Ben Jonson, and **Philip Massinger**. James Shirley seems to have revised *The Tragedy of Chabot*, a play Chapman wrote earlier but that was performed in 1639. His achievement in the tragedies included creation of heroic central characters, individualistic men of action whose experiences lead them from external knowledge to knowledge of themselves.

His work as a translator of Homer began in 1598 with *Seven Books of the Iliads*. In spite of bad luck with his patrons, Chapman continued with his translations of Homer, to publish, as we have seen, *The Whole Works of Homer* in 1616 and *The Crown of All Homer's Works*, which included *The Iliad, The Odyssey, The Batrachomyomachia, Hymns*, and *Epigrams*, in 1624.

CRITICAL RECEPTION

Through the centuries since Chapman wrote, critics' views of his works have varied. **Dryden** and other neoclassical writers of the late 17th century did not look on him favorably. Among the Romantics, Lamb praised his work, and so did Keats in the famous sonnet, but the Victorians gave him mixed reviews. Arnold criticized the ornateness and complexity of his translation of Homer. Swinburne offered the most thorough discussion of his work before the 20th century and probably set the tone for numerous critics of his poetry in the 20th century.

Today, as earlier, the quality of his lyric poems is seen to be inconsistent, but charges of obscurity have abated as critics have gained a better understanding of the Neoplatonic doctrines that influenced Chapman's poetry. His poems reveal substance and technical versatility, even though at times they seem labored. The monumental Homeric translations, or as Chapman said of the task, "the work that I was born to do," use striking language and display subtleties of character. Yet critics find fault with his occasional misreadings and expansions of Homer and generally view the scholarship underlying them as lacking by modern standards.

George Chapman is viewed to this day as among Elizabethan playwrights and poets who are second in rank to such figures as **Shakespeare** and **Donne**. Yet he held the highest aspirations for his drama, and in his own day, his notable achievement is evident in the words of Sir Francis Meres, who called him "among the best in comedy and tragedy." He made significant contributions to the drama of his time. In comedy, he brought to the stage the comedy of "humours" and the tragicomedy, which Beaumont and Fletcher would build on in the next decade. His tragedies bring to the stage larger-than-life heroes in the blank verse inherited from Marlowe. Even though his translations of the works of Homer are the least read today, at moments they show a strength and vitality lacking in many a translation of the same works since then.

BIBLIOGRAPHY

Works by George Chapman

Chapman's Homer. Ed. Allardyce Nicoll. 2 vols. New York: Pantheon Books, 1956.
The Comedies of George Chapman. Ed. Thomas Marc Parrott. London: Routledge and Kegan Paul, Ltd., 1913.
George Chapman's Minor Translations. Ed. Richard Corballis. Salzburg: Institut für Anglistik und Amerikanistic, 1984.
The Plays of George Chapman. Vol. 1: Ed. Allan Holaday and Michael Kiernan. Urbana: University of Illinois Press, 1970. Vol. 2: Ed. Allan Holaday, G. Blakemore Evans, and Thomas Berger. Woodbridge, United Kingdom, and Wolfeboro, NH: D.S. Brewer, 1987.
The Poems of George Chapman. Ed. Phyllis Bartlett. New York: Modern Language Association, 1941.

Studies of George Chapman

Eliot, T.S. *Selected Essays*. London: Faber and Faber, 1953.
Gordon, D.J. "The Renaissance Poet as Classicist: Chapman's *Hero and Leander*." In *The Renaissance Imagination*, ed. Stephen Orgel. Berkeley: University of California Press, 1975. 102–133.
Huntington, John. *Ambition, Rank, and Poetry in 1590s England*. Urbana: University of Illinois Press, 2001.
Lewis, C.S. "Hero and Leander." In *Elizabethan Poetry*, ed. Paul J. Alpers. New York: Oxford University Press, 1967. 235–250.
Lord, George de Forest. *Homeric Renaissance: The Odyssey of George Chapman*. New Haven, CT: Yale University Press, 1956.

MacLure, Millar. *George Chapman: A Critical Study*. Toronto: University of Toronto Press, 1966.

Rees, Ennis. *The Tragedies of George Chapman*. Cambridge: Harvard University Press, 1954.

Snare, Gerald. *The Mystification of George Chapman*. Durham, NC: Duke University Press, 1989.

Spivack, Charlotte. *George Chapman*. New York: Twayne Publishers, 1967.

Swinburne, Algernon Charles. *George Chapman, a Critical Essay*. London: Chatto & Windus, 1875.

Waddington, Raymond B. *The Mind's Empire: Myth and Narrative Form in George Chapman's Narrative Poems*. Baltimore: Johns Hopkins University Press, 1974.

❧ *Mary, Lady Chudleigh*
(1656–1710)

AMY WOLF

BIOGRAPHY

Mary, Lady Chudleigh's personal life is largely portrayed as deeply unhappy because her often bitter writing ends up being taken for the record of her life in the absence of much biographical fact. Verses like "To the Ladies" seem to expose dissatisfaction with her marriage, the essay "Of Grief" and some of her poetry mournfully express her grief over the death of her eight-year-old daughter Eliza Maria, and her physical suffering from rheumatism is delineated in the few letters to friends left behind. Chudleigh was born Mary Lee on August 19, 1656, in Devonshire and married George Chudleigh, later a baronet, in 1674. Little is known about Chudleigh's childhood or her marriage. She and her husband had six children, but only two sons survived childhood, and the death of Eliza Maria, one of two daughters, was especially agonizing. Lady Chudleigh was well versed in the philosophical and scientific debates of her time; she read the classics in translation, philosophy, history, science, and literature and celebrated the life of the mind.

Like many writers of her time, Lady Chudleigh circulated her work among family and friends for years before it was formally published. Her first published piece, *The Ladies Defence*, was written in 1701 as a response to a sermon by John Sprint on "Conjugal Duty." Sprint's sermon advocated utter obedience on the part of wives in decidedly misogynistic tones. Chudleigh's response, in the form of a poetic dialogue, was envisioned by her "as a Satyr on vice, and not, as some have maliciously reported, for an Invective on Marriage." *The Ladies Defence* established her as a devotee of **Mary Astell**, the writer and advocate for women's education, whom Chudleigh greatly admired. Lady Chudleigh's collected *Poems on Several Occasions* (1703) appeared a few years later and included "To the Ladies," her most anthologized poem; poems addressed to female friends and fellow writers ("To Almystrea," "To Clorissa," etc.); and several poems celebrating the retired intellectual life with which she would long be associated. Chudleigh's last book, *Essays Upon Several Subjects* (1710), appeared just before her death from the crippling rheumatism that had affected her for years on December 15, 1710.

MAJOR WORKS AND THEMES

Virtue, education, intellectual fulfillment, retreat, and female friendship were the themes Lady Chudleigh returned to again and again. One of the earliest overtly feminist writers, she was also one of the first to see herself writing to a specifically female audience. Marilyn Williamson praises her for "forging [her] anger into one of the first clear definitions of the social terms of [women's] condition" (94). To Chudleigh, knowledge allowed women to control their own lives, to determine the virtuous right, and to be better wives, friends, mothers, and human beings. She was less concerned with social change than with women being able to cope with the predicament of being women in a world in which that was a disadvantage. Using the pseudonym "Marissa," she celebrated female friendship while remaining skeptical of sexual love between men and women because of the opportunities for the abuse of power inherent in that relationship. Her retirement/retreat poems are interesting because, as Ann Messenger writes, "she does not so much retire *to* the countryside as *into* her own mind" (84). Chudleigh wields pastoral descriptions in a general, nondetailed way; she is more concerned with the freedom from care and the silence for intellectual pursuits that her pastoral world provides than with any sense of nature's beauty. And female friendship, rather than an ideal male companion, is an essential part of the perfect retreat.

The Ladies Defence (1701), considered her most important work in her time as well as in ours, was written in the form of a verse dialogue between three men and one woman: a misogynistic Parson, a dull and oppressive husband Sir John Brute, the chivalrous but condescending Sir William Loveall, and the feminist Melissa. Melissa criticizes the injustice of a world in which "Men command, and we alone obey, / As if design'd for Arbitrary Sway." But far from discouraging women from marrying, Melissa advocates unreproachable virtue as the antidote for male tyranny. She envisions a world in which women "Read and Think, and Think and Read again" until they move beyond "the gross Allays of Sense" and achieve a peace that transcends the physical world. "To the Ladies" is even less sympathetic to men and to marriage than *The Ladies Defence*. The couplet that begins the poem is notable for its strong voice and straightforward bluntness: "Wife and Servant are the same, / But only differ in the Name." Here, the speaker is unable to advocate virtue as a solution to women's situation—once they are married, women are "Like Mutes"—and instead concludes that women must "despise" men and "shun that wretched State" of marriage.

CRITICAL RECEPTION

In her lifetime, Chudleigh was admired as one of few published women writers. **John Dryden** praised her, and Chudleigh wrote commendatory verses on his translation of Virgil. Much of the subsequent attention paid to her has been because of her gender; for centuries she has been anthologized primarily as a "female poet," rarely making it into anthologies without gender as an emphasis. George Ballard's biography of Chudleigh in *Memoirs of Several Ladies of Great Britain* in 1752 was for a long time the primary source for information about Chudleigh's life, but contemporary scholars such as Margaret J.M. Ezell have challenged the assumption that Chudleigh's married life was unhappy by contextualizing her work as not simply autobiographical but as participatory in the intellectual debate of her time. Ezell and others conclude that, at the very least, the facts of Chudleigh's marriage and personal life are indeterminate and that her words need to be understood as "less a coherent autobiographical chronicle of the events of her life than a continuous philosophical exploration of human passions and the ways to live a truly harmonious life, at peace with one's passions" (Ezell xxiii).

BIBLIOGRAPHY

Works by Mary, Lady Chudleigh

The Poems and Prose of Mary, Lady Chudleigh. Ed. Margaret J.M. Ezell. New York: Oxford University Press, 1993.

Studies of Mary, Lady Chudleigh

Ballard, George. *Memoirs of Several Ladies of Great Britain who have been Celebrated for their Writings or Skill in the Learned Languages, Arts and Sciences.* [1752]. Ed. Ruth Perry. Detroit, MI: Wayne State University Press, 1985.

Barash, Carol. " 'The Native Liberty . . . of the Subject': Configurations of Gender and Authority in the Works of Mary Chudleigh, Sarah Frye Egerton, and Mary Astell." In *Women, Writing, History: 1640–1740,* ed. Isobel Grundy and Susan Wiseman. Athens: University of Georgia Press, 1992. 55–69.

Ezell, Margaret J.M. Introduction to *The Poems and Prose of Mary, Lady Chudleigh.* New York: Oxford University Press, 1993. xvii–xxxvi.

———. "The Politics of the Past: Restoration Women Writers on Women Reading History." In *Pilgrimage for Love: Essays in Early Modern Literature in Honor of Josephine A. Roberts,* ed. Sigrid King. Tempe: Arizona Center for Medieval and Renaissance Studies, 1999. 19–40.

Messenger, Ann. *Pastoral Tradition and the Female Talent: Studies in Augustan Poetry.* New York: AMS, 2001.

Smith, Hilda L. *Reason's Disciples: Seventeenth-Century English Feminists.* Urbana: University of Illinois Press, 1982.

Williamson, Marilyn L. *Raising Their Voices: British Women Writers, 1650–1750.* Detroit, MI: Wayne State University Press, 1990.

ટે John Cleveland
(1613–1658)

BIOGRAPHY

John Cleveland, a shrewd and witty British metaphysical poet and satirist, was born in Loughborough, Leicestershire. When his family moved to Hinckley in 1621, Cleveland came under the tutelage of Richard Vines, one of the most notable Puritan figures of the era. At fourteen, Christ's College, Cambridge, admitted Cleveland as a lesser pensioner. Despite being the son of a clergyman and the parliamentary flavor of his education, Cleveland became a staunch Royalist and later a championing voice of the Royalist camp at Oxford. His political leanings, coupled with his lyrical skills and poetic innovations, helped Cleveland become one of the most popular poets of his time, with at least twenty-five editions of his poetry appearing between 1647 and 1687.

At Cambridge, Cleveland was well regarded personally and intellectually. In 1629, though still an undergraduate, Cleveland delivered a Latin oration of welcome for the university's chancellor, Sir Henry Rich, and his guest, the French ambassador. Like fellow Christ's College student **John Milton**, Cleveland was named "Father" of the Cambridge revels (a yearly mock-pageant of student life). Cleveland received his B.A. in 1631 and three years later was elected to the Hebblethwaite Fellowship at St. John's College where he taught undergraduates, including two of his first editors, John Lake and Samuel Drake. Cleveland completed his M.A. in 1634.

In 1643 parliamentary soldiers occupied Cambridge, forcing Cleveland to relocate to Oxford. Embraced by the Royal party, Cleveland's popularity as a poet and satirist surged as his sardonic and aggressive wit found an appreciative environment in which to voice his extravagant attacks. His time in Oxford was the pinnacle of his career, with "The Rebell Scot" marking the most unified blend of his lyrical and satirical voices. Regardless of his success, Cleveland was ousted from his fellowship at St. John's for his refusal to take a 1645 parliamentary oath. Royalists immediately came to his aid, appointing him judge advocate of the garrison at Newark. This stability, however, was overturned quickly when, in 1646, **Oliver Cromwell** defeated Charles I.

The next nine years of Cleveland's life remain a mystery, some scholars suggesting that Cleveland relied on the means of more fortunate Royalists, others suggesting that Cleveland wrote for various underground London mercuries. Facts concerning Cleveland's biography do not reemerge until November 10, 1655, when he was arrested for his Royalist sympathies. After three months in Yarmouth prison, Cleveland successfully petitioned Cromwell for his release. Most scholars agree that by 1657 Cleveland resided at Gray's Inn. However, weakened physically following his stay in prison, Cleveland died of intermittent fever on April 29, 1658, leaving no known descendants.

MAJOR WORKS AND THEMES

Cleveland's poetry and prose are characterized by extremism and social topicality. His decadent style reflects mannerist influences and prefigures the doggerels and satires of the Restoration period. Using countless conceits, Cleveland pairs seemingly contrasting images and themes. These conceits are not linked in an orderly manner and thus create incredibly jarring literary effects. While **John Dryden** would later criticize Cleveland's catachresis, referring to it as "Clevelandism," this distinct style embodied the political and cultural climate of the looming English Civil War.

Cleveland, like Milton, was constantly aware of the current sociocultural trends and how these affected the psychological nature of his audience. His works focus on these concerns in a manner that, though not always pleasant, cannot be ignored. Ironically, the cacophonous pangs of his works "ring home" subtle undertones that illustrate the uncertainties of what appear to be common and straightforward issues (Jacobus). Both his lyrical and political works, then, not only shock but, more important, provide unique perspectives on the ordinary. For instance, in his mock-love lyric "A Young Man to an Old Woman Courting Him," Cleveland compares a loving embrace to a new cover put on an old book. In "The Rebell Scot," probably his most explicit satire, Cleveland envisions the invading Scots as a scourge of wolves upon England (Jaeckle). Whether mockingly clever or sarcastically demeaning, Cleveland's cynical wit shines throughout almost all of his works and exemplifies 17th-century satirical literary fashion.

Although Cleveland's poetry and prose went through numerous editions, the original dates of composition of many of his works remain unknown. Scholars speculate that the majority of his works were composed in Cambridge. Part of the uncertainty surrounding Cleveland's works arises from the fact that he was uninvolved in the publishing process, which, consequently, allowed publishers to contract or expand his canon to best suit financial rather than literary interests. In 1659, for example, Nathaniel Brook published *J. Cleveland Revived*, yet most, if not all, of the pieces are not Cleveland's. Cleveland's canon, then, remains uncertain at best. Though this lack of concern with the publication process was typical of 17th-century writers, it is particularly problematic in Cleveland's case in that it has prevented thorough scholarly examinations of his works. Furthermore, the specific social and political subjects of his works are not easily understood without a detailed knowledge of the history of the age.

CRITICAL RECEPTION

Although Cleveland was the most popular poet of his day, he has often been considered little more than a footnote trailing in the wake of the metaphysical poets' reign. However, though there is limited criticism of his works, the judgments made are impassioned and long-lasting (Jacobus). For instance, only ten years after Cleveland's death, John Dryden rebuked Cleveland's wit, considering him an example of a "Metaphysical gone bad" and calling his poetry a "clownish kind of raillery" (Jacobus). Samuel Johnson finds Cleveland's verses equally offensive, lacking any sense of poetic decorum. Unfortunately, the negative opinions of 18th-century critics proved to be enduring. Geoffrey Walton (1955) refers to Cleveland's works as superficial rather than poetical. A. Alvarez (1961) dismisses Cleveland as "simply trying to be amusing," claiming that Cleveland wrote for a small Cambridge coterie. Alvarez's reading, however, ignores Cleveland's immense public popularity. Moreover, Cleveland's cleverly combined conceits and satirical voice influenced many writers, including **Andrew Marvell** and **Samuel Butler**. Cleveland's 20th-century editors, John Berdan, Brian Morris, and Eleanor Withington, have helped revive his works, providing fresh, unbiased readings that emphasize the historical events surrounding and affecting Cleveland's works. Lee A. Jacobus provides a thorough biography and criticism, also calling attention to the importance of history in Cleveland's works and the need to read Cleveland as a poet seeking the most dramatic of rhetorical effects.

BIBLIOGRAPHY

Works by John Cleveland

The Character of a Country Committee-man, with the Earmark of a Sequestrator. London, 1649.

The Character of a Diurnal-maker. London, 1654.

The Character of a London Diurnall. Oxford: Printed by L. Lichfield, 1644.

The Character of a London Diurnall: With severall select Poems: By the same Author. London, 1647.

Clieveland Vindiciae; or, Clieveland's Genuine Poems, Orations, Epistles, &c. edited by Samuel Drake and John Lake. London: Printed by Nathaniel Brook, 1677.

J. Cleaveland Revived. London: Printed for Nathaniel Brook, 1659. 2nd ed., enlarged, 1660.

The Poems of John Cleveland. Ed. Brian Morris and Eleanor Withington. Oxford: Clarendon Press, 1967.

The Poems of John Cleveland: Annotated and Correctly Printed for the First Time with Biographical and Historical Introductions. Ed. John M. Berdan. New York: Grafton, 1903.

The Works of Mr. John Cleveland, Containing his Poems, Orations, Epistles, Collected into One Volume, With the Life of the Author. London: Printed by R. Holt for Obadiah Blagrave, 1687.

Studies of John Cleveland

Alvarez, Alfred. *The School of Donne*. New York: Pantheon Books, 1961.

Berdan, John M. *The Poems of John Cleveland*. New York: Grafton, 1903.

Cousins, A.D. "The Cavalier World and John Cleveland." *Studies in Philology* 78.1 (1981): 61–86.

Duffy, Helen. "Two Manuscripts of John Cleveland." *PMLA* 46 (1931): 1075–1086.

Gapp, S.V. "Notes on John Cleveland." *PMLA* 46 (1931): 1075–1086.

Jaeckle, Daniel P. "John Cleveland." In *Dictionary of Literary Biography*. Detroit, MI: Gale Research, 1982. 126.

Jacobus, Lee. *John Cleveland*. Boston: Twayne Publishers, 1975.

Withington, Eleanor. "The Canon of John Cleveland's Poetry." *Bulletin of the New York Public Library* 67 (1963): 307–327.

❧ *Arcangelo Corelli*

(1653–1713)

NANCY HAGER

BIOGRAPHY

Arcangelo Corelli was born on February 17, 1653, in Fusignano, a small town between Ravenna and Bologna where the Corellis were an old and respected family. His early years have been the subject of much fanciful speculation, but it seems safe to assume that his education included music because in 1670, at the age of seventeen, he was accepted at the prestigious Accademia Filarmonica of Bologna. From 1675 Corelli's name appears in the lists of various orchestras in Rome, soon rising to the position of first violinist. In 1679 he became a chamber musician to Christina, the witty, intelligent former Queen of Sweden, whose magnificent Palazzo Riario was a cultural rendezvous in Rome. Corelli dedicated to Christina what he described as the "first fruits of my studies," the opus 1 trio sonatas.

Corelli's following published collection was dedicated to another of Corelli's patrons, Cardinal Pamphili, a highly cultured man who authored some libretti set by Handel and was godfather to one of Alessandro Scarlatti's children. In 1684 Corelli became a violinist and sort of musical manager for Pamphili's academies, high points of Rome's musical life held at his Palazzo al Corso. Corelli, accompanied by his friend, the violinist Matteo Fornari, lived at this palace from 1687 to 1690. With Pamphili's transfer to Bologna, Corelli entered the service of Cardinal Pietro Ottoboni, the young nephew of Pope Alexander VIII.

Ottoboni's palace, the Cancelleria, which was to be Corelli's home for the rest of his life, was another center of Rome's artistic society and the scene of a legendary meeting between Handel and Domenico Scarlatti. Here Corelli, Fornari, and the Spanish cellist Lulier were often heard performing Corelli's trio sonatas or the solo parts in his concerti. In 1700 Corelli was named head of instrumental music of the Congregazione dei Virtuosi de S. Cecilia, of which he had become a member in 1684. Six years later, Corelli, the keyboard virtuoso Bernardi Pasquini, and the composer Alessandro Scarlatti were honored as the first musicians admitted to Rome's exclusive society of poets and noblemen, the Accademica dei Arcadi (Arcadian Academy).

In addition to composing and performing, Corelli often served as a leader or director, as when he led a force of 150 instrumentalists and 100 singers in an *accademia per musica* written by Pasquini for performance at Christina's palace. His standards of discipline were unusually strict, and Francesco Geminiani, a violinist and one of his students, recalled that

Corelli regarded it as essential to the ensemble of the band that their bows should all move exactly together, all up, all down; so that at his rehearsals, which preceded every performance of his concerti, he would immediately stop the group if he discovered one irregular bow.

From about 1710 Corelli no longer performed in public, but his activities continued to be of great interest to his admirers, one of whom reported in 1711 that "the greatest glory of the century . . . is at present occupied in bringing to perfection his sixth work of concerti, which will shortly be published and render his name forever immortal." Publication of this final collection during Corelli's lifetime was prevented by his final illness, but fortunately the process of revision and polishing had been completed. He died on January 8, 1713, and was buried in the Pantheon.

Judging from the inventory of possessions at his death, Corelli seems to have had little interest in material property, confining his passions to paintings and music. Handel, who met him in Rome in the early 1700s, reported with customary dryness that

his two dominant characteristics were his admiration for pictures, which they say he never paid for, and an extreme parsimony. His wardrobe was not extensive. Ordinarily he went about clothed in black, and he used to wear a dark cloak; he was always on foot, and protested vigorously if one tried to make him take a carriage.

Other contemporary evidence suggests that Corelli's abilities as a violinist had its limitations. According to the English composer and music historian Charles Burney, while an orchestra in Naples flawlessly read through one of Corelli's concerti at sight, he himself encountered difficulties in high passages that the Neapolitans managed with ease. In another instance, Corelli was said to be unable to execute his part in an overture by Handel because, as he protested, he did not understand the French idiom. Corelli's fame as a violinist was probably based on his performances of his own works, which are both thoroughly Italian in style and oriented toward lyricism and expressiveness rather than virtuosity. On the whole, his writing is technically conservative, eschewing intricate figuration and passages in high registers in favor of a style remarkable for its refinement, clarity, and classic simplicity.

MAJOR WORKS AND THEMES

Corelli is an anomaly among Baroque composers. At a time when composers routinely produced hundreds of works in all genres—vocal and instrumental; sacred and secular; solo and ensemble; church, chamber, and theater—Corelli's output was modest in both size and scope: six published volumes of twelve compositions each (four collections of trio sonatas, one of solo sonatas, one of concerti grossi), plus a handful of miscellaneous works, most of doubtful authenticity. Moreover, the published works are all scored for strings and continuo, the opus 1, 2, 3, and 4 trio sonatas for two violins and continuo, the opus 5 sonatas for violin and continuo, and the opus 6 concerti grossi for strings and continuo.

CRITICAL RECEPTION

During his lifetime, Corelli's name was almost synonymous with Italian instrumental music and his fame of almost legendary proportions. He was much sought after as a teacher. Geminiani, Gasparini, and Locatelli were among his many pupils, but the actual number was much inflated by the widespread practice of claiming study under the great master. As the English lawyer and amateur musician Roger North noted in his *Memoirs of Musick*, "[M]ost of the nobility and gentry that have traveled in Italy affected to learn of Corelli."

Although my own performance training was in keyboard instruments, violin music has played a special role in my life. My mother was a Juilliard-trained violinist, and one of my uncles, a professional artist, was an amateur violinist, violin maker, and author of *The Strad Facsimile*, a manual on violin building. One of my fondest childhood memories is accompanying my mother and uncle playing Bach's concerto for two violins. My particular interest in Corelli was awakened while I was preparing to teach a graduate seminar on the Baroque concerto. The concerto was largely the invention of Italian musicians who, during the 17th century, made considerable advances in instrumental technique and in the manufacture of instruments, especially the violin. The violin was invented around 1550 and quickly developed in the hands of Italian craftsmen such as Stradivarius and Amati into an instrument whose brilliant, penetrating tone was perfectly suited to the Baroque ideal of an intensely expressive instrumental melody supported by a bass line and accompanying harmonies. Indeed, throughout the 17th and 18th centuries, Italian composers of instrumental music devoted themselves almost exclusively to this new member of the string family.

Corelli figures as both a refiner and creator in the history of the concerto. In spite of the relatively late publication date of his one concerto collection—1714—he had been known and admired as a composer of concerti for several decades. Georg Muffat, a German composer and organist, stated in the preface to his own concerti grossi of 1701 that as a student of Corelli in the 1680s he heard "with astonishment some symphonies [i.e., concerti] of Signor Arcangelo Corelli, which were very beautiful and very well performed by a good company of musicians." He continued, "Having noticed the great variety which this style admits of, I began to compose some of these concerti, which I tried out with the aforesaid Arcangelo Corelli, to whom I am indebted for many useful observations in respect of his collection." Corelli's concerti are also singled out for praise in a 1689 treatise by the theorist Angelo Berardi, according to whom "concerti for violins and other instruments are called symphonies; those of Signor Arcangelo Corelli, the celebrated violinist, called the Bolognese, the new Orpheus of our time, are especially esteemed today." After their initial publication in 1714 by the Amsterdam firm Estienne Roger, the opus 6 concerti were reprinted over the next decades by other houses in London and Paris. They also appeared in various arrangements and transcriptions, for example, one rescored for two flutes, another adapted for organ, harpsichord, or piano "as they are performed by Mr. Cramer."

Corelli's concerti had enormous impact on the instrumental music of a long list of composers, including Handel, Bach, and Albinoni, in addition to his own pupils. The opus 6 concerti were still known and admired at the end of the 18th century when Charles Burney expressed a view of them echoed by critics today:

The Concertos of Corelli seem to have withstood all the attacks of time and fashion with more firmness than any of his other works. The harmony is so pure, so rich, and so grateful; the parts are so clearly and judiciously, and ingeniously disposed; and the effect of the whole . . . so majestic, solemn, and sublime that they preclude criticism and make us forget that there is any other music of the same kind existing.

BIBLIOGRAPHY

Works by Arcangelo Corelli

Concerti grossi, opus 6. Amsterdam, 1714.
Overture to S Beatrice d'Este. 1689.
Sonate a tre (Trio Sonatas), opus 1. Rome, 1681.
Sonate a tre (Trio Sonatas), opus 2. Rome, 1685.
Sonate a tre (Trio Sonatas), opus 3. Rome, 1680.
Sonate a tre (Trio Sonatas), opus 4. Rome, 1694.
Sonate (Solo sonatas), opus 5. Rome, 1700.

Studies of Arcangelo Corelli

Edwards, O. "The Response to Corelli's Music in Eighteenth-Century England." *Studia musicologica norvegica* (1976): 51–96.
Hutchings, A. *The Baroque Concerto*. 3rd ed. London: Faber, 1978.
Marx, H.J. "Die Musik am Hofe Pietro Kardinal Ottobonis under Arcangelo Corelli." *Analecta musicologica*, no. 5 (1968): 104–177.
Pincherle, M. *Corelli* (English translation). New York: Columbia University Press, 1956.
Talbot, Michael. "Corelli." In *New Grove Dictionary of Music and Musicians*. 4: 768–774. New York: Oxford University Press.

❧ *Abraham Cowley*

(1618–1667)

SHELLEY LePOUDRE WIEBE

BIOGRAPHY

In late 1618, the recently widowed Thomasine Cowley (pronounced Cooley) gave birth to her seventh child, Abraham, in London. Educated first at the famed Westminster School, he later entered Trinity College at Cambridge where Cowley took a B.A. and an M.A. During the Civil War, Cowley's Royalist leanings resulted in his expulsion from Cambridge, and he found a more congenial environment at the University of Oxford. His sojourn there, however, proved brief; 1644 saw Cowley's departure from England, and he settled in France, deciphering the coded messages that passed between the ousted King and his Queen. Cowley probably also worked as a Royalist spy, occasioning a short term of imprisonment in the year following his return to England in 1654.

After the Restoration, Cowley's relationship with the Royal Family was strained, primarily due to the "preface" of the 1656 *Poems*; here the author recommends reconciliation between Royalist and roundhead factions. A bitter Cowley never received the Mastership of the Savoy that both Charles I and Charles II had promised him, although he managed to acquire some leasehold land in Kent in recognition of his services to the Queen Mother. Life as a gentleman farmer beckoned, leading him ultimately to Chertsey in Surrey, where he hoped to live quietly in an atmosphere of solitude and peace. Cowley's dream, unfortunately, proved short-lived. He died on July 28, 1667, probably of pneumonia. Six days later, Cowley was buried in Westminster Abbey near Spenser and Chaucer. Although Charles II arguably did not treat him as well as befitted a man who had spent over a decade in service to the Royal Family, the King is said to have remarked at the poet's death that "Mr. Cowley had not left a better man behind him in England."

MAJOR WORKS AND THEMES

Cowley's juvenilia shows tantalizing poetic promise, but other genres also attracted him. To mark the young Prince Charles's visit to Cambridge in March of 1641–1642, Cowley penned his third play, *The Guardian*, a remarkably perceptive humors comedy taking gleeful delight in lampooning Puritan extremism and hypocrisy. A man who subscribed to a strong *via media* philosophy, Cowley continued to tackle the subject of religious excess in a subsequent poem, *The Puritan and the Papist.*

In 1656, Cowley responded to the unauthorized publication of some of his love poetry with an author-sanctioned folio titled *Poems.* In addition to the previously purloined verses of *The Mistress*, it included a "preface" (which won him no friends among the Royalists), the *Miscellanies*, an unfinished epic poem, *Davideis*, concerning itself with the life of the biblical David, and the Pindaric odes. The Greek poet Pindar inspired the latter group of poems as Cowley sought to recreate the ancient author's style, form, and manner.

A man quite unafraid of literary experimentation, Cowley dabbled in prose as well, creating the pre-Restoration piece *A Proposition for the Advancement of Experimental Philosophy*, a Baconian (see **Francis Bacon**) treatise on education that the Royal Society later considered but did not have the means to implement. Similar in tone and content to **Milton**'s *Of Education*, the *Proposition* does not favor the acquisition of scientific or natural knowledge over the arts' quest for the divine (an allegation some have hurled at the work) but rather holds that both endeavors are inextricably intertwined and necessary for the education of a well-rounded citizenry.

On the occasion of Restoration in 1660, publication of the saccharine "Ode, upon the Blessed Restoration," written to commemorate Charles II's return, appears not to have softened the King's attitude toward Cowley; the monarch apparently still smarted from the poet's 1656 prefatory acceptance of Cromwellian (see **Oliver Cromwell**) government. The following year **William Davenant**'s Duke's Company staged Cowley's *Cutter of Coleman Street*, a sparkling adaptation of the earlier Cambridge play *The Guardian*. The comedy's premiere received a somewhat hostile response from a few audience members who felt it unflattering to the King's Party. The preface to *Cutter*'s first publication in 1663 contains the dramatist's indignant rebuttal and a reassertion of his Royalist sympathies.

Cowley seems to have felt that a growing understanding of nature would enable a closer relationship with God; to explore this theme, he published over the next few years several numbered Latin poems, *Plantarum Libri*, detailing the uses and characteristics of various plants. He focuses here on their role within the unity of being while likewise recognizing humanity's unique place in creation. Most of these verses Cowley wrote while seeking a bucolic existence in the country, and now also appeared "Several Discourses by Way of Essays, in Verse and Prose," a thoughtful and reflective work that found favor with no less a critic than the curmudgeonly Samuel Johnson. Written at the end of Cowley's career and displaying an ease of composition and an unstudied grace appearing nowhere else in his writing, the essays are classic studies in understatement, often dealing with the salubrious qualities of nature, the delights of solitude, and the rewards of contemplation. But the self-styled "melancholy Cowley" had composed these pieces, and the author's darker moments at times surface in the display of an edge, a scarcely concealed disillusionment and a dissatisfaction with the vagaries of human nature. The many complexities the essays present require both a reader's intellectual engagement and a certain sensitivity of spirit.

CRITICAL RECEPTION

Few articles about Abraham Cowley do not contain this question and observation from Alexander Pope's *Imitations of Horace* (Bk. II, Epistle I): "Who now reads Cowley? If he pleases yet, / His moral pleases, not his pointed wit." John Milton's favorite contemporary poet, Cowley experienced a sharp decline in literary reputation mere decades after his death, and his oeuvre has not seen the renaissance enjoyed by many of his less-talented peers. While Johnson, in the "Life of Cowley," found him and the other metaphysicals pretentious ("more desirous of being admired than understood") and many modern critics consider Cowley's work imitative and derivative (particularly *The Mistress*, where one sees **John Donne**'s influence), the poet has always had admirers strongly expressing quite different views. Charles Lamb, writing in the century after Johnson, declares in *Mrs. Leicester's School*:

Donne and Cowley, by happening to possess more wit, and faculty of illustration, than other men, are supposed to have been incapable of nature or feeling . . . whereas, in the very thickest of their conceits,—in the bewildering mazes of tropes and figures,—a warmth of soul and generous feeling shines through.

Paradoxically, both Johnson and Lamb correctly assess Cowley's poetry; the man's literary output is so vast that one easily finds examples to prove either a shallow pretentiousness *or* an uncanny understanding of the human condition.

Although critics more often than not disdain his poetry, the pronouncements on Cowley's dramatic abilities have generally been positive, recognizing that the plays of his adulthood showcase the talents of a writer naturally attuned to the intricacies of structure, plot, and characterization. Alfred Harbage's *Cavalier Drama* lavishly praises Cowley's dramatic dexterity, and Kathleen Lynch, in *The Social Mode of Restoration Comedy*, maintains that *Cutter of Coleman Street* was instrumental in providing Restoration comedy with an ancestor for its fops and witwoulds. Some feel Cowley might well have rescued himself from literary obscurity if he had only chosen to concentrate his expertise on playwriting rather than on poetry.

Cowley's poetry may not please modern tastes, and his plays have occasionally found detractors, but the essays win universal praise. "No author ever kept his verse and his prose at a greater distance from each other," according to Johnson. And Edmund Gosse voices the majority opinion as he makes this declaration in *Books on the Table*: "If we read Cowley's chapter 'On Myself,' we find contained in it, as in a nutshell, the complete model and type of what an essay should be—elegant, fresh, confidential, and constructed with as much care as a sonnet." In the essays, more than anywhere else, one finds what Pope's *Imitations of Horace* so admires in the author's work—the language of Cowley's heart.

BIBLIOGRAPHY

Works by Abraham Cowley

The Collected Works of Abraham Cowley. Ed. Thomas O. Calhoun et al. Newark: University of Delaware Press, 1989–.

The Complete Works in Verse and Prose. Ed. Alexander B. Grosart. 2 vols. Edinburgh: Edinburgh University Press, 1881.

The English Writings of Abraham Cowley: Poems. Ed. A.R. Waller. Cambridge: Cambridge University Press, 1905.

Essays, Plays and Sundry Verses. Ed. A.R. Waller. Cambridge: Cambridge University Press, 1906.

Studies of Abraham Cowley

Hinman, Robert B. *Abraham Cowley's World of Order.* Cambridge: Harvard University Press, 1960.

Loiseau, Jean. *Abraham Cowley: Sa vie, son oeuvre.* Paris: Henri Didier, 1931.

———. *Abraham Cowley's Reputation in England.* Paris: Henri Didier, 1931.

Nethercot, Arthur H. *Abraham Cowley: The Muse's Hannibal.* 1931. Reprint, London: Oxford University Press, 1967.

———. *Reputation of Abraham Cowley, 1660–1800.* New York: Haskell House, 1970.

Taaffe, J.G. *Abraham Cowley.* New York: Twayne Publishers, 1972.

Trotter, David. *The Poetry of Abraham Cowley.* Totowa, NJ: Rowman and Littlefield, 1979.

❧ *Richard Crashaw*
(c. 1613–1649)

ALBERT J. GERITZ

BIOGRAPHY

Son of a Puritan minister, Crashaw was born in London during Advent Season in 1612 or near the Feast of the Epiphany in 1613. Whether his mother died during, soon after his birth, or while he was an infant is unknown. His stepmother, Elizabeth Skinner Crashaw, died in childbirth in 1620. After his father died in 1626, Crashaw became the charge of Sir Henry Yelverton and Sir Randolph Crew. In 1629, he was admitted to the Charterhouse School and completed his humanist education in the classics there. When, in 1631, he went to Peterhouse, Cambridge, a center of High Church thought, Crashaw became embroiled in theological controversy between the Puritans and Laudians. There, he produced his first volume of poetry in 1634, *Epigrammatum Sacrorum Liber*, a collection of Classical epigrams, and was elected to a fellowship. He took holy orders and was appointed to the Peterhouse curate of Little St. Mary's around 1638.

During the English Civil Wars (1642–1651), his position at Peterhouse became untenable because of his attraction to Catholicism, so he resigned it before the Puritans could evict him. He prepared the first edition of *Steps to the Temple: Sacred Poems, with Other Delights of the Muses*, which included religious and secular poems in Latin and English, for publication in 1646. The title is a tribute to **George Herbert**, whose sacred verse had been published in 1633 as *The Temple*. Crashaw's stay at Cambridge was the most idyllic time of his life, and the destruction of the Civil War forced him to sever himself from the security he found there.

His movement after his disappearance from Cambridge in 1643 remains mysterious. He next is heard of in Leiden on February 20, 1644. Soon thereafter, Crashaw possibly returned to England to take refuge at the Oxford court of Queen Henrietta Maria, wife of Charles I. Those who would help him were there—**Abraham Cowley**, another Cambridge friend and poet, and Susan Fielding, Countess of Denbigh. The Queen and her entourage fled to Paris in 1644; Crashaw may have remained on the run in England or adrift on the Continent. In 1645, Crashaw surfaced in Paris. Now converted to Catholicism, the poet entrusted his poems to Thomas Car for a new volume, *Carmen Deo Nostro*, published posthumously in 1652.

In September 1646, the Countess of Denbigh persuaded the Queen to recommend Crashaw to the Pope. Bolstered by the hope the English Catholic community abroad placed in him, Crashaw began his journey to Rome. For the next year, he struggled with poverty and sickness while waiting for some papal retainer. After renewed diplomatic entreaties to the Pope, Crashaw was given a post with Cardinal Palotto. Finally, in April 1649, the Cardinal procured him a cathedral benefice at the Virgin's Holy House, Santa Casa, at Loreto. Weakened by years of exile, Crashaw set out for Loreto in May and died there on August 21, 1649.

MAJOR WORKS AND THEMES

Joy and exaltation are the promised spiritual effects of Crashaw's verse. Almost all his poetry is some form of meditative exercise, aiming to guide readers toward the light of vision turned on God, with everything to do with the self abandoned. Typically, Crashaw's religious poems allow traditional Christian allusions and images to accumulate and transcend sensuous response. He often concludes with epigrammatic shifts that pull together allusions and images to focus on a devotional point their relationship implies. For Crashaw, as for **John Donne**, Herbert, and other metaphysical poets, the conceit is a principal poetic device. The difference between Crashaw's poetry and that of other metaphysicals is not that it is foreign, formless, lush, or excessively emotional but rather that his art, by its use of repeated, juxtaposed images, traditional Christian allusion, and limited structural design, is based on a more narrow scope than theirs.

His poetry also reflects the imagery of the continental Baroque poets and poetics of the Counter Reformation and its attempt to render the spiritual through the senses. Exuberant, rhetorical, and elaborately ornamented, the Baroque style uses sensuous metaphors for spiritual themes and seeks to transcend the limits of genre. Crashaw's favorite subjects are the Baroque artists' favorites: angels, cherubs, the infant Jesus, the bloody wounds of the crucified Christ, the sufferings of the Virgin Mary, the tears of Magdalene, the agonies of martyrs, and the ecstasy of Teresa.

The uniqueness of Crashaw's art comes from fusing aesthetic, theological, and personal influences, and it is eclectic and exhibits great variety in subject, meter, and form. In addition to Baroque art and poetics, the epigram, Renaissance classicism, Spenserianism, and native English traditions help shape Crashaw's poetry. Crashaw's verse also manifests conventions, themes, and styles of the lyric and mystic writers of the Spanish Golden Age. Finally, his verse developed from the religious, intellectual, and poetic environment he experienced at Cambridge.

Much influenced by Jesuit epigram style, Crashaw's Latin epigrams and later English versions display sophisticated rhetoric, puns, paradoxes, antithesis, and sometimes grotesque metaphors, as in the epigram on Luke II. One aim of his epigrams was to stun readers into awareness of the supernatural in earthly experience, and Crashaw was innovative in introducing spiritual and mystical subjects into the epigram in England, first in Latin (1634), then in English (1646).

Crashaw continuously revised his poems, usually making them longer. Especially noteworthy are the final versions of "Music's Duel," "Hymn in the Holy Nativity" and its companion piece "In the Glorious Epiphany," and "The Flaming Heart." In "Music's Duel," a contest between a nightingale and a lutenist, melody and harmony, Crashaw imitates musical sounds by means of liquid vowels, subtle syntax, repetition, onomatopoeia, and synesthesia. A recension of the Artusi-Monteverdi controversy, the poem debates whether music should be the servant of words or vice versa, and there are similarities between Crashaw's techniques in the poem and those of Monteverdi.

"Hymn in the Holy Nativity," the first of three Christmas hymns, would eventually appear as a trio in *Carmen Deo Nostro*. In it, the Nativity gospel of Luke inspires Crashaw to emulate the joyful song the shepherds improvised as they returned to their fields after beholding the Virgin and Child. As all shepherds' eyes are on the Infant asleep at His Mother's breast, Crashaw uses the Virgin and Baby as an icon that focuses upon the meditative purpose of his art, prayerful absorption in God. "Hymn in the Glorious Epiphany," which celebrates the Adoration of the Magi, uses oxymoron, syntactical manipulation, and sensuous images to convey the paradox of the bright darkness of God and the dark brightness of this world, thereby revealing the complexity of human relationships with God. The concept of the "dark night of the soul," or *via negativa*, found in the the writings of John of the Cross unifies its divergent elements, and parallels in language, structure, images, and symbolism between the saint's writings and Crashaw's poetry show how the poet was able to depict a sense of the mystical experience through his art.

Crashaw's poems in Teresa's honor—"A Hymn to St. Teresa," "An Apology for the Fore-going Hymn," and "The Flaming Heart"—which form a triptych, are perhaps his most sublime works. Part "Advice to a Painter" and part ecstatic hymn, the later poem critiques a painting of Teresa and the seraph, possibly conceived in the manner of Bernini's sculpture. His attitude toward the image and the word in these poems, especially in "The Flaming Heart," reveals the power of the word over that of the picture or image to capture and convey spiritual truth, and his interest is not in exalting poetry over painting, a common Renaissance theme, but in celebrating the saint's writing. At the end of "The Flaming Heart," he concedes both the verbal and visual image pale in the light of Teresa's writing about her mystical union with God. Thus, Crashaw's trilogy to Teresa becomes another part of his meditative and poetic life in which he saw God as the center and source of knowledge of the self and others.

CRITICAL RECEPTION

Readers need to understand that Crashaw's poetry was first admired as an extension of his prayer life and testimony to God's presence. In spite of his artistic efforts to increase spiritual fervor in himself and his readers, Crashaw remains perhaps the most misunderstood of 17th-century English poets and the least appreciated of the metaphysical poets. Condemned during the 18th and 19th centuries for its extravagance, Crashaw's art received sympathetic critical reading in the early 20th century, as T.S. Eliot, among the first to admire him, said, "There is brain work" behind his use of language. Even with revived interest in the metaphysicals, however, many critics preferred Donne and Herbert to Crashaw.

Because new materials have been added from manuscript collections, Crashaw's poems have recently experienced a revival of interest. Expanded understanding of

Baroque art has also contributed. Yet despite critical efforts to reevaluate Crashaw's work and to establish its place in 17th-century English poetics, some notions remain unchanged, and old negative tags continue to be attached to him. What is needed, in addition to a fully annotated edition of his works, is a comprehensive reading that, while accounting for continental influences, will stress the influences of classical Greece and Rome and native English Christian writers. Although separate studies have explored these traditions, no work integrates all of them. Hence, some features of Crashaw's poetry are emphasized to the exclusion of others, thereby opening the way to value certain aspects of his work outside the context of his complete achievement (Roberts, "Recent Studies" 439–440).

BIBLIOGRAPHY

Works by Richard Crashaw

Carmen Deo Nostro. Paris: Peter Targa, 1652.

The Complete Poetry of Richard Crashaw. Ed. George Walton Williams. Garden City, NY: Doubleday, 1970.

Epigrammatum Sacrorum Liber. Cambridge: T. Buck & R. Daniel, 1634.

The Poems, English, Latin, and Greek, of Richard Crashaw. Ed. L.C. Martin. Oxford: Clarendon, 1927; 2nd ed. rev., 1957.

Richardi Crashawi Poemata et Epigrammata. Cambridge: Ex Officina Joan Hayes, 1670.

Steps to the Temple: Sacred Poems, with Other Delights of the Muses. London: Printed by T.W. for Humphrey Moseley, 1646; 2nd ed. enlarged, 1648.

Studies of Richard Crashaw

Cooper, Robert M. *An Essay on the Art of Richard Crashaw*. Salzburg Studies in English Literature, Elizabethan & Renaissance Studies, no. 102. Salzburg: Universität Salzburg, 1982.

———, ed. *Essays on Richard Crashaw*. Salzburg Studies in English Literature, Elizabethan & Renaissance Studies, no. 83. Salzburg: Universität Salzburg, 1979.

Davis, Walter R. "The Meditative Hymnody of Richard Crashaw." *English Literary History* 50 (1983): 107–129.

Healy, Thomas F. *Richard Crashaw*. Medieval and Renaissance Authors, no. 8. Leiden: Brill, 1986.

Low, Anthony. *The Reinvention of Love Poetry: Politics and Culture from Sidney to Milton*. New York: Cambridge University Press, 1993.

Martz, Louis L. "Richard Crashaw: Love's Architecture." In his *The Wit of Love: Donne, Carew, Crashaw, Marvell*. Notre Dame, IN: University of Notre Dame Press, 1969. 113–147.

Parrish, Paul A. "The Feminizing of Power: Crashaw's Life and Art." In *"The Muses Common-Weale": Poetry and Politics in the Seventeenth Century*, ed. Claude J. Summers and Ted-Larry Pebworth. Columbia: University of Missouri Press, 1988. 148–162.

———. "Reading Poets Reading Poets: Herbert and Crashaw's Literary Eclipse." In *Literary Circles and Cultural Communities in Renaissance England*, ed. Claude J. Summers and Ted-Larry Pebworth. Columbia: University of Missouri Press, 2000. 115–127.

———. *Richard Crashaw*. Twayne English Authors Series, no. 299. Boston: Twayne Publishers, 1980.

Roberts, John R., ed. *New Perspectives on the Life and Art of Richard Crashaw*. Columbia: University of Missouri Press, 1990.

———. "Recent Studies in Richard Crashaw (1977–1989)." *English Literary Renaissance* 21.3 (1991): 425–445.

Sabine, Maureen. *Feminine Engendered Faith: The Poetry of John Donne and Richard Crashaw*. London: Macmillan, 1992.

Williams, George Walton. *Image and Symbol in the Sacred Poetry of Richard Crashaw*. Columbia: University of South Carolina Press, 1963.

Young, R.V., Jr. *Richard Crashaw and the Spanish Golden Age*. Yale Studies in English, no. 191. New Haven, CT: Yale University Press, 1982.

🙣 *Oliver Cromwell*

(1599–1658)

JOHN A. SHEDD

BIOGRAPHY

Oliver Cromwell was born on April 25, 1599, into a minor gentry family. In 1620 he married Elizabeth Bourchier, whose wealthy London relatives were in the fur trade. The couple went on to settle on Cromwell's small inherited estate in Huntingdon. In 1628 he was elected member of Parliament for Huntingdon, and in his first recorded speech, he argued for an end to royal policy prohibiting free-speaking Puritan ministers. Soon after, Charles I launched what has come to be known as his personal rule, resulting in an England that went without a Parliament for eleven years. Many members of the gentry class were frustrated by the King's decision to shut them out of central government, and some scholars believe Charles I's increasingly High Church religious initiatives tempted Cromwell to consider emigration to New England. In 1641 he was elected to the Long Parliament as a member for the town of Cambridge, site of his alma mater and what Archbishop Laud considered the birthplace of Puritanism. Certainly Cromwell's voice was among the most willing in Parliament to risk civil war with the King, which came in 1642.

Possessing no prior experience as a leader of armed forces, Cromwell nonetheless threw his body and soul into the conflict, quickly perfecting his skills as a cavalry commander. He displayed remarkable personal courage on the battlefield and played decisive roles in several victories for Parliament's forces, such as at Marston Moor and at Naseby, but he did not take a central position on the national stage as a political and military leader until the period between the defeat of the Royalist army in 1646 and the King's execution in 1649. He appears to have been content to work under the orders of Parliament's supreme army commander, Sir Thomas Fairfax, but the issue of putting Charles I on trial for his life caused anxiety in Fairfax, and he never found enough nerve or will to push England into a republic.

Almost everyone agrees that Cromwell, on the other hand, was endowed with plenty of both nerve and will, drawn in part from his unshakable Calvinism, and it was his determination to make of Britain a virtuous, reformed estate that shaped the political history of England, Ireland, and Scotland until his death. Cromwell was an inner-directed leader, which often made him unpredictable, and the three most important entities affecting the messages of his conscience were God's words and signs, the well-being of Parliament's soldiers, and gentry-class social assumptions. Unfortunately, starting in 1647 and thereafter, the army and the gentry were often at odds with each other, and not even Cromwell's considerable political skills could forge them into a stable, unified state.

From the King's execution in 1649 to 1653, England was a republican "Commonwealth," ruled by the Rump, the sitting portion of Parliament remaining after Parliament's army purged it of moderates in 1648. The Rump quickly developed a reputation among soldiers as self-serving, as it put off time and again dissolving itself and calling for an election of new members. In April 1653 Cromwell went to the House of Commons, berated its members, and dissolved the Rump by summoning two files of musketeers to enter the chamber. By this time, he was set upon the idea of an England ruled by the godly few who possessed the virtues needed to legislate a just society. Thus followed the Nominated Parliament, made up of Puritan notables, none of whom had political experience and who held much less in common than Cromwell had hoped. Persistent bickering on the floor of the Commons, occasionally broken by voting in a handful of measures too radical for the gentry to stomach, led Cromwell to dissolve Parliament for a second time in 1653. The rule of the saints lasted only five months.

Hoping to achieve stability by returning to old and familiar ways, Cromwell moved the government halfway back to the Stuart system by taking the title Lord Protector and working with a more traditional Parliament. But as the Protector, Cromwell had difficulties similar to Charles I's in dealing with Parliament, an annoyance that encouraged him to try yet another experiment in government, the rule of the Major Generals. Continuing Royalist plots to overthrow the Puritan government and replace it with a restored Charles II alarmed Cromwell who, in 1655, divided the nation into twelve military districts, each overseen by a general charged to work out security measures with local civilian leaders. This was Cromwell's greatest political blunder, as it intensified popular hatred of army rule and left him open to charges of military dictatorship from that time to this. Broadly speaking, however, the 1650s were marked by a drift back toward monarchy, as the Protector increasingly took on the trappings, roles, and obligations of a king. Parliament offered him the crown in 1657, but he declined it, apparently still hoping to avoid becoming that which he had been so instrumental in bringing down. He died of natural causes in 1658, and Charles II returned to London as King in 1660. As part of a widespread pattern of Royalist revenge, Cromwell's body was exhumed in January 1661 on the anniversary of Charles I's "martyrdom" and hanged at Tyburn.

All of the attempted political settlements of the 1650s failed, and Cromwell was an author of most of them. As a military leader, however, he was second to none, winning every battle he led. The fledgling Commonwealth of 1649 was beset by enemies within and without the British Isles. Cromwell took them on one at a time, defeating or neutralizing each. Throughout the period, plans from the European Continent for invading England and overthrowing the regicide regime were thwarted by a strong military. Cromwell invaded Ireland in 1649 and Scotland in 1650 to put down dissent;

his barbarous slaughter of civilians in Drogheda sealed forever his evil reputation among Irish Catholics. He led England into war in 1654 with a new overseas rival, Holland, and in 1655 with the old one, Spain, securing two hard-won truces that paved the way for extended international trading patterns for Britain. Cromwell, in fact, left England a stronger and more prosperous nation than he found it.

MAJOR WORKS AND THEMES

Cromwell became a published author with a wide audience two centuries after his death when eminent British historian Thomas Carlyle collected and edited his "letters and utterances" from "a hundred repositories." Like so many other Puritans, Cromwell sought to discern reflections of his predestined, elect status in the records he produced, choosing frequent letter writing to keeping a diary. His hundreds of surviving letters are thought to be only a fraction of the total, since throughout his life Cromwell spent time writing letters to an extent unusual even for the 17th century. Only a couple of times did he have his speeches printed and distributed as a means of recruiting support for his causes. The rest have been recovered as manuscripts taken down by eyewitnesses and scribes. Carlyle's collection was first printed in 1845. His efforts to bring Cromwell to the people were so impressive they helped bring about the traditional modern archives, setting up repositories in the counties and in London where old records could be stored, sorted, edited, and indexed. More of Cromwell's writings have been found since and published, pushing the total to nearly a thousand.

Taken at their face value, Cromwell's writings read as though they are products of a decent, sometimes self-effacing man struggling to ensure that his actions coincide with God's providential will. His speeches, delivered either with few or no notes, often amounted to thinking out loud, as he rambled toward the concluding admonition that both he and his audience should do what is right. The Venetian ambassador noted that he sounded more like a preacher than a statesman, and his speeches were peppered with quotes from the Bible to reinforce his points. Regardless of one's assessment of his sincerity, it is hard to conclude that Cromwell's words were those of a self-righteous religious bigot. One of the steadfast themes of his writings was his support for liberty of conscience, with an attendant respect for the beliefs of others. His toleration of Jews while he was Lord Protector is famous, and he once said of the many Protestant splinter groups that had multiplied greatly during the Civil War period: "Every sect saith, Oh, Give me liberty. But give him it, and to his power he will not yield it to anybody else."

Nevertheless, by the early 1650s Cromwell considered himself God's chosen instrument, albeit unworthy, and he habitually began his longer speeches with a summary of past events—from, for example, the victories of his armies to the abolition of monarchy and the House of Lords—as a means of discerning the pattern of God's will unfolding over time. He then went on to remind his audience of the role of wrong-minded people in forcing his hand so that he had to intervene into events, changing their course and bringing them into line with the series of blessings visited upon England since the bad old days of Stuart rule without a Parliament. What may appear today as a series of political experiments in the 1650s was to Cromwell a path to a more just society made winding and indirect by the many who resisted seeing the light.

CRITICAL RECEPTION

Opinions about the merits of Cromwell's writings cannot be detached from opinions about the man himself, and rarely has history produced a figure with a wider range of reputations than Oliver Cromwell. W.C. Abbott, editor of what is currently the most prevalent collection of Cromwell's writings, noted that during the 1700s "most Tories hated him because he overthrew the monarchy, most Whigs because he overthrew Parliament." At the turn of the 19th century, America's second president, John Adams, vehemently praised Cromwell to an English audience. In order to take on an entirely favorable reputation, Cromwell had to come to be seen as part of the process leading to popular parliamentary government. This was the task admirably achieved by influential Victorian authors such as Thomas Babington Macaulay and Thomas Carlyle. They and others interpreted his writings as products of a pious hero of the common man, defending ordinary people from religious and political tyranny. By the middle of the 19th century, a cult of Cromwell had caught on, so that the middle classes could read the words of their role model and embrace him as a supreme example of an independent-minded, self-made man. A noble bronze statue of Cromwell was erected on the very grounds of the Houses of Parliament, where it remains to this day. Even radicals of the time, such as the Chartists, as well as Marx and Engels and their followers, could celebrate him as a compelling example of a rising commoner, though for very different reasons. The cult of Cromwell eventually became thoroughly transatlantic when U.S. President Theodore Roosevelt published a favorable biography of him in 1901.

The monster dictators of the 20th century led to another rethinking of Cromwell's reputation, as he came to be seen by some as a precursor to modern ruthless ideologues who purge nonbelievers from politics and who are kept in power by a spoiled and loyal army. The same sorts of perspectives are sometimes used to interpret Napoleon, and comparisons between the two are tempting. In a recent biography, J.C. Davis notes that Trotsky, Stalin, and Hitler were Cromwell admirers and that both Hitler and Mussolini are rumored to have kept his portrait in their offices.

Most contemporary scholars of 17th-century Britain, however, reject presentism, leaving Cromwell's reputation in a muddle. The rancor of the late 17th and 18th centuries, as well as the glowing admiration of the 19th, have long since bled away. Nowadays, scholars wonder about the extent to which Cromwell shaped and was shaped by events as well as what motivated him, so that "his precise achievement" is a matter of "great dispute." He is a "puzzlement" whose motives, especially at key turning points in his life, are "hard to fathom" and his "feelings [hard] to discern." Cromwell's writings and speeches have never been considered masterpieces. Yet to his countless biographers, as well as to any serious student of the period, they are considered a primary source indispensable to our attempts to understand a complex man as well as his complex times.

BIBLIOGRAPHY

Works by Oliver Cromwell

Oliver Cromwell's Letters and Speeches. Ed. Thomas Carlyle. 2 vols. London, 1845.
Speeches of Oliver Cromwell. Ed. Ivan Roots. London: J.M. Dent & Sons, Ltd., 1989.

Speeches of Oliver Cromwell, 1644–1658. Ed. C.L. Stainer. London: Henry Frowde, 1901.
The Writings and Speeches of Oliver Cromwell. Ed. W.C. Abbott. 4 vols. Cambridge: Harvard
    University Press, 1937–1947.

Studies of Oliver Cromwell

Ashley, Maurice. *The Greatness of Oliver Cromwell.* Toronto: Macmillan, 1957.

Coward, Barry. *Oliver Cromwell.* London: Longman Publishers, 1991.

Davis, J.C. *Oliver Cromwell.* New York: Oxford University Press, 2001.

Hill, Christopher. *God's Englishman: Oliver Cromwell and the English Revolution.* New York:
    Harper & Row, 1970.

Howell, Roger. *Cromwell.* Boston: Little, Brown, 1977.

Knoppers, Laura Lunger. *Constructing Cromwell: Ceremony, Portrait, and Print, 1645–1661.*
    New York: Cambridge University Press, 2000.

Morrill, John. "Textualizing and Contextualizing Cromwell." *The Historical Journal* 33.3
    (1990): 629–639.

———, ed. *Oliver Cromwell and the English Revolution.* London: Longman Publishers, 1990.

Paul, Robert S. *The Lord Protector: Religion and Politics in the Life of Oliver Cromwell.*
    London: Lutterworth Press, 1955.

William Davenant

(1606–1668)

RON LEVAO

BIOGRAPHY

William Davenant (D'Avenant, D'avenant) had notable careers in the theater, politics, and the military, but the most widely broadcast legend was that he was the godson of **William Shakespeare** and perhaps more. The famous playwright was a frequent and amiable visitor to the family's Oxford tavern, reports **John Aubrey**, who describes a jovial Davenant in later years boasting to drinking companions that he wrote with "the very spirit [of] that Shakespeare . . . content enough to be thought his son." The legend, writes Aubrey, led to Davenant's beautiful, witty mother being called "whore"; among later Shakespeareans, it installed her as a leading candidate for the Dark Lady of the Sonnets. Ironically, Davenant would be "fired out" by his own Dark Lady in 1630. Again, according to Aubrey: "He got a terrible clap of a black handsome wench . . . which cost him his nose." This syphilitic deformity (a collapsed bridge rather than a complete loss) may have been traumatic, but it inspired numerous jaunty (and occasionally cruel) jokes, even by Davenant himself, whose sole portrait, an engraving in the posthumous folio of his works, features him with flowing robes and hair, laurel wreath, and flattened nose.

Educated at Oxford until the death of both parents in 1622, Davenant was sent to London, then became part of **Fulke Greville**'s household in Holborn (1624) while cultivating powerful friends and patrons. The seventy-year-old courtier poet/playwright was reportedly "much delighted" with the talented youth, who wrote the two tragedies while residing with him. When Greville was murdered by a disgruntled servant in 1628, Davenant moved to the Middle Temple and wrote *The Siege* (1629). Temporarily silenced in 1630 by that nearly fatal bout with syphilis, he was cured by a physician to Queen Henrietta Maria, and *The Wits* proved a comic success in 1634 when King Charles I, upon the advice of Davenant's patron, Endymion Porter, overruled objections by the Master of the Revels. Within a year, Davenant was a leading playwright for Shakespeare's old company, the King's Men, and collaborating with

Ben Jonson's old partner and antagonist, Inigo Jones, on opulent court masques under the Queen's patronage. The year 1638 saw the production of his most successful tragedy, *The Unfortunate Lovers*, the publication of a volume of poetry, and his appointment as poet laureate, succeeding Jonson and preceding **Dryden**. Two years later he was theater manager at the Cockpit in Drury Lane, replacing William Beeston when Charles I took offense at a play staged there.

Davenant's military career, begun during his years with Greville, also heated up. After serving in the two Bishops' Wars (1639–1640), he was arrested, together with his friend and fellow-poet **John Suckling**, for his part in the first Army Plot. Escaping a death sentence, he joined the Queen in France and was convicted of high treason by the House of Commons in 1641. For the rest of the decade he worked in England and on the Continent for the Royalist cause, and in 1649 he wrote the first two books of his epic, *Gondibert*. His political loyalty was rewarded by Charles I with knighthood (1643) and by Charles II, who named him treasurer of Virginia and lieutenant-governor of Maryland (1649–1650). His attempt to assume his American posts led to his capture at sea, and he was held prisoner on the Isle of Wight and in the Tower of London until released, possibly through the intervention of **Milton** and others. It was a favor he would return during the Restoration when, according to Jonathan Richardson, he intervened for Milton.

After his release, Davenant worked on covertly dramatic "entertainments," and with the Restoration, despite chilly relations with Charles II, his theater monopoly (shared with Thomas Killigrew) led to epochal innovations—popularizing movable scenery and employing female actors—as well as adaptations of Shakespeare's plays featuring the most celebrated Restoration actor, Thomas Betterton. He also presented works by other leading Jacobean and Caroline dramatists, as well as his own and George Etherege's. On a paving stone marking his grave in Westminster Abbey is written, notes Aubrey, "in imitation of that on Ben Jonson, '*O rare Sir Will. Davenant.*' "

MAJOR WORKS AND THEMES

Davenant began with revenge tragedies, replete with decadent Italian courts, sexual obsession, and blood-soaked plots. *Albovine* was not staged, but *The Cruel Brother* (1627) was. Echoing Jacobean tragedy, it may glance at the late James himself in its Duke's passion for a courtier. It also features a cruelly moralistic brother tying his twin sister to a chair and slitting her "wrist-veins" for the sake of honor after she has been raped, a twinly sadism reminiscent of *The Duchess of Malfi*. (Davenant would revive **Webster**'s play years later.) After two tragicomedies, Davenant produced his most successful comedy, *The Wits* (1634). Echoing Jonson and anticipating Restoration comedy, its lively action includes a rich, overconfident country brother gulled in London by his rakish city brother and by the clever heiress, Lady Ample, whom he finally marries once he has been amply humbled. A popular tragicomedy, the thematically explicit *Love and Honour* (1634), followed and the intriguing, if less popular, *Platonic Lovers* (1635), which catered to Queen Henrietta Maria's interest in Neoplatonism. The latter is respectful but generally skeptical of courtly idealization, even introducing a philosopher who denies that his "old friend Plato" ever invented so "fantastic" a notion. Davenant then reverted to the Italianate revenge play, *The*

Unfortunate Lovers (1638), a complex plot of lust and bloodshed that played three times before the Queen and court and would become a Restoration standard.

Amid the Commonwealth suppression of the theaters, Davenant staged what he called "representations" or "operas" in a hall in his home and possibly in other houses as well. *The First Day's Entertainment at Rutland House* (1656), featuring declamations interspersed with music composed by Henry Lawes (of *Comus* fame) and others, presents the cynic Diogenes and the poet Aristophanes self-reflexively debating the value of public entertainment, followed by a Parisian and a Londoner comically attacking each other's cities. Davenant then ventured the more ambitious *Siege of Rhodes* (1656), first at Rutland house, but eventually revised and expanded to two parts for the public theater. Concerned with the 1522 attack by Solyman the Magnificent, it is remembered for its numerous historical firsts or near-firsts: the first English "opera" with music and recitative (by Lawes and others), one of the first uses of a woman on the public stage (a minor role; the first major role was probably Mary Saunderson's Ophelia in Davenant's Restoration *Hamlet*), the first use of movable scenery on a public stage (employing sets designed by Inigo Jones's successor, John Webb), and providing an influential model for **Dryden**'s "heroic plays" in heroic couplets. Two more patriotic "operas" appeared during the Commonwealth: *The Cruelty of the Spaniards in Peru* and the *History of Sir Francis Drake*.

Davenant's experiments with movable scenery—relying on shutters running in grooves and background reliefs—would come to fruition in the Duke's Theatre, a former tennis court refitted in the Restoration; but many of his techniques stem from earlier Caroline masques at the royal court, where the ingenuity of scene changes was part of the spectacle. Davenant wrote five masques between 1635 and 1640, four in conjunction with Inigo Jones. These were scenic spectaculars, filled with Royalist mythologizing and Neoplatonic idealism—the former affirmed, the latter treated with irony. *Salmacida Spolia* ("the spoils [i.e., waters] of the fountain of Salmacis") is his grandest and the Caroline era's final masque. Beginning with a tempest and followed by a sequence of allegorical figures and grotesque antimasques, it finally reveals Philogenes ("lover of the people" played by King Charles on a seat of gold) assuring harmony in defiance of Discord, "adverse times," and "the people's giddy fury." The whole climaxes with elegant visions produced by machines and lavish costumes—magnificent buildings, deities, dancers, and a pregnant Henrietta Maria and her ladies as Amazons descending from the heavens on a "huge cloud of various colours." If such doomed fantasies are now the stuff of historical irony, the scenic techniques nurtured those of modern staging.

Better known are Davenant's Restoration adaptations of Shakespeare. As a theatrical manager expanding his repertory, Davenant sought to fit "ancient plays" for modern consumption. Simplifying and ennobling, he highlights his favorite didactic themes: the conflict between love and honor and the dangers of ambition. He also tightens structure, regularizes meter, and polishes language by updating vocabulary, deleting obscenity and profanity, and rewriting or excising obscure, suggestive verse. Particular examples have become notorious. *Hamlet* was probably always cut in Shakespeare's time, but Davenant's trimmed famous speeches and soliloquies in an intrusive adjustment of emphasis; he transformed *Measure for Measure* into *The Law against Lovers* by deleting the Mistress Overdone plot and importing Beatrice and Benedict from *Much Ado About Nothing* to take her place. Angelo is sanitized: He means only to test Isabella's virtue, and Mariana is excised altogether.

In *Macbeth*, Lady Macduff's role is expanded to counterbalance Lady Macbeth's, and with the addition of songs, dances, and flying machines, the witches become "operatic and acrobatic as well as merely prophetic," as Alfred Harbage remarks. The problematic *Two Noble Kinsmen* is resolved into a more joyous *The Rivals*. Best known is the adaptation of *The Tempest*, a joint effort by Davenant and John Dryden, with numerous plot changes, deletions of famous passages, and the invention of new characters to fulfill a taste for symmetrical couplings and contrasts, including a paramour for Ariel, a sister for Miranda, and a twin sister for Caliban. Once condemned by critics, these adaptations have recently been defended as a necessary response to, and lucrative accommodation of, new social and political conditions.

Davenant's early nondramatic poetry appears in *Madagascar* (1638), a slim volume by turns serious and witty, that includes poems to the King and Queen and prominent courtiers. The title poem encourages Prince Rupert, cousin to Charles I, to invade the East African island, a soon-forgotten plan that Rupert's mother compared to "one of Don Quixote's conquests." The volume ends with an early mock epic, *Jeffereidos*, on the capture and escape of the Queen's dwarf from pirates, including his combat with a turkey. More resolutely serious is *Gondibert* (1650), a philosophical-romantic-heroic poem in *abab* quatrains, published half completed when Davenant expected to be executed in the Tower. Planned for five books or acts, recalling Sir Philip Sidney's *Arcadia* and other works, it was called "a play in narrative" by Dryden. Set in 8th-century Lombardy, its hero is torn between the daughter of a king and the daughter of a philosophical wise man, and themes of love and honor abound within a medley of poetic forms, homages to learning, and according to some critics, coded political messages (see Potter).

Gondibert is noted chiefly today for its critical *Preface*, cast as a long and grateful letter to the author's friend and adviser **Thomas Hobbes**. It was first published in 1650 in Paris, together with the philosopher's sympathetic *Answer*, without the poem itself. It echoes Renaissance defenses of poetry with emphases that forecast a new kind of neoclassicism. Davenant champions harmony and warns against excessive love and ambition; he abjures the supernaturalism of ancient epic, preferring to "make great actions credible" so that they might instruct the high-born reader. Its definition of wit includes "dexterity of thought" but favors time, labor, and luck over far-fetched conceits and claims of "inspiration"—"a dangerous word" excusable among the ancients but presuming a "saucy familiarity with a true God." And there is a lengthy defense of poetic didacticism, derived from humanist interpreters of Aristotle, praising its living truth over the dead facts of history and insisting on the value of poetry to promote order and government when clergy, military, law, and politics have failed. Hobbes's compact *Answer*, despite some differences, generally supports Davenant's didacticism and the coupling of judgment with fancy. He allows a qualified supernaturalism but dismisses mystical afflatus: "inspiration" means only that one speaks "like a bagpipe."

CRITICAL RECEPTION

Davenant's historical importance usually overshadows consideration of his literary talents, which have been debated. His confession that "the desire of Fame made me a Writer" is often quoted, and his laureateship together with contemporary praise show fame in his own age. **Thomas Carew** admired his "strong fancies, raptures of the brain," which are caviar to the general; Milton's nephew, Edward Philips, noted "the great fluency of his wit and fancy"; and Dryden, in his preface to their *Tempest*, called him "a man of quick and piercing imagination" and professed delight in their collaboration ("my writing received daily his amendments"). **Pepys** found much of his theatrical work "most excellent."

Davenant's reputation suffered in the 18th and 19th centuries. Though occasionally praised, his works were usually forgotten, and if Sir Walter Scott thought *Gondibert* "majestic," William Hazlitt found its stanzas "aiming to be wise and witty" but on the whole "amounting to nothing." In the late 19th century David Masson, in his monumental biography of Milton, offered clear (if qualified) enthusiasm for the "undoubted power" of Davenant's "Elizabethan" energy: "something from Ben Jonson, something from **Massinger**, but more from Shakespeare." Important studies by Harbage and Nethercot in the 1930s focused academic interest. Harbage conceded Davenant's opportunism but defended him against personal attacks as a "court toady." Some modern critics see his writing as limp or derivative, or wince at his sententiousness; others admire his metaphorical wit and incorporation of cavalier and metaphysical styles.

Davenant seems to matter most in historical narratives, whether in tales of continuity, transformation, or appropriation. His crucial role in returning Shakespeare to the stage and reviving a devastated dramatic profession, as well as his introduction of movable scenery (as atmospheric counterpoints to plot rather than naturalistic settings) and women actors (he had eight in his company), always earn him a place in the story. For Douglas Bush, his correspondence with Hobbes constitutes "landmarks on the road from the Renaissance to the Augustan age." If Nethercot lamented his "violating hand rov[ing] murderously among the greatest lines in English literature," recent criticism is fascinated by what his changes reveal about Restoration culture. In Davenant's own day, the fascination was also with what he preserved. The implications are, in part, political. Betterton's wearing of Charles II's coronation robes in the revival of *Love and Honour* stages its author's renewed Royalism. They are also aesthetic. When Betterton's Hamlet created a sensation, the company's prompter credited Davenant's memory of Shakespeare's own version of the role and his teaching Betterton "every particle of it."

BIBLIOGRAPHY

Works by William Davenant

A Book of Masques in Honour of Allardyce Nicoll. Cambridge: Cambridge University Press, 1967.

The Dramatic Works of Sir William D'Avenant, with Prefatory Memoir and Notes. Ed. J. Maidment and W.H. Logan. 5 vols. 1872–1874. Reprint, New York: Russell & Russell, 1964.

Sir William Davenant: The Shorter Poems, and Songs from the Plays and Masques. Ed. A.M. Gibbs. Oxford: Clarendon Press, 1972.

Sir William Davenant's Gondibert. Ed. David F. Gladish. Oxford: Clarendon Press, 1971.

Studies of William Davenant

Bordinat, Philip, and Sophia B. Blaydes. *Sir William Davenant*. Boston: Twayne Publishers, 1981.

Collins, Howard S. *The Comedy of Sir William Davenant*. The Hague: Mouton, 1967.

Dobson, Michael. *The Making of the National Poet: Shakespeare, Adaptation and Authorship, 1660–1769*. Oxford: Clarendon Press, 1992.

Dowlin, Cornell March. *Sir William Davenant's "Gondibert," Its Preface, and Hobbes's Answer: A Study in English Neoclassicism*. Philadelphia, 1934.

Edmond, Mary. *Rare Sir William Davenant: Poet Laureate, Playwright, Civil War General, Restoration Theatre Manager*. Manchester: Manchester University Press, 1987.

Harbage, Alfred. *Sir William Davenant: Poet Venturer, 1606–1668*. Philadelphia: University of Pennsylvania Press, 1935.

Hotson, Leslie. *The Commonwealth and Restoration Stage*. Cambridge: Harvard University Press, 1928.

Nethercot, Arthur H. *Sir William Davenant: Poet Laureate and Playwright-Manager*. 1938. Reissue, New York: Russell and Russell, 1967.

Orrell, John. *The Theatres of Inigo Jones and John Webb*. Cambridge: Cambridge University Press, 1985.

Potter, Lois. *Secret Rites and Secret Writing: Royalist Literature, 1641–1660*. Cambridge: Cambridge University Press, 1989.

Raddadi, Mongi. *Davenant's Adaptations of Shakespeare*. Uppsala, 1979.

Southern, Richard. *Changeable Scenery: Its Origin and Development in the British Theatre*. London: Faber and Faber, 1952.

Spencer, Hazelton. *Shakespeare Improved*. Cambridge: Harvard University Press, 1927.

Welsford, Enid. *The Court Masque: A Study of the Relationship between Poetry and the Revels*. 1927. Reprint, New York: Russell and Russell, 1962.

❧ *John Dennis*
(1658–1734)

RICHARD J. SQUIBBS

BIOGRAPHY

John Dennis comes to us through literary history mainly among "the forms / Of hairs, or straws, or dirt, or grubs, or worms" preserved in the "Amber" of Pope's poetry (*Epistle to Dr. Arbuthnot*). But the relative prominence Pope accords him in his attacks testifies to Dennis's stature in the literary scene of early-18th-century London. Born on September 16, 1658, to a London saddler and his wife, Dennis early studied classics at Harrow and later entered Caius College, Cambridge. He received his M.A. in 1683 from Trinity Hall, after being expelled from Caius for wounding another student with a sword. Following a tour of the Continent (a near-requirement for an aspiring wit), Dennis returned to London and fell in with the crowd at Will's Coffeehouse. He there apparently befriended **Dryden** and during this time developed his reputation as a controversialist. His earliest critical piece of note, *The Impartial Critick* (1693), was an attack on Thomas Rymer, and throughout his life Dennis would engage in public squabbles with **Addison**, Steele, Swift, and Pope, among others. Coupled with his deep interest in the sublime, Dennis's brash, and at times hostile, authorial demeanor would earn him the epithet "Sir Tremendous Longinus" in *Three Hours after Marriage* (1717), a play credited to Pope, Gay, and Arbuthnot. In 1705, Dennis was appointed to a position in the London Custom House but was forced to sell it in 1715 out of financial necessity, a problem that would plague him for most of his life, leading to several stays in debtors' prison. Politically, he was a solid Whig, and though he wrote a number of forgotten panegyrics and pamphlets, these were likely motivated more by financial distress than outright sycophancy. Dennis continued to publish fractious criticism through the 1720s, but his health declined precipitously in the early 1730s, when he became almost completely blind. He died on January 6, 1734, a few weeks after Pope organized a benefit performance of Vanbrugh and Cibber's *The Provoked Husband* for him at the Haymarket. Aside from his perennial status as a target of Pope's satire, Dennis's critical writings—especially those on the sublime—give valuable insight into the various modes of critical thought in the early 18th century.

MAJOR WORKS AND THEMES

Dennis is most noteworthy for his development of an affective theory of art, which dovetails with his promotion of the sublime as the sine qua non of literature. His tragic theory in *The Impartial Critick* (1693) and *The Usefulness of the Stage* (1698) generally proves more interesting to modern readers than Thomas Rymer's, thanks to the emphasis Dennis places on the psychology of tragic response as opposed to neoclassical rules. But in the end, he agrees with Rymer in seeing reason as the arbiter of tragic experience. His analysis of tragic affect cites rational reflection in the wake of the pathetic spectacle of a suffering hero as that which reconciles the audience to their exclusion from power: their very anonymity and powerlessness spares them the tragic ends meted out to the great. Similarly, Dennis subscribes to the doctrine of poetic justice for its capacity to preserve social order through instantiating a predictable system of rewards and punishments. But the seeds of a new aesthetic theory sown in these tracts bear fruit in his subsequent work on the sublime.

In *The Advancement and Reformation of Modern Poetry* (1701), Dennis defines poetry as "an imitation of nature, by a pathetic and numerous [i.e., metrical] speech." However, he insists that "passion" is more necessary to poetry than "harmony," for while the latter distinguishes poetry from prose, passion is poetry's "very nature and character." For Dennis, religion is the greatest source of passion and, ultimately, of the sublime, a position that places him at odds with the rationalistic tenor of much literary criticism in the early 18th century. He further believes that true religion is revealed and not to be arrived at through rational inquiry; indeed, Dennis argues that by suppressing passional experience rationalistic religion and poetry throw the soul into disarray.

In assigning order a crucial role in his thinking, Dennis resembles other critics of his day, but he conceives order as inextricably bound up with passion and sensual experience. He posits a prelapsarian state of psychological balance in which reason, the passions, and the senses all worked together to render experience in a heightened form to suggest that with the Fall humanity's faculties were set against one another, leading to a myopic, conflict-ridden state of being. As the vehicle of passionate experience, poetry throws the soul into further disarray with an infusion of sublime energy, a "homeopathic" approach to psychological imbalance, as Shaun Irlam puts it, that shocks the soul into reordering itself after its primal state of dynamic, balanced unity. Dennis sees epic poetry as most suited to this task since it appeals to what he terms the "enthusiastic" passions, those that are "moved by . . . ideas in contemplation, or the meditation of things that belong not to common life," as opposed to the "vulgar" passions roused by tragic representations of "objects themselves, or by . . . ideas in the ordinary course of life" (*The Grounds of Criticism in Poetry* [1704]). In his writings on poetry per se and on tragedy in particular, Dennis shows himself concerned with the effects of art on civil society. Whether analyzing the palliating effects of tragedy on the masses or epic's sublime transportation of the soul, the right ordering of the passional individual through art remains his dominant concern.

CRITICAL RECEPTION

For literary critics interested in 18th-century drama and the sublime, Dennis has always merited at least a page or two, but his critical writings have seldom been the object of sustained study. Treatments of his drama criticism—and most especially of his tragic theory—tend to emphasize those elements of his thought that depart radically from the neoclassical criticism of his contemporaries in arguing for Dennis's prescience as a forerunner of aesthetics as we know it. Insofar as Dennis can be said to have inaugurated detailed investigation of the psychology of aesthetic response, such studies can be productive, but they sometimes obscure just how much of an early-18th-century critic Dennis really was. More recently, interest in the discourse of enthusiasm in the 18th century has prompted closer analyses of Dennis's theory of the passions, focused especially on the social and political valences of the distinction between "enthusiastic" and "vulgar" passions that grounds his later criticism. Given that enthusiasm was generally associated at the time with England's "vulgar" and that many viewed it with distrust bordering on paranoia following the Civil War, Dennis's role in trying to purge enthusiasm of its disreputable taint in formulating an aesthetics of the sublime merits deeper consideration for what it can tell us about the complicated class politics of early Modern print culture.

BIBLIOGRAPHY

Works by John Dennis

The Critical Works of John Dennis. Ed. Edward Niles Hooker. 2 vols. Baltimore: Johns Hopkins University Press, 1939.
The Plays of John Dennis. Ed. J.W. Johnson. New York: Garland, 1980.

Studies of John Dennis

Albrecht, W.P. *The Sublime Pleasures of Tragedy: A Study of Critical Theory from Dennis to Kant*. Lawrence: University Press of Kansas, 1975.
Barnouw, Jefferey. "The Morality of the Sublime." *Comparative Literature* 35 (1983): 21–42.
Grace, Joan C. *Tragic Theory in the Critical Works of Thomas Rymer, John Dennis, and John Dryden*. Rutherford, NJ: Fairleigh Dickinson University Press, 1975.
Heffernan, James A.W. "Wordsworth and Dennis: The Discrimination of Feelings." *PMLA* 82 (1967): 430–436.
Hooker, Edward Niles. "Pope and Dennis." *English Literary History* (1940): 188–198.
Irlam, Shaun. *Elations: The Poetics of Enthusiasm in Eighteenth-Century Britain*. Stanford, CA: Stanford University Press, 1999.
Morillo, John D. "John Dennis: Enthusiastic Passions, Cultural Memory, and Literary Theory." *Eighteenth-Century Studies* 34 (2000): 21–41.
———. *Uneasy Feelings: Literature, the Passions, and Class from Neoclassicism to Romanticism*. New York: AMS Press, 2001.
Morris, David B. *The Religious Sublime: Christian Poetry and Critical Tradition in Eighteenth-Century England*. Lexington: University Press of Kentucky, 1972.
Murphy, Avon Jack. *John Dennis*. Boston: Twayne Publishers, 1984.
Wheeler, David M. "John Dennis and the Religious Sublime." *CLA Journal* 30 (1986): 210–218.

&❧ *John Donne*
(1572–1631)

MAUREEN GODMAN

BIOGRAPHY

John Donne was born in London in 1572, the third child of the six children of John and Elizabeth Donne. Through his mother he claimed descent from Sir Thomas More; many contemporary family members were active in the "old faith," too, including his brother Henry, who died of the plague in Newgate prison, awaiting trial for harboring a Catholic priest, and his uncle Jasper Heywood, condemned but later released and banished for his activities as head of a Jesuit mission. His father was a prosperous citizen prominent in the Company of Ironmongers, his chosen trade. Donne was educated at Hart Hall, Oxford, and for a time at Cambridge. He matriculated at the age of fifteen without taking a degree, probably because of the requirement that all candidates over the age of sixteen subscribe to the Thirty-Nine Articles and take an oath recognizing the monarch as head of the Church in England. In 1592, after a short break during which time he may have traveled abroad, he entered Thavies Inn and, the following year, Lincoln's Inn. It was during this early period that he wrote most of the love elegies, some of the songs and sonnets, the satires, "An Epithalamion Made at Lincoln's Inn," and various epigrams and paradoxes and established his reputation as a witty and intellectual gallant. Early verse letters "The Storme" and "The Calme" reflect his experiences in military expeditions in 1596 to Cádiz and the Islands expedition in 1597.

On his return, Donne was appointed Secretary to the Lord Keeper, Sir Thomas Egerton, a position that he had every hope would lead to a bright career in public service or the law. Such hopes were disappointed, though, by what he later described as his "disorderlie proceedings"—his affair and secret marriage, in 1601, with Ann More, his employer's niece and the daughter of Sir George More. Donne hoped that his father-in-law would accept the match as a fait accompli; instead, Donne was imprisoned and dismissed from his post. While the period of imprisonment was brief, the impact on his chances of rising in the world was not. His subsequent attempts at gaining offices of substance were hampered by his reputation arising from that "intemperate and hastie act" of his marriage. For many years he and his wife and their increasing number of children lived dependent for financial support upon minor secretarial appointments and the patronage of courtiers and friends who recognized and encouraged Donne's talents.

During this period, however, Donne pursued his studies in the law, theology, languages, and any other subjects prompted by his broad intellectual interests. After initial reluctance, in part fueled by a belief in his own unworthiness, he took holy orders in January 1615; King James, who had urged him to this vocation, appointed him Chaplain-in-Ordinary to the King, a post that involved regular attendance at court and the ability to hold benefices that provided a substantial income. James also signed a royal mandate ordering the authorities of Cambridge University to appoint Donne a Doctor of Divinity. In 1617 he was chosen for the important position as Divinity Reader at his old Inn of Court—Lincoln's Inn—and received invitations to preach at Paul's Cross, an opportunity to test his skills in communicating to a wide cross section of the populace.

In 1617 Donne's wife Ann died at age thirty-three, a few days after the death of her stillborn twelfth child. His grief at her death caused his health and enthusiasm for life to falter, but an appointment as chaplain to an embassy to Germany in 1619 where he preached before the Prince and Princess Palatine helped to divert his mind to other matters. He returned to his position at Lincoln's Inn, and once more took up his preaching duties, preparing his sermons with rigor and extensive study.

In 1621, Donne was installed as Dean of St. Paul's. Besides his obligations there, he preached frequently at court, before both King James and his successor King Charles, at the request of friends and dignitaries on various occasions and, at regular intervals, at his livings under the care of curates. His status elicited other demands on his time—for instance, his knowledge and experience of the law were drawn upon when he was commissioned to sit in the Court of Delegates, hearing appeals from lower ecclesiastical courts and in other judicial capacities as well. In this latter period, his fortunes improving, he assisted financially many of those who had helped him in his impoverished earlier years, and as both priest and friend he earned a reputation for generosity and integrity. In the vocation that he initially considered himself unworthy to pursue he proved a compelling, inspired preacher driven by a strong moral, ethical, and religious imperative. He fell ill in 1630 and died in 1631 at age fifty-nine.

MAJOR WORKS AND THEMES

Judicious observers have noted that to all his work—the love poems, elegies and satires, the divine poems written during the earlier and middle part of his life, and the devotions and sermons toward the end, Donne brings the same kind of rigorous examination, delight in extension of intellectual thought, and vivid imagery. Intensity and passion, wit, and often humor characterize his writing. His voice is as individual and demanding as his train of thought, which to his admirers is a hallmark of genius and to his critics exasperating circumlocution. Although much of Donne's work is difficult to date with any accuracy, we can speculate that many of the poems later collected as the *Songs and Sonnets* (first published in 1633) together with the love elegies, most of the satires, several verse letters (for instance, "Epistle to I.L.") he probably completed by the time he left Lincoln's Inn in 1594 or in the period shortly thereafter. His "Epithalamion Made at Lincoln's Inn" obviously dates from that period. Some poems, such as "Twickenham Garden" and "Nocturnall Upon St. Lucie's Day," might suggest, by virtue of internal reference, a date from a later period when Lucy, Countess of Bedford, was his patron.

Some of Donne's *Songs and Sonnets* reveal a distinct anti-Petrarchanism and even a contempt for women: "Woman's Constancy" and "The Indifferent" seem to be good examples of such an attitude, although other poems demonstrate a warm, loving, and egalitarian attitude to the fictional or real beloved. His imagery, labeled by later commentators as "metaphysical" (a term first assigned by **Dryden** and later by Johnson in his "Life of **Cowley**"), describes the extension of an idea to, and even beyond, its logical conclusion to produce one that shocks and sometimes offends, or as Johnson vividly describes it, the process in which "heterogeneous ideas [are] yoked by violence together" (cited in Smith 1: 218). In "A Valediction: Forbidding Mourning," for instance, the speaker imagines two loves as inseparable; their absence from each other so unbearable that as they move away from each other, they stretch until they are like "gold to airy thinness beat," a metallic image that then transforms into a pair of compasses in which one part or "foot" cannot move without the other. These images, the fusing of intellectual tours de force with intensity of feeling, were judged by some too highly wrought—odd to the point of disgust or headache—yet others noted the individuality that forces the reader to acknowledge new aspects of a subject previously unseen.

The intellectual agility that Donne shows in these poems is no less arresting than his humor and ability to write in an easy conversational style; "For God's sake hold thy tongue, and let me love," the opening line of "The Canonization," is a good example of his ability to reproduce both a conversational voice and a strong impression of the presence of the writer. The elegies are generally of the type that enjoyed a fashion among Inns of Court students during the 1590s and show a daring wit that borders occasionally on the indecent. Great hardship characterized the fourteen years between his marriage in 1601 and his ordination in 1615, yet in it he produced some of his best work. He wrote *Biathanatos*, an odd defense of suicide, the unfinished *Metempsychosis* (1601), most of the *Divine Poems*, the prose *Problems, Verse Letters* to patrons and friends, and *Epicedes* and *Obsequies*, what Patrides describes as "nonpastoral funeral elegies" (373).

Donne's *Essays in Divinity* are private devotions, a record of his internal debate immediately prior to taking holy orders. Published during this period were *Pseudo-Martyr* (1610), a vindication of James's argument that Catholics should take the Oath of Allegiance; *Ignatius His Conclave*, a satire on the Jesuits (1611); *An Anatomy of the World* (1611) and *The Progress of the Soul* (1612) (known as *The First and Second Anniversaries*), poems commemorating the life and death of Elizabeth Drury, the young daughter of Sir Robert Drury; and *Elegy on Prince Henry* (1613), commemorating the death of James's eldest son and heir to the throne. After Donne's ordination in 1615, he wrote mostly sermons, although some of the Holy Sonnets and other religious poems such as "A Hymn to Christ, at the Author's Last Going into Germany" (1619), "Hymn to God my God, in my Sickness," "Hymn to God the Father" (1623), and *Devotions upon Emergent Occasions* belong to this period as well. *Death's Duell*, his last sermon, was preached before the court about a month before his death.

CRITICAL RECEPTION

Reference to the few poems (notably the first and second *Anniversaries*) published during his lifetime and the frequency with which his poetry appears in manuscript miscellanies give us the only indication of Donne's popularity with contemporary readers. Before the first edition of his poems in 1633 (two years after his death), he had what A.J. Smith calls "a devoted following," although a restricted one, as "very few people could have read any of Donne's poems during the greater part of his poetic career" (4). Works most frequently occurring in manuscript miscellanies before 1625 were the satires, the elegies, some epigrams, and individual lyric poems. As Smith points out, however, since readers could only copy into manuscript those works to which they had access, frequency of their occurrence in manuscript cannot be taken as an absolute indicator of audience preference for some of his works over others.

It was not until after the publication of the *Songs and Sonnets* in 1633 that Donne's reputation as a poet became firmly established. Six editions of the poems appeared in the next twenty years or so, testament to their popularity, but after that, demand petered out and editions in 1669 and 1719 were the last until the 19th century. **Thomas Carew** saw Donne's poetry as the forerunner of a new poetic movement; in "An Elegie upon the Death of the Dean of Paul's" he speaks of Donne's "masculine expression" and his "rich and pregnant phantasie" (cited in Larson 24), and his famous reference to Donne as "a King, that rul'd as hee thought fit / The universall Monarchy of wit" seems to sum up the prevailing attitude to Donne's poetic gifts until what Smith describes as "the turn against Donne" in the late 1660s. Izaak Walton in his biography admires him this side of idolatry and pictures him as a hypochondriac whose favorite word was "done." Dryden, an admirer and emulator of Donne, refers, in a generally praising comment, to Donne's "rough cadence," a phrase that was "for a hundred and fifty years [used] as a stick to beat Donne" (Smith 12).

By the late 1600s Donne no longer reigned supreme; Dryden's statement that Donne was "the greatest Wit, though not the best Poet of our Nation" established a mantra heard over the next century or more. Donne's poetic voice was deemed clever but too clever for his own good, witty but unable to express true human feeling. Dryden's comment that Donne "perplexes the Minds of the Fair Sex with nice Speculations of Philosophy, when he shou'd ingage their hearts, and entertain them with softnesses of Love" (Smith 13) resonated with the temper of the time, and although some 18th-century critics speak well of Donne's poetry, he was seen increasingly as a poet of the past. Smith sums up the complaints:

We hear of his confounding metaphysics with love and losing himself in his own subtleties and extravagances; of his blatant disregard of "Nature" in favor of spurious ornaments, out-landish effects, cold and childish quibbles, an ostentatiously affected learning; of his failure to be just, simple, obvious; of his vicious manners and disastrous corruption of taste; of his general disagreeableness which soon produces disgust in the reader; of his puerility, triviality, and, in short, total lack of any poetic merit. (15)

Samuel Johnson, although less damning and fairer than most, echoed many of earlier Restoration critics' concerns; his enormous influence as a literary critic shaped and even warped general perceptions of Donne's contribution to poetry. Many 19th-century critics shared the complaints of their 18th-century predecessors, but with increasingly strident comments on what they perceived as Donne's prurient sexual reference and morally questionable attitudes, particularly in the earlier love poetry (41). Even Grosart, editor of *The Complete Poems* (1872–1873), says in the preface:

I do not hide from myself that it needs courage . . . to edit and print the poetry of Dr. JOHN DONNE in our day. Nor would I call it literary prudery that shrinks from giving publicity to such sensuous things (to say the least) as indubitably are found therein. . . . I deplore that Poetry, in every way almost so memorable and potential, should be stained even to uncleanliness in sorrowfully too many places. (Grosart 1872, 1: ix, cited in Larson 41)

But in spite of these attitudes and detractions, among 19th-century luminaries such as Coleridge, the Brownings, de Quincy, and Dante Gabriel Rossetti, Donne's poetic style was admired and more completely understood, his "roughness" and perceived oddities seen in the context of their historical period and the poet's individual genius.

Coleridge, for instance, understood that "[t]o read Dryden, Pope, & you need only count syllables; but to read Donne you must measure *time*, and discover the time of each word by the sense of passion" (cited in Smith 1: 265). In part buoyed by such revaluations, Donne's reputation as a poet burgeoned in the earlier 20th century and especially after T.S. Eliot's championing of his poetry. New Criticism, in considering biography irrelevant to a poet's work, dampened the enthusiasm, for a time, for often-unproductive preoccupations with Donne's life as an index to the meaning of the poetry, or as a reason for disliking it. In the last half century, though, biographical interpretation—attempts to connect the poetic, often fictional world created by Donne with the real events of the author's life—has remained an important strand of criticism. Studies on his wit, language, learning, political and religious views, his historical context, as well as psychoanalytical studies and interpretations of individual works have all found their place in the now enormous collection of criticism. John R. Roberts points out that his first bibliography covering the years 1912 to 1967 contained 1,300 items; the second, in the ten-year period from 1968 to 1978, produced over a thousand (cited in Smith 2: xxxix). The Modern Language Association (MLA) bibliography from 1979 to June 2002 shows that 1,100 books and articles have Donne as their subject, an indication of an enduring interest in this perennially stimulating, demanding, and gifted writer.

BIBLIOGRAPHY

Works by John Donne

Biathanatos. Ed. E.W. Sullivan. Newark: University of Delaware Press, 1984.
The Complete English Poems of John Donne. Ed. C.A. Patrides. London: Dent, 1985.
Devotions upon Emergent Occasions. Ed. A. Raspa. Montreal: McGill–Queens University Press, 1925.
The Divine Poems. Ed. Helen Gardner. 2nd ed. Oxford: Oxford University Press, 1978.
The Elegies and the Songs and Sonnets. Ed. Helen Gardner. Oxford: Oxford University Press, 1963.
The Epithalamions, Anniversaries and Epicedes. Ed. W. Milgate. Oxford: Oxford University Press, 1978.

Essays in Divinity. Ed. Evelyn M. Simpson. Oxford: Oxford University Press, 1952.

Ignatius His Conclave. Ed. T.S. Healy. Oxford: Oxford University Press, 1969.

John Donne: A Critical Edition of the Major Works. Ed. John Carey. Oxford Authors Series. Oxford: Oxford University Press, 1990.

Paradoxes and Problems. Ed. Helen Peters. Oxford: Oxford University Press, 1980.

The Poems of John Donne. Ed. Herbert J.C. Grierson. 2 vols. 1912. Oxford: Clarendon Press, 1963.

The Satires, Epigrams and Verse Letters. Ed. W. Milgate. Oxford: Oxford University Press, 1967.

The Sermons. Ed. George R. Potter and Evelyn M. Simpson. 10 vols. Berkeley and Los Angeles: University of California Press, 1962.

Studies of John Donne

Bald, R.C. *John Donne: A Life*. Oxford: Clarendon Press, 1970.

Carey, John. *John Donne, Life, Mind and Art*. London: Faber and Faber, 1990.

Combs, Homer C., and Zay R. Sullens. *A Concordance to the English Poems of John Donne*. Reprint, New York: Haskell House, 1969.

Gosse, Edmund. *The Life and Letters of John Donne*. 2 vols. Dodd Mead, 1899. Reprint, Gloucester: Peter Smith, 1959.

Keynes, Sir Geoffery. *A Bibliography of Dr. John Donne*. 3rd ed. Cambridge: Cambridge University Press, 1958.

Larson, Deborah Aldrich. *John Donne and Twentieth-Century Criticism*. Rutherford, NJ: Fairleigh Dickinson University Press, 1989.

Leishman, J.B. *The Monarch of Wit*. 5th rev. ed. London: Hutchinson, 1962.

Roberts, John R. *John Donne: An Annotated Bibliography of Modern Criticism 1912–1967*. Columbia: University of Missouri Press, 1973.

———. *John Donne: An Annotated Bibliography of Modern Criticism 1968–1978*. Columbia: University of Missouri Press, 1982.

Smith, A.J. *John Donne: The Critical Heritage*. Vol. 1. London: Routledge, 1975.

———. *John Donne: The Critical Heritage*. Ed. Catherine Phillips. Vol. 2. London: Routledge, 1996.

Stringer, Gary A., gen. ed. *The Variorum Edition of the Poetry of John Donne*. 8 vols. Bloomington: Indiana University Press, 1995–.

❧ *Michael Drayton*

(1563–1631)

RICHARD F. HARDIN

BIOGRAPHY

Michael Drayton's world began in the countryside, first with his birth in Hartshill, near Atherstone, Warwickshire, in 1563, then in boyhood as a page in the nearby manor house of Henry Goodere. To this family he would always remain attached, despite enjoying a variety of patrons—Sir Walter Aston, Lucy Countess of Bedford, Edward Sackville Fourth Earl of Dorset, and James I's son Henry Prince of Wales. Goodere, soon to be Sir Henry, held some status in his time: soldier in the Netherlands, then a colonel in the Queen's defense forces after the Armada threat, then recusant-hunter in Warwickshire. Late in life Drayton wrote a letter to the Scots poet William Drummond—part of a correspondence that began in 1618—from the home of Anne Rainsford, Goodere's daughter. Newdigate informs his life of Drayton with the sup-position that the poet always carried a torch for his old master's daughter, and certainly Drayton's "Hymn to His Lady's Birthplace" (meaning Coventry, where Anne was born) indicates longtime admiration, perhaps friendship, but anything more is dubious.

Without a university education—merely a boyhood schooling from the "mild tutor" whom he recalls in the autobiographical poem "To Sir Henry Reynolds"—Drayton shows himself at no more of a disadvantage than **Shakespeare**. Beginning in 1591, when he came to London with Goodere, he published poetry of increasing variety and achievement during Elizabeth's reign and even had some "traffic" with the stage—again to use a word from the Reynolds poem. The years 1597 to 1602 find him in Philip Henslowe's stable of playwrights. The titles of his lost plays suggest that Dray-ton, always in collaboration, was writing comedies, tragedies, plays about Rome and about legendary English history, but we have only one remnant of this chapter in his career, *The First Part of Sir John Oldcastle* (1599), the work of several collaborators who are out to show that their man was a pious patriot, not the "pampered glutton" whose name was changed to Falstaff in *1 Henry IV*. One more theatrical episode bears mention here: In 1608, with several others, he took over the Whitefriars Playhouse and the Children of the King's Revels, a venture that soon failed.

When James I took the throne, he created Drayton's patron Walter Aston (and many others) Knight of the Bath, with the poet attending him as Esquire, a title Drayton continued to use despite its near meaninglessness by then. Within a few years he began to sound increasingly critical of the King and his court, not unlike his younger poet friend George Wither, who served time in prison for a collection of satires in 1613. Other London writing friends included William Browne, John Selden, John and Francis Beaumont, and George Sandys. Later, oral tradition in Stratford puts Drayton and **Jonson** with Shakespeare at a "merry meeting" there, supposedly leading to Shakespeare's death. Surely two poets of the same age from the same county would have known each other in London. Having become something of a literary personage in his later years (portraits show him wearing laurel), Drayton naturally took to self-reference in some of his poems then, especially his elegies, probably written in the 1620s. One of these indicates that the poet himself had been officially silenced about discussing state affairs. Wither again went to jail for his satires, this time implicating Drayton as someone with whom he had discussed his work. Testimony declares the poet a man of "vertuous disposition." Publishing new poems right up to the end, Drayton died in London on or about December 23, 1631, and was buried in Poets' Corner of Westminster Abbey, where a sculpted wall monument may still be seen.

MAJOR WORKS AND THEMES

From our distance, Michael Drayton appears as a poet of talent who, as he himself admits in one of his sonnets, "could not long one fashion entertain." He indulged, often excelling, in a variety of Elizabethan, Jacobean, and Caroline poets' fads. He wrote a collection of pastoral eclogues in the Spenserian style, *Idea the Shepherds Garland* (1593), later revised as *Pastorals*, then a sonnet sequence in 1594; a series of *Mirror for Magistrates*–stye historical poems; *Mortimeriados* (1596), later recast as *The Barons Warres*, a long poem about England's civil strife, following Samuel Daniel's *Civil Wars* by a year. *Endimion and Phoebe* (1595) followed Marlowe and others in the mythological narrative, though with a Platonism that is sui generis, and Drayton would pursue this myth into his last years with the rarified "Quest of Cynthia." Such recasting provides a clue to something more substantial than imitation, however, as witness the various editions of the sonnets. Drayton revised or dropped old sonnets and added new ones from the 1590s to the final state of the sequence in 1619, which includes, for the first time, two superb poems, "How many paltry, foolish, painted things" and "Since theres no helpe."

Drayton also introduced two classical conventions to English poetry. *Englands Heroicall Epistles* (1597) imagines verse letters exchanged between famous lovers in English history (Henry II and Matilda Fitzwater, the poet Surrey and his Geraldine— twelve pairs in all), subtly imitating Ovid's *Heroides*. In the best of these, Drayton matched Marlowe in his sure sense of what would become "heroic couplets," perhaps one reason why his stock held steady in the generations following 1660. A decade later Drayton published the first collection of English odes (1606), longer lyric poems modeled more or less on Horace and Ronsard. One of the best of these, "To the

Virginian Voyage," is quintessential bardic Drayton, being entered for publication when the patent for the Virginia colony was not yet two weeks old. As a poem celebrating "Earths onely paradise," it belongs to the foundation mythology of America. Another ode, "The Ballad of Agincourt," written not in Ballad meter but in an original martial stanza, evokes the emotions of the war scenes in *Henry V*. If a common core unites this collection it is that of celebration, the poetry of praise, whether in the "Hymn to His Ladys Birthplace" (a 1619 ode) or "An Ode Written in the Peak," extolling a tourist spot where one can find "Buckstons delicious baths, / Strong ale and noble cheer / T'assuage breme Winters scathes."

From this brief poem of place, we turn to something quite vast, *Poly-Olbion*, a geographical-historical celebratory poem on all the shires of England. The title plays on the Greek *olbios*, happy or blessed: England is a land of many blessings. The first installment appeared in late 1612 or 1613, dedicated to Henry Prince of Wales. It is a lavish book sporting, in addition to a handsome image of the young prince, maps of the shires spread throughout the book, with prominent topographical features like hills and forests personified as male and female figures. These images parallel Drayton's personifications of landscape features in the text, singing the "Songs" that comprise the sections of his book. The survey begins in the southwest, moving east and north—though it was interrupted for a decade while the publishers recouped their losses. It finishes covering the terrain with "Part Two" in 1622, though now without the learned notes of John Selden. Drayton may not have chosen wisely in casting his 15,000 lines in alexandrine couplets. At their best, however, as in Songs 10 and 13, the lines show a lyric color and variety evocative of Spenser; elsewhere, especially in the 1622 addition, they can be flat and monotonous. Stories of rivers and hills often employ the Ovidian myth-of-locality convention, and the poet often compares English legends with classical myths (England's naval heroes are Argonauts; Maid Marian of Sherwood is a Diana figure). In Song 3 "the Muse" (Drayton's chief narrative voice in the poem) regrets that England lacks an Arthurian epic to rival those of Homer. But by 1622 the weary, prosaic tone casts doubt about Drayton's stated plan to "go on with Scotland."

Drayton had a talent for raillery, for some readers perhaps his most immediately attractive feature. While it may erupt anywhere (as in the final song of *Poly-Olbion*), it works especially well in the narrative satires, *The Owl* and *The Moon-Calf*, poems of the early Jacobean and Caroline reigns, respectively, in the vein of Spenser's *Mother Hubberds Tale*. Not to be overlooked is "Nimphidia," a brief faerie epic that places Drayton beside **Herrick** in originating English diminutive fairy lore. His last poems, published in his sixty-sixth year, strike both a new note—narrative poems on Noah, Moses, and David—and an old—pastoral, in *The Muses Elizium*, though the reader will note a strong Caroline feeling about these poems alongside the traditional English eclogue.

CRITICAL RECEPTION

In dedicating his 1627 collection *The Battaile of Agincourt* to "the noblest gentlemen of these renowned Kingdoms of Great Britain," Drayton suggests that he saw himself as a public poet, a laureate, addressing literate, patriotic readers throughout England and Scotland. Allusions to him in his later years suggest that he was something of a living institution when he died, a sort of "last Elizabethan." His *Heroicall Epistles* continued to find an audience after the Restoration, as did his lyric poems, which appeared in Tonson's 1716 *Miscellany* and similar collections. Blake, Keats, and Tennyson read him, but with the 20th-century enthusiasm for "metaphysical" poets, Drayton, on record as disdaining that particular fad, nearly slips off the horizon. He profited, however, from the renaissance of Spenser studies and from the socio-historical approaches to literature that surfaced after mid-century. Perhaps his straddling of the 1600 dateline has sometimes worked against his inclusion in literary histories or anthologies of either period. Quite rightly, the *Oxford History of English Literature* treats him as a significant figure in both centuries.

BIBLIOGRAPHY

Works by Michael Drayton

The Works of Michael Drayton. Ed. J. William Hebel, Kathleen Tillotson, B.H. Newdigate, and B.E. Juel-Jensen. 5 vols. 1931–1941. Corrected ed., Oxford: Blackwell, 1961.

Studies of Michael Drayton

Brink, Jean R. *Michael Drayton Revisited*. Boston: Twayne Publishers, 1990.

Capp, Bernard. "The Poet and the Bawdy Court: Michael Drayton and the Lodging-House World in Early Stuart London." *Seventeenth Century* 10 (1995): 27–37.

Curran, John E. "The History Never Written: Bards, Druids, and the Problem of Antiquarianism in *Poly-Olbion*." *Renaissance Quarterly* 51 (1998): 498–525.

Ewell, Barbara C. "Unity and the Transformation of Drayton's Poetics in *Englands Heroicall Epistles*." *Modern Language Quarterly* 44 (1983): 231–250.

Galbraith, David Ian. *Architectonics of Imitation in Spenser, Daniel, and Drayton*. Toronto: University of Toronto Press, 2000.

Hardin, Richard F. *Michael Drayton and the Passing of Elizabethan England*. Lawrence: University Press of Kansas, 1973.

Harner, James L. *Samuel Daniel and Michael Drayton: A Reference Guide*. Boston: G.K. Hall, 1980.

Helgerson, Richard. "The Elizabethan Laureate: Self-Presentation and the Literary System." *Journal of English Literary History* 46 (1979): 193–220.

Hiller, Geoffrey. " 'Sacred Bards' and 'Wise Druids': Drayton and His Archetype of the Poet." *Journal of English Literary History* 51 (1984): 1–15.

La Branche, Anthony. "Drayton's *Barons Warres* and the Rhetoric of Historical Poetry." *Journal of Germanic Philology* 62 (1963): 82–95.

Newdigate, B.H. *Michael Drayton and His Circle*. Oxford: Blackwell, 1941.

Prescott, Anne Lake. "Marginal Discourse in Drayton's Muse and Selden's 'Story.' " *Studies in Philology* 88 (1991): 307–328.

Roberts, Josephine A. "The Imaginary Epistles of Sir Philip Sidney and Lady Penelope Rich (with Texts)." *English Literary Renaissance* 15 (1985): 59–77.

Tillotson, Kathleen. "Michael Drayton as a 'Historian' in the 'Legend of Cromwell.' " *Modern Language Review* 34 (1939): 186–200.

Westling, Louise Hutchings. *The Evolution of Michael Drayton's Idea*. Salzburg Studies in English Literature, Elizabethan and Renaissance, no. 37. Salzburg: Austria Institut Für Englische Sprache und Literatur, 1974.

❧ *John Dryden*

(1631–1700)

HUGH MACRAE RICHMOND

BIOGRAPHY

John Dryden was a versatile writer: poet, dramatist, translator, critic, and poet laureate. He was born in 1631 at Aldwinkle in Northamptonshire. His education began at the academically distinguished Westminster School and continued at Trinity College of Cambridge University. His shifting political interests were largely reflected in his verse, beginning with his *Heroic Stanzas*, a panegyric on the death of **Oliver Cromwell** in 1659, followed by *Astraea Redux* on the Restoration of King Charles II in 1660. With his loss of political standing as a Catholic, after the installation in 1688 of the staunchly Protestant Dutch King William III, Dryden directed more of his energies in verse to translation of the classics.

Dryden's principal writing however, was for the stage, in which venue he proved to be prolific and highly diversified, including comedies, tragedies, heroic plays, and several adaptations and collaborations. As a result of his composition of some thirty scripts, he became the leading playwright of the Restoration period, ranging through a variety of dramatic genres with varying success. His first play was in prose, *The Wild Gallant*, staged somewhat unsuccessfully in 1663, the year when he married Lady Elizabeth Howard (with whom he had three sons in 1666, 1667, and 1669). He switched to couplets in *The Rival Ladies* (1664), a successful tragicomedy, perhaps derived from Calderón, which **Samuel Pepys** called "a very innocent and most pretty witty play" (though later, in 1680, Dryden's play *The Kind Keeper* was banned for indecency). Dryden's first serious play in couplets, *The Indian Queen*, was a tragedy, written in collaboration with his brother-in-law, Sir George Howard, and spectacularly staged to great acclaim in 1664. The same year he defended his use of rhyme in the preface to an edition of *The Rival Ladies*. The success of *The Indian Queen* was followed the next year (1665) by its sequel, staged with identical flamboyance: *The Indian Emperor, or The Conquest of Mexico by the Spaniards*. Among his other successful heroic plays on the model of Corneille's *Le Cid* were *The Conquest of*

Granada (in two parts, 1669, 1670) and *Aureng-Zebe* (1675), followed by the more disciplined *All for Love* (1678), a neoclassical tragedy in blank verse indirectly derived from **Shakespeare**'s *Antony and Cleopatra*. In this period Dryden also wrote successful comedies, such as *Marriage à la Mode* (1672) and *The Spanish Friar* (1681). *Marriage à la Mode* has proved to be one of the most successful Restoration treatments of love and marriage, perhaps partly from contributions by the Earl of Rochester, to whom it was dedicated.

Thereafter, Dryden wrote *Secret Love or the Maiden Queen* (1667) about Queen Christina of Sweden (partly following an episode in *Le Grand Cyrus* of Mlle. de Scudery). In the first production of this play, Nell Gwyn triumphed in the role of Florimel, who (with her lover Celadon) echoes Shakespeare's Beatrice and Benedick, while anticipating Congreve's Millamant and Mirabel. Dryden's play *Sir Martin Mar-all* (1667) was a prose adaptation of the Duke of Newcastle's translation of Molière's *L'Étourdi*, composed in the Jonsonian (see **Ben Jonson**) vein, and successful largely from the virtuosity of Nokes in the title role. He also cooperated with Sir **William Davenant** in an adaptation of Shakespeare's *The Tempest* (including a new sister for Caliban, 1667), and himself adapted *Troilus and Cressida* (1679). In 1774, he even drafted the script of an opera (printed 1677) called *The State of Innocence, and the Fall of Man*, based on **Milton**'s epic of *Paradise Lost* (adapted with the author's permission); another of his operas, *King Arthur*, was orchestrated by **Henry Purcell**. Among the more significant of his other works for the stage are *Oedipus* (1679), *The Duke of Guise* (1683, with Nathaniel Lee, based on a scene from his failed early script of 1660), *Albion and Albianus* (an opera, 1685), *Don Sebastian* (a study of incest, in Shakespearean style, 1690), and *Amphitrion* (after Plautus, 1690). His last play was a comedy, *Love Triumphant* (1694).

After writing *Annus Mirabilis* (1667) about Prince Rupert's victory over the Dutch (and the Fire of London), Dryden was named poet laureate by the King in 1668 and Historiographer Royal in 1670. In 1688 he acquired shares in **Anne Killigrew**'s theater company and signed a contract to write plays for the Drury Lane Theatre. He had outlined his dramatic interests in his dialogue *Essay of Dramatic Poesy* (1668), following ideas derived from French dramatist Pierre Corneille. In this dialogue Eugenius (Charles, Lord Buckhurst, later Earl of Dorset) debates with three other critics, among whom Crites (Sir Robert Howard) defends the classical tradition of drama, Lisedeus (Sir Charles Sedley) approves of neoclassical French drama, while Neander (Dryden himself) defends the English theatrical tradition as seen in Ben Jonson's *The Silent Woman*, though conceding the need to combine its freedom with modern decorum. Beyond formal literary discussion, Dryden also excelled in prologues and epilogues for his own and others' plays, and close to a hundred of these have survived as further sources of insight into his dramatic and literary inclinations, as well as his views on the events of the day.

In 1671 Dryden's dramatic and literary pretensions had been ridiculed in the role of Bayes (mocking his poetic crown of laurel leaves) in *The Rehearsal*, a satirical comedy principally composed by his enemy, the Duke of Buckingham. Partially in response to this attack, in 1681 Dryden published *Absolom and Achitophel*, his verse satire on anti-Royalist politicians, including the Duke of Buckingham. This poem was followed in 1682 by *Mac Flecknoe*, a satire against rival poets and playwrights such as **Thomas Shadwell**. In 1682 Dryden also published his religious poem, *Religio*

Laici, affirming his Anglican faith. However, in 1687 he wrote another religious poem, *The Hind and the Panther*, defending his new commitment to Roman Catholicism (1685), adopting the religion of King James II, brother and successor to Charles II. After James II was deposed in the Glorious Revolution of 1688, Dryden's persistence in his Roman Catholicism ensured his loss of court favor through the succession of the staunchly Protestant King William III, as we have seen. After Dryden was replaced as Poet Laureate by his rival Thomas Shadwell, he turned his attention more readily to translation of the Classics (he had already published translations of *Ovid's Epistles* in 1680), working with the publisher Jacob Tonson from 1679. After various further translations of Ovid, Horace Lucretius, Theocritus, and Virgil (in *Miscellany Poems*, 1684; *Sylvae*, 1685; *Examen Poeticum*, 1693; *The Annual Miscellany*, 1694), in 1697 Dryden successfully published his translation of *The Works of Virgil*. In 1693 he had already published his translations of the *Satires* of Juvenal and Persius, and in that same year he also wrote his second *Ode on St. Cecilia's Day*, which he considered to be the best of all his works. In 1700 he published further translations (of Ovid, Boccaccio, and Chaucer) as *The Fables*, but he died in the same year and was buried in Westminster Abbey.

MAJOR WORKS AND THEMES

Dryden generally favored conversational ease in much of his poetry, midway between the suave tones of **Waller** and the dramatic flair of **Donne** (as seen in Dryden's earlier verse). This moderating tendency also appears in his sentimental but effective reworking of Shakespeare's subject in *Antony and Cleopatra* with *All for Love* (1678). Dryden compressed his tragedy into the format required by the neoclassical interpretation of Aristotle in the dramatic doctrine of the Unities of Time, Place and Action, which limited the treatment to one day, one place, and one action. For example, the whole action of Dryden's version of the story of Antony and Cleopatra takes place in Alexandria. He particularly stresses the need for unity of plot in the preface to his *Troilus and Cressida* (1679), in which he revised Shakespeare's *Troilus and Cressida* (1679). He also helped Davenant in "improving" *The Tempest* (1670), as well as drafting his own stage version of *Paradise Lost* (printed in 1677, though it was not performed).

Many of Dryden's other serious plays, however, fall into the far more flamboyant genre of the "heroic play" on romantic subjects, in the French vein of Pierre Corneille's *Le Cid*, for which Dryden's English precedent is Sir William Davenant's *The Seige of Rhodes* (1656). In his preface to *The Conquest of Granada* (*Part 1*, 1669; *Part 2*, 1670), Dryden says that he considers these plays "ought to be an imitation in little of an Heroik Poem," leading to the metrical term of "heroic couplets," in which these scripts were couched. He asserts that "Love and Valour ought to be the Subject" and that they should treat of such exotic figures as Montezuma of Peru (in *The Indian Queen*, 1664, and in *The Indian Emperor*, 1665) and a contemporary ruler in India (in *Aureng-Zebe*).

Dryden's comedies follow the neoclassical form of Jonsonian comedy as favored in scripts for the Restoration stage by Etherege, **Wycherley**, and Congreve. However, as a literary critic, Dryden emerged as one of the earliest defenders of Shakespeare's unruly genius, while still praising the suaver tones of Beaumont and Fletcher and the decorum of Ben Jonson, as seen in his *Essay on Dramatic Poesy* (1668) and in his numerous prologues and epilogues to his plays, including his "Defence of the Epilogue" at the end of *The Conquest of Granada*, which comments on Shakespeare and Fletcher.

In his verse satires, translations, and religious verse, Dryden accomplished the creation of a speaking voice as natural as Donne at his best but marked by a greater urbanity and coherence, perhaps attributable to the more formal effect of his rhyming couplets. This poised tone gave great authority to his attacks on the erratic careers and psychological eccentricity of his opponents, so that his ridicule of the volatility of the Duke of Buckingham as Zimri in his mock-heroic satire *Absolom and Achitophel* (1681) has generally been held to be a witty masterpiece, while his penetrating attack on the Whig leader, the **Earl of Shaftesbury**, as the sinister Achitophel achieves a tragic intensity (perhaps echoing Milton's Satan), which is still preserved in the popular aphorism derived from it, that "Great wits are sure to madness near allied." The whole poem dexterously redeploys the Old Testament story of King David and his son Absolom to the doomed rebellion of Monmouth, Charles II's illegitimate son. However, though Shaftesbury was portrayed as the insidious inspirer of the doomed Monmouth's rebellion, he ultimately emerged unscathed from the royal prosecution that Dryden had sought to reinforce. Dryden's controversial nature had already been confirmed in 1679 when he was assaulted in Covent Garden by thugs recruited by the **Earl of Rochester**, whom he had supposedly offended. His other satires are less consistently impressive than *Absolom and Achitophel* but contain some passages of irresistible force, such as the caricatures of Doeg (Elkanah Settle) and Ogg (Thomas Shadwell) in Dryden's contributions to **Nahum Tate**'s *The Second Part of Absolom and Achitophel* (1682), in which Dryden took revenge for attacks resulting from his further censure of Shaftesbury in *The Medal* (1682). Shadwell is also the comic hero of *Mac Flecknoe* (written in 1679; pirated in 1682; authorized edition, 1684). This poem was Dryden's climactic attack on his literary opponents and thus prefigured Pope's mock-heroic compilation of his literary vendettas in *The Dunciad*.

Dryden's translations are urbane, fluent, and remain readable, even if the originals' tone and individuality are perhaps best preserved in that of Lucretius, whose poetic temperament seems most closely to match Dryden's own, which was less readily accommodated to the distinctive art of Virgil or Chaucer. Dryden also shows great ease with ratiocination in his religious expositions, as seen in the suave opening of *Religio Laici* (1682), thus leading the way for much 18th-century didactic verse. In all these modes, Dryden provided an essential precedent for achievements of Alexander Pope, both as a translator and satirist. In his versatility, urbanity, and vocal incisiveness, Dryden remains one of the most important contributors to the evolution of the principal themes of English literature between the age of Shakespeare and that of Pope.

CRITICAL RECEPTION

The testimonies of authorities such as Congreve, **Addison**, Pope, and Johnson establish that Dryden became a figure of great authority in Restoration literary society, and he remained a crucial precedent throughout the 18th century, with his fame extending to France, as seen in the estimate of him by Voltaire as "un très-grand génie"

(Van Doren 234). However, by the Romantic period, Dryden became associated with the tradition of "poetic diction," which Wordsworth excoriated. His political trimming and basic conservatism have also been unfavorably viewed from that time (as in the case of Waller). Even so, an underlying respect can be detected among discriminating Romantics such as Coleridge. However, if many poets from Byron to Tennyson acknowledged the distinction of Dryden's verse, at the end of the century Matthew Arnold could still write: "The difference between genuine poetry and the poetry of Dryden and Pope, and all their school, is briefly this: their poetry is conceived and composed in their wits, genuine poetry is conceived in the soul" (Van Doren 256).

Whatever the fashionable judgments of his achievement, Dryden has remained an essential reference in the history of English literature, as reflected in the innumerable editions of his work in the 19th and 20th centuries, and he is a major focus for critics and scholars. It is true that in the period after his death, after a partial attempt (four volumes) at a collected edition of his works, in 1701, the next substantial edition was Tonson's, edited by Charles Broughton, in 1742 (though Congreve had collected the plays in his edition of 1717). The first complete edition of Dryden's works came only a century after his death, that by Sir Walter Scott (1808–1821), revised by George Saintsbury (1882–1892), and only now superseded by the University of California Press *Works of John Dryden* (edited by E.N. Hooker and H.T. Swedenborg). *The Poems* alone have been recently well edited by James Kinsey (1958), but since Dryden's time there have been innumerable selective editions of his works, so that his St. Cecilia odes found their way even into Palgrave's *Golden Treasury*, while Handel's setting of *Alexander's Feast* ensured its continued visibility.

In more general terms, Dryden's works became less conspicuous as their social and political context became more remote and therefore more obscure; his versatility, poise, and clarity, however, were never underestimated, and they have served to inspire a modern recovery of much of his prestige, led by such figures as T.S. Eliot and critic Mark Van Doren. Though Dryden has not once more become a broadly popular writer, as Swift has, Dryden's plays have shared in the general rehabilitation of Restoration drama, and they have been increasingly revived, notably *All for Love* and *Marriage à la Mode*. *All for Love*, in particular, has attracted a whole line of distinguished actors from Mrs. Oldfield and Booth (1718) to Edith Evans (1922). Dryden's translations, particularly that of Plutarch's *Lives*, have remained standard and have provided a solid basis for later versions.

BIBLIOGRAPHY

Works by John Dryden

Dryden: The Dramatic Works. Ed. M. Summers. 6 vols. London: Nonesuch, 1931–1932.
John Dryden: Essays. Ed. W. Ker. 2 vols. Oxford: Clarendon Press, 1900.
John Dryden: The Poems and Fables. Ed. Bruce Alvin King. London: Oxford University Press, 1970.
"Of Dramatic Poesy" and Other Critical Essays. Ed. G. Watson. 2 vols. London: J.M. Dent (Everyman), 1962.
The Poems of John Dryden. Ed. James Kinsley. 4 vols. Oxford: Clarendon Press, 1958.

The Works of John Dryden. Ed. E.N. Hooker and H.T. Swedenborg. 20 vols. Berkeley: University of California Press, 1956–1992.

The Works of John Dryden Now First Collected. Illustrated with Notes, Historical, Critical and Explanatory, and a Life of the Author. Ed. Sir Walter Scott. 18 vols. London: W. Millar, 1808. 2nd ed., Edinburgh: A Constable, 1821.

Studies of John Dryden

Aden, John. *The Critical Opinions of John Dryden: A Dictionary*. Nashville, TN: Vanderbilt University Press, 1963.

Atkins, G. Douglas. *The Faith of John Dryden: Change and Continuity*. Lexington: University of Kentucky Press, 1980.

Bredvold, L.I. *The Intellectual Milieu of John Dryden*. Ann Arbor: University of Michigan Press, 1934.

Eliot, T.S. *John Dryden: The Poet, the Dramatist, the Critic*. New York: Haskell House, 1966.

———. *Selected Essays*. 3rd ed. New York: Harcourt Brace, 1951.

Frost, William. *Dryden and the Art of Translation*. New Haven, CT: Yale University Press, 1953.

———. *John Dryden: Dramatist, Satirist, Translator*. New York: AMS Press, 1988.

Gelber, Michael W. *The Just and the Lively: The Literary Criticism of John Dryden*. Manchester: Manchester University Press, 2000.

Hammond, Paul, and David Hopkins, eds. *John Dryen: Tercentenary Essays*. Oxford: Clarendon Press, 2000.

Johnson, Samuel. "John Dryden." In *Lives of the Poets*. 2 vols. London: J.M. Dent (Everyman), 1950. 1: 181–264.

King, Bruce Alvin. *Dryden's Heroical Plays*. Lincoln: University of Nebraska Press, 1981.

———. *Dryden's Major Plays*. New York: Barnes and Noble, 1966.

———, ed. *Dryden's Mind and Art*. Edinburgh: Oliver and Boyd, 1970.

Kirsch, A.C. *Dryden's Heroic Drama*. Princeton, NJ: Princeton University Press, 1964.

McFadden, George. *Dryden: The Public Writer, 1660–1685*. Princeton, NJ: Princeton University Press, 1978.

Miner, Earl. *Dryden's Poetry*. Indianapolis: University of Indiana Press, 1967.

Osborne, James M. *John Dryden: Some Biographical Facts and Problems*. Rev. ed. Gainsville: University of Florida Press, 1965.

Pechter, Edward. *Dryden's Classical Theory of Literature*. London: Cambridge University Press, 1975.

Schilling, Bernard N. *Dryden and the Conservative Myth*. New Haven, CT: Yale University Press, 1961.

———, ed. *Dryden: Twentieth Century Views*. Englewood Cliffs, NJ: Prentice-Hall, 1963.

Van Doren, Mark. *The Poetry of John Dryden*. Indianapolis: Indiana University Press, 1960.

Ward, C.E. *The Life of John Dryden*. Chapel Hill: University of North Carolina Press, 1961.

Winn, James A. *John Dryden and His World*. New Haven, CT: Yale University Press, 1987.

———, ed. *Critical Essays on John Dryden*. Boston: G.K. Hall, 1987.

Zwicker, Stephen N. *Politics and Language in John Dryden's Poetry: The Art of Disguise*. Princeton: Princeton University Press, 1984.

❧ *Richard Fanshawe*

(1608–1666)

RON HARRIS

BIOGRAPHY

Although today he is noted mostly as a translator, during his life Richard Fanshawe was better known as a diplomat. When he was active politically, he wrote little. He seems to have considered translation to be a political, as well as literary, activity. Though Fanshawe was Laudist, his life was in many respects similar to **John Milton**'s. They were born within months of one another, attended Cambridge at the same time, served as Latin Secretary (Fanshawe succeeded Milton in that post), and devoted time in political exile to literary pursuits.

Fanshawe was born in June 1608, at Ware Park, Hertfordshire, the fifth son of Sir Henry Fanshawe. He was seven when his father died, and shortly thereafter his mother, Elizabeth, sent him to London to study at the school of Thomas Farnaby, where he would begin the serious study of languages. He entered Jesus College, Cambridge, in 1623, though his mother wanted him to study law. To that end, he entered the Inner Temple in 1626, but as his wife described it in her memoirs, "[I]t seemed so crabbed a study and disagreeable to his inclination, that he rather studied to obey his mother than to make any progress in the law." Consequently, he remained scarcely a year before going abroad to study languages in Paris and Madrid. In Spain, his facility with languages attracted the attention of Lord Walter Alston, the English ambassador, whose secretary he became in 1635.

He was a devoted Royalist, and he spent the last half of his life in service to Kings Charles I and Charles II. Around 1640, after his return to England, his brother Thomas offered him the position of King's Remembrancer, a post the Fanshawe family had held for generations, in exchange for a large sum of money, to be paid over seven years. At the outbreak of the Civil War, he joined Charles I at Oxford, where he met Anne Harrison (1608–1680), who later described herself as "a hoyting girle," on account of her love for dancing and parties. They married on May 18, 1644. Only five of their fourteen children survived to adulthood, perhaps due to the difficult and forgetful, overbusy life the family led during years of exile and imprisonment during the Civil War and Commonwealth. During the Civil War, the family served Charles in Ireland, Spain, France, Holland, and Scotland, until Fanshawe was captured at the battle of Worcester in 1651. After a period of detention, he was permitted to seek asylum at Tankersley Park, Yorkshire. He spent his time there writing, most notably the translations of Horace and Camöens, for which he is best known. After the Restoration, he succeeded John Milton in the position of Latin Secretary, when Milton would enter a period of internal exile devoted to literary pursuits.

Fanshawe spent the remaining years of his life in public service. He was elected to Parliament in 1661, appointed Ambassador to Portugal in 1662 and Ambassador to Spain in 1664. His life ended under a shadow, owing to political intrigue. He was sent to Madrid in 1664 to negotiate a trade treaty favorable to England. Although he was successful, the treaty included a controversial ratification clause, which led to his dismissal. It is unclear whether he overstepped his authority in negotiating the clause, as the Earl of Clarendon, then Lord Chancellor, charged. It is also possible that Clarendon held anti-Spanish sentiments and saw the clause as an opportunity to kill the treaty. While awaiting the arrival of his replacement in Madrid, Fanshawe became ill and died. In later years, Lady Anne, his widow, would write her memoirs, which are the main source of information about his life.

MAJOR WORKS AND THEMES

Richard Fanshawe is known primarily for his translations out of Italian, Spanish, Portuguese, and Latin as well as translations into Latin. His major influences were Horace, the Roman poet, and Edmund Spenser, the English poet. His first published work was a translation of Baptista Guarini's *Il Pastor Fido* in 1647. The Italian play, a tragicomedy in verse, was never intended for performance. Indeed, Fanshawe considered the play a political allegory of a torn and divided kingdom reunited by a royal marriage that reconciled the opposing factions. He underscored the play's relevance for England in his dedications (two poems and one letter) to King Charles I. In 1648, he published an expanded edition of *Il Pastor Fido*, to which he added twenty-five poems. Among those poems were some of the earliest translations into English of sonnets by Luis de Gongora y Argote, including "A Rose," which is frequently anthologized, "A Canto of the Progresse of Learning," and a translation of the fourth book of Virgil's *Aeneid*, the last two written in Spenserian stanzas. The volume also contained a short prose piece, *A Summary Discourse of the Civill Warres of Rome*, which addressed English political problems by way of Roman history. He argued that Augustus Caesar, who brought an end to civil war in Rome, offered a proper model for a prince to imitate.

In 1652, he published *Selected Parts of Horace, Prince of Lyricks, and of all the Latin Poets the Fullest Fraught with Excellent Morality*. The book featured both the Latin texts and facing-page translations—the Renaissance mode—of selections of Horace's Odes, Epodes, Epistles, and Satires, along with English translations of a poem by Ausonius and a selection from Virgil's *Georgics*. The translations of Horace are remarkable for their stanza forms, an English equivalent to Horace's Alcaic and Sapphic strophes. Essentially, he translated the form of the Latin ode, based on quantitative meter, into the conventional English accentual-syllabic meter. His translations, written between 1626 and 1650, anticipate the stanza forms employed by **Andrew Marvell** in *An Horatian Ode upon Cromwell's Return from Ireland*, though it is unknown whether Marvell knew of or borrowed directly from Fanshawe's poems.

Fanshawe's most famous work appeared in 1655, *The Lusiad, or Portugal's Historicall Poem*, the great Renaissance epic of Portuguese discovery written by Luis de Camöens. Modeled on Virgil's *Aeneid*, Camöens's poem takes as its central theme Vasco da Gama's discovery of the sea route to India. The poem weaves da Gama's adventures of discovery into the context of Portuguese history to create an epic of a small, poor, seafaring nation's destined trajectory toward greatness. Fanshawe translated the poem in 1653 and 1654, while confined to Tankersley Park. Though Camöens wrote in Portuguese, it is unclear whether Fanshawe knew the language. Given his facility with Latin and the Romance languages, he may have been able to read Portuguese. Regardless, it seems likely that he based his translation on the scholarly edition of the poem by Manuel de Faria e Sousa, *Lusiades de Luis de Camoens, principe de los poets de España* (Madrid, 1639). In this scholarly edition, each of Camöens's stanzas is followed by a prose translation in Spanish, a language Fanshawe knew well, and a detailed commentary.

His final publications were translations of plays. In 1658 he published *La Fida Pastora*, a translation into Latin of John Fletcher's *The Faithfull Shepherdess* (1608) and echoing Guarini's *Pastor Fido*, arguably the first English tragicomedy. His final works, published posthumously in 1670, were *Querer por solo Querer* and *Fiestas de Aranjuez*, translations of Spanish plays written by Antonio Hurtado de Mendoza. Fanshawe's diplomatic letters were published in 1701.

CRITICAL RECEPTION

Fanshawe's critical reception is largely a running commentary on the state of literary translation. His method in translation was an example of what **John Dryden** would later call "paraphrase," in which the translator attempts to recreate the original in modern language, an imitation of sorts. In a commendatory poem to the translation of *Il Pastor Fido*, John Denham described and praised Fanshawe's writing more precisely:

> That servile path thou nobly dost decline
> Of tracing word by word, and line by line.
> Those are the labour'd births of slavish brains,
> Not the effects of Poetry, but pains;
> Cheap vulgar arts, whose narrowness affords
> No flight for thoughts, but poorly sticks at words.
> A new and nobler way thou dost pursue
> To make Translations and Translators too.
> They but preserve the Ashes, thou the Flame,
> True to his sense, but truer to his fame.

Although Denham was speaking specifically about the translation of *Il Pastor Fido* (which actually follows the Italian fairly closely in metaphrase, not paraphrase), his remarks describe most of Fanshawe's work as a translator.

Fanshawe's translation of *The Lusiad* apparently was well received by his contemporaries. The few extant contemporary accounts are generally favorable. His translation effectively introduced Portugal and Portuguese poetry to British readers. In fact, the translation may have led to his appointment as Ambassador to Portugal in 1662, where he had been greeted as a national hero upon his arrival as a special envoy in the previous year.

His later literary reputation ebbed and flowed, depending on the currents in literary translation. Voltaire would write an "Essay on the Epic Poetry of European Nations" based largely on his reading of Fanshawe's translation of Camöens. Samuel Johnson would number Fanshawe (with Denham, **Waller**, and **Cowley**) as a pioneer translator who "broke the shakles of verbal interpretation and showed the way towards elegance and liberty." Much adverse criticism of Fanshawe was delivered by subsequent translators of *The Lusiad*, who often as not attempted to define the novelty of their own work in contrast to Fanshawe. In the introductory dissertation to his own 1776 translation of *The Lusiad*, William Julius Mickle severely criticized Fanshawe's translation as being "exceedingly unfaithful" to the original.

Robert Southey's 1822 review of John Anderson's *Life and Writings of Camöens*, on the other hand, argued that "the English reader who desires to see the plan and character of the Lusiad must still have recourse to Fanshawe." Sir Richard Burton, in his translation of 1880, called Fanshawe's *Lusiad* rugged, harsh, and bombastic and accused him of taking "improper liberties with his author." Such discussions of "fidelity" to the "original" display pejorative (and frequently sexist) attitudes toward translation, attitudes that cast aspersion on the important cultural work of translation. In light of recent scholarly arguments that Fanshawe's translation of the poem was based on the translation and commentary of Manuel de Faria e Sousa, the criticisms seem more a comment on the status of translation as a literary activity than on Fanshawe's translation.

In the last half of the 20th century, Fanshawe drew the attention of scholars, primarily in the fields of English literature, translation studies, and Portuguese literature. Scholars such as William E. Simeone and Roger Walker placed Fanshawe's translations into the context of the English Civil War and English literary relations with continental Europe. Still, much of the critical commentary on Fanshawe remains in the notes and commentaries of recent editors.

BIBLIOGRAPHY

Works by Richard Fanshawe

A Critical Edition of Sir Richard Fanshawe's 1647 Translation of Giovanni Battista Guarini's Il Pastor Fido. Ed. Walter F. Staton, Jr., and William E. Simeone. Oxford: Clarendon Press, 1964.

The Fourth Book of Virgil's Aeneid, *on the Loves of Dido and Aeneas, Done into English by the Right Honourable Sir Richard Fanshawe, Knight*. Ed. A.L. Irvine. Oxford: Basil Blackwell, 1924.

Il Pastor Fido = The Faithfull Shepherd / Battista Guarini; Translated (1647) by Richard Fanshawe. Ed. J.H. Whitfield. Austin: University of Texas Press, 1976.

Luis De Camões, The Lusiads, in Sir Richard Fanshawe's Translation. Ed. Geoffrey Bullough. Carbondale: Southern Illinois University Press, 1963.

The Lusiad, by Luis De Camoens, Translated by Richard Fanshawe. Ed. Jeremiah D.M. Ford. Cambridge: Harvard University Press, 1940.

Original letters of his Excellency Sir Richard Fanshaw, during his embassies in Spain and Portugal: which, together with divers letters and answers from the chief ministers of state of England, Spain and Portugal, contain the whole negotiations of the treaty of peace between the three crowns. London, 1701.

The Poems and Translations of Sir Richard Fanshawe. Ed. Peter Davidson. 2 vols. Oxford: Clarendon Press, 1997–1999.

Sir Richard Fanshawe: Shorter Poems and Translations. Ed. N.W. Bawcutt. Liverpool: Liverpool University Press, 1964.

Studies of Richard Fanshawe

Burton, Richard F. *Camöens: His Life and His Lusiads: A Commentary*. London: B. Quaritch, 1880.

Davies, Gareth Alban. "Sir Richard Fanshawe, Hispanist Cavalier." *University of Leeds Review* 20 (1977): 87–119.

Denham, Sir John. "To Sir Richard Fanshawe, Upon His Translation of Pastor Fido." In *The Poetical Works of Sir John Denham*, ed. Theodore Howard Banks, Jr. New Haven, CT: Yale University Press, 1928.

Loftis, John, ed. *The Memoirs of Anne, Lady Halkett and Ann, Lady Fanshawe*. Oxford: Clarendon Press, 1979.

Mackail, J.W. "Sir Richard Fanshawe." *Transactions of the Royal Society of Literature* 2nd ser. 28 (1908): 89–112.

Mickle, William Julius. *The Lusiad: or The Discovery of India, from Camöens*. Oxford, 1776.

Parry, Graham. "A Troubled Arcadia." In *Literature and the English Civil War*, ed. Thomas Healy and Jonathan Sawday. Cambridge: Cambridge University Press, 1990. 38–55.

Simeone, William Eugene. "Sir Richard Fanshawe: An Account of His Life and Letters." Ph.D. dissertation, University of Pennsylvania, 1950.

Southey, Robert. Rev. of John Anderson, *Memoirs of the Life and Writings of Luis de Camöens*. *The Quarterly Review* 27 (1822): 1–39.

Turner, James Grantham. *The Politics of Landscape*. Cambridge: Harvard University Press, 1979.

Walker, Roger. General note. In *The Poems and Translations of Sir Richard Fanshawe*, ed. Peter Davidson. Oxford: Clarendon Press, 1999. 2: 579–590.

———. "Sir Richard Fanshawe's *Lusiad* and Manuel de Faria e Sousa's *Lusiadas Comentadas*: New Documentary Evidence." *Portuguese Studies* 10 (1994): 44–64.

Whitfield, John H. "Sir Richard Fanshawe and the Faithfull Shepherd." *Italian Studies* 19 (1964): 64–82.

Anne Finch,
Countess of Winchilsea
(1661–1720)

AMY WOLF

BIOGRAPHY

Anne Finch, Countess of Winchilsea, was the third child of Sir William Kingsmill and Anne Haselwood. Little is known of her childhood, but she lost her father, mother, and then stepfather by the time she was ten. She met her husband Heneage Finch while he was gentleman of the bedchamber to James II (at the time, the Duke of York) and she was a maid of honor to Mary of Modena, and they married in 1684. While maid of honor, Finch participated in the courtly world of masques and performances, literature and translation, and began writing verse. After the Revolution in 1688–1689, she and her husband were exiled from the court as nonjurors who remained loyal to the Catholic Stuarts.

Finch and her husband apparently had a loving and supportive marriage; in an age when male poets wrote love poems to mistresses based on their physical qualities, she celebrated her spiritual, emotional, and physical love for her husband in challenging, loving verse. In a reversal of the traditional gender relationship, Finch's biographer Barbara McGovern calls Heneage "editor, transcriber, and muse" for his unfailing promotion of his wife's poetic gift (70). Finch's childlessness, her husband and family's support, and her comfortable life at the family estate in Eastwell (while Heneage's nephew was Earl of Winchilsea) gave her the time, leisure, and position from which to develop her poetic talents in a way that was unusual for women at the time. Finch's work began to appear anonymously in the late 1680s after she had left Mary's court, and "The Spleen," a well-received and popular Pindaric ode on the vagaries of depression and cultural assumptions about female "hysterical" ailments, appeared in 1701.

Around 1708 Finch and her husband returned to London with the shift in the political climate, and she became a more active participant in London's literary life, developing further her friendships with Jonathan Swift and Alexander Pope. Although her poems circulated in manuscript among her friends and a few appeared here and there in print, a major collection was not published until 1713 (after she became the Countess of Winchilsea) when her *Miscellany Poems, on Several Occasions* appeared. The strategy of positioning herself as an amateur, not a professional, allowed Finch to maintain her status as a virtuous lady, yet still publish. It allowed her to distance herself from the associations with prostitution that often trapped early professional women writers.

Much of Finch's best poetry, in fact, never appeared in print, only circulated among her friends and family, or remained in manuscript, unseen by the public until the 20th century. Yet despite her reluctance to publish or to be prideful about her abilities, Finch was creative and driven, producing poetry in most of the major Augustan genres and using her writing as a space to voice political and personal concerns in an intimate voice and with careful attention to details of the world around her. Finch suffered from depression for most of her life and around 1715 became increasingly physically ill. Her later poetry turned more firmly to religious themes and to a contemplative style. She died on August 5, 1720, in London, and her husband's eulogy praised her as wife, poet, royal servant, both "publick and private, so illustrious an Example of such extraordinary Endowments, both of Body and Mind, that the Court of England never bred a more accomplished Lady, nor the Church of England, a better Christian."

MAJOR WORKS AND THEMES

In an age of satire, Anne Finch carefully distanced herself from the negativity and aggression of that genre and turned to other modes of expression in her poetry. Not only was she out of place in her time in her rejection of satire, but merely being a woman in a literary tradition from which women were largely excluded shaped the themes and genres she chose. Much of her poetry is explicitly concerned with the difficulty of being a woman and a poet, and though "Ardelia" wrote in most of the major verse forms and styles of her time—love poetry, odes, lyrics, pastoral, occasional poems, fables, epistles, translations, emblems—she often self-consciously reflected on her position as a woman writing those forms. For example, her love poems "An Invitation to Dafnis" and "To Mr. F. Now Earl of W." reject the promiscuity and overt sexuality of much Restoration love poetry. As a lady she cannot write to a lover or describe sex, so she writes to her husband instead and emphasizes love beyond the physical.

Finch's "An Invitation to Dafnis" playfully handles pastoral conventions, working with the carpe diem tradition, but set in solid present reality and celebrating a feminine, nonsexual plea to seize the day with its refrain: "Come then, my Dafnis, and the fields survey, / And throo' the groves, with your Ardelia stray." Finch creatively responds to and reworks the various Augustan genres, undermining the pathetic fallacy and using classical allusions only to rework them, often with a distinctive feminist perspective. "The Unequal Fetters" gives the masculine metaphor of marriage as a ball and chain and the commonplace carpe diem theme a feminine twist in which the female speaker refuses to "Yield to be in Fetters bound / By one that walks a freer round." Finch also frequently celebrated female friendship and playfully satirized the false culture of coquetry foisted on women by society, not nature, in such poems as "Ardelia's Answer to Ephelia," which juxtaposes the sedate Ardelia, who longs for the "detraction free" countryside, with Almeria, who "flys round the Coach . . . /

Through ev'ry glasse, her sev'ral graces shows, / This, does her face, and that, her shape expose."

The fable, moreover, was a form within which Finch felt at home because it allowed her both to morally instruct—important to her as a Christian writer—and to indulge her imagination. "The Spleen," first published anonymously in 1709, was probably Finch's best-known work in the 18th century but was less interesting to later readers. In the form of a Pindaric ode, "The Spleen" was actually included in medical textbooks as a portrayal of the hysterical illness with which women were often diagnosed. "Nocturnal Reverie" first received attention because Wordsworth admired it, but his attention was amply justified by the poem's beauty, fluidity, and imagery. The entire poem is one sentence, mirroring the long, breathing interlude that the night gives the speaker from the cares and tyrannies of day. The night's beauty creates a scene of calmness where "silent Musings urge the Mind to seek / Something, too high for Syllables to speak / . . . Till morning breaks, and All's confus'd again; / Our Cares, our Toils, our Clamours are renew'd, / Or Pleasures, seldom reach'd, again pursu'd."

The sole collected edition of Finch's poems in her lifetime was the 1713 edition *Miscellany Poems, on Several Occasions*, and much of her greatest work remained in manuscript until the 20th century. Her drive to write was intense and deeply felt. Even when she doubted her authority, ability, or role as a writer who was also a woman, she always knew that she must write. Recently, several critical discussions have centered on the public and private split between Finch's published and unpublished work. Although the 17th- and 18th-century convention of circulating manuscripts without formal publication certainly complicates easy distinctions between "public" and "private" poems, scholars like McGovern see a "startling discrepancy between the passion and playful domesticity of her private love poems and the stark portrayal of contemporary marriages and the plight of women found in her more public poems" (34). Other scholars see in the manuscript poems a candid, satirical, feminist perspective absent from her published works.

CRITICAL RECEPTION

From her time to our own, Anne Finch has been consistently read and consistently considered an interesting and skillful, if minor, poet. William Wordsworth's admiration for Finch's "Nocturnal Reverie" influenced scholars from his time onward to characterize her poetry as a link between the metaphysical and the Romantics, but later-20th-century scholars primarily concerned themselves with critiquing the myth that so labeled Finch. Jonathan Swift playfully urged her to publish her poetry in his "Apollo Outwitted. To the Honourable Mrs. Finch, under her Name of Ardelia." He also showed her poetry to **Delarivier Manley** who included one of them with a portrait praising Finch in her *The New Atalantis*. Finch also exchanged poems and letters with Alexander Pope. John Middleton Murry's 1928 selection of her poems perpetuated Wordsworth's assumptions about Finch. Although Murry praised her "authentic poetry of distinct emotion" (20), he also deleted lines or omitted poems that challenged Finch's image as a pre-Romantic nature poet, cutting, for example, from "A Nocturnal Reverie" the lines that praised Finch's female friend "Salisbury." More recently, Katharine Rogers singles out Finch's love poems and poems on friendship and concludes that "the fact that her poems make a woman's consciousness the center of awareness distinguishes them in a literature where women generally appear only as an incidental part of life" (46). Because much of Finch's work has only recently been published, her reputation and importance to literary history are still being written, a process refueled by McGovern's recent biography and the recent critical edition of the Wellesley manuscript of her poetry.

BIBLIOGRAPHY

Works by Anne Finch, Countess of Winchilsea

The Anne Finch Wellesley Manuscript Poems: A Critical Edition. Ed. Barbara McGovern and Charles Hinnant. Athens: University of Georgia Press, 1998.

Poems by Anne, Countess of Winchilsea. Selected by John Middleton Murry. London: Jonathan Cape, 1928.

The Poems of Anne, Countess of Winchilsea. Ed. Myra Reynolds. Chicago: University of Chicago Press, 1903.

Selected Poems of Anne Finch, Countess of Winchilsea. Ed. Katharine Rogers. New York: Frederick Ungar, 1979.

Studies of Anne Finch, Countess of Winchilsea

Hinnant, Charles. *The Poetry of Anne Finch: An Essay in Interpretation*. Newark: University of Delaware Press, 1994.

Mallinson, Jean. "Anne Finch: A Woman Poet and the Tradition." In *Gender at Work: Four Women Writers of the Eighteenth Century*, ed. Anne Messenger. Detroit, MI: Wayne State University Press, 1990. 34–36.

McGovern, Barbara. *Anne Finch and Her Poetry: A Critical Biography*. Athens: University of Georgia Press, 1992.

Messenger, Ann. *Pastoral Tradition and the Female Talent: Studies in Augustan Poetry*. New York: AMS Press, 2001.

Rogers, Katharine. "Anne Finch, Countess of Winchilsea: An Augustan Woman Poet." In *Shakespeare's Sisters: Feminist Essays on Women Poets*, ed. Sandra M. Gilbert and Susan Gubar. Bloomington: Indiana University Press, 1979. 32–46.

Salvaggio, Ruth. *Enlightened Absence: Neoclassical Configurations of the Feminine*. Urbana: University of Illinois Press, 1988.

‟ *Phineas Fletcher*
(1582–1650)

RICHARD F. HARDIN

BIOGRAPHY

Brother of the poet Giles, cousin of the dramatist John Fletcher, and son of Giles the elder, who also wrote poetry, Phineas Fletcher received his education at Eton and King's College, Cambridge (M.A. 1608), before leaving the university to marry and serve as a minister in Norfolk. While still at Cambridge he developed a reputation as a poet in both Latin and English, his first published verse being included in a collection mourning the death of Queen Elizabeth I. On the occasion of James I's 1615 visit to the university, Fletcher wrote a "piscatory" play, *Sicelides*. After Cambridge he served as chaplain to Sir Henry Willoughby, who proved a generous patron. He knew Isaak Walton and the younger poets Francis Quarles and Edward Benlowes, the latter a sometime patron who shared Fletcher's interest in Neoplatonism. His later career in the Church led him to write two brief works of religious prose, *The Way to Blessedness* and *Joy in Tribulation*, both published in 1632.

MAJOR WORKS AND THEMES

Following the Sicilian poet Sannazaro, Fletcher wrote a collection of Latin and English "piscatory" eclogues—pastoral poems substituting fishermen and fish for shepherds and sheep. His play *Sicelides* continues this motif and is historically interesting in showing the early influence of **Shakespeare**'s *Tempest*. *Venus and Anchises*, in the mythological "epyllion" tradition of *Hero and Leander*, raises the bar for erotic titillation in that vein, and probably for that reason Fletcher never authorized its publication. In 1628 a pirated version, *Brittain's Ida*, underwent careless printing as a newfound work of Spenser, and the stanzas, with their alexandrine line-endings, might have fooled some readers then. The original manuscript, discovered by Ethel Seaton, represents one of the poet's best achievements, along with a few late, **Herbert**-like poems printed posthumously in *A Father's Testament* (1670). A long Latin poem on the Gunpowder Plot, complete with infernal council scene, appeared as *Locustae, vel Pietas Jesuitica* in 1611, perhaps influencing the adolescent **Milton**'s Latin poem on the same subject, "In Quintum Novembris." In 1627 Fletcher translated and expanded the poem, using a nine-line near-Spenserian stanza, as *The Locusts, or Apollyonists*.

The Purple Island (1633, but probably written by 1610) is a bizarre tome composed again in quasi-Spenserian stanzas. It builds on the House of Alma episode in *The Faerie Queene*, where the human body and soul are likened to a castle, though here it is an island. The bones are likened to rocks, the blood vessels to rivers, and so forth. The first half shows Fletcher to have been a serious student of human anatomy as it was known then. Passages on the structure and function of the eye and the heart reveal an arguably advanced knowledge of these subjects. The second, "soul" half of the poem employs the conventional psychology of the times, with personified sins and virtues engaged in a psychomachia, again resembling Spenser's Alma episode.

CRITICAL RECEPTION

Criticism has dwelt chiefly upon *The Purple Island*, which intrigued James Joyce, and upon Fletcher's role as a bearer of the Spenserian torch during the period between Spenser and Milton. Historians of English pastoral and mythological narrative poetry find his innovations in those fields worth consideration.

BIBLIOGRAPHY

Works by Phineas Fletcher

Locustae, vel Pietas Jesuitica. Supplementa Humanistica Lovaniensa, 9. Louvain: Leuven University Press, 1996.
Poetical Works. With Giles Fletcher. Ed. F.S. Boas. 2 vols. Cambridge: Cambridge University Press, 1908–1909.
Venus and Anchises. Ed. Ethel Seaton. Oxford: Oxford University Press, 1926.

Studies of Phineas Fletcher

Bouchard, Gary. *Colin's Campus: Cambridge Life and the English Eclogue*. Selinsgrove, PA: Susquehanna University Press, 2000.
————. "Phineas Fletcher: The Piscatory Link between Spenserian and Miltonic Pastoral." *Studies in Philology* 89 (1992): 232–243.
Brooks, Harold F. "Oldham and Phineas Fletcher: An Unrecognized Source for *Satyrs upon the Jesuits*." *Review of English Studies* 22 (1971): 410–22 and 23 (1972): 19–34.
Grundy, Joan. *The Spenserian Poets: A Study in Elizabethan and Jacobean Poetry*. London: Arnold, 1969.
Langdale, Abraham B. *Phineas Fletcher: Man of Letters, Science, and Divinity*. New York: Columbia University Press, 1937.
Nicolson, Marjorie Hope. *The Breaking of the Circle: Studies in the Effect of the "New Science" upon Seventeenth-Century Poetry*. Rev. ed. New York: Columbia University Press, 1960.
Piepho, Lee. "The Latin and English Eclogues of Phineas Fletcher: Sannazaro's Piscatories among the Britons." *Studies in Philology* 81 (1984): 461–472.

❧ *John Ford*
(1586–1639?)

KEITH M. BOTELHO

BIOGRAPHY

Caroline dramatist William Heminge's well-known lines about his contemporary John Ford give us insight into a life that we know relatively little about:

> Deep in a dumpe Jacke Forde alone was gott
> With folded Armes and Melancholye hatt.

Speculation always surrounds Ford's life beyond the few documented facts. He was born into a well-established Devonshire family in 1586; his great-grandfather obtained a coat of arms in 1524, and his father, Thomas, was a gentleman landowner. Evidence points to an unstable relationship between Ford and his father. In his will, Thomas Ford left larger sums to John's younger brothers than he did to John. Perhaps Thomas was displeased by Ford's expulsion from the Middle Temple in 1605 for failing to pay his buttery bill (he was reinstated in 1608); perhaps he disapproved of his budding literary aspirations; or, perhaps he was at odds with his "folded Armes and Melancholye hatt." Nevertheless, his older brother, Henry, who died in 1616, left Ford £20 a year for the rest of his life. This financial independence helped Ford to pursue his dramatic career, which would begin in 1621 and last for approximately twenty years.

To supplement his income, Ford may have practiced law or performed some legal work for a brief period in London, as records indicate that he was reprimanded by the Middle Temple in 1617, along with thirty-nine fellow members, for wearing hats in place of the traditional lawyers' caps. Ford is generally believed to have attended Oxford for a period of time. To conjecture further about Ford's early life is a fruitless endeavor, yet his career as dramatist is better documented, although there remains speculation about the authorship of works attributed to him and disagreement regarding the dating. After 1639, when *The Lady's Trial* was published under his name, Ford fell into obscurity—no concrete record of his death can be found.

MAJOR WORKS AND THEMES

John Ford is attributed with producing five nondramatic works, eleven independent plays (eight are extant), and numerous collaborations. Between 1606 and 1620, when Ford had not yet devoted himself to the theater, he composed an elegy, another lengthy poem, and three prose pamphlets. This early work, largely influenced by Stoicism and focusing on the themes of love and honor, or repentance and resolve, lacks the intensity of Ford's drama, although it does prefigure many of the themes that Ford would utilize again and again in his plays. The earliest of these writings, *Fame's Memorial*, is notable for its historical associations. Written upon the death of Charles Blount, Lord Mountjoy and Earl of Devonshire, in 1606, the elegy is dedicated to Penelope Rich, the model for Sir Philip Sidney's Stella in his 1582 sonnet cycle, *Astrophil and Stella*. Ford's first literary work is topical and displays sympathy for the love between Mountjoy and Rich, while glorifying Mountjoy's virtues. Ford's early attempts at writing focus on various aspects of love (courtly and Platonic) and seem to be attempts at securing a patron.

The period 1621–1628 represents Ford's collaborations with other established dramatists, namely, Dekker, **Webster**, Rowley, and possibly **Middleton**. Only two of these works are extant, *The Witch of Edmonton* (with Dekker and Rowley, 1621) and *The Sun's Darling* (a masque written with Dekker, 1624). Four productions attributed to Ford were entered into the Stationers' Register but were not printed. Scholars have also been inclined to attribute two other plays to Ford: *The Queen* and *The Spanish Gypsy*, both printed in 1653; however, evidence ultimately remains inconclusive.

Ford's collaborations with some of the leading Jacobean dramatists served as an influential apprenticeship before he began his own independent dramatic career in 1628 with the tragicomedy *The Lover's Melancholy*, which is strongly influenced by **Burton**'s *The Anatomy of Melancholy*. Parallels can also be drawn to **Shakespeare**'s *Hamlet*, *King Lear*, and *Twelfth Night*, yet Ford cannot match the rhetorical and psychological depth of his predecessor. The play sets forth the popular tale of love overcoming evil and couples this with the story of the physician Corax, who helps Meleander and Palador cure their respective melancholy. In one of the play's strongest scenes, Corax presents a masque of melancholic characters to get Palador to admit that he suffers from love melancholy.

Many of the plays that Ford wrote after *The Lover's Melancholy* focus on the implications of a disordered society and its inhabitants who must control passion with reason. Furthermore, Ford's characters demonstrate an acceptance of their ultimate fates, revealing a certain heroic victimization. In *The Broken Heart* (1631–1633), the final Ford play to be performed at Blackfriars, Ford utilizes the symbolic techniques of the masque as his characters' names are fitted to their qualities. Again, Ford depicts extremes of passion and melancholy: Penthea starves herself to death after her enforced marriage to the evil Bassanes; Ithocles is "butcher'd" at the hands of Orgilus; Orgilus chooses to bleed himself to death; and Calantha dies of a broken heart. The spectacle of many of the scenes of the play does not detract from some of Ford's finest speeches, and the four songs dealing with love provide a striking contrast to many of the horrors onstage.

The remaining five Ford plays were all performed at the Phoenix Theater in the final decade before the closing of the theaters. *'Tis Pity She's a Whore*, Ford's most intense and well-known work, presents the incestuous relationship between brother and sister Giovanni and Annabella. Despite the subject matter, Ford infuses Giovanni with a passion that is at once disturbing and appealing. In the opening scene, Giovanni relates to Friar Bonaventura (who seems to be modeled after the Friar in *Romeo and Juliet*) his love for Annabella, but the Friar calls for Giovanni's repentance for his sin. Later, after Annabella becomes pregnant by Giovanni, the Friar urges her to marry the nobleman Soranzo. Soranzo's evil servant Vasques orders that the eyes of Annabella's tutress, Putana, be "put out" after getting her to reveal the love of Annabella and Giovanni. In the final act, Giovanni stabs Annabella and enters a banquet with her heart on a dagger, killing Soranzo before being killed by the banditti. Vasques exclaims in the final scene, "I rejoice that a Spaniard outwent an Italian in revenge." Ford successfully rewrites earlier revenge tragedy conventions with his focus on incest and the extremes of passion, themes that many critics have labeled as decadent and "Jacobean."

Love's Sacrifice (1633) parallels Shakespeare's *Othello*: Iago-like D'Avolos convinces the Duke of Pavia that his wife, Bianca, is having an affair with his close friend, Fernando. Fernando later poisons himself at Bianca's tomb, and the Duke, remorseful for killing Bianca, stabs himself. The play examines Platonic love as well as the effects of lust within Pavia, yet unlike *'Tis Pity*, it does not examine more profound moral and religious questions.

Perkin Warbeck (1634) is a chronicle history that closely follows **Bacon**'s *History of King Henry VII* (1621) and Thomas Gainsford's *True and Wonderful History of Perkin Warbeck* (1618). The play is often regarded as one of the best historical plays outside of Shakespeare, and many have seen Ford's presentation as a critique of the divine right of Kings. Warbeck himself is inept and at times melancholic (as opposed to his dedicated wife Katherine Gordon), and, like many of Ford's tragic characters, he awaits his fate with resolution. Lisa Hopkins has recently remarked that the play is a Stuart succession play.

The final two plays, the domestic tragicomedies *The Fancies Chaste and Noble* and *The Lady's Trial*, have been viewed as careless and stylistically flat. Deception and misunderstanding permeate the plays' multiple plots, misleading readers for effect. *The Lady's Trial* is another nod to *Othello*, yet Auria and his young wife Spinella are able to reasonably reconcile by the conclusion of the play, due in part to Spinella's defense of herself at her trial. Ford is at his best when he presents resistant and spirited women, as he does in the case of Spinella, and her characterization should not be overlooked by critics.

CRITICAL RECEPTION

Despite writing in the years following the appearance of Shakespeare's First Folio in 1623, Ford seems to have managed to make a name for himself in Shakespeare's and other Jacobean dramatists' impressive shadows. The 17th-century religious poet **Richard Crashaw**, however, charged that Ford cheated his audience, while **Pepys** reacted unfavorably to witnessing *'Tis Pity* and *The Lady's Trial* in the 1660s. Serious criticism of Ford's work begins with Charles Lamb's 1808 *Specimens of English Dramatic Poets*, where he praises, among other things, Calantha's final speech in *The Broken Heart*. In the later 19th century, Swinburne noted that "the high figure of Ford stands steadily erect." Lamb and his supporters (notably Havelock Ellis and Swinburne) admire Ford's sympathetic portrayal of human behavior and his adept examination of human psychology. Hazlitt and his supporters (notably James Russell Lowell), however, contend that Ford's decadence and sensationalism highlight the immorality of his plays.

Much of his early criticism focused on the ethical and moral dimensions of Ford's work until T.S. Eliot's *Selected Essays* (1932) focused on the aesthetics of the plays. Eliot calls Ford's comic passages "quite atrocious," yet he does call *Perkin Warbeck* Ford's highest achievement. M. Joan Sargeaunt's central study of Ford (1935) relates that Ford was able to demonstrate man's resolve in the midst of horror. Ewing's study (1940) examines Ford's indebtedness to **Burton**, while Sensabaugh focuses on Ford's modernism. Among the other leading 20th-century critics of Ford, Leech, Stavig, and Anderson are most influential, while Neill's edited collection brings together eleven essays on topics from Ford's metatheatricality to his presentation of female authority. More recently, incisive work on Ford's drama and the political nature of his work has appeared in work by Butler, Clerico, and Hopkins, while Dyer examines *The Broken Heart* through the lens of psychoanalysis. The turn away from viewing Ford and his work as primarily decadent has allowed critical work on Ford and the Caroline Theater once again to show promise.

BIBLIOGRAPHY

Works by John Ford

The Fancies, Chast and Noble. Ed. Dominick Hart. New York: Garland Publishing, 1985.
John Ford's Love's Sacrifice. Ed. Herbert W. Hoskins, Jr. Washington, DC: University Press of America, 1978.
The Nondramatic Works of John Ford. Ed. L.E. Stock et al. Binghamton, NY: Medieval & Renaissance Texts & Studies, 1991.
'Tis Pity She's a Whore and Other Plays. Ed. Marion Lomax. Oxford: Oxford University Press, 1995.

Studies of John Ford

Anderson, Donald K., Jr. *"Concord in Discord": The Plays of John Ford, 1586–1986*. New York: AMS Press, 1986.
———. *John Ford*. New York: Twayne Publishers, 1972.
Anderson, Judith H. "But We Shall Teach the Lad Another Language: History and Rhetoric in Bacon, Ford, and Donne." *Renaissance Drama* 20 (1989): 169–195.
Barbour, Reid. "John Ford and Resolve." *Studies in Philology* 86.3 (1989): 341–366.
Barton, Anne. "He that plays the King: Ford's *Perkin Warbeck* and the Stuart History Play." In *English Drama: Form and Development*, ed. Marie Axton and Raymond Williams. Cambridge: Cambridge University Press, 1977.
Bentley, Gerald Eades. *The Jacobean and Caroline Stage: Plays and Playwrights*. Vol. 3. Oxford: Clarendon Press, 1956.
Bowers, Fredson Thayer. *Elizabethan Revenge Tragedy 1587–1642*. Gloucester, MA: Peter Smith, 1959.
Bueler, Lois E. "Role-Splitting and Reintegration: The Tested Woman Plot in Ford." *Studies in English Literature* 20.2 (1980): 325–344.

Burnett, Mark Thornton. "Marlovian Echoes in Ford's *Perkin Warbeck*." *Notes and Queries* 36.3 (1989): 347–349.

Clark, Ira. *Professional Playwrights: Massinger, Ford, Shirley, & Brome*. Lexington: University Press of Kentucky, 1992.

Clerico, Terri. "The Politics of Blood: John Ford's *'Tis Pity She's a Whore*." *English Literary Renaissance* 22.3 (1992): 405–434.

Comensoli, Viviana. *Household Business: Domestic Plays of Early Modern England*. Toronto: University of Toronto Press, 1996.

Dyer, William D. "Holding/Withholding Environments: A Psychoanalytic Approach to Ford's *The Broken Heart*." *English Literary Renaissance* 21.3 (1991): 401–424.

Eliot, T.S. *Essays on Elizabethan Drama*. New York: Harcourt, Brace and Company, 1956.

Ewing, S. Blaine. *Burtonian Melancholy in the Plays of John Ford*. Princeton: Princeton University Press, 1940.

Farr, Dorothy M. *John Ford and the Caroline Theater*. New York: Barnes & Noble Books, 1979.

Hopkins, Lisa. *John Ford's Political Theater*. Manchester: Manchester University Press, 1994.

Leech, Clifford. *John Ford and the Drama of His Time*. London: Chatto and Windus, 1957.

Leggatt, Alexander. *English Drama: Shakespeare to the Restoration 1590–1660*. London: Longman, 1988.

Logan, Terence P., and Denzell S. Smith, eds. *The Later Jacobean and Caroline Dramatists*. Lincoln: University of Nebraska Press, 1978.

McCabe, Richard A. *Incest, Drama, and Nature's Law 1550–1700*. Cambridge: Cambridge University Press, 1993.

Neill, Michael, ed. *John Ford: Critical Re-Visions*. Cambridge: Cambridge University Press, 1988.

Oliver, H.J. *The Problem of John Ford*. Melbourne: Melbourne University Press, 1955.

Sargeaunt, M. Joan. *John Ford*. Oxford: Basil Blackwell, 1935.

Sensabaugh, G.F. *The Tragic Muse of John Ford*. Stanford, CA: Stanford University Press, 1944.

Stavig, Mark. *John Ford and the Traditional Moral Order*. Madison: University of Wisconsin Press, 1968.

Wymer, Rowland. *Webster and Ford*. New York: St. Martin's Press, 1995.

✇ *Orazio and Artemisia Gentileschi*

(1563–1639 and 1593–1652/1653)

SONJA HANSARD-WEINER

BIOGRAPHY

Born in Pisa, Orazio di Giovanni Battista Lomi Gentileschi, the second son of a Florentine goldsmith, settled in Rome sometime around 1676–1678, adopting the matronymic Gentileschi by which both he and his daughter Artemisia would be known throughout their professional lives. Orazio's career began as a member of the vast crew of painters enlisted to complete the decoration of the Biblioteca Sistina in the Vatican and ended as court painter to Charles I and Henrietta Marie of England. Often grouped with the minor Caravaggisti, Orazio developed a personal style that reflected a much wider range of influences and competitors, as he painted religious, mythological, and allegorical subjects for a succession of popes and patrons including the Borghese and Sauli families in Fabriano and Genoa, Marie de'Medici, and the Duke of Buckingham.

Born in Rome, Artemisia was the only daughter and oldest child of Orazio and Prudentia Montoni. Orphaned at twelve, she lived and painted under her father's tutelage, completing her first dated painting, *Susanna and the Elders*, in 1610. In the next year, she studied with Agostino Tassi. In 1612, charges of rape were brought against Tassi, and though he was convicted, the scandal led to a hasty marriage to Pietro Antonio di Vicenzo Stiattesi. Artemisia and Pierantonio, as he preferred to be called, left for Florence where, over the next half dozen years, she bore two sons and two daughters and established a significant reputation as a painter, counting among her patrons Cosimo II. By 1621, she returned to Rome with her family and took up residence in her father's house; by 1623, Pierantonio, who had encouraged her career in Florence, left her. Artemisia's career, however, continued to flourish as she completed *commissions* for Philip IV of Spain, Cardinal Barberini, Francesco I d'Este, and Ferdinando II de'Medici, among others. In 1635, she declined an invitation to join her father and brother in England to work at the court of Charles I, although sometime between 1637 and 1639 she acquiesced. Sometime after 1640 she returned to Rome, then spent her last years in Naples where her last recorded work, ironically, was *Susanna and the Elders* (1652).

MAJOR WORKS AND THEMES

Both Gentileschi père et fille followed the Baroque interest in highly dramatic allegorical, biblical, and classical scenes including Aurora, Diana, Abraham and Isaac, Lot and His Daughters, David and Goliath, David and Bathsheba, Susanna and the Elders, Judith and Holofernes, Jael and Sisera, Cleopatra, and Lucrece. Unlike her father, however, who painted numerous martyrs and saints as well as scenes of the Holy Family and crucifixions, Artemisia is credited with very few. While contemporary accounts praise Artemisia's skill as both portraitist and still-life painter, only the *Portrait of a Condottieri*, from her adolescence, is undisputed. In England, Orazio is known to have worked on *Rest on the Flight to Egypt*, *The Finding of Moses* (presented as a gift from Charles I to Philip IV), and *Lot and His Daughters*. Gentileschi's major work in England, however, is *An Allegory of Peace and the Arts*, a series of nine canvases painted for the ceiling of the Queen's House in Greenwich (now installed at Marlborough House, London). Designed (probably in collaboration with Inigo Jones) around a central circular canvas, the figure of Peace along with figures representing the Liberal Arts, Victory, and Fortune sit in state. Four rectangular panels as well as four smaller circular panels present the nine Muses and personifications of Painting, Sculpture, Architecture, and Music. While some scholars have credited Artemisia with part of the work on the ceiling, no direct evidence supports the claim. Nonetheless, by 1637–1639, three paintings by Artemisia were inventoried in the Royal Collection (*Fame*, *Susanna and the Elders*, and *Tarquin and Lucretia*); a 1649 inventory recorded, in addition to these three, *Diana at Her Bath* and *A Saint Laying His Hand, on Fruite*. Despite their shared interests, Orazio's work is frequently described as theatrical and decorative, whereas Artemisia's tends to be characterized as personal and psychological.

CRITICAL RECEPTION

Keith Christianson and Judith W. Mann, in separate essays in their catalog accompanying the recent exhibition at the Metropolitan Museum of Art (New York), *Orazio and Artemisia Gentileschi*, argue persuasively that both Gentileschis' work has been overinterpreted in the light of Orazio's brief connection with Caravaggio and Artemisia's rape by Tassi. While there is no question that Artemisia's most widely acclaimed works are her stunningly powerful and graphic representations of Judith, before, during, and after the beheading of Holofernes, and her distraught *Susanna and the Elders*, the totality of her oeuvre deserves wider recognition, as it assuredly had in her lifetime. Similarly, while certain of Orazio's paintings exploit the tenebrous lighting of Caravaggio, few of his paintings share Caravaggio's interest in the intimate or the mundane, supporting Christianson's contention that Gentileschi's place as a pivotal figure between Caravaggio and **Vermeer** should be recognized. The Metropolitan's joint retrospective may have provided an opportunity to more closely evaluate their careers, but it is Artemisia who has captured the imagination of novelists, poets, and new generations of artists.

BIBLIOGRAPHY

Studies of Orazio and Artemisia Gentileschi

Bissell, R. Ward. *Artemisia Gentileschi and the Authority of Art: Critical Reading and Catalogue Raisonne*. University Park: The Pennsylvania State University Press, 1999.

———. *Orazio Gentileschi and the Poetic Tradition in Caravaggesque Painting*. University Park: The Pennsylvania State University Press, 1981.

Christianson, Keith, and Judith W. Mann, eds. *Orazio and Artemisia Gentileschi*. New Haven, CT: Metropolitan Museum of Art & Yale University Press, 2001.

Garrard, Mary D. *Artemisia Gentileschi*. New York: Rizzoli Art Series, 1993.

———. *Artemisia Gentileschi: The Image of the Female Hero in Italian Baroque Art*. Princeton: Princeton University Press, 1989.

———. *Artemisia Gentileschi around 1622: The Shaping and Reshaping of an Artistic Identity*. Berkeley: University of California Press, 2001.

❧ *Fulke Greville, Lord Brooke*
(1554–1628)

ANDREW D. WEINER

BIOGRAPHY

Fulke Greville's epitaph, published on the tomb he had constructed for himself in the chapter house of St. Mary's Church in Warwick, proclaims the occupant as "Fulke Greville, Servant to Queene Elizabeth, Concellor to King James, and Frend to Sir Philip Sidney. Trophaeum Peccati" (Rees 25). Under Elizabeth, Greville, the son of a wealthy Warwick landowner whose father had married a Neville heiress and inherited much property and a claim to the Brooke baronetcy, had attached himself to Sir Philip Sidney, whom he met on his first day at Shrewsbury School and who became his closest friend during his life. His second best friend was Sir Francis Walsingham, Secretary of the Privy Council and, after 1583, Sidney's father-in-law. Like them, he sought to influence the direction of the court toward an interventionist policy to restrain Catholic military power abroad and political influence at home. Greville sought to fight against the Spanish on land and at sea but was refused permission by the Queen either to sail with Drake (as was Sidney) or to accompany Sidney to the Netherlands, where, in 1586, Sidney lost his life.

Through the intervention of Sidney and Walsingham, Greville was awarded and confirmed in the position of Clerk of the Signet in the Council in the Marches of Wales (of which Sir Henry Sidney, Philip's father, was Lord President) and received a reversion to the position of Secretary of the Council. From the two positions, Greville would ultimately receive the greater part of his public income for the rest of his life (Rebholz 20–25). While Greville was appointed Treasurer of the Navy in 1598 and made a Rear-Admiral in 1599, he seems to have spent more time, as so many of the Queen's servants did, begging for the money necessary to outfit the ships and feed the sailors than profiting personally from the appointment.

Elizabeth's death and the ascent of Robert Cecil, later Earl of Salisbury under James I, put Greville's public career on hold. Greville's friendship with the Earl of Essex made him suspect to Cecil, and even though he was part of the force besieging Essex

House in 1601, from 1604 to 1612, when Cecil died, he found himself exiled from the inner circle at court. Greville used this time to work on his *Life of Sidney*, which simultaneously presented Sidney as a model of selfless service to his Queen and country, offered Sidney's philosophy of founding service to the Queen upon service to God, and was at one point apparently intended to serve as a preface to Greville's own literary works, both those written in his youth in conversation with Sidney's *Astrophil and Stella* (primarily the sequence of poems about love in *Caelica*, i.e., poems 1–72 and 74) and those more philosophical verse treatises written during his enforced idleness under Cecil. His *Life*, however, like his poetry was only published posthumously in 1652, and his literary career, though important to him—he kept a manuscript of all his poetry and tinkered with it throughout his life, especially during his final retirement from public service—was unknown until the publication of his poetry in 1633 and 1672.

After Cecil's death, Greville returned to the public eye, becoming Chancellor and Under-Treasurer of the Exchequer in 1614 and a Privy Councillor. In 1624 James made him Lord Brooke. He was one of those named to form a "noble household" for Charles I and served for three years on Charles's Privy Council (Rees 35–36). Greville died in 1628 at the hands of a servant, who stabbed him in a quarrel whose nature is unknown. His poetry was finally published in 1633 in a volume titled *Certaine Learned And Elegant Works of the Right Honourable Fulke, Lord Brooke, Written in his Youth, and familiar Exercise with Sir Philip Sidney*. His *Life of . . . Sidney* made it into print during the Commonwealth, appearing in 1652 as *The Life Of The Renowned Sir Philip Sidney. With the True Interest of England as it then stood in relation to all forrain Princes; and particularly for suppressing the power of Spain stated by him. Together with a short account of the Maximes and Policies used by Queen Elizabeth in her Government*, at a time when comparisons between Queen Elizabeth and her unhappy successors would not be held to be offensive to the Crown, and his final verse treatises were published in 1670 as *The Remains of Sir Fulk Grevill Lord Brooke: Being Poems of Monarchy and Religion*.

By this time, the publisher seemed to fear that his author might have been forgotten, so he added a brief "Advertisement" to introduce Greville to a post-Commonwealth audience:

The Author having dedicated all his Monuments to the Memory of Sir Philip Sidney, whose Life he did write as an intended Preface to these; it will not bee fit to add any other than a brief Advertisement to acquaint the Reader, he was that Sir Fulk Grevill whose Noble Line by Matches with the Honourable Families of Nevil, Beauchamp, and Willoughby Lord Brooke make good the observation of Hereditary advantages, of Mind as well as Body, by Descents purely derived from Noble Ancestors; the Excellency of his Qualities rendering him as eminent Courtier in Queen Elizabeths Raign, and in King James's time, under whom he had the Honourable emploiments of Chancellour of the Exchequer and Privy Councellor, and was by Letters Patent of that King, in consideration of services done to the Crown, made Lord Brooke; to the title of which Barony by Descent from Willoughby he had right: and having always lived a batchelor (which was no small advantage to the freedom of his mind). He died in the Seventy fourth year of his Age, Ann. Dom. 1628. having been also Counsellor of State for about Three years to King CHARLES the First. (Wilkes 33)

MAJOR WORKS AND THEMES

In his *Life Of The Renowned Sir Philip Sidney*, Greville observes of Sidney that like William of Orange, whom they both admired, "he made the Religion he professed, the firm Basis of his life: For this was his judgment (as he often told me) that our true-heartedness to the Reformed Religion in the beginning brought Peace, Safetie, and Freedome to us" (*Life* [1907] 35; henceforth *Life*). If this be true of Sidney, it is equally likely to be true of Greville, who modeled his life as much as he could upon that of his friend. But what kind of life would one construct upon the basis of the religion they both professed, Reformed Protestantism? Though a sincere Protestant, Sidney did not think himself a saint. According to his chaplain, George Gifford, Sidney, after sleeping poorly the night before he died, said to him,

I had this night a trouble in my mind: for searching myself, methought I had not a sure and firm hold in Christ. After I had continued in this perplexity a while, observe how strangely God did deliver me—for indeed it was a strange deliverance that I had! There came to my mind a vanity wherein I had taken delight, wherein I had not rid myself. It was my Lady Rich. But I rid myself of it, and presently my joy and comfort returned. (*Miscellaneous Prose of Sir Philip Sidney* [henceforth *MP*] 169)

Hypersensitive to those occasions when they could not help but violate the commands of their God, Renaissance Protestants built a spiritual life upon their knowledge of the sinfulness of their attraction to the "vanities" of the world, of their consciousness of their unworthiness, and of their inability to merit the gifts a gracious God had bestowed upon them, hence Greville's reference in his epitaph to his tomb and its contents as a Trophaeum Peccati. Unlike the stereotypical self-righteous Puritan constructed by their political opponents, whose condition could as easily be described as "sick of self love" as Olivia categorizes Malvolio in *Twelfth Night*, the best defense against such pride was a knowledge of what one was. As the narrator puts it in Sidney's *Old Arcadia*, "[T]rue it is that that sweet and simple breath of heavenly goodness is the easier to fall because it hath not passed through the worldly wickedness, nor feelingly found the evil that evil carrieth with it" (*The Old Arcadia* [henceforth *OA*] 95).

In his *Defense of Poetry*, Sidney goes so far as to make "the knowledge of a man's self, in the ethic and politic consideration" (*MP* 83) the "highest end of the mistress—knowledge, by the Greeks called architechtonike" (82). But the self-knowledge that is our end is predicated upon an understanding that all learning must begin by acknowledging the limitations in the "perfection" that "our degenerate souls, made worse by their clayey lodgings, can be capable of" (*MP* 82). Yet compared to Sidney, who believed that most people "are childish in the best things till they be cradled in their graves" (*MP* 92), Greville was a pessimist. In his *Life of . . . Sidney*, he distinguishes his "creeping Genius," which is "fixed upon the Images of Life," from Sidney's, which could reach to "images of Wit," and insists that he writes only for those "on whose foot the black Oxe [misfortune] had . . . already trod," those "that are weather-beaten in the Sea of this World, such as having lost sight of their Gardens, and groves, study to saile on a right course among Rocks, and quick-sands" (*Life* 224). This insistence upon trying to teach the lost how to find themselves again is especially clear in

Greville's *Treatie of Humane Learning*, written sometime during the decade following the completion of his *Life of . . . Sidney*. In this work, Greville begins with a survey of the mental world fallen man has created and ends by exploring the possibilities for a refashioning of "frail, fall'n human kind" (Bullough, stanza 143).

Like Sidney's discussion of learning in the *Defense*, Greville's *Treatie* begins by appealing to our desire for knowledge and then quickly undermines that desire:

> The mind of man is this worlds true dimension;
> And Knowledge is the measure of the minde:
> And as the minde, in her vast comprehension,
> Contains more worlds than all the worlds can finde,
>   So Knowledge doth itself far more extend
>   Than all the minds of Men can comprehend.
> A climbing Height it is without a head,
> Depth without bottome, Way without an end,
> A Circle with no line enuironed;
> Not comprehended, all it comprehends;
>   Worth infinite, yet satisfies no minde
>   Till it that infinite of the God-head finde.
>
> This Knowledge is that same forbidden tree
> Which man lusts after to be made his Maker. (stanzas 1–3)

The quest for knowledge, no longer a Thomist *imitatio dei*, is here seen as a Satanic attempt to become God, an attempt rendered even more ludicrous by the next stanza's insistence that, blinded by our desire to achieve something beyond our capabilities, we have become, like Ixion, grapplers with clouds we deem solid and real. Our "centaur-like affection"—our blindness to the world as it is rather than as we might desire it to be—is led on a guided tour through the faculties of the mind and the senses, and the narrator's conclusion, at stanza 16, reinforces our growing sense that there are less things in heaven and earth than are dreamt of in our philosophy: "man's bankrupt Nature is not free / By any Arts to raise it selfe againe."

If we are unable in ourselves, because of our "falne estate[s] the fatal stains" (stanza 19), to rise above our own "corruption" (stanza 15), it is only natural to wonder whether

>   all these naturall Defects perchance
> May be supplied by Sciences and Arts,
> Which wee thirst after, study, admire, advance,
> As if restore our fall, recure our smarts
>   They could. (stanza 21)

But they can't. As Greville mordantly observes,

> For if Mans wisdomes, lawes, arts, legends, schooles
> Be built vpon the knowledge of the evill,
> And if these Trophies be the onely tooles,
> Which doe maintaine the kingdome of the Diuell,

> If all these Babels had the curse of tongues,
> So as confusion still to them belongs:
>
> Then can these moulds neuer containe their Maker. . . .
>> These Arts, moulds, workes can but express the sinne
>> Whence by mans folie, his fall did beginne. (stanzas 46–47)

For Greville, man's fallenness is the essential fact: If knowledge cannot raise man back to that lost first estate, then all it does is "Word-magike," which as physicians know, "neuer helpeth the disease" (stanza 30). If our arts and sciences are merely created out of words (stanza 26), they may recreate us but not re-create us:

> Then, if our Arts want power to make vs better,
> What foole will thinke they can vs wiser make;
> Life is the Wisdome, Art is but the letter
> Or shell, which oft men for the kernell take. (stanza 35)

Our options, in fact, seem rather limited—the only thing we seem truly able to know is our own sense of how fallen we are: "In this Mortalitie, this strange priuation, / What knowledge stands but sense of declination?" (stanza 48). Abused by his "knowledge"—the arts and sciences he invents to hide from him the truth of his fallen condition—man neglects the only true knowledge that can tell him what he is.

Yet though Greville rejects those false knowledges, he rejects as well the idea that "Ignorance is the mother of Deuotion" (stanza 60), arguing instead that fallen man needs exercise more than idleness (stanza 67) and that the arts and sciences must be reformed by basing them on nature rather than allowing man to turn nature itself into a merely wordish phenomenon, the product merely of man's art (cf. stanzas 74, 27):

> Forme Art directly vnder Natures Lawes;
> And all effects so in their causes muold:
>> As fraile Man liuely, without School of smart,
>> Might see Successes coming in an Art. (stanza 74)

Though nature, too, is corrupt, "God made all for use" (stanza 71). But what use can fallen man make of fallen nature? Greville's answer seems to be that though the world is fallen, at least it has its own order—something more real than the fantasies of fallen man—and any order external to man is an improvement on our disorder:

> For though the World, and Man can neuer frame
> These outward moulds, to cast Gods chosen in,
> Nor giue his Spirit where they giue his Name,
> That power being neuer granted to the sinne:
>> Yet in the world those Orders prosper best
>> Which from the word, in seeming, vary least. (stanza 87)

Only God can frame his chosen, a class introduced briefly and strictly set apart from the rest of us in stanza 64. God's "Children," "pure soules (who only know his voice)" neither have nor need any art "but Obedience, for their test":

> A mystery betweene God, and the man,
> Asking and giving farre more than we can. (stanza 64)

The rest of us, lacking the art of obedience, must learn it even if only from those who cannot teach it well, institutions like the church, the law, physics, and philosophy, which "embrace" wisdom, though they "hate the good, / Since Power thus vayl'd is hardly understood" (stanza 89).

External systems of order seem to function like Una's black vestments, which veil her pure white robe so that we see her "as one that inly mourned" (Spenser I.i.5). If we cannot see the light, at least we can more clearly perceive the darkness that covers it. And in that contrast there seems to be at least some cause for optimism from time to time. If the sciences cannot make us better, at least they can teach us to feel our disease; if the arts cannot raise us out of our selves, at least they can teach us to see ourselves more clearly. Thus when discussing the "instrumentall following Arts, / Which . . . / Afford not matter, but limne out the parts" (stanza 102), Greville, warning us not to get trapped in the intricacies of grammar for their own sake, observes that

> whosoeuer markes the good, or euill
> As they stand fixed in the heart of Man,
> The one of God, the other of the devil,
> Feele, out of things, Men words still fashion can,
> So that from life since liuely words proceed,
> What other Grammar doe our natures need? (stanza 103)

Similarly, Greville notes that rhetoric has suffered from those who have used it to make reason captive with the "painted skinne / Of many words" (stanza 107), and he decries the excessive employment of the wings of metaphor to "express all things" (stanza 108). Yet he does not dismiss rhetoric as inherently useless. Greville asserts that although no earthly language contains "Sufficient Characters" to express things without the use of figurative language, language too having fallen (stanza 108), neither words nor speech per se are thereby invalidated:

> Whereas those words in every tongue are best
> Which doe most properly expresse the thought;
> For as of pictures, which should manifest
> The life, we say not that is fineliest wrought,
>   Which fairest simply showes, but faire and like:
>   So words must sparks be of those fires they strike.
> For the true Art of Eloquence indeed
> Is not this craft of words, but formes of speech,
> Such as from liuing wisdomes doe proceed;
> Whose ends are not to flatter, or beseech,
>   Insinuate, or perswade, but to declare
>   What things in Nature good, or euill are. (stanzas 109–110)

Even poetry has a role to play. Although, like music, poetry is "esteemed," an idle man's profession since both arts can "move" but not "remove or make impression" (stanza 111), Greville, like Sidney, stresses the utility of "moving": Church music can "move thoughts, while God may touch the hearts"; martial music "raiseth passions which enlarge the mind, / And keeps down passions of the baser kind" (stanza 113). Poetry can "serve . . . our hearts"

> if to describe, or praise
> Goodnesse, or God she her Ideas frame,
> And like a Maker, her creation raise
> On lines of truth, it beautifies the same;
> And while it seemeth onely but to please,
> Teacheth vs order vnder pleasures name;
>   Which in a glasse, shows Nature how to fashion
>   Her selfe againe, by ballancing of passion. (stanza 114)

That Greville would find any human art capable of raising a creation "on lines of truth" is perhaps as startling as the idea that he would suggest that words can be "sparks" of those fires they strike. Given that he has already bewailed the Babel that made language as fallen as its maker, given that he has repeatedly emphasized man's inability to comprehend his Maker, that he would suddenly suggest that poets can, as makers, praise their Maker in words that "beautifie" their creations or that they can, "in a glasse," show "Nature how to fashion / Her selfe again" is quite a turn from the argument he had been making. Like Sidney in *The Defense of Poetry*, Greville seems to be implying that poets are "makers" who can make a brazen world golden, perhaps, like Sidney, because he means us to "give right honor to the heavenly Maker of that maker, who with the force of a divine breath" (*MP* 79) can bring forth things better than those in nature or quite anew.

That Sidney's "right poet" can create is, Sidney says, a "great proof to the incredulous of that first accursed fall of Adam since our erected wit knoweth what perfection is and yet our infected will keepeth us from reaching unto it" (*MP* 79). That our infected wills keep us from reaching for the perfection we know is a rebuke to the so-called learned men whom Sidney mocks for "hav[ing] learnedly thought that where once reason hath so much overmastered passion as that the mind hath a free desire to do well, the inward light each mind hath in itself is as good as a philosopher's book" (*MP* 91). Sidney argues that although "in nature we know it is well to do well, and what is well, and what is evil" (*MP* 91), in nature we have not the ability to choose to do well and to avoid evil.

While our understanding of Greville's argument thus far suggests that he would happily join himself to the notion that we cannot choose to do well or to avoid evil, nothing before these stanzas had suggested that there were those among us with "erected wits" save for his one reference to God's children, so different from the rest of us. Indeed, even in Sidney's works, not all wits are erect (and I take as my example David, who has seen, as it were, God coming in his majesty through the eyes of his mind, "only cleared by faith" [*MP* 77]). But those whose spiritual eye is not opened by faith are more likely to see as the despairing Gynecia does in *The Old Arcadia*:

I am divided in myself; how can I stand? I am overthrown in myself; who shall raise me? Vice is but a nurse of new agonies, and the virtue I am divorced from makes the hateful comparison more manifest. No, no, virtue; either I never had but a shadow of thee, or thou thyself art but a shadow, for how is my soul abandoned! How are all my powers laid waste! My desire is pained, because it cannot hope; and if hope came, his best should be but mischief. O strange mixture of human minds: only so much good left as to make us languish in our own evils! (*OA* 160–161)

If the Sidneyan "right poet" is the chosen instrument of God, to be used as God used Nathan, to call so beloved a servant as David back to obedience, what is the Grevillian user of words?

In an interesting rhetorical move, Greville brings back "those pure humble Creatures," now seen as sharing, at least to some extent, in the common inheritance of "vaine, traducing, humane features" in order to "helpe Obedience" by defeating "pride" (stanza 128). Though chosen by God, his own children, they are still "in the world" even if "not of it" and must learn to "take"

> Onely those blessings of Mortality,
> Which he that made all, fashion'd for their sake:
>   Not fixing loue, hope, sorrow, care, or feare,
>   On mortal blossoms, which must dye to beare. (stanza 129)

Partakers though they may be of the "blessings of Mortality," they seem now to be a lot more like the rest of us than they were before. In fact, the only difference that now seems to be apparent is that they have learned to seek God "euen in the Faith He giues" (stanza 138), using God's gift of faith as the tool by which they can "cleave" like "shells" the "words of Art" and disclose "the lifes true wisdome" (stanza 139). To find the Word within the words, even the "liuely words [that] proceed" from life (stanza 103), the "formes of speech, / Such as from liuing wisdomes doe proceed" (stanza 110), for Sidney requires learning to see as David did, with the eyes of his mind "only cleared by faith," learning to see what our "erected wit" is trying to show us. In Greville, however, the seeing takes place not in our minds but in our hearts:

> Lastly, we must not to the world erect
> Theaters, nor plant our Paradise in dust,
> Nor build vp Babels for the Deuils elect;
> Make temples of our hearts to God we must. (stanza 147)

As the change from third person to first suggests, "we" have now become God's children, his chosen, our hearts, the temple for the Holy Spirit, now not the theater where the vanities of the world will be enacted but the stage on which God's drama is shown. "Our selues we may obserue, / To humble vs" (stanza 148), but the main action involves seeing God's "spiritual work" within:

> Thus are true Learnings in the humble heart
> A Spiritual worke, raising Gods Image, rased
> By our transgression, a well-framed art,
> At which the world, and error stand amazed,
>   A Light divine, where man sees ioy, and smart
>   Immortall in this mortall body blazed;

A wisdome, which the Wisdome vs assureth
With hers, euen to the sight of God endureth. (stanza 150)

In this penultimate stanza of the poem, Greville offers two interpretative choices: we can either read these words as abstractions or see them as lively images of the spiritual work that "gifts of Grace, and Faith" have begun in our hearts (stanza 149). If we attempt to cleave these words open, to find the fires of which they are sparks, we get a rather different picture. What Greville invites us to see is the crucified Christ spiritually resident in our hearts, God's image within to restore that image and likeness of God in which mankind was created by that was destroyed—razed out—when Adam turned from God at the Fall. As Christ says in **Herbert**'s "The Sacrifice," "Adam ate the apple but I must climb the tree." In this living monument to our sin, the "light divine" that entered our darkness to shine within, Christ's "ioy, and smart / Immortall" becomes for Greville our wisdom, our joy, our means of sharing in the amazement of "the world, and error" that we can find in God's word, God's Word, Christ, the wisdom of God, blazing within our humbled hearts. By assuming his mortal body and allowing Himself to be raised on our cross, Christ enables the Father to redeem us, to make us again his "Children" (stanza 64).

When our hearts are opened by grace and faith and we learn to see again "the good . . . / . . . fixed in the heart of Man" (stanza 103), we have found the "Grammar" that "our natures need," the grammar that enables "liuely words" in turn to proceed from us. Though Greville, like Sidney, is quite clear that only God can save us, the saved poet by being saved seems to be able to become the instrument (as Nathan's fable was for David) by which "Man may well professe / To studie God, whom he is borne to serve" (stanza 148). By letting us see God's children both as other and then as self, Greville's *Treatie of Humane Learning* offers us the chance to try both positions; by allowing us the chance to enact in his poem what God enacts in the hearts of those he chooses to redeem, Greville offers us the opportunity to see, as in a glass, whether poetry can indeed balance our passion. In these images from the life of Reformed Protestant humankind, Greville's *Treatie* claims its place as a Sidneyan work of "right" poetry and offers us a way to rejuvenate language itself.

CRITICAL RECEPTION

During his life, the only literary work with which Greville was publicly associated was the first publication in 1590 of Sir Philip Sidney's *The Countesse of Pembrokes Arcadia.* Sidney had left the unfinished manuscript of his revision with Greville before he left for the Netherlands in 1585 and instructed him to destroy it if anything happened to him. Learning from the publisher William Ponsonby that another publisher was planning to issue the original version of the work, Greville asked Sir Francis Walsingham to forbid the publication as not so fit as the final version, which he then edited and gave to Ponsonby to print. In his revisions, Sidney had begun moving poems from the eclogue into the body of each book. In his version, Greville, assuming that Sidney intended to eliminate the eclogues entirely, cut all of the poems that Sidney had not moved from the eclogues into the text, and since Sidney's work broke off in the middle of a sentence, that's where Greville's edition comes to a sudden stop. It was superseded in 1593 when Sidney's sister, the Countess of Pembroke, had Ponsonby publish a version that combined the unfinished revised version with the last three books of the original version in its earliest state and contained all of the eclogues, changing them only where Sidney had moved poems from the eclogues into the text, and it is her version that was known to readers until the publication in 1928 of the original version (*The Old Arcadia*).

Greville's own works had to wait until the 20th century for any kind of sustained literary analysis. Yvor Winters's assertion in "Aspects of the Short Poem in the English Renaissance," a revision and expansion of an essay published in *Poetry* in 1939, has had a major impact on Greville's literary reputation. Winters claimed that

in his later work he [Greville] became a greater poet than any of the associates of his youth. It is my opinion that he should be ranked with **Jonson** as one of the two great masters of the short poem in the Renaissance. In addition he is the main connection between the School of Gascoigne and the School of Sidney; and then again he is the main connection between the School of Sidney and the Schools of **Donne** and Jonson. He is thus a figure of considerable interest to the student of the history of method. (44)

After C.S. Lewis notoriously categorized 16th-century poetry as either "Drab" or "Golden," Winters's followers responded by proposing a different scheme for thinking about English Renaissance poetry—"Plain" and "Eloquent," with "Plain" being the preferred medium for serious poems and poets. In *The English Lyric from Wyatt to Donne*, Douglas L. Peterson devotes a chapter to Greville, discussing *Caelica*, Greville's lyric sequence composed over a period of at least thirty years, and arguing that the poems begin as a

more or less conventional group of praises, complaints, and petitions depicting the familiar role of suffering or admiring lover, but in the course of the sequence the poems grow increasingly critical of that role, until the neo-Platonic religion, along with the worship of Cupid as God or erotic desire, are renounced in favor of the divine love made available to undeserving man through Christ. (252)

Peterson sees *Caelica* as "a poetry of ideas, philosophical reflection, and scrupulous self-examination" that employs the "native plain style, although considerably refined by syntactical techniques developed within the eloquent tradition by experimentation with the 'schemes' of grammar" and void of any traces of the " 'sugared' style" (252).

Using Greville's *Treatie of Humane Learning* (stanzas 107–110) as a way of talking about Greville's ideas about poetic style, Peterson argues that for Greville

"[t]he true Art of Eloquenc" is devoted to the declaration of truth and the elimination of deceptive appearances. It seeks the means which "most properly express the thought" itself and not the means of clothing it in attractive language. It employs metaphor only when clarity of thought requires it. It is the art of direct statement, simple and unadorned. (253)

While I think that this undervalues Greville's urgent desire to cleave words (and hearts) open to reveal the truth within (*A Treatie of Humane Learning*, stanza 139), it offers a way of thinking about verse that is not golden but hardly drab and suggests a way of distinguishing Greville from both Jonson and Donne. It also invites us to think what the poetry of the first third of the 17th century might have looked like had Greville's poetry been as available as the works of Sidney, Spenser, **Shakespeare**, and Jonson.

BIBLIOGRAPHY

Works by Fulke Greville, Lord Brooke

Certaine Learned And Elegant Works of the Right Honourable Fulke, Lord Brooke, Written in his Youth, and familiar Exercise with Sir Philip Sidney. Printed by E.P. for Henry Seyle, and are to be sold at his shop at the signe of the Tygers head in St. Paul's Church-yard. London, 1633.

The Life Of The Renowned Sir Philip Sidney. With the True Interest of England as it then stood in relation to all forrain Princes; and particularly for suppressing the power of Spain stated by him. Together with a short account of the Maximes and Policies used by Queen Elizabeth in her Government. London: Henry Seile, 1652.

Poems and Dramas of Fulke Greville. Ed. Geoffrey Bullough. 2 vols. London: Oliver and Boyd, 1939.

The Prose Works of Fulke Greville, Lord Brooke. Ed. John Gouws. Oxford: Clarendon Press, 1986.

The Remains being Poems of Monarchy and Religion. Ed. G.A. Wilkes. London: Oxford University Press, 1965.

The Remains of Sir Fulk Grevill Lord Brooke: Being Poems of Monarchy and Religion. London: Henry Herringman, 1670.

Sir Fulke Greville's Life of Sir Philip Sidney etc. 1652. Introduction by Nowell Smith. Oxford: Clarendon Press, 1907.

Studies of Fulke Greville, Lord Brooke

Craft, William. *Labyrinth of Desire: Invention and Culture in the Work of Sir Philip Sidney*. Newark: University of Delaware Press, 1994.

Croll, Morris W. *The Works of Fulke Greville, a Thesis*. Philadelphia: J.B. Lippincott, 1903.

Hager, Alan. *Dazzling Images: The Masks of Sir Philip Sidney*. Newark: University of Delaware Press, 1991.

Miscellaneous Prose of Sir Philip Sidney. Ed. Katherine Duncan-Jones and Jan van Dorsten. Oxford: Clarendon Press, 1973.

The Old Arcadia, Ed. Katherine Duncan-Jones. New York: Oxford University Press, 1985.

Peterson, Douglas L. *The English Lyric from Wyatt to Donne: A History of the Plain and Eloquent Styles*. Princeton: Princeton University Press, 1967.

Rebholz, Ronald A. *The Life of Fulke Greville, First Lord Brooke*. Oxford: Clarendon Press, 1971.

Rees, Joan. *Fulke Greville, Lord Brooke, 1554–1628: A Critical Biography*. London: Routledge & Kegan Paul, 1971.

Spenser, Edmund. *The Faerie Queene*. Ed. J.C. Smith. Oxford: Clarendon Press, 1909.

Waswo, Richard. *The Fatal Mirror: Themes & Techniques in the Poetry of Fulke Greville*. Charlottesville: University Press of Virginia, 1972.

Weiner, Andrew D. *Sir Philip Sidney and the Poetics of Protestantism*. Minneapolis: University of Minnesota Press, 1978.

Winters, Yvor. "Aspects of the Short Poem in the English Renaissance." In *Forms of Discovery: Critical and Historical Essays on the Forms of the Short Poem in English*. [Denver, CO]: Alan Swallow, 1967.

❧ *William Harvey*
(1578–1657)

GLENN SUCICH

BIOGRAPHY

William Harvey, considered by many the father of modern physiology, was born in Kent, England, on April 1, 1578. The oldest of nine children born to Thomas Harvey and Joan Hawke, William received his early education from itinerant schoolmasters in his native town of Folkestone. In 1588, he entered King's School, Canterbury, where he followed a religious and classical curriculum that, ironically, excluded the natural sciences. Between 1593 and 1599, Harvey attended Gonville and Caius College, Cambridge, where he received the prestigious William Parker scholarship, established by the Archbishop of Canterbury himself. Although a serious illness— Geoffrey Keynes suggests it was malaria—caused Harvey's absence from the university for much of 1598–1599, he left Cambridge after taking his B.A. in 1599.

In 1600, he entered the medical school at the University of Padua, long renowned for its distinguished faculty. John Caius, Andreas Vesalius, and Girolamo Fabrizi d'Acquapendente (Fabricius) had all been educated and/or taught at the university. This rich tradition, combined with the university's cosmopolitan student body and liberal reputation, made Padua a natural choice for the aspiring doctor and English Protestant Harvey. He immediately distinguished himself as a student and was elected by his peers as *consiliarius*, or representative of the executive body, of the English Nation. After taking his doctorate in 1602, Harvey returned to London, where in 1604 the College of Physicians granted him permission to practice medicine in the city. That same year, Harvey married Elizabeth Browne, the daughter of Dr. Lancelot Browne, royal physician to both Queen Elizabeth and King James. William and his wife Elizabeth never had children, but in an episode that typifies Harvey's avid curiosity and experimental approach, he once dissected his wife's beloved pet, "an excellent, and a well instructed Parrat." Inside the bird's womb Harvey found "an egge almost completed," a discovery that surprised the young doctor because, as he later confessed, "I always thought him to be a Cock-parrat, by his notable excellence in singing and talking." This experience, recorded in *De generatione animalium*, was one of many that fueled Harvey's desire to explain the genesis and development of living creatures.

In 1607, after an unsuccessful attempt to become physician to the Tower of London, Harvey was admitted as a fellow to the Royal College of Physicians. Two years later, he became Physician at St. Bartholomew's Hospital, a post he held for more than thirty years before **Cromwell**'s government forced him to surrender his position. In 1618, he was appointed Physician Extraordinary to James, attending the King on his deathbed, and later to Charles, whom Harvey accompanied at the King's coronation in Scotland (1633) and during much of the English Civil War. In exchange for his loyal service and friendship, Charles granted Harvey access to all the deer in the royal parks, a gift that contributed significantly to Harvey's discovery of the circulation of the blood.

Following the execution of Charles in 1649, both Harvey's activities and his enthusiasm for medical research waned. In his later years, Harvey suffered from severe gout and kidney stones. **John Aubrey** reports that Harvey "had, towards his latter end, a preparation of Opium and I know not what, which he kept in his study to take, if occasion could serve, to putt him out of his paine." After a long and distinguished career, England's most eminent—and controversial—physician died on June 3, 1657. He was eighty years old.

MAJOR WORKS AND THEMES

Harvey's greatest achievement is *Exercitatio anatomica de motu cordis et sanguinis in amimalibus* (*An Anatomical Exercise Concerning the Motion of the Heart and Blood in Animals*). Published in 1628, *De motu cordis*, as it is commonly called, represents the culmination of research and experiments Harvey began while a lecturer at the Royal College of Physicians. Among the many seminal demonstrations offered in *De motu cordis*, Harvey proved definitively what the ancient anatomist Galen suggested more than a millennium earlier—namely, that the blood does not contain its own air—as well as the fact that the pumping of the heart, not the contraction and relaxation of the veins themselves, impels the blood through the body. He confirmed that blood does not pass through the septum, the muscular wall separating the right and left ventricles of the heart, and explicated how each of the four cardiac valves— tricuspid, pulmonic, mitral, and aortic—perform in regulating the flow of blood to and from the heart. These proofs were all part of Harvey's larger effort to demonstrate how the blood, as he himself put it, "doth go round, is returned, thrust forward, and comes back from the heart into the extremities, and from thence into the heart again, and so makes as it were a circular motion."

Harvey's other major works include *Exercitatio anatomica de circulatione sanguinis* (1649) and *Exercitationes de generatione animalium* or *Anatomical Exertations Concerning the Generation of Animals* (1651). The latter begins with a survey of Aristotle's and Galen's theories of generation, followed by seventy-two exercises that discuss, among other things, the reproductive organs of various animals, the development of the chick in the hen's egg, and the theory of spontaneous generation. Like his other works, *De generatione animalium* is run through with an implicit faith in providential design. In an interview with his friend and colleague George Ent, Harvey explained that "the examination of the bodies of animals has always been my delight; and I have thought that we might thence not only obtain an insight into the lighter mysteries of nature, but there perceive a kind of image or reflex of the omnipotent Creator himself." For Harvey, the best way to this insight was not through passive deference to ancient authority but through active observation and experimentation. The poet **Abraham Cowley** perhaps said it best when, in "On the Death of Mr. William Harvey," he wrote:

> Thus Harvey sought for Truth in Truth's own book,
> The Creatures, which by God himself was writ;
> And wisely thought 'twas fit,
> Not to read Comments only upon it,
> But on the th' Original itself to look.

CRITICAL RECEPTION

Thomas Hobbes, who along with Sir **Francis Bacon** was one of Harvey's most famous patients, asserted with some accuracy that Harvey was "the only man, perhaps, that ever lived to see his own doctrine established in his life-time." *De motu cordis* and *De generatione animalium* were, in fact, instantly celebrated by scientists, poets, and philosophers alike. Physicians such as Francis Glisson, Walter Charleton, and **Robert Boyle** all drew inspiration from Harvey's achievement; Cowley was joined by **John Dryden**, Henry More, and others in singing Harvey's praises in verse; and **John Locke** marked his copy of *De generatione animalium* with a paraph he reserved for works he esteemed. In 1668, Joseph Glanvill, writing on behalf of the Royal Society, expressed the sentiment of many when he wrote that "of all the modern Discoveries, Wit and Industry have made in the Oeconomy of humane Nature, the Noblest is that of the Circulation of the Blood, which was the invention of our deservedly-famous Harvey."

Of course, Harvey's works were not universally accepted. The French anatomist Jean Riolan and the English physician James Primrose were among the many distinguished scientists who rejected Harvey's theories. What these detractors ultimately objected to, however, was not the validity of Harvey's hypotheses—his proofs were difficult to refute—but rather the serious challenge Harvey posed to the time-honored ideas of Galen, Aristotle, and other ancient authorities. Unfortunately, many of Harvey's works and lecture notes were either seized by parliamentary forces during the Civil War or destroyed in the Great Fire of 1666. But Harvey's legacy survives. His commitment to rigorous experimentation and ocular proof, and the discoveries to which that commitment led, forever changed the field of medicine, both in theory and in practice.

BIBLIOGRAPHY

Works by William Harvey

The Anatomical Exercises: De Motu Cordis *and* De Circulatione Sanguinis *in English Translation*. Ed. Geoffrey Keynes. New York: Dover, 1995.

Disputations Touching the Generation of Animals. Trans. and ed. Gweneth Whitteridge. Oxford: Blackwell Scientific Publications, 1981.

Studies of William Harvey

Bylebyl, Jerome J., ed. *William Harvey and His Age: The Professional and Social Context of the Discovery of the Blood*. Baltimore: Johns Hopkins University Press, 1979.

French, Roger. *William Harvey's Natural Philosophy*. Cambridge: Cambridge University Press, 1994.

Fuchs, Thomas. *The Mechanization of the Heart: Harvey and Descartes*. Trans. Marjorie Grene. Rochester: University of Rochester Press, 2001.

Keynes, Geoffrey. *The Life of William Harvey*. Oxford: Clarendon Press, 1966.

McMullen, Emerson Thomas. *William Harvey and the Use of Purpose in the Scientific Revolution: Cosmos by Chance or Universe by Design?* New York: University Press of America, 1998.

Pagel, Walter. *New Light on William Harvey*. Basel: Karger, 1976.

Whitteridge, Gweneth. *William Harvey and the Circulation of the Blood*. New York: American Elsevier, 1971.

🙋 *George Herbert*
(1593–1633)

GREG KNEIDEL

BIOGRAPHY

George Herbert was born into a "generous, noble, and ancient" Welsh family, but as a younger brother in a minor branch, he spent most of his life as an academic in search of better employment (his family's wealth would pass down primarily through his eldest brother, the poet and philosopher Edward, Lord Cherbury). He was educated first at Westminster—perhaps learning Greek under **Lancelot Andrewes**, who later praised Herbert's facility in that language—and at Christ College, Cambridge. He remained affiliated with Cambridge in various capacities after taking his degrees (B.A. in 1613; M.A. in 1616) and in 1620 was appointed Public Orator, a position that involved composing official letters and delivering ceremonial orations, all in Latin. Although Cambridge would remain his primary intellectual milieu, Herbert also enjoyed the literary society that congregated around his mother, Magdalen Herbert, and his stepfather, Sir John Danvers. This society included **John Donne**, who exchanged verses with Herbert and preached his mother's funeral sermon, and **Francis Bacon**, who praised his "Divinitie" and "Poesie" and for whom Herbert seems to have collected a volume of commemorative verse.

The key biographical question for Herbert scholars is, When did Herbert abandon his hopes of secular promotion and undertake a career as a churchman? In his early biography, Izaak Walton states that the death of James I in 1625 dashed Herbert's "Court-hopes." But his sickly constitution and bookish disposition seem to have dissuaded him from pursuing the same career—gentleman soldier *cum* foreign diplomat—as his brothers. Moreover, as early as 1618 Herbert wrote to his stepfather that he was "setting foot into Divinity" (though holy orders and political power were not mutually exclusive). Herbert was ordained deacon in 1624 and priest with cure of souls in 1630; earlier in the same year he had taken a living in the country parish of Bemerton near Salisbury. It is usually assumed that a sophisticate like Herbert would have found the rural inhabitants of his parish distastefully uncultured, and thus that he was either exceptionally pious for deigning to live there or exceptionally unhappy about being forced to. At any rate, his tenure at Bemerton was short; Herbert died on March 1, 1633.

MAJOR WORKS AND THEMES

Around 1610 Herbert wrote to his mother that he would spurn "the vanity of those many love-poems, that are daily writ and consecrated to Venus" and that his "poor abilities in poetry, shall be all, and ever consecrated to God's glory." The only writing Herbert published during his life was a collection of Latin and Greek poems commemorating the death of his mother, *Memoriae Matris Sacrum* (1627), a few other encomiastic poems, and two of three extant Latin orations. Three other groups of Latin religious poems (*Musae responoriae*, *Passio discerpta*, *Lucus*), probably composed in the early 1620s, went unpublished until the 17th century and are generally more Baroque in style and theme than his vernacular verse. All his English works were printed posthumously and by 1652: a translation of Alvise (Luigi) Cornaro's 1558 *Treatise of Temperance and Sobriety* (1634); *Briefe Notes* on Juán de Valdés's 1550 *The Hundred and Ten Considerations* (1638); a compellation of adages first published as *Outlandish Proverbs* (1640); and the pastoral manual *A Priest to the Temple: Or, The Country Parson* (1652).

Herbert's literary legacy rests almost entirely on the English poems in *The Temple* (1633), which was published just after his death (a handful of other lyrics omitted from *The Temple*, as well as early drafts of poems included in it, survive in the so-called Bodleian and Williams manuscripts). *The Temple* is divided into three parts: (1) "The Church-Porch," a long didactic poem in heroic sestets on Christian ethics and social conduct emphasizing decorum and self-control (e.g., "Laugh not too much; the wittie man laughs least"; (2) "The Church," a collection of some 160 lyric poems (depending on how one counts what seem to be double poems); and (3) "The Church Militant," a survey in brisk couplets of the migration of the true church, from East to West and from Old Testament times to Herbert's own day when it stood on "tip-toe," "Readie to passe to the American strand" (lines that ran afoul of censors). The purpose, if there is one, of this tripartite structure remains unclear: some critics find in it the architectural design of a Hebrew temple, others a scriptural sequence moving from Old Testament to New Testament to Book of Revelations; others a parallel spiritual sequence moving from the Law to Grace to prophecy.

The lyrics in the largest part of *The Temple*, "The Church," resist the ready description of "The Church-Porch" and "The Church Militant" because of their enormous formal and generic variety. Herbert skillfully adapts poetic forms typically associated with secular poetry (dramatic monologue, sonnet, dialogue, ballad, epigram, and anagram) to religious subjects. He also invented new forms, ranging from the conspicuously shaped (the pattern poems "The Altar" and "Easter Wings") to the seemingly shapeless (such as "The Collar," written in something like modern *vers libre*) and including any number of arresting stanzaic forms ("Discipline" and "Love" [III], among many). The generic diversity of Herbert's lyrics—hymn, song, and prayer; poems of complaint, confession, petition, consolation, thanksgiving, and praise—is modeled on primarily Scripture, especially Psalms, but also incorporates elements from medieval and Reformation devotional literature as well as the religious emblem book.

Some of Herbert's lyrics fall easily into groups by title (e.g., five poems titled "Affliction") or by subject (e.g., poems on the Crucifixion, on the Eucharist, and on the limits of sacred poetics). But the two largest and loosest groups of lyrics concern what might be called the individual and the collective experience of belief. Because of the first of these two groups, Herbert's poems are described as devotional, intimate, or introspective. The heart is Herbert's topic, and his distinctive practice is to describe the heart's state in domestic or social scenes. Thus Herbert's God is by turn a friend, a parent, a host, and a king. Herbert's speakers often misunderstand, misapply, or simply resist a point of theology and are then corrected, gently or forcefully, comically or distressingly. Herbert's poems invoke and evoke a range of precisely conceived emotions—despair and assurance, confusion and understanding, anger and love—and the cumulative effect of reading "The Church" is to valorize all of them in the lived Christian life while ultimately subordinating them to service of the Lord. Herbert himself said that the poems in *The Temple* provide "a picture of the many spiritual conflicts that have passed betwixt God and my soul, before I could subject mine to the will of Jesus my master; in whose service I have now found perfect freedom."

If, however, Herbert's introspective lyrics move toward a mystical subjection of the human to the divine, paralleling or sometimes impeding this movement are the poems in the second main group, those concerned with the collective or public experience of belief. Thus, Herbert can write, "All Solomon's sea of brass and world of stone / Is not so dear to thee [God] as one good groan," but in other poems "stone" seems to trump "groan." Some of these poems give hints of autobiography, especially those on employment or vocation and on the nature of the priesthood. Others discuss and often vindicate sacramental piety and the liturgy, rituals, and visible structure of the established English Church, its *via media* between Roman Catholicism and radical Puritanism. A glance at some of Herbert's poems' titles—"Church-monuments," "Church-music," "The Church-floor," "The Windows," "The British Church," "Church-rents and Schisms"—shows that what were called the "externals" of religion preoccupied Herbert as much as the internal workings of the human heart and that order, decency, tradition, reverence, and beauty have a firm place in his religious vocabulary.

CRITICAL RECEPTION

If Donne founded a school and **Ben Jonson** headed a tribe, Herbert gathered a flock. In preface to the 1655 edition of *Silex Scintillans* (1st ed. 1650), **Henry Vaughan** would claim that Herbert's "holy life and verse gained many pious converts . . . and gave the first check to a most flourishing and admired *wit* [i.e., for secular love poetry] of his time." Within a decade of Herbert's death *The Temple* had gone through some six editions. In a show of reverence and marketing savvy, Christopher Harvey titled his collection of religious lyrics *The Synagogue . . . In imitation of Mr. George Herbert* (1640), and **Richard Crashaw** titled his collection *Steps to the Temple* (1646). Vaughan's *Silex Scintillans* and **Robert Herrick**'s *Noble Numbers* (1648) regularly rework Herbert's titles, imagery, wording, and themes. Herbert's initial readership ranged from Charles I, who is said to have read his copy of *The Temple* while imprisoned, to the Puritan nonconformist Richard Baxter, who lauded Herbert as a poet who "speaks to God like one that really believeth a God."

Already in 1655, however, Vaughan could complain that Herbert's "diverse" followers filled their pages with "lean conceptions," "productions of a common spirit," and "obvious ebullitions" of "light humour." Variations of these criticisms would, over the years, dog Herbert himself. His plain diction and quaint conceits compared unfavorably to Donne's and Crashaw's argumentative force and Baroque effects, even though Herbert can achieve metaphysical juxtapositions of even ordinary images (e.g., "My thoughts are all a case of knives"). When a taste for simple and unaffected poetry emerged in the 19th century, Herbert's fortunes improved. But the project of 20th-century Herbert criticism has been to reveal him to be a sophisticated poetic craftsman. Poetic forms that seemed common or just odd became innovative and complex; diction that seemed childish and ordinary became precise and even loaded; ideas, images, and themes that seemed clear and didactic became ironic and ambiguous.

Discovery of his poetic sophistication produced debates about Herbert's doctrinal beliefs that challenged the traditional portrait of "holy Mr. Herbert" as a saint of High Church Anglicanism. Noting his debt to medieval iconography and especially to the Ignatian and Salesian meditative practices, some critics argued for a more Catholic or continental Herbert. Other critics argued in response that these Catholic elements are frequently ironized and that Herbert's scripturalism, his emphasis on heartfelt emotion, and his attack on reason imply potentially radical Protestant beliefs. Still others argued that Herbert's piety, whatever its doctrinal foundation, cannot be understood apart from his courtly ambitions, aristocratic biases, and Royalist politics. Herbert's God is a king ("Nor let them punish me with losse of rime, / Who plainly say, *My God, My King*") who sometimes seems to act very much like a Stuart King, torturing and discreetly manipulating his beloved subjects. It is left for critics to speculate on if and why these jarring elements cohere in Herbert's literary corpus. Did Herbert's beliefs change over the dozen or so years during which he composed *The Temple*? Would these tensions have worked themselves out if Herbert had lived through the cultural upheaval of the English Civil War? Or do they reveal the inevitable ideological inconsistencies of early modern Christianity?

BIBLIOGRAPHY

Works by George Herbert

The Latin Poetry of George Herbert: A Bilingual Edition. Trans. Mark R. McCloskey and Paul R. Murphy. Athens: Ohio University Press, 1965.

The Temple: A Diplomatic Edition of the Bodleian Manuscript (Tanner 307). Ed. Mario Di Cesare. Binghamton, NY: Medieval & Renaissance Texts & Studies, 1995.

The Williams Manuscript of George Herbert's Poems. Ed. Amy Charles. Delmar, NY: Scholars' Facsimiles & Reprints, 1977.

The Works of George Herbert. Ed. F.E. Hutchinson. 1941. Rev. ed., Oxford: Clarendon Press, 1945.

Studies of George Herbert

Charles, Amy. *A Life of George Herbert*. Ithaca, NY: Cornell University Press, 1977.

Fish, Stanley Eugene. *The Living Temple: George Herbert and Catechizing*. Berkeley: University of California Press, 1978.

Lewalski, Barbara. *Protestant Poetics and the Seventeenth-Century Religious Lyric*. Princeton: Princeton University Press, 1979.

Martz, Louis. *The Poetry of Meditation*. New Haven, CT: Yale University Press, 1954.

Ray, Robert H., comp. and ed. "The Herbert Allusion Book: Allusions to George Herbert in the Seventeenth Century." *Studies in Philology* 83.4 (Fall 1986).

Roberts, John R., ed. *Essential Articles for the Study of George Herbert's Poetry*. Hamden, CT: Archon Books, 1979.

Schoenfeldt, Michael. *Prayer and Power: George Herbert and Renaissance Courtship*. Chicago: University of Chicago Press, 1991.

Strier, Richard. *Love Known: Theology and Experience in George Herbert*. Chicago: University of Chicago Press, 1983.

Summers, Joseph. *George Herbert: His Religion and Art*. Cambridge: Harvard University Press, 1954.

Tuve, Rosamond. *A Reading of George Herbert*. Chicago: University of Chicago Press, 1952.

Vendler, Helen. *The Poetry of George Herbert*. Cambridge: Harvard University Press, 1975.

❧ *Robert Herrick*
(1591–1674)

REGINA MASIELLO

BIOGRAPHY

Baptized in London on August 24, 1591, Robert Herrick was the seventh child of London goldsmith Nicholas Herrick. When Herrick was only fourteen months old, his father fell from a fourth floor window in an apparent suicide. According to English law, a suicide's property was forfeit to the Crown, and for a month after Nicholas Herrick's death, the Privy Council examined the circumstances of his fall. The Herricks were well connected in London, however, and eventually the Almoner decided to free Nicholas Herrick's estate to his family. Nicholas Herrick's estate (a hefty £5,000) was split between his seven children and his widow. Herrick's mother abdicated her portion of the money (she apparently had money from her own family), and the children shared the inheritance under the watchful eyes of executors.

At age sixteen, Herrick was apprenticed to his uncle Sir William Herrick (one of the men responsible for managing the Herrick children's money). Like Herrick's father, Sir William Herrick was also a goldsmith in London's Cheapside. But unlike so many of his family members, Robert Herrick did not take to the trade, and after only six years he left his ten-year apprenticeship to go to school instead. A good deal older than his classmates, Herrick matriculated at St. John's College, Cambridge, at age twenty-two. Although he entered St. John's College as a wealthy student, he soon found that living at Cambridge was quite costly. He often wrote to his uncle asking for money but eventually tired of begging for funds (his uncle was determined to force the college student to live on a budget). He transferred from the costly St. John's College to the more economic Trinity Hall by 1617.

In 1617 Herrick graduated from Trinity Hall with a B.A. and received his master's three years later. It is unknown when Herrick first met **Ben Jonson**, but after leaving Trinity Hall Herrick certainly made his acquaintance and attended several drinking parties at which Jonson was present. Herrick's relationship with Jonson left a lasting impression on him, an impression best seen in poems like "Upon Master Ben. Johnson.

Epigram," "Another," "His Prayer to Ben. Johnson," "Upon Ben. Johnson," and "An Ode for him." In 1623 Herrick took orders as a deacon and priest in the Anglican Church, and in 1627 he served as a chaplain in the first Duke of Buckingham's disastrous crusade to the Isle of Rhé.

In 1629 Herrick accepted a nomination to the vicarage of Dean Prior in Devonshire (far southwest of London). He was installed in rural Devonshire on October 29, 1630, where he served as Dean Prior for a total of thirty-one years. Herrick's stay in Devonshire did not continue without interruption. In 1647, the Anglican and Royalist Herrick, along with 142 other clergymen, was expelled from Devonshire by a largely Puritan and Parliamentarian populace. Herrick headed back to London, where in 1648 he personally supervised the publication of his only book *Hesperides: Or, The Works Both Humane and Divine of Robert Herrick Esq.*, a volume composed of over 1,400 separate poems. In 1660, the year of Charles II's Restoration to the English throne, Herrick personally petitioned to return to his priorship in Devonshire. His petition was granted, and Herrick lived, unmarried, for another fourteen years in his modest arrangements in Devonshire until his death in 1674.

MAJOR WORKS AND THEMES

Herrick's sprawling *Hesperides: Or, The Works Both Humane and Divine of Robert Herrick Esq.*, consists of 1,130 separate poems. It contains an astounding 1,402 poems if his collection of religious pieces, *His Noble Numbers*, appended to the end of *Hesperides* and printed along with it in 1648, is included in such an inventory. Given the sheer number of poems, it is no surprise that its subject matter is highly varied, ranging from pastoral to occasional poems. Herrick's "The Argument of the book" offers perhaps the best catalog of the book's contents:

> I Sing of *Brooks*, of *Blossomes*, *Birds*, and *Bowers*:
> Of *April*, *May*, of *June*, and *July*-Flowers.
> I sing of *May-poles*, *Hock-carts*, *Wassails*, *Wakes*,
> Of *Bride-grooms*, *Brides*, and their *Bridall-cakes*.
> I write of *Youth*, of *Love*, and have Accesse
> By these, to sing of cleanly-*Wantonnesse*. (lines 1–6)

But while his catalog seems exhaustive, in reality "Flowers," "Birds," and "Love" make up only a portion of the poems. Some of his poems are scatological, nearly grotesque pieces, like the fifth poem of the collection, "Another." This four-line entry finds Herrick damning the reader who dares to use the pages of *Hesperides* as toilet paper, the buttocks being unflatteringly described as "that place, where swelling *Piles* do breed" (line 2). Likewise, Herrick's catalog in "The Argument of his book" does not cover the many seduction poems in the collection, aimed at many of Herrick's (mostly fictive) mistresses. Julia makes the most appearances in *Hesperides*, but Corinna, Perilla, Anthea, and Lucia (among others) make numerous appearances as well.

Whether the poems in *Hesperides* are about flowers or not, they are all undoubtedly the property of Robert Herrick. Herrick's involvement in collecting and publishing his own work was unusual for a day invested in often anonymous manuscript circulation and riddled with taboos about men (not to mention women) who dared to publish their work. But Herrick's devotion to his publication (a devotion rivaled only by Herrick's mentor Ben Jonson, who also published a collection of his works during his lifetime) manifests itself in the many poems bearing his imprint of ownership. Indeed, the reader encounters "The Argument of *his* book," a poem "To *his* Muse," several poems "To *his* Booke," and even a poem directing the reader how the poet "would have *his* verses read" (emphases mine). These titles, paired with an engraving of Herrick done by William Marshall, mark the book as unmistakably authored by Robert Herrick.

But Herrick's claim to authorship is never exclusive; indeed, the book also belongs to Charles I, the ill-fated monarch, beheaded just after the book's publication. The prefatory poem is "to the Most Illustrious and Most Hopefull Prince, Charles, Prince of Wales," and in it, Herrick claims that Charles is his "Works *Creator*, and alone / The *Flame* of it, and the *Expansion*" (lines 3–4). Poems dedicated to the monarch and his Queen, Henrietta Maria, appear throughout the collection, each set off with a larger font and often written in capitalized letters. And the title of the book itself also acts as a tribute to the King. On the day of Charles's birth, the evening star Hesperus appeared, leading his subjects and poets forever to associate the King with its strange appearance. *Hesperides* is then another play on the appearance of what came to be known as the King's star.

Herrick's dedication to the King often leads critics—notably Leah S. Marcus—to discuss his work in terms of his Royalist sympathies. Thus, his poems about English festivals and country pastimes, especially "Corinna's going a Maying," are often read as protests of the Puritan desire to repress such activities. Indeed, in 1618 James I published his *Book of Sports*, encouraging the public to take part in English customs, suggesting that it was their duty as loyal subjects to do so. Charles I reissued his father's book in 1633, investing the participation in festivities with Royalist loyalty during a time of political strife. When Herrick instructs one of his mistresses, Corinna, to get out of bed "while we are in our prime" because "Our life is short," he is then not merely the cavalier poet attempting to seduce the girl but the staunch Royalist following royal decree (lines 57–61). Due to political readings of this kind, Herrick's poems have shed some of their assumed "triviality" (his poems about boils and flowers often led readers to the conclusion that Herrick's poetry was light stuff, never to be taken seriously) and are finally being understood not as poems by a deacon separated from England's political conflict by country life but as poems by a writer enmeshed in his country's affairs.

To approach Herrick's book with an eye only for its political fervor would be as foolhardy as reading it only for its lightheartedness. Indeed, Herrick's book is both of these things at times and more, for it is truly a varied and often puzzling collection of work. Anthologized excerpts thereby do his massive work little justice, for by isolating individual poems, anthologies rob the pieces of their complicated context. Reading Herrick's *Hesperides* as a whole certainly seems best, and over the past forty years, critics have produced delightful readings of his poems that understand each as part of a larger project.

CRITICAL RECEPTION

While some critics maintain that Robert Herrick was as well known to 17th-century readers as **Carew** and **Marvell**, other critics insist that Herrick was virtually unheard of. This disagreement makes any estimate of Herrick's 17th-century popularity inherently speculative. Before the publication of his book, several of his poems certainly circulated in manuscript, and Henry Lawes had set a few of his poems to music for the King. But, unlike other highly celebrated poets of the day, Herrick was already thirty-four by the time he received his first printed compliment in Richard James's *The Muses Dirge*, a volume published in honor of King James's death. The compliment places Herrick in a category with Ben Jonson, the premier poet and playwright of the day, a categorization that certainly argues that Herrick had earned favor in some quarters. Yet despite this bit of praise, Herrick's *Hesperides* apparently did not sell well in 1648, for the book did not appear in a second edition until 175 years later. While it is possible that the first printing of Herrick's book was unusually large (making a second edition unnecessary), it is perhaps more possible that a public battered by a bitter civil war had no appetite for poetry. Yet other books of poetry sold edition after edition despite the turbulent times, and so the debate over Herrick's reputation rages on.

What can be said with certainty is that Herrick's poems were often anthologized after *Hesperides* appeared but that anthologies just as often failed to attribute the poems to Herrick or shamelessly edited (and even rewrote) his poems without Herrick's input. In 1675 Edward Philips, **John Milton**'s nephew, published his survey of English poets and placed Herrick in a category with the little-known poet Robert Heath. In the 1680s, William Winstanley confirmed this classification of Herrick as an obscure author by again comparing Herrick to Robert Heath in his *Lives of the English Poets*. After these dismissive classifications, Herrick disappeared entirely and was not mentioned either in censure or in praise.

In 1796 an English periodical, the *Gentleman's Magazine*, received a request for information about a group of obscure poets. Robert Herrick was among this group, and the magazine's editor (John Nichols) published a reply discussing Herrick. This mention sparked interest in the poet, and by 1810 the *Quarterly Review* (another periodical) declared that Herrick had been unjustly neglected. Editions of his poems started to appear, and by the end of the 19th century, Charles Algernon Swinburne was calling Herrick the "greatest English song writer" ever to live.

Despite 19th-century interest in Herrick, however, the early 20th century marked another period of relative neglect of his work. Once F.R. Leavis dubbed his talent "trivial," and T.S. Eliot proclaimed that he was the paradigmatic "minor poet," Herrick appeared in anthology only, his more than 1,400 poems being pared down to three or four pretty pastorals. But critics in the 1960s and 1970s have rediscovered Herrick all over again, and many have argued against the long tendency to read Herrick only in terms of his anthologized songs. Indeed, critics have pointed to the beauty of Herrick's sprawling work as a whole and have started to see Herrick not as a minor songwriter but as a major 17th-century figure, grappling with and echoing in his works the tensions and concerns that characterize the 17th century in literary history.

BIBLIOGRAPHY

Works by Robert Herrick

The Complete Poetry of Robert Herrick. Ed. J. Max Patrick. Garden City: New York University Press, 1963.
The Poems of Robert Herrick. Ed. L.C. Martin. London: Oxford University Press, 1965.

Studies of Robert Herrick

Chute, Marchette. *Two Gentle Men: The Lives of George Herbert and Robert Herrick*. New York: Dutton, 1959.

Coiro, Ann Baynes. *Robert Herrick's "Hesperides" and the Epigram Book Tradition*. Baltimore: Johns Hopkins University Press, 1988.

————, ed. *Robert Herrick: A Special Issue of the George Herbert Journal* 14.1–2 (1991): 1–77.

Corns, Thomas. *Uncloistered Virtue: English Political Literature 1640–1660*. Oxford: Clarendon Press, 1992.

Marcus, Leah S. *The Politics of Mirth: Jonson, Herrick, Milton, Marvell and the Defense of Old Holiday Pastimes*. Chicago: University of Chicago Press, 1986.

Rollin, Roger B., and J. Max Patrick, eds. *Trust to Good Verses: Herrick Tercentenary Essays*. Pittsburgh: University of Pittsburgh Press, 1977.

☙ *Thomas Hobbes*
(1588–1679)

LOUIS A. GEBHARD

BIOGRAPHY

Thomas Hobbes was born at Westport, near Malmesbury, about eighty-five miles west of London. His birth, as he later related (Rogow 17), took place just before the arrival of the Spanish Armada in the English Channel. He died about nine years before the "Glorious Revolution," the ousting of James II and the accession of William and Mary, and about eight years before Sir Isaac Newton published his epoch *Principia*, marking the culmination of the "Scientific Revolution." In his long life, Hobbes was acquainted with **Francis Bacon**, René Descartes, King Charles II, **Robert Boyle**, **William Harvey**, and Galileo Galilei. He was well aware of the scientific breakthroughs taking place in Europe, which included Kepler's discovery of the laws of planetary motion, Harvey's theory of the circulation of the blood, and Galileo's laws describing the behavior of falling bodies. In his lifetime, he witnessed the constitutional struggle in England, the civil wars in France (the "Fronde"), and the Thirty Years War in Germany, disturbing events for Hobbes. Fear, personal and immediate, seems to have contributed in an important way to Hobbes's political theory.

Hobbes was the second son of a dissolute Anglican clergyman who abandoned the family when Thomas was about fifteen. But Hobbes was able to receive an Oxford education through the generosity of an uncle, an education that he completed in 1608. A few months after graduation he entered the service of the Devonshire family. For most of the rest of his life he remained associated with the Devonshires, sometimes as a traveling companion and tutor, then later as secretary and adviser, living at Hardwick Hall or their residence in London. Hobbes's responsibilities began in 1608 as a tutor and traveling companion of William Cavendish, son of William Cavendish, first Baron of Hardwick, then first Earl of Devonshire (Rogow 20–57).

After about three years on the Continent (mostly France and Italy) the pair returned to England. Hobbes then found the opportunity for a brief time to become the companion and translator (from English to Latin) for Francis Bacon, philosopher and former Chancellor, living in exile (and disgrace) from the court. Despite the friendship that developed, Hobbes never accepted Bacon's belief in induction (Rogow 65–67). After the death of his pupil (the second Earl of Devonshire) in 1628, Hobbes took service for about two years with the Clifton family, again as a tutor and traveling companion, visiting France and Switzerland.

At about this time, Hobbes published his first significant political work (he had already published a travelogue, a description of the "Peak district" in Derbyshire), a translation of the Peloponnesian War of Thucydides, a work that was to be reissued again and again with commercial success. Probably around 1630 he discovered (or rediscovered) Euclid's *Elements*, a discovery, as his biographer **John Aubrey** later wrote, that "made him in love with geometry" (Rogow 100). The geometric approach, rationalistic, deductive, logical, would remain a major and crucial part of his method. But also, probably influenced by Galileo, Kepler, and Harvey, by 1636 he concluded that motion was a key concept, not only in physics but in anatomy and indeed in perception. But despite his respect for Galileo and the successes of Kepler and Harvey and his own work in optics and ballistics, he remained skeptical (as did many of the leading minds of the time) of the reliability of perception and experience. Exactly what influenced Hobbes's thinking has puzzled commentators. As Rogow puts it, "Throughout his life Hobbes tended to establish or try to establish the maximum possible distance between himself and those among the eminent thinkers of his time whom he most resembled and to whom he was philosophically closest" (Rogow 107).

In 1631, Hobbes returned to England and service with the Devonshires. He was also associated (probably through the Devonshires) with their cousin the Earl of Newcastle who was the center of a group of amateur mathematicians and scientists known as the "Wellbeck Academy," after the residence of the earl, Wellbeck. He was also in contact with the "Great Tew" circle, theologians and poets, who were friends and acquaintances of Lucius Cary, Viscount Falkland, whose house "Great Tew" gave its name to the group (Sorell, *Companion* 22–23).

In 1634, Hobbes returned to the Continent, traveling again, in France and Italy, meeting Galileo around 1636, but spending most of his time with Marin Mersenne (1588–1648), friar and resident at the Convent de l' Annonciade in Paris where his "cell was a kind of salon" (Rogow 141) for a group of savants that included Descartes, Gassendi, and others. Gassendi and Mersenne were both members of the Catholic clergy; Hobbes's deep regard for both of them remained separate from his strong antipathy to Roman Catholicism.

In 1636, he was back in England where the political conflict between the King and Parliament was moving toward violence. Hobbes, along with the Devonshires and the Newcastles, was a Royalist (Laird 4–5). Indeed, he actually assisted in the raising of a forced loan for the King back in 1626 (Skinner 216). In 1640, he wrote an introduction to his philosophy called *Elements of Law*, which included a defense of absolutism. In manuscript form it circulated among the Royalists in the parliamentary debates of 1640 (Sorell, *Companion* 26) and probably made Hobbes a marked man. Thoroughly frightened by the situation, he fled to Paris, taking up residence there for the next eleven years, during the Civil Wars in England that resulted in the defeat and execution of Charles I in 1649. In Paris he was joined by a number of Royalist emigrés, including the future King, Charles II (Rogow 122–126).

In Paris, Hobbes renewed his association with Mersenne and his circle, became a tutor for the future King, and worked out his philosophical system. As completed, it was divided into three parts: (1) *Corpus* or Body; (2) *Homo* or Man; (3) *Cives* or Citizenship. But Hobbes decided to publish his work on citizenship (*De Cive*) first because of the turmoil in England (Hobbes, *English Works* 2: xix). Appearing in 1642, it marked the beginning of his European reputation, a reputation that remained despite the notoriety that became associated with his name among the English (Sorell, *Companion* 29).

If *De Cive* "raised eyebrows" (Sorell, *Companion* 29), the publication of *Leviathan* in 1651 provoked outrage (Tuck ix). Hobbes, despite his good rapport with Charles, was banned from the court in exile. The outrage only deepened when Hobbes, after making his peace with the Puritan government, returned, or, indeed, fled, to England, arriving in February 1652 (Tuck xxxiv). I say "fled" because *Leviathan*, among other things, contained a lengthy scathing attack on Catholicism, an attack that provoked the French clergy into attempting to have Hobbes arrested (Sorell, *Companion* 33).

Cromwell's government left Hobbes to his own devices in the 1650s, but the decade for Hobbes was filled with personal and extended scholarly controversy. One of his antagonists was John Bramhall (1594–1663), Bishop of Londonderry, who skirmished with Hobbes over the existence of free will (which Hobbes denied), Hobbes insisting on predestination. Other antagonists included Seth Ward and John Wallis, Oxford professors who bested Hobbes, bringing him into ridicule and discredit, as Hobbes, among other things, attempted, literally, to square the circle. Hobbes, it is agreed, overestimated his own grasp of mathematics. He also became involved in a controversy with **Robert Boyle**, Hobbes denying the possibility of a vacuum. These controversies may have contributed to Hobbes's exclusion from the newly founded (1660) Royal Society, an exclusion that wounded him, as he considered himself a major scientist and philosopher. But it seems the controversies and his sometimes bizarre opinions were not so much a bar as the notoriety of his philosophy. By the 1660s he was widely, if inaccurately, considered an atheist, finding it difficult and sometimes impossible to publish in England (Sorell, *Companion* 33–37; Laird 18–20; Rogow 151–201).

The Restoration in 1660 created some difficulties for Hobbes, despite his good personal relationship with Charles II. For one thing the court and the Anglican establishment remained incensed at his ideas. The disasters of the mid-1660s (the Great Fire, the Plague, defeat at the hands of the Dutch) led to a measure of hysteria and seemed Divine retribution for what was thought to be rampant irreligion. Hobbes received some of the blame, and in 1666 Parliament began to consider trying him for heresy or atheism. He responded with a short tract denying the right of Parliament the right to do anything of the sort. Fortunately for Hobbes, the hysteria subsided, and he remained unmolested (Laird 18–22; Rogow 184–206).

Although he found it impossible to publish his philosophical work, he did write a translation of Homer. Until the effects of Parkinson's disease took hold, he remained active, physically and intellectually, eschewing alcohol and meat. Despite his dogmatism, he was usually genial and courteous (Wernham 566–567). In 1675, as his health began to fail, he left London to reside at Hardwick. Despite his royalism, he seems to have supported the attempt to exclude the Catholic James from the throne (Tuck xl). He died at Hardwick Hall in December 1679, leaving "a modest estate"

(Rogow 224), part of which went to a woman who may have been a natural daughter (Laird 28).

MAJOR WORKS AND THEMES

In 1629, Hobbes produced his first major work, as we have seen, a work consistent with his political theory, a translation of Thucydides's *Peloponnesian War* wherein he gives a Hobbesian emphasis in his translation on the evils of democracy, implying that the parliamentary opposition in England were democrats or demagogues (*English Works* [hereafter *EW*] VIII, ix). After completing a number of short pieces on ballistics and optics, he completed his first philosophic work, *Elements of Law*, in 1640. The work contains two essays, *Human Nature or the Elements of Policy* and *De Corpore Politico or the Elements of Law* (*EW* IV). Both essays, relatively short (together about 230 pages), introduced nearly all of Hobbes's thought. As mentioned, the work circulated in manuscript and then was published in 1650.

In his treatment of human nature, he discusses "sense" (perception). Although he accepts the empiricist's view of the origin of sensory data ("conceptions"), he casts doubt on its validity. Images, colors, and sounds are not there but are "apparitions into us of the motion, agitation or alteration which the object worketh on the brain" (*EW* IV, 4). Furthermore, "the remembrance of succession of one thing to another, that is, of what was antecedent, and what consequent, and what concomitant, is called an experiment; . . . To have had many experiments is what we call experience" (*EW* IV, ch. 3, para. 6). [But] "we cannot from experience conclude, that any thing is to be called just or unjust, true or false, or any proposition universal whatsoever" (*EW* IV, ch. 4, para. 11).

What, however, is the way to truth? For Hobbes, as has been mentioned, it was through reason, in particular, the method of geometry, or as he puts it in his dedication to the Earl of Newcastle in 1640, he sees two kinds of learning:

mathematical and *dogmatical* (his emphasis): the former is free from controversy and dispute, because it consisteth in comparing figure and motion only; in which things, *truth*, and the *interest of men* (his emphasis) oppose not each other: but in the other (dogmatical) there is nothing indisputable, because it compareth men and meddleth with their right and profit; in which, as oft as reason is against a man, so oft will a man be against reason. And from hence it cometh, that they who have written of justice and policy in general, do all invade each other and themselves with contradictions. To reduce this doctrine (dogmatical learning) to the rules and infallibility of reason, there is no way, but, first to put such principles down for a foundation, as passion, not mistrusting may not seek to displace; and afterwards to build thereon the truth of cases in the law of nature . . . by degrees, till the whole [*sic*] have been inexpugnable. (*EW* IV, xiii)

The essay on *Human Nature* goes beyond epistemology, treating also psychology (mostly emotions), ethics, and theology. God exists but for Hobbes is "incomprehensible" (*EW* IV, ch. 10, 259). We can have no conception of Him. Is Scripture the word of God? Is Jesus the Son of God? These are matters of "faith" (ch. 10, 64), not of "evidence."

In the second essay, *De Corpore Politico or the Elements of Law*, Hobbes introduces, in about 150 pages, his political theory. Men, he states, are essentially equal in strength and "wit." And they are individualistic, egocentric, and not the social animals as Aristotle believed. So they are possessed of "vain glory" and in competition with each other. In a natural state (without the state or government) they live in mutual fear, a fear of violent death because they dwell in a state of war. The only right a man has is the right of self-preservation. There is no right on the part of the individual to property; everyone owns everything. But men are possessed of reason, "no less than passion" (Part 1, ch. 2, para. 1), and so men divest themselves of the right to all things and to protect themselves they "covenant" with one another to create a "commonwealth" (the state or civil society).

Part 2 describes the three traditional forms of government: democracy; aristocracy; monarchy. The last is best. The monarchy that Hobbes wants is an absolute monarchy, although he doesn't use the word *absolute*. Hobbes does not want the monarch to be subject to the law; he should have the right to establish the religion he sees fit; he has the right (and should exercise it) to root out seditious opinion. Hobbes did believe in natural law (*Lex*, in his view), supposedly known to us through reason and essentially God's law and therefore revealed through Scripture. Natural law expresses itself in certain precepts and includes the injunction to forgive (Part 1, ch. 3, para. 9) and to forego revenge (Part 1, ch. 3, para. 10); to treat others with respect (Part 1, ch. 3, para. 11); to acknowledge others as equals (Part 1, ch. 4, para. 1); to practice fairness in the treatment of commerce and trade (Part 1, ch. 3, para. 12); to respect messengers of peace (Part 1, ch. 3, para. 13). Hobbes sums it up with the phrase, "*Quod tibi non vis, alteri ne feceris*" (Part 1, ch. 4, para. 9). However, given man's egoism, natural law in the state of nature is insufficient; the state (a "commonwealth") is necessary to keep everyone "in awe," as Hobbes says in *Leviathan* (Tuck edition 88).

In 1642, Hobbes published *De Cive* (*Latin Works*, II, hereafter *LW*), the third "section" of his philosophy. As mentioned, Hobbes decided to publish it first because of the civil strife in England (*EW* II: xix). Several Latin editions were printed, and an English version, *Philosophical Rudiments Concerning Government and Society*, appeared in 1650 (*EW* II). The work is a greatly expanded version (from 150 to 300 pages) of *Elements of Law*. The message is the same, but with much more attention to natural law (*leges naturae*), to the causes of dissolution of the commonwealth, and to religion. He includes the advice of St. Paul, urging obedience (*LW* II: Caput xi) and concludes with his own advice to have faith and practice obedience (to the sovereign power) in order to enter the Kingdom of Heaven (*LW* II: Caput xvii).

Hobbes's masterpiece *Leviathan* was published in London in English in 1651. It was followed by a Latin version (somewhat different) in Amsterdam in 1668, Hobbes regarding the Latin version as definitive (Laird 33). The title is drawn from the Book of Job, which mentions a mythical sea monster who rules the oceans (Rogow 163). *Leviathan* restates the themes of *De Cive* and of *Elements of Law* but in unforgettable prose. As he says in his description of the state of nature, "[I]t is manifest, that during the time men live without a common power to keep them all in awe, they are in a condition which is called Warre; a such a warre, as in of every man, against every man" (Tuck edition 88). So the result

is no place for industry; because the fruit thereof is uncertain; and consequently no Culture of the Earth, no Navigation, . . . no commodious Building; no Instruments of moving, and . . . ; no knowledge of the Face of the Earth, no account of Time, no Arts; no Letters; no Society; and which is worst of all, continual feare; and danger of violent death; and the life of man, solitary, poore, nasty, brutish and short. (Tuck edition 89)

Did such conditions ever exist? Generally not, thought Hobbes (Tuck edition 89), but in his own time, he thought they existed in America. *Leviathan* is longer than *De Cive*, some 490 pages in a modern edition, and includes a lengthy final section (about a third of the work), the famous attack on Catholicism. *Leviathan* also criticizes the English universities and certain preachers for bringing on the Civil War. There are also passages where he argues for more humane, more rational treatment of criminals (240) and even defends the right of the destitute to steal food, even by force (208). But he also believes that punishment, including capital punishment, sometimes with "torment," is a deterrent to crime (217). The last part, "Review and Conclusion," contains a passage suggesting submission to the Puritan regime in England.

In 1654, Hobbes's essay *On Liberty and Necessity* (*EW* IV) appeared, marking the beginning of his controversy with Bishop Bramhall. It grew out of a discussion in Paris in 1645 or 1646 on the issue of free will versus predestination. Hobbes, invited to set down his views, did so, but with the understanding that they not be published. Somehow his statements fell into the hands of one of his admirers, one John Davys, who, without the permission of either man, not only published them but added an introduction twitting the English divines, calling them "black cats" and "ignorant tinkers" (*EW* IV: 235). As for Hobbes, he not only denied free will but used the occasion to restate his view of God, all of whose actions are "justified" because of his "irresistible power" (*EW* IV: 250).

In 1655, in the midst of his quarrel with Bishop Bramhall, Hobbes finally completed the first "section" of his trilogy titled *Elementorum Philosophiae. Sectio Prima: De Corpore* (*LW* I). The first part is devoted to logic and includes a discussion of the syllogism. The second deals with such basic concepts as time, place, body, accident (in the Aristotelian sense), cause, effect, potentiality, actuality. There is also a discussion of lines, angles, curves, and figures. The third deals with motion, magnitude, then reflection and refraction. The fourth part, *Physica, sive de naturae phenomenis*, returns to "sense" along with light, heat, color, a bit of astronomy (and astrology), and some meteorology.

About two years later Hobbes published the second "section" of his philosophy, *De Homine sive Elementorum Philosophiae Sectio secunda* (*LW* II). The work, relatively short, about 130 pages, represents a revision of the first portion of *Elements of Law* of 1640 and remained untranslated into English until the 20th century. After commenting briefly in the first chapter on human physiology, he launches into a discussion of perception, largely vision. Chapters three through nine deal with optics, followed by a brief statement on science (*sciencia*). (He believes that it is made up of theorems and general propositions and includes the study of politics and ethics.) He then proceeds, after enumerating a whole gamut of emotions, to discuss religion and ethics.

Hobbes's only major historical work, *Behemoth or the Epitome of the Civil Wars of England* (1640–1660) (*EW* VI), is pretty much a polemic against the parliamentarians and their allies, the city of London, and certain ministers who seduced the people, who were "ignorant of their duty." But he also blames the "papists," despite the fact that most Catholics supported the King.

Notorious in the mid-1660s and faced with a parliamentary inquiry, Hobbes published a short article in self-defense titled *An Historical Narration Concerning Heresy and the Punishment Thereof* (*EW* IV: 383–408), a deft and readable resume of the issue from Hellenistic times to 16th-century England. Hobbes argues cogently that he could not be charged with heresy because there was no longer any legal statement as to what it was. He ends with a rueful comment on how men seem all too eager to crucify someone, forgetting St. Paul's advice to be gentle to all men.

In 1677, Hobbes produced a translation of the *Iliad* and the *Odyssey* (*EW* X), apparently for the fun of it. As he writes in the introduction: "Because I had nothing to do. Why publish it? Because I thought it might take off my adversaries from showing their folly upon my serious writings, and set them upon my verses to show their wisdom."

CRITICAL RECEPTION

Hobbes has been the subject of a wide range of judgments and interpretations. In his own time he enjoyed great respect on the Continent, but in England he was attacked by a number of prominent authors (Bowle), reviled as an atheist, and ridiculed for his gaffes in mathematics. In the 18th century he was eclipsed by **Locke**, despite the fact that on the Continent, at least, it was an age of absolutism and deism. But he began to have an impact in the 19th century when "his ideas were incorporated in the radicalism of the Utilitarians and in John Austin's theory of sovereignty" (Sabine 457).

In the 20th century, Leo Strauss, writing in the 1930s, remarks, "His morality is the morality of the bourgeois world. Even his sharp criticism of the bourgeoisie has, at bottom, no other aim than to remind the bourgeoisie of the elementary condition of its existence" (Strauss 121). Similarly, C.B. MacPherson in the 1960s sees Hobbes's morality as essentially a bourgeois morality (MacPherson, "Bourgeois Man" 169–183).

What merit is there to Hobbes's thought? Not much, argues the Jesuit Frederick Copleston in his multivolume *History of Philosophy* (V: 51), concluding that his political philosophy is "one sided and inadequate." Bertrand Russell seems to agree, writing that Hobbes's philosophy has "grave defects," and thus he was "not a thinker of first rank" (546). Even a recent sympathetic biographer, Arnold A. Rogow, writing in the mid-1980s, admits his deficiencies, noting "[h]is impatience with detail work and his preference for generalization, his marked indifference to scientific methodology and experimentation, his confusion of inference and evidence and his tendency to treat hypotheses as facts" (101).

On the other side is Archibald Wernham, who, writing in the *Encyclopedia Brittanica* (XL: 564), rates him as "perhaps the greatest thinker of his nation." And then an earlier biographer, John Laird, writing in the early 1930s, calls him the father of British ethics, notes his work in optics, and calls him "a psychologist of genius" (v–vi). Despite the strictures mentioned above, Rogow still considers him "perhaps the greatest, certainly the most original, of the British philosophers." His originality, Rogow writes, is "in having political authority not in God's will or popular consent, but on sheer necessity" (Rogow 9).

George H. Sabine, onetime professor of philosophy at Cornell University, writing in the mid-1930s, also concedes that Hobbes never mastered mathematics or physics but notes that he did recognize the pervasiveness of the increased legal power of the state and the role of "self interest as the dominant motive in life." He goes on to say "that Hobbes made [these] the premises of his system and followed them through with relentless logic is the true measure of his philosophical insight and of his greatness as a thinker" (Sabine 457, 475).

Whatever his merit, however, "Hobbes remains permanently important, not least because his adoption of a vigorously minimal metaphysics (materialism) and ethics (a kind of egoism), and his impatience with theory that does not confront these truths squarely, make him the permanent model for skeptical and pragmatic philosophies" (Blackburn 176–177).

BIBLIOGRAPHY

Works by Thomas Hobbes

The Clarendon Edition of the Works of Thomas Hobbes. Ed. Howard Warrender et al. Oxford: Clarendon Press, 1983–.

Elements of Law. Ed. Ferdinand Tonnies. London, 1889.

The English Works of Thomas Hobbes of Malmesbury. Ed. William Molesworth. 11 vols. London: John Bohn, 1839–1845.

Leviathan. Ed. Richard Tuck. New York: Cambridge University Press, 1991.

Thomae Hobbes Malmesburiensis. Opera Philosophica Quae Latine Scripsit, Omnia In Unum Corpus Nunc Primum Collecta. Ed. Gulielmi Molesworth. 5 vols. London: John Bohn, 1845.

Thomas Hobbes: The Correspondence. Ed. Noel Malcolm. 2 vols. Oxford: Clarendon Press, 1984.

Studies of Thomas Hobbes

Archive de Philosophie. *Bulletin Hobbes*. Arsen, the Netherlands: Van Gorcum, 1988. (Appears biennially.)

Aubrey, John. *Brief Lives, Chiefly of Contemporaries, Set Down by John Aubrey Between the Years 1669 and 1696*. Ed. A. Clark. 2 vols. Oxford, 1898.

Blackburn, Simon. *The Oxford Dictionary of Philosophy*. New York: Oxford University Press, 1994.

Bowle, John. *Hobbes and His Critics: A Study in Seventeenth Century Constitutionalism*. New York: Barnes & Noble, 1951.

Brown, Keith C., ed. *Hobbes Studies*. Cambridge: Harvard University Press, 1965.

Chappell, Vere, ed. *Essays on Early Modern Philosophers: Thomas Hobbes*. New York: Garland Publishing, 1992.

Copleston, Frederick C. *A History of Philosophy*. Vol. 5. Westminster, MD: Newman Press, 1961.

Hinnant, C.H. *Thomas Hobbes: A Reference Guide*. Boston: G.K. Hall, 1980.

Laird, John. *Hobbes*. New York: Russell and Russell, 1934.

MacPherson, C.B. "Hobbes's Bourgeois Man." In *Hobbes Studies*, ed. Keith C. Brown. Cambridge: Harvard University Press, 1965. 169–183.

———. *The Political Theory of Possessive Individualism: Hobbes to Locke*. 1962. New York: Oxford University Press, 1985.

Rogers, G.A.J., and Alan Ryan, eds. *Perspectives on Thomas Hobbes*. Oxford: Clarendon Press, 1988.

Rogow, Arnold A. *Thomas Hobbes: Radical in the Service of Reaction*. New York: W.W. Norton, 1986.

Russell, Bertrand. *A History of Western Philosophy*. New York: Simon and Schuster, 1963.

Sabine, George H. *A History of Political Theory*. 1937. Rev. ed., New York: Henry Holt, 1951.

Sacksteder, William. *Hobbes Studies (1879–1979)*. Bowling Green, OH: Bowling Green State University, Philosophy Documentation Center, 1982.

Skinner, Quentin. *Reason and Rhetoric in the Philosophy of Hobbes*. New York: Cambridge University Press, 1996.

Sorell, Tom. *Hobbes*. London: Routledge, 1986.

———, ed. *The Cambridge Companion to Hobbes*. New York: Cambridge University Press, 1996.

Strauss, Leo. *The Political Philosophy of Thomas Hobbes: Its Basis and Its Genesis*. Trans. E.M. Sinclaire. 1936. Reprint, Chicago: University of Chicago Press, 1952.

Tuck, Richard. *Hobbes*. New York: Oxford University Press, 1989.

Warrender, Howard. *The Political Philosophy of Hobbes: His Theory of Obligation*. Oxford: Clarendon Press, 1957.

Wernham, Archibald G. "Hobbes." In *Encyclopedia Brittanica*. 1967. 11: 564–567.

❧ *Ben Jonson*
(1572/1573–1637)

RICHARD HARP

BIOGRAPHY

More is known about Ben Jonson than many other English Renaissance authors. There are a number of reasons for this. For one, Jonson was not shy in making autobiographical allusions in some of his poetry. He commemorated, for example, the death of his first daughter and his eldest son in touching epigrams, told of "my mountaine belly, and my rockie face" when he was forty-seven years old in "My Picture left in Scotland," and wrote numerous other epigrams and verse epistles to his friends and patrons indicating his admiration for their accomplishments or occasionally asking for or thanking them for relief of his financial distress. He also was brutal in castigating those whom he despised in his epigrams, although he did not name who they were, hoping that generic criticism would move many to reform. His candid and unguarded comments about some details of his life, along with his off-the-cuff judgments about men and books that he knew or read, were surreptitiously copied down by the Scot William Drummond during Jonson's visit to his home in 1619 and is a document of the greatest interest. We also know many of the books he liked because of the prefaces that he wrote for some of them and for the approximately 200 books that we know he owned, many of which contain his marginalia—Robert Evans's book on this subject provides much intriguing discussion of this. He kept a commonplace book (*Discoveries*) in which he made his own the judgments of others about arts and letters and where he also made occasional remarks about his contemporaries, such as **Shakespeare** ("I lov'd the man, and do honor his memory [on this side idolatry] as much as any"). Jonson was a man who lived fully, drank deeply from the muses' Pierian spring, and was at once the most magisterial and most controversial English writer of his time.

Jonson was born in 1572 or 1573, the son of a Scottish minister who died before he could see his new baby boy. Jonson later in effect acknowledged his Scottish roots by taking a walking tour to Scotland in 1619 and also there showed, perhaps, something of his paternal genealogy by telling his host Drummond that if he could ever preach a sermon before the King, he should not flatter. Indeed, he also said to Drummond that the adjective he liked best applied to him was "honest," a word encompassing in Jonson's case both candor and virtue. He was fortunate as a boy to be sent to the excellent Westminster school where the noted William Camden was master, who Jonson later memorialized in an epigram as he "to whom I owe / All that I am in arts, all that I know." He was made to learn the craft of bricklaying, the profession of the stepfather his mother had given him when he was quite young. Jonson did not care for this work, and probably in 1591 or 1592, he volunteered to fight in Flanders against the Spanish where he defeated an opponent in single combat—Jonson's pen and sword were both mighty.

Jonson married, perhaps in 1594, Anne Lewis, a woman that he told Drummond was a "shrew yet honest." By 1597 his theatrical career had begun, as there is a record that the theatrical manager Philip Henslowe then loaned him money. One of his first extant plays is *Every Man in His Humour*, acted in 1598, which created the "comedy of humors" so long associated with his name. He did this in the midst of some considerable personal turmoil. He had been imprisoned in 1597 for his partial authorship of a now lost play, *The Isle of Dogs*, judged to be politically subversive by governmental authority, and was again in jail in 1598, this time for having killed Gabriel Spencer, a fellow actor, in a duel. This was a capital offense, but Jonson pled "benefit of clergy" (i.e., he was able to recite a biblical verse in Latin) and escaped the gallows: his intellectual capacity was adjudged to make him of benefit to the kingdom, a law that in this case at least proved more farsighted than did many other laws of the time. Dramatically Jonson now turned to satire, composing *Cynthia's Revels* and *The Poetaster* (both 1601), which strongly criticized life at court and which also directed particular censure at fellow playwrights Thomas Dekker and John Marston, who had also attacked Jonson in their own work, provoking the so-called War of the Theaters.

After his foray into classical historical drama with *Sejanus* (1604), Jonson found his firmest dramatic footing with the completion of *Volpone* in 1606. Over the next eight years he was to write his almost universally acknowledged masterpieces which, in addition to *Volpone*, include *Epicoene* (1609), *The Alchemist* (1610), and *Bartholomew Fair* (1614). In all there are eighteen extant plays by Jonson (including the fragmentary but excellent *The Sad Shepherd*); those written after *Bartholomew Fair* have sometimes been referred to dismissively as his "dotages" (the phrase was originally **John Dryden**'s), but criticism of the past twenty years has found substantial worth in many parts of these works, especially in *The Devil Is an Ass* as well as, perhaps, in *The Staple of News* (1626) and *A Tale of a Tub* (1633). Those written after 1628 are all the more remarkable in that Jonson suffered a paralytic stroke in that year.

As befits a Renaissance man, though, Jonson by no means limited himself to work in one genre. Between 1603 and 1634 he wrote more than thirty-five masques and entertainments, short dramatic works that emphasized spectacle and scenery (and thus were the forerunner of modern lavish theatrical productions) as well as dialog and action and that were performed for courtly or aristocratic audiences, who frequently acted in them as well. He was also the first author to oversee the publication of a volume of his collected works, superintending the production of a folio volume in

1616. He also had more to say about literary criticism, in his *Discoveries*, than any Englishman of letters of his time except Sir Philip Sidney. Above all, he was one of the world's great lyric poets. He collected his poems under the titles of *Epigrams* (1616), which he called the "ripest of my studies," *The Forest* (1616), and *The Underwood* (1640–1641); this final volume was posthumously published by his literary executor Kenelm Digby after Jonson died in 1637.

MAJOR WORKS AND THEMES

In his "humor" plays Jonson created characters that were dominated by a particular "humor" or disposition, such as melancholy that caused them to act in an unwieldy or exaggerated manner. The plays were successful, but to his credit Jonson did not continue to repeat himself in this particular vein but soon turned to other dramatic forms. His courtly satires were not popular, perhaps because of the particularity of their criticism, but in *Volpone* he created a satire that carried universal import. Here a Venetian grandee and onetime actor with an insatiable appetite for money was both comic and reprehensible in his feverish pursuit of wealth. Thus he illustrated the medieval commonplace that evil was as naughty as it was ludicrous, and that at bottom the "devil is an ass"—a proverbial phrase Jonson was to use as the title of his later play in 1616.

Punishments for greed were harshly appointed in *Volpone*, but greater charity is shown to characters of equally great folly in other plays of Jonson's "great decade" (1606–1616) of dramatic work. Jonson excelled in showing a society nearly consumed with vice and silliness, in which charlatans and confidence tricksters are barely able to keep up with the demand of those gullible enough to believe that they can get something for nothing. The comic devil Pug in *The Devil Is an Ass* finds London so teeming with vice that he exclaims "why, Hell is / A grammar school to this." Targets of Jonson's acidic but always funny satire in the plays of this creative period included Puritan hypocrisy, henpecked husbands and men lusting after virtuous—or not-so-virtuous—women, the ability of an alchemical philosopher's stone to provide youth and wealth to the most heterogeneous of supplicants (*The Alchemist*—1610), fanatical desire for a quiet life (Morose in *Epicoene*), and a collection of characters in *Bartholomew Fair* (1614) whose names denote their character, such as "Littlewit," "Dame Purecraft," "Quarlous," "Wasp," "Grace Wellborn," and "Winwife," among others.

Jonson's later drama chose ever-new objects of satire, the success of such plays depending to a large degree on how universal those objects were and how genial was the author's tone. *The Staple of News* (1626) has particular modern relevance, as Jonson attacks the news industry for pandering to trivial and low tastes. He also showed in later life a surprising taste for fantastic reunions and romantic comedy, a quality he had criticized in the Shakespearean drama but that he found himself practicing in *The New Inn* (1629), showing there also an ability to draw a sympathetic female character, the lady's maid Prudence, who lives up to her name in believable ways. This romantic vein was continued compellingly in Jonson's final, unfinished play, *The Sad Shepherd*, an updating of the story of Robin Hood and Maid Marian.

In his poems Jonson showed remarkable range. As has been mentioned, he wrote well about children, and he also paid tribute to friends that was praise and not flattery. He could speak both feelingly and rationally about subjects such as politics and friendship, and he could of course write scathing satire in a few lines. Longer poems present moving depictions of the "good life," such as that lived by the Sidney family at their country estate of Penshurst, where inanimate, animate, and human nature live in generous interdependence reminiscent of the Creation recounted in Genesis. Shakespeare is praised in a famous tribute for being "not of an age but for all time," and women are frequently presented as models of virtue and intellectual capacity, counterbalancing what has been perceived (not altogether justly) as his slighting of women in his dramas.

Jonson was famous for gathering into his orbit a group of younger writers who composed the "Tribe of Ben." He made a set of "rules" for them and others to follow who cared to drink with him at the Apollo Room of the Devil and St. Dunstan Tavern. This urban sociability was as much a part of the cavalier "good life" as was retired country living, and Jonson sent one of his most famous epistles to "one that asked to be sealed of the Tribe of Ben." Here Jonson was explicit about the requirements of friendship and declared his own character to be one that dwelled "as in my Center, as I can, / Still looking to, and ever loving heaven." Jonson was a poet of society— remembering that this word derives from the Latin *socius*, which means "companion"—but this did not mean that he did not also have a regard for God (his few but quite moving religious poems testify as much). And his versatility as a poet is further evidenced by the fact that while not considered at all a love poet, his poem "To Celia," which begins, "Drink to me only with thine eyes," is one of the age's—and the world's—supreme love lyrics.

Jonson's masques made even more obvious than the plays his interest in symbolic characters, many of whom were drawn from mythology. Jonson's masques show in excellent fashion the Renaissance ability to combine classical and Christian themes and also to reflect at the same time current political realities concerning royalty and court. *Pleasure Reconciled to Virtue* (1618) is a relatively typical masque, which brings on stage first the glutton Comus, the antitype of the virtue of temperance embodied by the masque's hero Hercules. Comus celebrates his vice by roaring "Room, room! Make room for the bouncing belly" before being eventually routed by Hercules, whose virtue knows how to enjoy pleasure in moderation. The end of the masque is a dance in which the audience participates; it figures, in its maze, that is, in its intricate steps (the leader of the dance is Dedalus), the complexity of the action previously portrayed. Reconciling virtue with pleasure, as Horace's joining instruction and delight, might be considered Jonson's whole poetic enterprise.

CRITICAL RECEPTION

Jonson was extremely highly regarded in his own time and throughout the 17th century, although his individual dramas received varying degrees of popularity. Shakespeare acted in *Every Man in His Humour* in 1598, and the title page of its publication says that it was acted "sundry times." The play had staying power, too, as it, along with several others (including *Every Man Out of His Humour, Bartholomew Fair,* and *The Devil Is an Ass*) were "stock" plays in the revival of the English theater that took place after the Restoration of the English monarchy in 1660. *Volpone* was first acted at the Globe Theater in 1606, then at Oxford and Cambridge, and continued to be performed periodically in the decades thereafter. But there were flops; Jonson's most notorious failures were *The New Inn*, which played only once, and *Catiline*. The latter Roman tragedy was acted in 1611, the heart of Jonson's most creative period, but the audience did not like the lengthy oration by Cicero in the fourth act. This play did achieve, however, great popularity later in the 17th century. And through most of the time he was writing for the public stage, Jonson was also finding great acceptance at court in the masques he composed.

The year 1616 was in many ways the pinnacle of Jonson's acceptance by his public. Then he published the great folio edition of his *Works* (and he made history by considering his plays as part of his serious "*Works*") and also received the unofficial poet laureateship of England from King James in the form of an annual pension of 100 marks (approximately £66).

That he was not forgotten at his death is clear from the posthumous group of poetic tributes published in 1638 under the title of *Jonsonus Virbius*. Here his admirers, some of whom had been of the "Tribe of Ben," paid him homage. Jasper Mayne appreciated Jonson's observance of poetic decorum and said his plays were free "from Monsters [and] no hard Plot / Called down a God t'untie th'unlikely knot." Before he died, and upon the occasion of the failure of his play *The New Inn*, the poet **Thomas Carew** was even able to tactfully praise him while honestly acknowledging that his latest play was not his best work: "The wiser world doth greater thee confess / Then all men else, than thyself only less." One of the most famous of Jonson's "sons," the poet **Robert Herrick**, gives us a picture of the convivial Jonson in taverns, saying that those "lyric feasts" did make "us nobly wild, not mad; / And yet each verse of thine / Outdid the meat, outdid the frolic wine." But perhaps the consensus and most poignant view of Jonson after his death is best expressed by the eloquent four-word epitaph on his grave in Westminster Abbey: "O rare Ben Jonson!" The greatest English critic of the later 17th century would certainly have agreed. John Dryden called Jonson "the greatest man of the last age" and said that "while he was himself . . . I think him the most learned and judicious writer which any theatre ever had."

The 18th and 19th centuries depreciated Jonson in part by making unnecessarily invidious comparisons with Shakespeare, so much so that T.S. Eliot remarked, with some exaggeration, of course, in 1920 that Jonson was read only by "historians and antiquaries." Eliot did predict, though, that "the present age," if it were more familiar with Jonson, would find him of great interest. Twentieth-century criticism, in works too numerous to mention here, helped to fulfill this prophecy.

BIBLIOGRAPHY

Works by Ben Jonson

Ben Jonson. Ed. Ian Donaldson. Oxford: Oxford University Press, 1985. (For the poetry and two plays, *Volpone* and *The Alchemist*.)

Ben Jonson. Ed. C.H. Herford and Percy and Evelyn Simpson. 11 vols. Oxford: Oxford University Press, 1925–1952. (The standard scholarly edition.)

The Complete Masques. Ed. Stephen Orgel. New Haven, CT: Yale University Press, 1969.

Jonson's Plays and Masques. Ed. Richard Harp. New York: Norton, 2001. (Includes *Volpone*, *Epicoene*, *The Alchemist*, and selected criticism.)

Studies of Ben Jonson

Barish, Jonas A. *Ben Jonson and the Language of Prose Comedy*. Cambridge: Harvard University Press, 1960.

Barton, Anne. *Ben Jonson, Dramatist*. Cambridge: Cambridge University Press, 1984.

Brooks, Douglas. " 'If He Be at His Book, Disturb Him Not': The Two Jonson Folios of 1616." *Ben Jonson Journal* 4 (1997): 81–101.

Evans, Robert C. *Ben Jonson's Major Plays: Summaries of Modern Monographs*. West Cornwall, CT: Locust Hill Press, 2000.

Harp, Richard, Stanley Stewart, and Robert C. Evans. *Ben Jonson Journal*. Westport, CT: Locust Hill Press, 1994. (Annual publication.)

Kay, W. David. *Ben Jonson: A Literary Life*. New York: St. Martin's Press, 1995.

Knights, L.C. *Drama and Society in the Age of Jonson*. London: Chatto & Windus, 1937.

Orgel, Stephen. *The Jonsonian Masque*. Cambridge: Harvard University Press, 1965.

Riddell, James, and Stanley Stewart. *Jonson's Spenser: Evidence and Historical Criticism*. Pittsburgh: Duquesne University Press, 1995.

Summers, Claude J., and Ted-Larry Pebworth. *Ben Jonson*. Twayne's English Authors Series. Boston: Twayne Publishers, 1999.

Trimpi, Wesley. *Ben Jonson's Poems: A Study of the Plain Style*. Stanford, CA: Stanford University Press, 1962.

❧ Anne Killigrew
(1660–1685)

LORRAINE MELITA

BIOGRAPHY

Born the daughter of Dr. Henry Killigrew, master of the Savoy and a prebendary of Westminster in 1660, Anne Killigrew's social level determined an education consisting of poetry and painting. Samuel Lowndes, the publisher of her single volume of poetry, *Poems*, felt that she was "A GRACE for Beauty and a MUSE for Wit." **John Dryden** in his "To the Pious Memory of the Accomplished Young Lady, Mrs Anne Killigrew, Excellent in the two Sister-Acts of Poesie and Painting. An ODE," applauded her efforts in both areas (Hurley 112).

At a young age, she was appointed as a Maid of Honor to Mary of Modena, the Duchess of York. Her attendance in this household exposed her to and schooled her in the opposition of the profligacy of King Charles II and his court. Her attendance to the Duchess made her aware of the general and courtly attitude that regarded women as only a necessity for the pleasure of men (Hobby 156). Her painting abilities were lauded by Horace Walpole. He noted that "with a print of her, taken from her portrait drawn by herself, which with the leaves of the authors I have quoted, is in a much better style than her poetry and evidently the manner of Sir Peter Lely" (Walpole 107).

A short battle with smallpox in 1685 ended Killigrew's life at the age of twenty-five. She died in her father's quarters in Westminster Abbey and was buried in the chancel of St. John the Baptist's Chapel in the Savoy. The Killigrew family permitted the formal publication of her work in late 1685. The book was prefaced by the publisher's note, John Dryden's ode, and the Latin epitaph, translated, from her tomb (Hurley 112).

MAJOR WORKS AND THEMES

Anne Killigrew's only work was a collection of poems of approximately 100 pages containing thirty-three poems. A facsimile version from 1967 also contained an introduction by Richard Morton. Thirty of these poems are credited to Mrs. Killigrew. Her father and publisher felt the final three poems were not hers, but Ann Messenger and Harriette Andreadis disagree (Killigrew 84). These critics contend that the content, although controversial, and style of these final poems point to Killigrew as the writer.

To understand the themes of Anne Killigrew's work, the status of upper-middle-class women in the 17th century needs a brief comment. During this century, women were generally expected to preserve their families' "honor" through sexual chastity or honesty and focus their attention on concerns such as household duties rather than on divinity or political matters. They could not travel alone, go to college, enter government, practice law, enter the Church, or initiate on their own relationships with men, had few opportunities to earn or manage money, and were gradually removed from being midwives. If a woman published in this era, she was considered to be competing with men and, therefore, "immodest" (Rogers, XIV, XV). Clearly these limits initiated a theme of depression in a number of Killigrew's poems. "A Farewel to Worldly Joys," "The Complaint of a Lover," "An Invective against Gold," "The Miseries of Man," "Upon the saying that my Verses were made by another," "The Discontent," and all of the Pastoral Dialogues give particular evidence to this theme.

A second influence on her poetry was the debauched conduct at the court of Charles II. Sexual pleasures and clear, open misogyny among the male population of the court promoted the degradation of women. Because of this attitude, several of Killigrew's poems reflect a rejection of sexuality as a way of life (Hobby 156). This rejection is apparent in the last few lines of "Alexandreis," "The Second Epigram, on Billinda," "St. John Baptist Painted by her Self in the Wilderness, with Angels appearing to him, and with a Lamb by him," and "A Farewel to Worldly Joys." She also incorporates this theme in the final stanza of "To the Queen."

An often referenced but rarely critiqued segment of Killigrew's work is her successful use of wit and specific poetic style including alliteration and imagery. "On Galla" displays her frequent use of wit combined with satire to produce the picture of a group of people on a cold frosty night with everyone feeling the effects except Galla, thanks to her makeup (Messenger 21). Her use of pronounced imagery continues in "Alexandreis," "On Death," "The Third Epigram, On an Atheist," and "The Complaint of a Lover."

The poem "Herodias's Daughter presenting to her Mother St. Johns Head in a Silver Charger, also Painted by her self" demonstrates Killigrew's wit. She has used twelve lines of verse to describe a painting of the head of St. John being presented to Herodias's wife. She compares St. John's lifeless lips to a lover's gaze. She lightly states that he has been seduced by "her Victorious Charms, / See how his Head reposes in my Arms." The reader can almost see her eyes twinkling with mirth. She has entertained us with a very interesting image of love from one who denies physical love.

CRITICAL RECEPTION

Richard Morton states that Killigrew's poems "have an appealing wit, a picturesque imagination and a touching personal candor." Morton's statement at the time was accurate. Killigrew's works had only been reviewed when referencing John Dryden's "To a Pious Young Woman." In chronological order, Ann Messenger, Kristina Straub, Elaine Hobby, and Harriette Andreadis have researched Anne Killigrew's works in conjunction with the condition of women in the 17th century and the issue of the rejection of sensuality and sexuality.

Messenger maintained that Dryden was drawn to Killigrew because of similarities in their writing experiences and lives. Both attempted to write epic poems, were criticized for not writing their own work, and completed works not complimentary to their respective political affiliations. Dryden had been a family friend and probably watched Anne grow to a young woman and profoundly mourned her untimely death (Messenger 38).

Straub considers the sexual sensitivity issue by using the metaphor of rape in her critique of Killigrew's "Upon the saying that my Verses." Relying on a description of rape as an act infused with overtones of sexual humiliation that leads to domination and victimization of one human being by another, Straub explains how Killigrew's readers' attribution of her work to another poet reversed her expectations of "honor." These false accusations were viewed as an assault on Killigrew's honor, thus dominating and victimizing her (32). Thus, Dryden, in his Ode, although he is seemingly complimentary, made remarks that could be construed to be a type of domination and victimization.

Hobby uses the rejection of sensuality and sexuality in discussions of "To the Queen" and "The Miseries of Man," to illustrate Killigrew's reason for writing poetry. According to Hobby, poetry, for Killigrew, was an escape from the constraints of sexual exploitation and upheld the "honour" requirement for women of that age (159). And lastly, Andreadis employs the rejection of sensuality and sexuality in discussions of Dryden's "To the Pious Memory . . . ," "On Billinda," "The Miseries of Man," "The Discontent," "Cloris Charms Dissolved by Eudora," "Upon a Little Lady under the Discipline of an Excellent Person," and "On the soft and gentle motions of Eudora." Andreadis's critiques display various views of Killigrew's works. These examples identify Killigrew's constant struggle for self-discipline and control of her passions, her chosen cynical view of friendship, her fear of realizing her passions, acceptance of that passion, and finally embracing the pleasure that passion brings (119–124). Modern feminist criticism of Killigrew's poetry thus adds an interesting perspective to a traditional reading of her poems and her "canonization" by John Dryden.

BIBLIOGRAPHY

Works by Anne Killigrew

Poems by Mrs Anne Killigrew. Printed for Samuel Lowndes. London, 1686 [i.e., 1685]. Facsimile published as *Poems (1686) by Mrs. Anne Killigrew, a Facsimile Reproduction with an Introduction*. Ed. Richard Morton. Gainesville, FL: Scholars' Facsimiles & Reprints, 1967.

Studies of Anne Killigrew

Andreadis, Harriette. *Sappho in Early Modern England: Female Same-Sex Literary Erotics 1550–1714*. Chicago: University of Chicago Press, 2001.
Dryden, John. "To the Pious Memory of the Accomplisht Young LADY Mrs Anne Killigrew,

Excellent in the two Sister-Acts of Poesie, and Painting. An ODE." In *Poems (1686) by Mrs. Anne Killigrew, a Facsimile Reproduction with an Introduction*, ed. Richard Morton. Gainesville, FL: Scholars' Facsimiles & Reprints, 1967.

Ezell, Margaret J.M. *The Patriarch's Wife: Literary Evidence and the History of the Family.* Chapel Hill: University of North Carolina Press, 1987.

Hobby, Elaine. *Virtue of Necessity: English Women's Writing 1649–88.* Ann Arbor: University of Michigan Press, 1989.

Hurley, Ann. "Anne Killigrew." In *Dictionary of Literary Biography. Volume 131: Seventeenth Century British Nondramatic Poets*, ed. M. Thomas Hester. Detroit, MI: Gale Research, 1993. 112–119.

Messenger, Ann. *His and Hers: Essays in Restoration and Eighteenth-Century Literature.* Lexington: University Press of Kentucky, 1986.

Mulvihill, Maureen E. "Essential Studies of Restoration Women Writers: Reclaiming a Heritage, 1913–1986." *Restoration: Studies in English Literary Culture, 1660–1700* 11 (1987): 122–131.

Pohli, Carol Virginia. "Formal and Informal Space in Dryden's Ode, 'To the Pious Memory of Anne Killigrew.' " *Restoration: Studies in English Literary Culture, 1600–1700* 15 (1991): 27–40.

Rogers, Katherine M., and William McCarthy, eds. *The Meridian Anthology of Early Women Writers: British Literary Women from Aphra Behn to Maria Edgeworth, 1660–1800.* New York: New American Library, 1987.

Silber, C. Anderson. "Nymphs and Satyrs: Poet, Readers, and Irony in Dryden's Ode to Anne Killigrew." *Studies in Eighteenth Century Culture* 14 (1985): 193–212.

Staves, Susan. *Players' Scepters: Fictions of Authority in the Restoration.* Lincoln: University of Nebraska Press, 1979.

Straub, Kristina. "Indecent Liberties with a Poet: Audience and the Metaphor of Rape in Killigrew's 'Upon the saying that my Verses' and Pope's 'Arbuthnot.' " *Tulsa Studies in Women's Literature* 6 (1987): 27–45.

Walpole, Horace. *Anecdotes of Painting in England with Some Account of the Principal Artists.* Vol. 2. London: Chatto and Windus, Piccadilly, 1876.

❧ *Sarah Kemble Knight*
(1666–1727)

GAIL WOOD

BIOGRAPHY

The presence of Sarah Kemble Knight, or Madame Knight as she is called, in the literary and social history of America rests on the publication of one small journal chronicling her travels from Boston to New York in 1704 and 1705. Not much is known about her life, and there is no full-length biography. The documentary evidence of her life is scant and fragmented. She was born the daughter of Elizabeth Trerice Kemble and Thomas Kemble, a Boston merchant. There is no record of her marriage except a document stating Richard Knight's intention to marry her in 1688. Their only child, Elizabeth, was born in 1689. Her husband, a shipmaster and London agent for an American company, was frequently away from home, and Madame Knight worked to support the family.

Knight supplemented the family income in a variety of ways. She copied legal documents, kept a shop, ran a lodging house, and taught school. It has been reported that Benjamin Franklin and Samuel Mather were among her students. There is no mention of Richard Knight after 1706, and it is assumed that he died around that date. In 1712, she sold the Boston property and moved to Connecticut where she ran several businesses including farming, shopkeeping, innkeeping, and Indian trading. The remainder of the documents about her indicate that she was fined for selling liquor to Indians, a charge she denied, and she was given permission in 1717 to sit in a designated pew in the Norwich church meeting house. It is also documented that after her husband died, her daughter moved in with Knight and her mother. When she died in 1727, she left an impressive estate of £1,800.

MAJOR WORKS AND THEMES

Sarah Kemble Knight's journal was published in 1825, nearly 100 years after her death. According to the editor, Theodore Dwight, much of the journal was written in her personal shorthand, so the entire work has never been published. The manuscript has since disappeared.

At the age of thirty-eight, Knight embarked on a journey from New York to Connecticut. The journal is a series of observations and commentaries on her journey and the people she encounters. Critics argue whether her journal is a faithful recording of the people and conditions of the time or a developed story interlaced with social commentary. The journal does reveal that she has created a lively narrative with herself as the main character. She reveals herself to be a no-nonsense traveler, assured, dignified, demanding. In private, through the pages of her journal, she reveals herself to be ascerbic, tart-tongued, and conscious of her economic status. She is superior to many of those she meets and slightly martyred by the primitive conditions of the colonial frontier.

Knight's journey was unusual for women of the times since the colonial frontier was still unexplored and dangerous travel for anyone. Her narrative reflects her middle-class, merchant-class attitudes of gender, class, and race. The journal provides a window on the American colonial social and economic world. Her references to classical works reflect a strong literary education. The journal also shows shrewd observations of the myriad of people she encountered. Her work reflects a keen sense of appreciation for a good story, often written in the dialect of her fellow travelers. She reflects, moreover, her own biases toward Indians, slaves, and women. These biases are tempered by her sharp sense of humor and vivid storytelling.

CRITICAL RECEPTION

Knight's journal is considered one of the beginning points for women writers and for American writers in the areas of humor and social commentary. Even so, the body of literary critique is small. Hollis L. Cate compares her journal to Mark Twain in her observations of other classes and use of figurative language. John L. Mahoney writes that Knight was not writing a journal as an accurate record of her travel but as a classic heroic journey in the Homeric tradition. Peter Thorpe and Kathryn Zabelle Derounian-Stodola discuss Knight's use of the picaresque literary tradition, with which Knight was, no doubt, familiar. Derounian-Stodola also discusses how Knight's journal provides a female picaresque perspective on the American frontier. Michaelson writes that Knight's use of storytelling provides a commentary on the socioeconomic changes of her time. Julia Stern writes on Knight's struggles as a woman in a man's world and on the class differences between herself and those she encounters on her travels.

BIBLIOGRAPHY

Works by Sarah Kemble Knight

The Journals of Madam Knight, and Rev. Mr. Buckingham. From the Original Manuscripts Written in 1704 & 1710. Ed. Theodore Dwight, Jr. New York: Wilder & Campbell, 1825.

Studies of Sarah Kemble Knight

Bush, Sargent, Jr. "Sarah Kemble Knight (1666–1727)." *Legacy: A Journal of American Women Writers* 12 (1995): 112–120.

Cate, Hollis L. "The Figurative Language of Recall in Sarah Kemble Knight's Journal." *CEA Critic* 43 (1980): 32–35.

———. "Two American Bumpkins." *Research Studies* 41 (1973): 61–63.

Derounian-Stodola, Kathryn Zabelle. "The New England Frontier and the Picaresque in Sarah Kemble Knight's Journal." In *Early American Literature and Culture: Essays in Honor of Harrison T. Meserole*, ed. Kathryn Zabelle Derounian-Stodola. Newark: University of Delaware Press, 1992. 122–131.

Dietrich, Deborah. "Sarah Kemble Knight." In *Dictionary of American Biography, Vol. 200: American Women Prose Writers to 1820*, ed. Carla Mulford, Angela Vietto, and Amy E. Winans. Detroit, MI: Gale Group, 1999. 221–227.

Latashaw-Foti, Elizabeth Anne. "Social Agendas in the Eighteenth-Century Travel Narratives." Ph.D. dissertation, University of South Florida, 1999.

Michaelson, Scott. "Narrative and Class in a Culture of Consumption: The Significance of Stories in Sarah Kemble Knight's Journal." *College Literature* 21 (June 1994): 33–46.

Stanford, Ann. "Three Puritan Women: Anne Bradstreet, Mary Rowlandson, and Sarah Kemble Knight." In *American Women Writers: Bibliographic Essays*, ed. Maurice Duke, Jackson R. Bryer, and M. Thomas Inge. Westport, CT: Greenwood Press, 1983. 3–20.

Stephens, Robert O. "The Odyssey of Sarah Kemble Knight." *College Language Association Journal* 7 (1964): 247–255.

Stern, Julia. "To Relish and to Spew: Disgust as Cultural Critique in the Journal of Madam Knight." *Legacy: A Journal of American Women Writers* 14 (1997): 1–12.

Thorpe, Peter. "Sarah Kemble Knight and the Picaresque Tradition." *College Language Association* 10 (1986): 114–121.

Madame de Lafayette

(c. 1634–1693)

NHORA LUCÍA SERRANO

BIOGRAPHY

Born in April 1634 in Paris to a family whose social and economic status bordered between the middle class and the minor aristocracy—her father tutored one of the Cardinal de Richelieu's nephews, and her mother came from a wealthy Provence family—Marie-Madeleine Pioche de la Vergne, Comtesse de Lafayette, was both a participant and an observer of 17th-century French court life. Like other privileged young women of her time, she was privately tutored and developed important friendships that provided her access to the court milieu and established her social position within aristocratic circles. One such friendship was with Mother Angélique de Lafayette, the mother superior of the convent of Chaillot, whose brother Count François de Lafayette would become Lafayette's husband in 1655. This marriage would produce two sons while she lived with her husband in their estates in Auvergne, the mountainous region of south-central France. During this period, she was intensely embroiled with her husband's legal problems and assisted in their resolution. In 1659, she relocated to Paris without her husband and would remain there until her death in 1693.

At the convent of Chaillot, Lafayette would also make the acquaintance of Henriette-Marie, the Queen consort of England, and her daughter Henriette. When in 1661 Henriette of England married Phillippe d'Orléans, the younger brother of Louis XIV, Lafayette became part of Henriette's royal entourage and gained direct access to the royal court. Lafayette would set forth her friend's biography in the historical memoir *Histoire de Madame Henriette d'Angleterre*, published posthumously in 1720. After Henriette's death in 1661, Lafayette continued to participate actively in court life.

Lafayette's involvement with the literary and intellectual circles of the elite salons, specifically the feminocentric salons—*ruelles*—provided, however, other crucial friendships that initiated her into the creative Parisian milieu of the 17th century.

Among her closest friends in these salons were Daniel Huet, Gilles Ménage, Marie de Rabutin Chantal de Sévigné, Madeleine de Scudéry, François de Marcillac—Duke of La Rochefoucauld, Madame du Plessis-Guénegaud, Jean Regnault de Segrais, and Madame de Sablé. These social gatherings of salon *habitués* witnessed the collaborative composition, revision, and discussion of erudite letters, poetry, and prose whose publication was either anonymously or under a masculine nom de plume for women.

MAJOR WORKS AND THEMES

With the single exception of a literary "portrait" of Marie de Sévigné for Montpensier's *Recueil des portraits et éloges* to which Lafayette playfully signed her name, during her lifetime she refused to acknowledge authorship to those compositions that many critics then and now have attributed to her. For example, Lafayette's *Nouvelles: La Princesse de Montpensier* (1662) and *Zaïde, Histoire espagnole* (1670) originally were published under the name of her fellow *habitué* Segrais, and the renowned *La Princesse de Clèves* (1678) was an anonymous publication. Her other lesser-known works, *Mémoires de la cour de France* (1731), *La Comtesse de Tende* (1724), and *Histoire de Madame Henriette d'Angleterre* (1720), were all published posthumously. Present throughout all of these works, though, is a similar and complex thematic tapestry of politics, love, *histoire* (meaning both history and story in French), and propriety. This unique literary arrangement where reality is fused with fiction, and history with storytelling, is actually representative of the *habitués'* efforts to experiment with a new narrative structure. Yet what strongly attests to Lafayette being a major contributor if not the sole composer of most of these works is the distinctive manner in which a new narrative is spun, through the lens of a unique heroine whose progression into adulthood runs alongside its narrative. In fact, her famous and influential *La Princesse de Clèves* is considered to have heralded in a new genre because it was an early model of a Bildungsroman, the story of a young person's education and development out of childhood.

Prior to the mid-17th century, there was a vast difference between the two dominant genres, romance (*roman*) and novella (*nouvelle*). The earlier *roman* dealt with the amorous, spiritual, and physical journeys of long ago knights and princes in faraway places whose adventures were sprinkled with supernatural elements. In contrast, the French *nouvelle* took place in a more recent time and concerned itself with establishing and upholding the socially recognized principles of truth and conduct of the day. With the publication of *La Princesse de Clèves* these very categories were, however, put to question because, according to many later critics, it catalyzed with its new narrative form the birth of the modern novel (a revised definition of *roman* incorporating reality).

To begin with, the story of the *La Princesse de Clèves* is staged within the historical court of Henri II (1527–1559) and recounts the thought processes behind the actions of an inexperienced and young noblewoman's entry into court life. First, since the independent female protagonist is a fictive character woven into the court life of well-known historical figures, the narrative itself complicates the gap that lay between history and fiction. Second, it refuses to be a traditional *roman* even though at the beginning the newly married *Princesse*, who is caught in the web of amorous court politics and political interpersonal conduct, finds herself regrettably in love with another man. After an uncharacteristic confession by the *Princesse* to her husband, followed by her husband's death, she chooses to separate herself forever from the court and renounce romance. Third, by providing the *Princesse*'s inner psychological musings of what she should do or not do about her adulterous sentiments, Lafayette also inaugurates the psychological novel. And last, by situating these themes within the woman's domain of love and marriage, couched in a mother-daughter relationship, and highlighted by internal narratives of other women to which the heroine compares herself, Lafayette endows the *Princesse* and all of these women with political and amorous power. Moreover, for some current feminist scholarship, Lafayette liberates the heroine and her narrative from a traditional ending and genre.

CRITICAL RECEPTION

The anonymous 1678 publication of *La Princesse de Clèves* initially sparked debates about how to classify the text, who wrote it, and why the writer(s) permitted the *Princesse* to confess her love of another man to her husband. By 1679 it was translated into English, and two critical books were written about it, Valincour's *Lettres à Madame la marquise de *** sur le sujet de* La Princesse de Clèves and Charnes's response to Valincour, *Conversations sur la critique de* La Princesse de Clèves. Valincour would accuse the *Princesse* of being "la prude la plus coquette et la coquette la plus prude que l'on ait jamais vue" (the most coquettish prude and the most prudish coquette anyone has ever seen) (272–273). Even the Parisian literary magazine of the day, *Le Mercure Galant*, published readers' opinions regarding the *Princesse*'s behavior and sense of propriety, thus fashioning critics out of the public readers. As to the question of authorship, Mme de Sévigné identifies in a letter that Lafayette and La Rochefoucauld were the collaborators, although some later critics suspect that Segrais was a third contributor. In 1780, the first edition with Lafayette's name appeared, forever legitimizing her as the author. Yet its most lasting impact has been the controversy that it first provoked over genres. With its new twist on the concept of *histoire*, *La Princesse de Clèves* creatively opened the door to a new type of writing where fiction could confront cultural reality, and history is storytelling.

BIBLIOGRAPHY

Works by Madame de Lafayette

Correspondance. Ed. André Beaunier. 2 vols. Paris: Gallimard, 1942.
Histoire de Madame Henriette d'Angleterre. Ed. Claudine Herrman. Paris: Femmes, 1979.
Oeuvres complètes. Ed. Roger Duchêne. Paris: Bourin, 1990.
Oeuvres complètes de Mesdames de La Fayette, de Tencin et de Fontaines. Ed. M. Auger. 4 vols. Paris: Lepetit, 1820.
Oeuvres de Madame de Lafayette. Paris: Garnier, "Bibliothêque amusante," 1864.
La Princesse de Clèves. Ed. Antoine Adam. Paris: Garnier, 1966.
La Princesse de Clèves. Ed. Jean Mesnard. Paris: Garnier, 1996.
The Princess of Clèves. Trans. John D. Lyons. New York: Norton, 1994.
Zaïde, Histoire espagnole. Paris: Nizet, 1982.

Studies of Madame de Lafayette

Beasley, Faith E., and Katherine Ann Jensen, eds. *Approaches to Teaching Lafayette's* The Princess of Clèves. New York: Modern Language Association of America, 1998.

Beaunier, André. *L'amie de la Rochefoucauld*. Paris: Flammarion, 1927.

Charnes, Jean-Antoine, Abbé de. *Conversations sur la critique de* La Princesse de Clèves. [1679.] Ed. François Weil et al. Tours: Université de Tours, 1973.

Henry, Patrick, ed. *An Inimitable Example: The Case for* The Princesse de Clèves. Washington, DC: Catholic University of America Press, 1992.

Hirsch, Marianne. "A Mother's Discourse: Incorporation and Repetition in *La Princesse de Clèves*." *Yale French Studies* 62 (1981): 67–87.

Kamuf, Peggy. *Fictions of Feminine Desire*. Lincoln: University of Nebraska Press, 1982.

———. "A Mother's Will: *The Princess of Clèves*." In her *Fictions of Feminine Desire*. Lincoln: University of Nebraska Press, 1982. 67–96. Reprinted in Madame de Lafayette, *The Princess of Clèves*. Trans. John D. Lyons. New York: Norton, 1994. 206–230.

Lyons, John D., and Mary B. McKinley, eds. *Critical Tales: Studies of the Heptaméron and Early Modern Culture*. Philadelphia: University of Pennsylvania Press, 1993.

Miller, Nancy K. "Emphasis Added: Plots and Plausibilities in Women's Fiction." *Publication of the Modern Language Association (PMLA)* 96 (1981): 36–48.

Paulson, Michael G. *A Critical Analysis of de La Fayette's* La Princesse de Clèves *as a Royal Exemplary Novel: Kings, Queens, and Splendor*. Lewiston NY: Edward Mellen, 1991.

Valincour, Jean Trousset de. *Lettres à Madame la marquise de *** sur le sujet de* La Princesse de Clèves. [1678.] Ed. Jacques Chupeau. Tours: Université of Tours, 1972.

❧ *Aemilia Lanyer*
(1569?–1645)

ERIKA L. FARR

BIOGRAPHY

Aemilia Lanyer, the first known Englishwoman to publish a volume of original verse, lived a life marked by ambition and disappointment. Born to Baptist Bassano, a court musician, and his common-law wife Margaret Johnson, Aemilia was christened in the parish church of St. Botolph, Bishopsgate, on January 27, 1569. By the age of eighteen, Lanyer found herself orphaned with a dowry of £100 and the profits from several rental properties. Family ties to the court placed Lanyer in the midst of her social betters, where, presumably, she first met Henry Cary, Lord Hunsdon, Queen Elizabeth's Lord Chamberlain. After spending several years as Hunsdon's mistress, her pregnancy in 1592 necessitated Aemilia's marriage to court musician Alphonso Lanyer, a union arranged by Hunsdon. Her son Henry was born in 1593, and in 1598 Lanyer gave birth to a daughter, Odillya, who died in infancy. Though her husband's service to the court produced little social advancement, it was not completely without reward; James I granted Alphonso a hay and grain patent in 1604.

The apex of Lanyer's literary career occurred in 1611 when she published *Salve Deus Rex Judæorum*. The poetic ambitions expressed in this volume enjoyed no recorded success, with Lanyer's pleas for patronage going unanswered. Alphonso's death in 1613 introduced legal struggle into Lanyer's life, as she entered into decades of litigation with Alphonso's relatives over the rights to his patent. In another attempt to attain financial security, Lanyer opened a school in a wealthy London suburb in 1617, but the venture failed within two years. Lanyer spent her remaining years near her son, Henry, a court flautist, and his family. Upon her death in 1645, Lanyer was listed as a "pensioner," suggesting that she enjoyed a stable income and respectable social standing.

MAJOR WORKS AND THEMES

Lanyer's literary career rests on her one published work, *Salve Deus Rex Judæorum*, which considers both religious and secular topics. Published in 1611, *Salve* introduces an aspiring female voice into the early modern book trade, a public space rarely entered by women writers of the period. The volume consists of three sections, with an afterword directed at the "doubtfull Reader." The first section includes eleven dedications, nine of which address individual royal and noble ladies, while the other two dedications are aimed at a more general readership. In these dedications, Lanyer introduces the scope of her title poem, requests support and "grace" from her readers, and attempts to construct a community of moneyed women around her text. Composed of four sections, including "The Passion of Christ," "Eves Apologie in Defence of Women," "The Teares of the Daughters of Jerusalem," and "The Salutation and Sorrow of the Virgine Marie," the title poem recounts the story of Christ's suffering from a distinctly female perspective, highlighting the unwavering loyalty of Christ's female followers.

Lanyer creates polemically driven scenes in which women defend, support, and mourn Christ, while their male counterparts doubt, betray, and crucify him. The final section of the volume includes the first published country-house poem in English, "The Description of Cooke-ham," which beat **Ben Jonson**'s country-house poem "To Penshurst" to print by five years. This poem depicts a small community of learned women, including the poet Margaret the Countess Dowager of Cumberland and Margaret's daughter Anne Clifford. The tone is elegiac and the setting pastoral, as Lanyer mourns the loss of this Edenic female community.

A recurring theme throughout *Salve* is the necessity of female community, a topic that has received much attention by critics. Lanyer attempts to foster female community in varied ways; she employs a feast metaphor throughout the dedications, inviting worthy ladies to her feast and relying on conventions of hospitality and gift-giving to entice her readers. She continues her efforts in the title poem, most pointedly when Lanyer takes on the female cause, defending Eve and all womankind by placing the blame for Christ's crucifixion specifically on men. Cooke-ham's idealized sorority of learned women comes closest to realizing the female community for which Lanyer yearns.

Lanyer questions, moreover, the restrictions of social rank that structured 17th-century England. She acknowledges the distance between her and her dedicates throughout her prefatory material. Within "Salve," Lanyer scorns society's divisions, arguing that all of humanity "sprang from one woman and one man." Lanyer's most eloquent and pointed lamentation of social difference occurs in her final poem, "Cooke-ham." While addressing the primary dedicatee of her volume, Margaret Countess Dowager of Cumberland, she complains:

> Unconstant Fortune, thou art most to blame,
> Who casts us downe into so lowe a frame:
> Where our great friends we cannot dayly see,
> So great a difference is there in degree.

Frustrated ambitions and unyielding social stratification prove relentless adversaries to an ambitious poet.

By addressing women in her dedications and proclaiming that her volume is "for the generall use of all vertuous Ladies and Gentlewomen of this kingdome," she introduces readers to her politics and rhetoric. This protofeminism, as some critics have termed it, colors the entire volume, appearing as a defense of women in "Salve" and shaping her depiction of an ideal, though lost, female community. This feminist rhetoric takes a radically revisionist turn in "Salve" when she exclaims:

> But surely Adam can not be excused,
> Her faulte though great, yet hee has more to blame.

Lanyer reinterprets traditional biblical rhetoric, affixing the responsibility for the Crucifixion and the Fall to man. Thus, Lanyer's one surviving text adeptly negotiates literary and social conventions, employing and sustaining elevated rhetoric, while also registering the struggles of women writing and publishing in early 17th-century England.

CRITICAL RECEPTION

After languishing in obscurity for over 350 years, Lanyer's *Salve* entered into critical debate in the 1970s when the Shakespearean (see **William Shakespeare**) critic A.L. Rowse encountered her name in a notebook of Renaissance astrologer Simon Forman. After realizing that Lanyer had been Hunsdon's mistress while Hunsdon was the master of the Lord Chamberlain's Men, Shakespeare's theater company, Rowse argued that Lanyer was the Dark Lady of Shakespeare's *Sonnets*. While Rowse performed a service to Lanyer's verse by publishing an edition of *Salve* in 1978, his portrayal of her as Shakespeare's Dark Lady obscured her literary merit. *Salve* came under more fruitful scrutiny in the 1980s, however, as literary critics began recovering the works of early modern women writers. Critics such as Barbara Lewalski, Susanne Woods, Elaine Beilin, and Wendy Wall examine Lanyer's concern with community, her text's feminist bent, her engagement with Renaissance literary conventions, and her responses to social expectations and oppressions, to name but a few critical pursuits.

BIBLIOGRAPHY

Works by Aemilia Lanyer

The Poems of Aemilia Lanyer: Salve Deus Rex Judæorum. Ed. Susanne Woods. New York: Oxford University Press, 1993.
Salve Deus Rex Judæorum. London: Printed by Valentine Simmes for Richard Bonian, 1611.

Studies of Aemilia Lanyer

Beilin, Elaine V. "The Feminization of Praise: Aemilia Lanyer." In her *Redeeming Eve: Women Writers of the English Renaissance*. Princeton: Princeton University Press, 1987.
Goldberg, Jonathan. "Canonizing Aemilia Lanyer." In his *Desiring Women Writing: English Renaissance Examples*. Stanford, CA: Stanford University Press, 1997.

Grossman, Marshall, ed. *Aemilia Lanyer: Gender, Genre, and the Canon*. Lexington: University Press of Kentucky, 1998.

Lewalski, Barbara. "Imagining Female Community: Aemilia Lanyer's Poems." In her *Writing Women in Jacobean England*. Cambridge: Harvard University Press, 1993.

Schnell, Lisa. " 'So Great a Difference Is There in Degree': Aemilia Lanyer and the Aims of Feminist Criticism." *Modern Language Quarterly* 57.1 (1996): 23–35.

Wall, Wendy. "Our Bodies/Our Texts? Renaissance Women and the Trials of Authorship." In *Anxious Power: Reading, Writing, and Ambivalence in Narrative by Woman*, ed. Carol J. Singley and Susan Elizabeth Sweeney. Albany: State University of New York Press, 1993.

Woods, Susanne. *Lanyer: A Renaissance Woman Poet*. New York: Oxford University Press, 1999.

ॐ *John Lilburne*
(1615–1657)

BRYAN A. HAMPTON

BIOGRAPHY

The man nicknamed "Free-born John," following his refusal to swear the ex officio oath before Star Chamber in 1638, spent much of his adult life in prison. His obstinate commitment to the liberty of conscience; his uncanny ability to promote personal sufferings in the cause of securing liberty on behalf of others; his vigorous defense of clear laws that would extend to all persons; and his passionate belief in the contractual nature of government—all contributed to his enormous popularity and his being named among the leaders of the Levellers.

Despite pandemic fears that the Leveller program included social and economic leveling, John Lilburne advocated no such agenda. He came from a well-established gentry family in Durham: his father, Richard, once served the Earl of Northumberland; his mother, Margaret, was the daughter of Thomas Hixon, who served at the palace at Greenwich; and his paternal great-grandfather had attended Henry VIII. Unlike his contemporary Gerrard Winstanley, Lilburne was careful to link his notion of personal liberty with the freedom of private possession.

During the 1630s Lilburne was apprenticed to a clothier in London where he was inundated with Puritan nonconformist rhetoric. Early in 1638 he was summoned to Star Chamber for the illegal printing and distribution of John Bastwick's antiprelatical pamphlet *Letany*. **Oliver Cromwell** aided his release more than two years later, and Lilburne thereafter married Elizabeth Dewell, a woman of extraordinary resilience. Restless and idealistic, he abandoned a promising brewery business to enlist in the army under Robert, Lord Brooke, in 1642. Subsequently, Lilburne served with distinction under the Earls of Essex and Manchester and attained the rank of Lieutenant Colonel of the Dragoons in 1644—a title he consciously maintained after his resignation in 1645 when he refused the Solemn League and Covenant.

He met Levellers Richard Overton and William Walwyn in 1645. The next seven years were spent mostly in prison, as he continued to write tracts attacking Parliament and Cromwell's Council of State and inciting mutiny among the Agitators in the Army, as well as contributing to the Leveller newspaper *The Moderate* (June 1648–September 1649). Consequently, he was brought to trial for high treason in October 1649. Before a packed audience at Guildhall, Lilburne mounted a brilliant defense and secured an acquittal, causing shouts of celebration to ring in the London streets.

During 1650–1651 Lilburne worked unsuccessfully as a soap-boiler but could not stay far from the press. He was brought before Parliament for libel in December 1651, fined an exorbitant £7000, and in January he was sentenced to banishment. In exile for seventeen months among the Dutch, Lilburne returned to England following the dissolution of the Rump. Arrested and tried, he mounted yet another compelling defense in July 1653 and avoided the death penalty, but Cromwell ordered him to life imprisonment at Jersey and Dover Castle. Late in 1655 he converted to Quakerism and was allowed parole visits to his family, who had settled in Dover. During one of these visits in the late summer of 1657 he fell ill and died on August 29, the day he was ordered to return to confinement.

MAJOR WORKS AND THEMES

Nearly all Lilburne's writings emanated from prison. The majority of his eighty vindictive pamphlets include letters of appeal, disputations with those in the public eye (among them William Prynne, the Earl of Manchester, and Cromwell), and narrations of his numerous arrests and trials. Throughout, Lilburne presents himself as a martyr for the English people against the tyranny of the old and new regimes. He frequently quotes from the Bible, the Magna Carta, Parliament's books of *Remonstrances* and *Declarations*, the *Institutes* of Sir Edward Coke, and his own writings.

His early tracts, including *The Christian Mans Triall* (March 1638) and *A Poore Mans Crye* (December 1638), detail his arrest, trial, and imprisonment by Star Chamber and are also anti-Episcopal. The watershed of his career is *Englands Birth-right Justified* (October 1645). Here Lilburne argues that the rule of law is everyone's birthright, one that has been repeatedly compromised by Parliament. He demonstrates the need for a vernacular translation of English law; outlines the proper proceedings of a legal trial; attacks the monopolies of preaching, trade, and printing; advocates the abolition of tithes; and demands annual Parliaments in order to keep electors accountable to the people. Many of these themes remain a constant throughout his career.

Accountability is the partial subject of *Londons Liberty In Chains discovered* (October 1646). For Lilburne, English law is consonant with the law of reason and contingent on the will of the people. English citizens, however, have been deluded by the lawyers and the clergy, "captivated to the Lawes, covetous Lusts, and the Arbitrarie unlimited power and dominion of your illegally imperious lording Magistrates" (6). In denying London's citizens the right to vote annually for city officers, these "lording Magistrates" violate liberties guaranteed by the Magna Carta.

Lilburne returns to this theme of arbitrary power in *Plaine Truth without Feare or Flattery* (April/May 1647). He begins by arguing against the "new formed Monster" (11) of Scottish Presbyterianism, but the pamphlet quickly blossoms into an attack on individual members of Parliament whose "Arbitrary wills are become Englands Lawes" (21) and for whom "expulsion is too little, and beheading is too honourable"

(16). So critical of Parliament's power is Lilburne that in *Jonahs Cry out of the Whales belly* (July 1647), he asserts, "Parliament tyrannizeth ten times more over us than ever the King did" (4). This contempt for Parliament culminates in *Strength out of Weaknesse* (September 1649), narrating his trial and debate with Attorney General Edmund Prideaux, who defends the Commonwealth as the people's government. With characteristic vehemence, Lilburne questions how Parliament can belong to the people and yet act without their consent. "I tell you Sir," declares Lilburne, "the same principle that led me to hate [Arbitrary and Tyrannical] Will in the King, leads me a thousand times more to hate Will in you, seeing you have promised better things, ye absolute freedom, and yet perform nothing, but do worse than ever he did" (12). Like **John Milton**, whom he admired, Lilburne consistently defended the covenantal relationship between civil magistrates and the people—a notion developed in later decades by **John Locke**.

Despite Lilburne's rational appeals and biting invective, the Leveller program was defeated. Years of imprisonment and poverty exacted a hard toll on his family, and in his last pamphlet, Lilburne abandons politics. *The Resurrection of John Lilburne* (May 1656)—his military title has been self-consciously effaced—describes his conversion to Quakerism. Likening the drama of his conversion to Paul's, Lilburne declares, "I am already dead, or crucified, to the very occasions, and real grounds of all outward wars, and carnal swordfightings & fleshly . . . contests" (13). The man formerly so passionate about constitutional reform, so restless for liberty, and so driven by combative polemics seemed to find peace at last in the "loving kindness of God" (6), for which "my soul many yeers hath sought diligently after, and with unsatisfied longingness, thirsted to injoy" (14)—much to the discontent of his peers.

CRITICAL RECEPTION

Lilburne's legacy is multihued. Many English commoners saw Lilburne as their champion and reportedly flocked after him; those in power, however, saw him as the pestilential symbol of anarchy and rebellion. Indeed, Lilburne's enemies must have been overwhelmed by his charisma and impudence, his productivity and influence. Early on, Cromwell was impressed with the young man's poise and resilience; later, he was increasingly frustrated by them and grew to resent the man he once defended before the Long Parliament. Oddly, during his exile several Royalists thought they had found an ally in Lilburne, who reportedly said he would embrace a prince as long as he subscribed to the demands made in the Leveller manifesto *An Agreement of the People* (May 1649). It is no wonder that just before Cromwell sentenced him to life imprisonment, the Council of State judged his writings "scandalous, seditious and tumultuous"—ultimately incompatible with the aims of the fledgling Republic.

Because the majority of Lilburne's writings are personal vindications and appeals, they are often neglected, adumbrated by the writings of his peers: Winstanley compellingly reinvigorates biblical myth, foreshadowing William Blake; Overton and Walwyn are much more systematic thinkers. But Lilburne is rhetorically at his best during these moments of persecution and often displays a gift for storytelling. While some scholars observe that Lilburne is not an original thinker, and that his writings are limited in their scope, these compelling qualities of his work are just beginning to be reassessed by literary scholars and historians, and there remains much to do as scholars seek to understand both this complex and dynamic man and his turbulent time.

BIBLIOGRAPHY

Works by John Lilburne

The Christian Mans Triall. March 1638.
Englands Birth-right Justified. October 1645.
Jonahs Cry out of the Whales belly. July 1647.
Londons Liberty In Chains discovered. October 1646.
Plaine Truth without Feare or Flattery. April/May 1647.
A Poore Mans Crye. December 1638.
The Resurrection of John Lilburne. May 1656.
Strength out of Weaknesse. September 1649.

Studies of John Lilburne

Achinstein, Sharon. "Revolution in Print: Lilburne's Jury, *Areopagitica*, and the Conscientious Public." In her *Milton and the Revolutionary Reader*. Princeton: Princeton University Press, 1994.

Aylmer, G.E., ed. *The Levellers in the English Revolution*. Ithaca, NY: Cornell University Press, 1975.

Frank, Joseph. *The Levellers: A History of the Writings of Three Seventeenth-Century Social Democrats: John Lilburne, Richard Overton, and William Walwyn*. Cambridge: Harvard University Press, 1955.

Gibb, M.A. *John Lilburne the Leveller*. London: L. Drummond, 1947.

Gregg, Pauline. *Free-born John: A Biography of John Lilburne*. London: George G. Harrap & Co., 1961.

Haller, William, ed. *Tracts on Liberty in the Puritan Revolution*. 3 vols. New York: Columbia University Press, 1934.

Haller, William, and Godfrey Davies, eds. *The Leveller Tracts, 1647–1653*. New York: Columbia University Press, 1944.

Loewenstein, David. "Lilburne, Leveller Polemic, and the Ambiguities of the Revolution." In his *Representing Revolution in Milton and His Contemporaries*. Cambridge: Cambridge University Press, 2001.

Smith, Nigel. "Discourse from Below: The Levellers, the City and the Army." In his *Literature and Revolution in England, 1640–1660*. New Haven, CT: Yale University Press, 1994.

Webber, Joan. *The Eloquent "I": Style and Self in Seventeenth-Century Prose*. Madison: University of Wisconsin Press, 1968.

Wolfe, Don M. ed. *Leveller Manifestoes of the Puritan Revolution*. New York: Nelson & Sons, 1944.

❧ *John Locke*
(1632–1704)

LOUIS A. GEBHARD

BIOGRAPHY

John Locke was born in 1632 at Wrington, about eight miles south of Bristol. It was a time of growing tension between King Charles I (1624–1649) and the increasingly restive and increasingly Puritan Parliament. Locke was the elder of two sons of a country gentleman attorney, a Puritan in persuasion who joined the Parliamentary army in the Civil Wars of the 1640s against the King (Aaron 3), serving as a captain in a regiment raised by a more wealthy friend and neighbor. One result of the friendship was Locke's nomination to the prestigious Westminster School, where Locke enrolled in 1647. Locke was still there two years later when the defeated King was executed nearby, though it seems that Locke did not witness it (Cranston 20). A promising student, he was "elected" to Christ Church at Oxford in 1652, residing there for the next fifteen years, during **Cromwell**'s Commonwealth (1649–1660) and during the early years of the Restoration, which began with the return of Charles II in 1660. During these years, Locke advanced from student to teacher, beginning his teaching in 1660 when most Englishmen, Locke included, welcomed the return of Charles II and the restoration of the old constitution (Milton 7).

Locke was well schooled in the classical languages, not only in Latin and Greek but in Hebrew as well. Much of his education was "scholasticism," Aristotelian thought, especially his logic, combined with Christian theology, taught by lecture, syllogism, and "disputation" (formal debate). Thoroughly put off by both method and content (Jenkins x), and coming under the influence of **Robert Boyle** (1627–1691), Locke turned more and more to the natural sciences. Another influence was Thomas Sydenham (1624–1689), who relied on careful observation rather than on ancient authority, hoary maxims, or deduction. Locke, disinclined to take holy orders or a legal degree, embarked on the study of medicine, ultimately receiving his B.A. (but never an M.D.). He remained a practitioner of sorts for many years but more of a well-informed "amateur" than a professional (Aaron 4–6).

Science and philosophy, still interwoven, were both in flux. The work of Andreas Vesalius (d. 1564), **William Harvey** (d. 1657), William Gilbert (d. 1603), Johannes Kepler (d. 1630), and Galileo Galilei (d. 1642), to name a few, were posing a mortal challenge to traditional Aristotelian science. Methodology, too, was a matter of debate. What was the way to truth? Through reason? Through observation? Observation was still somewhat suspect, with René Descartes in his *Discourse on Method* (1637) using systematic doubt and careful reasoning to build a philosophical system on his famous *Cogito ergo sum* (I think therefore I am). Despite his later reputation as an empiricist, Locke accepted much of Descartes's rationalism, employing it in his *Essay Concerning Human Understanding* to prove the existence of God. But he also read Descartes's critics, most notably Pierre Gassendi (1592–1653), French priest and philosopher. Contrary to Descartes, Gassendi argued that "nothing is in the intellect which has not been in the senses." Well, almost. As with the later Locke, he was willing to admit that the mind was able to discover some truths a priori, that is, without experience. Locke has, indeed, sometimes been called a "good Gassendist" (Aaron 9), but the appellation may be misplaced.

Locke's politics—and religion—at this time, in 1660, were still conservative (Cranston 66), but his views were about to undergo change. In 1665, he sought and received a diplomatic assignment joining the mission of Sir Walter Vane to Brandenburg (later known as Brandenburg-Prussia, and ultimately, Prussia). Its ruler was a Calvinist, but the populace included large numbers of Lutherans and even Catholics. Sir Walter's mission, attempting to enlist Brandenburg in England's war against the Dutch, accomplished nothing. All returned home (Locke to Oxford) after a few months. But the episode may have helped change Locke's views on religious toleration. As he noted, the three religions seemed to coexist in the country without tension (Cranston 82).

A more decisive influence on Locke appeared a year later when he was introduced to Anthony Ashley Cooper (later, in 1672, **first Earl of Shaftesbury**). The two soon became close friends, Locke leaving Oxford in 1667 to take up residence in the Shaftesbury household in London. Through Shaftesbury, Locke entered public service, serving from 1668 to 1671 as Secretary to the Lords Proprietors of Carolina. As Secretary, Locke seems to have had some influence (how much has been debated) in drawing up the "constitutions" [sic] of the new colony—a constitution be it noted that placed important checks to a "numerous democracy." The constitution provided for aristocratic domination with a large measure of religious freedom, although atheism was proscribed (Cranston 120).

Locke also saw service under Shaftesbury as Secretary of Presentations when Shaftesbury become Lord Chancellor. Locke recorded both the petitions of clergymen for positions in the Church and Shaftesbury's decisions. Locke also served on the Council of Trade and Plantations (the forerunner of the Colonial Office) in 1673 and 1674. His fortunes improving, he was able to invest in the Royal African Company and in the Bahama Adventurers, making him, unfortunately, an accomplice of sorts in one of the worst atrocities of modern history, the Atlantic slave trade. Locke would later condemn slavery as a "vile and miserable estate" (*Works* V: Book I, ch. 1, 212) and was opposed to enslavement of the Amerindian population of Carolina (Tully 171). But he was willing to accept slavery as a consequence of a "just war" (*Works* V: ch. 7, 88). Was the enslavement of the people of West Africa the consequence of a "just war"? Did Locke ever confront the question? We do not know.

In 1668, Locke joined the newly constituted Royal Society, an association devoted to advancing scientific knowledge. Locke does not seem to have participated much in the formal sessions, preferring rather the smaller informal gatherings devoted to the discussion of intellectual issues. One of these took place in Locke's quarters when the discussion turned to "knowledge." As Locke wrote later (Fraser, *Essay Concerning Human Understanding*, "Epistle to the Reader" 9), an impasse was soon reached. This set Locke to pondering, reading, discussing, writing, and revising over the next twenty years during travel, political turmoil, illness, flight, exile, and other distractions. The result was the epoch-making *Essay Concerning Human Understanding*, finally published in 1690, just after the "Glorious Revolution"—the ousting of James II and the accession of William of Orange.

The political temperature was moving upward in the 1670s. Shaftesbury was in opposition by 1673, and in the summer of 1675 an anonymously authored pamphlet appeared titled *A Letter From a Person of Quality to His Friend in the Country*. It dwelt on a possible conspiracy in high places that, it claimed, aimed at establishing absolutism. Shaftesbury and Locke were both suspects, and indeed the pamphlet was printed in a 1720 edition of Locke's work. Locke somewhat evasively denied authorship but, possibly fearing arrest, left the country for France, remaining there for about three years. Shaftesbury, getting into deeper trouble, was jailed in the Tower for about a year, from February 1677 to February 1678.

Locke returned in 1679, the furor over the pamphlet having subsided, but the political situation was more tense. At issue was the succession. Charles did not have a legitimate male heir and under the Constitution, James, his brother, would succeed. This, Shaftesbury was determined to prevent. For Shaftesbury and his "Country Party" (beginning to be called "Whigs"), James was impossible for two reasons: (1) his Catholicism; (2) his absolutism. The atmosphere deteriorated drastically when in September 1678 one Titus Oates, a reputable university professor (Van der Zee and Van der Zee 148) and former Baptist preacher (Smith 361), informed the King and his Privy Council of a "Popish Plot" to kill him, massacre Protestants, and reintroduce Catholicism in the country. The story was a fabrication but was widely believed. In the resulting hysteria, a wave of arrests followed, and several executions of innocent victims were carried out to which Shaftesbury (and Locke?) acquiesced. Indeed, Shaftesbury exploited the situation to introduce in 1679 a bill providing for the exclusion of James from the throne. But after a second reading, in May 1679, Charles prorogued the session and then in July ordered a dissolution. Matters went from bad to worse, and talk of a new civil war began to be heard. Charles jailed Shaftesbury again in July 1679 and then placed him on trial for treason. He was acquitted, but his health was now gone and his power broken. In the fall of 1682, he went into exile to the Netherlands, where he died the following year.

A second scare, the Rye House Plot of June 1683, involved a plan to assassinate both Charles and James and place the Duke of Monmouth, a Protestant and one of Charles's illegitimate sons, on the throne. The plot was given away before it could materialize, an investigation was launched, some executions took place, and Locke came under suspicion. Again, fearful of arrest, Locke left the country in September, this time for the Netherlands. These events were part of the milieu of another of Locke's major works, his *Two Treatises of Government* (to use the short title), which were published anonymously in 1690 but were written, for the most part, around 1681.

The laudatory comments on William of Orange together with some other remarks were added just prior to publication.

James, prevailing for the moment, ascended the throne in 1685 but, as his late brother had predicted, lost it within four years (Van der Zee and Van der Zee 173), after alienating not only the Whigs and the general public but the Tories as well. The birth of a male heir in 1688 raised the prospect of an indefinite succession of Catholic rulers. He—and his heir—had to go. Whig and Tory emissaries invited William of Orange, a grandson of Charles I, married to Mary, one of the Protestant daughters of James and at the time *Stadholder* of the Netherlands, to come to England, where he arrived with a small army in the fall of 1688. As resistance evaporated, James and his family fled the country, and William and Mary were crowned cosovereigns in the spring of 1689, with Locke returning to England a few months earlier (Aaron 23).

During his exile in the Netherlands, Locke completed his famous *Essay*, publishing it in 1690, this time with his name displayed. Locke, now in favor, was offered an embassy but declined it, resuming his position on the Board of Trade, where he remained until his deteriorating health (asthma, mostly) forced his retirement in 1700. In the meantime, in the 1690s, he published a number of lengthy essays and wrote the usual lengthy rejoinders to his attackers. Locke wanted to write a thorough revision of the *Essay*, but overwhelmed with work and failing health, the best he could do was a succession of editions containing minor revisions. He was, however, able to oversee a French translation and did write an addendum called the *Conduct of the Understanding*, which appeared posthumously in 1706.

Locke had met Newton in 1680 and wrote a review of Newton's *Principia* of 1687, a truly daunting task, but after great effort and study, he seemed to have mastered the physics and received help with the mathematics (Axtell 165–182). After 1700, Locke (like King William), racked by asthma, could endure London no longer and attempted to retire permanently with the Masham family at Oates in Sussex. He returned briefly to London on the summons of the King, but the trip proved taxing, and after returning to Oates, he steadily weakened, passing away toward the end of the summer of 1704 while Lady Masham read him the Psalms.

MAJOR WORKS AND THEMES

The *Essay Concerning Human Understanding* (1690) was Locke's major work, and for the rest of his life, he remained proud of it, although he did admit that it needed revision (Rogers 3; Cranston 263). It is composed of four books, together with an "Epistle to the Reader" and a dedication to Thomas Herbert (1656–1733), Earl of Pembroke, a patron, friend, and in 1690, President of the Royal Society. Book One is an attack on the belief in the existence of "innate" ideas—ideas in the mind independent of any experience. In using the word *idea* broadly (too broadly in the view of most critics), ideas for Locke are "whatsoever is in the object of the understanding when a man thinks" (Introduction, para. 8; all citations from the *Essay* are from the Alexander Campbell Fraser edition) including any principle, proposition, "phantasm," or "notion," true or false (Introduction, para. 8, Book Two, ch. xxxii). The "understanding is the power of thinking" and is one of the "powers" or abilities or a "faculty" in the mind (Book Two, ch. 7). Reminding us that "general assent" (the general belief of the existence of innate ideas) "proves nothing" (Book One, ch. 1, para. 2-4), Locke insists that all children and idiots have not the least apprehension "of ideas" (Book One, ch. 1, para. 5), nor is the idea of God innate and therefore "it is hard to conceive how there should be innate principles" (Book One, ch. 3, para. 8).

Book Two describes how we acquire ideas. Here Locke uses his famous (if ill chosen) metaphor comparing the mind to a "white paper, void of all characters, without any ideas" (ch. 1, para. 2). It acquires "all the materials of reason and knowledge" from "experience" (Book Two, ch. 1, para. 2). For Locke there are two aspects or "fountains" of experience: "sensation" and "reflection" (Book Two, ch. 1, para. 2). He then takes the remainder of Book Two to analyze various kinds of ideas as well as a number of concepts including space, time, cause, effect, substance, and infinity. But he adds a discussion in a chapter on "Identity" (ch. 27), making an important (but not altogether successful) effort in addressing the question as to when a thing or person is the same thing and when not.

Book Three is devoted to words and language, a subject that gave Locke a great deal of difficulty. For Locke words are signs of ideas in the mind (ch. 1, para. 2). Speech, given to man by God (ch. 1, para. 1), conveys the "thoughts of men's minds" to others (ch. 1, para. 2) but not well. Probably attacking scholasticism, he charges that language all too often is "abused willfully" (ch. 10). In the final chapter (ch. 11), Locke offers "remedies," including the refraining from meaningless words, defining words clearly, and using (in the natural sciences) pictures. A dictionary would be desirable, but he considers it too costly to produce (ch. 11, para. 25).

Book Four deals with knowledge and probability. Here at the outset, he writes "*knowledge* then seems to me to be nothing but *the perception of the connection of and agreement or disagreement and repugnancy of any of our ideas*" (Locke's emphasis). In this alone, it consists (ch. 1, para. 2) and "whenever we perceive the agreement or disagreement of any of our ideas, there is certain knowledge" (Book Four, ch. 4, para. 18). Further, "for when we know that white is not black, what do we else perceive that these two ideas do not agree?" He goes on to list the "sorts" of agreement and disagreement (ch. 1, para. 2), degrees of our knowledge (ch. 2), and the extent of human knowledge (ch. 3) (which he considers "very narrow") (ch. 3, para. 22). Chapter five in Book Four includes a discussion of "truth" (ch. 7) and comments about "our knowledge of the existence of God." Departing from his empiricism, here he offers an essentially "ontological" proof of the existence of God (essentially, I exist, therefore God exists) (ch. 10, para. 1–4). Chapter 15 deals with probability; chapter 17 with reason. Locke, predictably, finds reason and faith complementary.

The year 1690 was a banner year for Locke; in addition to the *Essay*, there appeared his now classic *Second Treatise on Civil Government*. But the *Second Treatise* was published (anonymously) along with the largely forgotten *First* under the title, *Two Treatises of Government, in the Former the False Principles and Foundation of Sir Robert Filmer, and His Followers are Detected and Overthrown and the Latter is an Essay Concerning the True Original Extent and End of Civil Government*. In the preface, he states that "these (treatises) which remain I hope are sufficient to establish the throne of our great restorer our present King William to make good his title in the consent of the People which being the *only* (my emphasis) one of all lawful government" (*Works* V: preface, 209).

The *First Treatise* (*Works* V)—much of which was lost—is an attack, sometimes shrill, on Filmer's contention that Kings are heirs to Adam and as such own everything and, indeed, everybody. This total dominion comes from God. Locke, deploying his mastery of Scripture, classical languages, a bit of reason, and some name calling, attempts to refute this. In the *Second Treatise*, a landmark work and relatively short (146 pages), Locke attempts, among other things, to lay down the philosophical basis of a legitimate government. Government originates, he argues, when men decide to put an end to the "state of nature" (the absence of government) and create a civil society (government). The chief end of government is to eliminate the inconveniences of the state of nature and to better protect man's natural rights. Natural rights include the right to one's life and—especially for Locke—to property. Natural rights stem from the existence of natural law, law that our reason teaches us. When men create a government or civil society, they agree to live under majority rule. The majority rules through the legislature. But neither the majority nor the legislature can legitimately violate natural rights. If it or the executive or the monarch does so, resistance and revolution (though Locke does not use the term) are justified; the people have the right to change the government.

Locke's third major work, the *Epistola de Tolerantia*, originally in Latin, was the first of four *Letters on Toleration*, published in Gouda in the Netherlands in 1689. Addressed to a European readership, it seems to have been provoked by the persecution of the Huguenots by Louis XIV. Locke, again, was at pains to conceal his authorship and was greatly vexed when it became known that the tract was his (Cranston 332). The *Epistola* provoked the predictable rejoinder, and a long public exchange took place with one Jonas Proast, Anglican clergyman and controversialist (Vernon 95–106). Quite possibly the controversy was sharpened by William Popple, who not only translated the *Epistola* into English but added (most probably without Locke's consent) a preface calling for "absolute [religious] liberty" (Locke, *Works* VI; Cranston 259–260).

Locke's major points in four long public letters (all together some 570 pages) may be summarized as follows:

1. Persecution is inconsistent with—and counter to—true Christianity.
2. Government ("the magistrate") does not have the authority to legislate on religious matters; the Church does not have the right to legislate on civil matters. Church and State are separate entities.
3. True religion does not need force to prevail; "truth will shift for herself."
4. All Protestants, Jews, Moslems, even "idolators" have the right to toleration but not Catholics or atheists. The latter two groups are a threat to society.

Locke found time after returning to England to publish a tract titled *Some Thoughts Concerning Education*, which appeared in 1693, although it had been composed some twenty years earlier. It is designed as a guide for the rearing of a "gentleman" and covers a gamut of suggestions. Anticipating the humanitarianism of the Enlightenment, it advises against corporal punishment (*Works* IX: 57) and urges the teaching of kindness "to all sensible creatures" (113) as well as "civility toward inferiors and meaner sorts of people, particularly servants" (114). Locke's choice of words here as well as his advice about keeping a young gentleman away from the "taint of servants and meaner sorts of people" (59) is significant and suggests that Locke was, despite the rhetoric of the *Second Treatise*, hardly a democrat in the modern sense but rather a class-conscious if Whiggish member of the English gentry.

He also published a tract titled the *Reasonableness of Christianity* (1695), which again irked the more orthodox theologians as Locke seemed to accept the Socinian (or Unitarian) position on the nature of Christ (He was human, not divine). But Locke would not say as much. Other publications written in the 1670s dealing with political economy found their way into print in the 1690s with Locke urging the government to forego lowering interest and in a separate tract urging it not to debase the currency. In addition, he somehow found time to write a commentary on the Epistles of St. Paul.

CRITICAL RECEPTION

Locke's work from the very beginning sparked enormous interest; the *Essay* was an immediate success and indeed was more widely read than any other book of his generation (Lamprecht xxxv). He was a participant in the scientific revolution, and his empiricism was vindicated by his difficult friend Isaac Newton. The scientific revolution helped set in motion the so-called Enlightenment of the 18th century and the revolutions of 1776 and 1789, with Locke's rhetoric from his *Second Treatise* easily appropriated by democratic revolutionists, then and ever since. All this despite the fact that Locke was not the thoroughgoing empiricist, no believer in democracy (in the modern sense), and doubtful as to the possibilities of scientific progress. The deeds of the French Revolution and the "death of God" of the late 19th century would have filled him with horror.

Locke's influence on the American Revolution has been the subject of debate. Writing in 1943, John C. Miller wrote that the "American Revolution had a ready made philosophy," its ideology inspired "above all by the political writings of John Locke" (169–170). "[C]olonial clergy served their parishioners John Locke and Holy Writ in equal measure" (187). But by the 1960s another view had developed that argued that the *Two Treatises* had little influence on 18th-century American political thinking (Dunn 45–80). More recently, however, S.M. Dworetz, after reviewing the issue, argues convincingly that Lockeian ideas were indeed influential, providing both the ideas and the rhetoric of the revolutionists. Moreover, it is probably relevant that his work formed a significant part of the curricula in America's universities in the 18th century, only to disappear in the 19th (Scholes 12, 182–185).

For three centuries Locke has had his critics. Indeed, he himself was one of them, referring to himself as "lazy" and as a "mediocrity" (Jenkins xii). He admitted that the *Essay*, despite his pride in it, was "repetitious" and "confused" and "needed to be reduced to better order" (Cranston 263; Joad 42). Though revised three times in Locke's lifetime, it never received a sufficiently thorough revision. Thus, even friendly critics have found his doctrine of ideas "muddled" and "incomplete" (Cranston 274); "ambiguity" in the whole work has been "a staple of criticism for centuries" (Milton 25) and a cottage industry as Lockeian scholars continue to debate "what Locke meant."

Bishop Stillingfleet and other divines found his work dangerous to faith; the *Essay* was "censored by some Heads of College at Oxford in 1703" (Yolton, *Introduction*

4) but later in the century became part of the curriculum (Bill 265). Locke went into eclipse in the 19th century, receiving some of the blame for the French Revolution, condemned by such luminaries as Samuel Taylor Coleridge and Joseph de Maistre. Even his style, once applauded for its "elegance" (*Essay* xiii), was derided, and his integrity was called into question, with the charge of plagiarism leveled at him (Aarsleff 278). He was considered "out of fashion" in the 1960s (Martin and Armstrong 1). But a revival began in the 1970s, coinciding with the publication of his correspondence and the launching of the *Locke Newsletter*. Locke was again "in fashion" by the end of the decade.

Portions of the *Essay* continue to meet with mixed reviews. His attempt to treat the problem of personal identity, for example, has been called "justly famous" (Jenkins 103) but his specific answers "generally repudiated" (Allison 105). Some critics have been more severe; the late Oxford professor Gilbert Ryle has called his definition of knowledge "notorious" (Ryle 31), and some critics have been contemptuous of his linguistic theory as "not as bad as it looks" (Kretzman 125).

But the *Essay*—and indeed all his work—needs to be seen in the historical context. The *Essay* was written in everyday language over two decades by a busy, often distracted man whose interests (and sometimes contributions) extended to epistemology, political theory, political economy pedagogy, medical science, and linguistics. On the third centenary of Locke's birth, despite his strictures, Ryle offered this:

What, then was Locke's achievement? If I am not mistaken, it was something much greater than is usually allowed him. He was not merely the plain spoken mouth piece of the age or the readable epitome of its development, nor was it his task merely to anglicize and popularize the philosophical and scientific concepts and theories of his day.

Instead, I claim for Locke that he did achieve a part of his ambition "to be an underlabourer," in clearing ground a little and removing some of the rubbish that lies in the way to knowledge. He taught the educated world the lesson that there are differences in kind between mathematics, philosophy, natural science, theology, inspiration, history, and commonsense acquaintanceship with the world around us. In a word, his achievement is that he gave us not a theory of knowledge but a theory of the sciences. As Ryle puts it, "he taught us to distinguish the types of our inquiries, and thus, made us begin to understand the questions we ask" (38–39).

BIBLIOGRAPHY

Works by John Locke

The Correspondence of John Locke. Ed. E.S. De Beer. 9 vols. London: Oxford University Press, 1976–.

An Essay Concerning Human Understanding. Ed. Peter Nidditch. 1975. Reprint, Oxford: Oxford University Press, 1979.

An Essay Concerning Human Understanding by John Locke. Ed. Alexander Campbell Fraser. 2 vols. New York: Dover Publications, 1959.

John Locke's of the Conduct of the Understanding. Ed. Francis W. Garforth. New York: Teachers College, Columbia University Press, 1966.

Two Treatises of Government. Ed. Peter Laslett. 2nd ed. Cambridge: Cambridge University Press, 1967.

The Works of John Locke. Corrected. 10 vols. London, 1823. Reprint, Aalen, Germany: Scientific Verlag, 1963.

Studies of John Locke

Aaron, Richard I. *John Locke*. 3rd ed. Oxford: Clarendon Press, 1971.

Aarsleff, Hans. "Locke's Influence." In *The Cambridge Companion to Locke*, ed. Vere Chappell. New York: Cambridge University Press, 1994. 252–289. (Chappell contains an excellent bibliography and brings together the most recent scholarship.)

Allison, Henry E. "Locke's Theory of Personal Identity: A Re-examination." In *Locke on Human Understanding: Selected Essays*, ed. I.C. Tipton. Oxford: Oxford University Press, 1977. 105–122.

Ashcraft, Richard. *Revolutionary Politics and Locke's Two Treatises of Government*. Princeton: Princeton University Press, 1986.

Axtell, James L. "Locke, Newton and the Two Cultures." In *John Locke: Problems and Perspectives: A Collection of New Essays*, ed. John Yolton. Cambridge: Cambridge University Press, 1969. 165–182. (Yolton is one of the leading Locke scholars.)

Bill, E.W.G. *Education at Christ Church Oxford 1660–1800*. Oxford: Oxford University Press, 1988.

Copleston, Frederick. *A History of Philosophy*. Vol. V: *Hobbes to Hume*. Westminster, MD: Newman Press, 1961.

Cranston, Maurice. *John Locke: A Biography*. New York: Macmillan, 1957.

Dunn, John. "The Politics of Locke in England and America in the Eighteenth Century." In *John Locke: Problems and Perspectives: A Collection of Essays*, ed. John Yolton. Cambridge: Cambridge University Press, 1969. 45–80.

Dworetz, S.M. "John Locke on Government: The Two Treatises and the American Revolution." *Studies in Eighteenth Century Culture* 21 (1991): 101–127.

Jenkins, John J. *Understanding Locke: An Introduction to Philosophy through John Locke's Essay*. Edinburgh: Edinburgh University Press, 1983.

Joad, C.E.M. *Guide to Philosophy*. New York: Dover, 1957.

Kretzman, Norman. "The Main Aspects of Locke's Semantic Theory." In *Locke on Human Understanding: Selected Essays*, ed. I.C. Tipton. Oxford: Oxford University Press, 1977. 123–140.

Lamprecht, Sterling P., ed. *Locke: Selections*. New York: Scribner's, 1928.

Marshall, John. *John Locke: Resistance, Religion and Responsibility*. Cambridge: Cambridge University Press, 1994.

Martin, C.B., and D.M. Armstrong, eds. *Locke and Berkeley: A Collection of Critical Essays*. Notre Dame, IN: Notre Dame University Press, 1968.

Miller, John C. *Origins of the American Revolution*. Boston: Little, Brown, Company, 1943. Reprint, Stanford, CA: Stanford University Press, 1959.

Milton, J.R. "Locke's Life and Times." In *The Cambridge Companion to Locke*, ed. Vere Chappell. New York: Cambridge University Press, 1994. 5–25.

Russell, Bertrand. *A History of Western Philosophy and Its Connection with Political and Social Circumstances from the Earliest Times to the Present Day*. New York: Simon and Schuster, 1963.

Ryle, Gilbert. "John Locke on Human Understanding." In *Locke and Berkeley: A Collection of Critical Essays*, ed. C.B. Martin and D.M. Armstrong. Notre Dame, IN: University of Notre Dame Press, 1968. 38–39.

Sabine, George H. *A History of Political Theory*. Rev. ed. New York: Henry Holt and Company, 1950.

Scholes, Robert. *The Rise and Fall of English: Reconstructing English as a Discipline*. New Haven, CT: Yale University Press, 1958.

Skalweit, Stephen. "Political Thought." In *The New Cambridge Modern History*. Vol. V: *The Ascendancy of France*, ed. E.L. Carsten. New York: Cambridge University Press, 1961. 96–121.

Smith, Goldwyn. *A History of England*. 2nd rev. ed. New York: Scribner's, 1957.

Tully, James. "Rediscovering America: The Two Treatises and Aboriginal Rights." In *Locke's Philosophy: Context and Context*, ed. G.A.J. Rogers. Oxford: Clarendon Press, 1994. 166–196.

Van der Zee, Henry, and Barbara Van der Zee. *William and Mary*. New York: Alfred A. Knopf, 1973.

Vernon, Richard. "Locke's Antagonist Jonas Proast." *Locke Newsletter*, no. 27 (1993): 95–106.

Von Leyden, W. "Philosophy." In *The New Cambridge Modern History*. Vol. V: *The Ascendancy of France*, ed. E.L. Carsten. New York: Cambridge University Press, 1961. 73–95.

Yolton, John S. *John Locke: A Descriptive Bibliography*. Bristol: Thoenmer Press, 1998.

———. *Locke: An Introduction*. Oxford: Basil Blackwell, 1985.

❧ *Richard Lovelace*

(1618–1657)

THOMAS HOWARD CROFTS III

BIOGRAPHY

The poet Richard Lovelace was a scion of an old Kentish family that distinguished itself in the court of Elizabeth I. His great-grandfather, Sir William, Sergeant-at-Law, represented Canterbury in Parliament in 1562 and 1572. The following Sir William, the poet's grandfather, was knighted either by Queen Elizabeth or the Earl of Essex in Dublin in 1599. The poet's father, called Sir William of Woolwich (knighted by James I in 1609), was an outstanding soldier in the Low Countries. At the age of forty-four, Sir William was killed at the siege of Groll in Holland (1627), leaving his widow Anne (née Barne) in charge of their eight children: Richard, Thomas, Francis, William, Dudley Posthumus, Anne, Elizabeth, and Johanna. To Richard fell a great portion of his father's and grandfather's estates.

Lovelace matriculated at Gloucester Hall, Oxford, in 1634. While there he wrote and had produced a comedy entitled *The Scholar* (or *The Scholars*) of which only the prologue and epilogue survive. After only two years, Lovelace—apparently by means of the intervention of one of Queen Henrietta's ladies—was created Master of Arts. The next year Lovelace was in residence at Cambridge where he made the acquaintance of **Andrew Marvell**. About 1639, Lovelace "retired in great splendour" (Wilkinson xx) to Charles's court, where he soon found soldierly occupation, following George, Lord Goring, on both Scottish campaigns (i.e., in the Bishops' Wars of 1639 and 1640). During the second expedition, he wrote a play, *The Soldier*, which was apparently suppressed and, at any rate, is not extant; at this time he also wrote the lines "To Generall Goring, after the pacification of Berwicke."

Returning from the North, Lovelace repaired to his ancestral properties in Kent and was active in the not-inconsequential politics of that region. In 1642 he presented the Royalist Kentish to Parliament, thereby aligning himself with such notorious Royalist upstarts as Sir Edmund Dering (whose own such petition had already landed him in jail). For this offense, Lovelace was imprisoned in Westminster Gatehouse from April

30 to June 21, 1642. On his release, he immediately began mustering and financing troops with the help of his brothers Francis and William and sent another brother, Dudley, to Holland to study the arts of war (Wilkinson xl). Lovelace himself went to London where he lived extravagantly and wrote much poetry.

During this period some of Lovelace's lyrics were set to music by Henry Lawes. Lovelace was again on the field, marching with Charles to Oxford, in 1646. When Charles was captured and imprisoned there (effectively ending his rule), Lovelace went to France, raised a militia, and fought for the French King, then at war with Spain. Lovelace left the field when he was wounded at the battle of Dunkirk. On his return to (**Cromwell**'s) England in 1648, he was promptly jailed at Petre's House at Aldergate. He remained a prisoner until April 1649. By this time, Lovelace had exhausted his patrimony. In his *Athenae Oxoniensis* (1691–1692) the antiquarian Anthony Wood gives the following account of Lovelace's last days:

After the Murther of K[ing] *Ch*[arles], *Lovelace* was set at liberty, and having by this time consumed all his Estate, grew very melancholy, (which brought him at length to Consumption) became very poor in body and purse, was the object of charity, went in ragged Cloaths (whereas when he was in his glory he wore Cloth of gold and silver) and mostly lodged in obscure and dirty places, more befitting the worst of Beggars, than poorest of servants, &c . . . he died in a very mean Lodging in *Gun-Powder Alley* near Shoe-lane, and was buried . . . in sixteen hundred fifty and eight.

This account cannot be counted on for accuracy, but it does express the passing of the Cavalier era with a certain poetic force. Lovelace died—in some degree of poverty—in 1657, and was buried at St. Bride's Church (which was destroyed in the Great Fire of 1666).

MAJOR WORKS AND THEMES

Lovelace's songs to Lucasta and Althea are some of the finest lyrics of the period, notable for wit, soldierly nobility, and a high level of craftsmanship. "Song to Lucasta, Going to the Wars" is one of the most representative lyrics of the age, which, according to Bush, states a chivalric theme far older than its century, "is Jonsonian [see **Ben Jonson**] in its logical brevity and completeness" (122). Lovelace, like **Suckling** and **Carew**, saw military action in the Royalist effort, and his lyrics, too, are those of a soldier-poet. His most famous lines, however, are not of the field but of the dungeon. "Stone walls do not a prison make, / Nor iron bars a cage" ("To Althea from Prison"). This lyric, with pieces such as "Gratiana Dancing and Singing," "Elinda's Glove," and "Lucasta Laughing," all brilliant carpe diem poems, record in their own way the feeling among those loyal to Charles that upheaval was looming and that moments of happiness were to be savored and preserved.

CRITICAL RECEPTION

The *sprezzatura*, or self-irony, of Lovelace's poems gave way to foreboding. The longer poem "The Lady A.L.: My Asylum in Great Extremity," probably addressed to the poet's cousin Anne Lovelace, manages, among other things, an ingenious synthesis of the experience of a deposed King and that of an ordinary person broken by hard fate. It is a particularly good example of that propensity in the Cavaliers to shift easily from the brief, witty lyric to the carefully crafted pathos of the soliloquy. One of Lovelace's best pieces is the lovely, lilting poem "The Grasshopper," which, taking up an image from Anacreon, takes a uniquely philosophical view of the pressing "winter" of Cromwell's England; the poem also displays the poet's subtle sense of humor and eye for natural imagery. Like Suckling, Lovelace produced only a small body of work, published first by the poet in *Lucasta* (1649) and subsequently by his brother Dudley as *Lucasta. Postume Poems* (1660), but it is a telling achievement.

BIBLIOGRAPHY

Works by Richard Lovelace

The Poems of Richard Lovelace. Ed. Cyril Hackett Wilkinson 1930. Rev. ed., Oxford: Clarendon Press, 1953.

Studies of Richard Lovelace

Bush, Douglas. *English Literature in the Earlier Seventeenth Century*. 2nd ed. Oxford: Clarendon Press, 1962. pp. 122–123.
Hartmann, Cyril Hughes. *The Cavalier Spirit and Its Influence on the Life and Work of Richard Lovelace (1618–1658)*. 1925. New York: Haskell House Publishers, 1973.
Jones, George Fenwick. " 'Love'd I not Honour More': The Durability of a Literary Motif." *Comparative Literature* 2 (1959): 131–143.
Weidhorn, Manfred. *Richard Lovelace*. New York: Twayne Publishers, 1970.

🏵 *Delarivier Manley*

(1672?–1724)

AMY WOLF

BIOGRAPHY

Much of what we know about Delarivier Manley comes from her own writing. Her life story is different each time she writes it, either playfully reconstructed to make her a persecuted romance heroine or shaped into the story of a brilliant, influential, and savvy Tory political writer—or somewhere in between. She is most often portrayed by others as neither but instead as a scandalous, fallen woman with loose morals, a woman who prostituted both her body and her writing. Probably born in 1672, but perhaps as early as 1663, she was the daughter of Sir Roger Manley. Her father authored translations and histories and valued a literary education for his children. When her father died, she and her sister were left in the care of her father's nephew John Manley, who posed as a widower and convinced her to enter into a bigamous marriage with him. She had a son with her cousin and remained with him for at least three years, while he spent what little fortune she had. Her writing career began when she left John Manley and needed to survive in a world in which her reputation had been sullied. After a brief interlude as a companion to the Duchess of Cleveland, King Charles II's former mistress—and a possible source for some of the scandalous stories of which Manley would later make use—in 1696 she went to London with two plays, a comedy, *The Lost Lover; or, The Jealous Husband*, and a tragedy, *The Royal Mischief*. The latter play was relatively successful, having at least six performances.

Around this time Manley met John Tilly, a warden at the Fleet Prison, and they openly became lovers. Manley declared Tilly the great love of her life and probably had at least one child with him, but he was married and neither of them had much money. When his wife died, Manley freed him to marry someone else for money, and they ended their relationship. She turned again to writing, publishing *The Secret History, of Queen Zarah, and the Zarazians* in 1705. One of the first English romans à clef, this secret history savagely satirized Sarah and John Churchill and was a popular success and a major piece of Tory propaganda.

In 1706, Manley's tragedy *Almyna; or, The Arabian Vow* was performed, and the next two years saw the publishing of two small collections of letters appended to translations of works by Marie Catherine d'Aulnoy. Manley's greatest success was *Secret Memoirs and Manners of Several Persons of Quality, of Both Sexes from the New Atalantis, an Island in the Mediterranean*. Usually referred to as *The New Atalantis*, this scandal chronicle was an immediate success but led to Manley's imprisonment and trial for libel. The charges were dropped, and Manley brought out two more volumes of *The New Atalantis* in 1710 called *Memoirs of Europe*, capitalizing on the same formula of real-life scandal and illicit sex barely veiled by pseudonyms.

Subsequently, Manley collaborated with Jonathan Swift on the *Examiner*, and in 1710 he chose her as his successor as editor. In 1714 Manley wrote her autobiography *The Adventures of Rivella* for printer Edmund Curll in order to prevent the publication of an unauthorized version of her life under that same title by Grub Street writer Charles Gildon. With the death of Anne in 1714 and the Hanoverian succession, many Tory writers turned away from politicized scandal fiction, and Manley was no exception. She moved to the country around this time and never returned to "the town." Manley's literary career ended with a play, *Lucius, the First Christian King of Britain* (1717), and a collection of tales, *The Power of Love: In Seven Novels* (1720). During this time she lived with the printer John Barber, possibly as his mistress, but probably an arrangement of their professional and friendly relationship. Her scandalous life continued to be as interesting to most people as her work, and her quest for legitimate financial independence was never fulfilled. She died at Barber's printing-house on July 11, 1724, requesting in her will that any remaining unpublished writings be burned.

MAJOR WORKS AND THEMES

Manley's plays are little read today but notable for their candid and explicit portrayal of female sexual desire and ambitious women. Like the heroines in her novels, the women in her plays are victims of sexual and moral seduction, but they often achieve the power to seduce others. Government and family are closely linked, and corrupt male seducers are representative of the disaster of failed government. *The Lost Lover* and *The Royal Mischief* both appeared in 1696 and were moderately successful. *Almyna* (1706) is usually considered the best of her plays because of its tight, coherent plot borrowed from the *Arabian Nights*.

The domestic and private are inextricably linked to the political and public in Manley's scandal chronicles. Zarah's (Sarah Churchill's) intrigues in *The Secret History of Queen Zarah* are sexual ones that have political consequences, and the various treacherous relationships that the Churchills have are not merely allegories for political miscreance but are basically the same thing. It is Zarah's desire for love "which has always made her life one continued scene of political intrigue" (60). The preface to *Zarah* gestures to realism and history as alternatives to the Romance form that had dominated the previous century. *The New Atalantis* made Manley famous in her own century and still receives the most critical attention. Like *The Secret History of Queen Zarah*, *The New Atalantis* works on both an allegorical and a narrative level and uses the Churchills as the central villains. As Catherine Gallagher points out, "[S]uch doubleness, moreover, makes the defamation all the more pleasurable, effective, and, indeed, *explicit*" (103).

Manley's Astrea, the goddess of Justice, tours earth in order to learn its vices so she may protect her ward, a young prince. Intelligence is her guide, a knowing satirical goddess who often stands in for Manley herself in her access to scandal and stories. In the midst of several stories of incest and abuse of guardianship with innocent young women as persecuted heroines, Manley/Intelligence also gives another version of her own seduction by John Manley veiled as the story of "Delia." The repetition of the seduction plot and its allegorical function as a story of abused political power can be seen as "an attempt to figure the possibility of female political agency" and as "a series of attempts to destabilize the structuring oppositions of contemporary ideology . . . in order to privilege the woman as commentator upon and actor in the political realm" (Ballaster 131). Both her scandal fictions are important for their emphases on private life, the tension between the political and personal, their obsession with the theme of persecuted innocence, and their move from earlier forms of fiction and toward dialogue and realistic detail.

CRITICAL RECEPTION

Despite the many personal insults flung at Delarivier Manley in typical 18th-century fashion, many of her contemporaries praised her as an important and talented writer. But for over two centuries after her death, Manley was infamous for her personal life and attacked for the supposed shamelessness of her writing, seen as inappropriate especially for a woman. However, she has been reclaimed and reevaluated in the second half of the 20th century, especially by historians of the novel and feminist critics. In her lifetime she was named as one of the "Female Wits" and savagely satirized in a play of that name along with Catherine Trotter and Mary Pix, but the title was also used in other contexts as a nonironic compliment.

In the third canto of "The Rape of the Lock," Alexander Pope used the fame of *The New Atalantis* as a benchmark for eternity, "as long as *Atalantis* shall be read." Jonathan Swift respected her enough to choose her, as we have seen, as his successor as editor of the *Examiner*, and in a letter to Stella he gave her the mixed compliment that "she has very generous principles, for one of her sort; and a great deal of sense and invention." And Daniel Defoe was inspired to write his own imitation of Manley's most famous work, his *Atalantis Major*, in 1710. But within a few decades of her death, her works and her life were largely ignored because they did not mix with a new morality or fit the expected role of a woman writer. Generations later Winston Churchill was still disgusted by her treatment of his ancestors and derided her as shameless and immoral. *The Dictionary of National Biography* used the same sort of language when discussing the *New Atalantis* in which she "exhibited her taste for intrigue, and impudently slandered many persons of note." By 1978 Dolores Palomo could feel as if she was discussing an "almost unknown writer" who needed to be reclaimed, but by the close of the 20th century, Manley was happily a key figure in most histories of the novel.

BIBLIOGRAPHY

Works by Delarivier Manley

The Adventures of Rivella. [1714.] Ed. Katherine Zelinsky. Peterborough, Ontario: Broadview, 1999.

The New Atalantis. [1709.] Ed. Rosalind Ballaster. New York: New York University Press, 1992.

The Novels of Mary Delariviere Manley. Ed. Patricia Koster. Gainesville, FL: Scholars' Facsimiles and Reprints, 1971.

Studies of Delarivier Manley

Ballaster, Ros. *Seductive Forms: Women's Amatory Fiction from 1684 to 1740.* Oxford: Clarendon Press, 1992.

Gallagher, Catherine. *Nobody's Story: The Vanishing Acts of Women Writers in the Marketplace 1670–1820.* Berkeley: University of California Press, 1994.

McDowell, Paula. *The Women of Grub Street: Press, Politics, and Gender in the London Literary Marketplace 1678–1730.* Oxford: Clarendon Press, 1998.

Morgan, Fidelis. *A Woman of No Character: An Autobiography of Mrs. Manley.* London: Faber and Faber, 1986.

Palomo, Dolores. "A Woman Writer and the Scholars: A Review of Mary Manley's Reputation." *Women and Literature* 6.1 (1978): 36–46.

🐦 *Andrew Marvell*

(1621–1678)

HUGH MACRAE RICHMOND

BIOGRAPHY

In his own time Andrew Marvell was noted primarily as a civil servant, parliamentarian, and political writer. He was initially associated with the Puritan faction that attained power during the Commonwealth period, but he usually took a moderate position, which left him in a position of influence even after the Restoration. He was born in 1621 at Winestead, just outside the port city of Kingston on Hull, moving to the latter city when his Calvinist father became lecturer at Holy Trinity Church. In 1633, Marvell progressed from Hull Grammar School to Trinity College, Cambridge, a university then closely associated with the Puritan faction (while Oxford was Royalist); but Marvell contributed to an anthology of Greek and Latin verse congratulating King Charles I on the birth of a daughter. In 1638 his mother died, and his father remarried. The following year Marvell was briefly converted to Catholicism, but after running away to London, he was recovered by his father (who was drowned in the River Humber in 1641). From 1642 to 1648 Marvell traveled in Holland, France, Italy, and Spain, acquiring languages and seeming deliberately to avoid most of the tensions and sufferings of the Civil War in England. On his travels he met such exiles as the poet Richard Flecknoe in Rome and himself composed the pastoral *Dialogue between Thyrsis and Dorinda* (set to music by William Lawes by 1645).

By the time of his move to Yorkshire to take up an appointment in 1650 as tutor of Mary Fairfax (daughter of the Puritan leader General Fairfax), Marvell had advanced his career as a poet and political writer in such poems as *An Horatian Ode upon Cromwell's Return from Ireland*. During his stay in the Fairfax establishment Marvell probably wrote many of his best-known poems, "The Garden," *Upon Appleton House*, and the Mower poems. In 1653 he became tutor to **Cromwell**'s protégé William Dutton and moved to the home of John Oxenbridge, whose travels inspired Marvell to write "The Bermudas." In 1658, after many other poems in the same vein, he wrote *A Poem upon the Death of Oliver Cromwell*. In 1659 he was first elected

Member of Paliament for Hull, which he continued to represent until his death. He served on several foreign missions, to Holland, Russia, Sweden, and Denmark. He may have served as a secret agent in his eleven months in Holland, judging by his later critique of the secret services in 1668 and his covert work for the Dutch in 1673–1674. After assisting and then replacing **John Milton** (after his blindness) as Latin Secretary in charge of correspondence for Cromwell's government, Marvell may have maintained enough influence following the Restoration to help protect John Milton from persecution as a defender of regicide, for Marvell had by then become an admired Parliamentarian with progressive political views. During 1662–1665 he represented Britain in Holland, Denmark, Sweden, and Russia. On his return he continued to write political prose and verse, some of it politically provocative enough to be published anonymously to avoid persecution. In his last year, 1678, he briefly became a Warden of Trinity House, which handled nautical concerns in British waters relevant to Hull's interests. In 1681, three years after his death, his collected verse (excluding the post-Restoration satires) was published as *Miscellaneous Poems* by a Mary Palmer, who claimed to be his wife (without any surviving proof). The political poems appeared later in various anthologies, culminating in *A New Collection of Poems Relating to State Affairs* in 1705.

MAJOR WORKS AND THEMES

Andrew Marvell has been chiefly remembered in modern times for his lyric verse, despite the greater length and early recognition of his contentious writings in verse and prose. Among his early works, his pastorals focused on the figure of the Mower have remained popular because of their qualities of urbanity and wit that they share with comparable poems of **Herrick** and **Herbert**. One, at least, "The Mower against Gardens," achieves a larger significance in its attack on the tightly formal gardens of the Renaissance that reached a kind of mathematical perfection in France with the horticulture of Le Notre. Marvell's Mower anticipates the more irregular landscapes that Capability Brown made representative of English rural taste. Similarly elegantly conventional verse is seen in other popular poems, such as "On a Drop of Dew," "Mourning," and "The Coronet." His greatest success in this vein may be his rehearsal of the carpe diem convention in "To His Coy Mistress," which delicately fuses pagan tradition with contemporary references in the vein of **Ben Jonson**. While this poem appears personal in its Yorkshire allusion to the Humber, its aetheistic vision cannot be reconciled with the Puritan theology of Marvell's ilk, and the poem may therefore be seen to be in the tradition of the amoral Volpone's attempt to debauch Celia in Jonson's comedy and thus as a study in misguided sophistication. More personally revealing may be the two "Dialogues": "between the Resolved Soul and Created Pleasure" and "between the Soul and the Body," in which a greater tension can be detected between temptation and moral orthodoxy, perhaps anticipating the moderate position Marvell was later to take politically in an equally polarized society.

In his other verse, Marvell can be seen to progress toward his political career to which he ultimately devoted himself wholeheartedly. Such later poems explore other alternative points of view that may seem to be more personally relevant: "The Garden" proposes an Epicurean retreat from disordered society, of which a further more truly Christian variant appears in "The Bermudas," showing how many Puritans evaded

English political strife by emigration. These options achieve an implicit resolution in *Upon Appleton House*, which also follows a Jonsonian model in "Penshurst" but with a far more political relevance. While Marvell luxuriates in the lush landscape of his patron's estate, as he did in "The Garden," he begins to recognize that General Fairfax's retreat from metropolitan politics to his idyllic estate is an evasion and one that even his daughter Mary Fairfax will be less likely to undertake with her prospect of a political marriage (she became the wife of the Duke of Buckingham).

Granted this flow of thought, it is not surprising to find Marvell's acceptance of the role of Latin Secretary to the Commonwealth's Council of State, in succession to John Milton, who showed a similar progression from art to politics. As a poet he had already addressed such political themes as his *Horation Ode upon Cromwell's Return from Ireland*, but the poem avoided a narrowly partisan point of view. Thus, unlike Milton, Marvell was discreet enough to bridge the gap between the Commonwealth and the Restored monarchy, for his political support in Parliament was even solicited by Charles II with the offer of a substantial bribe. Marvell's subsequent writing reflected a moderate position in the pursuit of liberty, which made him a model for what became the Whig position (and perhaps ultimately that of the modern liberal). This conciliatory posture appears in his *Rehearsal Transpros'd*, a witty defense of toleration against the authoritarianism of Anglican cleric Stanley Parker, in which Marvell's moderate position was famously expressed in his review of the Civil War: "I think the cause was too good to be fought for. Men ought to have trusted God; they ought and might have trusted the king with the whole matter." Nevertheless, his post-Restoration political satires often seem intemperate in their attacks on the royal court generally and the King and his principal minister, Clarendon, in particular. His witty parody of the King's Speech to Parliament (1675) anticipates the comic bravura of Swift, who considered him "a great genius."

CRITICAL RECEPTION

Marvell's poems were not collected until 1681, three years after his death, and only his political verse achieved prominence in his lifetime. As for his prose, the two parts of *The Rehearsal Transpros'd* were praised by Gilbert Burnett in 1678 as "the wittiest books that have appeared in this age." Even Charles II read them "over and over again," and they also won the praise of an author as stylish as the **Earl of Rochester** (John Wilmot). Marvell's prose continued to be generally admired after his lifetime; indeed, John Carey calls Swift "his pupil in style." An anonymous account "On his Excellent Friend Mr. Anth [sic] Marvell" in 1697 calls Marvell "this island's watchfull sentinel."

The contemporary lack of comment on Marvell's lyrics indicates that they were largely unknown despite their posthumus publication in 1681. John Carey compares their obscure status to that of **Vermeer**'s paintings, which remained equally obscure until the 20th century. The highly finished delicacy of both artists failed to catch popular attention. However, new interest in Marvell's verse began in the Romantic period with praise in Charles Lamb's *Essays of Elia* and Tennyson's enthusiasm inspired Palgrave to include *An Horatian Ode*, "The Bermudas," and "The Garden" in his famous *Golden Treasury*. Marvell's poetic status soared in the 20th century, sharing the popularity of the "metaphysical poets" with whom he was grouped by scholars such as H.J.C. Grierson in his influential anthology of metaphysical verse, which in turn led to the enthusiastic advocacy of T.S. Eliot and intense attention from the New Critics, such as Cleanth Brooks and John Crow Ransome, as well as William Empson. Their close textual scrutinies yielded heightened appreciation of the lyrics' social subtlety and of their verbal agility and nuance. However, the supposed contrast of the "Metaphysicals" with the "Cavalier" poets was never fully valid, and Marvell offers proof of their compatibility by fusing **Donne**'s ingenious style of imagery with a Jonsonian decorum and elegance, reflected in Marvell's overt indebtedness to **Waller**'s style and themes. Marvell's complex literary career has recently been set in this more comprehensive context, stressing the relevance of the precedents not only in Jonson and his followers but also in French poets such as Ronsard, St. Amant, and Théophile de Viau, who share his amatory themes and delight in landscape, even his mystical evocation of "green shades." Marvell's political significance remained evident throughout the 18th century but is only now being thoroughly explored and reevaluated.

BIBLIOGRAPHY

Works by Andrew Marvell

The Complete Poems. Ed. E.S. Donno. Harmondsworth: Penguin, 1972.

The Complete Poetry. Ed. George de Forest Lord. New York: Random House (Modern Library), 1968.

A Critical Edition of the Major Works. Ed. Frank Kermode and Keith Walker. Oxford: Oxford University Press, 1990.

The Latin Poetry of Andrew Marvell. Ed. William A. McQueen and Kiffin A. Rockwell. Chapel Hill: University of North Carolina Press, 1964.

The Metaphysical Lyrics and Poems of the Seventeenth Century, Donne to Butler. Ed. H.J.C. Grierson. Oxford: Clarendon Press, 1921.

Miscellaneous Poems. 1681. Reprint, London: Nonesuch Press, 1923.

The Poems and Letters of Andrew Marvell. Ed. H.M. Margoliouth. 2 vols. Oxford: Clarendon Press. 3rd ed. revised by Pierre Legouis and E.E. Duncan Jones, 1971.

"The Rehearsal Transpros'd" and "The Rehearsal Transpros'd, the Second Part." Ed. D.L.B. Smith. Oxford: Clarendon Press, 1971.

Studies of Andrew Marvell

Brett, R.L., ed. *Andrew Marvell: Essays on the Tercentenary of His Death*. Oxford: Oxford University Press, 1979.

Carey, John, ed. *Andrew Marvell: A Critical Anthology*. Harmondsworth: Penguin, 1969.

Chambers, A.B. *Andrew Marvell and Edmund Waller: Seventeenth Century Praise and Restoration Satire*. University Park: Pennsylvania State University Press, 1991.

Chernaik, Warren L. *The Poet's Time: Politics and Religion in the Work of Andrew Marvell*. Cambridge: Cambridge University Press, 1983.

Chernaik, Warren L., and Martin Dzelzainis, eds. *Marvell and Liberty*. Basingstoke: Macmillan, 1999.

Colie, Rosalie L. *"My Echoing Song": Andrew Marvell's Poetry of Criticism*. Princeton: Princeton University Press, 1970.

Collins, Dan S. *Andrew Marvell: A Reference Guide*. Boston: G.K. Hall, 1981.

Eliot, T.S. "Andrew Marvell." In his *Selected Essays*. 3rd ed. New York: Harcourt Brace, 1950.

Empson, William. *Some Versions of Pastoral*. London: Chatto and Windus, 1935.

Friedman, Donald F. *Marvell's Pastoral Art*. Berkeley: University of California Press, 1970.

Griffin, Patsy. *The Modest Ambition of Andrew Marvell*. London: Associated University Presses, 1995.

Hodge, R.I.V. *Foreshortened Time: Andrew Marvell and Seventeenth Century Revolutions*. Cambridge: Cambridge University Press, 1978.

Legouis, Pierre. *André Marvell: Poète, Puritain, Patriote, 1621–1678*. Paris: Didier, 1928. 2nd ed. translated and abridged as *Andrew Marvell: Poet, Puritan, Patriot*. Oxford: Clarendon Press, 1968.

Leishman, J.B. *The Art of Marvell's Poetry*. 2nd ed. London: Hutchinson, 1966.

Patterson, Annabel M. *Marvell and the Civic Crown*. Princeton: Princeton University Press, 1978. 2nd ed. London: Longman, 2000.

Richmond, H.M. *Renaissance Landscapes*. The Hague: Mouton, 1973.

———. *The School of Love: The Evolution of the Stuart Love Lyric*. Princeton: Princeton University Press, 1964.

Rees, Christine. *The Judgment of Marvell*. London: Pinter Publishers, 1989.

Røstvig, Maren-Sophie. *The Happy Man: Studies in the Metamorphosis of a Classical Ideal*. 2nd ed. Oslo: Norwegian Universities Press, 1971.

Scoular, Kitty. *Natural Magic: Studies in the Presentation of Nature in English Poetry from Spenser to Marvell*. Oxford: Clarendon Press, 1965.

Turner, James Grantham. *The Politics of Landscape: Rural Scenery and Society in English Poetry, 1630–1660*. Cambridge: Harvard University Press, 1979.

Wallace, John M. *Destiny His Choice: The Loyalism of Andrew Marvell*. Cambridge: Cambridge University Press, 1968.

Wilcher, Robert. *Andrew Marvell*. Cambridge: Cambridge University Press, 1985.

❧ *Philip Massinger*
(1583–1640)

BRIAN WALSH

BIOGRAPHY

In 1620, Philip Massinger's name appeared in John Taylor's poem "The Praise of Hemp-Seed" as part of a catalog of the most prominent playwrights of the day. In Taylor's poem, "Messenger" (a common variant spelling) takes his place with **Jonson**, Heywood, Fletcher, **Middleton**, and others as one whose "true worth" is evinced by his work. Massinger's subsequent place in the canon of Stuart drama has been considerably more volatile. The vicissitudes of his reputation aside, Massinger is an important figure in early English drama, who worked prolifically alongside some of the most renowned figures of his time and who wrote both within and against the political and dramatic conventions of his age.

Taylor's 1620 reference suggests that Massinger had established himself as a significant dramatist by that time, although it is unclear what he had produced before that date. Somewhat like **Shakespeare** and other figures from the Elizabethan and Stuart theater, Massinger's biography contains considerable gaps, particularly between his early adulthood and the time of being established on London's theatrical scene. Scholars have worked assiduously to establish Massinger's links to plays before the 1620s, either as a collaborator or as sole author, but these theories remain conjectural. A greater degree of certainty is possible in regard to Massinger's family background and early years. Massinger was born in 1583 in Salisbury to Anne and Arthur Massinger. Arthur Massinger was a servant and adviser to the Pembroke family, first Sir Henry Herbert and later to his son Sir William Herbert, a family connection to the nobility that influenced Philip's writing and remained a source of pride throughout his life.

Massinger followed his father in attending St. Alban Hall, Oxford, beginning in 1602, but did not complete a degree. Arthur Massinger died in 1603, and it is possible that remaining at Oxford was no longer financially feasible for Philip. There are no records of his whereabouts or activity between his enrollment at Oxford in 1602 and

1613, by which time it is clear he was working in the London theater world. This is established by the "tripartite" letter that links him to famed theater entrepreneur Philip Henslowe and his stable of playwrights. In the letter, Massinger, Nathan Field, and Robert Darborne collectively wrote Henslowe from debtor prison, asking for an exculpatory loan. Further financial dealings between Massinger and Henslowe are recorded during the 1610s, verifying Massinger's continued association with the lively but often impecunious career of professional playwright during these years.

It is generally postulated that before the 1620s Massinger worked mainly as a collaborator or as a reviser of older plays. In 1623, three years after Taylor's poem, Massinger's name first appeared as sole author of a published play, *The Duke of Milan*, written for the King's Men and performed at the Blackfriars. Massinger seems in this period to have been working on his own and in collaboration with Fletcher for the King's Men, as well as contributing plays to Christopher Beeston's Queen's Men at the Phoenix (or Cockpit) in Drury Lane. With the death of Fletcher in 1625, Massinger became the principal playwright for the King's Men, thus succeeding both Fletcher and Shakespeare in that distinguished position. With one exception, all Massinger's known works between 1625 and his death in 1640 were written for the King's Men, beginning in 1626 with what Massinger himself considered his greatest achievement, *The Roman Actor*.

Most scholars conjecture that Massinger was involved in the writing of roughly fifty-five plays, more than twenty of which are now lost. Of extant plays to which he is associated, it is estimated that fifteen were his own and eighteen were written with one or more joint authors. Ten plays solely authored by Massinger were printed in his lifetime, and from his comments in several dedicatory epistles and prefaces, he appears to have been actively involved in their publication. A surviving collection of eight printed plays, now at the Folger Library, contains corrections in Massinger's hand and suggests he may have been planning to bring out a collection of his plays, either for a patron or for commercial sale, that was never completed.

Massinger seems to have never secured financial stability. He made repeated requests to noble families for patronage throughout his career, including during the time of his long association with the King's Men. Whether such requests were due to indigence or a desire to leave the commercial playwrighting circuit is not known, although the latter is suggested in an epistle to the Earl of Pembroke circa 1615. Massinger died in 1640 at age fifty-six (*not* of the Plague, reports **Aubrey**) and was reputedly buried in Southwark in the same grave as his old friend John Fletcher, an odd but fitting final place for a man who spent much of his professional career working in collaboration.

MAJOR WORKS AND THEMES

Despite a critical tendency to oversimplify Massinger's writing as banally moralistic, there is a skillful breadth and complexity to his plotting and characterizations that is evident throughout his generically diverse plays. A careful examination of Massinger's work reveals a self-conscious playwright who was invested in presenting and manipulating the dramatic conventions he inherited. For instance, in *A New Way to Pay Old Debts* (1625), Massinger's most enduring play, the covetous Sir Giles Overreach's very name displays his connection to the great, egomaniacal "overreachers" of Marlowe and others, and his demonic obsession with lucre makes him a clear descendant of Shylock. Structural parallels exist between *A New Way* and *The Merchant of Venice* and many city comedies, but Massinger's play both imitates and exceeds its predecessors. This is particularly evident in Overreach's hunger not merely to take advantage of the old aristocracy that scorn him (even as they find themselves in financial need) but actually to instigate their ruination and then force them to serve him. In a sense, Overreach combines Tamburlaine with Shylock, becoming a new, hybrid stage villain.

Massinger shows a horrified fascination with the "new rich" class of social climbers in other city comedies, notably *The City Madam* (1632). He was also an accomplished writer of tragedies. *The Roman Actor*, his most important tragedy, is at first glance a typical "fall of a tyrant" play, but upon closer examination it is a complex investigation of the overlaps between theatrical and political power and presents an intriguingly ambivalent defense of the practice of playing. While Massinger's political plays are generally conservative and Royalist in tone, they were controversial nonetheless. His political tragedy *Believe as You List* (1631) provoked the censor and had to be rewritten to avoid engaging with political controversies between England and Spain, and a now-lost play called *The King and the Subject* (1638) reportedly was censored at the direct insistence of King Charles I because it presumed to depict a monarch raising money through coercion, a touchy subject as the Civil War loomed.

CRITICAL RECEPTION

The extent to which Massinger's literary worth is a matter of controversy is perhaps the most striking feature of his critical reception. Nearly every important critical work on Massinger in the past 100 years or so contains either a damning dismissal, a lukewarm apology for its subject, or a polemical defense. Massinger received some scattered praise from fellow poets in his own time, and his plays were regularly put on when the theaters reopened after the restoration of Charles II. *A New Way to Pay Old Debts* proved particularly enduring. It was frequently produced from the Restoration through the late 19th century, and Sir Giles Overreach held place with Shylock and Hamlet as one of the great roles prominent actors used as "star vehicles." While the Romantics, particularly Coleridge, approved of Massinger, his critical fortunes declined throughout the 19th century, a move that culminated in T.S. Eliot's 1922 essay on Massinger that declared his work "dreary" and anemic. Eliot saw what he considered Massinger's stylistic and intellectual deficiencies as the starting point for the decline in English poetry that he famously characterized as a "dissociation of sensibility." While much too subjective and polemical to be a useful critical model for Massinger studies, Eliot's essay has nonetheless been influential in pushing Massinger's work to the margins of literary history.

The publication of Philip Edward's and Colin Gibson's *The Plays and Poems of Philip Massinger* in 1976, answering the need for a modern and accessible version of Massinger's oeuvre, initiated something of a Massinger renaissance, helped in part by Anne Barton's review of the edition in the *Times Literary Supplement*. In that piece, Barton wrote of the need for a "critical re-evaluation" of Massinger, a call that partly served as the impetus to Douglas Howard's important collection *Philip Massinger: A Critical Reassessment* (1985). Containing eight original essays by a range of distinguished scholars (as well as a reprint of Barton's *TLS* review), Howard's book is perhaps most notable for the entirely normalized way in which the authors approach Massinger from a range of methodological and historical perspectives. In a word, Howard's collection, helping to inaugurate a salutary trend that has continued to the present, takes Massinger *seriously*.

BIBLIOGRAPHY

Works by Philip Massinger

The Plays and Poems of Philip Massinger. Ed. Philip Edwards and Colin Gibson. 4 vols. Oxford: Clarendon Press, 1976.

Studies of Philip Massinger

Adler, Doris. *Philip Massinger*. Boston: Twayne Publishers, 1987.

Clark, Ira. *The Moral Art of Philip Massinger*. Lewisburg, PA: Bucknell University Press, 1993.

Dunn, T.A. *Philip Massinger: The Man and the Playwright*. London: Thomas Nelson and Sons, Ltd., 1957.

Eliot, T.S. "Philip Massinger." In his *Elizabethan Essays*. New York: Haskell House, 1964. 153–176.

Garrett, Martin, ed. *Massinger: The Critical Heritage*. New York: Routledge, 1991.

Howard, Douglas, ed. *Philip Massinger: A Critical Reassessment*. Cambridge: Cambridge University Press, 1985.

Neill, Michael. "Massinger's Patriarchy: The Social Vision of a *New Way to Pay Old Debts*." *Renaissance Drama* 10 (1979): 185–213.

❧ *Thomas Middleton*
(1580–1627)

MIMI YIU

BIOGRAPHY

The son of a prosperous citizen bricklayer, Thomas Middleton was born a Londoner and remained firmly oriented in the city for most of his life. After the death of his father, William, in January 1586, Middleton's mother rashly remarried scant months later to a down-and-out adventurer, Thomas Harvey, who would soon embroil the whole family in legacy disputes. Middleton's new stepfather had lost all his money in Ralegh and **Greville**'s failed colonization project in Roanoke. Having returned to London from Virginia in July 1586, Harvey was married by November of that same year. His entrance into the Middleton family launched a string of complicated lawsuits over property that would dog Middleton, his sister Avice, and his mother Anne for many years to come. As a consequence of Harvey's persistent and litigious demands, Middleton's family was forced to learn how to manipulate the intricacies of London's legal system. At one juncture, Middleton's mother took the extreme measure of having herself arrested so that her husband would be forced to pay her bond and appear in court. Although Harvey left for the Low Countries and Portugal, he returned in 1590 to pester the family for money. Undoubtedly, these protracted legal battles marked the young Middleton's conception of urban community, surfacing later in his city comedies as the petty squabbles and maneuvers of London's citizenry.

Middleton's financial and legal difficulties followed him to Queen's College, Oxford, where he matriculated in 1598. By 1600, he had left university without a degree and was again in London, "daily accompanying the players." Middleton began to write plays professionally, although his earliest works seem not to have been very successful. By 1602, Middleton had joined the stable of writers associated with Philip Henslowe, the influential impresario and actor. Henslowe's company, the Admiral's Men, was one of the two major theater companies of late Elizabethan times; its main rival, the Lord Chamberlain's Men, boasted **Shakespeare** as an actor and shareholder. Although some of Middleton's plays during this period are believed lost, it is known that he collaborated with other London playwrights such as Dekker, **Drayton**, Greene, Munday, and **Webster**. Sometime in this period as well, Middleton married Maria (Magdalen) Marbeck, granddaughter of the Calvinist composer and organist John Marbeck. Their son Edward was born in 1603 or 1604.

Besides his work for the Admiral's Men, Middleton was also busy producing works for the boys' companies of Blackfriars and Paul's. When theaters closed due to plague in 1603, Middleton resorted to pamphlet writing to sustain himself. By 1604, however, he had turned his hand to the adult companies, writing for diverse groups including Prince Charles's Company, Lady Elizabeth's Men, and even the King's Men (the renamed Lord Chamberlain's Men from Shakespeare's day). Rowley becomes a principal collaborator in Middleton's works, participating in perhaps four theatrical pieces. Despite a steady stream of works, Middleton continued to suffer from financial problems, running into debt in 1610–1611. Perhaps it was financial need that prompted him, beginning in 1613, to write civic entertainments; if this was indeed the case, Middleton received his reward in 1620 when he was appointed city chronologer of London. This lucrative post, which Middleton apparently took seriously, required keeping city annals, writing occasional speeches, and organizing public pageants. When Middleton died, in debt once again, his widow petitioned for and received a grant from the city government. Middleton was buried in the parish church of Newington Butts, near Southward, where he had lived almost all of his life.

MAJOR WORKS AND THEMES

Middleton's output includes roughly thirty plays in a variety of genres, plus an assortment of masques, civic entertainments, pageants, pamphlets, and poems. At age seventeen, he composed a didactic poem titled *The Wit of Solomon Paraphrased* (1597); two other early poems, *Micro-Cynicon* and *The Ghost of Lucrece* (a sequel to Shakespeare's *Lucrece*), seem not to have met with particular success. Because Middleton chose to pursue writing as a profession, his mature output was often determined as much by commercial viability as by artistic merit. This necessity to support himself and his family accounts for his prolific output, especially minor works such as the civic entertainments and pamphlets that are perhaps of less literary value. Nevertheless, Middleton's major works—the plays that he wrote by himself and in partnership with other playwrights—were successful enough to earn him a considerable reputation within his lifetime. Unfortunately, some of his plays are now lost, and in any event, attribution in many cases is open to dispute. Since Middleton worked in an age just beginning to recognize authorship at all, the issue of collaboration remains an area of much debate for present-day scholars. Most controversially, perhaps, some commentators believe that Middleton collaborated with Shakespeare on *A Yorkshire Tragedy* (with others, 1605) and even *Timon of Athens* (1607).

Not only did Middleton collaborate with other playwrights, but he also drew upon diverse generic sources ranging from jest-books and cony-catching pamphlets to interludes and Italian intrigue comedy. Truly a playwright of many stripes, Middleton broadened his repertoire with works of comedy, tragedy, tragicomedy, satire, history, and political allegory. In the trajectory of his career, however, his early work for the boys' companies of Blackfriars and Paul's were mainly comedies, while his major tragedies date from a later period. Numbering among his best comedies are *A Mad World, My Masters* (1604–1606), *The Roaring Girl* (with Dekker, 1604–1608), and *A Chaste Maid in Cheapside* (1611–1613). These "city comedies" or "citizen comedies," which draw upon the New Comedy tradition established by the Roman playwrights Plautus and Terence, typically revolve around a romantic plot filled with various obstacles but resolving happily. Intrigues abound in multiple intersecting plots that converge toward the union of young lovers. Often, legal tribulations form one of the major hindrances to this final resolution: Here, Middleton was evidently able to draw upon his own extensive dealings with the law. Indeed, Middleton's immersion into the London scene allowed him to create such a vivid cityscape in his comedies, displaying to viewers both its surface gloss and seamy underside, its outward pageantry and inward immorality.

Perhaps the most notable feature of Middleton's city comedies is their colorful depiction of the diverse social strata characterizing urban life in the 17th century. Whether set in his native London or locales abroad, Middleton's comedies involve a cast drawn from different classes—merchants, nobles, mayors, cutpurses, bawds—thrown together on the streets, in city dwellings, in shops. Also inhabiting the same city spaces are foreigners, immigrants, and provincials, all distinguished by their peculiar accents, dress, or habits. Despite the sometimes stereotypical portrayals of various human types, Middleton's plays derive much of their comic impact from the transgression of traditional gender roles, familial structure, and class hierarchy. Moll, the "roaring girl," boldly dons masculine attire and blazes through public spaces with total disregard for feminine propriety. In *A Chaste Maid in Cheapside*, the decayed Sir Walter Whorehound undermines several marriages while secretly surviving on an expected inheritance. Although some sort of equilibrium usually emerges by the end, the fluidity of social movement throughout the play necessarily raises questions about the validity of current societal structures.

After 1613, Middleton ceased to write city satires, instead turning his attention to the tragic mode: *Women Beware Women* (1621) and *The Changeling* (with Rowley, 1622) are arguably his greatest achievements in this genre. While the comedies generally resolve tensions with a happy pair of lovers united, the tragedies present a darker vision where transgressions of social order lead only to complete moral corruption, despair, and irremediable chaos. Women and their sexuality seem to play important roles in setting off this tragic downfall, and women often constitute both the victims and perpetrators. In *Women Beware Women*, the chaste Bianca is raped through the scheming of her neighbor, Livia; in *The Changeling*, the desire of Beatrice for Alsemero leads to murder and the selling of her body to a man she detests. Avarice and pride also seduce the characters into piling sin upon sin, distorting their worldview so that cynicism, cruelty, and solipsism seem to be the only viable responses.

Other works by Middleton include a political allegory, *A Game at Chess* (1624), which took an anti-Catholic stance against James's alliance with Spain; Middleton, forced to go into hiding from the political fallout, sent his son instead to answer before the Privy Council. Less politically dangerous but also less successful were *The Witch* (1615), a type of melodrama, and *The Widow* (1616), a tragicomedy. His civic entertainments and masques are almost entirely overlooked today.

CRITICAL RECEPTION

Although Middleton was able to sustain a fairly successful career as a writer, he never enjoyed the stature of a Shakespeare, **Jonson**, or Marlowe. His characters were considered stiff types, while his dialogue lacked the lyricism of Shakespeare or the brilliance of Jonson. Nevertheless, his commissioned plays were popular, and *A Game at Chess* had the longest known run of any Jacobean play. His reputation fell into serious neglect following his death and suffered almost a complete lack of interest until the 20th century. Within the past few decades, however, Middleton's work has undergone such a significant reevaluation that he now stands among the foremost ranks of Renaissance playwrights. This current rehabilitation of Middleton owes at least a partial debt to T.S. Eliot, who considered *The Changeling*'s moral tragedy second only to Shakespeare's. A substantial body of criticism now exists on the Middleton canon; in fact, simply defining which works are solely or partly Middleton's has occupied a great deal of critical attention. A corollary direction of interest lies in establishing the genres of his plays, since Middleton worked in an unusually broad variety of literature. Margot Heinemann's pioneering work on Puritanism and theater has brought to light another aspect of Middleton's work, namely, the conflict between the playwright's Calvinist influences and his satire of Puritan principles. New Historicist readings of Middleton tend to focus on his city comedies and their exposition of Jacobean urban relations. In bringing Middleton to life from literary oblivion, even contemporary playwrights such as Howard Barker have adapted some of Middleton's dramas, exploring the works' 17th-century moral outlook from a 20th-century point of view.

BIBLIOGRAPHY

Works by Thomas Middleton

The Changeling. With William Rowley. 1622.
A Chaste Maid in Cheapside. 1611–1613.
A Game at Chess. 1624.
A Mad World, My Masters. 1604–1606.
The Revenger's Tragedy. With Cyril Tourneur? 1606–1607.
The Roaring Girl. With Thomas Dekker. 1604–1608.
A Trick to Catch the Old One. 1604–1606.
The Widow. 1616.
Women Beware Women. c. 1621.

Studies of Thomas Middleton

Barker, Richard. *Thomas Middleton*. New York: Columbia University Press, 1958.
Corvatta, Anthony. *Thomas Middleton's City Comedies*. Lewisburg, PA: Bucknell University Press, 1973.
Eliot, T.S. *Elizabethan Essays*. New York: Haskell House, 1964.
Ellis-Fermor, Una. *The Jacobean Drama*. New York: Vintage Books, 1964.
Empson, William. *Some Versions of Pastoral*. Norfolk, VA: New Directions, 1950.

Farr, Dorothy. *Thomas Middleton and the Drama of Realism*. Edinburgh: Oliver and Boyd, 1973.

Friedenreich, Kenneth, ed. *"Accompanyinge the Players": Essays Celebrating Thomas Middleton, 1580–1980*. New York: AMS Press, 1983.

Heinemann, Margot. *Puritanism and Theatre: Thomas Middleton and Opposition Drama under the Early Stuarts*. Cambridge: Cambridge University Press, 1980.

Holmes, David M. *The Art of Thomas Middleton*. Oxford: Clarendon Press, 1970.

Howard-Hill, T.H. *Middleton's "Vulgar Pasquin": Essays on* A Game at Chess. Newark: University of Delaware Press, 1995.

Lake, David. *The Canon of Thomas Middleton's Plays*. London: Cambridge University Press, 1975.

Rowe, George E., Jr. *Thomas Middleton and the New Comedy Tradition*. Lincoln: University of Nebraska Press, 1979.

Schoenbaum, Samuel. *Middleton's Tragedies: A Critical Study*. New York: Columbia University Press, 1955.

❧ *John Milton*
(1608–1674)

MARGARET J. ARNOLD

BIOGRAPHY

After **Shakespeare**, John Milton is probably the best known of all English poets. In addition to major works in English, he leaves a reputable body of work in Latin and Italian. In addition to his poetry, he contributed vigorously to religious and political controversies surrounding the English Civil War and its aftermath. Both poetry and prose have inspired later writers to cite him and also react to his style and major ideas about theology, marriage, and education.

The son of a prosperous London scrivener and musician, Milton grew up in a stimulating environment. He entered St. Paul's School in about 1615, where he continued his humanistic and Puritan tutoring under Thomas Young, an advocate of religious reformation. Also at St. Paul's the young Milton met his closest friend, Charles Diodati, the addressee of many Latin verse letters and the subject of a later pastoral lament, *Epitaphium Damonis* (1639). Milton entered Christ's College, Cambridge, in 1625, receiving a B.A. in 1629 and an M.A. in 1632. After graduation he supplemented his formal education with five additional years of private study, completing his preparation, like many contemporaries, with a continental tour during which he met the Dutch humanist Hugo Grotius and reported visiting Galileo. During his formative years he confirmed his vocation as a poet, initially participating in college exercises and later sharing his work with associates he encountered at home and in Italy. At a time when many Cambridge graduates were entering the ministry, Milton petitioned his father to accept a dedicated career of writing prophetic poetry as a worthy vocation (*Ad Patrem*, c. 1631).

By 1639, when he cut the Italian journey short in order to respond to events culminating in the English Civil War, he had already composed a respectable body of English, Latin, and Italian poetry. These works, selected and revised, appeared in 1645. Their topics and importance are discussed below. Upon his return, Milton penned a series of pamphlets supporting his former tutor, Thomas Young, and others who protested the increasing alliance of King and Church advocated by Archbishop William Laud. Milton argued that this alliance threatened the freedom of individual congregations and believers. During this period he supported himself in part by tutoring young men, including his nephews Edward and John Phillips, writing "Of Education" (1644). In place of current practices beginning with grammatical rules, this work advocated the gradual exposure of future leaders to a sequence of humanistic and Christian works that fostered their capacity for moral choice. So trained, they would stand ready to lead others in public service. To his educational reform, Milton added the topic of domestic reform. His 1642 marriage to Mary Powell, whose political and religious background differed from his own, was followed by separation in the same year with eventual reconciliation in 1645. Within these three years Milton authored tracts on divorce for incompatibility and advocated the free licensing of books (*Areopagitica*, 1644).

From 1649 to about 1658, Milton served as Secretary for Foreign Tongues to the Council of State, originally headed by **Oliver Cromwell**. In this position he defended the regicide of Charles I to audiences of English and continental leaders. His first Latin defense earned him recognition in Europe in its response to an attack by the noted French humanist Claude de Saumaise (Salmasius). On behalf of Cromwell and the Council of State, he also corresponded with foreign diplomats to express governmental policies, especially in a series of negotiations with the Dutch. By 1652 Milton was totally blind, continuing his study and writing through amanuenses. After the death of Mary Powell Milton in 1652, he married Katherine Woodcock in 1658, who died in childbirth two years later.

After the Restoration of Charles II, Milton spent some time under house arrest. During the rest of his life, he published his three most famous works, *Paradise Lost* (1667, 1674), *Paradise Regained*, and *Samson Agonistes* (1671). He continued to write political and educational treatises up to the time of his death in 1674. A controversial prose work on Christian doctrine, discovered in a public record office in 1823, is also generally attributed to him. He was survived by his third wife, Elizabeth Minshull, who he married in 1663, and by three daughters.

MAJOR WORKS AND THEMES

Milton's self-conscious examination of a poet's vocation, expressed in his transformation of several genres—lyric, dramatic, and epic—helps to unify his poetic works. His early poems reflect his growing dedication to writing prophetic poetry rather than entering the Anglican ministry, the option of many Cambridge graduates. He assumes the prophetic mantle in the early ode, *On the Morning of Christ's Nativity* (1629), his tribute to the infant Christ as the mighty child who vanquishes pagan deities. The list of banished gods looks forward to the catalog of fallen angels in *Paradise Lost*. His early companion poems, *L'Allegro* and *Il Penseroso*, written shortly after his Cambridge years, balance the active and contemplative lives, concluding with a prophetic vision. When his classmate Edward King drowned, he contributed *Lycidas* (1637) to a commemorative volume. This pastoral elegy examines the value of a poet's vocation as well as attacking clerical corruption. Milton's early dramatic work *A Mask Performed at Ludlow Castle* (*Comus*) was first performed in 1634. Milton's associate, the musician Henry Lawes, enlisted his services for ceremonies honoring the installation of John Egerton, Earl of Bridgewater, as President of Wales and the Marches. The masque emphasizes the value of resisting temptation as essential to strengthening virtue, a consistent theme throughout all of Milton's work. In *Comus* he also advocates temperate use of the divinely created natural world. During this period, too, his Latin epistles and elegies reveal his friendships and vocational concerns. Italian sonnets and odes gained him a favorable reputation outside of England.

Milton's early religious treatises are compatible with contemporary endeavors to reform the doctrine and discipline of the Anglican Church. He opposes the imposition of creeds and the close alignment of royal and ecclesiastical power. Under the Long Parliament, which Presbyterian reformers dominated, Milton opposed censorship in *Areopagitica* (1644), again defending the strength of a tested virtue and stressing his lifelong concern with free choice among even erroneous opinions. His polemics advocating domestic liberty, permitting divorce for incompatibility, had met Parliamentary opposition. His gradual disillusionment with the Presbyterian regime led him toward support of Independent congregations as he moved toward his ultimate belief that no worldly barrier should stand between a believer's conscience and God.

The divorce tracts as well as Milton's defenses of the revolution assume a contract between the rulers and the citizens governed by them. He defends the execution of Charles I by arguing that Charles has broken his contract with his people, becoming a tyrant no longer worthy of their obedience. A continuing sequence of prose tracts during the Interregnum consistently protests civil interference with a citizen's freedom to express ideas and to follow his conscience in religious matters. Milton evidently considered Oliver Cromwell the most adequate available defender of these rights, opposing any steps toward the alignment of church and state. Documents Milton wrote as Cromwell's secretary fall short of approving more radical groups, although recent scholars (Corns, Loewenstein) have noted his increasing tolerance of many "leftist" views just before the Restoration and especially after it. As the Restoration approached, he sometimes assumed a prophetic persona in treatises advocating a free commonwealth governed by leaders responsible to the best interests of the public. Increasingly, his prose and later poetry emphasize the difficulty most of his countrymen have in taking responsibility for their own freedom. Without faith and strenuous effort on the part of its citizens, a nation returns to captivity.

Milton's major poetry after the Restoration repeats and expands such early concerns as the poet's prophetic vocation. *Paradise Lost* breaks with rhyme as Milton publishes the first English epic in blank verse, emulating Homer and Virgil but also aiming to transcend them. He casts his narrator as both a prophet and a vulnerable human being. His voice pleads for divine inspiration while it acknowledges the risks of representing God in a hostile society. When he assigns language to God and allows the angel narrators to describe heavenly struggles, Milton draws on the doctrine of accommodation, the comparison of spiritual events to earthly analogs. Milton has also moved away from the Calvinism of many Puritan reformers to the Arminian doctrine of free will. Milton's God explains that all rational creatures are endowed with free choice and sufficient strength to obey God as the only true source of continuing liberty. Satan, other heavenly beings, and humans are responsible for their own disobedience and separation from the integrity with which they are created. God allows Satan to act freely and powerfully throughout the work in order to give meaning to one's voluntary choice of goodness. Milton also moves toward an Anti-Trinitarian view of God's Son. The Son is a created being through whom the material universe takes shape and life. As a willing agent rather than a part of the Trinity he makes the voluntary choice to take Adam's place, becoming finally man's judge and redeemer. As a creative agent the Son shapes chaos into physical and organic order. Milton thus aligns himself with philosophic materialism.

Characterizing Adam and Eve allows Milton to explore such larger concerns as the need for education in virtue through experiencing temptations and making choices when they learn of alternatives from each other and from angelic messengers. Their commandment to tend Eden assigns them the stewardship of Edenic resources in extending the process of creation. Their marriage exemplifies Milton's model of pre-lapsarian union, affirming their spiritual and physical union. Whether their relationship is complementary or socially hierarchical (Nyquist), they allow each other freedom before the Fall and also receive instruction in the temperate use of knowledge. Their separate decisions to disobey God's commandment exemplify the strenuous responsibility accompanying freedom of choice. Their separation, repentance, and reconciliation introduce them to a world in which good and evil are intertwined. Although they are expelled from Eden, they may seek an internal Paradise wherever their journey takes them. Paradise moves from a place to a state of mind. The entire epic, through narration and allusion, includes all time from the creation through the apocalypse. At death, both body and soul "sleep" until the general resurrection, aligning Milton with theological mortalism.

In the major poems and prose following *Paradise Lost*, Milton's diction is simpler and his heroic figures more isolated than Adam and Eve. *Paradise Regained* fulfills Milton's early hope to write a "brief epic" modeled in part on the Book of Job. It chronicles Jesus' temptation in the wilderness following his baptism, reifying Milton's emphasis on the importance of a tested virtue. Christ's refusal of military, national, imperial, and humanistic power leads to the affirmation that a kingship of the spirit is the only ultimate authority chosen by God's Son and, by implication, by the individual believer. Jesus's rejection of classical learning also exemplifies the idea that knowledge is not itself an end but must be evaluated with respect to its source.

Although the date of Milton's dramatic poem *Samson Agonistes* is disputed, he published it and *Paradise Regained* in the same volume (1671). Many critics see them as companion poems, often contrasting Christ's pacifism with Samson's anger and violence. Because *Samson Agonistes* lacks a narrator or a theophany, its characters convey many differing views regarding heroic action, marriage, and the appropriate use of divine gifts. Many readers view Samson's movement from despair through a state of affirmation as a form of self-integration or even regeneration. Others consider his verbal and physical violence the mark of tragic emotional and physical blindness. Several readers stress the many uncertainties—sources, dating, and ambiguous terms—surrounding its text and its interpretation (Shawcross). The work reinforces Milton's concern with the difficult exercise of free will, the appropriate conditions under which to dissolve a marriage, and the ease with which citizens accept servitude.

In addition to the major poems, Milton completed the composition of histories of Britain and Muscovy as well as additional trreatises on religion and education. The British historical work reflects the difficulty of maintaining civic freedom, while the final publications on religious issues, especially *Of True Religion, Heresy, and Schism* . . . (1672), broaden the base of tolerance even beyond the limits of *Areopagitica*.

CRITICAL RECEPTION

Again with the exception of Shakespeare, Milton has influenced a larger number of critics, authors, artists, and musicians than any other English poet. His contemporary **John Dryden** dramatized an orthodox Eden in his *State of Innocence* and drew upon Milton's portrayal of Satan in *Absalom and Achitophel*. Although some early editors objected to the Arianism of *Paradise Lost*, **Joseph Addison** defended the work's classical and literary excellence in a series of essays for *The Spectator* (1728). Samuel Johnson admired Milton's sublimity but found flaws when he applied neoclassical criteria to his predecessor's works. The Romantics in particular admired the heroic energy of Milton's Satan, revising the figure in Shelley's *Prometheus* and Byron's *Cain*. William Blake added a series of illustrations to *Comus*, *Paradise Lost*, and *Paradise Regained*, commenting in his own *Marriage of Heaven and Hell* that Milton was of the devil's party. Both Coleridge and Wordsworth admired Milton's craft and his republican politics.

In England Milton's views on liberty and the separation of church and state influenced early Whig thinkers (Lewalski, *Life* 451). Early American colonists cited him as they sought to fashion an Eden in the New World. Later, preceding the American revolution, Benjamin Franklin and Thomas Jefferson quoted his poetry as well as his antiprelatical and antimonarchical tracts. In the 19th century early Unitarians admired his Arianism, while such Transcendentalists as Emerson identified with his prophetic role.

In the early 20th century Milton's political and religious views drew initial attacks from T.S. Eliot, who later modified his hostility. Stylistically, a series of New Critics preferred the compressed conceits of **John Donne** to the longer periods of Milton's longer works, especially *Paradise Lost*. Debating Milton's theology, C.S. Lewis defended the poet's orthodox Christianity, while William Empson mounted an attack on Milton's God. More recent criticism has linked him with the political, theological, and social issues of his time. In the final decades of the 20th century, many fine studies have pointed toward Milton's adaptation of classical genres to introduce Protestant allusions and issues. His poetry and prose have drawn critics' attention to his place in debates about theology, political theory, education, and family life in the 17th century. Both religious and scientific associates including early Quakers and such early scientists as **Robert Boyle** appear in recent discussions. At least two particular controversies have currently engaged Milton's readers. William B. Hunter and others have debated his authorship of *De Doctrina Christiana*, but most interpreters now verify Milton's authorship. A second point of concern is Milton's position on the ethics of violence, particularly in his characterization of Samson. Whether Dalila voices an acceptable position and whether Samson's liberation of his tribe was legitimate rather than a misuse of power remain open to debate.

BIBLIOGRAPHY

Works by John Milton

Complete English Poems, Of Education, Areopagitica. Ed. Gordon Campbell. 4th ed. London: J.M. Dent, 1990.

The Complete English Poetry of John Milton. Ed. John Shawcross. 1963. Rev. ed. New York: Anchor, 1971.

The Complete Prose Works of John Milton. Ed. Don M. Wolfe (gen. ed.). 8 vols. New Haven, CT: Yale University Press, 1953–1982.

John Milton: Complete Poems and Major Prose. Ed. Merritt Y. Hughes. New York: Odyssey Press, 1957.

The Poems of John Milton. Ed. John Carey and Alastair Fowler. London: Longman, 1980.

The Riverside Milton. Ed. Roy Flannagan. Boston: Houghton Mifflin, 1998.

The Works of John Milton. Ed. Frank A. Patterson (gen. ed.). 18 vols. New York: Columbia University Press, 1931–1938.

Studies of John Milton

Achtinstein, Sharon. *Milton and the Revolutionary Reader*. Princeton: Princeton University Press, 1994.

Benet, Diana Treviño, and Michael Lieb, eds. *Literary Milton: Text. Pretext, Context*. Pittsburgh: Duquesne University Press, 1994.

Bennett, Joan S. *Reviving Liberty: Radical Christian Humanism in Milton's Great Poems*. Cambridge: Harvard University Press, 1989.

Campbell, Gordon. *A Milton Chronology*. London: Macmillan, 1995.

Campbell, Gordon, Thomas N. Corns, John K. Hale, David I. Holmes, and Fiona J. Tweedie. "The Provenance of *De Doctrina Christiana*." *Milton Quarterly* 31 (1997): 67–121.

Corns, Thomas. *Uncloistered Virtue: English Political Literature, 1640–1660*. Oxford: Clarendon Press, 1992.

Dobranski, Stephen. *Milton, Authorship, and the Book Trade*. Cambridge: Cambridge University Press, 1999.

Fallon, Robert T. *Divided Empire: Milton's Political Imagery*. University Park: Pennsylvania University Press, 1995.

Fallon, Stephen. *Milton among the Philosophers: Poetry and Materialism in Seventeenth-Century England*. Ithaca, NY: Cornell University Press, 1991.

Ferry, Anne D. *Milton's Epic Voice: The Narrator in* Paradise Lost. Chicago: University of Chicago Press, 1983.

Fish, Stanley. *Surprised by Sin*. 1967. Cambridge: Harvard University Press, 1997.

Frye, Northrop. *The Return of Eden*. 1965. Toronto: University of Toronto Press, 1975.

Hale, John K. *Milton's Languages*. Cambridge: Cambridge University Press, 1997.

Hill, Christopher. *Milton and the English Revolution*. London: Faber and Faber, 1977.

———. *The World Turned Upside Down: Radical Ideas during the English Revolution*. New York: Viking, 1972.

Hunter, William B. *Visitation Unimplor'd: Milton and the Authorship of De Doctrina Christiana*. Pittsburgh: Duquesne University Press, 1998.

Kerrigan, William. *The Prophetic Milton*. Charlottesville: University of Virginia Press, 1974.

———. *The Sacred Complex: On the Psychogenesis of* Paradise Lost. Cambridge: Harvard University Press, 1983.

Knoppers, Laura Lunger. *Historicizing Milton: Spectacle, Power, and Poetry in Restoration England*. Athens: University of Georgia Press, 1994.

Lewalski, Barbara K. "Innocence and Experience in Milton's Eden." In *New Essays on* Paradise Lost, ed. Thomas Kranidas. Berkeley: University of California Press, 1960. 80–117.

———. *The Life of John Milton: A Critical Biography*. London: Blackwell, 2000.

———. *Milton's Brief Epic: The Genre, Meaning, and Art of* Paradise Regained. London: Methuen, 1966.

———. Paradise Lost *and the Rhetoric of Literary Forms*. Princeton: Princeton University Press, 1985.

Lieb, Michael. *Milton and the Culture of Violence*. Ithaca, NY: Cornell University Press, 1994.

Lieb, Michael, and John T. Shawcross, eds. *Achievements of the Left Hand: Essays on the Prose of John Milton*. Amherst: University of Massachusetts Press, 1974.

Loewenstein, David. *Milton and the Drama of History*. Cambridge: Cambridge University Press, 1990.

Loewenstein, David, and James Grantham Turner, eds. *Politics, Poetics, and Hermeneutics in Milton's Prose*. Cambridge: Cambridge University Press, 1990.

Masson, David. *The Life of John Milton: Narrated in Connection with the Political, Ecclesiastical and Literary History of His Time*. 7 vols. 1881–1894. Reprint, Gloucester, MA: Peter Smith, 1965.

McColley, Diana. *A Gust for Paradise: Milton's Eden and the Visual Arts*. Urbana: University of Illinois Press, 1993.

———. *Milton's Eve*. Urbana: University of Illinois Press, 1983.

Mueller, Janel M. "Contextualizing Milton's Nascent Republicanism." In *Of Poetry and Politics: New Essays on Milton and His World*, ed. Paul G. Stanwood. Binghamton, NY: MRTS, 1993. 263–282.

Norbrook, David. *Writing the English Republic: Poetry, Rhetoric, and Politics, 1627–1660*. Cambridge: Cambridge University Press, 1999.

Nyquist, Mary. "The Genesis of Gendered Subjectivity in the Divorce Tracts and *Paradise Lost*." In *Re-membering Milton: Essays on the Texts and the Traditions*, ed. Mary Nyquist and Margaret Ferguson. New York: Methuen, 1987. 99–127.

Parker, William Riley. *Milton: A Biography*. 2 vols. 1968. Rev. ed., Oxford: Clarendon Press, 1996.

———. *Milton's Debt to Greek Tragedy in Samson Agonistes*. Baltimore: Johns Hopkins University Press, 1937.

Patterson, Annabel. *Censorship and Interpretation: The Conditions of Writing and Reading in Early Modern England*. Madison: University of Wisconsin Press, 1984.

Radzinowicz, Mary Ann. *Milton's Epics and the Book of Psalms*. Princeton: Princeton University Press, 1989.

———. *Toward Samson Agonistes: The Growth of Milton's Mind*. Princeton: Princeton University Press, 1978.

Revard, Stella P. *Milton and the Tangles of Naera's Hair: The Making of the 1645 Poems*. Columbia: University of Missouri Press, 1997.

Rosenblatt, Jason P. *Torah and Law in* Paradise Lost. Princeton: Princeton University Press, 1994.

Rumrich, John P., and Stephen Dobranski, eds. *Milton and Heresy*. Cambridge: Cambridge University Press, 1998.

Shawcross, John T. *John Milton: The Self and the World*. Lexington: University Press of Kentucky, 1993.

———. *The Uncertain World of Samson Agonistes*. Cambridge: D.S. Brewer, 2001.

Turner, James Grantham. *One Flesh: Paradisal Marriage and Sexual Relations in the Age of Milton*. Oxford: Clarendon Press, 1987.

Walker, Julia M., ed. *Milton and the Idea of Woman*. Urbana and Chicago: University of Illinois Press, 1988.

Wittreich, Joseph A., Jr. *Interpreting Samson Agonistes*. Princeton: Princeton University Press, 1987.

Wood, Derek N.C. *"Exiled from Light": Divine Law, Morality, and Violence in Milton's* Samson Agonistes. Toronto: University of Toronto Press, 2001.

&a Thomas Otway
(1652–1685)

JOHN HUNTINGTON

BIOGRAPHY

Thomas Otway was a reckless and self-destructive man, and as steeply as his reputation rose, his health and finances declined. He went from obscurity in 1675 to fame
and notoriety in 1680 to destitution and a pathetic, lonely death in 1685. As the son
of a clergyman, his beginnings were modest. Though he entered Oxford in 1669, he
did not take a degree. As a young man in London he managed to get the attention of
important people in the theater world. He played the King in **Aphra Behn**'s *The
Forc'd Marriage*, but after a humiliating episode of stage fright he gave up his acting
career. In 1675 his own play, *Alcibiades*, was staged, and thereafter, in fairly quick
succession, he produced a series of nine plays in a variety of genres. The romantic
heroic tragedy *Don Carlos* (1676) gained him recognition. It was followed quickly
by a double-bill of *Titus and Berenice*, based on Racine, and *The Cheats of Scapin*,
based on Molière (1676), and an English comedy, *Friendship in Fashion* (1678). After
a short stint as a soldier in Flanders, he returned to London. *The History and Fall of
Caius Marius* (1680) established his reputation as a tragedian. In the next two years
The Orphan (1680) and *Venice Preserv'd* (1682) solidified his fame. In this period
he also wrote two more comedies, *The Soldier's Fortune* (1680) and *The Atheist: or
the Second Part of the Soldier's Fortune* (1683).

Financial success did not accompany fame, and by the time of this last play, Otway
had entered a life of impoverished debauchery. He was described by contemporaries
as very fat, and at his death his largest debt was to his vintner. As one might expect
from the extremely delicate sense of honor exhibited in his plays, he was sensitive
about his name and reputation and at least once engaged in a duel. On another occasion
he called out Settle in revenge for lines satirizing him in a lampoon later shown to
have been written by the **Earl of Rochester**. In 1697, long after his death, six letters
attributed to him were published that testify to a futile *amore* with Mrs. Barry, the
great tragic actress who created the roles of Lavinia in *Caius Marius*, Monimia in *The*

Orphan, and Belvidera in *Venice Preserv'd*. Otway died, so one story goes, choking on a too-hastily-swallowed piece of bread, bought with a shilling given him on the street by a friend distressed at seeing the great author destitute. According to another story, he died from a fever incurred while chasing a friend's murderer to Dover. One thing is sure: He died poor despite the success of his tragedies.

MAJOR WORKS AND THEMES

Otway's fame as a playwright rests on his rendering of "feeling," and in his own time he was said to surpass **Shakespeare** in this respect. He was also capable of writing the most politically interesting plays of the period. He allied himself with the Royalists, as his dedications attest, but his tragedies, while seldom discomforting the Tory position, always speak to a darker vision than a simple propagandist could attain.

In the early *Don Carlos* Otway established the mode of distressful emotional conflict that was to become identified with him. The King of Spain has married the woman he had originally intended for his son, Don Carlos, to marry. Unfortunately, the Queen and Don Carlos have already fallen deeply in love, and now, try as they may to obey their various obligations, Don Carlos to his father, the Queen to her husband, they cannot repress their affection. The static, triangular structure of the character relations given at the beginning does not change, but it offers the actors the opportunity to give vent to a variety of strong and violently conflicting feelings.

The Orphan works from a similarly static, triangular beginning. Twin brothers, Castalio and Polydore, love their father's ward, Monimia, but in this play Castalio initiates change by secretly marrying Monimia. Polydore, unaware of the marriage, "possesses" Monimia on her wedding night by pretending to be Castalio. Castalio, angered at being refused access to his bride's chamber, denounces Monimia, and later Polydore, a rake but not a scoundrel, but is distraught when he discovers what he has done. Castalio takes the blame for the tragedy by confessing disloyalty for not telling his brother about his marriage. The overwhelming sense of honor felt by all the parties leads to a catastrophe in which both Monimia and Castalio die. The play's subplot involving Monimia's brother, Chaumont, and the twins' sister, Serina, hardly matters.

The tragedy that precedes *The Orphan*, *Caius Marius*, adds a political element to marital-familial difficulties. While the plot poses clear political differences—the aristocratic senate against Marius Senior, the plebeian general—the play's ideology is interestingly complicated. The senators prove corrupt, and Marius has a genuine nobility. He moves from being a man of Tamburlaine-like single-mindedness to a complex figure of despair and repentance who is still able brutally to execute his enemies. Further distancing the play from pure Tory propaganda is the secondary plot, the love between Marius Junior and Lavinia, the daughter of a senator. This plot is taken, as the Prologue openly acknowledges, from *Romeo and Juliet*, and many passages are close renderings of Shakespeare.

Venice Preserv'd, Otway's masterpiece, combines the political complexity of *Caius Marius* and the homosocial difficulties of *The Orphan*. Jaffeir, the impoverished husband of Belvidera, commits himself to his friend Pierre's plot to bring corrupt Venice to its knees by slaughtering the Venetian senate. In London right after the Popish plot, one would expect such a story to reveal clear political alignment, but the revolutionary plot is treated quite sympathetically, and the Venetian rulers are shown as corrupt. In a set of startling scenes, senator Antonio (a clear satire of the **Earl of Shaftesbury**) demeans himself in sadomasochistic play with the prostitute Aquilina. "Nicky Nacky," Antonio's nickname for Aquilina, became a common allusion in the period, much like **Wycherley**'s china. In the middle of the play, swayed by Belvidera's pity and humanity, Jaffeir betrays the plot. The situation, like those of earlier plays, pits friends against each other, and Jaffeir at one time threatens his wife for causing him to betray Pierre. Jaffeir saves Pierre from the humiliation of public execution by killing him on the scaffold before stabbing himself. On hearing of the men's deaths, Belvidera goes mad and dies. The period's common themes of honor and love are here rendered with intelligence and with a ruthlessness that is elsewhere unmatched.

Otway is very much a creature of his age. He speaks to the exaggerated sense of the obligations of honor, both masculine loyalty and feminine chastity, that are common in the period's tragedy, but he presses the dilemmas almost beyond endurance. His verse, especially in some of the more operatic moments, displays powerful emotions directly and in strong language. His satiric language can be extraordinarily vigorous.

CRITICAL RECEPTION

Early in the 18th century our author was christened "the tender Otway," and so he was known throughout the period of his popularity. For more than a century after his death *The Orphan* and *Venice Preserv'd* were regularly performed as part of the standard stage repertory in London, though modifications were often made to tame their suggestive language and provocative situations. Productions of *The Orphan* turned Polydore into a melodramatic villain and focused on the destructive triangle by diminishing the minor characters' roles. Mid-18th-century productions of *Venice Preserv'd* treated Pierre as an Iago-like schemer, but by the end of the century he had become so much the heroic first role, with audiences cheering his revolutionary sentiments, that the play was banned from the London stage from 1795 to 1802. By 1800, however, the situation of *The Orphan* had become incomprehensible, and the tragedy could not be staged without laughter. *Venice Preserv'd* continued as part of the repertory until the 1840s when the shift from a heroic to a natural acting style made it, too, impossible for audiences to understand. By the end of the 19th century, Otway's work had come to have only academic interest.

BIBLIOGRAPHY

Works by Thomas Otway

The Works of Thomas Otway: Plays, Poems, and Love-Letters. Ed. J.C. Ghosh. Oxford: Clarendon Press, 1932.

Studies of Thomas Otway

Ham, Roswell Gray. *Otway and Lee: Biography from a Baroque Age*. New Haven, CT: Yale University Press, 1931.

Munns, Jessica. *Restoration Politics and Drama: The Plays of Thomas Otway, 1675–1683.* Newark: University of Delaware Press, 1996.

Taylor, Aline Mackenzie. *Next to Shakespeare, Otway's* Venice Preserv'd *and* The Orphan. Durham, NC: Duke University Press, 1950.

Warner, Kerstin P. *Thomas Otway.* Boston: Twayne Publishers, 1982.

❧ *Samuel Pepys*
(1633–1703)

JAMES GRANTHAM TURNER

BIOGRAPHY

A quintessential representative of the arriviste "middling sort," Samuel Pepys was the son of a London tailor but built a career in naval administration, thanks to his cousin and employer Edward Mantagu (made Baron by **Cromwell** and Earl of Sandwich by Charles II, whose Restoration he helped to engineer). At St. Paul's School, Pepys rejoiced in the execution of Charles I, and at Cambridge he earned a reputation as both a drinker and a "great Roundhead." Between 1655 and 1669 he was married to the daughter of a feckless Huguenot immigrant; the marriage was stormy, passionate, and childless, before and after his 1658 operation for bladder-stone that probably sterilized him by accident. Like his patron, Pepys made a smooth transition of allegiance from Cromwell to the Crown in 1660, sailing on the ship that brought Charles II home. He rapidly acquired a number of official "places," administering the finances and supplies of the Royal Navy and eventually turning it into an efficient national defense. He was a Fellow (later President) of the Royal Society and an eloquent speaker several times elected to Parliament, though his close association with the papist Duke of York twice led to his imprisonment on trumped-up charges of leaking classified information to France.

Though his frenetic sexual activity probably subsided after 1669 (when fears of going blind rose to a climax), he remained throughout his life an avid theatergoer, amateur musician, and collector of books, pictures, and manuscripts (including Middle English literature and Renaissance music). He appreciated virtually every cultural and material pleasure, from madrigals to mutton pies.

MAJOR WORKS AND THEMES

Pepys dabbled in songwriting and fiction (*Love a Cheat*, manuscript destroyed on January 3, 1664), took Charles II's autobiography down from dictation, wrote many letters and official reports, published *Memoires Relating to the State of the Royal Navy* in 1692, and founded an important library—still intact at Magdalene College, Cambridge—that includes popular ballads, chapbooks, and other "penny merriments." But his significance for literature resides in his million-word diary. Written in shorthand between 1659 and 1669, this private journal is now the most famous diary in the world. An astonishing profusion of vivid details, down to the number of times he ejaculated and the precise kind of cheese he buried during the Great Fire, creates the illusion of a knowable "modern" person, even though he is in fact largely unreflective. With his keen sensuality, feverish metabolism, and passion for all kinds of "telling" and "reckoning," Pepys seems to combine two characters who are opposed in **Wycherley**'s *Country-Wife*—Sir Jaspar Fidget, for whom business is pleasure, and Horner, for whom pleasure is business (2.1).

Beneath the regularity of the daily diary entries, with their breathless account of shopping, home improvement, masturbation, and other business, we perceive a double construction of time, private and public, subjective and chronometrical. Writing begins with Elizabeth's menstrual period (dispelling hopes for a child, which the journal in a sense replaces), juxtaposed to the momentous state of the nation as it prepared to restore the monarchy. But public and private are intimately related. As his best critics perceive, his narrative is often structured like a virtuoso dramatist's, and his bravura polyglot language implies the scrutiny, even the applause, of an audience. Pepys does not cast himself as the flawless dashing hero or the pious Christian but rather as the rising man who for all his faults gains social recognition.

The actual writing of the diary, worked up from rough notes some time after the event, shows how even the most naive and spontaneous-seeming language is rhetorically constructed. Generally Pepys strikes an easy conversational tone, with little asides ("God forgive me") to cover his more embarrassing confessions. But his syntax sometimes interlaces past and present in complex ways, and his sentences sometimes loop and subdivide revealingly. Describing his arousal by *L'Escole des filles*, "a lewd book, but what doth me no wrong to read for information sake (but it did hazer my prick para stand all the while, and una vez to decharger)," Pepys's irresolute grammar encloses his sex in a double binder, a parenthetical "but" clause nesting inside another "but" clause. Here and in all his guilty pleasures, he splits himself into a "sober man informing himself" and a libertine bent on sexual tomfoolery. These pleasures are often vicarious, as he identifies with and agonizes over the King's irresponsible frolics with his mistress the Countess of Castlemaine. Even in his dreams, Pepys imagines himself copulating with Castlemaine while simultaneously meditating on death by plague, applying Hamlet's "To be or not to be" soliloquy to his own wishful thinking (August 15, 1665).

In the conventional reading of "bourgeois" experience, the private sphere of the home is isolated from the larger pressures of society, whether it is seen as a crucible of guilt and repression or as a shelter from the heartless forces of court corruption and "business." But Pepys's household clearly resembles the larger national world in its unstable mingling of politics and personal emotion. He buys *L'Escole des filles* in response to Elizabeth's complaints about her lack of "money and liberty," the very issues that convulsed the political nation. The central concept in his condemnation of King Charles merges the political and the personal, and the same concept lies at the heart of Pepys's gender relations, both with his wife and with his servants: Charles "is at the *command* of any woman like a slave" and "cannot *command* himself in the presence of a woman he likes" (July 27, 1667); Pepys cannot "*command* himself in the pleasures of his eye" (April 25, 1666), and when jealous of his wife confesses "I fear, without great discretion, I shall go near to lose too my *command* over her"—something that "the rest of the world" might see (May 21, 1663).

The diary ends ostensibly because Pepys fears for his eyesight, but a psychological interpretation can be obtained quite cheaply, thanks to the repeated associations of sex and optics: After one bout with the "very bad" Mrs Martin he declares that "it is dangerous to have to do with her, nor will I see any more a good while," accidentally leaving out the object "her" (February 28, 1666, Ash Wednesday); one particularly furtive and conflicted encounter with his wife's ex-companion Deborah Willett takes place in a "blind alehouse" (April 15, 1669). What grieves him is having to renounce the secret libertine part of his writing, having to

be contented to set down no more than is fit for . . . all the world to know, or if there be anything (which cannot now be much, now my amours to Deb are past . . .) I must endeavour to keep a margin in my book open, to add here and there a note in short-hand with my own hand. (May 31, 1669)

He never did.

CRITICAL RECEPTION

Though Pepys was valued as a speaker and connoisseur by contemporaries like Evelyn, his literary reputation had to await the transcription of the diary. Readers devoured the bowdlerized but increasingly complete editions of *Lord Braybrooke* (1825), *Mynors Bright* (1884), and *Henry Wheatley* (1893–1899), many times reprinted and abridged. The Victorians relished the teeming Dickensian particularity and appetite for life but generally regarded the diary as an unmediated transcription of reality. They were further inhibited by the scandalous sensuality apparent even in the censored editions. Even Leslie Stephen, in an original *DNB* article that pays tribute to Pepys's "lively" if unromantic interest in the arts, his "shrewd" observation and "boundless curiosity," his "piquancy" and "frankness" in confessing commonplace emotions, can only hint mysteriously at "weaknesses," "tastes for enjoyment of a not very refined kind," and "passages which cannot possibly be printed."

Appreciating Pepys came to be part of general literary culture. Joyce includes a Pepysian passage in the "Oxen of the Sun" chapter of *Ulysses*, his parodic history of English prose. Virginia Woolf devoted a typically perceptive essay to "Papers on Pepys." Mr. and Mrs. Pepys, King Charles, and assorted actresses feature in J.B. Fagan's *"And So to Bed"* (1927), a sexy farce well sprinkled with Egads and Odsbluds. Dozens of books extract from the diary a portrait of the man and his age, and dozens of specialist articles mine it for information on theater, science, weather, music, or bladder-stones. Anthologies and recordings feature famous passages like the description of the Great Fire, presented as direct reportage rather than the complex, metaphorical text it is.

The full Latham-Matthews edition of the diary restores every account of genital fumbling and sexual daydreaming, written in a vivid, jumbled mixture of French,

Spanish, Latin, and English. Starting with Lawrence Stone's citations in *Family, Sex, and Marriage in England* (1977), Pepys has become an essential figure in the history of sexuality. Bowdlerized selections for school and popular consumption still circulate, however, and one of them forms the basis for Francis Barker's unconvincing attempt to make Pepys a prototypical nervous, repressed bourgeois, "silent" on sexual matters (*The Tremulous Private Body* [1984], uncorrected in the 2nd edition [1995]).

Scholars and biographers now read the diary itself less transparently. Sherman acutely reconstructs Pepys's sense of time, his love of intricate watches and precise measurement, conceiving the diary as a way of pacing himself as he walks endlessly through London. My own work explores the intersection of sex and politics in Pepys, the mingled fear and joy of spectatorship in his response to riots and crowds, his complex relation to pornography (in the often-quoted episode where he reads, then burns, *L'Escole des filles*), and the importance of sexual self-portraiture in Pepys's conception of the diary itself. Berger analyzes the performative, flaunting element in the language (which he compares to "stage whispers"), showing us a Pepys who "selectively lives a writable life," driven by "documentary desire." Tomalin's biography makes similar points ("Pepys the man" feeding "Pepys the writer") but in plain, commonsense language aimed at the general reader. Dawson, writing to historians, admonishes them to look at "textuality (not sexuality)": Pepys actually wrote up his notes into several parallel texts (official memorandum books, financial accounts), selecting and pitching them according to the occasion and the narrative point. The diary does not simply reveal but *creates* the character of the bustling, appetitive, get-ahead Pepys.

BIBLIOGRAPHY

Works by Samuel Pepys

Boscobel [by Thomas Blount] to which Is Added the King's Own Account of his Adventures, Dictated to Mr Samuel Pepys. Ed. Charles G. Thomas. London: Tylston and Edwards, 1894.

The Diary of Samuel Pepys: A New and Complete Transcription. Ed. Robert Latham and William Matthews. 11 vols. Berkeley and Los Angeles: University of California Press, 1970–1983. (Vol. 1 includes an introductory essay on "the diary as literature.")

Letters and the Second Diary of Samuel Pepys. Ed. R.G. Howarth. London: Dent, 1932.

Studies of Samuel Pepys

Berger, Harry, Jr. "The Pepys Show: Ghost-Writing and Documentary Desire in *The Diary*." *English Literary History* 65 (1998): 557–591.

Bryant, Arthur. *Samuel Pepys*. 3 vols. 1933–1938. Cambridge: Cambridge University Press, 1948.

Dawson, Mark S. "Histories and Texts: Refiguring the Diary of Samuel Pepys." *The Historical Journal* 43 (2000): 407–431.

Pearlman, E. "Pepys and Lady Castlemaine." *Restoration* 7 (1983): 43–53.

Sherman, Stuart. *Telling Time: Clocks, Diaries, and English Diurnal Form, 1660–1785*. Chicago: University of Chicago Press, 1996.

Tomalin, Claire. *Samuel Pepys: The Unequalled Self*. New York: Knopf, 2002.

Turner, James Grantham. *Libertines and Radicals in Early Modern London: Sexuality, Politics and Literary Culture, 1630–1685*. Cambridge: Cambridge University Press, 2001.

———. "Pepys and the Private Parts of Monarchy." *Culture and Society in the Stuart Restoration: Literature, Drama, History*, ed. Gerald MacLean. Cambridge: Cambridge University Press, 1995. 95–110.

———. *Schooling Sex: Libertine Literature and Erotic Education in Italy, France, and England, 1534–1685*. Oxford: Oxford University Press, 2003.

ʑ❧ *Samuel Pufendorf*
(1632–1694)

LOUIS A. GEBHARD

BIOGRAPHY

Samuel Pufendorf was born in Chemnitz, Saxony, about 100 miles south of Berlin. The son of a Lutheran pastor, he came of age during one of the worst periods in German history, the Thirty Years War (1618–1648). The war's end left the country in economic, political, and cultural ruin; population losses ranged from 40 percent in some regions to 62 percent in others and as high as 70 percent in still others (Sagarra 3). The peace settlements of Westphalia left the states of the empire (approximately 300) virtually sovereign. Exacerbating matters was the religious divide that very generally left the south and west of the country Catholic and the north and east Protestant, either Lutheran or Calvinist ("Reformed"). The empire was still headed by the Emperor (*Kaiser*) elected by eight hereditary princes, the Electors (*Kurfursten*). The Kaiser continued to reside at Vienna, ruling directly only his Austrian dominions. There were other imperial institutions such as the *Reichstag*, but that body resembled an international conference rather than a national legislature. In addition, there were two judicial bodies that were largely ineffectual. It was this empire that Pufendorf described in such critical terms in his famous *De Statu Imperii Germanici* in 1667.

In 1650, he began his study for the ministry at the University of Leipzig. Put off by "scholastic" philosophy, he abandoned theology—and the University of Leipzig—moving to the University of Jena, where he came under the influence of Erhard Weigel (1625–1699), "the greatest authority on mathematics and natural science" in Germany (Hochstrasser 24), who introduced him to the work of Descartes and Galileo. Following Descartes, Weigel was attempting to build science anew, on the "mathematical" (deductive) method, eschewing all authority. It was this method that Pufendorf attempted in his first major work, *Elementa Jurisprudentia Universalis* (Behme 14). In 1658, Pufendorf completed his studies but rejected the doctor's degree, settling instead for the *Magister*, his decision reflecting his contempt for both the academic guild and scholastic philosophy. He then left Jena to seek "fame and patronage" (Krieger, *Politics* 16). Both were to come in due course.

Pufendorf's initial appointment was as a tutor in the household of Baron Peter Coyet, Swedish envoy to the Danish court. Pufendorf arrived in Copenhagen in 1658, just in time to be trapped in the city when the Swedes suddenly laid siege to it (Behme 22). Since 1630, when the redoubtable King Gustavus Adolphus (reigned 1611 to 1632) landed his army in Germany, Sweden, allied with France, was the dominant power in the Baltic region. Now in 1658, during the "First Northern War" (1655–1660), King Charles X Gustavus (reigned 1654–1660) broke off his campaign in Poland, attacked Denmark, and laid siege to Copenhagen. The attack proved unsuccessful, but the Swedes did acquire Scania (the southern portion of modern Sweden), a region, however, that was largely Danish in culture. This region was to figure decisively on Pufendorf's subsequent career.

During the siege, Pufendorf and the rest of the household staff of the baron were confined to the city hall, where Pufendorf, relying on memory, composed his first important work, *Elementa Jurisprudentia Universalis*. Written to demonstrate his talents, the work, despite its deficiencies, was "well received" (Hochstrasser 47). With the end of hostilities, Baron Coyet was assigned to the Netherlands, he and Pufendorf arriving there in the autumn of 1659. It was in the Netherlands that Pufendorf saw to the publication of his *Elementa* and won the favorable attention of Elector Karl Ludwig of the Palatinate, a small principality athwart the Rhine, with the University at Heidelberg. Ludwig was a moderate Calvinist, tolerating both Lutherans and Catholics. It was to him that Pufendorf dedicated his *Elementa*. In 1661, Pufendorf was offered—and accepted—a teaching position at the university (Behme 16).

What Pufendorf wanted, however, was a professorship on the prestigious law faculty. Rebuffed (Behme 16), his response was his famous work on the German Empire, *De Statu Imperii Germanici* (1667) under the pseudonym of Severinus de Monzambano (!), a fictitious Italian traveler. Pufendorf was careful to obtain the permission of Karl Ludwig (Krieger, *Politics* 21) and for many years would not publicly admit his authorship. He was a popular teacher, but his professional relations were becoming strained. His ambition, his combative nature, and his book on the German constitution were probably all contributing factors. In any case, in the late 1660s, he accepted an offer of a professorship at the new university of Lund in Scania, Sweden. The university was part of a policy of conciliating the local Danish population (Von Treitschke 251).

The trend in Sweden—as in most of Europe at the time—was toward absolutism, culminating in the Declaration of Sovereignty of 1693 wherein the Riksdag "recognized him (the ruler) as an absolute sovereign king, whose commands are binding upon all, and who is responsible to no one on earth for his actions" (Lockyer 449). Pufendorf arrived in Sweden in the summer of 1668 and remained there for the next seventeen years. After seven years of effort, he published his most important work, *De Jure Naturae et Gentium Libro Octo* (*On the Law of Nature and Nations in Eight Books*). The next year he published *De Officio Hominis et Civis . . .* (*On the Duty of Man and the Citizen . . .*). This was both a condensation and a textbook. It was a smashing commercial success, going through 145 editions and translated into eight languages before 1800 (Döring, in Schmidt-Biggemann). Pufendorf was famous.

However, Pufendorf was infamous to some. Outraged by his more secular rationalistic approach to natural law, theologians at Lund published attacks that were both scholarly and personal. Pufendorf eventually found his work banned both in Lutheran Saxony and in Catholic Rome. But he struck back, his articles eventually collected under the title *Eris Scandica* (Scandinavian Polemics), which appeared in 1686. In the meantime, in 1672, another major war broke out, the "Dutch War," in which Louis XIV assailed the Netherlands. The war in time drew in the English, the empire, Spain, Denmark, and Brandenburg in support of the Dutch. But not Sweden. True to her long-standing alliance, she joined the fray in support of France. The war did not go well; Scania was invaded by the Danes, and Lund was overrun. Thanks to French diplomatic assistance, the Swedes eventually recovered the region, but in the interval Pufendorf had to leave, ultimately to Stockholm where he was appointed Court Historiographer with the rank of State Secretary.

Pufendorf never returned to the university and instead dedicated many of the next several years to history. In 1682, he published his only work in German, *Einleitung zur Historie der Vornehmsten Reiche so Itziger Zeit in Europa Sich Befinden*, a product of his lectures at Lund. Three years later he reverted to Latin with his work on Swedish history. But by the late 1680s Pufendorf's relations with elements at the court were becoming strained. Pufendorf's personality as well as the alliance with France were both probably important. Indeed, in 1681, Pufendorf wrote a formal memorandum (reprinted and translated into German by Döring, *Kleine Vorträge*) urging that the alliance be dropped. By the late 1680s, he was thoroughly outraged by French persecutions of the Huguenots. At this juncture, the Calvinist Elector of Brandenburg, Frederick William (ruled from 1640 to 1688, known in time as the "Great Elector"), issued the Edict of Potsdam, offering refuge to his coreligionists (Behme 19; Von Treitschke 269–270, 286).

By this time, Pufendorf seems to have been angling for a position in Brandenburg. In 1687, he published *De Habitu Religionis Christianae ad Vitam Civilem* (*On the Relation of the Christian Religion to Civil Life*), dedicated (of course) to Frederick William. Brandenburg, ruled by the Hohenzollern since the 15th century, was centered around Berlin but possessed scattered holdings in western Germany, a sizable compact bloc of territory farther east (East Prussia), as well as small holdings in the south. Like Sweden it was relatively efficient and moving toward absolutism. This was, of course, the principality that became in the 19th century the nucleus of the modern German state.

In 1688, Pufendorf was invited to Berlin and commissioned to write a history of the Great Elector. The Swedes were put out; he had not finished his work on Charles Gustavus; Brandenburg had developed into a dangerous rival. After some delay, he was permitted to leave but had to leave his manuscript in Stockholm. He arrived in Berlin in February 1688, just after the death of the Great Elector. But in short order, he produced his history and then began a work on his successor, Elector Frederick III, who in 1701 assumed the title "King in Prussia." He also found time to write an essay on Lutheran-Calvinist relations. By 1694, a reconciliation seems to have taken place with the Swedes, and in May he was welcomed back to Stockholm, raised to the rank of baron, and saw to the completion of his work on Charles Gustavus. But the strain may have been too much, for he suffered a stroke. With difficulty, he returned to Berlin, where he died near the end of October. Buried with high honors, his frequently quoted epitaph reads (in translation) as follows:

His bones rest here
His soul has been taken into Heaven
His fame has spread to the entire world
(Döring, in Geyer, Goerlich, and Schliebe 34–37; Krieger, *Politics* 27–33; Behme 19–
20; Von Treitschke 285–300)

MAJOR WORKS AND THEMES

Pufendorf's *Elementa Jurisprudentia Universalis* (1660) states the same themes as his major work of 1672, *De Jure Naturae et Gentium* and the textbook *De Officio Hominis et Civis*. But *Elementa* is the more rationalistic, deductive work, written without drawing on other authorities or deduction from Scripture. *De Jure*, a much more massive tome, is "eclectic," that is, replete with hundreds of references, both ancient and modern.

For all of his "secularism" Pufendorf was still a 17th-century Lutheran. God is the author of natural law (*De Officio*, Book I, ch. 111, para. 11, Moore trans.), law that man can discern through his reason (*De Jure*, Book II, ch. III, para. 13, citations from the Oldfather translation). Man is not only a rational but, as intended by the Creator, a "social animal" (*De Jure*, preface, IX). But men differ from animals; they are more complex and sometimes "more fierce and uncontrolled" (*De Jure*, Book VII, ch. I, para. 4). The chief precept of natural law is to live in peace with other men (*De Jure*, Book II, ch. II, para. 9). In his "natural state" (the absence of any government), which Pufendorf believed never existed (*De Jure*, Book II, ch. II, para. 4), man lives in peace (*De Jure*, Book II, ch. II, para. 9).

The state, however, is "the most perfect society" providing the "greatest safety for mankind" (*De Jure*, Book VII, ch. I, introduction). The state is ruled by a sovereign power, whose chief *duty* is the "welfare" of the people, Pufendorf emphasizing "duty" in the entire chapter (*De Jure*, Book VII, ch. IX). "All men are accounted as naturally equal" (Chapter heading, *De Jure*, Book II, ch. II), but they have obligations as well as rights. Men have the right of self-defense (*De Jure*, Book II, ch. V) and to property, though this right seems to be hedged about with qualifications (*De Jure*, Book II, ch. V, VI; Book VIII, ch. V). Private property is a more convenient institution than communal ownership. Men do not have much religious freedom; atheism must be forbidden (*Elementa*, Definition 12, para. 16), and magistrates can rightly silence dissent (*Elementa*, Book II, Observation I, para. 2). Uniformity in religion within the state "is desirable," but force to achieve it is not "appropriate" (*Elem*, Book II, Observation I, para. 2).

The highest degree of freedom is possessed by those who are exempt from the civil law, the sovereign power. If the Supreme Sovereign abuses his authority, citizens do not have the right to rebel: "It is foolish and impudent to rise in revolt against a prince *for any grievance*" [my emphasis] (*De Jure*, Book VII, ch. VIII, para. 5). In short, Pufendorf is a prophet of equality before the law but also of despotism. Pufendorf's other major work, his book on the German Empire, resembles in its modern German edition a small pocket-sized book of about 225 pages. It provides a brief history of the German people from ancient times to the 17th century together with a careful description of the organs of government and the various princely houses and their holdings. In his characterization of the Reich, he uses the word "monstrosity" to describe the constitution (Ch. VI, para. 9, 106, in Denzer), a characterization that, added to his other sarcastic comments, provoked widespread outrage.

Other less significant works by Pufendorf include his *Einleitung zu der Historie der Vornehmsten Reiche und Staaten* . . . , designed as a textbook for future statesmen. It describes the rise and fall of the ancient empires and carries the story of Europe to the Peace of Nymwegen of 1679, which ended the "Dutch War" (Krieger, *Politics* 181). He eventually completed two works on Swedish history, spanning the reigns of Gustavus Adolphus, Christina and Charles X Gustavus, one work on Frederick William, the "Great Elector" of Brandenburg. A sequel devoted to his successor Frederick III was never completed. Of interest is a long digression in it devoted to the "Glorious Revolution" (1688) in England, a revolution that Pufendorf defends (Krieger, *Politics* 197–199). Pufendorf's response to his attackers was published under the title of *Eris Scandica*; his views on church–state relations are discussed in *De Habitu Religionis Christianae ad Vitam Civilem*; Lutheran–Calvinist relations are treated under the title *Jus Feciale Divinum Sive de Censensu et Dissensu Protestantium*, published posthumously in 1695.

CRITICAL RECEPTION

Pufendorf died famous, his work exercising enormous influence on legal thinking in the 17th and 18th centuries, helping shape, for example, the Prussian and Austrian legal codes. He is generally recognized as one of the leaders of the early German Enlightenment. **Locke** recommended the reading of his work, and he was cited by the American revolutionists. But by the mid-19th century, he was almost forgotten. One biography was written in 1710, but it was not until the mid-19th century that another appeared, that of the Prussian historian Gustav Droysen.

Pufendorf's most enthusiastic partisan was probably Heinrich Von Treitschke (1834–1896), also a Saxon and later professor at the University of Berlin. Writing in 1875, he saw Pufendorf as a "brilliant energetic courageous German patriot who first exposed the rottenness of the old Empire" and "who seized the right to think freely of the secular nature of the State" (IV: 303). But in his own lifetime not everyone was so impressed, Leibniz dismissing him "as not enough of a lawyer and scarcely a philosopher at all" (Derathé 80). And "most French historians . . . have considered him a thinker of second rank" ("un penseur de second plan") (Derathé 78), though Derathé himself believes this judgment should be revised (78).

Equally unimpressed is the American historian Leonard Krieger. Writing in 1965 he concludes that Pufendorf did contribute his "mite" "to the secularization of politics and the growth of absolutism" (*Politics* 1). Indeed, Krieger was of the opinion "that he was not a particularly rigorous thinker" (218). Nonetheless, interest in Pufendorf has revived since World War II, and again, as Krieger has pointed out (Rev. 674), he has received some attention in each decade. A commemorative symposium was held at Lund in 1992 and again in Leipzig in 1994. His legacies and achievements are fairly clear, but there are other details that remain to be brought out. As Detlef Döring has pointed out, there is not yet a modern edition of his work nor of his correspondence, nor an adequate up-to-date biography (*Pufendorf-Studien* 7). And as Pufendorf himself wrote in a letter to Christian Thomasius in March 1688, "I have not sufficient courage to publish [my real opinions]" (Krieger, *Politics* 34).

BIBLIOGRAPHY

Works by Samuel Pufendorf

"Briefe Pufendorfs an Falaiseau, Friese und Weigel." Ed. K. Varrentrapp. *Historische Zeitschrift* 73 (1894): 59–67.

Briefe Samuel Pufendorfs an Christian Thomasius (1687–1693). Ed. E. Gigas. Munich and Leipzig, 1897.

"Briefe von Pufendorf." Ed. K. Varrentrapp. *Historische Zeitschrift* 70 (1893): 1–51, 193–232.

Briefwechsel. Ed. D. Döring. Vol. I of *Samuel Pufendorf: Gesammelte Werke*. Ed. W. Schmidt-Biggemann. Berlin: Akademie Verlag, 1996–.

Commentarium de Rebus Suecicis Libri XXXVI ab Expeditione Gustavi Adolphi in Germanium ad Abdicationem Usque Christianae. Utrecht, 1686.

De Habitu Religionis Christianae ad Vitam Civilem. Bremen, 1687.

De Jure Naturae et Gentium Libri Octo. London, 1672.

De Officio Hominis et Civis Juxta Legem Naturalem Libri Duo. 1673.

De Rebus a Carolo Gustavo Sueciae Rege Gestis Commentarium Libri VII. Nuremberg, 1696.

De Rebus Frederici Wilhelmi Magni Electoris Brandenburgici Commentarium Libri XIX. Berlin, 1695.

De Rebus Gestis Frederici III, Electoris Brandenburgici Post Primus Borussiae Regis Libri III Complectentes Annas 1688–1690. Berlin, 1784.

De Statu Imperii Germanici ad Laelium Fratrem, Dominum Trezolani, Liber Unus. Geneva, 1667.

Die Verfassung des Deutschen Reiches. Ed. and trans. Horst Denzer. Stuttgart: Philip Reclam jun, 1994.

Dissertationes Academicae Selectiores. Uppsala, 1677.

Divine Feudal Law. Trans. Theophilus Dorrington. London, 1703.

Einleitung zu der Historie der Vornehmsten Reiche und Staaten so Itziger Zeit in Europa Sich Befinden. Frankfurt-am-Main, 1682.

Elementa Jurisprudentia Universalis. Hague, 1660.

Eris Scandica qua Adversus Libros de Jure Naturali et Gentium Objecta Diliuntur. Frankfurt-am-Main, 1744.

An Introduction to the History of the Principal Kingdoms and States of Europe. Trans. J. Crull. London, 1702.

Jus Feciale Divinum Sive de Consensu et Dissensu Protestantium Exercitatio Posthuma. Lübeck, 1695.

Kleine Vortäge und Schriften, Texte zu Geschichte, Pädagogik, Philosophie, Kirche und Völkerrecht. Ed. D. Döring. Frankfurt-am-Main, 1995.

The Law of Nature and of Nations. Ed. J. Barbeyrac. Trans. B. Kennett. London, 1749.

The Law of Nature and of Nations. [2nd ed. of 1688.] Trans. C.H. Oldfather and W.A. Oldfather. 2 vols. Oxford: Oxford University Press, 1934.

On the Duty of Man and Citizen According to Natural Law. Ed. J. Tully. Trans. M. Silverthorne. Cambridge: Cambridge University Press, 1991.

On the Duty of Man and the Citizen. Trans. F.G. Moore. Oxford, 1927.

On the Relation of the Christian Life to the Civil Life. Trans. J. Crull. London, 1698.

Political Writings of Samuel Pufendorf. Ed. Craig L. Carr. Trans. Michael J. Seidler. New York: Oxford University Press, 1994. (Selections from *Elementa* and *De Jure Naturae*.)

The Two Books of the Elements of Universal Jurisprudence, Together with an Appendix on the Moral Sphere. Trans. W.A. Oldfather. Oxford, 1931.

Studies of Samuel Pufendorf

Behme, Thomas. *Samuel von Pufendorf. Naturrecht und Staat. Eine Analyze und Interpretation Seiner Theorie, Ihrer Grundlagen und Probleme.* Göttingen: Vandenhoek und Rupprecht, 1995.

Burns, J.H. *The Cambridge History of Political Thought.* Cambridge: Cambridge University Press, 1991.

Denzer, Horst. "Leben, Werk und Wirkung Samuel Pufendorfs." *Zeitschrift für Politik* 30 (1983): 160–186.

Derathé, Robert. *Jean-Jacques Rousseau et la Science Politique de Son Temps.* Paris: Presses Universitaires, 1950. (Contains extensive bibliography including French translations of Pufendorf's works.)

Döring, Detlef. *Pufendorf-Studien: Beiträge zur Biographie Samuel von Pufendorf und zu Seiner Entwicklung als Historiker und Theologischer Schriftsteller.* Berlin: Duncler u. Humbolt, 1992.

Droysen, Gustav. "Zur Kritik Pufendorfs." In *Abhandlungen zur Neueren Geschichte.* Leipzig, 1876.

Fiorilla, Vanda. *Tra Egoismo e Socialitá. Il Giusnaturalismo di Samuel Pufendorf.* Naples, 1992.

Geyer, Bodo, Helmut Goerlich, and Gerol Schliebe, eds. *Samuel Pufendorf und Seine Wirkungen Bis Auf Die Heutige Zeit.* Baden-Baden: Nomas Verlags-Gesellschaft, 1996.

Hochstrasser, T.J. *Natural Law Theories in the Early Enlightenment.* New York: Cambridge University Press, 2000.

Krieger, Leonard. *The Politics of Discretion: Pufendorf and the Acceptance of Natural Law.* Chicago: University of Chicago Press, 1965.

————. Rev. of Horst Denzer's *Moralphilosophie und Naturrecht bei Samuel Pufendorf. American Historical Review* 78 (June 1973): 674–676.

Lockyer, Roger. *Habsburg and Bourbon Europe 1470–1720.* London: Longman's, 1974.

Modéer, Kjell A., ed., and the Institut für Rättshistorisk Forskning Grundat av Gustav och Carin Olin. *Samuel von Pufendorf, 1632–1982. Ett Rättshistorisk Symposium i Lund 15–16 Januari 1982.* Stockholm: A-B Nordiska Bibliotek, 1986.

Palladini, Fiammetta. *Samuel Pufendorf Discepolo di Hobbes.* Bologna, 1990.

Sagarra, Eda. *A Social History of Germany, 1648–1914.* London: Methuen, 1977.

Schroder, Peter. "The Constitution of the Holy Roman Empire after 1648: Samuel Pufendorf's Assessment in His Monzambano." *The Historical Journal* 42 (1999): 961–983.

Tuck, Richard. *Natural Rights Theories: Their Origin and Development.* Cambridge: Cambridge University Press, 1979.

Von Treitschke, Heinrich. *Historische und Politische Aufsätze.* Vol. IV. Leipzig, 1897.

⁊♠ *Henry Purcell*
(1659–1695)

NANCY HAGER

BIOGRAPHY

Most of what is known about the life of Henry Purcell derives from official documents recording the positions to which he was appointed and commissions he was awarded. His father was probably Thomas Purcell, a gentleman of the Chapel Royal, one of the institutions reestablished after the fall of **Cromwell**'s Commonwealth and the Restoration of the monarchy in 1660. At some point in his youth, Henry himself became a member of the Chapel Royal as one of the twelve carefully selected boys brought from all over England to constitute the boys' section of the Westminster Abbey choir. The Chapel's master was Henry Cooke, a singer and composer who was described by a contemporary as England's best singer "after the Italian manner." Cooke's duties included the musical training of the choristers, providing instruction on the lute, organ, harpsichord, violin, and in Latin and other general subjects, as well as ensuring the boys were housed, clothed, and fed. In addition to Purcell, Pelham Humphrey and **John Blow** were also pupils of Cooke who later emerged as major musical figures of Restoration England.

When his voice broke at about age fifteen, Purcell took his first paid position as tuner of the organ at Westminister Abbey. In 1677 he succeeded Matthew Locke as composer for the royal violins, and in 1679 he was appointed as one of the organists of the Chapel Royal as well as organ maker and keeper of the King's instruments. These appointments under Charles II were renewed by James II and William III. Chapel Royal organists were also members of the choir, and contemporary records indicate that Purcell performed as a bass and as a countertenor.

In the absence of diaries, letters, and other informal records, very little is known of Purcell's personal life or character. He married in 1680 or 1681 and died in 1695 on the eve of St. Cecilia's Day, the name day of the patron saint of music. He was survived by his wife Frances and two sons, one of whom, Edward, became an organist. Purcell's funeral was held in Westminister Abbey, where he was buried near the organ.

MAJOR WORKS AND THEMES

Purcell's creative output is remarkable with respect to quantity, breadth, and compositional craftsmanship. The works list at the end of the article on Purcell in *New Grove Dictionary of Music and Musicians* lists one opera and five semioperas, incidental music and songs for over forty plays, about 110 anthems, services, and other sacred works, twenty-four odes and welcome songs, hundreds of songs and catches, plus instrumental overtures, suites, and dance movements, voluntaries, fantasies, marches, and trumpet tunes.

Purcell's studies in composition as a boy of the Chapel Royal included copying sacred works of late Renaissance composers such as Thomas Tallis and William Byrd. This rich repertory of *a cappella* choral polyphony provided the models for Purcell's more conservative "full anthems," most of which are early works. Through his teacher, Henry Cooke, Purcell was also introduced to the more modern "operatic" style of Italian composers, whose choral works incorporated instrumental overtures and ritornellos and florid settings for solo voice. The majority of Purcell's anthems and services are of the latter "verse" type, the most elaborate being *My heart is inditing*, composed for the coronation of James II in 1685.

Works written in connection with his official duties at court include odes and welcome songs for such occasions as royal birthdays and important holidays. Purcell's settings of the texts, which were often obsequious and of dubious literary quality, could be quite operatic in character, with virtuosic writing for solo singers, instruments employed in a concertato texture, and choral movements. The earliest such work, from 1680, was written to honor Charles II, the latest, from 1695, for a birthday celebration of the Duke of Gloucester. The most often performed today are *Hail, bright Cecilia*, performed at a St. Cecilia's Day celebration in 1692, and *Come, Ye sons of art* from 1694, the last of the five odes Purcell composed for the birthday of Queen Mary II.

Music for the stage occupies a very prominent place among Purcell's creative output and reflects an English passion for theater that was rooted in rich traditions of the court masque and the remarkable flowering of staged drama during the Elizabethan period. Masques were hybrid entertainments involving spoken dialogue, songs, instrumental music, lavish costumes, and spectacular effects. Songs, dances, fanfares, and so on, were also incorporated into the stage works of **Shakespeare** and other Elizabethan playwrights but, in their pursuit of greater dramatic unity, as more integrated theatrical elements.

During Purcell's lifetime, London had two principal theaters, one presenting plays performed by the King's company, the other by the company of the Duke of York. Purcell's first stage music probably dates from 1680 and consisted of songs, ensembles, and choruses for a play entitled *Theodosius, or The Force of Love*. Over the remaining fifteen years of his life, Purcell contributed such incidental music to over forty plays by Beaumont, **Dryden**, Congreve, Fletcher, and D'Urfey as well as lesser-known authors. The publication of many of Purcell's theater songs, sacred songs, catches, and solo songs and duets written for private entertainment attests to their popularity with the English public. The range of styles is enormous, from coloratura arias and declamatory settings to folklike tunes and pastoral songs, as determined by the subject of the text.

Five of the plays to which Purcell contributed music constitute a distinctive category of stage works, labeled "semioperas" by a contemporary. Two are adaptations of Shakespeare (*The Fairy Queen*, after *Midsummer Night's Dream*, and *The Tempest*), two were created in collaboration with Dryden (*King Arthur* and *The Indian Queen*), and one was an adaptation of a play by Beaumont and Fletcher (*Dioclesian*). All date from the 1690s, and the unusually prominent role given to music is probably a testament to Purcell's reputation as England's leading composer for the theater. Although these productions all incorporated abundant airs, choruses, dances, instrumental overtures, and interludes, none is classified as opera because the dialogue was spoken rather than set as recitative.

Experiments in setting all the words of a drama to music were an Italian innovation dating from around 1600. The earliest successful manifestation of this new genre, which became known as opera, is generally considered to be Monteverdi's *Orfeo* of 1607. At the time of Purcell's birth, the center of world opera was Venice, where Monteverdi had worked from 1613 to his death in 1643 and where the first public opera house had opened in 1636. The acceptance of opera in France was accomplished primarily by the Italian-born Lully, who developed a style of recitative that followed the rhythms and nuances of spoken French and also incorporated numerous ballets, a passion of Louis XIV, who is known himself to have danced in these elaborate *divertissements*.

The earliest attempt by an English composer to declaim dialogue in music may have been the now-lost score by Nicolas Lanier for **Ben Jonson**'s *Lovers Made Men* of 1617. Two subsequent works considered to be operas are John Blow's *Venus and Adonis*, composed for the entertainment of Charles II, and *Siege of Rhodes* of 1656, subtitled "A Representation by the art of Perspective in Scenes and the Story sung in Recitative Music," with several composers contributing music that has not survived. *Siege of Rhodes* was revived in 1661 but "acted as a just *Drama*." The implication that it had been transformed from an opera to a play with music is likely attributable to a deep-seated distaste among the British for setting dialogue in English to music, as noted by many commentators of the time.

Purcell did compose one true opera, *Dido and Aeneas*, commissioned in 1689 for performance by students at a girls' boarding school. The libretto is an adaptation by **Nahum Tate** of the episode in Virgil's *Aeneid* in which Aeneas and his crew have been driven by a storm to Carthage, which is ruled by Queen Dido. Aeneas and Dido fall in love, but in obedience to fate, he abandons her and she dies presumably of a broken heart, with a hint of Virgil's fire. In Purcell's setting, dialogue is sung in recitative, while more musically elaborate arias are the vehicle for dramatic characterization and emotional expression. Dido's moving lament, "When I am laid to rest," from the end of Act III, is probably Purcell's best-known aria today. Choruses and dances are also important theatrical elements: for example, the chorus of the witches as they engineer Aeneas's departure by conjuring an evil spell, the sailor's chorus as they prepare to depart from Carthage, and the concluding chorus of mourners for Dido's death.

A year after the composition of *Dido and Aeneas*, the following statement appears in the preface to Purcell's music for *Dioclesian*:

Musick and Poetry have ever been acknowledg'd Sisters, which walking hand in hand, support each other; As Poetry is the harmony of Words, so Musick is that of Notes; and as Poetry is a Rise above Prose and Oratory, so is Musick the exaltation of Poetry. Both of them may excel apart, but sure they are most excellent when they are joyn'd, because nothing is then wanting to either of their Perfections: for thus they appear like Wit and Beauty in the same Person. Poetry and Painting have arrived in their perfection in our own Country: Musick is yet but in its Nonage, a forward Child, which gives hope of what it may be hereafter in England, when the Masters of it shall find more Encouragement.

This vision of the imminent flowering of a union of music and drama that might have led to an English tradition of opera was not to be, perhaps because Purcell's life was so tragically short. Less than two decades after his death, opera was all the rage in London, but it was a foreign import, Italian opera in the Neapolitan style composed by the German-born George Frederick Handel. It would be almost 200 years before England produced another great composer for the English theater, Sir Arthur Sullivan. However, as with most of Purcell's theater music, his collaborations with Gilbert are classified as operettas, not operas, because they again employ spoken dialogue.

Practically all Purcell's orchestral music consists of the overtures, dances, and other instrumental movements composed for his stage works, anthems, and odes. Among his important chamber compositions are fifteen early works for from three to seven viols written in a serious, old-fashioned style. More modern are twenty-two trio sonatas, twelve published in 1683, the other ten shortly after his death, in which Purcell "faithfully endeavor'd a just imitation of the most fam'd Italian masters." Despite his appointments as organist of Westminster Abbey and the Chapel Royal and as harpsichord player to James II, Purcell's extant keyboard music is relatively small: one verse and five voluntaries for organ and, for harpsichord, suites, miscellaneous dances, and arrangements of movements from the odes and stage works.

In addition to music intended for the royal court and chapel, Purcell's music was also performed at public concerts that were becoming popular during the 17th century, for example, those presented by the musician John Banister and the coal merchant Thomas Britton. According to a contemporary commentator, Roger North,

Here was consorts, fugues, solos, lutes, hautbois, trumpets, kettle drumes, & what not . . . & here it was that the masters began to display their powers afore the wise judges of the towne, and found out the grand secret, that the English will follow musick & drop their pence freely.

Purcell's style, both vocal and instrumental, is often described as a fusion of English, Italian, and French elements. English folk dance is recalled in his instrumental hornpipes and gigs, and the influence of folksong is evident in the freshness of his melodies. Even when foreign influence is detectable in his vocal writing, his text settings sensitively reflect the inflections and rhythms of English speech. But his awareness and adoption of modern continental practices were what won him the admiration of contemporary critics and observers.

Italy was regarded by the English as the source of the most progressive musical trends in the second half of the 17th century. An almost obsessive fascination with Italy had also been rampant during the Elizabethan period, when Italian madrigals were the rage and Shakespeare chose Italy as the setting for many of his plays. Later, Italian names were in fashion among musicians, exemplified by the composers Orlando Gibbons, Ferdinando Richardson, and Giovannni Coperario (born John Cooper).

In the years following the end of the Commonwealth, Italian operas were enthusiastically received at court, and documents record the appearance of numerous Italian musicians, including the castrato Siface, the inspiration for Purcell's eponymous harpsichord work titled "Sefauchi's Farewell." Purcell himself acknowledged his emulation of Italian music in several prefaces, two of which are cited above, and Roger North noted "his Great skill before the reforme of musick al Italliana." Clear but chromatically inflected tonality and florid writing for the voice are pronounced Italianate features of Purcell's compositional language.

French influence in the music of Purcell and other Restoration composers is especially evident in orchestral overtures modeled on those of Lully and in dance pieces and descriptive symphonies of stage works. Charles II, who as a child had gone into exile in France and lived at the court of Louis XIV, returned to England with ideals of taste and decorum he had known at Versailles. Louis's *Vingt-quatre violons du Roi* were the model for The King's Violins, to which Purcell was appointed composer in 1677 and which performed at meals and other court functions. A witness to a performance in chapel reported hearing "a concert of 24 violins between every pause, after the French fantastical light way, better suiting a tavern or playhouse than a church." In 1666 Charles appointed a Frenchman, Louis Grabu, as master of the King's music, the highest musical post in England. In 1673, Grabu was succeeded by another Frenchman, Robert Cambert. Charles also sent a number of young English musicians to study under Lully. Pelham Humphrey, one of Purcell's early masters, was among those who traveled on the Continent after leaving the Chapel Royal in 1664, according to **Pepys**, returning "an absolute Monsieur."

Analysis and description of Purcell's music with reference to the materials and compositional practices of contemporary Italian and French composers is not a construct imposed by modern scholars. In one of his prefaces, Purcell himself acknowledged the dominance of these two national styles and expressed his conviction that the future of English music lay in the emulation and assimilation of their distinctive musical languages.

'Tis now learning Italian, which is its best Master, and studying a little of the French Air, to give it somewhat more of Gayety and Fashion. Thus being farther from the Sun, we are of later Growth than our Neighbour Countries, and must be content to shake off our Barbarity by degrees. The present Age seems already dispos'd to be refin'd, and to distinguish betwixt wild Fancy, and a just, numerous Composition.

CRITICAL RECEPTION

Purcell is indisputably regarded today as the most important English composer of the second half of the 17th century. This judgment was shared by Purcell's contemporaries, one of whom pronounced him the "Orfeus Britannicus." He was especially esteemed for the care and precision of his settings of poetic texts, in the words of the music publisher John Playford, possessing "a peculiar Genius to express the Energy of *English Words*, whereby he mov'd the Passions as well as caus'd Admiration in all his Auditors." Dryden praised him in the introductions to two of his plays for which Purcell had composed incidental music. With respect to the comedy *Amphitryon*, Dryden writes, "What has been wanting on my Part, has been abundantly supplyed by the Excellent Composition of Mr. *Purcell*: in whose Person we have at length found an *English-man*, equal with the best abroad. At least my Opinion of him has been such." Similarly in the preface to *King Arthur*, Dryden asserts, "There is nothing better, than what I intended, but the Musick; which has since arriv'd to a greater Perfection in *England*, than ever formerly; especially passing through the Artful Hands of Mr. *Purcel*, who has Compos'd it with so great a Genius, that he has nothing to fear but an ignorant, ill-judging Audience." One of Purcell's death notices states, "He is much lamented, being a very great Master of Musick." And he was hailed as "one of the most Celebrated Masters of the Science of Musick in the Kingdom & scarce Inferior to any in Europe." In the opinion of Roger North, a lawyer, amateur musician, and author of several books about music, "A greater musical genius England never had." And the 18th-century historian Charles Burney declared Purcell to be "as much the pride of an Englishman in music, as Shakespeare in productions of the stage, **Milton** in epic poetry, **Locke** in metaphysics, or Sir Isaac Newton in philosophy and mathematics."

BIBLIOGRAPHY

Works by Henry Purcell

The Catch Book. 153 Catches Including the Complete Catches of Henry Purcell. Ed. Paul Hillier. Oxford: Oxford University Press, c. 1987.

Dido and Aeneas. Ed. Curtis Price. New York: W.W. Norton, c. 1986.

Eight Suites: newly transcribed and edited from A choice collection of lessons for the harpsichord or spinnet (1696). Ed. Howard Ferguson. London: Stainer & Bell, c. 1968.

Fantasias and in nomines. Ed. Thurston Dart. London: Novello, c. 1959.

Ode for St. Cecilia's Day (1692). Ed. Michael Tipett and Walter Bergmann. London: Schott, c. 1955.

Orpheus Britannicus: a collection of the choicest songs for one, two, and three voices compos'd by Mr. Henry Purcell. Facsimile ed. Ridgewood, NJ: Gregg Press, 1965.

The Works of Henry Purcell. The Purcell Society. 1878–1965. Rev. ed., London: Novello, 1961–.

Studies of Henry Purcell

Harley, John. *Music in Purcell's London: The Social Background.* London: Dobson, 1968.

Harris, Ellen. *Henry Purcell's Dido and Aeneas.* New York: Oxford University Press, 1987.

Holman, Peter. *Henry Purcell.* Oxford: Oxford University Press, 1994.

Holst, I., ed. *Henry Purcell (1659–1695): Essays on His Music.* London: Oxford University Press, 1959.

Hutchings, Arthur. *Purcell.* London: British Broadcasting Corporation, c. 1982.

Keates, Jonathan. *Purcell: A Biography.* Boston: Northeastern University Press, 1996.

Moore, Robert. *Henry Purcell and the Restoration Theatre.* London: Heinemann, 1961.

Price, Curtis. *Henry Purcell and the London Stage.* New York: Cambridge University Press, 1984.

———, ed. *Purcell Studies.* New York: Cambridge University Press, 1995.

Westrup, Jack. "Henry Purcell." In *New Grove Dictionary of Music and Musicians.* 15: 457–475. London: Oxford University Press, 1980.

———. *Purcell.* Rev. ed. London: Oxford University Press, 1980.

Zimmerman, F.B. *The Anthems of Henry Purcell*. New York: American Choral Foundation, 1971.

———. *Henry Purcell, 1659–1695: His Life and Times*. Philadelphia: University of Pennsylvania Press, 1983.

❧ *Allan Ramsay*
(1686–1758)

HUGH MACRAE RICHMOND

BIOGRAPHY

Allan Ramsay the Elder is noted as a poet, anthologist, and dramatist. He was born in Leadhills, Lanarkshire, Scotland, son of an Edinburgh lawyer who was a local estate manager. After starting a career as a wigmaker Ramsay progressed to bookseller, and he is considered to be the creator of the first circulating library in Britain. His exceptional personal amiability and conversational finesse secured his acceptance to the Easy Club (of Jacobite predictions) where he acquired the pen name of Isaak Bickerstaff and later of Gawin Douglas. His poems reflect a Jonsonian (see **Ben Jonson**) range of social dynamism, from sentimental songs and pastorals to literary satire, and familiar epistles addressed to socially prominent members of Edinburgh society, who are often treated with Jonson's mode of mockery and faintly concealed didacticism. Ramsay's interest in drama was best expressed in his pastoral play *The Gentle Shepherd*, but his attempt to establish a theater in Carruber's Close failed after closure by the Edinburgh Town Council. His octagonal House at Ramsay Garden, Castlefield (at the top of the Golden Mile in Edinburgh), was mockingly called "Goose Pie" by his friends and still survives. We are further indebted to Allan Ramsay the Elder for the heritage of his son, Allan Ramsay the Younger, whose paintings are considered among the great achievements of Scottish culture. The father was buried in Greyfriars churchyard, and a statue was set up on Princes Street at the Mound. There are three portraits of him in the National Gallery at Edinburgh, one by William Aikman; a copy by Alex Carse of an original by Smibert; and an anonymous one.

MAJOR WORKS AND THEMES

Ramsay's *Scots Songs* (1718, 1719) delightfully echo the love poems of the Tribe of Ben's tradition. "The Happy Lover's Reflections" matches **Richard Lovelace**'s "To Lucasta. Going to the Wars"; "Delia, to the Tune of Greensleeves" parallels

Waller's "Go lovely Rose"; and "The Yellow Haired Laddie" pursues the pastoral vein of **Marvell**'s Mower poems, a vein in which Ramsay reaches perfection in "The Lass of Patie's Mill." Ramsay's pastoral vein achieves its major climax in *The Gentle Shepherd*, which pursues the mode of pastoral drama stemmimg from Guarini's *Il Pastor Fido*, with its English imitation by John Fletcher in *The Faithful Shepherdess*. Ramsay's script mutates the style into the vernacular of Lowland Scots dialect (or Lallans), just as Italian Renaissance comedy exploits regional dialects. It was performed by the boys of Haddington Grammar School in 1729.

Ramsay also wrote fables in the style of La Fontaine, as collected in *Fables and Tales* (1722, 1730)—perhaps a tribute to Henryson's efforts—but his collected verse in *Poems* (1721), though addressed "To the most beautiful Scots Ladies," includes familiar epistles, pastorals, funeral elegies, occasional verse (sometimes scurrilous, often trivial), comic epics (adding two more Rabelaisian cantos about a village festival to the anonymous first one of *Christ's Kirk on the Green*), religious expositions, Horatian odes ("Content"), literary satires (*The Scribblers Lashed*), and epigrams. The style is varied and versatile, from Jonsonian urbanity to Swiftian scathing wit. Ramsay often echoes Pope, as in "On the most Honorable the Marquis of Bowmont Cutting off his Hair," which parallels *The Rape of the Lock* in miniature. The style ranges from neoclassical purity to idiomatic Lallans, for which Ramsay actually provided a detailed glossary or "explanation of the Scots words us'd by the Author, which are rarely or never found in the Modern English Writings."

CRITICAL RECEPTION

Ramsay was well known and much admired in his own day, and *The Gentle Shepherd* has run through many editions. He continued to be popular throughout the 19th century, and his best works (particularly the lyrics) remain a notable part of the Scottish literary tradition to this day. Ramsay's reliability as an anthologist and editor of earlier Scottish texts in his collections *The Evergreen* and *The Teatable Miscellanies* has been questioned by his scholarly successors, for his inexactitude and bold freedom of adaptation. However, he is a significant modulating figure between the native Scottish tradition, with its Lallans vernacular, and the imported neoclassical style of English courtly verse, leading unmistakably to the later achievements of the now higher-profiled Robert Burns.

BIBLIOGRAPHY

Works by Allan Ramsay

The Evergreen, Being a Collection of Scots Poems, Wrote by the Ingenious Before 1600. 2 vols. Edinburgh: Thomas Ruddiman, 1724.

Fables and Tales. 1722. Edinburgh: [Thomas Ruddiman] at the Mercury, 1730.

The Gentle Shepherd. Edinburgh: Thomas Ruddiman, 1725. (And many subsequent editions)

Poems. Edinburgh: Thomas Ruddiman, 1721–1728.

Poems, Epistles, Fables, Satires, Elegies, and Lyrics by Allan Ramsay after the 1721–28 Edition. Ed. H. Harvey Wood. Edinburgh: Oliver and Boyd (for the Saltire Society), 1940.

The Poems of Allan Ramsay. Ed. George Chalmers. 2 vols. London: Cadell and Davies, 1800.

Scots Songs. 1718. Edinburgh: Mercury, 1720.

The Teatable Miscellany, or a Complete Collection of Scots Songs. 3 vols. Edinburgh: Thomas
Ruddiman, 1723–1727.

The Works of Allan Ramsay. Vols. 1 and 2 ed. B. Martin and J. Oliver. Vols. 3–6 ed. Alexander
M. Kinghorn and A. Law. Edinburgh: William Blackwood for the Scottish Text Society,
1951–1974.

Studies of Allan Ramsay

Burns, Martin. *Allan Ramsay: A Study of His Life and Works.* Cambridge: Harvard University
Press, 1931.

———. *Bibliography of Allan Ramsay.* Glasgow: Jackson, Wylie, and Co., 1931.

Chalmers, George. "The Life of Allan Ramsay." In *The Poems of Allan Ramsay*, ed. George
Chalmers. Vol. I. London: Cadell and Davies, 1800.

Gibson, Andrew. *New Light on Allan Ramsay.* Edinburgh: William Brown, 1927.

Rembrandt van Rijn

(1606–1669)

CLAIRE I.R. O'MAHONY

BIOGRAPHY

Rembrandt's artistic formation stemmed from the classical education instilled both at the Latin school and at the University at Leiden and his tutelage with Italianate painter Jacob van Swanenburgh. His apprenticeship to the Amsterdam history painter Pieter Lastman, of whom he was later an assistant, was instrumental, as was the influence of his peers, in particular, Jan Lievens, with whom he shared not only a studio but also models and a mutually stimulating passion for similar motifs.

Rembrandt's intimate links to the art market reflected a fluctuating but ultimately successful "enterprising" nature (Alpers). Returning to Amsterdam in 1631, Rembrandt not only resided with the art dealer Hendrick van Uylenbergh but also invested in the business both financially and through his own labor, teaching pupils and executing Uylenbergh's steady stream of portrait commissions. Throughout his life Rembrandt extravagantly collected the antiques, prints, and paintings that appear in his paintings. Rembrandt's unsuccessful attempts at art dealing, coupled with inept speculative ventures, forced his bankruptcy in 1656. The slumped art market of the 1650s meant Rembrandt's collection was auctioned off for less than he had paid for one print in his heyday; nonetheless, he died in relative comfort surrounded by a considerable and newly amassed collection.

Much of the inspiration but also the complexity of Rembrandt's art and life resides in the family members who were his usual models. The second youngest of ten children of a Leiden miller and a baker's daughter, Rembrandt was born into prosperity. He often painted his parents in his early works, deploying various atmospheric settings and costumes. Saskia van Uylenbergh (1612–1642) was a socially advantageous bride, orphaned daughter of a mayor of Leeuwarden and the art dealer's niece. Three children died in infancy, but a healthy son Titus (1641–1668) would become one of the artist's favorite models. Rembrandt had an amorous relationship with Geertge Dircx (1600?–1656), employed to care for Titus when Saskia died of tuberculosis, but their separation led to an acrimonious battle in the courts and Dircx's incarceration in a reform institution in Gouda. Rembrandt had left Dircx for Hendrickje Stoeffels (1626–1663), who bore him a daughter Cornelia, married him in 1660, and, with Titus, ran his art business after he declared himself insolvent. Rembrandt, Hendrickje, and Titus van Rijn are buried side by side.

MAJOR WORKS AND THEMES

A prolific artist, creating over 400 paintings, a thousand drawings, and 290 etchings, Rembrandt typifies the complex intermingling of artistic currents in the 17th century. His oeuvre reinterprets the classical and biblical tradition as transmitted by Italian Renaissance exemplars by participating in both the sensual extremities of the Baroque and the naturalistic representation of the beauties of the ordinary and the individual, typical of the Dutch Golden Age and the Northern tradition. In a work on an unusually large scale, *The Blinding of Samson* (1636) (Städelsches Kunstinstitut, Frankfurt am Main) with its visceral physicality and theatrical contrasts of illumination—the straining flesh and glistening metal have particularly engaged many Freudian critics—ensures Rembrandt's central place within any understanding of the Baroque. *The Hundred Guilder Print* (1639–1649) encapsulates the multiple stylistic allegiances and aesthetic tensions at the heart of his many drawings and etchings visualizing the life of Christ. Rembrandt's works on paper comfortably deploy the disparate strategies of minutely detailed rendering, as in the physiognomies of the humble crowd or of naturalistic setting, and the contrasts of light that absorb these passages into a synthesized dramatic moment suggesting the harmony of the mundane and the divine by material as well as metaphorical means.

Rembrandt often envisioned his interpretation of great historical and biblical themes through a quiet celebration of personal observation and experience, evocative of debates about individuality aroused by the Protestant Reformation. *Aristotle Contemplating the Bust of Homer* (1653) (Metropolitan Museum of Art New York), for example, not only captures the paths opened before the person of intellect, decorated with a gilt chain of honor—Aristotle turns his back on the portrait of Alexander who holds mere earthly triumphs to contemplate the gentler humanist virtues of Homer—but also conceives of the great philosopher as a man of tactile and individualized flesh. Rembrandt's creation of the "tronie," figural composition poised between portraiture and history painting in which friends, family, or the artist himself are exoticized through dress and props, evoked a fascination with individual psyche and expressivity as much as antique exemplars. Equally he transformed the group portrait from an amalgamation of traditional didactic gestures and awkwardly dislocated figures into involving dramatic narratives as with the guild of surgeons in *The Anatomy Lesson of Professor Tulp* (1632) (Mauritsuis, The Hague) enthralled by a dissection. In the highly prestigious commission for Kloveniersdolen, the arquebusier's hall, *Militia Company of Capt. Frans Banning Cocq and Lt William van Ruytenburch*, known as *The Nightwatch* (1642) (Rijksmuseum, Amsterdam), Rembrandt visualizes each figure, its physiognomy, gesture, and attributes, and the details of setting to serve dramatic coherence and narrative engagement as much as the more mundane ambitions of portraiture.

The involving complexity of Rembrandt's paintings of women resides in their emulation of pastoral poetry's intermingling the languages of art and close observation, redolent in *Saskia as Flora* (1634) (Hermitage, St. Petersburg). *Bathsheba at Her toilet* (1654) (National Gallery, London) and *Naked Woman on a Mound* (c. 1631) (etching, British Museum, London) couple a sensitivity to the beauties of the natural rather than idealized proportions of the female form with an attentive evocation of the psychological depth of the women, be they contemplative or coy, who inhabit these sensual bodies. Rembrandt's many exquisite pen and ink drawings reveal a fascination with life drawings, capturing the fleeting gestures, facial expression, and posture through which psychological states radiate in every part of the anatomy with unique sensitivity and alertness.

The self-portraits are for me Rembrandt's greatest achievement, exploring the distinct physical and psychological manifestations of different stages of maturity reminiscent of **Shakespeare**'s role-playing and introspection, from Taming of the Shrew to the Tempest, and **Milton**'s Puritan self-analysis: the ambitious yet thoughtful youth of *Painter in his Studio* (c. 1629) (Museum of Fine Arts, Boston); the drunken dandy of *Self Portrait with Saskia* (1635) (Gemäldegaerie AlteMeister, Staatliche Kunstsammlungen, Dresden); the self-confidant master artist emulating Titian's *Ariosto* (1510–1515) (National Gallery, London) of *Self Portrait Leaning on a Stone Sill* (1639) (etching, Teylers Museum, Haarlem); and the moving introspection of the wiser, older man of *Self Portrait* (1657) (National Gallery of Scotland, Edinburgh).

CRITICAL RECEPTION

Surviving portraits by fellow artists and the early date of the first biography attest to Rembrandt's standing within his own lifetime, which he sought and achieved as a court artist, an art collector, and property owner. As a teacher of a younger generation of Dutch artists, most famously Gerrit Dou, Rembrandt influenced an unusually large number of pupils attracted by his less regimented tuition based on the Italian studio tradition. Although several early commentators such as Joachim van Sandrart (1675) or the Frenchman A de Piles (1699) derided Rembrandt's inattentiveness to Italian conventions, his Old Master status was assured particularly by Adam von Bartsch's cataloguing of the complete etchings in 1797.

Like many of his contemporaries, Rembrandt often signed his students' work and thus began centuries of violent debate about attribution. The controversial re- and deattributions made by the Rembrandt Research Project (RRP), formed by five Dutch scholars in 1968 and their findings published in 1993, solicited both great acclaim and outcry. Whatever the ultimate outcome of these connoisseurial debates, Rembrandt's intrinsic reputation remains firm in the recognition of his ability to bridge the core artistic, spiritual, and political dichotomies of the 17th century, interweaving the classical and Catholic Italianate tradition with a Protestant attention to individualism.

Surely subsequent artists' emulation of Rembrandt's techniques and concerns are the greatest testament to his relevance and achievement. His self-portraits inspired a fellow Dutchman, Vincent Van Gogh, to scrutinize the multifaceted nature of the artistic persona. Rembrandt's unheroic beauty motivated 19th-century Realist preoccupations with both the observable world and the problems of its evocation through painterly means, typified by the Barbizon landscapists and the peasant painter Gustave

Courbet. The expressive brushwork and subject matter *Slaughtered Ox* (1655) (Louvre) provided a vehicle for the tortured experiences of 20th-century painters Chaim Soutine and Francis Bacon, while Charles Laughton's film characterisation popularized the artist. Rembrandt's relevance and expressivity in his own age and ours are uncontested.

BIBLIOGRAPHY

Studies of Rembrandt van Rijn

Alpers, Svetlana. *Rembrandt's Enterprise: The Studio and the Market.* Chicago: University of Chicago Press, 1988.

Bomford, David, Christopher Brown, and Roy Ashok. *Art in the Making: Rembrandt.* London: National Gallery, 1988.

Broos, B.P.J. *Index to the Formal Sources of Rembrandt's Art.* Maarssen: Schwartz, 1977.

Bruyn, J., B. Haak, S.H. Levie, P.J.J. van Thiel, and E. van de Wetering. *A Corpus of Rembrandt Paintings.* Rembrandt Research Project. The Hague: Martinus Nijhoff, 1982–.

Chapman, H.P. *Rembrandt's Self Portraits: A Study in Seventeenth-century Identity.* Princeton: Princeton University Press, 1990.

Clark, Kenneth. *Rembrandt and the Italian Renaissance.* London: Murray, 1966.

Munz, L. *A Critical Catalogue of Rembrandt's Etchings.* 2 vols. London: Phaidon, 1952.

Williams, Julia Lloyd, ed. *Rembrandt's Women.* Royal Academy of Arts. London: Prestel, 2001.

Second Earl of Rochester (John Wilmot)

(1647–1680)

JAMES GRANTHAM TURNER

BIOGRAPHY

John Wilmot was born on April Fool's Day and near his deathbed, at the age of thirty-three, wondered about entering heaven "in disguise." His mother tended to Puritanism, while his father spent long periods in exile with the defeated Charles II (who gave him the title Earl of Rochester but conveyed no wealth with it). According to the critic Thomas Rymer, the young poet later "found no Body of Quality or Severity so much above him, to challenge a Deference"—a phrase that applies equally to his writing and his behavior; this can partly be explained by the early death of his real father (1658) and Charles's rakish unwillingness to take on the role of patriarchal authority-figure. Rochester junior entered Wadham College, Oxford, at the age of twelve, welcomed the Restoration with coached Latin verses, took the Grand Tour of France and Italy in 1661–1664, volunteered for the Second Dutch War, and lost his religious faith when a dead comrade failed to return as a ghost despite his promise. Though he fought valiantly in this campaign, he later gained a reputation for cowardice by fighting the police and running away, leaving a friend dead; typically, he admits and neutralizes the scandal in the memorable witticism "all men would be cowards if they durst" (*Satyr against Mankind*). With no profession and little inherited estate, Rochester lived partly off his heiress-wife Elizabeth Malet (abducted 1665, married 1667, four children by her and one by the actress Elizabeth Barry), and partly off royal favor. Though the King rarely paid his courtiers' salaries, Rochester's appointment as Gentleman of the Bedchamber allowed him to live and frolic in the inner circles of Whitehall, with occasional rest periods in his native Oxfordshire.

As a brilliant, seductive, yet unstable courtier, Rochester kept the gossip mills turning throughout the 1670s. Even in his own brief lifetime the Rochester myth, or "Rochester-effect," loomed large. He seems to have encouraged it by acting out the worst aspects of his reputation half-mockingly and by pouring out his unorthodox beliefs in candid celebrity interviews with the Scots clergyman Gilbert Burnet. From

Burnet's memoir (published shortly after the wicked Earl's deathbed repentance), we learn that "for five years together he was continually Drunk," that his two ruling passions were "a violent love of Pleasure and a disposition to extravagant Mirth" reinforced by the carnival disorder of the Restoration, that he particularly "took pleasure to disguise himself as a Porter, or as a Beggar, . . . to follow some mean Amours, which, for the variety of them, he affected." Burnet records many of Rochester's opinions, presumably sincere even if stated for effect: Christianity is a fraud necessary to keep the lower classes in order; though genuine believers are happy, belief itself cannot be induced by authority; a benevolent God would never prohibit the promiscuous "use of women" (for elite males, it goes without saying); all pleasure is legitimate, provided it does no harm to oneself or others, and should be "indulged as the gratification of our natural Appetites." Other sources, including his own letters to friends, confirm his drunken and often violent "Frollicks"—embroidered first by Rochester himself and then by a shocked and fascinated public.

Rochester made fitful attempts to enter public life (taking his hereditary seat in the House of Lords while still underage, caballing with the Duke of Buckingham), but his chief roles were those of unofficial court jester, impromptu Wit, and cultural patron. Several times imprisoned, banished from the court, or sent abroad for his impulsive behavior, he always managed to regain the King's personal favor. His "unaccountable charm" and talent to amuse saved him on these occasions, dissolving censure into "extravagant Mirth" by some dazzling one-liner or shapely verse; he describes himself, as well as his King, in his famous epigram about the unreliable ruler "Who never said a foolish thing / And never did a wise one." But syphilis, alcohol, and religion caught up with him on July 26, 1680.

MAJOR WORKS AND THEMES

Rochester's writings were mostly intended for manuscript circulation among a coterie of courtiers who valued wit and extremity, violent debauchery, and polished epigrams. They range from conventional love-lyrics to hair-raisingly obscene songs and include a number of extended couplet satires on literary, political, social, and sexual themes. He never sought print publication, though some of his less salty lyrics show up in miscellanies and more philosophical poems—"Upon Nothing," *A Satyr against Reason and Mankind*—appeared in unauthorized pamphlets and inspired hostile responses. The great *Satyr* launches a series of "paradoxes" against the world, provoking it to show why humans are better than animals and why faith is better than sense; Rochester's most scandalous proposition is that abstract reason drops us in the dirt, whereas "right reason" devotes itself to heightening sensual pleasure. Alongside his libertine coterie verse he prepared a few texts for public performance—including a mountebank's speech (brilliantly proving himself genuine because he seems fake), prologues, epilogues, and extra scenes for other writers' plays, and a complete rewrite of John Fletcher's tragedy *Valentinian*. Through his stage orations and formal satires, Rochester becomes a new Horace or Petronius, punctuating aesthetic and social pretension ("My Lord All-Pride," "Timon," "Tunbridge Wells"), defining true wit and sketching a theory of "mannerly obscene" poetics ("An Allusion to Horace").

Rochester was not always successful at hiding his keen intelligence and wide reading under the "disengaged" languor required of aristocrats. His poetry, though suitably sketchy and miscellaneous, includes translations from Lucretius's Latin, informed "allusions" to Horace and Ronsard, and deceptively casual verifications of agonizing moments in philosophy: "Love and Life" turns **Hobbes**'s demonstration of the insubstantiality of past and future into a plea that he only be expected to remain faithful for "the present moment"; "The Fall" rewrites St. Augustine's vision of paradisal sexuality, an unattainable, ideal fusion of mind and body. Biblical echoes give a frisson of familiar blasphemy to his letters and to his most accomplished lyrics, such as "An Age in her Embraces Passed" (or "The Mistress"). The effect is strangely moving, despite the studied cynicism. Startling shifts of affect move below the polished surface, expressing from moment to moment sadism, wistfulness, boredom, and adoration. Rochester laments (or perhaps celebrates) the separation of volition, desire, and performance, the fleeting nature of feeling, the compulsion to betray true love ("Absent from thee I languish still"), the paradox of "art" as it both heightens and destroys desire ("A Young Lady to her Antient Lover"), and the philosophical doubts that force lovers to torture one another: "Love raised to an extream" through anguish and jealousy gives them epistemological security, since "pain can ne'er deceive."

"Faire Cloris in a Pigsty Lay" makes a charming pastoral out of the pig-girl's masturbatory dream (her slop-pails are ivory), and even the violent *Ramble in St James's Parke* has a moment of pathos, when the jealous lover recalls the former "tender hours" that Corinna has now "betrayed,"

> When leaning on your Faithless Breast,
> Wrapt in security and rest,
> Soft kindness all my powers did move,
> And Reason lay dissolved in Love.

In other poems (and in other parts of the long *Ramble*) obscene words and images are thrown in the reader's face. A courtesan is savagely attacked for her power to enslave men—or more accurately, to arouse men so that their own "Bollox" make them "slaves" to her ("On Mrs Willis"). In drinking songs and monologues, Rochester's various personae strive to "Raise pleasure to the topp" by alternating bouts of wine, boys, and "Cunt."

Rochester added a sexual twist to almost everything he wrote. When he revised Fletcher's *Valentinian*, for example, he wove in extra details about the emperor's love for eunuchs and boys and retitled the play *Lucina's Rape*. But his poems (like his letters) often express the absurdity of sex, the incongruous mismatch of "head" and "tail." The unpredictable autonomy of the genitals haunts Rochester's longer poems of debauchery. A *Ramble* proclaims, "There's something generous in mere Lust" and yet reduces the faithless mistress to a "Cunt" that speaks in her mouth and "came spewing home, / Drencht with the Seed of half the Town." "The Disabled Debauchee" celebrates drunken brothel riots and bisexual orgies, but in the voice of a syphilitic, impotent man. Impotence is the classic theme of *The Imperfect Enjoyment*, where the penis becomes in rapid succession an "all-dissolving Thunderbolt," a spear that "Where e're it pierced, a Cunt it found or made," a withered flower, a "wishing, weak, unmoving lump," a cowardly street hooligan, and "a Common Fucking Post." The phallus is at once the raison d'être of Rochester's poem and the "worst part of me."

Despite this fascination with misogynistic and impotent male voices, Rochester's most complex and sympathetic poem is a monologue by a female persona, sharply but intelligently exploring women's problems—the excesses of freedom, the waste of intelligence in superficial chatter, the difficulty of choosing between men and monkeys, the economic perils of failing in sexual adventure, and the constraints on her literary ambitions. At first she hesitates to write because "Whore is scarce a more reproachfull name / Than Poetesse," but this recognition then makes her all the more eager, like her author "Pleased with the Contradiction and the Sin" ("A Letter from Artemiza in the Towne to Chloe in the Countrey"). Transgression itself is the chief spur to writing. In the *Satyr*, Rochester himself explores the similarities between literature and the kind of sex he knows best, the scandalous and illicit variety: whores and men of wit are alike because their patrons first "enjoy" them and then "kick them out of doors," but "a threatening doubt remains" in both cases, since the satirist's sting lingers on like the burning of syphilis.

Many of Rochester's more outrageous poems interconnect sex and politics. The ingenious ode "Upon Nothing" brackets together Kings' promises and whores' vows. One notorious lampoon, slipped "by mistake" into Charles II's pocket, asserts that the monarch's "sceptre and his prick" are not only the same length but equally manipulable by whoever lays her hand on them. Again, far from glorifying the "peremptory Prick" (and the absolutism it represents), Rochester makes the genitals ridiculous. The royal testicles, the locus of authority in a hereditary monarchy, become "graceless Ballocks," uncultured plebeians who destroy any pretension to stylish eroticism. Throughout his brilliantly various oeuvre, Rochester cultivates the disjunction between extreme matter and elegant manner. He can seem a postmodern *avant la lettre*, all contradictory attitude and ironized performance. In a revealing verse fragment he expressed the desire to "make my wishes insolent, / And force some image of a false content"; he would harness both insolence and wine for the creative process, raising the heat of fancy by any means necessary.

CRITICAL RECEPTION

Rochester was luridly imitated during his lifetime—for example, by Etherege and Oldham—and extravagantly praised after his much-publicized conversion and death. Even critics who strongly disapprove of his morals endow his "disorders" with an aura of seductive glamor. Burnet, however severe on his "excesses" and "irregular appetites," links them directly to the wine-heated brilliance and individuality of his imagination: "He had a strange Vivacity of thought and vigour of expression; his Wit had a subtilty and sublimity both, that were scarce imitable." Funeral tributes confirm Burnet's hyperbole: Rochester was "fam'd for high Extreams," "one of the *greatest of Sinners*," utterly "singular," raised "above the reach and thought of other men" by "the heightening and amazing circumstances of his sins." Women poets like **Aphra Behn** and Anne Wharton (his niece, adopted sister, and reputed lover) explicitly celebrate Rochester for embodying, and fusing together, "all the charms of Poetry and Love." In his preface to the rewritten *Valentinian* (1685), Robert Wolseley explicitly defends Rochester's "Obscenity" as "the chief power, the main weight and stamp of the Poet's Expression," the baseness of the material being transfigured by "Wit," "Genius," or "poetical Daemonianism"; Wolseley freely admits that Rochester's loose poems might "offend Age and corrupt Youth," but while he dismisses the issue as irrelevant to artistic quality. He became the prototype for Richardson's Lovelace, indeed, for every brilliantly wicked rake in English literature.

Publishers rushed to cash in on Rochester's notoriety from 1680 onward. Any obscene or erotic poem they could find was posthumously printed as his, and, for this reason, it is still difficult to know precisely what he wrote. Most of the poems in underground editions can be attributed to other writers, as David Vieth proved long ago, but a few pseudoautobiographical lyrics ("To the Post Boy," "I Rise at Eleven") still divide the best scholars. In his great edition of 1999, Harold Love has shown convincingly that Rochester had no connection with the bawdy classics "Signior Dildo" and *Sodom* (treated as his in popular works like Jeremy Lamb's 1993 biography or Stephen Jeffreys's comedy *The Libertine*, 1994). The mock-heroic drama *Sodom*, evidently written by an individual or group of would-be wits outside the court circle, imitates Rochester at certain points (for example, when the absolutist King Bolloxinian declares "with my Prick I'le governe all the land"). But it rarely rises above a banal and schoolboyish nastiness. The version entitled *Sodom and Gomorah*—published only in Love's appendix of spurious works—is more extreme and more coherent.

Rochester's works were reprinted throughout the 18th century in two quite different canons, one respectable and one clandestine. Selected cleaner writings were included in the uniform edition of British poets for which Johnson wrote a severe but perceptive "Life." Hazlitt recognized the sublimity of Rochester's offensiveness, and Tennyson would recite to great effect the gloomy lines from the *Satyr* that end "Huddled in dirt the reasoning Engine lies, / Who was so proud, so witty, and so wise." Scholars still cannot decide whether Rochester is a libertine poet (the most striking example in English literature) or an antilibertine, who exposes the emptiness of desire and the futility of misogyny by acting out their contradictions in extreme personae. But this uncertainty is a fruitful one, stimulating the critical essays and monographs cited below. Rochester now fascinates students the way **Donne** and **Marvell** did a generation or two ago.

BIBLIOGRAPHY

Works by the Second Earl of Rochester (John Wilmot)

The Letters of John Wilmot, Earl of Rochester. Ed. Jeremy Treglown. Oxford: Blackwell, 1980.
The Works of John Wilmot Earl of Rochester. Ed. Harold Love. Oxford: Oxford University Press, 1999. (Includes works unreliably attributed to Rochester ["Appendix Roffensis"], with full scholarly evidence for authorship and distribution)

Studies of the Second Earl of Rochester (John Wilmot)

Burns, Edward, ed. *Reading Rochester*. Liverpool: Liverpool University Press; New York: St. Martin's Press, 1995.
Chernaik, Warren. *Sexual Freedom in Restoration Literature*. Cambridge: Cambridge University Press, 1995.
Coltharp, Duane. "Rivall Fopps, Rambling Rakes, Wild Women: Homosocial Desire and Courtly Crisis in Rochester's Poetry." *The Eighteenth Century: Theory and Interpretation* 38 (1997): 23–42.

Combe, Kirk. *A Martyr for Sin: Rochester's Critique of Polity, Sexuality, and Society*. Newark: University of Delaware Press; London: Associated University Presses, 1998.

Farley-Hills, David, ed. *Rochester: The Critical Heritage*. London: Routledge, 1972. (Essential documents on his contemporary reception and influence, including funeral tributes, Gilbert Burnet's *Some Passages of the Life and Death of John Earl of Rochester*, and Robert Wolseley's preface to *Valentinian*.)

Fisher, Nicholas, ed. *That Second Bottle: Essays on John Wilmot, Earl of Rochester*. Manchester: University of Manchester Press; New York: St. Martin's Press, 2000.

Greene, Graham. *Lord Rochester's Monkey, Being the Life of John Wilmot, Second Earl of Rochester*. New York: Penguin, 1974. (Brilliant insights but uses works almost certainly not by Rochester.)

Griffin, Dustin H. *Satires against Man: The Poems of Rochester*. Berkeley: University of California Press, 1973.

Thormählen, Marianne. *Rochester: The Poems in Context*. Cambridge: Cambridge University Press, 1993.

Treglown, Jeremy, ed. *Spirit of Wit: Reconsiderations of Rochester*. Oxford: Blackwell, 1982.

Turner, James Grantham. *Libertines and Radicals in Early Modern London: Sexuality, Politics and Literary Culture, 1630–1685*. Cambridge: Cambridge University Press, 2001.

———. *Schooling Sex: Libertine Literature and Erotic Education in Italy, France, and England, 1534–1685*. Oxford: Oxford University Press, 2003.

Vieth, David M. *Attribution in Restoration Poetry: A Study of Rochester's "Poems" of 1680*. New Haven, CT: Yale University Press, 1963. (Essential information on authorship.)

The Works of the Earls of Rochester, Roscomon, Dorset, Etc. 4th ed. London: Edmund Curll, 1714. (Numerous similar editions, each one with more smutty "Rochester" poems.)

❧ *Mary Rowlandson*

(c. 1637–1711)

GAIL WOOD

BIOGRAPHY

Mary White was born in England to John and Joane White, one of seven children, around 1637. In 1638, the Whites emigrated to Salem, Massachusetts, and in 1653 moved to Lancaster, where John White was the wealthiest landowner in this frontier town. In 1656, Mary married John Rowlandson, the Harvard-educated first minister of Lancaster parish. She had four children, one died in infancy, a daughter who died in the Lancaster raid, a son, and a daughter. In 1676, the frontier settlement of Lancaster was raided by Narragansett Indians, and Rowlandson was captured along with thirteen members of her family. Her status as a wife of the minister and the daughter of a wealthy man accorded her great value as a captive. She was ransomed nearly three months later for an exchange of goods estimated to be around £20.

The Rowlandsons lived for a year in Boston and then in 1677 moved to Wethersfield, Connecticut, where she wrote her *Narrative*. John Rowlandson died in 1678, and it was assumed that Mary Rowlandson died shortly thereafter because her widow's pension was never collected. In 1985, however, David Greene published an article in *Early American Literature* that revealed through genealogical records that Mary Rowlandson married Captain Samuel Talcott in 1679. After his death, she lived with her son until her own death on January 5, 1711.

MAJOR WORKS AND THEMES

Mary Rowlandson wrote the first book by an Anglo-American woman, securing her place in American history and literature. Titled in its entirety *The Soveraignty and Goodness of GOD, Together with the Faithfulness of His Promises Displayed; Being a Narrative of the Captivity and Restauration of Mrs. Mary Rowlandson*, the book provides a rich resource of information and critical reflection on the cultural, political, religious, and historical events of the American frontier. Her prominence and education placed her in a place to observe and reflect on Indian captivity, while at the same time revealing her emotions and cultural attitudes.

While her Puritan worldview did not provide Rowlandson with the context to understand the wildness of captivity in the frontier or the ability to understand her captors, the wilderness became a spiritual and psychological metaphor for the anguish and hardship she endured during the weeks of her captivity. She turned to Scripture as a resource for comfort and spiritual, if not physical, rescue. She learned to survive in this physical and spiritual wilderness and to thrive. Her captors did not abuse her sexually, and this provided a means for her to remain intact and aided her in her ability to move back into her life as a Puritan wife and mother. She remained womanly and courageous without destroying the sphere that defined her role in society.

CRITICAL RECEPTION

Rowlandson's *Narrative* was widely read in the Americas and was thought to have been read widely in England. This book created a genre of captivity narratives, being the most highly praised of its kind and much anthologized. Her status in the white world accorded her status as a captive and has provided historians with valuable source material on the times. Moreover, her reaction and attitudes about her captivity and her captors has provided critics with fertile ground. Many historians place her work in its historical context, enriching the study of the American frontier. Feminist critics study her grief at the death of her daughter, reflected in the narrative; and her behavior during her captivity included her religious reflections, her resourcefulness, and her reflections both inside and outside of the Puritan woman's sphere. Many critics study the role and attitude toward the wilderness as a religious journey and as a metaphor for the life of a woman's body and spirit.

BIBLIOGRAPHY

Works by Mary Rowlandson

The Sovraignty and Goodness of GOD, Together with the Faithfulness of His Promises Displayed. Being a Narrative of the Captivity and Restauration of Mrs. Mary Rowlandson. 2 add. corr. and amended. Green, 1682.

Studies of Mary Rowlandson

Arnold, Laura. " 'Now. . . . Didn't Our People Laugh?' Female Misbehavior and Algonquian Culture in Mary Rowlandson's *Captivity and Restauration*." *American Indian Culture and Research Journal* 21 (1997): 1–28.

Derounian, Kathryn Zabelle. "The Publication, Promotion and Distribution of Mary Rowlandson's Indian Captivity Narrative in the Seventeenth Century." *Early American Literature* 23 (1988): 239–261.

Dietrich, Deborah J. "Mary Rowlandson's Great Declension." *Women's Studies* 24 (1995): 427–439.

Faery, Rebecca Blevins. *Cartographies of Desire: Captivity, Race and Sex in the Shaping of an American Nation.* Norman: University of Oklahoma Press, 1999.

Greene, David L. "New Light on Mary Rowlandson." *Early American Literature* 20 (1985): 24–38.

Henwood, Dawn. "Mary Rowlandson and the Psalms: The Textuality of Survival." *Early American Literature* 32 (1997): 169–186.

Howe, Susan. *The Birth-mark: Unsettling the Wilderness in American Literary History.* Hanover, NH: Wesleyan University Press, 1993.

Salisbury, Neal. "Contextualizing Mary Rowlandson: Native Americans, Lancaster and the Politics of Captivity." In *Early America Re-Explored: New Readings in Colonial, Early National and Antebellum Culture*, ed. Klaus H. Schmidt and Fritz Fleischman. New York: Peter Lang, 2000. 107–150.

Stanford, Ann. "Three Puritan Women: Anne Bradstreet, Mary Rowlandson, and Sarah Kemble Knight." In *American Women Writers: Bibliographic Essays*, ed. Maurice Duke, Jackson R. Bryer, and M. Thomas Inge. Westport, CT: Greenwood Press, 1983. 3–20.

Toulouse, Teresa A. " 'American Puritanism' and Mary White Rowlandson's *Narrative*." In *Challenging Boundaries: Gender and Periodization*, ed. Joyce W. Warren and Margaret Dickie. Athens: University of Georgia Press, 2000. 137–158.

———. " 'My Own Credit': Strategies of (E)valution in Mary Rowlandson's Captivity Narrative." *American Literature: A Journal of Literary History, Criticism and Bibliography* 64 (1992): 655–676.

Wesley, Marilyn C. "Moving Targets: The Travel Text in 'A Narrative of the Captivity and Restauration of Mrs Mary Rowlandson.' " *Essays in Literature* 23 (1996): 42–58.

Peter Paul Rubens
(1577–1640)

CLAIRE I.R. O'MAHONY

BIOGRAPHY

The son of a Protestant legal counselor and a Catholic textile merchant's daughter, Rubens was immersed in a patrician social climate, serving as a court page and receiving a classical and multilingual education. His apprenticeship to Otto van Veen helped him to become master painter to the Guild of Saint Luke in 1598. The Duke of Mantua brought Rubens as his protégé to the humanist and artistic center of the Italian Renaissance, awakening him to the coloristic tradition, copying works in the Gonzaga collection, the churches and palaces of Venice, Genoa, Rome, and Spain. Rubens's eight-year sojourn ended in 1608 when the illness of his mother recalled him to Antwerp, where he remained fulfilling a vast array of commissions encouraged by the affluence and confidence of the Twelve Year Truce (1609–1621). Rubens's two marriages were both happy, first to Isabella Brandt in 1609, who died in 1626, and to Hélène Fourment in 1630, producing three and five children, respectively.

Rubens possessed innate charm and diplomacy, a man "born to please and delight in all he says and does" (Nicholas-Claude Fabri de Peiresc, 1637). He was a key architect of the peace negotiations undertaken from the 1620s, culminating personally in his appointment as Secretary of the Privy Council of Philip IV of Spain in 1629 and in the achievement of the Anglo-Spanish peace accords of 1630.

Rubens's rigorous and committed work patterns reflected his links to the revival of Stoicism in the humanist circles of Antwerp; however, his affluence, royal patronage, and accolades meant he enjoyed an aristocratic lifestyle typified by his houses—the Antwerp house and studio refurbished as a Genoese palazzi and "Het Steen," a castle in pastoral Elewijt—as well as his art collection of Old Master drawings, which included examples of the classical sculpture at the heart of his pictorial idioms.

MAJOR WORKS AND THEMES

Rubens's extraordinary versatility blended an attentive study of nature, classical narratives, and the effulgence of Baroque sensuality. He executed his favored themes of biblical narratives, historical allegories, and portraits in a wide range of forms including altarpieces, decorations, easel paintings, and tapestry cartoons. His religious and allegorical paintings evoke artistic and ecclesiastical debates of the Counter-Reformation. Rubens's eclectic assimilation of Italian influences, as in *The Mocking of Christ* (1602) (for Santa Croce in Gerusalemme, now Grasse Cathedral), which synthesizes the rich palette of Titian, Raphaelesque confidence of draughtsmanship and the dramatic spatial effects of Tintoretto, has been likened by some critics to the theoretical approaches of Annibale Carracci.

Among the torrent of religious commissions Rubens received, two triptychs for Antwerp, center of the Counter-Reformation, *The Raising from the Cross* (1610–1611) and *The Descent from the Cross* (1612–1614) (now both in situ Antwerp Cathedral), succinctly indicate Rubens's ability to respond imaginatively to the exigencies of a work's destination, deploying diverse pictorial strategies to elucidate contemporary theological positions. *The Elevation*, intended as a high altarpiece, achieves a fevered pitch of dramatic and spiritual engagement through the torsion of flesh, *chiaroscuro*, and vertiginous compositional movement. The three panels immerse the worshipper in a single compelling moment from the commanding centurion through the act of raising of the cross surging into the viewer's space to the imploding sorrow of Mary, St. John, and the Women.

By contrast, *The Descent*, conceived for the meditational space of a side chapel, achieves its impact through an elegiac mode. It evinces through night effects the subtle complementing of the theme of "Christ bearing" in the side panels (*The Visitation* and *The Presentation in the Temple*) and the gentle coalescing of gesture within the collective act of retrieving the body. Thus it suggests both the patrons'—a municipal shooting club—civic friendship and the Jesuit Carolus Scribianus's account of the Descent in his treatise on Christ's Passion.

Rubens declared his "natural instinct, better fitted to execute very large works." Thus his secular decorations achieve a virtuosity of execution and the capacity to juxtapose historical and allegorical modes effectively. Note the twenty-four painting cycle of *The Life of Marie de' Medici* (1625) (Louvre, Paris) and his nine-part ceiling decoration of 1634–1635 celebrating James I for the Banqueting House of Whitehall Palace. This palace designed by Inigo Jones was the site of the performance of **Thomas Carew**'s masque, *Coelum Britannicum* (1633), and Charles I's execution (1549). Evocatively described by Burkhardt as the "eternal and unforgettable frontispiece to the Thirty Years' War," *The Horrors of War* (1637–1638) (Pitti Palace, Florence), with its billowing drapery, impassioned gesture, and loving attention to voluptuous and vulnerable flesh. This work eloquently visualizes the political climate of this age of absolute monarchy and brutalizing warfare in a manner resonant with **Milton**'s divine battles or the extremities of **Webster**'s Jacobean tragedies.

By contrast, Rubens's portraits and genre paintings achieve an engaging intimacy while still elucidating larger discursive qualities, as in *The Family of Jan Brueghel the Elder* (c. 1612–1613) (Courtauld Gallery, London), which is both a tender testament to a treasured colleague and a pictorial treatise on the family unit as a microcosm of Flemish social order. While Baroque epic was clearly Rubens's most accomplished rhetoric, his closest literary affinity resides in his celebration of sensuality and patrician amusements, as in *Conversations à la Mode* (c. 1633) (Prado, Madrid), key precursors to the Rococo *fêtes galantes* of Watteau and analogous to the court masques and affairs of the Cavalier love poetry of **Herrick**, Carew, **Marvell**, and **Waller**. I find Rubens's less celebrated late landscapes such as *The Castle at Steen Autumn* (1636) (National Gallery, London) of lasting resonance, not only for their wistful introspective quality, the private indulgence of old age in the pleasure of looking and describing rather than decrying, but also their reminiscence of the golden pastoralism of Milton's *Comus* and the poetry of Herrick and **Herbert**.

CRITICAL RECEPTION

In his epitaph, Jan Caspar Gevaert praised Rubens as he "who among the other gifts by which he marvellously excelled in the knowledge of ancient history and all other useful and elegant arts, deserved also to be called the Apelles, not only of his own age but of all time." Rubens's preeminence in artistic and diplomatic circles across Europe was reflected in his patrons, which included Charles I, Philip IV, Archduke Albert and Isabella, both Maria de Medici and Louis XIII, as well as aristocratic and burgher collectors such as Nicholas Rockox. *Justus Lipsius and His Pupils* (1611) (Pitti Palace, Florence) attests to Rubens's links to the Stoical humanists through his brother Philip (who appears with his arm raised). Although the theologian Georg Calixtus derided Rubens's diplomacy as nonpartisanship, literary figures such as the Leiden professor Domenicus Baudius penned laudatory poems about Rubens's painting (*Poematum nova editio* [1616].

Through his collaborations with Frans Snyders and Jan Brueghel, and with influential pupils and assistants such as **Anthony Van Dyck**, Rubens was unprecedentedly prolific and acclaimed. I feel his greatest artistic legacy was to grant weight and intensity to the coloristic and lyrical tradition. The Romanticism of Géricault and Delacroix derives its luxuriance, its brutality, and its impact from the study of Rubens; Cézanne envisioned his own bathers through the prism of his early copies of Rubens's paintings in the Louvre. Moreover, the Fauvist celebration of color as equally significant as line in the artist's tools of expression was unthinkable without Rubens.

BIBLIOGRAPHY

Works by Peter Paul Rubens

The Letters of Peter Paul Rubens. Ed. R.S. Magnum. Cambridge: Harvard University Press, 1955.
Original Unpublished Papers Illustrative of the Life of Sir Peter Paul Rubens as an Artist and Diplomatist. Ed. W. Sainsbury. London, 1859.

Studies of Peter Paul Rubens

Corpus Rubenianum Ludwig Burchard. London: Phaidon, 1968–.
Glen, T.-L. *Rubens and the Counter-Reformation: Studies in His Religious Paintings between 1609 and 1620*. New York: Garland, 1977.

Held, J.S. *The Oil Sketches of P.P. Rubens*. 2 vols. Princeton: Princeton University Press, 1980.

Millen, R.F. and R.E. Wolf. *Heroic Deeds and Mystic Figures: A New Reading of Rubens's "Life of Marie de' Medici."* Princeton: Princeton University Press, 1989.

Rubens, P. *Vita Petri Pauli Rubenii*. Antwerp, 1676.

Stechow, W. *Rubens and the Classical Tradition*. Cambridge: Harvard University Press, 1968.

Sutton, P.C., ed. *The Age of Rubens*. Boston: Museum of Fine Arts, 1993–1994.

Warnke, Martin. *Peter Paul Rubens, Life and Work*. Woodbury, NY: Barron's, 1980.

❧ *Thomas Shadwell*

(c. 1642–1692)

MICHAEL BRYSON

BIOGRAPHY

Though the matter is not certain, Thomas Shadwell was probably born at Stanton Hall in Norfolk somewhere between 1640 and 1642 (1642 is the most commonly accepted date). According to the preface of his play *The Libertine*, he had the "Birth and Education, without the Fortune, of a Gentleman." In 1656 he entered Caius College, Cambridge, studied law at the Middle Temple in London in 1658, and spent 1664–1665 in travel abroad, most notably in Ireland and France. Sometime between 1663 and 1667, he married an actress, and he began his career as a playwright in 1668 with a comedy of humors titled *The Sullen Lovers*, which met with reasonable success. In 1674, he was asked by **John Dryden** to transform his comedy *The Tempest* (adapted from the **Shakespeare** original) into an opera. But the relationship between Shadwell and Dryden was tense even during the best of times, and the dispute that developed between the two men was to have lasting and destructive effects on Shadwell's reputation as a dramatist and poet. What was at first a virulent—if relatively inconsequential—dispute over theories of comedic writing for the stage became deadly serious when politics entered the picture. Throughout the early and mid-1680s, Shadwell was virtually banned from the stage (likely through the influence of Dryden) as he defended the growing Whig movement, eventually becoming a supporter of the "bloodless" revolution of 1688. Dryden, in the meantime, as the poet laureate of Charles II and James II, had taken a firmly Tory position.

The political dispute is little remembered today, however, as it is the vivid terms of Dryden's poetic caricature of Shadwell that have survived the specific politics of time and place to enter the much more nearly permanent realm of satire and ridicule. Shadwell has the unique misfortune of being remembered almost exclusively in the terms of his poetically powerful detractor—the John Dryden who wrote *Mac Flecknoe* and *Absalom and Achitophel*, in which Shadwell appears as the heir apparent to the throne of poetic "dullness" and as Og, respectively. In *Mac Flecknoe*, Dryden brilliantly and unfairly satirizes Shadwell's supposed shortcomings as a poet and play-wright. In *Absalom and Achitophel*, Dryden castigates him for his Whig politics, his drinking, and his obesity. Snide comments about Shadwell's weight are a common item in contemporary references to the poet, leading me to believe that Falstaff was right in *1 Henry IV* when he feared that "to be fat is to be hated."

However, despite the effect Dryden's humorous, if mean-spirited, invective has had on Shadwell's posthumous reputation, it was Shadwell who had the last laugh in his lifetime. For a period of several years between 1682 and 1688, he produced no plays for the stage. That Shadwell viewed himself as having been deliberately prevented from the stage is made clear in his prologue to *Bury-Fair*: "Our author then oppressed, would have you know it, / Was silenced for a Noncomformist poet." With the rise of William and Mary, however, he triumphed over his adversary Dryden by being ap-pointed to the very office Dryden had held under the Stuart monarchs, Charles II and James II. Shadwell's term as poet laureate is short (1689–1692) and filled with un-remarkable poetry—primarily panegyrics to the monarchs. However, he writes four plays during this period, including one of his most successful, *Bury-Fair*. Increasingly ravaged by illness in his later years, Shadwell turned to opium to relieve the chronic pain from which he suffered. His death in 1692 is thought to have resulted from an overdose.

MAJOR WORKS AND THEMES

Shadwell wrote seventeen plays overall, beginning with *The Sullen Lovers* in 1668 and going on to include such works as *Epsom-Wells* (1673), *The Libertine* (1676), *The Virtuoso* (1676), *The Lancashire Witches* (1682), *The Squire of Alsatia* (1688), *Bury-Fair* (1689), and *The Volunteers* (produced posthumously in 1693). Never strongest as a pure dramatist or poet, he had the most success with comedy combined with musical segments, as was then popular with theatergoers. A wildly enthusiastic devotee of **Ben Jonson** (**Samuel Pepys** recounts his own bemusement at the experi-ence of attending one of Jonson's plays with Shadwell), he was also a lover of French theater and was influenced by the works of Molière and Corneille, among others.

Shadwell's success as a playwright, while artistically uneven, was sufficient to make his Jonsonian comedies of humors popular with the play-going public. Shadwell him-self defined such humors as a "Byas of the mind" that "makes our Actions lean on one side still" and used these humors in creating broadly recognizable "type" char-acters, such as the misanthropes of *The Sullen Lovers*. As the leading Restoration proponent of the Jonsonian "humours" comedy, Shadwell often found himself at odds with other playwrights and with contemporary playgoers. His most popular plays were often those that departed from his theory of comedy, as the invective of his prologues often notes. His ambition, as he states in the preface to *The Squire of Alsatia*, is to write comedy "Which does not monsters represent, but men, / Conforming to the rules of Master Ben."

Though Shadwell's work never reaches the verbal heights of such contemporaries as Congreve, Etherege, or **Wycherley**, he is nonetheless an important figure from a literary historical perspective as one of the precursors of the sentimental comedies of the 18th century. His plays are especially valuable today as keen observations of the manners, attitudes, and expressions of Shadwell's contemporaries. Despite Dryden's description of his "dullness," moreover, Shadwell's most lasting strength, and most important contribution to the history of English literature, is probably as an observer with a sharp eye and keen ear who described his contemporaries in accurate detail.

CRITICAL RECEPTION

Perhaps due to the influence of *Mac Flecknoe*, Shadwell has long been dismissed as the poet who "never deviates into sense," whose "genuine night admits no day." The corpulent Shadwell is remembered in Dryden's terms as Og, "A monstrous mass of foul corrupted matter" who was born with "this prophetic blessing: *Be thou dull.*" Beginning with the early 20th century, some scattered attempts have been made to reconsider Shadwell's work in a notably less Drydenesque light. Ernst Ammann (1905) praises Shadwell for having democratic attitudes that he sees as similar to those of his own day. Albert Borgman (1928) considered Shadwell's entire career and declared him to be in "the line of the great tradition of English drama" (253) as a writer of "moral purpose" (252). Michael W. Alssid (1967) tries to reconstruct Shadwell as a "highly conscious" artist who "intelligently and perceptively . . . translated into his plays many of the profound and ironic views of man, society, and art which he and his age held" (7).

BIBLIOGRAPHY

Works by Thomas Shadwell

The Amorous Bigotte: With the Second Part of Tegue O Divelly. A Comedy. London: James Knapton, 1690.
Bury-Fair. A Comedy. London: James Knapton, 1689.
The Complete Works of Thomas Shadwell. Ed. Montague Summers. 5 vols. London: The Fortune Press, 1927.
A Congratulatory Poem To the Most Illustrious Queen Mary Upon Her Arrival in England. London: James Knapton, 1689.
A Congratulatory Poem upon His Highness the Prince of Orange His Coming into England. London: James Knapton, 1689.
The Dramatick Works of Thomas Shadwell, Esq. 4 vols. London: Knapton and J. Tonson, 1720.
Epsom-Wells. A Comedy. London: Henry Herringman, 1673.
Epsom-Wells and The Volunteers or The Stock-Jobbers. Ed. D.M. Walmsley. Boston: D.C. Heath and Company, 1930.
The History of Timon of Athens, The Man-Hater. London: Henry Herringman, 1678.
The Humorists: A Comedy. London: Henry Herringman, 1671.
The Lancashire Witches, and Tegue O Divelly The Irish Priest: A Comedy. London: John Starkey, 1682.
The Libertine. In *The Theatre of Don Juan: A Collection of Plays and Views, 1630–1963*, ed. Oscar Mandel. Lincoln: University of Nebraska Press, 1963.
The Libertine: A Tragedy. London: Henry Herringman, 1676.
The Medal of John Bayes: A Satyr Against Folly and Knavery. London: Richard Janeway, 1682.
The Miser, A Comedy. London: Thomas Collins and John Ford, 1672.
Ode on the Anniversary of the King's Birth. London: James Knapton, 1690.
Psyche: A Tragedy. London: Henry Herringman, 1675.

The Royal Shepherdess. A Tragi-Comedy. London: Henry Herringman, 1669.

The Scowrers. A Comedy. London: James Knapton, 1691.

Some Reflections Upon the Pretended Parallel in the Play Called The Duke of Guise. London: Francis Smith, 1683.

The Squire of Alsatia. A Comedy. London: James Knapton, 1688.

The Sullen Lovers: or, The Impertinents. London: Henry Herringman, 1668.

The Tempest, or The Enchanted Island. A Comedy. London: Henry Herringman, 1674.

The Tenth Satyr of Juvenal, English and Latin. London: Gabriel Collins, 1687.

Thomas Shadwell (Mermaid Series). Ed. George Saintsbury. London: T. Fisher Unwin, n.d.

Thomas Shadwell's Bury-Fair: A Critical Edition. Ed. John C. Ross. New York: Garland Publishing, 1995.

A True Widow. A Comedy. London: Benjamin Tooke, 1679.

The Virtuoso. A Comedy. London: Henry Herringman, 1676.

The Volunteers, or The Stock-Jobbers. A Comedy. London: James Knapton, 1693.

Votum Perenne. A Poem to the King on New-Years-Day. London: Samuel Crouch, 1692.

The Woman-Captain: A Comedy. London: Samuel Carr, 1680.

The Works of Tho. Shadwell, Esq. London: James Knapton, 1693. (Collection of seventeen plays in one volume that leaves out *The Tempest*.)

Studies of Thomas Shadwell

Alssid, Michael W. *Thomas Shadwell*. New York: Twayne Publishers, 1970.

Ammann, Ernst. *Analysis of Thomas Shadwell's Lancashire Witches and Tegue O'Divelly the Irish Priest*. Bern: Gustav Grunau, 1905.

Borgman, Albert S. *Thomas Shadwell: His Life and Comedies*. New York: New York University Press, 1928.

Elwin, Malcolm. *The Playgoer's Handbook to Restoration Drama*. London: Jonathan Cape, 1928.

Fujimura, Thomas H. *The Restoration Comedy of Wit*. Princeton: Princeton University Press, 1952.

Gagen, Jean Elizabeth. *The New Woman: Her Emergence in English Drama, 1660–1730*. New York: Twayne Publishers, 1954.

Harris, Brice. *Charles Sackville, Sixth Earl of Dorset, Patron and Poet of the Restoration*. Urbana: University of Illinois Press, 1940.

Hopkins, Kenneth. *The Poets Laureate*. New York: Library Publishers, 1955.

Lloyd, Claude. "Shadwell and the Virtuosi." *PMLA* 44 (1929): 472–494.

Nicoll, Allardyce. *A History of English Drama, 1660–1900*. Vol. 1. 4th ed. Cambridge: Cambridge University Press, 1955.

Perry, Henry Ten Eyck. *The First Duchess of Newcastle and Her Husband as Figures in Literary History*. Boston: Ginn and Company, 1918.

Smith, John Harrington. *The Gay Couple in Restoration Comedy*. Cambridge: Harvard University Press, 1948.

———. "Shadwell, the Ladies, and the Change in Comedy." *Modern Philology* 46 (1948): 22–33.

Smith, R. Jack. "Shadwell's Impact upon John Dryden." *Review of English Studies* 20 (1944): 29–44.

Steiger, August. *Thomas Shadwell's "Libertine": A Complementary Study to the Don-Juan Literature*. Bern: A. Francke, 1904.

Stroup, Thomas B. "Shadwell's Use of Hobbes." *Studies in Philology* 35 (1938): 405–432.

Summers, Montague. *The Playhouse of Pepys*. London: Kegan Paul, Trench, Trübner and Company, Limited, 1935.

"Thomas Shadwell." *The New Monthly Magazine* n.s. 3 (1873): 292–297, 353–361.

Towers, Tom H. "The Lineage of Shadwell: An Approach to *Mac Flecknoe*." *Studies in English Literature* 111 (1963): 323–334.

Ward, Adolphus William. *A History of English Dramatic Literature to the Death of Queen Anne*. Vol. 3. London: Macmillan, 1899.

Third Earl of Shaftesbury (Anthony Ashley Cooper)
(1671–1713)

RICHARD J. SQUIBBS

BIOGRAPHY

Anthony Ashley Cooper, Third Earl of Shaftesbury, was born in Dorset on February 26, 1671. His grandfather was the notorious First Earl of Shaftesbury, a radical Whig who vigorously backed the Duke of Monmouth during the Exclusion Crisis and was subsequently demonized for all time in **Dryden**'s *Absalom and Achitophel*. The First Earl legally adopted Anthony when he was four years old and had the boy educated by tutors schooled in **Locke**'s comprehensive pedagogy. Shaftesbury would feel a connection with Locke throughout his life, though one marked by a mixture of admiration and conflict. When, in 1682, the First Earl fled England for Holland for political reasons, Anthony's father placed him at Winchester College, an odd choice given its High Church affiliations and staunchly Tory politics. After two miserable years there, Shaftesbury embarked on a continental tour, where he defied convention by actually using it to expose himself to culture and history and to cultivate manners appropriate to his noble lineage.

Shaftesbury returned to London in May 1689 but set off for Rotterdam in 1697 to tend to poor health, a problem that dogged him for the rest of his short life. In 1699, following his father's death, Anthony became the Third Earl of Shaftesbury and quickly plunged into the electioneering on behalf of country Whigs that later earned him the ire of Queen Anne's administration. At the same time, Shaftesbury began to publish those works in moral philosophy and aesthetics that have secured him a permanent place in the canon of 18th century British thinkers. His first major work, *An Inquiry Concerning Virtue, in Two Discourses* (1699), argues for the existence of an innate moral sense in every individual. He expounded this notion at great length, and from different methodological angles, throughout subsequent essays, which were published together in 1711 as the *Characteristicks of Men, Manners, Opinions, and Times*. Shaftesbury married Jane Ewer in August 1709, and an heir was born in February 1711. Stricken ill yet again, the couple traveled to Chiaia, Italy, for the sake of Shaftesbury's health, where he began work on *Second Characters*, an unfinished treatise on the imbrication of morality and aesthetics, and commissioned the emblematic illustrations for the second edition of the *Characteristicks*. He died at Chiaia on February 15, 1713.

MAJOR WORKS AND THEMES

Shaftesbury's optimistic moral philosophy directly challenges **Hobbes**'s notion of humanity as irreducibly self-interested and antisocial. In order to argue for natural sociability and benevolence in humankind, Shaftesbury also rejected Locke's *tabula rasa*, positing instead the existence of innate ideas of beauty and harmony that, if properly cultivated, would establish the pleasures of mutual benefit as a guiding principle of social existence. In explicating this process of cultivation, Shaftesbury roots all questions of morality in motivation, arguing that since acts (and their consequences) can be calculated to serve ends dictated by external constraints, they cannot be reliable indicators of moral virtue. He then distinguishes three types of affection out of which moral motivation can spring: self-love, natural affection, and unnatural affection. Natural affection is "suited to the publick Good, or Good of the Species," while unnatural affection involves antisocial delight in observing torment, destruction, and other degrading spectacles. While it seems at first glance that natural affection and self-love would oppose one another, Shaftesbury's deistic belief in the order and harmony of cosmic design provides him a means to conceive self-love as but a subset of natural affection.

Since human beings possess a universal inclination to goodness, Shaftesbury rejects egoism, revelation, and Locke's Will of God as bases for moral action, substituting instead the pleasures stimulated by perceiving the beauty of order, harmony, and balance. Virtue is "no other than the Love of Order and Beauty in Society," he writes. Each part in the universal cosmic order has its role to play in relation to all others, and by performing this role to its fullest potential, one ensures that the whole functions properly and thus acts morally. But while, in social terms, fulfilling one's public role generally produces private benefits, Shaftesbury insists that self-interest has no part in socially beneficial acts. Conflating morality with aesthetics—and thereby providing future commentators endless grist for their critical mills—Shaftesbury argues that the perception of balance and harmony made possible by performing one's role in the universal order carries with it a natural, innate pleasure that is ultimately disinterested. Rational reflection upon this pleasure then creates ideas of right and wrong in accord with God's design and so constitutes a moral sense. Through such reflection, we can also see that pernicious fashions and customs produce unnatural affections through twisting our natural ones into depraved, self-obsessed channels.

While the highly digressive and repetitive character of Shaftesbury's *Characteristics* had long been viewed as a stylistic flaw, critics are beginning to recognize that the work as a whole formally replicates a conversational dialectic in accord with that promoted in his *Sensus Communis*. An inveterate enemy of fanaticism of all kinds, Shaftesbury ascribed to conversation, and especially to humor, the power to free individuals from obstinate adherence to a sense of their own rectitude. Such humorous intercourse performs the dialectical task of stimulating pleasure and prompting rational reflection on one's beliefs, forging in the process a sociable morality. The blend of optimism, sentimentalism, rationalism, and organicism in his philosophy locates Shaftesbury in the center of a number of competing intellectual currents in the early 18th century, rendering him an object of increasingly deep critical interest across several disciplines.

CRITICAL RECEPTION

In his own day, Shaftesbury signaled his connection with the Cambridge Platonists by publishing an edition of Benjamin Whichcote's sermons, for which Shaftesbury provided an introduction as well. The Cambridge Platonists sought to refute Hobbes with their argument for the existence of an objective moral order, a position that was clearly foundational for Shaftesbury's own moral philosophy. Bernard Mandeville remarked that Shaftesbury's "notions . . . are generous and refined" and "a high compliment to human-kind," before archly adding, "What a pity it is that they are not true!" Nevertheless, the sentimentalist aspects of Shaftesbury's thought were amplified and given a broader audience by Francis Hutcheson, though Hutcheson introduced a subjectivist dimension to the moral sense wholly alien to Shaftesbury's objectivist morality. Diderot, Voltaire, d'Holbach, and Rousseau all looked to Shaftesbury in their different ways in challenging received notions of divinity in the name of rational freedom.

When the *Second Characters* was published in 1914, it stimulated new critical interest in Shaftesbury, and he began to be regarded as a crucial forerunner of modern aesthetic theory. The publication of newly discovered correspondence around this time also led to a revaluation of the sentimentalist character of his philosophy, bringing to the fore the crucial role of rational reflection in the development of the moral sense. In addition to Shaftesbury the Platonist, the sentimentalist, and the aesthetician, we now have Shaftesbury the Stoic as well. Current interest in the discourse of politeness as one of the constitutive elements in the codification of civil society in 18th-century Britain is sending literary critics and cultural historians back to Shaftesbury in increasing numbers, ensuring the addition of yet another face to the already multifaceted Third Earl.

BIBLIOGRAPHY

Works by the Third Earl of Shaftesbury (Anthony Ashley Cooper)

Characteristics of Men, Manners, Opinions, Times. Ed. Lawrence E. Klein. Cambridge: Cambridge University Press, 1999.

The Life, Unpublished Letters, and Philosophical Regimen of Anthony Earl of Shaftesbury. Ed. Benjamin Rand. Cambridge: Cambridge University Press, 1914. Includes *Second Characters, or the Language of Forms*.

Select Sermons of Dr. Whichcot[e]. Ed. with a preface by Shaftesbury. London: Printed for Awnsham & J. Churchill, 1698.

Studies of the Third Earl of Shaftesbury (Anthony Ashley Cooper)

Bernstein, John Andrew. "Shaftesbury's Optimism and Eighteenth-Century Social Thought." In *Anticipations of the Enlightenment in England, France, and Germany*, ed. Alan Charles Kors and Paul J. Korshin. Philadelphia: University Press of Pennsylvania, 1987.

Brett, R.L. *The Third Earl of Shaftesbury: A Study in Eighteenth-Century Literary Theory.* London: Hutchinson's University Library, 1951.

Brook, Garland P. "Shaftesbury and the Psychological School of Ethics." *Dalhousie Review* 62 (1982): 431–440.

Grean, Stanley. *Shaftesbury's Philosophy of Religion and Ethics: A Study in Enthusiasm.* Athens: Ohio University Press, 1967.

Klein, Lawrence E. *Shaftesbury and the Culture of Politeness: Moral Discourse and Cultural Politics in Early Eighteenth-Century England.* Cambridge: Cambridge University Press, 1994.

Mortensen, Preben. "Shaftesbury and the Morality of Art Appreciation." *Journal of the History of Ideas* 55 (1994): 631–650.

Schlegel, Dorothy B. *Shaftesbury and the French Deists.* Chapel Hill: University of North Carolina Press, 1956.

Stolnitz, Jerome. "On the Significance of Lord Shaftesbury in Modern Aesthetic Theory." *Philosophical Quarterly* 11 (1961): 97–113.

Townsend, Dabney. "From Shaftesbury to Kant: The Development of the Concept of Aesthetic Experience." *Journal of the History of Ideas* 48 (1987): 287–305.

Voitle, Robert. *The Third Earl of Shaftesbury.* Baton Rouge: University of Louisiana Press, 1984.

Weinsheimer, Joel. "Shaftesbury in Our Time: The Politics of Wit and Humor." *Eighteenth-Century Theory and Interpretation* 36 (1995): 178–188.

Wolf, Richard B. "Shaftesbury's Just Measure of Irony." *Studies in English Literature* 33 (1993): 565–585.

———. "Shaftesbury's Wit in *A Letter Concerning Enthusiasm.*" *Modern Philology* 86 (1988): 46–53.

❧ *William Shakespeare*
(1564–1616)

VICKI JANIK

BIOGRAPHY

As in his plays, William Shakespeare's life juxtaposes a series of opposites that begs resolution of ambiguity. He lived in the country and city, as an artist and a business-person, with his wife and children in his youth and his retirement but apparently as something of a bachelor during his professional years in London. He was a burgher and an actor during the reigns of the last Tudor Queen and the first Stuart King, in a country still medieval yet feeling the spirit of the modern floating in through un-guarded cracks in the culture. Shakespeare could observe for himself an increasing population, mercantilism, religious variation, literacy in women, and a British global outlook. These were insistently edging out an agrarian economy dominated by regional nobility and based on religious conformity, marketable daughters, the commonplace death of offspring, and a vision of the world several miles in diameter.

Furthermore, existing evidence of the life of this greatest of writers clouds our understanding with further ambiguity. Although many legal and church documents record the boyhood and retirement of William Shakespeare in Stratford and his pro-fessional years in London, they are annoyingly pedestrian, recording births, deaths, and marriages, or financial and legal transactions, usually successful, of an ordinary man and his family. Except for the few written observations by his contemporaries that usually praise and rarely condemn him, deeds, contracts, and other minor legal papers record a life too shallow, pale, and petty, it seems, to suggest the canon of a Shakespeare.

The genealogy of Shakespeare's mother, Mary Arden, extends back from her father, Robert, a prosperous farmer of Wilmcote, to ancestors living on the lands near Strat-ford before the Norman Conquest. Shakespeare's paternal grandfather, Richard, died a yeoman farmer near Stratford in 1561, and soon after his death in the mid-16th century, his son John, Shakespeare's father, moved to Stratford, a town of 1,500 residents about ninety-six miles northwest of London. Although no nobles or high-born government officials lived in the immediate area, it was relatively prosperous, and John became a successful glover, landowner, moneylender, and dealer in agricultural goods. When he married Mary Arden, he gained even more acreage. He bought additional land, enlarged his businesses, and became a leading figure in the town, serving as ale taster, constable, burgess, and bailiff (a leading ceremonial position similar to that of mayor) between 1556 and 1586. In 1576 his fortunes began to decline, however, for unknown reasons, although some speculate that he may have been discriminated against for remaining loyal to Catholicism.

The couple had eight children; William was the third child and oldest son, christened in the Church on April 26, 1564. The Feast of St. George, the patron saint of England, is celebrated on April 23, which is the likely and usual date given for Shakespeare's birth. Besides William, three siblings survived into adulthood—Gilbert, a haberdasher in Stratford, who died in 1612; Edmund, an actor in London, who died in 1608; and Joan, who died in 1646, living with her family and her mother in her childhood home on Henley Street.

Shakespeare was born when the family was enjoying increasing prosperity, living in one of the larger houses in town. Although no records remain, at the age of four or five William almost certainly began attending the petty school in town, since he belonged to one of the most prestigious and affluent families, and the school was only a short walk from his house. The petty school was attached to the grammar school, the King's New School, taught at the time by Thomas Jenkins, an Oxford graduate. The school was good, paying a higher-than-average salary to its teacher and having a long history of excellence. It was established as a free school in the 13th century and reorganized during the reign of Edward VI (1547–1558). In the petty school, Shakespeare learned religion and reading and writing in English. Then at the age of seven, he began study in the grammar school, where Latin was the core curriculum— grammar, rhetoric, and logic, Aesop, Apuleius, and Ovid. The school day was long, beginning at six or seven in the morning and continuing until five, with only a few days' respite at three holiday times each year. Corporal punishment was the default incentive for learning.

Shakespeare never went to university, and his limited formal education was a recurrent theme in his contemporaries' comments about him, but his absorption of learning was profound. The reflections in his works of what he had gathered from books does not seem distinct from what he observed in nature and society. They are similarly incorporated with ease. Learning does not stand out as learning, an artificial construct of a human mind; in Shakespeare's art, learning itself becomes the natural world.

Church records in Stratford note Shakespeare's marriage to Ann Hathaway, a twenty-six-year-old woman from Shotterey, a village near Stratford, on November 1582 after only one (rather than the requisite three) readings of the banns in subsequent weeks in Church. That Ann was pregnant when the couple was married is perhaps less interesting than the centuries of often embarrassed responses to the fact, ranging from the young eighteen-year-old's seduction by an older woman to the sanctity of their "troth-plight," which would neutralize any hint of fornication. Their daughter Susannah was born on May 26, 1583, and their twins, Judith and Hamnet, were christened on February 2, 1585. Hamnet died as an eleven-year-old child and was buried on August 11, 1596. Both daughters remained in Stratford for their entire lives. In 1607 Susannah married John Hall, a Paracelsian physician of excellent reputation, and they had one daughter, Elizabeth, who married twice but died childless in 1670. Judith married Thomas Quiney, a vintner, in 1616 but suffered a sad life, since two months after her marriage her father died and Thomas soon after confessed to carnal intercourse with a woman who died along with her newborn child. Quiney was fined for a variety of misdemeanors, and finally in about 1652 he left Judith, who died in 1662. They had three sons, all of whom Judith survived by many years, and two of whom died within a month of each other. Thus William Shakespeare's family had died out by 1670.

No record exists concerning Shakespeare from 1585, when records show him as a twenty-year-old father of three with no known means of earning a living, and 1592, when he is described as a playwright in London apparently living away from his family. Various historians of the later 17th century record personal recollections or remembered stories of others, describing the young Shakespeare variously as a schoolmaster in the country, an ale drinker, a deer poacher, or a prompter's attendant, perhaps joining an acting company as it passed through Stratford.

Thanks to Robert Greene, however, we know that in 1592 Shakespeare was working as a playwright in London. Greene, a dying London dramatist, poet, and pamphleteer, called him a plagiarist in his *Groats-worth of Wit*:

Yes, trust them not: for there is an upstart crow, beautified with our feathers, that with his *Tiger's heart wrapt in a player's hide*, supposes he is as well able to bombast out a blank verse as the best of you; and being an absolute *Johannes Factotum*, is in his own conceit the Shakes-scene in a country.

Parodying a line from *3 Henry VI*, mocking Shakespeare's varied jack-of-all-trades career, and punning on his name in a way to indicate haphazard scene-creation (probably in the chronicle plays), Greene's comments elicited scorn from Thomas Nash and an apology from the printer of the document, Henry Chettle, who himself is sometimes considered the actual author of the diatribe. In any case, we can conclude that by 1592 Shakespeare had been in London long enough to arouse envy from at least one other brilliant writer and win praise from others.

Owing to the municipal Puritan and plague-driven theater closings in London during much of the following two-year period, the next record of Shakespeare is the publication of his first narrative poem, *Venus and Adonis*, in 1593, printed with care by Richard Field, a fellow Stratfordian living in London and four years Shakespeare's senior. Field's father was an acquaintance of Shakespeare's father. Shakespeare dedicated the popular poem to Henry Wriothesley, the Third Earl of Southampton and Baron of Titchfield, who Shakespeare hoped would become a patron. The following year he published *The Rape of Lucrece*, again with a dedication to Wriothesley. Because the genre of the narrative poem carried greater prestige than drama, these two poems gained wide popularity and praise; in fact, they were Shakespeare's most frequently printed works during his lifetime. During the 1590s, Shakespeare also likely wrote his 154-poem sonnet cycle, which was published without his supervision by Thorpe in 1609. Many biographers take from its content hints of Shakespeare's life—his relationship with "the rival poet," his idolatry of the "fair-haired youth," and his romance with "the dark lady." Although such circumstances may have occurred, they are not substantiated in other documents; and, of course, that poetry accurately reveals events from the poet's life cannot be assumed.

At first Shakespeare probably wrote as a freelance playwright, like others in London, so that his scripts were performed by more than one company. But his talent must have soon led to his lifelong affiliation with the Lord Chamberlain's Men. In 1598, Francis Meres, a writer and later a schoolmaster, wrote a 600-page commonplace book titled *Pallis Tamia, Wit's Treasury*, in which he compares the "mellifluous and honey-tongued Shakespeare" to the Romans—Ovid, Plautus, and Seneca—for his two minor epics, his "sugared sonnets," and eleven plays. Although this does not establish the transcendence of Shakespeare's reputation at the time, since Meres praises a total of 126 contemporary artists, it implies success and, for later scholars, establishes a *terminus ad quem* for eleven plays in the canon through 1598. The publication of his plays, too, continued, indicating dedicated readers: *Titus Andronicus* in 1594, *Richard III* and *Richard II* in 1597, *Love's Labour's Lost* in 1598, and *Romeo and Juliet* in 1599.

During the 1590s, Shakespeare also became a successful part-theater-owner, producer, and actor, as well as a popular playwright. He worked with the Lord Chamberlain's Men, a troupe formed in March 1594 from the defunct Lord Strange's Men, which might have been the first acting company with which he was affiliated. Court records in 1594 show that Shakespeare, Will Kempe, and Richard Burbage, representing the Lord Chamberlain's Men, received payment for productions before the Queen over the past Christmas. With his financial successes in London, in 1596 he was able to pay the fees to the College of Heralds for a coat of arms for his father, who had been suffering at least languishing fortunes since 1576, so that both he and his father were henceforward referred to as "gentlemen." In 1599, Nicholas Brend leased the site of the brand-new Globe Theater, stating that the land was "in the occupation of William Shakespeare and others." Shakespeare had become a principal shareholder in the acting troupe itself, and between then and 1612 he held between one-fifth and one-fourteenth of a moiety (between 10 percent and about 3.5 percent) of the lease on the Globe, depending on the inclusion of other shareholders.

Shakespeare also acted in his own plays, and he is listed first in the First Folio of 1623 among "the Principall Actors in all these Plays." He is also recorded first among the principal comedians in **Ben Jonson**'s *Every Man in His Humour* in 1598 and as an actor in Jonson's tragedy *Sejanus His Fall* in 1603, which were produced by the Admiral's Men, the company for which Jonson wrote and which was the chief rival of Shakespeare's company. The fact that he played Tiberius and Hamlet's Ghost indicate a predilection for old men's parts.

In 1601, Richard Burbage and Shakespeare, notably with the term "Gent." appended to his name, were selected as the tenants of the Globe. The troupe thrived into the next century, becoming the King's Men. After only twelve days when King James arrived in London to accept the crown, they received a formal Patent under the Great Seal of England on May 19, 1603, given to them at the command of King James, and the acting troupe wore new red liveries in the coronation procession of the King.

Shakespeare's financial success in London extended back to Stratford. Shakespeare bought the second largest house in town, New Place, in 1597, soon after his son's death. A home sixty feet by seventy feet, with a gable rising twenty-eight feet, it was called the Great House. Other real estate investments followed. In 1601, he inherited his father's large house where his mother, sister, and her family had lived, and the following year he bought 107 acres of land for £320 from the richest man in town, the moneylender John Combe, who charged the going rate of "ten in the hundred." Shakespeare also obtained a small cottage near his house and, in 1605, the lease of tithes. Although records say that he was renting quarters in London in 1604, he added to his fortune with London property in 1613, when he purchased a dwelling house in Blackfriars in London for £140 as an investment. But by then we know Shakespeare was residing in Stratford, thanks to records of his testimony in a civil lawsuit, as a resident of Stratford upon Avon.

In the summer of 1608 the King's Men signed a twenty-one-year lease on the Blackfriar's Theater, an indoor private theater constructed by James Burbage and after his death, by his son Richard, in a building that had once belonged to the Black Friars, the Dominicans, and had more recently housed another theater where the children's theaters had performed. Tickets were more expensive than those for the public Globe performances, but the popularity of outdoor public performances was waning, thanks to persistent Puritan propaganda that condemned theater as evil and sinful. Further-more, some playwrights parodied the rigid Puritans. Thus Shakespeare's company made the shrewd decision to perform more frequently for the more sophisticated, and sympathetic, audiences of this private indoor theater. Additionally, many of Shake-speare's plays were performed at court before the King, according to court revel accounts and title pages of quarto editions, including *Othello*, *King Lear*, and *The Tempest*. Based on the dramaturgy or theatrical elements of the plays, *Cymbeline*, *The Winter's Tale*, and *The Tempest* were likely written for the private indoor theater, although, simultaneously, these plays and others continued to be performed at the Globe, most memorably a performance of *Henry VIII* that led to the fire—without loss of life—that destroyed the Globe on June 29, 1613. Although he was spending less time in London, he returned for theater events and business dealings and remained a proprietor of the Globe and owner of the house in Blackfriars.

That Shakespeare was ill before his death on April 23, 1616, is supported by his three shaky signatures on each of the three pages of his will, signed on March 25, a month before he died. In February, his daughter Judith had married, and anecdotal evidence indicates that Shakespeare may have become ill at the wedding. John Ward, the vicar of Holy Trinity in Stratford, recorded in his diary fifty years later that Shakespeare, Jonson, and the poet **Michael Drayton** "had a merry meeting, and it seems drank too hard, for Shakespeare died of a fever there contracted."

Shakespeare's will indicates that his daughter Judith received a dowry of a few hundred pounds and other gifts; friends, relatives, the poor, and even business ac-quaintances were remembered with small portions of several shillings or pounds; and Shakespeare's eldest daughter Susannah received the remainder of the estate, New Place, the tithe incomes, and other assets. Most revealing to scholars is the meager attention Shakespeare showed to his wife Ann, who inherited only "the second best bed." This, combined with the seemingly forced youthful marriage, the twenty-five years or so of living apart, and hints of infidelity, implies to many that the marriage was less than idyllic. Others note, however, that Ann was due one-third of the estate by law anyway, and Shakespeare did return to Stratford and apparently lived with her for the last years of his life. We might imagine that for Ann, marital bliss was unlikely; options were unavailable; but security, status, and peace were assured; and for William, the comfort of a hard-earned prosperity was to be enjoyed in Stratford and particularly at New Place, a home where Ann lived also. For a lack of heirs, Shakespeare's estate—his worldly goods—was dissolved by 1670, just as his canon was beginning to be eternalized.

In examining the life of Shakespeare, we must note the anti-Stratfordian movement, originating in the 18th century, that holds that William Shakespeare did not write the plays attributed to him: first, because of what is deemed insufficient evidence and, second, because the facts of Shakespeare's life describe far too ordinary a man—a man who was country educated and could never have been exposed to, let alone absorbed, all the legal, governmental, political, medical, religious, scientific, historical, and military knowledge that the author of the plays possessed. So common a life supposedly could not support the canon. In the 19th and 20th centuries, the anti-Stratfordians, including Mark Twain and Sigmund Freud, described vast conspiracies in which one or another of Shakespeare's more high-born or university-educated contemporaries secretly wrote the plays and attributed them to him to avoid personal association with the disreputable public theater and the low art form of theater scripts. Historic individuals such as Edward de Vere, Christopher Marlowe, **Francis Bacon**, and Henry Wriothsley are said to have used the name of Shakespeare, the actor or glover or linen merchant, who agreed to serve as pawn, offering his identity to protect the genius of another far more learned man. We may conclude that, for some, a complicated conspiracy is the necessary means to a world-changing end—a grand effect *must* derive from a grand cause. But little in Shakespeare's canon itself supports so predictable a plan for human events. And the improbable schemes must have worked astonishingly well.

MAJOR WORKS AND THEMES

The theater of 1592 in which Shakespeare was already a successful playwright had developed from a variety of dramatic traditions that are apparent in Shakespeare's earlier and even some later dramas. English morality plays of the 15th and 16th centuries, with their allegorical battles over the soul of Mankind, fought by personifications of Virtue and the antic Vice, were performed by traveling troupes in towns throughout England. Miracle plays, dramatizing the lives of saints, had evolved into the newly popular chronicle history plays, which replaced the central character of the saint with a figure from English history, didactically drawn to encourage nationalism. Besides these quasi-religious influences, writers who were known as university wits, and were inspired by their classical Oxford or Cambridge education, wrote plays in the tradition of the Romans, the tragedian Seneca, and the comic writers Plautus and Terence. Besides this were the influences of comic continental genres, the witty *debat*, and the comic interlude of the French and *commedia dell'arte*, which had evolved in Italy as an improv comic theater about love with a set of stock characters wearing masks. Among the university wits were Robert Greene, John Lyly, Henry Chettle, and the innovative Christopher Marlowe, born in the same year as Shakespeare but killed in a tavern fight in 1594.

The performance spaces in which Shakespeare acted and for which he wrote discouraged scenery as well as act and scene breaks; they were at once bare and adaptable. The theater we usually associate with Shakespeare is the Globe, a public outdoor theater built in 1599 by James Burbage and his two sons Cuthbert and Richard on the Bankside or southern side of the Thames, just outside the boundary of the city of London and its controlling Puritan censors. Although public theaters were sometimes closed by government decree and the acting companies were forced to tour outside London, theaters thrived and became a glory of Britain. The Globe had been constructed from the dismantled Theatre, built in 1576 in Cheapside also by Burbage. It was probably the first purpose-built theater in London, and soon it was followed by the construction of the Curtain, the Swan, and the Rose. Based on theater records, a few drawings—mostly from foreigners—and archeological digs, scholars conclude that the Globe was similar to the other theaters, perhaps bigger and polygonal. Like the others, it had three tiers of galleries surrounding a central pit about seventy feet in diameter, all of which could hold an audience of up to about 3,000.

The audience of the Globe comprised the so-called groundlings—including graduate students and low school dropouts who became the great lyric poets of the next generation, who paid a penny for standing room in the pit, and those who paid two or three pence for a seat on the tiers of benches. On one end of the well was a rectangular platform stage resting on posts, raised from the ground about five and a half feet and almost entirely covered by a roof supported by columns at its four corners. At the back of the stage was a wall with two doors separating it from the tiring (dressing) house behind. The stage floor had a trapdoor; the roof was covered by a hut that probably held a suspension system for a *deus ex machina*, the lowering of a god to the stage. The back wall was only rarely covered by a curtain; and the back of the stage had a balcony that could be used as an acting space but more usually was saved for more expensive audience seats. With no curtain and proscenium arch, scenery changes were not used, nor were there pauses in the action.

When the acting company performed indoors at court or in the indoor private theaters, so called because the tickets were more expensive, the stage area was similar, unless the actors performed in the center of a room at court during a feast. There was a lower raised stage at the end of a rectangular room with doors on two sides and a gallery area where musicians often accompanied the performance. Such theaters became popular during the reign of King James. The Blackfriars Theater, leased by the King's Men in 1608, as we have seen, had this design and so was more conducive to musical numbers including entr'actes, masques, and songs like those in *The Winter's Tale* and *The Tempest*. Because Queen Elizabeth enjoyed the theater and King James enjoyed it even more, players regularly performed at court.

Plays were performed by repertory acting companies, groups of men and boys who risked arrest because of their trade. In order to avoid so dire a fate, groups of actors gained the protection of powerful men—lords, dukes, even King James himself—who gave their protection and their names to a company. These groups regularly formed, lost protection, disbanded, and re-formed with somewhat different personnel and a new protector. By the end of the century, the number of acting companies had diminished, but those remaining had gained greater security. The King's Men enjoyed the greatest prestige, performing regularly at court; but others were popular also, including the Admiral's Men, for whom Ben Jonson sometimes wrote, and the Children's companies, which very successfully reopened in 1598–1599 and specialized in satires produced in the private theaters. Wealthy and educated audiences—and tourists from the Continent—took great pleasure in theater. The new King James recognized this in his charter to the King's Men, saying that the company was to perform for "the recreation of our lovinge Subjectes as for our Solace and pleasure when wee shall thincke good to see them duringe our pleasure" (Schoenbaum, *Documentary Life* 195).

By 1600, perhaps twelve or so years into his writing career, Shakespeare had completed about twenty-two, or over half, of the existing plays we attribute to him as well as his poems. This first group primarily comprises romantic comedies and English histories, while the great tragedies, so-called problem plays, Roman plays, and romances, comprise the second group—a phenomenon perhaps resulting from Shakespeare's changing interests, his personal circumstances, or the enthusiasm of public, private, and courtly audiences. Readers, however, must show caution in grouping the plays into genres, as foolish Polonius might have done. Shakespeare's plays consistently override conventional genres, fusing tragic, comic, ironic, satiric, and romantic elements into most of the plays, thereby expanding their dimension and ambiguity.

During Shakespeare's lifetime, only about half, or eighteen, of his plays and his several poems were published. When a playwright wrote a play for performance, it became the property of the acting company, which allowed publication only after the script had lost popularity on stage or when the company wished to gain extra income. The eighteen plays printed singly between 1594 and 1616 in the smaller quarto format have been categorized by editors into two groups: (1) "good" quartos, copied by typesetters from authoritative manuscripts—performance scripts or final drafts called "fair copies"; (2) and "bad" quartos, supposedly reproduced from illegal memorial transcriptions, corrupt versions of the plays remembered by actors who had played perhaps only minor roles.

Seven years after Shakespeare's death, in 1623, John Heminges and Henry Condell, two actors who had long worked with Shakespeare in the King's Men, oversaw the publication of the complete plays, which then totaled thirty-six. Motivated by friendship, by respect for the works themselves, and by the precedent-setting publication of the *Complete Works* of Ben Jonson in 1616, Heminges and Condell created nearly exactly what remains today as the canon of Shakespeare's plays, which also now traditionally includes *Pericles, Prince of Tyre*, *The Two Noble Kinsmen*, and two sections of *Sir Thomas More*, a fragment of which is widely thought to be written in Shakespeare's own hand. The poems are regularly included today also. The large folio edition of 1623, the First Folio, then, has the only version of eighteen plays, and the authoritative version of six plays that had been previously printed as "bad" quartos and *Othello*, first printed in 1622. Thus, it contains the best versions of twenty-five of the thirty-eight plays. Modern editions are normally composites.

The sixteen extant plays Shakespeare wrote in the second half of his professional career in the 17th century are among the finest he wrote. Nearly all are directly created from source stories in historical chronicles of the classical world, like those of Plutarch's *Lives* (trans. North 1579), or of Britain, like Raphael Holinshed's *Chronicles of the History of England, Scotland, and Wales* (2nd ed. 1587), and from English translations of Roman or Italian stories by authors including Ovid, Giraldi Cinthio, Giovanni Boccacio, or Robert Greene(!).

Most scholars list *Hamlet* (1601) as Shakespeare's first play of the new century; the three other great tragedies followed within five years: *Othello* (1604), *King Lear* (1605), and *Macbeth* (1606) (the unproduced *Timon of Athens* and *Antony and Cle-*

opatra, both based on Plutarch's *Lives*, were completed within the next two years). These four plays, each named for its tragic hero, explore questions of political power and romantic, sexual, and family bonds amid the wrongdoing of the entire surrounding world or of particular individuals within it and the consequent suffering and death. It is noteworthy that the hero in each successive play is less noble than the last, more distant from an Aristotelian norm. From the ethical intellectual Hamlet there is a descent to the noble but passionate boasting soldier Othello, the vain flower child King Lear, and finally the murderous tyrant Macbeth. While the high-minded, idealistic Hamlet debates the morality of suicide, hypothesizing that it holds the threat of an afterlife of eternal pain, Macbeth observes that death is merely the end of a life, itself "signifying nothing" (5.5.28). Shakespeare experiments with the shaping of a hero, almost challenging himself to mold a tragic hero from less and less heroic substance, and in each case, succeeding in the rescue of action that could easily slip into the superficial, melodramatic victory of virtue over evil.

Hamlet seems to be based, in part, on the revenge formula developed by Seneca and popularized in England by Thomas Kyd in *The Spanish Tragedy* (c. 1587). Probably a reconstruction of an Ur-*Hamlet* also written by Kyd, *Hamlet* includes many of the conventions of the genre: supernatural forces, a play-within-a-play, feigned madness, and a troubled and almost inadvertently violent quest by an avenger. Shakespeare, however, transcended the genre, with a tragic hero of modern humanity. More than any other character, Hamlet fulfills Harold Bloom's observation that Shakespeare "compelled aspects of character to appear that previously were concealed or not available to representation" (Bloom, x). Such characters evolve, "overhear" themselves, and encourage literary analysis—which Bloom argues is itself Shakespearean invention. These characters do not simply represent, but rather they inspire the modern world.

In the play, Hamlet must respond to the command of his father's ghost—if that's what he is—for ancient, unquestioned revenge, but he must accomplish this while trapped in a mind of wit and reason and periodic bursts of passion. His is the inevitable and endless human quest to shape order from disorder even when he understands it cannot be done. As a tragic hero, he is splendid, and although that splendor derives from the same stuff that comprises all of us; he is slightly more than we—an unreasonably, richly, brilliantly compressed intellect. Still, his challenge is too great, as he moves in a world where the divide between illusion and reality is bridged only because they become equivalent. "Metadramatic" critic James Calderwood says the play represents "a world whose operant principle is 'seems.' " Illusion—false-seeming—is reality. Hamlet adds to it with his own plotting and feigned madness; yet he solves no mysteries. Neither he nor we know whether Fortinbras is an invader or whether Gertrude is an innocent or whether Hamlet himself is a true lover or even whether old Hamlet is culpable for the disorder in the kingdom. Everyone is like Polonius, hiding, watching, and seeing only shadows. As in life, never does the play answer Bernardo's opening question: "Who's there?"

Othello is less a tragedy of considered revenge or retribution than of misdirected naive passion. The successful mercenary Commander Othello wins his wife with persuasive language telling her of his war stories, but ironically these same seductive powers of language bring his downfall when they are directed at him. It has been said that if Hamlet and Othello were to exchange plays, there would be no plays—Othello would revenge his father's murder without question, and Hamlet would be clever enough to see Iago's cunning. But to Othello, Iago's malevolent words—their innuendo, their implicit meaning, their hints of tainted love—yield intended misimpressions and consequent mistaken action. What Othello lacks in wisdom he compensates for in passion, exploding almost as if he were a tragic, fully realized Prince of Morocco, the dark-skinned Moor of *Merchant of Venice*, a non-Venetian "Other," whose value in that slippery world lies in his marketable military skill, not in his shared humanity. His nemesis Iago derives less from classical tragedy than from the metaphoric Vice, a stage personification of evil, seeking to capture human souls and destroy lives through deception and seduction. Unlike Hamlet's Elsinore, where false-seeming is the norm, Venice and Cyprus are more ordered places, and false-seeming is the strongest weapon with which the villain—with the complaints of career and love melancholy—destroys the innocent. Iago refashions events so that a perverse image of truth poisons and dissolves reality for the unwise innocent who comes to see good and evil as inversions of one another.

Lear, like Othello, is neither perceptive nor a strong intellect, and worse, he is vain. He encourages flattery from his daughters, which leads to his destruction, and he at first misperceives the love of his youngest daughter, the silent woman, Cordelia, which eventually brings on her death. The play, recounting a story from 800 B.C.E. in pagan Britain, tells of the disastrous end of Lear's kingship. Even though his obligation is maintaining the kingdom, he indulges himself with retirement and divides his kingdom among his three daughters. But as a prelude, in what is an oddly comic scene, he desires to bask in the flattery of his daughters. All this is flawed, however—his decision to divide the kingdom at all and his refusal to grant Cordelia her portion when she refuses to flatter. In return for his terrible errors, Lear is cast out into the world, not the false black world of *Hamlet*, or the villain-infested world of Othello, but rather the natural world, hideous and agonizing, where cold wracks the naked body, blindness strikes the innocent, and fortune ensures that those of evil intent and cruel means—Goneril, Regan, and Gloucenter's "natural" son, Edmund—gain worldly wealth and power. What does it all mean? It is not that Lear's life means so little; it is that his suffering is vast. The play shows death, not the death by murder in *Hamlet*, that cries for the balance of revenge, or the passionate killing of the innocent in *Othello*. These deaths are moral wrongs, and they invite a response from the living. But in *King Lear*, death holds the immediacy of life itself—naked, irreversible—a leveling void over which we can only wail, not speak. Its pain explodes blindingly, dwarfing language. It is a mute finality saved only by the humor of fool, Kent, and oddly, Edmund.

As the successive heroes in these four plays are progressively less noble, Macbeth, the last, is the lone tyrant, almost a mirror image of Hamlet's antagonist, the lethal Claudius. Like the Dane (and Prince Hamlet) he commits regicide and is well aware of the monstrosity of his crime, which, unlike Claudius, he has the opportunity to repeat. Macbeth's own ambition, primed and encouraged by the witches and his wife (could Gertrude ever have been so malignant?), seduces him to his ruin. The witches are not metaphors of evil but rather images of false-seeming itself—the reality of one's inner vision as it contrasts the external self, pointing out the paradox of identity. Calderwood argues that Macbeth's honesty in acknowledging his sin, coupled with his refusal to name scapegoats, elevates him from melodramatic monster to tragic hero. Still, his fragility in the face of desire, his lust, is central. Who was the tyrant in the beginning, frighteningly, is everyman.

The so-called problem plays include *Troilus and Cressida* (1601–1602), *All's Well That Ends Well* (1602–1603), and *Measure for Measure* (1604). These plays are so designated because of their unusual moral and generic contamination. *Troilus and Cressida*, published in very different versions in the 1609 quarto and the 1623 Folio edition (where the play is the only one unlisted in the table of contents), presents a version of the Trojan War, arguably the war with the greatest tradition in Western culture. But Shakespeare uses a tone of cynicism to describe what Homer had cast as a noble fight between Achilles and Hector, and Chaucer had glorified as the reaches of sublunary love, and emphasizes the troubled political and sexual relationships and the suspension of morality that pervade this and, by extension, all other wars.

All's Well That Ends Well would seem to be comic and is so listed in the First Folio, since lovers unite at the end, but only as the result of the inversion of the more traditional plot, in which the heroine is the prize to be won by the hero. Here the hero Bertram is a reluctant prize, and unlike female prizes in stories past, he refuses to consummate the marriage unless the impossible occurs—a marriage ring appears on his finger and the heroine Helena becomes pregnant with his child. Although Helena succeeds in meeting these challenges, audiences cannot but be surprised over the implied joy resulting from this love match.

Measure for Measure, first published in the *Folio*, presents another jaundiced vision of sexual relationships. Based on a story by Cinthio, it cynically represents the implicitly popular view that fornication among the powerful is an expected perquisite, but among the poor it is a punishable sin. The play does not end in a happy union of lovers, and the heroine, Isabella, justly is cold to the Duke, who wishes to marry her, even though it was Angelo, his deputy, who had tried to extort sex with her in exchange for the life of her brother. The play portrays panderers, prostitutes, johns, and venereal disease in the sickened world of Vienna. None of these problem plays project a sunny world in which lovers will live in pleasure and society will thrive; yet to see them merely as condemnations of sexual appetite would be shortsighted. That lust supplants love and that self-serving politics trumps orderly government are omens of persistent disorder among humankind, implicit in Shakespeare from the beginning.

The romances briefly revive a fading literary genre, one in which other writers, like Thomas Greene, had formerly succeeded. Romances include magical events and characters, the return to life of characters who have been presumed dead, settings that are both real and magical, events that are life-threatening to children, mythic characters, the *deus ex machina*, and the music and dance of the mosque. Some contemporaries of Shakespeare found fault with the genre because it creates a world of improbability, unnaturalness, and incredibility and strays far from the neoclassical unities of time, place, and action.

Of Shakespeare's four or five romances, *The Winter's Tale* (1610–1611) and *The Tempest* (1611) are grouped among the comedies in the First Folio; *Cymbeline* (1609–1610) is among the tragedies; *Pericles* (1606–1608), possibly written with an unknown collaborator, was not included until the Folio of 1663–1664; and *The Two Noble Kinsmen* (1613), a possible collaboration with John Fletcher, is among the collected plays of Beaumont and Fletcher published in 1679. Written late in Shakespeare's career, these plays were doubtlessly intended for private theater and court performance as well as performance at the Globe. They were indeed popular, even with the King, who, records show, particularly liked *Cymbeline* and requested a performance of *The Tempest* at the Princess Elizabeth's wedding in the winter of 1612–1613. Furthermore, despite Ben Jonson's labeling *Pericles* "a mouldy tale," it was the first Shakespearean play to be produced after the Restoration.

Perhaps the most frequently produced among the romances is *The Tempest*, one of the few plays in the canon with no known source, save some references to travel accounts first appearing in England in the autumn of 1610. This is unlike *The Winter's Tale*, which follows the novel *Pandosto* (1588) by Robert Greene; *The Two Noble Kinsmen*, which dramatizes "The Knight's Tale" of Geoffrey Chaucer; *Pericles*, which follows the ancient story of Apollonius of Tyre remembered separately by John Gower and Laurence Twine; and *Cymbeline*, woven from stories recorded by Raphael Holinshed and Boccacio. Also like *The Winter's Tale* and *Cymbeline*, no authoritative edition of *The Tempest* was published before the First Folio (1623), where the play is placed first, although it was one of the last Shakespeare completed. This placement may result from the excellence of its scribal copy made by Ralph Crane, a scrivener for the King's Men, who included a *dramatis personae* at the end and complete act and scene division, or other reasons. The plot is simple and comes close to honoring the three classical unities, as most other Shakespearean plots do not. But the dramaturgy is elaborate with the storm at the beginning, magic, masques of goddesses, a monster, invisible characters, and an artist-as-hero who devises theatrical effects and music, all of which suggest a private theater production.

The Tempest stretches beyond the genre of romance, raising questions about imagination, art, colonialism, and empire. In *The Tempest*, the hero Prospero is at once scholar and all-powerful purveyor of white magic and a dictator. With his indentured worker-of-fantasy Ariel, he controls the future of all other characters on the magical island somewhere in the Mediterranean Sea, but still near Bermuda—a nonexistent place much like the setting of *The Winter's Tale* on the coast of (landlocked) Bohemia. Prospero is at once a ruler with the hubris allowed only to the divine and, in a postmodern mode, an artist consorting sometimes disingenuously in a world of his own creation. Because *The Tempest* is one of Shakespeare's final plays, some scholars are persuaded that Prospero speaks with the voice of Shakespeare himself, explaining the power of the artist, illusionist, and imperialist, which can make drowned sons reappear, churning tempests leave clothes newly clean, banquets appear to the hungry, and lovers avoid all missteps. But a curious reminiscence of "Virginia" remains.

CRITICAL RECEPTION

Although the full bloom of bardolatry did not appear until the 18th century, Shakespeare's works have always been received with popular success and praise, despite the qualifications or silence of a few of his contemporaries and those who immediately followed him. University wits, like Ben Jonson, belabored his lack of a university education—his "want of Learning and Ignorance of the Antients"—as evidence of the imperfection of his art, even as they recognized his popular success in those very areas. He used too many words: "[W]ould he had blotted a thousand," Jonson wrote, and even claimed, "That Shakeperr wanted Arte." The plays were considered odd admixtures of genres, "Shake-scenes," failing to honor the three classical unities of time, place, and plot and filled with indecorous characters.

After his death, however, published opinions began to change, including Jonson's, with the publication of the First Folio where he describes Shakespeare in an opening encomium as the "Soule of the Age," "the Sweet Swan of Avon!" and "Starre of Poets!" Writers, theatergoers, scholars, and antiquarians began to view Shakespeare with increasing respect, often in print, so that by 1765 Samuel Johnson could write in the preface to his edition of the plays that Shakespeare is the poet of nature "who holds up to his readers a faithful mirror of manners"; his characters "are not modified by the customs of particular places, unpracticed by the rest of the world"; rather, each is "commonly a species."

In the 17th and 18th centuries, a notion of mimesis (realism) reigned. Thus we find Nicholas Rowe (1674–1718), a dramatist and early editor of Shakespeare's plays, commenting on the purity of imitation in Shakespeare's art, predictably regretting, however, that "some of his Comedies, are really Tragedies, with a run or mixture of Comedy amongst 'em." He concludes that the works are "beautifully written." Other theatergoers praise the moral instruction of the plays; Francis Gentleman writes in 1770 that from many passages "useful, instructive inferences may be drawn" as well as the particular lessons on the nature of good and evil. Thus according to the mimetic aesthetic, which holds that art is the mirror of nature and moral guide, Shakespeare is the highest standard.

New Critical Theory developed in the 1940s and 1950s, in part in response to Historicism, placing a renewed emphasis on the plays themselves rather than on their historical background. This challenges the notion that literature takes meaning from the world of the author, or even from the author's own intent; rather, readers must look only to the words of the text for "meaning." In her analysis of the American New Critics, including William K. Wimsatt and Cleanth Brooks, Catherine Belsey explains that such critics view the text "as belonging to the public because language is public" (16). This means that the text itself offers an experience; it is not mimetic— a representation of a "real" experience—nor the author's expression of her or his own world or personal response to experience. Some of the most insightful commentary of the mid-century analyzes the plays as if they were dramatic poems, paying close attention to symbolism, imagery, word choice, metrical and syntactic structure, and the patterning and variation of themes or ideas within the play. Among the most influential New Critics are Carolyn Spurgeon (*Shakespeare's Imagery and What It Tells Us* [1935]), Harold C. Goddard (*The Meaning of Shakespeare* [1951]), and Sigurd Burckhardt (*Shakespearean Meanings* [1968]).

Dividing 20th century literary criticism at the beginning of the eighth decade is in some ways arbitrary, since the later commentary depends upon methods of analysis developed earlier, and the observations themselves from earlier decades remain persuasive. Yet in or around 1970, commentators change direction. Inspired by philosophy, linguistics, psychology, and perhaps political science, they often base their observations on continental theory, political and gender-based hegemony, and skepticism about the independence of authorship. A particularly fruitful critical approach in recent Shakespearean criticism is New Historicism. Like the more traditional historicism of the earlier decades of the 20th century, it clarifies the world in which the play was written in order to shed light on the play itself. Developed primarily by Stephen Greenblatt, Louis Montrose, and others, New Historicism deals less with well-known historic events, royal or noble figures, and broad philosophic ideas than with the details of the lives of common people, which are thought to more accurately inform our understanding of the entire period. As James Shapiro writes, "[New Historicism deals] with the history of the Other in the Renaissance" (86); and that might include witches, hermaphrodites, Moors, Turks, prophets—those who existed among the mainstream but were overlooked in general historical or literary studies.

Recent commentators have shown interest in performance history, generated from the notion of mutability in meaning, since changes in signifying systems occur in many aspects of performance in addition to language—dress, gesture, sets, script editing, music, lighting, and acting style. A production reworks the ambiguities of a play, edits, highlights, and reorders it to reflect prevailing values, in order to present a favored interpretation while shrouding others. For over 400 years, theatrical decisions have been made, first, by acting companies during the Elizabethan and Jacobean periods, then by the actor-manager who served as director and producer as well as lead actor in the 18th and 19th centuries, and finally by the theater or film director in modern productions. Valuable 20th-century studies of performance range from the classic four-volume work of E.K. Chambers, *The Elizabethan Stage*, to the examinations of performances such as those by George C.D. Odell, Charles H. Shattuck, James C. Bulman, and Jonathan Bate and Russell Jackson.

BIBLIOGRAPHY

Works by William Shakespeare

The Arden Shakespeare. Harold F. Brooks and Harold Jenkins, gen. eds. Cambridge: Harvard University Press, various years.

The Complete Oxford Shakespeare. Ed. Stanley Wells and Gary Taylor, with John Jowett and William Montgomery. 3 vols. Oxford: Oxford University Press, 1987.

The Complete Pelican Shakespeare. Ed. Alfred Harbage. New York: Penguin, 1969.

The Complete Pelican Shakespeare. Ed. Stephen Orgel and A.R. Braunmuller. New York: Penguin, 2002.

The Complete Works of Shakespeare. Ed. David Bevington. 4th ed. New York: Longman, 1997.

Mr. William Shakespeare's Comedies, Histories, & Tragedies. A Facsimile Edition Prepared by Helge Kökeritz. New Haven, CT: Yale University Press, 1954.

The New Cambridge Shakespeare. Philip Brockbank and Brian Gibbons, gen. eds. Cambridge: Cambridge University Press, 1984–.

A New Variorum Edition. Horace Howard Furness, gen. ed. Philadelphia: J.B. Lippincott, various years.

The Norton Shakespeare: Based on the Oxford Edition. Ed. Stephen Greenblatt. New York: W.W. Norton, 1997.

The Riverside Shakespeare. G. Blakemore Evans, gen. ed. 2nd ed. 1974. Boston: Houghton Mifflin, 1997.

Shakespeare Quarto Facsimiles. Ed. W.W. Greg. Oxford: Clarendon Press, 1963.

William Shakespeare: The Complete Works. Ed. Stanley Wells and Gary Taylor. Oxford: Clarendon Press, 1986.

Studies of William Shakespeare

Auden, W.H. *"The Dyer's Hand" and Other Essays*. 1948. New York: Vintage, 1968.

Baldwin, T.W. *The Organization and Personnel of the Shakespearean Company*. 1927. New York: Russell and Russell, 1961.

Ball, Robert Hamilton. *Shakespeare on Silent Film: A Strange Eventful History*. New York: Theater Arts, 1968.

Barker, Deborah, and Ivo Kamps. *Shakespeare and Gender: A History*. London: Verso, 1995.

Barton, John. *Playing Shakespeare*. London: Methuen, 1984.

Bate, Jonathan, and Russell Jackson, eds. *Shakespeare: An Illustrated Stage History*. Oxford: Oxford University Press, 1996.

Bevington, David. *From Mankind to Marlowe: Growth of Structure in the Popular Drama of Tudor England*. Cambridge: Harvard University Press, 1962.

———, comp. *Shakespeare. Goldentree Bibliographies in Language and Literature*. Arlington Heights, IL: AHM, 1978.

Bloom, Harold. *Shakespeare: The Invention of the Human*. New York: Riverhead Books, 1998.

Bradley, A.C. *Shakespearean Tragedy*. London: Macmillan, 1904.

Bullough, Geoffrey, ed. *Narrative and Dramatic Sources of Shakespeare*. 8 vols. London: Routledge, 1957.

Burckhardt, Sigurd. *Shakespearean Meanings*. Princeton: Princeton University Press, 1968.

Chambers, E.K. *The Elizabethan Stage*. 4 vols. 1923. Oxford: Clarendon Press, 1961.

Crowl, Samuel. *Shakespeare Observed: Studies in Performance on Stage and Screen*. Athens: Ohio University Press, 1992.

Dubrow, Heather. Introduction to *The Riverside Shakespeare*, ed. G. Blakemore Evans. 1974. Boston: Houghton Mifflin, 1997.

Erickson, Peter, and Coppelia Kahn, eds. *Shakespeare's "Rough Magic": Renaissance Essays in Honor of C.L. Barber*. Newark: University of Delaware Press, 1985.

Garber, Marjorie. *Coming of Age in Shakespeare*. New York: Routledge, 1981.

Girard, Rene. *A Theater of Envy: William Shakespeare*. New York: Oxford University Press, 1991.

Goddard, Harold C. *The Meaning of Shakespeare*. Chicago: University of Chicago Press, 1951.

Greenblatt, Stephen. *Renaissance Refashioning: From More to Shakespeare*. Berkeley: University of California Press, 1980.

———. *Shakespearean Negotiations: The Circulation of Social Energy in Renaissance England*. Berkeley: University of California Press, 1988.

Greenwood Guides to Shakespeare. Westport, CT: Greenwood Press, various years.

Greg, W.W. *The Editorial Problem in Shakespeare: A Survey of the Foundation of the Text*. Oxford: Clarendon Press, 1954.

———. *The Shakespeare First Folio*. Oxford: Clarendon Press, 1955.

Hager, Alan. *Shakespeare's Political Animal: Schema and Schemata in the Canon*. Newark: University of Delaware Press, 1990.

Hazlitt, William. *Shakespeare's Library: A Collection of the Plays, Romances, Novels, Poems, and Histories Employed by Shakespeare in the Composition of His Works*. 1875. New York: AMS Press, 1965.

Irving, Henry. *Impressions of America*. London, 1884.

Jorgens, Jack. L. *Shakespeare on Film*. Bloomington: Indiana University Press, 1977.

Kolin, Philip C., comp. *Shakespeare and Feminist Criticism: An Annotated Bibliography and Commentary*. New York: Garland, 1991.

Manly, John Matthews, ed. *Specimens of the Pre-Shakespearean Drama*. 2 vols. New York: Dover, 1967.

Mazer, Cary M. *Shakespeare Refashioned: Elizabethan Plays on Edwardian Stages*. Ann Arbor: University of Michigan Research Press, 1980.

Miriam Joseph, Sister. *Shakespeare's Use of the Arts of Language*. New York: Columbia University Press, 1947.

Muir, Kenneth. *Shakespeare's Sources*. 1957. London: Methuen, 1961.

Novy, Marianne. *Love's Argument: Gender Relations in Shakespeare*. Chapel Hill: University of North Carolina Press, 1984.

Odell, George. *Shakespeare from Betterton to Irving*. 2 vols. 1920. New York: Benjamin Blom, 1963.

Rabkin, Norman. *Shakespeare and the Problem of Meaning*. Chicago: University of Chicago Press, 1981.

Richmond, Hugh M. *Shakespeare's Political Plays*. New York: Random House, 1967.

Ridler, Anne, ed. *Shakespearean Criticism: 1935–1960*. London: Oxford University Press, 1970.

Schoenbaum, Samuel. *Shakespeare's Lives*. Oxford: Clarendon Press, 1970.

———. *William Shakespeare: A Documentary Life*. Oxford: Oxford University Press, 1975.

Schwartz, Murray M., and Coppelia Kahn, eds. *Representing Shakespeare: New Psychoanalytic Essays*. Baltimore: Johns Hopkins University Press, 1980.

Shapiro, James. *Shakespeare and the Jews*. New York: Columbia University Press, 1995.

Shattuck, Charles H. *Shakespeare on the American Stage*. 2 vols. Washington, DC: Folger Library, 1987.

Spivack, Bernard. *Shakespeare and the Allegory of Evil*. New York: Columbia University Press, 1958.

Sprague, Arthur Colby. *Shakespeare and the Actors: The Stage Business in His Plays (1660–1905)*. Cambridge: Harvard University Press, 1948.

Spurgeon, Carolyn. *Shakespeare's Imagery and What It Tells Us*. Cambridge: Cambridge University Press, 1935.

Stoll, E.E. *Shakespeare Studies: Historical and Comparative in Method*. 1927. New York: Frederick Ungar, 1960.

Trewin, J.C. *Going to Shakespeare*. London: George C. Allen, 1978.

———. *Shakespeare on the English Stage 1900–1964: A Survey of Productions*. London: Barrie and Rockliff, 1964.

Wells, Stanley. *Shakespeare: A Life in Drama*. 1995. New York: Norton, 1997.

———, ed. *The Cambridge Companion to Shakespeare Studies*. Cambridge: Cambridge University Press, 1986.

Wells, Stanley, and Gary Taylor. *William Shakespeare: A Textual Companion*. Oxford: Clarendon Press, 1987.

Winter, William. *Shakespeare on the Stage: First Series*. 1911. New York: Benjamin Blom, 1969.

Willis, Susan. *The BBC Shakespeare Plays: Making the Televised Canon*. Chapel Hill: University of North Carolina Press, 1991.

Woodbridge, Linda, comp. *Shakespeare: A Selective Bibliography of Modern Criticism*. West Cornwall, CT: Locust Hill, 1988.

❧ *Baruch de Spinoza*
(1632–1677)

MICHAEL T. MASIELLO

BIOGRAPHY

Spinoza, one of the towering figures in the history of philosophy, was born into the Spanish-Portuguese Jewish community in Amsterdam in 1632. His parents were *converso* immigrants from Portugal. In his youth, he studied at the synagogue schools under the teachers Saul Levi Morteira and Menassah ben Israel. He does not, however, appear to have completed his rabbinical training, perhaps because he had already begun to develop the unorthodox religious and philosophical opinions that characterize his works. By 1656, such opinions had caused his excommunication from the Jewish community. Afterwards, Spinoza was for some time affiliated with a group of radical Protestants known as the Collegiants.

Spinoza moved from Amsterdam to Rijnsburg in 1660, and from there to Voorburg in 1663; he spent his final years (1670–1677) at the Hague, subsisting on slender means. His career as a "lens-grinder" is well known, but that description understates his skill in optics: He fashioned telescopes and microscopes admired by the likes of Leibniz and Huygens. Most of his philosophical works remained unpublished when he died of phthisis in 1677.

MAJOR WORKS AND THEMES

Spinoza's work is early evidence of a sea change in Western thinking about the nature of God and human understanding. He rejects the supernaturalism of popular religion in favor of a scientist's confidence in the "natural light" of reason: for him, divine law and the laws of science are identical, and human beings learn about God by rightly understanding natural phenomena. The mysterious events frequently attributed to God's unknowable will are, in truth, no more than natural occurrences for which science has yet to discover correct explanations. "God exists," in other words, "but only philosophically." This dismissal of traditional pieties led to accusations of atheism during his lifetime but clearly anticipated the theological and intellectual crises of the Enlightenment.

Spinoza is, in a sense, a deeply religious thinker—Novalis called him a "God-intoxicated man"—but his God is vastly different from that of the Judeo-Christian tradition. In his most famous and influential work the *Ethics*—completed by 1675 but left unpublished at the time of his death for fear of violent reception—he defines God as "an absolutely infinite being; that is, a substance consisting of infinite attributes, each of which expresses eternal and infinite essence." "Substance," a term with a long and complicated history in Western philosophy, means for Spinoza "that which is in itself and is conceived through itself; that the conception of which does not require the conception of another thing from which it has to be formed." The very nature of substance necessarily includes existence; consequently, no substance has a beginning or can be caused by anything else. The first part of Book One of the *Ethics* is devoted to proving that the universe can contain only one such substance, which is God. Any other claim, Spinoza demonstrates, results in contradiction and absurdity. This variation upon the "ontological" argument for God's existence is the foundation upon which the rest of the *Ethics* is built.

God, the sole existing substance, contains infinite attributes. An attribute is "that which the intellect perceives of substance as constituting its essence." While God contains an infinite number of these, the human intellect recognizes only two, Thought and Extension. By locating these two attributes "in" a single substance, Spinoza resolves the problem of Cartesian dualism. Descartes had been unsuccessful in explaining how body and mind, which seem to have totally different characteristics, could possibly influence one another. Spinoza's answer is that Thought and Extension are simply two aspects of the same eternal unity: "whatever is, is in God, and nothing can be or be conceived without God." All "modes"—that is, determinate manifestations of attributes whether "infinite" (i.e., "motion and rest") or "finite" (i.e., an individual human being)—are "in" God, the one all-containing substance. Any mode of Extension—a chemical, physical, or biological event—will have its precise counterpart in Thought.

"Nothing in nature is contingent, but all things are from the necessity of the divine nature determined to exist and to act in a definite way." Anything that can exist—that is, anything the existence of which is not prevented by something else—*does* exist. (This is a strong variant of the Aristotelian principle of plenitude: for Spinoza, all possibles are actual at all times.) The divine nature does not determine anything to exist, however, by an act of *free will*. Willing is a mode of Thought. All volitions are finite and exist in time and are therefore caused; they "bear the same relationship to God's nature as motion-and-rest and, absolutely, as all natural phenomena that must be determined by God." Since individual volitions, like all modes, rely on prior causes, they are necessarily "constrained" rather than "free." Consequently, God does not act with free will: "things could not have been produced by God in any other way or in any other order than is the case."

God, therefore, is not an anthropomorphic deity who experiences desire, changes his mind, or exerts providential guidance over creation; he is simply substance containing infinite attributes, each expressing infinite essence, and modes, the finite and determinate manifestations of these attributes. Everything that exists and occurs is determined to do so by God's very nature.

Popular piety is, by such an account, absurd. For Spinoza, much human error—and human misery—can be chalked up to human beings' imposition of their own subjective moral categories, such as "good" and "bad," upon the objective natural order that God creates necessarily and from his nature alone, irrespective of human wishes and desires. As long as mistaken expectations are nourished, human beings are in bondage in the "citadel of ignorance." A kind of freedom becomes available to them only when they begin to understand and exercise rational control over their emotions and thereby begin to accept the necessity of the natural order, including those aspects of it that tend to cause them pain. We come to see that difficulties like the "problem of evil" are unreal the moment we apprehend the true nature of God and begin to view the universe *sub specie aeternitatis*, "under an aspect of eternity." Spinoza's God cannot love man; but man is blessed, and in a sense free, when he cultivates *amor intellectualis Dei*, the "intellectual love of God."

Spinoza's attempted reconciliation of determinism and free will is a form of what modern philosophers tend to call "compatibilism." The nature of freedom in Spinoza is much debated, but this much is clear: for Spinoza, an understanding of God—that is, of nature—will lead to a better understanding of humankind. The natural light of reason can mitigate the extremity of human response to predetermined volitions of the mind. Moreover, the natural light illuminates the value of ethical virtues like kindness and mercy. Spinoza's rejection of Judeo-Christian revelation is not a wholesale rejection of all Judeo-Christian ethics. Spinoza seeks, rather, to show that the validity of some such ethical claims—though by no means all—can be demonstrated scientifically.

A scientifically oriented philosophy is nonetheless far superior to any system based on prophecy. This is the central contention of the most important work Spinoza published during his lifetime, the *Theological-Political Treatise*. The enormous outcry caused by this work explains why the *Ethics* remained unpublished at Spinoza's death. In it, Spinoza had argued that prophetic vision is a mode of "imagination," far inferior to the rational understanding attainable through philosophy; prophecy was, in fact, an instrument of social control, designed to persuade the stiff-necked and superstitious Hebrews to obey. The treatise's focus on historical analysis and textual scrutiny anticipates the crisis soon to overtake biblical interpretation.

The geometrical proofs of the *Ethics* and the historicized rejection of prophecy in the *Theological-Political Treatise* exemplify the generally scientist character of Spinoza's thought. These, as well as his lesser-known philosophical treatises—the early *Principles of Descartes' Philosophy*, the *Short Treatise on God*, the *Treatise on the Emendation of the Intellect*, and the *Political Treatise*—are the work of a philosopher deeply interested in the physical laws governing natural phenomena. Spinoza's philosophical beliefs cannot be separated from his interest in the science of optics or his study of language (Spinoza also composed a Hebrew grammar). As W.N.A. Klever remarks, Spinoza's philosophy was "not a kind of 'armchair philosophy,' far away from the center of natural science. On the contrary, he conceived and practiced a kind of philosophy which was continuous with what we call today 'natural science' " (Klever, quoted in Garrett).

CRITICAL RECEPTION

For more than a century after his death, Spinoza was widely characterized as an atheist. Even Leibniz, Spinoza's correspondent and admirer, denounced Spinoza whenever it proved useful; the Calvinist Pierre Bayle, meanwhile, portrayed Spinoza as a "virtuous atheist" in his *Dictionnaire historique et critique*, even as he criticized Spinoza's doctrines. Through much of the 18th century, Spinoza's work languished in obscurity.

His fortunes have, however, rebounded since the Enlightenment. The German Romantics rethought Spinoza's reputation as an atheist; Novalis called him a "God-intoxicated man," while Goethe went so far as to call him "*christianissimus.*" A formidable list of philosophers testify to Spinoza's influence, including Leibniz, Diderot, Schopenhauer, Hegel, Nietzsche, and Marx. In the 20th century, Spinoza received careful study from thinkers as diverse as Harry Austryn Wolfson, Edwin Curley, Leo Strauss, Richard Popkin, Luce Irigaray, and Gilles Deleuze.

BIBLIOGRAPHY

Works by Baruch de Spinoza

The Collected Works of Spinoza. Trans. E. Curley. Vol. 1. Princeton: Princeton University Press, 1985.
Ethics and Selected Letters. Trans. S. Shirley. Indianapolis: Hackett, 1982.
Spinoza Opera. Ed. Carl Gebhardt. 4 vols. Heidelberg: Carl Winter, 1925.
Theological-Political Treatise. Trans. S. Shirley. Indianapolis: Hackett, 1998.
The Works of Spinoza. Trans. R.H.M. Elwes. 2 vols. New York: Dover, 1951.

Studies of Baruch de Spinoza

Curley, E. *Behind the Geometrical Method*. Princeton: Princeton University Press, 1988.
Curley, E., and P.-F. Moreau, eds. *Spinoza: Issues and Directions*. Leiden: E.J. Brill, 1990.
Deleuze, G. *Expressionism in Spinoza*. Trans. M. Joughin. Cambridge: MIT Press, 1992.
Garrett, D., ed. *The Cambridge Companion to Spinoza*. Cambridge: Cambridge University Press, 1996.
Grene, M., ed. *Spinoza: A Collection of Critical Essays*. Garden City, NY: Doubleday/Anchor, 1973.
Strauss, L. *Spinoza's Critique of Religion*. New York: Schocken, 1965.
Wolfson, H.A. *The Philosophy of Spinoza: Unfolding the Latent Processes of His Reasoning*. 2 vols. New York: Schocken, 1969.

❧ *John Suckling*
(1608/1609–1642)

THOMAS HOWARD CROFTS III

BIOGRAPHY

John Suckling was born at Whitton, Middlesex, in the parish of Twickenham and baptized on February 10, 1608/1609. His grandfather Robert Suckling (d. 1589) was mayor and parliamentary representative of Norwich. Robert's children, by Elizabeth née Barwick, were Edmond (the poet's uncle), the Dean of Norwich, and John, the poet's father, who entered Gray's Inn in 1590 and thereafter held the offices of MP (Member of Parliament), secretary to the Lord Treasurer (then Sir Robert Cecil), and receiver of fines on alienation. Knighted by James I on January 22, 1615/1616, the poet's father continued to accumulate posts (and lands), eventually rising to Secretary of State. With his wife Martha (née Cranfield) he had five children, John, Martha, Anne, Mary and Elizabeth.

The poet entered Trinity College, Cambridge, on July 3, 1623. Accounts as to his academic proficiency differ, though apparently he had a fine ear for music and languages. Finally, he did not take a degree. He was admitted to Gray's Inn on February 23, 1626/1627, and his father's death in March of that year left Suckling in command of a considerable estate. Having a large fortune and possessing good looks and a lively spirit, Suckling was an admired presence at court from the age of eighteen. He was knighted by Charles on September 19, 1630. In the summer of 1631 he was involved in a military effort backing Gustavus II Adolphus of Sweden in the latter's Bavarian campaign (in which Gustavus himself was killed on the battlefield). On his return to London in 1632, Suckling is said to have entered into drinking and gambling with prodigal enthusiasm, and, with other poets, he frequented the Bear Tavern.

Sir John's courtship of the daughter of Sir Henry Willoughby—which proceeded with Charles I's approval—was brought to a painful end when that lady prevailed on a rival suitor, who was also an accomplished duelist, to obtain Suckling's signature on a document renouncing his claim to her hand. On the poet's refusal to sign, the other suitor, Sir John Digby, cudgeled him severely. Some connect this defeat with the poet's subsequent interest in philosophy and debate. In 1639, however, during the first Bishops' War, Suckling marched with his own contingent of a hundred troops in the Scottish Campaign, accompanying Charles in his advance to the border (and subsequently in his retreat from it).

Though Sir John Suckling was ridiculed by London wits for outfitting his militia with gorgeous scarlet coats and ostrich-plumed hats, his performance in the field raised him in the estimation of his King, who in 1639/1640 made him captain of the carabineers. In the winter of 1640/1641, Suckling wrote a letter of counsel to Charles thinly disguised as a note to one of the Queen's friends, one Henry German. The letter was printed in 1641 as "A coppy of a Letter found in the Privy Lodgeings at Whitehall" and later in the 1646 edition of Suckling's *Fragmenta*. The letter is remarkable for urging on the King just such actions as led—if obliquely—to his eventual deposition.

Suckling enjoined the King to "doe something extraordinary" (Clayton 163) and by "reall [that is, *royal*] and kingly resolutions" (164) to reform law and religion and to take a strong personal hand in dispensing justice. The king should rise above his counselors "by doing more, doing something of his owne: as throwing away things they call not for, or giving things they expected not," since "the People are naturally not valiant, and not much Cavalieir" (165). This letter was followed shortly by another that recommended that the King seize the nation's military power for himself and also outlined a plan for doing so.

This supposed "first army plot" by Suckling was discovered and exposed by opponents of the Royalist movement, making Suckling a fugitive. By May the poet was hiding in France. Suckling's further adventures are enough to fill a book: amorous intrigues in Paris necessitating flight from the country; near-execution in Spain on (false) charges of conspiring to murder Philip IV; and according to some reports, torture at the hands of the Inquisition. He is then said to have married and settled in Holland for the remainder of his life. Accounts of Suckling's death in 1642 are split. One tradition holds that he was murdered by a servant who placed an open razor in his boot so that, pulling the boot on, the poet sliced an artery and bled to death. The other account holds that, reduced in means and crushed by debt, Suckling committed suicide by poison. The latter version has the authority of **Aubrey** and of the poet's family. Suckling was buried in the Protestant cemetery in Paris sometime in the summer of that year.

MAJOR WORKS AND THEMES

During his lifetime, Suckling was perhaps most noticeable as a dramatist. His first play, *Aglaura*, was produced in 1637. It fared badly with critics but, like his other dramatic works, *The Sad One* (1637; unfinished), *The Goblins* (1638), and *The Discontented Colonel* (1640; printed in 1646 as *Brennoralt*), yielded some fine lyrics, such as "Why so pale and wan fond lover?" (from *Aglaura*). *The Goblins*—acted by the King's Men at Blackfriars in 1638 and revived at the Theatre Royal in 1667—had the best reception. It is the action-packed tale of Tamoren and his gang of noble thieves whose pranksterism throws the fictional land of Francelia into confusion. Remarking on the traditional critique of this play—that it is heavily indebted to **Shakespeare**'s *Tempest*—its most recent editor writes:

The Goblins is surely more romance than comedy, for here is the typical long separation of children from their relatives, the outlaws in the forest, the tokens, idyllic love in a cave, sudden reversals, and spectacular recognition scenes. Suckling's most characteristic addition to a conventional story is the description of a country wedding through the eyes of cynical courtiers. . . . He is best at this kind of oblique representation of the simple, reflected by a sophisticated mirror; or the sophisticated reflected by the naïve. (Beaurline, *Plays* 275)

CRITICAL RECEPTION

The lyrics for which Suckling is best known today seem not to have had much life independently of the plays, though a few appeared in manuscript or chapbook form. Suckling's first poem of note, "Sessions of the Poets," was circulated in manuscript in 1637; the poem, which presents a lively rogue's gallery of Suckling's courtly and literary associates, has been often imitated. The famous epithalamion "Ballade on a Wedding" was printed in *Witt's Recreations* (1640). The "Letter sent by Sir John Suckling from France deploring his sad Estate and Flight, with a Discoverie of the Plot and Conspiracie intended by him and his adherents against England," printed as a tract in 1641, recounts in cavalier fashion the poet's life as an exile. Some lyrics, including "Sessions of the Poets" and "Prithee send back my heart" were set to music by Henry Lawes.

Most of Suckling's work first appeared in the posthumous volume titled *Fragmenta Aurea: A Collection of All the Incomparable Peeces written by Sir John Suckling; and Published by a Friend to Perpetuate His Memory. Printed by his owne copies, London: for Humphrey Mosely* (1646). Suckling's verse, of course, smacks of the Stuart court: It is, like Suckling himself, witty, decorous, naughty, all stock in trade for the Cavalier poet. But these qualities alone would not have sufficed to "perpetuate his memory." It should be remembered that the court swarmed with now-forgotten versifiers.

Suckling had his own voice, a deft, conversational ease often mixed with a certain hauteur or swagger, qualities not incompatible with his high birth and military preoccupations. In fact, though this is to some extent true of all the Cavaliers, Suckling especially favored military imagery and subject matter, and in poems like "Tis now, since I sate down before" and "A Soldier," he cultivates the persona of the Cavalier perfectly. Though his oeuvre is comparatively small, Suckling is an exemplary lyric poet whose trenchant urbanity presaged the literary and dramatic achievements of the Restoration.

BIBLIOGRAPHY

Works by John Suckling

The Works of Sir John Suckling. Vol. 1: *The Non-Dramatic Works*. Ed. Thomas Clayton. Vol. 2: *The Plays*. Ed. L.A. Beaurline. Oxford: Clarendon Press, 1971.

Studies of John Suckling

Anselment, Raymond A. " 'Men Most of All Enjoy, When Least They Do': The Love Poetry of John Suckling." *Texas Studies in Literature and Language* 14 (1972): 17–32.

Beaurline, L.A. " 'Why So Pale and Wan': An Essay in Critical Method." *Texas Studies in Literature and Language* 4 (1962): 53–63.

Henderson, F.O. "Traditions of 'Précieux' and 'Libertin' in Suckling's Poetry." *English Literary History* 4 (1937): 274–298.

❧ *Nahum Tate*

(1652–1715)

BRIAN WALSH

BIOGRAPHY

Poet laureate of England from 1692 until his death in 1715, Nahum Tate has shared the subsequent obscurity and ignominy of other poet laureates such as **Thomas Shadwell** and Colley Cibber. Somewhat sturdier than those others, Tate's reputation today rests largely on his revisions of **Shakespeare**, as well as on his involvement in some enduring collaborative projects ranging from an opera libretto to a translation of the Psalms. Tate strove to use his official position as poet laureate didactically, and despite his inclusion in Pope's *Dunciad*, his career had its share of brilliant controversy and excitement.

Tate was educated at Trinity College in Dublin. Upon entering Trinity in 1668, Tate claimed Dublin as his birthplace, although there is some speculation that he may have been born in England. Tate's father and grandfather (both named Faithful) were Puritan ministers, and the future poet laureate would carry with him a certain proselytizing impulse throughout his life. Tate completed a degree in 1672, and the details of his biography are fuzzy between his departure from Trinity and the start of his literary career. By 1676 he was living and working in London and had begun to establish connections to prestigious literary circles there and was soon noticed and befriended by **John Dryden**.

By 1678 Tate produced his first play, *Brutus of Alba*, a version of the Aeneas and Dido story. The play followed a trend for classically themed plays, and Tate would turn to the tale again in composing the libretto for **Henry Purcell**'s successful opera *Dido and Aeneas*. Tate's second play, *The Loyal General*, was published in 1680 and included a preface by Dryden. Tate's association with Dryden, the period's preeminent poet, was deepened two years later when the two wrote *The Second Part of Absalom and Achitophel*. Dryden contributed some important portions of this poem, but the bulk of the work was done by Tate.

New adaptations of Shakespeare came into vogue, and Shadwell, Dryden, and others had reworked plays like *Antony and Cleopatra* and *Troilus and Cressida*. Tate contributed his own series of Shakespeare adaptations, including *Coriolanus*, *Richard II*, and most famously *King Lear*. Tate's *Richard II*, which he dubbed *The Sicilian Usurper* to avoid the censor, provoked controversy for raising succession questions near the volatile time of the Exclusion Crisis. Tate's adaptation had a rocky production history, and its run was terminated. When Tate's *Richard II* was published in 1682, the author added an explanatory preface in which he defended his work against charges that it was subversive. Tate's revamped *King Lear* remains his most notable accomplishment, however dubious it appears to us now, a subject I will address below.

Throughout the 1680s, Tate's place among the prominent literary figures of his day was solidified, and he was increasingly associated with Tory poets such as Dryden and Elkanah Settle. During this decade, Tate continued writing and adapting plays, as well as producing new poetry and translations, and in 1689, as we have seen, he contributed the libretto for Purcell's *Dido and Aeneas*. In 1686, he came out with a translation of Fracastoro's *Syphilus: A Poetical History of the French Disease*. He was also perhaps experimenting with more "public" themed poetry, producing an elegy upon the death of Charles II in 1685. In the late 1680s and early 1690s, flush with enthusiasm for the Glorious Revolution, Tate produced laudatory verses on the ascension of William and Mary.

Thomas Shadwell died in 1692, and within a month Tate was named the new poet laureate. Tate's rise to the position was no doubt due to his association with Dryden and other Tory poets, as well as the support of Charles Sackville, Earl of Dorset, who was a longtime friend and patron of Tate, and of Shadwell and Dryden before him. Despite the financial security such a post would ostensibly afford a professional writer, Tate often suffered financial difficulties that would worsen as he grew older. Compounding what some scholars believe to be Tate's general lack of economy was the strange fact that he received a less generous stipend than previous poet laureates. Although Tate petitioned on different occasions for more money, he was seemingly happy in his position and produced much new work in his initial years as laureate. He wrote celebratory verses for the King and Queen, as well as a tract in defense of women in 1693. By the 1690s, Tate had begun the massive project of producing new translations of the Psalms in collaboration with Nicholas Brady. *A new version of the Psalms of David* was published in 1696 and was immediately put to use in church services.

Tate believed that as poet laureate he was responsible for promoting morality through literary forms. In 1698, he published a tract on the immorality of the theater and called for several reforms, including (ironically, considering his own past) stricter censorship. Consistent with his own interventions in earlier plays by Shakespeare, **Webster**, and others, Tate also called on extant plays to be rewritten to have more perspicuously moral themes and outcomes.

During the reign of Queen Anne, beginning in 1702, Tate continued to publish poems to celebrate events of public importance, such as the union of Scotland and England and in praise of various public figures, such as parliamentarian Robert Harley. He was involved in a short-lived periodical endeavor, *The Monitor*, but seems to have encountered increasing financial difficulties in the early years of the 18th century, despite being appointed Historiographer Royal under Anne, a post that provided additional income. He died in 1715, by which time his literary output had dropped off and when he was apparently deep in debt, to be succeeded by Nicholas Rowe as poet laureate.

MAJOR WORKS AND THEMES

Tate strove to produce morally edifying poetry and drama. His commendatory poems on the great public acts and figures of his time display Tory politics mixed with his moralistic Puritan upbringing. Tate's work encompassed the religious, the political, the panegyric, and the playful. His work on *The Second Part of Absalom and Achitophel*, as well as some of his other poetry (*A Congratulatory Poem on the New Parliament Assembled on This Great Conjuncture of Affairs*, *The Kentish Worthies*, both 1701) and dramas (his *Coriolanus* and *Richard II*), show an involvement in his age's pressing political questions from a Tory perspective. Tate's involvement with Brady in translating the Psalms is an indication of his commitment to putting literary efforts in the service of religious devotion. His libretto for Purcell's *Dido and Aeneas*—altering Virgil's story into something more romantic—demonstrates his taste for classical themes and his interest in music. His best-known work is his *King Lear* (1681), which has become notorious for its shocking revision of Shakespeare's ending. In Tate's version, Lear and Gloucester live, Cordelia survives and marries Edgar, and the caustic and funny voice of the fool is omitted altogether. In the last words of the play, Edgar proclaims that "truth and virtue shall at last succeed," giving an indication of how radically Tate's *Lear* reimagined Shakespeare's in order to provide something like pointed moral clarity. Tate's version proved to be immensely popular and for many years was the only *King Lear* that was put on in London. But Tate was not without a light side. His most celebrated poem is the mock-heroic *Panacea: A Poem Upon Tea* (1700), a witty investigation into the history and variable uses of what was fast becoming England's beverage of choice.

CRITICAL RECEPTION

Tate's work increasingly considered tedious and mediocre, he was a target of satirical attacks by the Scriblerus circle and other early-18th-century wits, and since that time he has fallen into the worse fate of near oblivion. Best known still as a "botcher" of Shakespeare, Tate's lack of standing in literary history can be attested by the fact that only one book-length study on his work exists, a Twayne Authors Series survey by Christopher Spencer. There is of yet no complete or standard edition of his output. The most interesting work on Tate appears in scattered articles and as part of broader studies of his period, as well as in the numerous collections of work devoted to the critical study of Shakespeare adaptations. Tate benefits somewhat from the increasing availability of more obscure older works of literature through Internet databases, so that now many of his poems and plays that would have been more difficult to access even ten years ago are readily available online through most research library computers.

BIBLIOGRAPHY

Works by Nahum Tate

Brutus of Alba, or, The Enchanted Lovers, A Tragedy Acted at the Duke's Theatre, Written by N. Tate. London: Printed by E.F. for Jacob Tonson, 1678.

A Congratulatory Poem to His Royal Highness Prince George of Denmark, Lord High Admiral of Great Britain, Upon the Glorious Successes at Sea. By N. Tate; To Which is Added A Happy Memorable Song, On the Fight Near Audenarde, Between the Duke of Marlborough and Vendome, &c. London: Printed by Henry Hills, 1708.

Dido and Aeneas: An Opera. With Henry Purcell. London: Novello, 1961.

The History of King Lear, adapted from Shakespeare by Nahum Tate. Ed. James Black. Lincoln: University of Nebraska Press, 1975.

A new version of the Psalms of David: Fitted to the Tunes Used in Churches, by N. Brady and N. Tate, Esq. London: Printed by T. Harrison for the Company of Stationers, 1785.

An Ode Upon His Majesty's Birth-Day. London: R. Baldwin, 1694.

An Ode Upon Her Majesty's Birth-Day, April the Thirtieth. London: R. Baldwin, 1693.

Panacea: A Poem Upon Tea: In Two Cantos. London: J. Roberts, 1700.

Poems by N. Tate. London: Printed by T.M. for Benj. Tooke, 1677.

The Second Part of Absalom and Achitophel. London: J. Tonson, 1682.

Selected Writings of the Laureate Dunces, Nahum Tate (Laureate 1692–1715), Laurence Eusden (1718–1730), and Colley Cibber (1730–1757). Ed. Peter Heaney. Lewiston, NY: E. Mellen Press.

Studies of Nahum Tate

Astor, Stuart L. "The Laureate as Huckster: Nahum Tate and an Early Eighteenth Century Example of Publisher's Advertising." *Studies in Bibliography: Papers of the Bibliographical Society of the University of Virginia* 21 (1968): 261–266.

Craven, Robert R. "Nahum Tate's Third *Dido and Aeneas*: The Sources of the Libretto to Purcell's Opera." *World of Opera* 1.3 (1979): 65–78.

Hardman, C.B. " 'Our Drooping Country Now Erects Her Head': Nahum Tate's *History of King Lear*." *Modern Language Review* 95.4 (2000): 913–923.

Johnson, Odai. "Empty Houses: The Suppression of Tate's *Richard II*." *Theatre Journal* 47.4 (1995): 503–516.

Massai, Sonia. "Nahum Tate's Revision of Shakespeare's *King Lear*." *Studies in English Literature 1500–1900* 40.3 (2000): 435–450.

Olsen, Thomas G. "Apolitical Shakespeare: Or, The Restoration *Coriolanus*." *Studies in English Literature 1500–1900* 38.3 (1998): 411–425.

Sharkey, Peter L. "Performing Nahum Tate's *King Lear*: Coming Hitherley Going Hence." *Quarterly Journal of Speech* 54 (1968): 398–403.

Shershow, Scott Cutler. " 'Higlety, Piglety, Right or Wrong': Providence and Poetic Justice in Rymer, Dryden and Tate Restoration." *Studies in English Literary Culture, 1660–1700* 15.1 (1991): 17–26.

Spencer, Christopher. *Nahum Tate*. New York: Twayne Publishers, 1972.

John Taylor ("The Water Poet")

(1578–1653)

LAURIE ELLINGHAUSEN

BIOGRAPHY

Through the novel combination of two trades—rowing and writing—John Taylor made himself a celebrity in seventeenth-century Britain. Born in the parish of St. Ewen's, Gloucester, he was apprenticed to a London waterman at age thirteen. His early years on the Thames brought him into contact with noblemen, artisans, and the players that he transported to the South Bank theaters. He also improved on his grammar-school education by reading classical and contemporary literary works. This wide exposure to literary and cultural life inspired him to begin a forty-year career that would result in approximately 150 works, many of which he printed at his own cost and sold by the then unusual strategy of public subscription.

Taylor closely imitated **Ben Jonson**'s self-publicizing activities. Like Jonson, Taylor published a massive folio of his complete works and, shortly after Jonson's famed walk to Scotland, completed one of his own. Yet Taylor embraced his lowly roots in ways that Jonson did not by weaving them into an authorial persona that gained the bemused notice of audiences. Styling himself "the king's water poet," he undertook such attention-grabbing stunts as rowing down the Thames in a brown paper boat. The journey succeeded in attracting interest if not admiration: when he landed the boat, crowds surged upon it to take pieces as souvenirs.

As a company officer during the 1640s, Taylor saw the influence of radical religion within his own Waterman's Company when a "democratic revolution" against the company's oligarchic rule resulted in his expulsion from office. A fervent Anglican and Royalist, he classed these changes among larger rebellions against church and king. He devoted his last years to satirizing nonconformist religion and writing impassioned defenses of Charles I. By the end of the war, he no longer worked as a waterman and had only his writing as income. He opened a tiring house called the "Poet's Head Tavern" and hawked his last verses to customers. Taylor is believed to have died of starvation shortly thereafter.

MAJOR WORKS AND THEMES

Taylor took interest in everything: religion, politics, tavern life, women and, of course, the waterman's life. He also published in a staggering array of genres: travel writing, verse satires, epigrams, jest books, and political prose, to name a few. The waterman's persona is especially prominent in his early career. In his first book, *The Sculler* (1612; rev. ed. 1614 as *Taylors Water-worke*), he explicitly announced this identity to readers with the illustration of a sculler who carries a "hotch-potch, or Gallimawfrey of Sonnets, Satyres, and Epigrams" to whomever will buy. *Taylors Motto* (1621) personalized this strategy in an illustration of the author standing on a rock in a storm-tossed sea with an oar in one hand, an empty purse in the other, and a book balanced between his legs. The satirical *Nipping and Snipping of Abuses* (1614) defended the reputed bad behavior of watermen in the "Apologie for Water-men." Other writings took an activist bent. *Taylor on Thame Isis* (1632) used a lively description of the two parts of the river to argue against the private use of public waterways; *The World Runnes on Wheeles* (1632) comically publicized the company's suit against the spread of hackney-coaches.

Throughout his career, Taylor directly engaged his public in contractual relationships. When subscribers failed to pay, he excoriated them in print, as in *A Kicksey-Winsey: or a Lerry Come-Twang* (1619; rev. ed. 1624 as *The Scourge of Basenesse*). He packaged his travel writing in particular as saleable information and entertainment. In the epilogue to *The Pennyles Pilgrimage* (1618), Taylor binds the writer and his audience in a contract of horizontal exchange: "Thus Gentlemen, amongst you take my ware, / You share my thankes, and I your moneyes share." Taylor based his writer's labor, like that of the waterman, on a premise of services for money that relied on good faith between the producer and his purchasers. Although he also sought patronage from nobles, Taylor profited most from the market model, and he was keenly aware that he wrote in an atmosphere of intense competition.

All the Workes of John Taylor The Water Poet (1630) was an ambitious undertaking that required the work of four different printers. The title page presents a self-portrait flanked by oars and fish, with another picture of two rowers ferrying a man across the waters. In the dedication "To the World," Taylor declares, "I a poore worme of your own breeding; doe (in waie of retribution) give you here the encrease of my Tallent, which I have beene almost 60 yeeres a gathering." This passage epitomizes Taylor's language of authorial labor, as he asks the world merely for a set of good clothes and for readers without prejudice. Accompanying verses by other authors stressed the novelty of a poet from the uneducated classes. Taking this class stigma into account, Taylor's collected works, like Jonson's folio, sought to establish him as an authoritative poet of prodigious talent.

During the war, Taylor turned his attention to satirizing sectarians, particularly mechanics who took up preaching. *The Whole Life and Progress of Henry Walker the Ironmonger*, the product of a feud between Taylor and the ironworker-cum-preacher, "exposed" Walker as unlearned, treasonous, and heretical. Perhaps the humor of pamphlets such as *A Swarme of Sectaries* (1641) and *New Preachers New* (1641) veiled Taylor's anxiety over his own position as a laborer who presumed to speak publicly. In either case, the democratic potential of the market that he explored in his early works is contradicted in his later writings, which increasingly insist on social hierarchy.

Because Taylor published some of his civil war pamphlets anonymously to avoid censorship, the *Short Title Catalogue* contains works that may not be accurately attributed to him.

CRITICAL RECEPTION

Contemporaries often classified Taylor as a ballad-rhymer. Jonson took the popularity of "the Water-rimers workes" as evidence of a public who favored cheap entertainment over serious poetry. But criticism also stemmed from Taylor's fondness for inciting feuds with contemporaries such as writer and entertainer William Fennor and humorist Thomas Coryate. Nonetheless, his best-sellerdom testifies to his overall success. In addition to his popularity among common readers, he found encouragement at James I's court, where he made numerous contacts. On the whole, both Taylor the poet and Taylor the man provoked awe and amusement. **John Aubrey** remembered him as "very facetious and diverting company; and for stories and lively telling them, few could outdo him" (298)

The "popular" quality of his writings has kept Taylor out of the canon. Robert Southey numbered him among "uneducated poets" who overcame "low breeding and defective education" (15). More recently, scholars have examined his career within the context of early modern print culture. Bernard Capp regards him as "the first 'modern' personality" who, through aggressive self-marketing, made himself his own project (*World*, 196). Alexandra Halasz, in a discussion of Taylor's "subscription scenario," identifies him as one of the first authors to conceptualize writing as a form of marketplace labor. Even if his verse is of dubious quality compared to more celebrated early-seventeenth-century poets, Taylor's works are nonetheless valuable as a vast record of commentary on culture, politics, and everyday life in the civil war period.

BIBLIOGRAPHY

Works by John Taylor

Hindley, Charles, ed. *Miscellanea Antigua Anglicana.* Vol. III. London: Reeves and Turner, 1871–1873.
———. *Works of John Taylor, the Water-Poet.* [Reprints of 21 separately issued pieces.] London: Reeves and Turner, 1872.
Works of John Taylor The Water Poet. Spenser Society Reprints. New York: Burt Franklin, 1868–1869, 1870–1878.

Studies of John Taylor

Aubrey, John. *Brief Lives.* Ed. Richard Barber. Totowa, NJ: Barnes and Noble, 1983.
Caldecott, J.B. "John Taylor's Tour of Sussex in 1653." *Sussex Archaeological Collections* 81 (1940): 19–30.
Capp, Bernard. "John Taylor 'The Water Poet': A Cultural Amphibian in Seventeenth-Century England." *History of European Ideas* 11 (1989): 537–544.
———. *The World of John Taylor the Water-Poet.* Oxford: Clarendon Press, 1994.
Chandler, John. "John Taylor Makes a Voyage to Salisbury in 1623." *The Hatcher Review* 40 (1995): 19–34.

————, ed. *Travels Through Stuart Britain: The Adventures of John Taylor, The Water Poet*. Thrupp: Sutton, 1999.

Halasz, Alexandra. *The Marketplace of Print: Pamphlets and the Public Sphere in Early Modern England*. Cambridge: Cambridge University Press, 1997.

————. "Pamphlet Surplus: John Taylor and Subscription Publication." In *Print, Manuscript, and Performance: The Changing Relations of Media in Early Modern England*, ed. Arthur F. Marotti and Michael D. Bristol. Columbus: Ohio State University Press, 2000. 90–102.

Humpherus, Henry. *History of the Origin and Progress of the Company of Watermen and Lightermen of the River Thames, with numerous historical notes*. Sudbury, Suffolk: Lavenham, 1999.

Notestein, Wallace. *Four Worthies: John Chamberlain, Anne Clifford, John Taylor, Oliver Heywood*. London: Jonathan Cape, 1956.

Southey, Robert. *The Lives and Works of the Uneducated Poets*. Ed. J.S. Childers. London: Humphrey Milford, 1925.

❧ *Cyril Tourneur*
(1575?–1626)

PATRICK D. ENRIGHT

BIOGRAPHY

Not much is known about Cyril Tourneur's life. He was born perhaps sometime between 1570 and 1580. His father may have been Captain Richard Turnor, who served the Vere and Cecil families, with whom Cyril Tourneur is also associated. Cyril Tourneur died in Ireland in 1625/1626 (Morris and Gill vii).

Tourneur's contributions to Elizabethan literature are small in number and, for the most part, not well known. He wrote one play that has come down to us as undisputably his, *The Atheist's Tragedy* (1611?). A second play, *The Revenger's Tragedy* (1607?), was attributed to Tourneur in 1656, though modern scholarship is of mixed mind whether the play was written by Tourneur or—most often mentioned—**Middleton**. Two other plays, both lost, are attributed to Tourneur, *The Nobleman* (1611/ 1612?) and *The Bellman of London* (1613?) (Ribner xix–xxiii).

Like so many other Renaissance playwrights, Tourneur was also a poet, the author of what Morris and Gill call "a long and obscure poem," *The Transformed Metamorphosis*, as well as four other works, "A Griefe on the Death of Prince Henrie" (1612), "On the Succession," "On the death of a child but one year old," and "Of My Lady Anne Cecill, the Lord Burleigh's Daughter." Tourneur also wrote a prose essay, *Character of Robert Earle of Salesburye* (1612) (Morris and Gill vii–viii).

MAJOR WORKS AND THEMES

Tourneur's *The Atheist's Tragedy* handles, in an unusual way, the revenge motif, with a very unSenecan ghost *restraining* his son from bloody revenge. Brian Morris and Roma Gill have called it the last original revenge tragedy, seeing later plays as going "over and over the old ground" (xxiv). Fredson Bowers, in *Elizabethan Revenge Tragedy, 1587–1642* (1940), calls the play "one of the last of the Kydian tragedies" (143).

Kydian—or more properly, Senecan—revenge tragedy employs an aspect of the Roman poet's closet dramas, the counseling scene, or what Robert S. Miola calls the domina-nutrix (i.e., mistress-nurse or lady-nurse) convention, "that dialogue between passionate protagonist and restraining confidant" (27). Seneca uses three versions of this scene, the "straight" counseling scene, in which the counseling figure advises the protagonist to avoid passion but is ignored, the protagonist carrying out his/her passionate will and causing a disaster; the reversed counseling scene, in which the advice (such as young Tantalus's to Thyestes) directly leads to disaster; and the successful counseling scene, in which the protagonist heeds the counselor's good advice and shuns passion, thus preventing further disaster, as when Hercules listens to Amphitryon in *Hercules Furens*.

A survey of English Renaissance revenge tragedies shows playwrights from the time of Kyd using and varying the first two kinds of scenes for dramatic effects. *The Atheist's Tragedy*, however, unexpectedly uses the successful counseling scene; the protagonist, Charlemont, is confronted by his father's ghost, who tells him,

> Return to France, for thy old father's dead
> And thou by murder disinherited.
> Attend with patience the success of things,
> But leave revenge unto the King of kings. (4.6.19–22)

This message is a shock for anyone familiar with revenge-tragedy conventions; the ghost of Hamlet's father, after all, if that's what he is, is but one of a host of specters demanding revenge. Although, like King Hamlet's ghost, the shade of Montferrers has to appear a second time to reinforce his message, he is successful, and Charlemont does refrain from getting revenge. The villain D'Amville's accidental braining of himself with an axe must be seen as the King of Kings carrying out His own revenge.

Consequently, one can see Tourneur's play as the logical end of development for the Elizabethan revenge tragedy. Revengers in earlier plays had ignored the biblical admonition "Vengeance is mine, saith the Lord," or "turn the other cheek," but once Tourneur introduced a hero who followed that exhortation, there was nowhere else to develop the revenge theme, and thus Morris and Gill's conclusion is apt—only "the old ground" remained, and the dramatic genre's days were numbered (Enright 169–178).

Critics have proclaimed various themes present in *The Atheist's Tragedy*. According to Charles R. Forker, Michael H. Higgins identifies "the secret providence of God" as the play's "central theme" (qtd. in Forker 263). Clifford Leech sees a conflict between "the supreme individualist" and "the man suspicious of action" (qtd. in Forker 264). Glen A. Love suggests as a theme "a world divided into irreconcilable opposites" (qtd. in Forker 265). Irving Ribner identifies the central conflict of the play as between the themes of "animalism, mechanism, and determinism . . . and Christian transcendence" (Forker 265). It is true, however, that Tourneur's play made brilliant and final use of a genre.

The other extant play attributed to Tourneur, *The Revenger's Tragedy*, is far more problematic, and its authorship is disputed. Using statistical analysis of key words in plays by Marston (also sometimes connected with *The Revenger's Tragedy*) and Middleton, as well as both *The Atheist's Tragedy* and *The Revenger's Tragedy*, M.W.A.

Smith concludes that "Middleton is . . . more likely to be the author of *The Revenger's Tragedy* than Tourneur" (511). L.C. Salingar, on the other hand, finding the play's "imagery and moral tone . . . consistent" with Tourneur's *The Transformed Metamorphosis*, asserts that "[w]ith Tourneur, then, rests the benefit of the doubt" (443). Inga-Stina Ewbank succinctly summarizes scholarly disagreement on the authorship problem and admiringly points out Samuel Schoenbaum's conclusion in *Internal Evidence and Elizabethan Dramatic Authorship* that "the evidence is inconclusive" (122). Perhaps the best indication of scholarly incertitude is that even those critics who believe Middleton or some other playwright wrote *The Revenger's Tragedy*, nonetheless, often refer to its author as Tourneur.

More has been written about this disputed play than about *The Atheist's Tragedy*. Jonas Barish sees two of *The Revenger's Tragedy*'s themes as "good versus evil" and "good contaminated" (qtd. in Hallett and Hallett 223). Charles and Elaine Hallett see as a major theme the idea that "the act of lust [is] the offense which sets revenge raging in the world" (228). Similarly, Salingar sees all the Italianate revenge plays (including this one) dealing with "lust and moral corruption" (438).

CRITICAL RECEPTION

Forker points out that works of Tourneur other than *The Atheist's Tragedy* and *The Revenger's Tragedy* have received "scant attention" (256). He goes on to note that the reception of the latter play has been mixed, mentioning Felix E. Schelling and Alfred Harbage among those who dispraise it and, among those who have been "more sympathetic," L.C. Salingar, R.J. Kaufmann, Norman Rabkin, Samuel Schoenbaum, Robert Ornstein, Alvin Kernan, and many others.

Huston Diehl, after observing that *The Atheist's Tragedy* has been seen by other critics variously as "a failed tragedy, a flawed revenge drama, and an outmoded allegory" (47), explains the differing readings as resulting from the characters' differing perceptions of their world, seeing the play as "interested in exploring the ways in which men see and interpret their darkened universe" (48). Irving Ribner, while asserting that *The Revenger's Tragedy* is "the greater artistic achievement," also acknowledges that *The Atheist's Tragedy* "has considerable merit of its own" and is "worthy of study" (xxxii). Morris and Gill, in their edition of *The Atheist's Tragedy*, call it a "very plain play" that "offers a thesis, and a demonstration of that thesis" (x). Noting the unusual use of the ghost to forbid the hero's revenge, they conclude that in this play "the Elizabethan revenge play, inaugurated so spectacularly by Kyd, committed a rational, predictable, and rather undistinguished suicide" (xxiv).

BIBLIOGRAPHY

Works by Cyril Tourneur

The Atheist's Tragedy. Ed. Brian Morris and Roma Gill. London: Benn; New York: Norton, 1976.

The Atheist's Tragedy. Ed. Irving Ribner. London: Methuen, 1964.

The Revenger's Tragedy. Ed. R.A. Foakes. London: Methuen, 1966.

The Revenger's Tragedy. Ed. Lawrence J. Ross. Lincoln: University of Nebraska Press, 1966.

The Works of Cyril Tourneur. Ed. Allardyce Nicoll. London: Fanfrolica Press, 1930.

Studies of Cyril Tourneur

Bowers, Fredson Thayer. *Elizabethan Revenge Tragedy, 1587–1642*. Princeton: Princeton University Press, 1940.

Diehl, Huston. " 'Reduce Thy Understanding to Thine Eye': Seeing and Interpreting in *The Atheist's Tragedy.*" *Studies in Philology* 78 (1981): 47–60.

Enright, Patrick D. "The Senecan Counselling Scene in English Renaissance Drama." Ph.D. dissertation, University of Kansas, 1994.

Ewbank, Inga-Stina. "Webster, Tourneur, and Ford." In *English Drama (Excluding Shakespeare)*, ed. Stanley Wells. London: Oxford University Press, 1975. 113–133.

Forker, Charles R. "Cyril Tourneur." In *The New Intellectuals: A Survey and Bibliography of Recent Studies in English Renaissance Drama*, ed. Terence P. Logan and Denzell S. Smith. Lincoln: University of Nebraska Press, 1977. 248–280.

Hallett, Charles A., and Elaine S. Hallett. *The Revenger's Madness: A Study of Revenge Tragedy Motifs*. Lincoln: University of Nebraska Press, 1980.

Morris, Brian, and Roma Gill, eds. Introduction to *The Atheist's Tragedy*. By Cyril Tourneur. London: Benn; New York: Norton, 1976.

Ribner, Irving, ed. Introduction to *The Atheist's Tragedy*. By Cyril Tourneur. London: Methuen, 1964.

Salingar, L.C. "Tourneur and the Tragedy of Revenge." In *The New Pelican Guide to English Literature*. Vol. 2: *The Age of Shakespeare*, ed. Boris Ford. Harmondsworth, England: Penguin, 1982. 436–456.

Smith, M.W.A. "The Authorship of *The Revenger's Tragedy.*" *Notes and Queries* (December 1991): 508–513.

&. *Thomas Traherne*
(1636?–1674)

GARY BOUCHARD

BIOGRAPHY

Given the transcendent nature of his poetry, it is appropriate that nearly all of the knowable details of Thomas Traherne's biography concern the inner life of the author. His prose meditations and verse furnish us with the astoundingly detailed unfolding of a young consciousness, yet we do not know with certainty exactly where or when he was born. He was likely born in Hereford or Ledbury in 1636 or 1637. The son of a shoemaker, he was also descended from a locally famous relative, Philip Traherne (1566–1645), twice mayor of Hereford and a loyalist to King Charles I.

Precisely how young Thomas spent his childhood we cannot know with certainty. There may have been little on the exterior that distinguished his daily work and play from that of other children. But if we trust even partially in the author's *Centuries of Meditations*, which he recorded as a grown man, we gain a picture of a child whose precocious intellectual curiosity and spiritual ponderings kept him apart, even remote, from the normal play and discourse of other children and even adults. Consider these brief samplings: "Once I remember (I think I was about four years old), when I thus reasoned with myself" (XVI). "Sometimes I should soar above the stars, and inquire how the Heavens ended, and what was beyond them" (XVIII). "Being swallowed up therefore in the miserable gulf of idle talk and worthless vanities, thenceforth I lived among shadows, like a prodigal son feeding upon husks with swine" (XIV). That the dawn of consciousness came earlier in Thomas Traherne than in most is, I think, apparent.

We speculate that his zeal for the life of the mind led his parents to somehow find the means to send him to Oxford, but one way or the other the *Athenae Oxonienses* records nearly everything else there is to know of the outward events of Traherne's short life:

Thomas Traherne, a shoemaker's son of Hereford, was entered a Commoner of Brasen-nose College on the first day of March, 1652, to one degree in Arts, left the house for a time, entered into the sacred function and in 1661 he was actually created Master of Arts. About that time he became Rector of Credinhill, commonly called Crednell, near to the city of Hereford . . . and in 1669 Bachelor of Divinity.

Traherne remained rector at Credinhill for nine and a half years when he was summoned to London to become the private chaplain to Sir Orlando Bridgman, who in 1667 was made Lord Keeper of the Seals. He remained in Sir Bridgman's service and died only three months after Bridgman in 1674 at the age of thirty-eight. Only in the last year of his life were any of his writings published. His tract *Roman Forgeries* was published in 1673, part of the veritable flood of partisan theological debate, and his manuscript *Christian Ethics* had been sent to the publishers, but its author died before it came to print. His poems would not be printed for the first time until 1903 and his meditations in 1908.

MAJOR WORKS AND THEMES

Louis Martz's bold claim that "the two greatest representations of paradise in English literature" were "composed within the same quarter century" prompts the obvious query: "**Milton**'s *Paradise Lost* and what else?" Martz's resolute reply: Traherne's masterpiece *A Century of Meditations*. Some readers might, after indulging in all 400-plus *Meditations*, disagree with Martz's assessment, but all would concur, I believe, that a zealous, Augustinian exploration of "all that is Great or Good in Blessedness" ("Silence") as exemplified within the author's own interior life is the unrelenting theme of all of Traherne's meditations and verse.

Inspiring to some and wearisome to others, Traherne's 400-plus prose meditations (numbered paragraphs of various lengths), seek to explain "the mystery that hath been hid in God since the Creation," the third "century" depicting in detail the inner paradise of the author's early childhood, as well as the causes for this innocence lost. His verse relies upon the very same themes as the titles of some of his more successful poems indicate: "Wonder," "Desire," "Goodness," "The Choice," "The Person," "The Recovery," "Love," and "Thoughts." Though it is not among his most commonly anthologized works, I would direct any firsttime reader of Traherne to the poem "Silence." An argument for the contemplative life is made with a clarity, simplicity, and beauty that elucidates everything else that he writes.

Traherne's unapologetic and experiential belief in God and the God-like nature of man, his unabashed Christian Platonism, and his enthusiastic individual pursuit of Grace, if startling to ecclesiastical orthodoxy and improbable to the religious skeptic, ought to be impressive to anyone with a literary mind. A century before Blake's *Songs of Innocence*, Traherne had fashioned a veritable canon of such songs, and a century and a half before Wordsworth's *Prelude*, he demonstrated how an epic-length reminiscence of childhood episodes could be Theo- rather than egocentric. Two centuries before Hopkins coined the term *inscape*, Traherne mapped that spiritual topography with detail that modern psychologists have not surpassed. Regarding his formal innovations, I would note that long before contemporary poet Charles Simic rediscovered the power of the brief prose narrative to explore versions of reality, Traherne had showed the way.

CRITICAL RECEPTION

That Thomas Traherne enjoys any literary life today is due entirely to Professor Bertram Dobell. Traherne died, as Dobell put it, "utterly out of the minds and memories of men" with his unpublished representations of paradise destined to be shadowed within manuscript collections until exactly 100 years ago. Dobell's discovery of Traherne after his manuscripts were rescued from a London bookstall, and his subsequent proof that the works were not the work of **Henry Vaughan**, as Dr. Gossart had supposed, brought to light a poet whom Dobell believed "destined to shine with undiminished luster as long as England or the English tongue shall endure." Dobell's initial assessment that Traherne was "not in the front ranks of poets, but, excluding Milton, in the front ranks of his class" still holds true.

With the assistance of Martz and others, Traherne still holds his place among Vaughan, **Crashaw**, and **Herbert**, but his reputation suffers, I think, from his unfortunate and long absence; for his manuscripts lay hidden during the literary era that might have made him its champion. Coming to light as he did at the beginning of the 20th century, he was destined, in a world of modernism and postmodernism, to find a small place among the minor poets of his age, his depictions of inner paradise regarded by most as curious eccentricities rather than inspired revelations. He remains the greatest pre-Romantic poet whom the Romantic poets never read.

BIBLIOGRAPHY

Works by Thomas Traherne

Centuries of Meditations. Ed. Bertram Dobell. London: Bertram Dobell, 1908.

Centuries, Poems and Thanksgivings. Ed. H.M. Margoliouth. Oxford: Oxford University Press, 1958.

Christian Ethics, or, Divine Morality, by Thomas Traherne, author of the Roman Forgeries. London: Printed by Jonathan Edwin, 1675.

Of Magnanimity and Charity. Ed. John Rothwell Slater. New York: King's Crown Press, 1942.

Poems of Felicity. Ed. H.I. Bell. London: Clarendon Press, 1910.

The Poetical Works. Ed. Bertram Dobell. London: Betram Dobell, 1903.

Roman Forgeries. 1673.

Select Meditations. Ed. Julia Smith. Manchester: Carcanet Press, 1997.

Traherne, Thomas. A Serious and Pathetical Contemplation of the Mercies of God, in several most devout and Sublime Thanksgivings for the Same. London: Printed for Samuel Keble, 1666.

Studies of Thomas Traherne

Allchin, A.M. *Profitable Wonders: Aspects of Thomas Traherne*. Harrisburg, PA: Morehouse, 1991.

Ames, Kenneth John. *The Religious Language of Thomas Traherne's Centuries*. New York: Revisionist Press, 1977.

Birt, Richard. " 'Sweet Infancy!' The Affinities between the Vaughans and Thomas Traherne." *Scintila* 3 (1999): 80–90.

Clements, A.L. *The Mystical Poetry of Thomas Traherne*. Cambridge: Harvard University Press, 1969.

Martz, Louis. *The Paradise Within*. New Haven, CT: Yale University Press, 1964.

Reid, David. "Traherne and Lucretius." *Notes and Queries* 45.243 (1998): 440–441.

Wöhrer, Franz. *Thomas Traherne: The Growth of a Mystic Mind*. Amherst, NY: Prometheus Books, 1983.

❧ *Anthony Van Dyck*
(1599–1641)

CLAIRE I.R. O'MAHONY

BIOGRAPHY

Anthony Van Dyck created a unique testament of the elegance of 17th-century courtly life through his painted and engraved portraits. His parents, an Antwerp silk merchant and a mother who excelled as an embroiderer and died when he was eight, instilled a sensitivity to the delights of fabric and patrician life. Several of Van Dyck's siblings entered religious life, and he himself was a member of the Antwerp Jesuit Confraternity of Bachelors. He apprenticed with Hendrick van Balen I at the Antwerp Guild of St. Luke. His reputation came early, and following the example of **Rubens**, Van Dyck set up a large studio with assistants. The preponderance of portrait commissions precluded his ambitions to become primarily a history painter, although he worked as Rubens's assistant for the thirty-nine ceiling paintings for the new Jesuit Church of St. Charles Borromeo in Antwerp as well as executing numerous direct commissions from religious orders and municipal fraternities and some secular mythological scenes for private patrons.

After a brief sojourn in England, in 1621 Van Dyck set off for Italy, traveling around for six years, remaining principally in Genoa and Rome but visiting all the major Italian artistic centers, despite repeated outbreaks of plague, and later he visited France. He made copious sketches before the great Masters of Italy, most prolifically of the work of Titian. He executed numerous portrait and altarpiece commissions for cardinals and aristocrats as well as visiting the painter Sofonisba Anguissola in her ninetieth year to converse about the art of portraiture (recorded by a portrait drawing and notes of their conversation in his Italian sketchbook, British Museum, London, f110r). The death of his father, who had lost his fortune, forced Van Dyck to return to Antwerp to ensure the financial security of his siblings. Rubens's return to Antwerp encouraged Van Dyck to seek his own fortune and fame at the Stuart court of Charles I.

Apart from sporadic visits to Antwerp, Brussels, and Paris, Van Dyck spent most of his mature life in England, residing in Blackfriars, London. He married Mary Ruthven, lady-in-waiting to Queen Henrietta Maria and granddaughter of the 1st Earl of Gowrie; their daughter Justiana was baptized on the day of his death; he also had an illegitimate daughter Maria Teresa. Van Dyck was himself a courtier, amassing an impressive art collection that included the work of Titian, whom he so admired and emulated. His personal elegance and charm can be evinced from the Earl of Newcastle's letter thanking the artist for "the Blessinge of your Companye, & Sweetnes off Conversation."

MAJOR WORKS AND THEMES

Although Van Dyck did paint ecclesiastical and secular themes, he is rightly best known for his gifts as a portraitist. His works on paper including atmospheric life drawings and engravings are engaging and significant, in particular, his *Iconography*, published by Martin van Enden in 1640, which comprised eighty portraits of illustrious men of learning, art, and political influence such as Inigo Jones.

The lasting power of Van Dyck's court portraits resides not only in the artistic and political panorama of the age implicit in their vast array of sitters but also in the elegance of their execution, particularly Van Dyck's bravura in capturing the lavish refinements of Caroline dress and the delicate tonalities and volumes of faces and hands. His most frequent and celebrated sitters were Charles I, his French Catholic Queen Henrietta Maria, and their children. Van Dyck captured an extraordinary multiplicity of facets to the royal personae as in the equestrian portraits that create contrasting and engaging visions of Charles I. *Charles I on horseback* (1636) (National Gallery, London), reminiscent of the bronze statue of Marcus Aurelius in Rome and Titian's portraits of Charles V, conveys the image of a King of martial prowess and presence. By contrast in *Le Roi à la chasse* (c. 1635) (Musée du Louvre, Paris) through his exquisite coloration, delicately executed finish, and imaginatively conceived setting, Van Dyck constructs an arresting glimpse of Charles I as a dandified man of fashion, while indulging in a touch of gentle humor at royal expense, which Holbein, **Velázquez**, and later Goya would also allow themselves. In his images of the royal family subtly evoking conjugal and familial informality, Van Dyck achieved equally sensitive modulations of physiognomy, gesture, and surrounding symbolic attributes such as peaceful and amorous laurel and evergreen leaves in *Charles I and Henrietta Maria* (1632) (Archiepiscopal Castle and Gardens, Kromeriz Czech Republic) and the contrasting heroic mastiff and endearing spaniel in *The Five Eldest Children of Charles I* (1637) (Royal Collection).

Van Dyck also executed a number of allegorical works for the royal family including *Cupid and Psyche* (Royal Collection) based on Shakerley Marmion's masque of 1637. Malcom Rodgers argues persuasively that the extravagances of fancy dress costumes popularized by masques and their basis in Neoplatonic beliefs that temporal beauty connoted celestial perfection, not vanity, encouraged Van Dyck's use of extravagant and exoticized dress. The fanciful luxurience of Van Dyck's depiction of Caroline court costume harmonizes perfectly with **Herrick**'s celebration of the sensuality of silk—"That liquefaction of her clothes" ("Upon Julia's Clothes," *Hesperides*)—and the sexual invitation that materials and their movement imply—"A sweet disorder in the dresse / Kindles in clothes a wantonnesse" ("Delight in Disorder").

Van Dyck painted paeans to many of the courtly ladies admired by the Caroline lyricists such as *Lady Dorothy Sidney, Countess of Sunderland* (Petworth) (1617–1684), who inspired **Edmund Waller**'s "Saccharissa" or *Venetia Stanley, Lady Digby as Prudence* (Private collection), whose cheeks were described by **John Aubrey** as "just that shade of Damaske rose, which is neither too hott nor too pale." After her tragic death, Van Dyck created the arresting *Lady Digby on her deathbed* (1633) (Dulwich Picture Gallery), which inspired William Habington's lines "she past away / So sweetly from the world, as if her clay laid onely down to slumber" ("To Castara, upon the death of a Lady").

Van Dyck captured masculine character with equal dexterity through a variety of tropes, alleviating the potentially monotonous black and gray of much male costume through greater attention to the arrangement of the drapery folds and the sitters' hands and hair as in *Sir Thomas Hammer* (1638) (Weston Park Foundation) or by indulging in celebrations of finery and texture as in *Lord John Stuart and his brother Lord Bernard Stuart* (c. 1638) (National Gallery, London), a lavish testament to the haughty, dandified elegance for which the Cavaliers would soon pay the highest price. These sitters' biographies are emblematic of the era. His father was a leading Puritan in Parliament, but Thomas Hammer, one of England's first great plantsmen and a regular correspondent with John Evelyn, raised Royalist troops, while Charles I's cousins would have their flamboyant youth cut down in the Civil Wars.

Van Dyck created a unique testament to the age's artistic flowering and its patrons such as *Philip Herbert 4th Earl of Pembroke* (c. 1634) (National Gallery of Victoria, Melbourne), Lord Chamberlain, who controlled the licensing of plays and theaters and to whom **Shakespeare**'s *First Folio* (1623) is dedicated. *Thomas Killigrew and a Man* (1638) represents the Royalist playwright who served both Charles I and II, evoking the loss of his wife Celia Crofts through a subtle set of symbolic cues eloquently visualizing the Counter-Reformation rejection of Puritan iconoclasm. Walpole seconded Vertue's identification of the second man as the lyricist **Thomas Carew** who had composed "On the marriage of T.K. and C.C. the morning stormie" in honor of the Killigrews' marriage. Thomas's sister Anne, who was Henrietta Maria's Dresser, played "Camena" in Montagu's *The Shepherd's Paradise* at Somerset House in 1633 and inspired Henry Glapthorne's elegy, also sat for Van Dyck, *Anne Killigrew with an unidentified Lady* (1638) (The Hermitage).

CRITICAL RECEPTION

Charles I not only knighted but also erected a monument in St. Paul's to his favorite painter inscribed: "Anthony Van Dyck, who while he lived gave immortality to many." Royal and aristocratic patrons who showered Van Dyck with commissions, pensions, and gifts extended far beyond his special relationship with the Caroline court, including James I, Infanta Isabella, Cardinal-Infante Ferdinand, as well as soldiers and burgher collectors such as Jacomo de Cachiopin who had a whole room of his house devoted to his collection of Van Dyck paintings. In 1640 the Guild of St. Luke made Van Dyck Dean of the Guild *honoris causa*, an accolade only previously awarded to Rubens. William Sanderson praised Van Dyck as the first painter "that e're put ladies' dress into a careless romance" (*Graphice*, London, 1658). Poetic tributes included not only Herrick but also Edmund Waller's "To Van Dycke." Van Dyck was admired but not directly emulated in his own time in England, although Sir Peter Lely collected Van Dyck's work. Van Dyck's artistic legacy impacted principally upon the 18th-century painters Reynolds and Gainsborough, who embraced his deployment of landscape settings and the elegance of his drapery and poses.

BIBLIOGRAPHY

Studies of Anthony Van Dyck

Brown, C., and H. Vlieghe. *Van Dyck 1599–1641*. London: Royal Academy of Arts, 1999.

Howarth, D., ed. *Art and Patronage in the Caroline Courts: Essays in Honour of Sir Oliver Millar*. Cambridge: Cambridge University Press, 1993.

Millar, O. *Van Dyck in England*. London: National Portrait Gallery, 1982.

Parry, G. "Van Dyck and the Caroline Court Poets." *Studies in the History of Art* 46 (1994).

Sutton, P.C., ed. *The Age of Rubens*. Boston: Museum of Fine Arts, 1993–1994.

Walpole, Hugh. *Anecdotes of Painting in England*. London, 1762–1771.

❧ *Henry Vaughan*
(1621?–1695)

GARY BOUCHARD

BIOGRAPHY

Henry Vaughan was born in 1621 or early 1622 in Newton, surrounded by scenic beauty and Welsh culture. He would spend the greater portion of his life there and would emphasize his own Welsh extraction by writing the word *Silurist* after his name, identifying himself as a descendant of the local British tribe known as *Sillures*.

Henry and his twin brother Thomas were tutored by a local clergyman, Matthew Herbert. They then attended Jesus College, Oxford. As he recollected to a friend: "I stayed not at Oxford to take any degree, butt was sent to London beinge then designed by my father for the study of the Law, which the sudden eruption of our late civil warres wholie frustrated." During his brief time in London he seems, from allusions in his poems, to also have served in the military on behalf of the king. Some time in the 1640s he married Catherine Wise and settled once more in Newton. He published his first book in 1646, *Poems, With the tenth Satyre of Juvenal Englished*.

From a literary point of view, the most significant time in Vaughan's life occurred sometime in the late 1640s. Troubled by the political upheavals of the 1640s and grieved by the death of his beloved younger brother William in 1648, Vaughan read the poetry of **George Herbert** and was so impacted by the verse that he resolved to set aside all "idle books" including, apparently, the one he was about to publish. Instead, *Silex Scintillans* (Sacred Poems) was published in 1650 and an expanded version of the same in 1655. These spiritual mediations in imitation of Herbert's are the work for which Vaughan is best remembered.

Sharing his brother's interest in Hermetic teachings, he would later publish quasi-scientific works on Hermetical medicine as well as some religious mediations and translations. In 1678 he published a collection of early and later poems called *Thalia Rediviva*. Vaughan seems to have devoted little time during the second half of his life to writing poetry. Instead, he apparently cultivated an active medical practice, and though no evidence exists that he obtained a formal medical degree, he accompanied his name with M.D. by 1677. When his wife died around 1653 he married her sister. He had four children by each marriage, and this poet whose verse celebrates worldly transcendence ironically spent his latter years battling legal suits brought against him by the children of his first marriage. As a result, he relinquished his Newton property to his eldest son and repaired with his wife to a cottage at Scethrog, where he died on April 23, 1695. He is buried in the Llansantffreead Churchyard.

MAJOR WORKS AND THEMES

An admirer and imitator of Herbert and a precursor to Blake and Wordsworth, Henry Vaughan is the best known and most prolific of the later-17th-century devotional poets. For two centuries, in fact, his poetry could be regarded as a unique foreshadowing of the Romantic era. When a 17th-century manuscript of thematically similar poems was discovered in the 1890s, it was presumed to be the previously undiscovered work of Vaughan and would have been published as such if not for an astute critic who recognized internal differences and pursued external evidence leading to the discovery of **Thomas Traherne**. Because of their overlapping life spans, common Welsh heritage, and shared influence from earlier devotional poetry, these two poets are frequently studied in tandem, though their poetry and persons were apparently unknown to one another.

Vaughan was explicit about his imitation of Herbert, assigning to his collection of poems the identical subtitle as Herbert's *Steps To Temple*. Emphatically religious and introspective, the "private ejaculations" of Vaughan's *Silex Scintillans* (or Sacred Poems) certainly echo Herbert in their spiritual yearnings, but the mystical chords they touch go beyond Herbert's orthodoxy. With a characteristically Welsh emphasis on the innocence of early childhood and communion with nature, the poems have a pre-Romantic quality that distinguishes them from the more conventional, scriptural piety of Herbert's verse. Consider, for example, the colloquial mysticism that characterizes the opening couplets of three Vaughan poems. First, from his well-known poem "Retreat": "Happy those early dayes! When I / Shin'd in my Angell-infancy." Or these lines that could mistakenly be attributed to Emily Dickinson: "I saw Eternity the other night / Like a great Ring of pure and endless light." And finally from "Peace": "My Soul, there is a Countrie / Far beyond the stars, / Where stands a winged Centrie / All skilfull in the wars." The tone is casual, the thoughts transcendent. Vaughan's Welsh eccentricity is best recognizable in such yearnings as "I would I were a stone, or tree, / Or flower by pedigree" or "I would I were some *Bird*, or *Star*, / flutt'ring in woods, or lifted far / Above the *Inne* / and rode of sin!" ("Christ's Nativity").

Categorizing Vaughan as a late metaphysical or a pre-Romantic helps us to comprehend the peculiarity of his verse, but it also causes us, I think, to overlook the most important aspect of his poetry, not just where the religious lyric is concerned but the evolution of English verse in general. Some forty years ago, Louis Martz observed that since Southwell, Alabaster, **Donne**, and Herbert had all entered into holy orders, the 1650 publication of *Silex Scintillans*, along with **Milton**'s *Poems* in 1645, marked "the emergence of the layman as central force in religious poetry of the period" (4). The death of the Catholic exile **Richard Crashaw** in 1649, the year before the publication of *Silex*, Martz declared, was the end of an era. "With Crashaw's death the power of liturgical and eucharistic symbols died away in English poetry of the seventeenth century" (3).

Whether or not Martz overstates the case, I think it is important to recognize that Henry Vaughan's poetry is different from that which came before it and that one essential difference is the displacement of sacramental symbol and energy with a more generic emphasis upon the Self, Nature, and Scripture. Vaughan writes about "Holy Communion," but his predecessors may be said to have come very near performing it in their verse in a way that England would not see again until Gerard Hopkins.

A century and a half after Vaughan's death, when the influence of Scripture and liturgy had greatly diminished, Nature and the Self would take hold as the central meditative ingredients of Romantic poetry. Therefore, while Vaughan's poetry serves to forecast the English literary future, it also preserves, along with the poetry of Traherne, a brief time of literary confluence when High Church orthodoxy, hermetic philosophy, scientific theory, childhood reminiscence, and infatuation with nature combined in the imaginations of a few poets whose "metaphysics" were unique, even among those we used to call the metaphysicals.

CRITICAL RECEPTION

Enjoying no popular or critical reception in his lifetime (is it any wonder he turned to medicine?), nor during the 18th century, Vaughan's literary stock began to rise in the latter part of the 19th century. An edition of his *Complete Works* was published in 1871, and his possible influence on Wordsworth sustained him enough attention to find a place among the "metaphysicals" identified by 20th-century critics. Even so, what was written in the 1968 edition of his *Complete Works* remains true: "[T]he value of Vaughan's contribution to English literature has yet to be fully assessed." I would begin such an assessment in the verse of Emily Dickinson who explicitly acknowledged Vaughan's influence and then turn once more to the English Romantics who did not.

BIBLIOGRAPHY

Works by Henry Vaughan

The Works of Henry Vaughan. Ed. L.C. Martin. 2nd ed. London: Oxford University Press, 1957.

Studies of Henry Vaughan

Cadogan, Alex. "Vaughan and the Mundus Imaginalis." *Scintilla* 6 (2002): 110–121.
Martz, Louis. *The Paradise Within*. New Haven, CT: Yale University Press, 1964. chap. 1.
Mathias, Roland. "A New Language, a New Tradition." *Scintilla* 6 (2002): 161–182.
Nauman, Jonathan. "Toward a Herbertian Poetic: Vaughan's Rigorism and 'the Publisher to the Reader' of Olor Iscanus." *George Herbert Journal* 23.1–2 (1999–2000): 80–104.

Rudrum, Alan. "Paradoxical Persona: Henry Vaughan's Self-Fashioning." *Huntington Library Quarterly: Studies in English and American History and Literature* 62.3–4 (2001): 351–367.

Young, R.V. *Doctrine and Devotion in Seventeenth-Century Poetry: Studies in Donne, Herbert, Crashaw and Vaughan.* Cambridge: Brewer, 2000.

❧ *Diego Velázquez*
(1599–1660)

HUGH MACRAE RICHMOND

BIOGRAPHY

Diego Velázquez was born in Seville in 1599 to parents of minor nobility deriving from Portugal. He was apprenticed in 1611 to the local master painter Francisco de Herrera the Elder, who sponsored a salon of intellectuals and artists. Velázquez won membership of the local painters' guild in 1617, when he also married the daughter of his master. Before he left for Madrid in 1622, Velázquez had signed about twenty paintings, including portraits, genre studies of low-life, and religious subjects. In 1623 he was summoned to the royal court in Madrid by King Philip IV's principal officer, the Count-Duke Gaspar Guzmán de Olivares, and there he painted the famous poet Don Luis de Gongora. Later he was commissioned to paint a portrait of the King, successful enough to secure him official appointment as court painter. He alone was permitted to paint the King. In 1627 he won a competition between the four painters at the court and became Usher of the Chamber.

When **Peter Paul Rubens** visited Madrid in 1628, Velázquez became familiar with his work. This influence was enriched by a visit to Italy in 1629, where he saw the art of Genoa, Venice, Florence, and Rome. On his return Velázquez earned much credit for paintings in the Bel Retiro palace, particularly *The Surrender of Breda*. Similar contributions to the décor of the royal hunting lodge at Torre de la Parada won him the office of Assistant to the Wardrobe in 1636. Shortly before the fall of Olivares in 1643, Velázquez was appointed to the post of Chamberlain to the King and Assistant Superintendant of royal building projects. From this time he painted some of his greatest pictures, such as *Venus at her Mirror* and *The Fable of Arachne* (*Las Hilanderas*). Velázquez visited Italy again in 1650 and was admitted to the Academy of Rome. On his return in 1651 he was appointed Supreme Court Marshal, and in 1656 he began work on *Las Meninas*, his best-known work. In 1659 he was admitted to the knightly order of Santiago, but he died the following year. A fire at the royal palace in Madrid destroyed or damaged many of Velázquez's works in 1734, but most of his best paintings survive in the Prado Museum of Madrid.

MAJOR WORKS AND THEMES

As a court painter Velázquez was chiefly concerned with innumerable portraits of the royal family, their associates such as Olivares, and comparable figures such as Pope Innocent III. He also painted the kind of religious subjects favored in the Counter Reformation, notably *Christ at the Column*, the *Canonization of the Virgin*, and *St. Antony Abbot and St. Paul the Hermit*. However, he also painted more mundane treatments of biblical subjects such as *The Supper at Emmaus* and *Christ in the House of Mary and Martha*. The domestic settings in these paintings match his genre studies of proletarian life in *Old Woman frying Eggs* and *The Waterseller*. His portraits also show unfashionable subjects, such as in the much admired portrait of his mestizo (or half-caste) servant, *Juan de Pereja*, which treats this mundane figure as the equal of any in dignity and intensity.

Velázquez shared Renaissance interest in classical themes (such as the Ovidian stories equally favored by **Shakespeare**) in such mythological paintings as *The Feast of Bacchus* and *The Forge of Vulcan*, not to mention the so-called *Rokeby Venus* (or *Venus at her Mirror*). The first two subjects are not treated very respectfully, though in his more historical and occasional paintings Velázquez favors occasions reinforcing official policy, as in *The Surrender at Breda*. Nevertheless, his interest in ordinary life counterbalances his official work; and he shows concern with the impoverished, the excluded, and the disadvantaged, as in his portraits of the "buffoons" of the court, often quite pathetic dwarfs, and unconventional personalities as seen in *The Buffoon Calabasas* and *Dwarf Holding a Tome on his Lap*.

His powers of empathy appear in these sympathetic studies of court clowns and grotesques akin to Shakespeare's fools. One of his portraits shows a saturnine clown in the role of Don John of Austria, the same figure whom Shakespeare presents in *Much Ado about Nothing* as the pathological Bastard Don John. A similar challenge to a heroic stereotype appears in his rueful study of a disarmed Mars. The presumptuousness of weavers is another shared theme of the two artists, who both follow Ovid (in *A Midsummer Night's Dream* and *Las Hilanderas*, respectively) with equal complexity of levels and perspectives. The more realistic vein in such works can be detected in the official portraits of Velázquez, which often include provocative lower-class elements, even in dealing with the royal family, as in his *Prince Baltazar Carlos with a Dwarf*. These traits appear in his most famous painting, *Las Meninas*, for the seeming portrait of the little princess also favors her attendants—the maids of the title, the dwarfs, a professional like Velázquez, and even a dog. The King and Queen, whom Velázquez is apparently involved in painting, appear only in the mirror.

CRITICAL RECEPTION

During his lifetime Velázquez was admired at the Spanish court, but limited access to his paintings elsewhere meant they were not widely appreciated thereafter. The range of Velázquez is still only fully recognizable in the Prado collection. There his fluency is visible for close study of the lightness and ease of his brushwork, antici-pating that of the Impressionists, so that some of his paintings seem unfinished, like *The Needlewoman*. Only in the late 19th century was there a full recognition of his distinction. This partly resulted from the anticipation of Impressionism in his imme-diacy of effect, perhaps deriving from his lack of much preliminary draughtsmanship and his frequent avoidance of achieving highly finished surfaces. Manet judged Ve-lázquez "the greatest painter of all" and praised his lively portrait of the performer *Pablo de Valladolid* as the ultimate vision of the actor.

Velázquez was appreciated from his own time as the ideal royal portraitist, blending the energy of Rubens and the elegance of **Van Dyck**, with whom he has many affin-ities. Of some 120 known paintings attributable to Velázquez (of the 200–250 he may have painted) about 80 are portraits, mostly of the royal family, the court, the socially prominent, or celebrities like the fashionable poet Gongora. The portraitist John Singer Sargent (1856–1925) trained himself by study and copying of Velázquez works in the Louvre and the Prado. Even Pablo Picasso painted numerous variations of *Las Men-inas*.

Recently Velázquez's Shakespearean range of empathy has been recognized not only in his "genre" studies of ordinary life but in elements of his more formal works, such as *Las Hilanderas*, because of the weavers in the foreground, while more elevated mythological personalities are relegated to an inset at the rear. The complexity of this painting was recognized by the Spanish critics Diego Angulo in 1948 and Maria Cartula in 1952, helping to restore its title as *The Fable of Arachne*, with the impli-cations about artistic pretensions of Arachne that Ovid's tale raises. Its multilayered construction is characterstic of the other greatest paintings of Velázquez: *The Surren-der at Breda*, and *Las Meninas*, in both of which the eye is led from a socially diverse foreground, through differing levels of detail into a deep perspective that lends richer meaning to the nominal subject. Even the portrait of the buffoon Don John has an impressionistic inset of the battle of Lepanto to the rear, a sea battle in which the original Don John was the Christian leader. However, the pathological elements of the portrait imply that this leader's manic bravura had elements of madness.

Velázquez has always been admired, but his reputation as one of the greatest of all painters still advances. His active career as a courtier afforded him distinctive oppor-tunities for psychological observation that are generally recognized. Yet his courtly role notably failed to inhibit his confident self-expression that remains an important attraction for modern taste in such paintings as *Las Meninas*, even if his administrative duties may often have distracted him from concentration on his art.

BIBLIOGRAPHY

Studies of Diego Velázquez

Recent bibliography covering Velázquez is vast and mainly not in English, and it is detailed in the López-Rey *Complete Works* below. The following are representative recent works in English.

Alpers, Svetlana. *The Decoration of the Torre del Parada*. Brussels: Arcade Press, 1971.
Brown, Jonathan. *Velázquez: Painter and Courtier*. New Haven, CT: Yale University Press, 1986.

López-Rey, José. *Velázquez: Catalogue Raisonné of His Oeuvre*. London: Faber and Faber, 1963.

———. *Velázquez, Painter of Painters: The Complete Works*. Köln: Benedict Taschen Verlag, 1997.

———. *Velázquez' Work and World*. London: Faber, 1968.

White, John Manchip. *Diego Velázquez: Painter and Courtier*. London: Hamish Hamilton, 1969.

Wolf, Norbert. *Velázquez, 1599–1660: The Face of Spain*. Köln and London: Taschen, 1999.

🐦 *Johannes Vermeer*

(1632–1675)

VELMA BOURGEOIS RICHMOND

BIOGRAPHY

Johannes Vermeer was born in 1632. His father Reynier Jansz, who had trained in Amsterdam as a weaver of fine fabric, belonged to the Guild of Saint Luke in Delft and was a picture dealer and keeper of the Mechelen inn, where Vermeer spent his boyhood. Vermeer's artistic training remains a subject of debate. His admission as a master to the Guild of Saint Luke in Delft on December 29, 1653, meant that he had served at least six years as an apprentice, but his teachers are unknown. One likely possibility was Abraham Bloemart, a distant relative of his wife Catharina Bolnes, whom he married on April 20, 1653. Catharina and her mother Maria Thins, who came from a distinguished family, were practicing Roman Catholics. Vermeer, whose parents were Reformed Protestants, converted to Roman Catholicism before his marriage, which took place in Schipluy, a strong Catholic center outside Delft. By 1660 the Vermeers and their increasing number of children lived in Maria Thin's house on the Oude Langendijk (part of the "Papists' Corner," with its Jesuit church) in Delft. A single patron, Pieter Claesz van Ruijven and his wife Maria de Knuijt, bought many of Vermeer's paintings; but his financial difficulties, heightened by the economic turmoil of the French wars, led to a severe distress that his widow, left with eleven children, blamed for her husband's early and sudden death.

MAJOR WORKS AND THEMES

Although Vermeer's early work shows influences of painters such as Gerard ter Borch and Pieter de Hooch, and a knowledge of Italian work, his unmistakable characteristics are regarded as self-taught and distinctively his own. Vermeer's genre painting, scenes of everyday life that create a consummate illusion of reality, are most numerous. Women are his principal subject, usually evoking a private way of life in an enclosed world where there is a single figure, as in *Girl with a Pearl Earring* and

The Girl with a Red Hat, both dated c. 1665–1666, and *Woman in Blue Reading a Letter* (c. 1663–1665). These paintings celebrate the wonder of ordinary existence, a secular counterpart to the religious subjects of his initial history paintings, *Saint Praxedis* and *Christ in the House of Mary and Martha*, both c. 1665. Vermeer's luminosity so exceeds that of other painters as to become numinous, prayer as the accomplishment of ordinary acts—reading, writing, making lace, pouring from a jug, gazing at the viewer. Vermeer's white walls, a mark of Dutch cleanliness, show his fascination with the effects of light within an interior and sign of austerity and purity, a wholesomeness in 17th-century Dutch painters that replaced the darkness of Bosch and Breughel.

Genre paintings lack a narrative, so that they are often deemed "poetic," but much of their fascination is imagining a story. Beautiful and precise details of props and furnishings, not least paintings within a painting, have inspired many interpretations. Take *A Lady Standing at the Virginal* (c. 1672–1674) where a large Cupid dominates the wall behind the Lady, and small cupids decorate the tiles that border the floor. Several paintings feature musical instruments, an analog in visual art for the tie between song and lyric.

Much more complex is *Woman Holding a Balance* (c. 1662–1664). On the table before the woman are Vermeer's favorite pearls, but the balance contains only light. On the wall is a painting of *The Last Judgment*, a favorite subject of 15th-century Dutch painters like Jan van Eyck and Rogier van der Weyden, as is the Virgin Mary. With this iconography the secular, perhaps pregnant, woman in the painting can be read as a refiguring of Catholic veneration of Mary, the Mother of God, through whose pregnancy Jesus the Savior entered the world; since the woman stands between the saved and damned, her child is not predestined as Calvinists argued. Alternatively, she stands alone as a manifestation of Vermeer's favorite motif of woman in whom is found life's meaning and an affirmation.

Several paintings, such as *The Girl with the Wine Glass* (c. 1661–1662) and *The Girl Interrupted at Her Music* (c. 1660–1661), show two or three figures, including men, in scenes that echo the popular amatory subjects of 17th-century poetry and romance, ultimately derived from Petrarch. The men and women appear conflicted, part of little dramas like those in **John Donne**'s lyrics. Similarly, Vermeer's two paintings of men alone reflect contemporary interest in science. In Vermeer's characteristic light and amidst objects that ask for interpretation, *The Astronomer* (1668), with his celestial globe, and *The Geographer* (1669), with a terrestrial globe, are idealized portraits that express the moral dimension of New Science in the 17th century.

Vermeer's interest in the outer world had earlier found expression in landscape, notably *View of Delft*, by some considered his most brilliant painting. He creates a lovely world of light and color, so vibrant that it seems to change as if the viewer were looking at the water and boats and the precisely delineated cityscape under clouds and sky. *The Little Street*, also dated c. 1660–1661, is an exterior scene; houses dwarf the women who go about their ordinary tasks of cleaning and sewing without noticing the viewer.

Vermeer's self-definition is most explicit in *The Art of Painting* (c. 1666–1667) and *The Allegory of Faith* (c. 1672–1674). In the first the painter, with his back to the viewer, sits at his easel while his female model, shown with attributes of Clio, muse of history, stands at the center; she inspires his passion to create a new Dutch art, rooted in the past but contemporary. That the task of living in the world is not easy finds expression in *The Allegory of Faith*, where a huge painting of the Crucifixion dominates the center wall, while other objects (the chalice, Mass book and crucifix on the table/altar, the suspended heavenly glass sphere) place the female figure of Faith in a context of Catholic belief, especially the doctrine of transubstantiation.

CRITICAL RECEPTION

Although there are only thirty-six extant paintings, from a career of but twenty years, Vermeer today ranks among the greatest Dutch artists. However, his fame has come only in the last 150 years. In his lifetime a single patron bought most of his work, and twenty-one paintings were listed in the family estate at the end of the 17th century. Thus Vermeer's work was not widely seen. Recognition came late in the 19th century, especially from wealthy collectors in the United States. The appeal was the immediate humanity and reassuring directness of Vermeer's paintings—unencumbered, since no surviving studies or comments from Vermeer survived. The availability of color reproductions, unusually successful for Vermeer, made his work familiar. The enthusiasm of painters, Pissarro and Van Gogh, soon spread to a huge audience. Millions viewed the Vermeer exhibition at the National Gallery of Art, Washington, DC, and Mauritshuis, The Hague, in 1995–1996. Today both Vermeer's original images and similarly posed figures are to be found on magazine covers, so that few artists have greater recognition.

BIBLIOGRAPHY

Studies of Johannes Vermeer

Alpers, Svetlana. *The Art of Describing: Dutch Art in the Seventeenth Century.* Chicago: University of Chicago Press, 1983.

Blankert, Albert. *Vermeer of Delft: Complete Edition of the Paintings.* Oxford: Phaidon Press, 1978.

Exhibition Catalogue. *Johannes Vermeer.* Washington, DC: National Gallery of Art and Mauritshuis, The Hague, 1995–1996.

Exhibition Catalogue. *Masters of Seventeenth-Century Genre Painting.* Philadelphia: Philadelphia Museum of Art, 1984.

Finlay, Ian F. "Musical Instruments in Seventeenth-Century Dutch Paintings." *The Galpin Society Journal* 6 (1953): 52–69.

Franits, Wayne, ed. *The Cambridge Companion to Vermeer.* Cambridge: Cambridge University Press, 2001.

———. *Looking at Seventeenth-Century Dutch Art: Realism Reconsidered.* Cambridge: Cambridge University Press, 1997.

Gaskell, I., and M. Jonker, eds. *Vermeer Studies.* Washington, DC: National Gallery of Art; New Haven, CT: Yale University Press, 1998.

Hedquist, Valerie. "The Real Presence of Christ and the Penitent Mary Magdalen in the *Allegory of Faith* by Johannes Vermeer." *Art History* 23 (2000): 333–364.

Hertel, Christiane. *Vermeer: Reception and Interpretation.* Cambridge: Cambridge University Press, 1996.

Littlejohn, David. "What's So Great about Vermeer? Reflections on the Washington Exhibition." *The Hudson Review* 49 (1996): 259–272.

Montias, John Michael. *Artists and Artisans in Delft: A Socio-Economic Study of the Seventeenth Century*. Princeton: Princeton University Press, 1982.

Schama, Simon. *The Embarrassment of Riches: An Interpretation of Dutch Culture in the Golden Age*. Berkeley: University of California Press, 1988.

Snow, Edward. *A Study of Vermeer*. 2nd rev. ed. Berkeley: University of California Press, 1994.

Steadman, Philip. *Vermeer's Camera: Uncovering the Truth behind the Masterpieces*. Oxford: Oxford University Press, 2001.

Wheelock, Arthur K., Jr. *Vermeer and the Art of Painting*. New Haven, CT: Yale University Press, 1995.

Wheelock, Arthur K., Jr., et al. *The Public and the Private in the Age of Vermeer*. London: Philip Wilson Publishers, 2000.

❧ *Edmund Waller*
(1606–1687)

HUGH MACRAE RICHMOND

BIOGRAPHY

Edmund Waller was born in the family manor house at Coleshill but moved with his family to Beaconsfield, where he is still commemorated by a public monument. He was educated at Eton, King's College, Cambridge, and Lincoln's Inn. He entered Parliament as a member of the opposition to King Charles I. After working for a political reconciliation of the King and Parliament, he became a Royalist to the point of leading a plot to seize London for the King in 1643. On its discovery by Parliamentarians, Waller was imprisoned, fined, and banished to France, having escaped execution by betraying his associates. However, he was reconciled to **Cromwell** in 1651 and allowed to return to England. Thereupon he composed "A Panegyric to My Lord Protector," subsequently offset by his "To the King, upon his Majesty's Happy Return." Despite these vacillations he was returned to Parliament after the Restoration and became a courtier and intimate of King Charles II. As a noted wit, Waller deflected the King's censure of his welcoming poem to Charles as inferior to the Cromwell panegyric by diplomatically responding: "Poets, sir, succeed better in fiction than in truth." On another occasion he was reproached for flattering the Duchess of Newcastle by saying he would give all his own compositions to have written her mediocre verses "On the Death of a Stag," only to riposte, "Nothing was too much to be given that a lady might be saved from the disgrace of such a vile performance."

His own verse was first published in 1644 (the authoritative edition is that of 1664), and it covered a wide range of topics, from amatory flattery of court ladies (the most favored of whom he addresses as Sacharissa) to occasional poetry. He rose to mock-heroic narrative with three cantos about the capture of a whale in the Bermudas, *The Battle of the Summer Islands*. His idyllic description of these islands influenced **Marvell**'s better-known verses about the Bermudas. Similarly, Waller's flatteries of Sacharissa in two poems "At Penshurst" (following **Jonson**'s more famous "To Penshurst") provided a model for Marvell's country-house poem about Mary Fairfax,

Upon Appleton House. Waller wrote a revision of *The Maid's Tragedy* of Beaumont and Fletcher, and he also translated Corneille's *Pompée* as *Pompey the Great*, with Charles Sackville, Sir Charles Sedley, and others (1664). Waller died at an advanced age in 1687 without loss of verbal mastery, as seen in "Of the Last Verse in this Book."

MAJOR WORKS AND THEMES

Waller was a precocious and prolific poet, developing as early as 1625 the meter of "heroic couplets" in his complimentary piece on *His Majesty's Escape at Santander* (about Prince Charles's escape from shipwreck). His flattering poems addressed to Sacharissa (such as "At Penshurst)" were much admired, and at least two elegant examples in this vein have survived in the popular esteem: "Go lovely Rose" and "On a Girdle." His political satire, *Instructions to a Painter*, was also influential, and his last poem, "Of the Last Verse in this Book," has always been much admired.

Dryden went so far as to say of Waller: "Unless he had written, none of us could write." This surprising assertion reflects the qualities to which Waller aspired, urbanity, clarity, and decorum. These defined the goals of the Augustan Age from Dryden to Pope. It is not accidental that almost all Waller's verse is complimentary and usually occasional, ranging from affairs of state to domestic events.

CRITICAL RECEPTION

During his lifetime Waller's social dexterity with its delicately nuanced tone of voice was greatly admired, and he was praised for his metrical correctness: Bell's edition (1861) observes, "His principal merit is that of having been the first who uniformly observed the obligations of a strict metrical system," and "There are very few of his lines that do not read smoothly, and but one in which a syllabic defect can be detected." However, for the Romantics he illustrated the supposed artificiality and insincerity of much neoclassical literature. As late as 1928 J.B. Emperor called him "the insipid and time-serving Waller. . . . He is a thoroughly bad poet. His love verse is cold, artificial and absurd." This critical view persisted into the middle of the 20th century because of critics' preference for the intense, even dislocated attitudes and style of **John Donne** and the metaphysical poets, as seen in T.S. Eliot's criticism.

In the second half of the 20th century, beginning with the occasional verse of their master Ben Jonson, the standing of the Cavalier poets as a group, including Waller, was enhanced. Their poetry was reviewed more favorably, not least because the two schools were perceived to be less distinct than previously believed. Such poets as Jonson, **Carew**, and **Herrick** were shown to share many virtues with their "metaphysical" contemporaries such as Marvell and **Herbert**. Waller has gained somewhat from this shift, so that the analogies in his work to that of Marvell and Carew are now recognized. His urbanity is generally admitted. Waller will never regain the definitive status as the master of an era that his correctness earned him from Dryden's point of view, and his political girations remain distasteful to moderns. However, he can now be credited with the verbal poise and social alertness in his best work, despite its limited scale.

BIBLIOGRAPHY

Works by Edmund Waller

The Poems of Edmund Waller. Ed. G. Thorn Drury. 2 vols. London: Lawrence and Bullen, 1893.

The Works of Edmund Waller in Verse and Prose. Ed. Elijah Fenton. Glasgow: Robert and Andrew Foulis, 1752.

Studies of Edmund Waller

Bateson, F.N. "A Word for Waller." In *English Poetry: A Critical Introduction*. London: Longmans, Green, 1950.

Chernaick, Warren L. *The Poetry of Limitation: A Study of Edmund Waller*. New Haven, CT: Yale University Press, 1968.

Gilbert, Jack G. *Edmund Waller*. New York: Twayne Publishers, 1979.

Johnson, Samuel. "Edmund Waller." In *Lives of the Poets*. 2 vols. 1779. London: J.M. Dent (Everyman), 1925. 1: 145–179.

Judkins, David C. "Recent Studies of the Cavalier Poets: Thomas Carew, Richard Lovelace, John Suckling, and Edmund Waller." *English Literary Renaissance* 7 (1977): 243–258.

Miner, Earl. *The Cavalier Mode from Jonson to Cotton*. Princeton: Princeton University Press, 1971.

Richmond, H.M. "The Fate of Edmund Waller." *South Atlantic Quarterly* 60.2 (Spring 1961): 230–238.

———. *The School of Love: The Evolution of the Stuart Love Lyric*. Princeton: Princeton University Press, 1964.

Sharp, R.L. *From Donne to Dryden: The Revolt against Metaphysical Poetry*. Chapel Hill; University of North Carolina Press, 1940.

Williamson, George. *The Proper Wit of Poetry*. Chicago: University of Chicago Press, 1961.

❧ *John Webster*
(1579?–1633?)

D. SUSAN KENDRICK

BIOGRAPHY

In the 1999 film *Shakespeare in Love*, Queen Elizabeth asks a boy if he liked the performance of *Romeo and Juliet*. He replies sincerely, "I liked it when she stabbed herself." Identifying himself as "John Webster," this character's dark humor contrasted with the pathos of the tragedy. Although the scene is fictional, it represents the playwright well. In Webster's tragedies, even the greatest honors, virtues, and beauty serve only as *memento mori*; as T.S. Eliot noted, "Webster was much possessed by death and saw the skull beneath the skin." He was born on or about 1579 to Elizabeth Coates Webster, the daughter of a blacksmith, and John Webster, Sr., a carriage-maker and member of the Merchant Taylor's Company. Records containing the exact dates of birth for John Jr. and his brother Edward were destroyed in the Great Fire of 1666, so birthdates are conjectural. Webster may have been educated at the Merchant Taylor's school and may have been admitted to the Middle Temple from New Inn in 1598. Webster's plays reveal knowledge of the law, and he condemns corrupt lawyers, praising honest ones. The first mention of John Webster the playwright appears in the diary of Philip Henslowe, the theater manager, who recorded payment in 1602 to Webster and others for plays. The date of his death is also conjectural: 1632 to 1634.

MAJOR WORKS AND THEMES

Webster collaborated with Munday, **Middleton**, **Drayton**, Dekker, Heywood, and Smith on several plays, none of which are extant. He also contributed prefatory verses to works by Munday, Middleton, and Harrison. In 1604–1605, Webster and Dekker collaborated on *Westward Ho!* and *Northward Ho!* Both plays focus on economic and social issues while presenting comedies of sexual escapades and marital relations; the women of these plays struggle against the double standard. A third collaboration with Dekker, *Sir Thomas Wyatt*, may contain sections from the earlier play *Lady Jane*

Grey; Jane and her husband Guildford Dudley are viewed as innocent victims of their parents' ambitions. Though Lady Jane is juxtaposed in religion and monarchy with Queen Mary I, the playwrights do not condemn either character, and the play, in fact, offers a critique of political ambition.

In 1612, Webster published the first of his three independent plays, *The White Devil*. In 1623, he published his other two plays, *The Duchess of Malfi* and *The Devil's Law-Case*. After that year, he contributed small verses to various collections, collaborated with John Ford on the now-lost *The Late Murder of a Son upon the Mother, or Keep the Widow Waking*. His last work was a collaboration with Heywood, the Roman tragedy *Appius and Virginia*.

Webster is generally interested not in the beauty of the world or its inhabitants, but the inherent corruption and despair of humanity. In his view, nothing in the world is as it seems, and there is no moral center to guide the characters. Good and evil are thus inverted, and the only motivation for any character is self-interest. In *The White Devil*, Webster creates a singular woman who refuses to abide by social standards of morality; her beauty covers a Machiavellian soul. Vittoria allows no one to dissuade her from her passion for Duke Brachiano, and the murder of her husband Camillo is presented as not only necessary but entirely unavoidable and justified. Despite her corruption, Vittoria's courage and strength inspires respect.

Another brave heroine, the title character of Webster's masterpiece *The Duchess of Malfi*, follows her own moral compass and ignores social and political pressures, yet remains the epitome of virtue. Her brothers, the Cardinal and Duke Ferdinand, reflect common Jacobean prejudices; they are the embodiment of (Catholic) Church and (Italian) state, vehicles transporting the vices of lust, greed, obsession, and cruelty in a soft coating of hypocrisy. Contrasted with the seeming purity of the Duchess, the two brothers represent the ultimate in human and spiritual corruption. Despite the Duchess's dignity and refusal to succumb to their influence, her own actions do not escape suspicion, as she vows to overthrow patriarchal authority by choosing Antonio as her husband. Her lady Cariola, awed by this vow, wonders which is more powerful in the Duchess: "the spirit of greatness / or of woman." Even in the most horrific circumstances, the Duchess remains the most honorable and courageous character in the play, her virtue revealed through her dignity in the face of death. So noble is she that even the ruthless Machiavellian villain Bosola is inspired to avenge her. For Webster, even the most honorable characters still bear the taint of human corruptibility, immorality, and decay. Both plays, based on actual events, represent the ultimate in revenge tragedy, the "tragedy of blood," wherein all characters—the dishonorable as well as the virtuous—are unavoidably drawn to their horrific fate.

Webster's third independent play, *The Devil's Law Case*, is a convoluted tragicomedy of lust, pride, and greed. Lord Contarino wishes to wed Jolenta and needs the consent of her brother Romelio and mother Leonora. Romelio wishes Jolenta to wed Ercole, a knight, and when Jolenta refuses, Romelio forces her betrothal to him, despite her protests. Contarino challenges Ercole to a duel for Jolenta, and both supposedly die of their wounds. Informing Jolenta that she is Contarino's heir, Romelio tries to convince her to pretend to be with child by Ercole in order to inherit his estates as well. In order to claim his estate for herself, Leonora decides to declare herself an adulteress and her son a bastard in open court in order to disinherit and shame him publicly. The honest judge Ariosto resolves all conflicts; the recovered

Contarino is betrothed to Leonora, and Jolenta to Ercole. Romelio must wed his pregnant mistress. The men must maintain a ship against the Turk for seven years, and the women are ordered to build a monastery. Leonora, like the Duchess and Vittoria, follows her own moral compass, but her defiance of traditional feminine behavior is presented as more sinister, since her primary motivation seems to be simple lust. Because she has no nobility to commend her, her character is considerably less admirable, and less sympathetic, than Webster's great tragic heroines.

CRITICAL RECEPTION

Probably more than any other Elizabethan or Jacobean dramatist, Webster adapted borrowed passages from a variety of sources. In 1617, Henry Fitzjeffrey satirized him in *Certain Elegies Done by Sundry Excellent Wits*: his slow and deliberate work habits earned him the nickname of "Crabbed *Websterio*" whose work "will be so obscure / That none shall understand him." However, not all his contemporaries disparaged him; Thomas Middleton wrote, "Thy monument is raised in thy life-time" . . . and "Thy epitaph only the title be, / Write DUCHESS." **John Ford** exclaimed, "Crown him a poet," and William Rowley praised Webster's creation of the Duchess, who "might speak more, / But never in her life so well before." Throughout the 17th century, *The White Devil* and *The Duchess of Malfi* kept Webster's name alive, although *The Devil's Law-Case* was never well received in performance. In 1651, Samuel Sheppard links Webster with Euripides and Sophocles. By the end of the 17th century, his name was rarely mentioned.

Critics of the 18th century recognized Webster's plays, but only in their need for extensive revision. **Nahum Tate** turned *The White Devil* into *Injured Love: or, The Cruel Husband* in 1707. In that same year *The Duchess of Malfi* became *The Unfortunate Duchess, or The Unnatural Brothers*. Lewis Theobald adapted it in 1735 as *The Fatal Secret: A Tragedy*, complete with a happy ending and a reunited family, more acceptable to contemporary tastes. Theobald commented that Webster had "a strange and impetuous Genius, but withal a most wild and undigested one." After Theobald, criticism on Webster virtually halted for the remainder of the century.

The 19th century saw the reformation of Webster's reputation. Charles Lamb succeeded in reviving interest in 1808. The Impressionist criticism of Lamb and William Hazlitt was enthusiastic about Webster, and other critics began to look again at the plays. Webster was found to be energetic, but gloomy, and critics emphasized the horrors of the plays. In 1838 Nathan Drake classified Webster as fourth behind **Shakespeare**, **Massinger**, and Ford, and by 1852 Edwin Whipple praised Webster as a Shakespearean imitator of great talent, and his regard strengthened the playwright's critical reputation. Victorian moralists, namely, Canon Charles Kingsley, attacked Webster's plays as unfit for the stage because of their horrific and immoral characterizations. The poet Algernon Charles Swinburne, however, believed Webster to be superior to Euripides in his creation of noble and tragic figures, notably female. The theater critic William Archer was Webster's greatest opponent in the 19th century; though he praised Webster's verse, he criticized his drama as haphazard and melodramatic. George Bernard Shaw found most Elizabethan drama to be horrific, and Webster was not eliminated from that judgment. James Russell Lowell's 1877 lectures recognize *The Duchess of Malfi* and *The White Devil* as moving, despite their horrors.

Edmund Gosse's 1883 *Seventeenth Century Studies* praises Webster's work, particularly the two independent tragedies. Though he saw Webster's work as lacking style, his criticism did much to solidify Webster's reputation. Webster was perceived in general as talented, but imperfect, as his plays did not appeal to the tastes of the Romantic period.

Cultural changes of the 20th century, however, brought about a new envisioning of Webster. The 19th-century self-assurance metamorphosed into the insecurity, displacement, and fractured consciousness of the 20th; while Webster was too horrific for a Victorian audience, to a 20th-century audience his dark vision seemed altogether too accurate. As Don Moore pointed out in 1966, "Eliot's Wasteland—our twentieth century—is remarkably similar to the charnel house atmosphere of Webster, and the equation follows through" (75). Inspiring new interest, F.L. Lucas's 1927–1928 edition of the plays praised "the courage of despair" that permeates the tragedies. Muriel Bradbrook's 1935 study of Elizabethan tragedy, followed the next year by Una Ellis-Fermor's study of Jacobean drama, perceived Webster as powerful but somewhat confused in methodology. Critics then turned their attention to Webster's "borrowings"; Robert W. Dent and Gunnar Boklund explored Webster's extensive sources. Critical focus then turned to the "moral vision" of Webster; F.P. Wilson viewed Jacobean dramatists as moralists, and Lord David Cecil praised Webster's plays as lessons in morality that emphasized the price of sin. Postmodern critics point out that Webster's characterizations reveal significant expectations regarding gender roles, particularly in the representations of women. Charles Forker's 1986 study is the most extensive treatment of the playwright's life.

BIBLIOGRAPHY

Works by John Webster

The Duchess of Malfi. Ed. Elizabeth M. Brennan. New Mermaids. 3rd ed. London: A&C Black; New York: Norton, 1993.

The Duchess of Malfi. Ed. Brian Gibbons. New Mermaids. 4th ed. London: A&C Black; New York: Norton, 2001.

The Works of John Webster: An Old Spelling Critical Edition. Ed. David Gunby et al. 2 vols. Cambridge: Cambridge University Press, 1995.

BIBLIOGRAPHY

Studies of John Webster

Berry, Ralph. *The Art of John Webster.* Oxford: Clarendon Press, 1972.

Bliss, Lee. *The World's Perspective: John Webster and the Jacobean Drama.* New Brunswick, NJ: Rutgers University Press; Brighton: The Harvester Press, 1983.

Boklund, Gunnar. The Duchess of Malfi: *Sources, Themes, Characters.* Cambridge: Harvard University Press, 1962.

Bradbrook, M.C. *John Webster, Citizen and Dramatist.* New York: Columbia University Press, 1980.

Brooke, Rupert. *John Webster and the Elizabethan Drama.* London: Sidgwick and Jackson, 1916.

Callaghan, Dympna. *Woman and Gender in Renaissance Tragedy: A Study of* King Lear, Othello, The Duchess of Malfi *and* The White Devil. New York: Harvester Wheatsheaf, 1989.

Dent, R.W. *John Webster's Borrowing*. Berkeley: University of California Press, 1960.

Edmond, Mary. "In Search of John Webster." *Times Literary Supplement*, December 24, 1976, 1621–1622.

Ekeblad, Inga-Stina. "The 'Impure Art' of John Webster." *Review of English Studies* 9 (1958): 253–267.

Forker, Charles R. *Skull beneath the Skin: The Achievement of John Webster*. Carbondale: Southern Illinois University Press, 1986.

Freer, Coburn. *The Poetics of Jacobean Drama*. Baltimore: Johns Hopkins University Press, 1981.

Haworth, Peter. *English Hymns and Ballads and Other Studies in Popular Literature*. Oxford: Basil Blackwell, 1927.

Jardine, Lisa. *Still Harping on Daughters*. 1983. New York: Harvester Wheatsheaf, 1989.

King, Bruce. *Seventeenth-Century English Literature*. A. Norman Jeffares, gen. ed. New York: Schocken, 1982.

Leech, Clifford. *John Webster: A Critical Study*. London: Hogarth, 1951.

Lever, J.W. *The Tragedy of State*. London: Methuen, 1971.

Luckyj, Christina. *A Winter's Snake: Dramatic Form in the Tragedies of John Webster*. Athens: University of Georgia Press, 1989.

Moore, Don D. *John Webster and His Critics: 1617–1964*. Baton Rouge: Lousiana State University Press, 1966.

Murray, Peter B. *A Study of John Webster*. The Hague: Mouton, 1969.

Peterson, Joyce E. *Curs'd Example*: The Duchess of Malfi *and Commonweal Tragedy*. Columbia: University of Missouri Press, 1978.

Ranald, Margaret Loftus. *John Webster*. Boston: Twayne Publishers, 1989.

Zimmerman, Susan, ed. *Erotic Politics: Desire on the Renaissance Stage*. New York: Routledge, 1992.

❧ *Henry Wotton*

(1568–1635)

MIMI YIU

BIOGRAPHY

Born in 1568 at Bocton Hall, Kent, Henry Wotton descended from a long lineage of landed gentry. His ancestor Nicholas Wotton, Lord Mayor of London during Henry V's reign, had acquired an estate through marriage; Bocton Hall had been the family seat for roughly 150 years when Henry Wotton was born. For generations even before this Nicholas Wotton, the family had distinguished itself primarily through public service and diplomacy. Although his father refused to join Elizabeth's court, Henry was no exception to the family trade: he and his older three brothers would all be knighted for various services to the Crown. Indeed, beyond his illustrious family connections, Wotton's own accomplishments make him a noteworthy figure on the political and cultural scene of late Elizabethan and early Jacobean times. Wotton's stature was such that Izaak Walton devoted an essay on him—alongside others on **John Donne**, Richard Hooker, and **George Herbert**—in the collected *Four Lives* (the essay on Wotton was originally intended for a separate volume, the *Reliquiae Wottonianae*. Indeed, a touching portrait of Wotton appears in Walton's own opus *The Complete Angler*, in which the two friends fish and converse, whiling away tranquil summer afternoons. Much of our contemporary knowledge of Wotton's life derives from Walton's biography sketch, accounts by his wide circle of friends, and his own extant letters.

According to Walton, Wotton's father, Thomas, was a "gentleman excellently educated, and studious in all the Liberal Arts" (245). Wotton, too, received a liberal education, first at Winchester, then at New College, Oxford, where he enrolled in 1584. He quickly transferred to Hart Hall, where he encountered the young John Donne and formed a strong, lifelong friendship. By age eighteen, Wotton had transferred yet again to Queen's College and written a play, the tragedy of *Tancredo*, whose performance at the college was apparently deemed promising. He earned a Master of Arts by age twenty, reading optics and picking up Italian along the way. In 1589,

Wotton capped his gentleman's education by embarking on a prolonged journey through France, Germany, Italy, and the Low Countries.

Returning to England in 1594, Wotton quickly found employment as secretary to Robert, Earl of Essex, accompanying him on voyages to Cadiz in 1596 and the Azores in 1597. When Essex took up a post as Lord Lieutenant of Ireland in 1599, Wotton acted as emissary in peace negotiations with the rebellious Earl of Tyrone. The subsequent unauthorized treaty and Essex's unexpected return to England so angered Queen Elizabeth that she committed Essex to the Tower, where he was later executed. Fearing royal censure, Wotton once again traveled to the Continent, putting to work the knowledge and connections acquired during his previous tour by becoming secretary to the Great Duke of Tuscany.

In 1601, the Great Duke intercepted letters in Florence ostensibly detailing a plot to poison James VI of Scotland. Wotton, traveling under the assumed Italian name of Ottavio Baldi, departed immediately for Scotland with a special dispatch and antidotes from the Duke. James received Wotton favorably outside Stirling; this felicitous messenger would reap the benefits when, several months after Wotton's return to Florence, James acceded to the English throne. Sending for Wotton, James knighted him and appointed him as ambassador to Venice, a post he would hold three times, keeping him in Italy for almost twenty years. Wotton's diplomatic savvy and experience stood him in good stead in a country that had become his second home. He sought to further the Anglican cause in the Venetian Republic, angled for the marriage of Prince Henry to the Infanta Maria of Savoy, and negotiated in various missions abroad in Germany and France. In one famous episode, however, Wotton endangered his privileged status with James by declaring, "An Ambassador is an honest man, sent to lie abroad for the good of his country": to remedy this politically unwise remark, Wotton wrote apologies both publicly and directly to his sovereign.

Returning to England in 1619, Wotton faced financial exigencies and was obliged to seek a post yet again. He quickly won an appointment as provost of Eton, taking holy orders as deacon two years afterward. By all accounts, he was a conscientious educator and administrator at the "public" school, where he remained for the next fifteen years until his death. Wotton served, moreover, as Member of Parliament in 1625, as he had before in 1614. His financial difficulties persisted, unfortunately, leading to his arrest for debt in 1635 and confinement by bailiffs in his lodgings. Nevertheless, according to Walton, visitors to the provost always found that at Wotton's table "his meat was choice, and his discourse better" (275). In October 1639, after a prolonged period of intermittent ill health, Wotton fell into a lingering fever that ultimately led to his death in December of that year. At his own request, his body lies in the chapel of Eton College, marked simply by his motto on a plain gravestone.

MAJOR WORKS AND THEMES

Wotton was widely admired for the breadth of his learning—he was knowledgeable in classical and modern languages, literature, art, philosophy, and sciences—as well as for his involvement in current political and cultural circles. As his letters demonstrate, Wotton enjoyed an enduring friendship with Donne, among other men of letters, and his advice on all sorts of aesthetic matters was highly regarded. Although not a major literary figure himself, Wotton can count among his works "two or three beautiful lyrics which are to be found in every anthology" (Smith I: iii). Much of Wotton's work was collected posthumously in the *Reliquiae Wottonianae* (1651), a compendium that includes his more known poems "Character of a Happy Life," first found in Thomas Overbury's *Sir Thomas Overbury His Wife*, and "On His Mistress the Queen of Bohemia," written in praise of James I's daughter Elizabeth. Walton also quotes some of Wotton's lyrics, with debatable attribution, in dialogues at the end of the *Complete Angler*. These poems speak of flying from cares and woes to the pleasures of nature, from courtly sophistication to rustic life. Despite being conventional tropes of the lyric genre, these concerns reflect Wotton's own eventual turning away from the turbulence and excitement of public life to a more private life of "holy melancholy" (Walton 178). Not surprisingly, this portrait of Wotton in the *Complete Angler* derives from the last period of his life, when he had left public service for the more contemplative pastures of Eton.

During his lifetime, however, Wotton himself published only three works. The first of these was a 1612 Latin letter to Velserius (Marc Welser), which was widely distributed and reprinted as a pamphlet. Prompted by a malicious political adversary, Scioppius, who tried to scuttle the Anglican camp by publicizing Wotton's indiscreet assertion that an ambassador is a liar for his country, this letter was a piece of statesmanship designed to rectify Wotton's miscue by justifying his intentions and reaffirming his dedication to James I. Wotton's *Ad Regem e Scotia reducem Henrici Wottonii plausus et vota* was a similar piece of literary diplomacy. Composed in honor of Charles I's coronation in Edinburgh, this panegyric was published in 1633 and is generally of interest only to scholars.

Wotton's major literary effort, published in 1624, was his *Elements of Architecture*. Preceded only by John Shute's *The First and Chief Grounds of Architecture* (1563), this book-length work was one of the first and most significant architectural treatises published in Britain. In contrast to **Francis Bacon**'s roughly contemporaneous essay "On Building," Wotton's book counsels going beyond the purely utilitarian purposes of housing to consider the harmonious relationship between the microcosmic building and the macrocosmic surrounding and universe. Doubtless, Wotton's familiarity with Italian culture contributed to his undertaking this project and his desire to articulate a poetics of architecture. During the Italian Renaissance, the rediscovery of Vitruvius had led to a spate of architectural treatises that attempted to theorize the function and aesthetics of the built environment. For the first time, buildings were conceived as works of art requiring consideration of proportion, harmony, utility, and context. Theorists such as Leon Battista Alberti and Filarete had published important works elaborating and expanding upon classical Vitruvian ideals; architectural pattern books by Serlio, Scamozzi, and Vredeman de Vries had greatly influenced Elizabethan and early Jacobean building schemes. Wotton's *Elements of Architecture*, by importing this Italian Renaissance avenue of inquiry across the Channel, formalized the study of continental ideas of architecture and aesthetics, a trend that reached its full flowering in Inigo Jones. Nevertheless, in describing the process of building a country house, Wotton was also sensitive to the specific demands of English culture and environment; in one instance, he deplored the wholesale adoption of the Italian "view-through" plan as incompatible with the cold and windy climate of England. The second part of Wotton's book expands in scope to include meditations on painting, sculpture, and the role of the artist.

The *Reliquiae Wottonianae* contains, moreover, several short essays or fragments of prose pieces never completed, including a history of England commissioned by Charles I and a survey of education promised at the end of *Elements*. More important, however, are the collected letters of Wotton as selected by Izaak Walton for publication. Addressed to a wide range of correspondents for both personal and business purposes, these letters display a direct, unaffected writing style, products of an agile and cultivated mind. They not only shed light on the inner workings of Jacobean culture but also trace the course of a remarkable life, revealing an individuality marked by wit, grace, and tact.

CRITICAL RECEPTION

Wotton's learning and sophistication was duly appreciated by his peers, whose number included many of the age's most influential political and artistic figures. Indeed, it was perhaps more as a friend and counselor, rather than as a prime mover, that Wotton left his greatest impression upon 17th-century England. John Donne, Francis Bacon, Richard Baker, **Robert Boyle** and Johannes Kepler were among his circle of friends, acquaintances, pupils, and admirers. By acquiring art while abroad for aristocrats such as the Duke of Buckingham, Wotton helped to synchronize English tastes with continental trends; Wotton himself presented a Fialetti painting to Eton and bequeathed numerous artworks to friends. His diplomatic legacy is considerable, especially in establishing relations with Italian states and in the Essex fiasco(s). One of twelve pallbearers at James I's funeral, Wotton saw his greatest rise to power under James and a subsequent wane in influence under Charles I. As provost of Eton, Wotton advised the young **Milton** on his poetic endeavors; his letter to the budding poet, commenting on the masque *Comus*, made such an impact that it was reprinted in Milton's 1645 edition of *Poems*. Walton's biography of Donne and the *Complete Angler* were both projects proposed and begun by Wotton but left unfinished upon his death. The *Reliquiae Wottonianae*, which includes a funeral elegy by **Abraham Cowley**, was also undertaken by Walton in appreciation of his friend and addressing the lack of Wotton literature.

Although Wotton's life and works has enjoyed sustained commentary since the 17th century, modern scholarship has largely relegated this figure to a supporting role of interest primarily in historical context. The *Reliquiae Wottonianae* was reprinted several times in the 1600s but has not seen a contemporary revival; *The Elements of Architecture* has been reprinted in the 20th century, however, and remains an important part of the historical discourse on English architecture.

BIBLIOGRAPHY

Works by Henry Wotton

"Character of a Happy Life." In *Sir Thomas Overbury His Wife. With Additions of New Characters*. London, 1614.

The Elements of Architecture. 1624. Reprint, Charlottesville: University Press of Virginia, 1968.

A Philosophical Survey of Education; or, Moral Architecture, and the Aphorisms of Education. Ed. H.S. Kermode. London, 1938.

Reliquiae Wottonianae. London, 1651.

Studies of Henry Wotton

Hard, Frederick, Introduction to *The Elements of Architecture*. By Henry Wotton. Charlottes-
　　ville: University Press of Virginia, 1968. xi–lxxxiii.

Novarr, David. *The Making of Walton's Lives*. Ithaca, NY: Cornell University Press, 1958.

Pearsall Smith, Logan. *The Life and Letters of Sir Henry Wotton*. 2 vols. Oxford: Clarendon
　　Press, 1907.

Sells, A. Lytton. "Sir Henry Wotton and the Venetian Embassy." In his *The Paradise of Trav-
　　ellers*. Bloomington: Indiana University Press, 1964. 52–76.

Walton, Izaak. *The Complete Angler and The Lives of Donne, Wotton, Hooker, Herbert, and
　　Sanderson*. 1653. Reprint, London: Macmillan, 1906.

Ward, Adolphus William. *Sir Henry Wotton: A Biographical Sketch*. Westminster: Archibald
　　Constance and Co., 1898.

🐘 *William Wycherley*
(1641–1715)

JAMES GRANTHAM TURNER

BIOGRAPHY

Born to minor Shropshire gentry and enrolled in the Inner Temple, William Wycherley drifted into the circle of fashionable London wits and courtiers. His successful first play (1672) earned him the attention (and sexual favors) of the King's mistress, the Duchess of Cleveland. When her cousin the Duke of Buckingham flew into a jealous fit and threatened to "ruine" the young poet, Wycherley gained admission to the Duke's company, through the intercession of the **Earl of Rochester** and Sedley, seducing him with a display of physical and mental talent; from 1672 to 1674 Buckingham bestowed patronage on Wycherley, making him a court equerry and lieutenant (later captain) in his regiment. In his writing and in his person Wycherley was perceived as a hunk, "masculine" and even "brawny." He had been sent to be polished in the very heart of *préciosité* and refined breeding, the *salon* of Julie de Montausier (née Rambouillet), but his typical form of expression was blunt, even savage. The misanthropic Manly, in his fourth and final play *The Plain-Dealer* (published 1677), became his alter ego—hence **Dryden**'s compliment to "The Satire, Wit, and Strength of Manly *Witcherly*."

After his brief and dazzling career as a dramatist Wycherley stumbled aimlessly into what Macauley called "the life of an old boy about town." Charles II offered him a vast salary for tutoring the bastard Duke of Richmond, paid him a personal visit during a bout of brain fever, and funded a restorative trip to France, but all such favor ceased abruptly when Wycherley shirked his appointment and embarked on a ruinous marriage with an Irish countess. (According to conversations later written down by **John Dennis**, she had gone to a bookshop in search of *The Plain-Dealer* and instead picked up the author himself.) The result was mutual disappointment: rumors of Wycherley's sexual prowess turned out to be unfounded, and the widow's fortune never materialized—even after her death in 1685 her family contested the inheritance. Years of bitter complaint, litigation, and imprisonment for debt followed, alternating with periods of solvency spent in the coffee-house. Wycherley did write vast amounts of prose and satiric verse couplets (published to no acclaim in 1704) and at sixty-four entered into a correspondence with the very young Alexander Pope, eager to cultivate this living monument of Restoration wit. Pope eventually reedited the poems with extensive revision, though he wanted to extract the flashes of wit from the rambling verse and publish them as maxims. Encephalitis had apparently ruined Wycherley's short-term memory, and the same repetitiveness marred his conversation and his writing. Acutely aware of his decline, he compared the youthful-looking portrait in front of his collected poems (engraved after Lely) to a shop sign that palms off spoiled goods. In old age he married a much younger woman (apparently to cheat a nephew of his inheritance) and died three days later, on the last day of 1715.

MAJOR WORKS AND THEMES

One, perhaps two, of Wycherley's four plays have become indispensable specimens of Restoration comedy, defining, and distorting, the entire genre. Though the thorny *Plain-Dealer* offers more challenge to interpretation, his reputation rests securely on the intricate sex farce *The Country-Wife* (published 1675). Wycherley's first publication was not a drama but a poem, *Hero and Leander in Burlesque* (1669). In the spirit of Scarron's *Virgile travesti*, every heroic detail is converted into something bawdy or plebeian; Leander falls asleep after his supper of stewed prunes, and Hero advertises her desire like a fishwife. Instead of the beautiful paintings in the Temple of Venus, Wycherley promotes graffiti, pub signs made by a common "Dawber," and the pornographic engravings known as "Aretino's Postures"—touchstones of naturalism in art because they expose the "craveing chincke 'tween maiden thighs." This might seem like a juvenile excess on Wycherley's part, but the same themes recur in his best-known drama, associated with vigor and peculiar honesty. The praise of the "coarse Dawber" and the aggressive exposure of women (equated with "Life and Nature") recur in the forematter of *The Plain-Dealer*, an aggrieved diatribe against the hypocrisy of aristocratic seductresses.

In his first comedy, *Love in a Wood*, generally known by its subtitle *St. James's Park*, Wycherley represents the carnivalesque social mingling of that zone of fashionable recreation. He cobbles together disparate plot elements (libertine seduction, romantic courtship, anti-Puritan satire, mockery of the aspiring "Dapperwit," Spanish intrigue from Calderón), but tow motifs hold them together: the machinating City bawd, Mrs. Joyner, and the park itself. Echoing (or anticipating) Rochester's notoriously obscene poem *A Ramble in Saint James's Parke*, Ranger proposes "a Ramble" to the park in search of sexual "Game," finding there a twilight zone where "no woman's modest," where (by a double paradox) a man "may bring his bashful Wench, and not have her put out of countenance by the impudent honest women of the Town" (1.2, 2.1). In a later park scene the predatory City widow Lady Flippant, sister to Alderman Gripe, pretends to be a libertine in order to snare a husband—peering through the mongrol light in search of her prey (5.1). The same pseudorakish character sings a song that condemns marriage and asserts the superiority of bastardy—the cue for Cleveland to initiate her sponsorship and seduction of the playwright, shouting at him in the street, "*You*, Wycherley, *you are a Son of a Whore.*" He acknowledged these "favors" in an ambiguous dedication. The play ends with another punning paradox, typical of Wycherley's wit: Matrimony now leads not to bondage but to "liberty, / And two are bound . . . to set each other free" (5.2).

The less successful *Gentleman Dancing-Master* (1673), produced in the shadow of the Dutch War where Wycherley may have seen action, similarly grafts light courtship comedy onto Jonsonian (see **Jonson**) humors and a disguise motif from Calderón. The blocking father of the sexy ingénue Hippolita is the pseudo–Don Diego, obsessed with Spanish habits, who wants her to marry the pseudo-French "Monsieur de Paris." Comic energy derives from the eruption of the lower urban stratum: The "midnight Ramblers," Flounce and Flirt, terrorize the West End, "hunt out the men," and burst into fashionable restaurants, expertly identifying the worn-out lechers ("the hot Service you have been in formerly, makes you unfit for ours now") and wolfing down new customers with the same fresh appetite that they bring to the menu (1.2). In the end, however, they settle for City merchants.

Moving away from the convention of parallel plots on different social levels, *The Country-Wife* interlocks three distinct stories without subordination, each involving prose-speaking gentry characters. In the opening scene the notorious rake Horner establishes a new confidence trick to gain access to "right" women, pretending that surgery has removed his genitals and made him "harmless." Hordes of acquaintances including his rakish companion Harcourt and a respectable City couple, then reveal their reaction to the news, mocking his lost masculinity, dangling their womenfolk in front of him, offering him employment as a eunuch to guard the harem. Describing himself as a "Machiavel in love," Horner picks precisely those women who express the most revulsion and makes secret assignations under cover of his eunuch disguise— though he seems equally concerned to get rid of them after a single conquest. Trickery and satirical exposé rather than erotic desire become his prime motive, as he keeps up the conspiracy of silence among an increasing number of partners: he mocks them as high-class whores, and they in turn name him Harry Common (a male prostitute) and reveal their consumeristic desires, making him a piece of luxury china or a gourmet treat ("we think wildness in a man, as desirable a quality, as in a Duck, or Rabbet," 5.4).

Meanwhile, the obtuse Pinchwife—like Molière's Arnolphe obsessed with avoiding cuckoldry by marrying an innocent country girl—works desperately to keep his bumpkin wife out of Horner's clutches. Conveniently, he has not heard the eunuch rumor and still continues to warn her against the devilish seducer in such detail that she learns everything she needs. Margery Pinchwife's country directness turns Horner on at first but then endangers the conspiracy that keeps his plot going; in the end the new lover shuts her up much as the old husband had done. Horner desires women only as they belong to another man, packing Margery off to Pinchwife again after a single bout.

In the third plot, Pinchwife's sister Alithea is contracted to the idiotic fop Sparkish, who displays his would-be cool by pretending to lack jealousy and introducing her to his libertine friends. Harcourt falls violently in love, but Alithea, whose name suggests "Truth," insists on keeping her word even while fully aware of Sparkish's emptiness. These plots mirror one another: excess versus deficiency of jealousy; natural versus forced wit; true versus false honor—a theme that ignites dazzling conceptual fireworks. And each plot affects the others as the action hurtles forward. At one of the play's climaxes, Horner is forced to betray Alithea to save the naive country-wife from exposure; Harcourt reveals his true nobility by refusing to believe him, while Sparkish breaks off the hated engagement in a jealous fury. In the final scene Horner's eunuch cover is about to be blown, bringing down the entire house of cards, only to be saved when all the female characters (even the virtuous Alithea) join in a ring to perjure themselves on his behalf, confirming his false eunuch facade and thus protecting his sexual game.

Wycherley himself encourages us to read Horner as a true lover of women, as he insists in the actress's epilogue and in *The Plain-Dealer*: in a scene modeled on Molière's *Critique de l'École des femmes*, the discredited and prudish Olivia denounces Horner's rampant priapism, at the same time advertising by her disapproval the famously bawdy china scene in the earlier play (2.1). Much of *The Plain-Dealer* consists of staged rants against hypocrisy, loosely connected to the story of Manly—a seacaptain, distantly related to Molière's misanthrope, who bursts into fashionable London like a bull into a china shop. His hatred of pretence does not save him from being utterly cheated by his false and sadistic friend Vernish and his faux-prude mistress Olivia, whom he pursues with a horrible mixture of lust and rage. These static elements are linked by two characters borrowed from romance rather than satire or sex comedy, the true male friend Freeman and the true lover Fidelia, who dresses as a cabin boy to follow Manly to sea, and even breaks into the occasional blank-verse soliloquy. If Manly's jealous outbursts sometimes sound like a prose *Othello*, Fidelia's maneuvers to avoid Olivia and win Manly resemble *Twelfth Night* played in a brothel.

The Plain-Dealer brings together a broad range of genres and social types, if not always convincingly. The main story alternates with a Jonsonian humor plot in which Freeman pursues a wealthy widow obsessed with the law by way of her rustic son. The Plain-Dealer himself seems split in two, so that critics remain confused about Wycherley's characterization. Is he an uncompromising truth-teller or a pathological fool? Is he conceived from the inside or the outside? Wycherley seems to endorse the positive view when he signs his preface "The Plain Dealer," but this only deepens the potential irony: this last play is dedicated, outrageously, to the infamous brothel keeper "Lady" Bennett, extravagantly praised at the expense of her aristocratic counterparts.

Like his friend Rochester, Wycherley belonged to what Pope would call "the Mob of Gentlemen," but he never "wrote with ease." Despite revealing and even brilliant moments in the lesser-known poems and essays, the reader feels bludgeoned. Wycherley takes on the key themes of Restoration satire in *Miscellany Poems* (London, 1704), a large, ambitious folio (of which numerous presentation copies survive but no praise): the prostitution or spaniellike dependence of courtiers like himself; female authorship as venereal disease; impotence; the paradoxical "honor" of pimps and whores; the hypocrisy of the virtuous; hatred of "mercenary" women and "the worst sort of Jilts, Wives"; the "Drudgery" of sex, both marital and libertine; the superiority of animals over humans "curst with constant Sensuality." But he cannot bring these themes to the verve and polish of *The Country-Wife*.

CRITICAL RECEPTION

Wycherley never quite regained the glory assigned by his contemporaries. Rochester admitted him to his literary inner circle, and Dryden flattered his wit, judgment, amiability, and "useful satire" as early as the 1674 *State of Innocence*, maintaining his praise of "Manly Wycherley" in the epoch-making poem "To my Dear Friend, Mr Congreve, on his Comedy called *The Double Dealer*." Congreve himself, in the prologue to *Love for Love* (1696), makes Wycherley a paragon of moral courage: "Since the Plain Dealer's scenes of manly rage / Not one has dared to lash this crying age." His friend Lord Lansdowne remarked that in his writing "every Syllable, every Thought is masculine," a judgment that many feminist critics would endorse. Though the bawdy Restoration ethos was waning, the public still craved scraps of Wycherley's memoirs and letters; the carcass of his literary reputation was fought over by those bitter rivals Dennis, Theobald, Curll, and Pope.

On stage, *The Country-Wife* remained intermittently popular up to 1747 but then started to fade, being replaced by more genteel adaptations (like Garrick's 1766 *The Country Girl*). Numerous reprints kept his drama in circulation. Literary commentary includes Steele's *Tatler* (number 3, reviewing a 1709 revival) and *Spectator* (number 266). Steele views the gentleman-libertine character as already historical evidence for a bygone era and tries to persuade us that Wycherley's intentions were moral: The country-wife offers "instructive satire" on female miseducation, and the dedication of *The Plain-Dealer* to a prostitute is "a masterpiece of raillery on that vice." This last play was also much reprinted but performed in adapted versions. Voltaire admired its wit and power (later revising it as *La Prude*) but found it far coarser than Molière. This was to become the standard complaint in the 19th century, even though (paradoxically) *The Plain-Dealer* was then considered his absolute masterpiece, worth ten volumes of sermons according to Hazlitt.

Leigh Hunt edited Wycherley's plays in 1849 (with those of Congreve, Vanbrugh, and Farquhar), and W.C. Ward presented an "unexpurgated" text with notes and introductions in the Mermaid Series (*William Wycherley*, London, 1888, often reprinted). Wycherley stimulated Macaulay to heights of rhetorical splendor: "[T]he most nauseous libertinism and the most dastardly fraud" replaces Molière's "purity"; *The Country-Wife* is "one of the most profligate and heartless of human compositions . . . protected against the critics as a skunk is protected against the hunters." But Macaulay's essay on Wycherley (prefaced to Ward) also stresses the constructed unreality of his "*simulacra*" and the beneficial effects of his laughter, an antidote to sensuality. Another critic compares the prismatic, "dazzling" brilliance of *The Plain-Dealer* to "the miasmatic radiance of a foul ditch shimmering in the sun." The old *DNB* epitomizes the late-Victorian consensus, eulogizing the vigor and brilliance but lamenting the indecency.

Wycherley enjoyed a revival in the anti-Victorian atmosphere of the 1920s— marked by Montague Summers's deluxe editions of the plays and the *Complete Works*—and he is discussed in every 20th-century academic survey of the drama. But it was the 1960s that reinvented him. Holland psychologized Wycherley's plays, presenting them as "modern comedies" about the right and wrong way to achieve personal authenticity in a problematic world. Birdsall celebrated Horner and his ilk as liberating surges of the life force (in which she was followed by Weber). Fujimura engaged the Hobbesian philosophy of the libertine. Wycherley did publish his plays with mottos from the classical satirists, suggesting high literary purpose, and Zimbardo accordingly interpreted them as formal satires à la Juvenal. Vernon detrivializes him by emphasizing his didactic passion for maxims and his serious engagement with "social problems," particularly the problem of devising new social bonds in an age of emergent "capitalism." Vieth initiated the study of masculinity in Wycherley's characters, continued by Rogers (with a feminist inflection) and Kaufman.

The semiotic and linguistic turn produced many studies of language, the body, and performance in Wycherley (some listed below). Critics have long noticed that virtually all the central issues in *The Country-Wife* exploit the opacity of the sign: Horner resorts to his eunuch trick because *all* women, "right" or not, have adopted a fashionable air of sexy complaisance; Harcourt and Alithea, the only characters engaged in marital courtship, must decide whether to take marriage as a "sign of interest" or a "sign of love"; even the dupe character Sparkish banters Horner as "a sign of a Man" (1.1, 2.1). Sedgwick, bringing out the homoerotic implications of womanizing and cuckolding in *The Country-Wife*, argues that the kinds of sign manipulation available to the female characters are more limited and static than those available to the men, who alone posses "cognitive mastery."

Interest in Wycherley remains keen, to judge from paperback editions, stage performances, and Internet links. In scholarly criticism, Horner and Manly continue to inspire a bewildering range of responses, from Dionysiac liberator to "nightmarish" demon. My own solution is to emphasize Wycherley's epistemic experiments, especially in the sexual realm: Against the author's apparent intentions, Horner truly becomes the eunuch he pretends to be. In the larger context, I present Wycherley as an ambiguator or "infiltrator" of scandalous and pornographic material into elite culture.

BIOGRAPHY

Works by William Wycherley

Complete Plays. Ed. Gerald Weales. New York: New York University Press, 1967.

Complete Works. Ed. Montague Summers. 4 vols. 1924. Reprint, London: Nonesuch Press, 1964.

Hero and Leander in Burlesque. 1669. Victoria and Albert Museum, London: Dyce 17.P.55, with censored passages completed in MS by Wycherley.

Miscellany Poems. London, 1704. Reprint, 1706.

Plays. Ed. Arthur Friedman. Oxford: Clarendon Press, 1979.

Posthumous Works. Ed. Alexander Pope. Vol. 2. London, 1729.

Posthumous Works . . . to which Are Prefixed Some Memoirs of Mr Wycherley's Life, by Major Pack. Ed. Lewis Theobald. London, 1728.

Studies of William Wycherley

Avery, Emmett L. "*The Country Wife* in the Eighteenth Century." *Research Studies of the State College of Washington* 10 (1942): 141–172.

Birdsall, Virginia Ogden. *Wild Civility: The English Comic Spirit on the Restoration Stage*. Bloomington: Indiana University Press, 1970.

Canfield, J. Douglas. *Tricksters and Estates: On the Ideology of Restoration Comedy*. Lexington: University Press of Kentucky, 1997.

Connely, Willard. *Brawny Wycherley, First Master in English Modern Comedy*. 1930. Reprint, New York: Scribner's, 1969.

Dennis, John. "To the Honourable Major Pack, Containing some remarkable Passages of Mr.

Wycherley's Life." Reprinted in *Critical Works*, ed. Edward Niles Hooker II. Baltimore: Johns Hopkins Press, 1943.

Ford, Douglas. *"The Country Wife*: Rake Hero as Artist." *Restoration* 17 (1993): 77–84.

Fujimura, Thomas H. *The Restoration Comedy of Wit*. Princeton: Princeton University Press, 1952.

———, ed. *The Country Wife*. Lincoln: University of Nebraska Press, 1965.

Gill, Pat. *Interpreting Ladies: Women, Wit, and Morality in the Restoration Comedy of Manners*. Athens: University of Georgia Press, 1994.

Holland, Norman. *The First Modern Comedies: The Significance of Etherege, Wycherley and Congreve*. Cambridge: Harvard University Press, 1959.

Hynes, Peter. "Against Theory? Knowledge and Action in Wycherley's Plays." *Modern Philology* 94 (1996): 163–189.

Kaufman, Anthony. "Wycherley's *The Country Wife* and the Don Juan Character." *Eighteenth-Century Studies* 9 (1975–1976): 216–231.

Knapp, Peggy A. "The 'Plyant' Discourse of Wycherley's *The Country Wife*." *Studies in English Literature* 40 (2000): 451–477.

Lansdowne, George, Lord. *Memoirs of the Life of William Wycherley Esquire, [with] Some Familiar Letters Written by Mr Wycherley*. London: Edmund Curll, 1718.

Markley, Robert. *Two-edg'd Weapons: Style and Ideology in the Comedies of Etherege, Wycherley and Congreve*. Oxford: Oxford University Press, 1988.

Marshall, W. Gerald. *The Great Stage of Fools: Theatricality and Madness in the Plays of William Wycherley*. New York: AMS Press, 1993.

McCarthy, B. Eugene. *William Wycherley: A Biography*. Athens: Ohio University Press, 1979.

———. *William Wycherley: A Reference Guide*. Boston: G.K. Hall, 1985.

Neill, Michael. "Horned Beasts and China Oranges: Reading the Signs in *The Country-Wife*." *Eighteenth-Century Life* 12.2 (May 1988): 3–17.

Novak, Maximillian E. "Margery Pinchwife's 'London Disease': Restoration Comedy and the Libertine Offensive of the 1670s." *Studies in the Literary Imagination* 10 (1977): 1–23.

Payne, Deborah C. "Reading the Signs in *The Country Wife*." *Studies in English Literature* 26 (1986): 403–419.

Pope, Alexander. *Correspondence*. Ed. George Sherburn. Vol. 1. Oxford: Clarendon Press, 1956. (Pope's altered versions of his letters to and from Wycherley, collated where possible with the originals.)

———. *Pastorals*. 1709. (Number 3 is dedicated to Wycherley.)

Rogers, Katherine M. *William Wycherley*. New York: Twayne Publishers, 1972.

Sedgwick, Eve Kosovsky. *Between Men: English Literature and Male Homosocial Desire*. New York: Columbia University Press, 1985.

Shepherd, Simon. " 'The Body,' Performance Studies, Horner and a Dinner Party." *Texas Studies in Literature and Language* 14 (2000): 285–303.

Sherman, Sandra. "Manly, Manliness, and Friendship in *The Plain-Dealer*." *Restoration* 20 (1996): 18–30.

Thompson, James. *Language in Wycherley's Plays: Seventeenth-Century Language Theory and Drama*. Tuscaloosa: University of Alabama Press, 1984.

Turner, James Grantham. *Libertines and Radicals in Early Modern London: Sexuality, Politics and Literary Culture, 1630–1685*. Cambridge: Cambridge University Press, 2001. 201–218.

———. *Schooling Sex: Libertine Literature and Erotic Education in Italy, France, and England, 1534–1685*. Oxford: Oxford University Press, 2003. 240–259.

Vance, John A. *William Wycherley and the Comedy of Fear*. Newark: University of Delaware Press, 2000.

Vernon, P.F. *William Wycherley*. London: The British Council, 1965.

Vieth, David M. *"The Country Wife*: An Anatomy of Masculinity." *Papers on Language and Literature* 2 (1966): 335–350.

Weber, Harold M. *The Restoration Rake-Hero: Transformations in Sexual Understanding in Seventeenth-Century England.* Madison: University of Wisconsin Press, 1986.

Zimbardo, Rose A. *Wycherley's Drama: A Link in the Development of English Satire.* New Haven, CT: Yale University Press, 1965.

❧ List of Authors by Birth Year

Fulke Greville, Lord Brooke (1554–1628)

Lancelot Andrewes (1555–1626)

George Chapman (1559?–1634)

Francis Bacon (1561–1626)

Michael Drayton (1563–1631)

Orazio Gentileschi (1563–1639)

William Shakespeare (1564–1616)

Thomas Campion (1567–1620)

Henry Wotton (1568–1635)

Aemilia Lanyer (1569?–1645)

John Donne (1572–1631)

Ben Jonson (1572/1573–1637)

Cyril Tourneur (1575?–1626)

Robert Burton (1577–1640)

Peter Paul Rubens (1577–1640)

William Harvey (1578–1657)

John Taylor ("The Water Poet") (1578–1653)

John Webster (1579?–1633?)

Thomas Middleton (1580–1627)

Phineas Fletcher (1582–1650)

Philip Massinger (1583–1640)

Elizabeth Cary (c. 1585–1639)

John Ford (1586–1639?)

Thomas Hobbes (1588–1679)

Robert Herrick (1591–1674)

George Herbert (1593–1633)

Artemisia Gentileschi (1593–1652/1653)

Thomas Carew (c. 1595–1639)

Anthony Van Dyck (1599–1641)

Oliver Cromwell (1599–1658)

Diego Velázquez (1599–1660)

Thomas Browne (1605–1682)

William Davenant (1606–1668)

Rembrandt van Rijn (1606–1669)

Edmund Waller (1606–1687)

Richard Fanshawe (1608–1666)

John Milton (1608–1674)

John Suckling (1608/1609–1642)

Anne Bradstreet (1612–1672)

Samuel Butler (1612/1613–1680)

John Cleveland (1613–1658)

Richard Crashaw (c. 1613–1649)

John Lilburne (1615–1657)

Richard Lovelace (1618–1657)

Abraham Cowley (1618–1667)

Andrew Marvell (1621–1678)

Henry Vaughan (1621?–1695)

Margaret Cavendish, Duchess of Newcastle (1623–1673)

John Aubrey (1626–1697)

Robert Boyle (1627–1691)

John Bunyan (1628–1688)

John Dryden (1631–1700)

Johannes Vermeer (1632–1675)

Baruch de Spinoza (1632–1677)

Samuel Pufendorf (1632–1694)

John Locke (1632–1704)

Samuel Pepys (1633–1703)

Madame de Lafayette (c. 1634–1693)

Thomas Traherne (1636?–1674)

Mary Rowlandson (c. 1637–1711)

Aphra Behn (1640?–1689)

William Wycherley (1641–1715)

Thomas Shadwell (c. 1642–1692)

Second Earl of Rochester (John Wilmot) (1647–1680)

John Blow (1649–1708)

Thomas Otway (1652–1685)

Nahum Tate (1652–1715)

Arcangelo Corelli (1653–1713)

Mary, Lady Chudleigh (1656–1710)

John Dennis (1658–1734)

Henry Purcell (1659–1695)

Anne Killigrew (1660–1685)

Anne Finch, Countess of Winchilsea (1661–1720)

Sarah Kemble Knight (1666–1727)

Mary Astell (1666–1731)

Third Earl of Shaftesbury (Anthony Ashley Cooper) (1671–1713)

Joseph Addison (1672–1719)

Delarivier Manley (1672?–1724)

Allan Ramsay (1686–1758)

✒ Selected General Bibliography

Bush, Douglas. *English Literature in the Earlier Seventeenth Century: 1600–1660*. Oxford: Clarendon Press, 1962.

Colie, Rosalie. *Paradoxia Epidemica: The Renaissance Tradition of Paradox*. Princeton: Princeton University Press, 1966.

Fish, Stanley Eugene. *Self-Consuming Artifacts: The Experience of Seventeenth Century Literature*. Berkeley: University of California Press, 1972.

Gay, Peter. *The Enlightenment: An Interpretation*. New York: Time-Life, 1969.

Greenblatt, Stephen. *Renaissance Self-Fashioning from More to Shakespeare*. Chicago: University of Chicago Press, 1980.

Hall, Rupert. *The Scientific Revolution, 1500–1800*. New York: Longmans, Green, 1954.

Hayden, Hyram Collins. *The Counter-Renaissance*. New York: Grove Press, 1960.

Hill, Christopher. *The Century of Revolution*. Edinburgh: T. Nelson, 1961.

Lewalski, Barbara. *Writing Women in Jacobean England*. Cambridge: Harvard University Press, 1993.

Lewis, C.S. *English Literature in the Sixteenth Century: Excluding Drama*. Oxford: Clarendon Press, 1954.

Loewenstein, David. *Representing Revolution in Milton and His Contemporaries: Religion, Politics, and Polemics in Radical Puritanism*. Cambridge: Cambridge University Press, 1990.

Lovejoy, Arthur O. *The Great Chain of Being: A Study of the History of an Idea*. Cambridge: Harvard University Press, 1933.

New, John F. *Anglican and Puritan: The Basis of Their Opposition, 1558–1640*. Stanford, CA: Stanford University Press, 1964.

Norbrook, David. *Writing the English Republic: Poetry, Rhetoric and Politics, 1627–1660*. Cambridge: Cambridge University Press, 1999.

Patterson, Annabel. *Censorship and Interpretation: The Condition of Writing and Reading in Early Modern England*. Madison: University of Wisconsin Press, 1984.

Pocock, J.G.A. *The Ancient Constitution and the Feudal Law*. 1957. Rev. ed., Cambridge: Cambridge University Press, 1987.

Richmond, Hugh. *Renaissance Landscapes: English Lyrics in a European Tradition*. The Hague: Mouton, 1973.

Scholes, Robert. *The Rise and Fall of English: Reconstructing English as a Discipline*. New Haven, CT: Yale University Press, 1958.

Shuger, Debora. *Habits of Thought in the English Renaissance: Religion, Politics, and the Dominant Culture*. Berkeley: University of California Press, 1990.

Stone, Lawrence. *The Family, Sex and Marriage, 1500–1800*. New York: Harper and Row, 1977.

Thomas, Keith. *Religion and the Decline of Magic: Popular Beliefs in Sixteenth- and Seventeenth-Century England*. New York: Scribner's, 1971.

Tillyard, E.M.W. *The Elizabethan World Picture*. New York: Vintage, 1966.

Turner, James Grantham. *The Politics of Landscape: Rural Scenery and Society in English Poetry, 1630–1660*. Cambridge: Harvard University Press, 1979.

⟋♠ *Index*

Note: Page numbers in **boldface** refer to the main entries in the encyclopedia.

❧ About the Editor and Contributors

ALAN HAGER is a professor of English specializing in Shakespeare and Renaissance comparative literature at the State University of New York at Cortland.

MARGARET J. ARNOLD is a professor of English specializing in Milton and the 17th century at the University of Kansas.

KEITH M. BOTELHO is a Ph.D. candidate specializing in 17th-century literature at the University of New Hampshire.

GARY BOUCHARD is the executive vice president specializing in administration and Renaissance pastoral and religious verse at Saint Anselm College.

DOUGLAS S. BRUSTER is a professor of Renaissance English literature at the University of Texas at Austin.

MICHAEL BRYSON is a visiting assistant professor of English specializing in the Renaissance at DePaul University.

GERALD EDWARD BUNKER is a medical doctor with a Ph.D. in history in Annapolis, Maryland.

THOMAS HOWARD CROFTS III is a Ph.D. candidate specializing in 17th-century authors and music at the University of Wisconsin at Madison.

RIKA DREA is a Ph.D. candidate specializing in 17th-century lyric at American University.

LAURIE ELLINGHAUSEN is a professor of English specializing in Renaissance literature at the University of Missouri-Kansas City.

PATRICK D. ENRIGHT is a professor of English specializing in Jacobean drama and 17th-century literature at Northeastern State University.

RICHARD EVERSOLE is a professor of English specializing in 17th- and 18th-century literature at the University of Kansas.

ERIKA L. FARR is a Ph.D. candidate specializing in 17th-century literature at Emory University.

LOUIS A. GEBHARD is an emeritus professor of English specializing in 17th-century thought at the State University of New York at Cortland.

ALBERT J. GERITZ is a professor of English specializing in Renaissance literature at Fort Hays State University.

MAUREEN GODMAN is a professor of English specializing in John Donne and 17th-century poetry at Washburn University of Topeka.

NANCY HAGER is a professor of music specializing in music of the Baroque through Early Romantics at Brooklyn College of the City University of New York.

BRYAN A. HAMPTON is a Ph.D. candidate in the English Renaissance at Northwestern University.

SONJA HANSARD-WEINER is an instructor of English at Madison Area Technical College in Wisconsin, specializing in early modern texts and art.

RICHARD F. HARDIN is a professor of English specializing in Renaissance comparative literature at the University of Kansas.

RICHARD HARP is a professor of English specializing in Ben Jonson and Jacobean literature at the University of Nevada at Las Vegas.

RON HARRIS is a Ph.D. candidate specializing in 17th-century translation and thought at the University of Wisconsin at Madison.

JOHN HUNTINGTON is a professor of English specializing in Renaissance English literature and Victorian romance at the University of Illinois at Chicago.

VICKI JANIK is a professor of English specializing in Shakespeare and Renaissance comparative literature at the State University of New York at Farmingdale.

D. SUSAN KENDRICK is a professor of English specializing in Renaissance literature at Emporia State University.

ADAM KITZES is a Ph.D. candidate specializing in 17th-century poetry and prose at the University of Wisconsin at Madison.

GREG KNEIDEL is an assistant professor of English specializing in Herbert and the metaphysical poets at the University of Connecticut, Greater Hartford Area.

RON LEVAO is a professor of English specializing in Shakespeare and Renaissance comparative literature at Rutgers University.

MICHAEL T. MASIELLO is a Ph.D. candidate specializing in 17th-century thought at Rutgers University.

REGINA MASIELLO teaches early modern literature at Rutgers University, New Brunswick, New Jersey.

ELLEN THOMPSON McCABE is a librarian specializing in Renaissance literature and periodicals at the Memorial Library of the State University of New York at Cortland.

LORRAINE MELITA is a librarian specializing in 17th-century women authors at the Memorial Library of the State University of New York at Cortland.

ERIN MURPHY is a Ph.D. candidate in Renaissance English literature at Rutgers University.

CLAIRE I.R. O'MAHONY is a professor of art history at Bristol University in England.

HUGH MACRAE RICHMOND is an emeritus professor of English specializing in 16th- and 17th-century comparative literature at the University of California at Berkeley.

VELMA BOURGEOIS RICHMOND is an emeritus professor of English specializing in English and Scottish medieval and Renaissance literature and art history at Hope College.

NHORA LUCÍA SERRANO is a Ph.D. candidate in the Department of Comparative Literature specializing in 17th-century English and French literature at the University of Wisconsin at Madison.

PAMELA K. SHAFFER is a professor of English specializing in 17th-century poetry and prose at Fort Hays State University.

JOHN A. SHEDD is a professor of history at SUNY Cortland, specializing in the Early Modern Period.

JULIE ROBIN SOLOMON is an independent scholar specializing in 17th-century thought and literature in Washington, D.C.

RICHARD J. SQUIBBS is a Ph.D. candidate specializing in Restoration literature and thought at Rutgers University.

GLENN SUCICH is a Ph.D. candidate in Renaissance literature at Northwestern University.

JAMES GRANTHAM TURNER is a professor of English specializing in 17th- and 18th-century comparative literature at the University of California at Berkeley.

BRIAN WALSH is a Ph.D. candidate specializing in 17th- and 18th-century drama at Rutgers University.

ANDREW D. WEINER is a professor of English at the University of Wisconsin-Madison, specializing in the Sidney Circle and theology.

SHELLEY LePOUDRE WIEBE is a Ph.D. candidate specializing in 17th-century poetry at the University of Saskatchewan.

AMY WOLF is a professor of English specializing in 17th-century literature at Canisius College.

GAIL WOOD is a librarian specializing in American women authors and library administration at the Memorial Library of the State University of New York at Cortland.

MIMI YIU is a Ph.D. candidate in the English Renaissance at Cornell University.